Philosophy and Contemporary Issues

FOURTH EDITION

John R. Burr
Milton Goldinger

University of Wisconsin—Oshkosh

Macmillan Publishing Company
NEW YORK

Copyright © 1984, Macmillan Publishing Company, a division of Macmillan, Inc.
Printed in the United States of America.

Earlier editions copyright © 1972 and 1976, and copyright © 1980 by Macmillan Publishing Company.

Macmillan Publishing Company
866 Third Avenue, New York, New York 10022

Collier Macmillan Canada, Inc.

Library of Congress Cataloging in Publication Data

Main entry under title:

Philosophy and contemporary issues.

   Bibliography: p.
   1. Philosophy—Addresses, essays, lectures.
I. Burr, John Roy, l933–   . II. Goldinger, Milton, 1936–   .
BD41.P47 1984   190′.9′04   83-7969
ISBN 0-02-317250-9

Printing: 2 3 4 5 6 7 8   Year: 4 5 6 7 8 9 0 1 2

ISBN   0-02-317250-9

Preface to the Fourth Edition

The purpose of this anthology is to show how philosophy illuminates and in some measure helps solve some of the important problems troubling contemporary man. The editors intend it to be an introductory text. Unfortunately, many introductory texts in philosophy are flawed by one of two major defects: (1) they are too difficult for the beginning student or (2) they are too simple for the beginning student. Some introductory philosophy texts are introductory in name only because they demand of the philosophically innocent student a mastery of technical philosophical language and a knowledge of the history of philosophy one could reasonably expect only from a professional philosopher. No wonder students struggling to understand such books become convinced of the truth of the popular view that philosophy is a subject wholly unintelligible to all except a few compulsive adepts and completely irrelevant to life outside of the classroom. On the other hand, in an attempt to eliminate excessive philosophical sophistication, other introductory philosophy texts are philosophical in name only because they contain no technical philosophy. Not surprisingly, students reading such books in order to learn about philosophy as a distinct discipline find them hollow and conclude philosophy is not worth serious study.

In designing the structure of this book, in selecting the readings, in writing the introductions to the various parts, and in choosing the books to be listed in the bibliographies, the editors have striven to produce a work avoiding both defective extremes. Throughout, the guiding aim has been to make philosophy interesting and intelligible to students undertaking their first sustained study of the subject and, above all, to encourage them to engage in philosophizing themselves. To achieve this end, each part of this volume contains pro and con articles on provocative contemporary issues, which in turn raise fundamental philosophical issues. In addition to the material dealing directly with contemporary issues, each part includes other selections discussing at length and in depth some of the philosophical problems raised by the contemporary controversies. Therefore, each part forms a coherent unit of mutually relevant sections rather than a miscellaneous grouping. Every effort has been made to pick readings for their substance, their intelligibility, and their freshness for the beginning student of philosophy. Since the editors planned a single volume and not a library, not all philosophical issues, positions, movements, and methods could be included. It should also be pointed out that the readings in one part often will throw light on the material dealt with in other parts. Of course, the decisions as to what material is covered in this course and in what order it is taken up are those of the individual instructor. Nothing is implied by the order in which the parts of this book are arranged.

This introductory text in philosophy is a mutual enterprise, each editor sharing equally in the work of its production and benefiting from the comments and suggestions of his colleagues.

About a third of the content of this fourth edition is fresh and, we believe, an improvement over that of the last edition. The editors have made every effort to choose philosophically significant selections that beginning students of philosophy will find interesting and understandable. Unfortunately, limitations of length have forced the elimination from this edition of the section on art and society included in the previous editions.

We wish to thank Gene Panhorst, who became philosophy editor of Macmillan while this fourth edition was in preparation, and his immediate predecessor, Kenneth J. Scott, as well as our colleague Marshall Missner; the Oshkosh Public Library, the Library of the University of Wisconsin-Oshkosh, and Mrs. Nathalie Moore. Finally, we have benefited from the thoughtful comments and criticisms of the many users of the previous three editions of *Philosophy and Contemporary Issues.*

J.R.B.
M.G.

Contents

General
Introduction

Many university and college students take their academic courses in the same way that travelers visit Eufaula, Alabama; Sweetgrass, Montana; or Passadumkeag, Maine. They simply pass through and go on their way. After a short passage of time, memory fades out and the experience leaves no detectable trace. Obviously, in such cases the students have wasted their time in class and the professor has squandered his. On the contrary, if a course of study is to be worthwhile, the subject matter must be assimilated by the student. Worthwhile philosophy courses provide no counterinstances to this generalization.

This process of assimilating a subject means more than diligently and doggedly memorizing names, dates, and definitions—more than the accumulating of inert information long enough to pass examinations and then allowing it to scatter, soon to be lost. A student who truly assimilates a subject finds himself changed in significant ways at the conclusion of his course. In this respect, taking a philosophy course should be analogous to undergoing battle in war, getting married, or giving birth to a child. At least some of the beliefs, values, methods of thinking, and general attitudes of the students should be altered.

But altered in what way? The editors of this volume think the change should be from less to more intellectual independence on the part of the student. An introductory philosophy course cannot transform a neophyte into a professional philosopher, a sophomore into a profound thinker. Still, it can strengthen students' courage and skill in thinking for themselves. An introductory philosophy course can advance the enlightenment of students. Immanuel Kant, one of the great philosophers, wrote an essay entitled "What is Enlightenment," in which he defined *enlightenment* in the following words:

> Enlightenment is the emergence of man from the immaturity for which he is himself responsible. Immaturity is the inability to use one's understanding without the guidance of another. Man is responsible for his own immaturity, when it is caused, by lack not of understanding, but of the resolution and the courage to use it without the guidance of another. *Sapere aude!* Have the courage to use your own reason! is the slogan of the Enlightenment.

Of course, Kant was trying to articulate the spirit of the eighteenth-century Enlightenment. Nevertheless, such "enlightenment" is not something appropriate only to a past historical period. It must be renewed in every age, particularly in our own, which the classical scholar Gilbert Murray has dubbed an "age of lying." And we must remember that in the story it was a youngster who dared to

3

say out loud that the Emperor was wearing no clothes. Often young people have not become as hopelessly habituated to hypocrisy and intellectual conformity as have their elders. Many university or college students have not degenerated as yet to the state of the average American who reacts to new ideas much like he reacts to the onset of Asian flu and who denounces all critical thinking concerning fundamental assumptions as sheer cynicism. The youthfulness of students, in short, argues a certain plasticity, a willingness to change. At least occasionally many students, however vaguely, recognize their immaturity in Kant's sense of the term. They know they possess the understanding but need the courage and resolution to use their reason "without the guidance of another."

Students tend to distrust authority, be it political, moral, aesthetic, scientific, religious, parental, academic, or that of the adolescent herd. Chaotic visions and confused indignations afflict them. However dimly and erratically, students want "enlightenment," intellectual independence; at least the best among them in their best moments desire to be bold and skeptical, not timid and believing. Therefore, however unconsciously, they desire to philosophize, to clarify and criticize basic assumptions in all fields, to free themselves from conventional pictures of reality by constructing new ones and defending them by argument.

Philosophy has performed many different functions in the course of its long history. Certainly not the least of these in importance has been the encouragement of intellectual independence. Because of their advocacy and practice of intellectual independence, philosophers again and again have appeared dangerous to their fellows and as a consequence have been persecuted by them. The ancient Greeks invented philosophy as they did so many other cultural disciplines. The ancient Greeks also were typical of "good" citizens in all times and places for they distrusted many of their best men, considered them subversive, persecuted them, exiled them, and even executed some of them. All educated people know the fate of Socrates, who questioned the soundness of conventional morality, ironically exposing the bogus "wisdom" of politicians, priests, and prominent citizens, and casting doubt on the superior virtue of democracy. Socrates attempted to substitute the authority of reason in place of the authority of tradition, myth, and majority opinion and to quicken the torpid intellectual life of the community by his probing questions.

However, the task of intellectual vivification to which Socrates devoted himself must be undertaken anew by every generation. Contemporary "good" citizens closely resemble those of ancient Athens in their distrust of unconventional ideas and their opposition to the assertion of intellectual independence. A prominent American educator recently declared:

> There seems to be nothing in the study of chemistry that makes you feel like a superior order of being, but you study Plato and you begin to believe

you're a philosopher—and a philosopher should be king. This is a dangerous trend, and it jeopardizes the democratic principles on which this country was founded.[1]

In the *Apology,* Plato represents his teacher, Socrates, defending himself
against the charges of corrupting the youth and introducing strange gods by
saying:

> Men of Athens, I honor and love you; but I shall obey God rather than you,
> and while I have life and strength I shall never cease from the practice and
> teaching of philosophy, exhorting anyone whom I meet and saying to him
> after my manner: You, my friend,—a citizen of the great and mighty and
> wise city of Athens,—are you not ashamed of heaping up the greatest
> amount of money and honor and reputation, and caring so little about wis-
> dom and truth and the greatest improvement of the soul, which you never
> regard or heed at all?

This is the most fundamental contemporary issue confronting every thinking individual personally: Are you on the side of Socrates or on that of his accusers?

The argument against the development of intellectual independence claims that
it will result in anarchy, destroying law and order. Socrates, on the contrary,
contended that a society where reason is sovereign will be more stable and just
than any other because such a rational collective life will rest on knowledge, not
on ignorance, fear, fraud, and force. Socrates further seemed to hold that truth
is consistent and unchanging. Therefore, to the extent that men know the truth,
they will agree. Men disagree through ignorance. Hence, the ideal or "real"
community, being based on full knowledge of all the truth, would be free of internal dissension and perfectly stable, having taken on the characteristics of
truth. The hegemony of reason will produce the only enduring social unity and
harmony, the only "real" law and order. Appeal to authorities other than reason
produces only a temporary and therefore illusory simulacrum of social order and
harmony. Socrates was tried and condemned to death for introducing strange
gods and corrupting the youth. He was found guilty by a jury of his peers and
probably rightly so. Reason is a strange god and corrupts provincial ignorance
and complacency.

This book of introductory readings in philosophy now in your hands has been
designed in the spirit of Socrates. The readings have been selected and arranged in order to encourage the student to use his own reason. Socrates
counted men and women truly his followers, not because they agreed with his
conclusions but because they dared to "follow the argument wherever it may
lead." The son of a father who was a stonecutter and of a mother who practiced the trade of midwife, Socrates neglected stonecutting, in which he had

---

[1] Dr. Samuel I. Hayakawa, "The Playboy Panel: Student Revolt," *Playboy,* September 1969, p. 98. Reprinted
by permission of *Playboy.*

been trained, and in a sense adopted the vocation of his mother. Socrates called himself an intellectual midwife, helping others to give birth to the new ideas with which their minds already were pregnant. Nearly every day Socrates could be found in the busy public square of ancient Athens, where all day long he buttonholed the rich politicians, poets, generals, businessmen, actors, philosophers, and all the Rotarians and intellectuals and "beautiful people," all the shrewd old men of power and the clever young men of ambition of his time, and asked them searching questions about what they were doing; what they wanted; what they believed; and why they were doing, wanting, believing it. As the great and powerful, the talented, the learned, the old, and the young passed by, Socrates asked them: What do you really want? Riches, power, happiness, knowledge? Is the Good pleasure and Evil pain? Does might really make right? What is love and what is worthy of love? Should children always obey their parents? How do you know your teacher really is wise? What can be taught and learned and what not? Can anything be taught? Who should rule the city: politicians, wealthy families, soldiers, intellectuals, artists? Do the gods really exist? Is there a life after death? Or is religion a confidence game perpetrated by clever priests? Who knows the truth: philosophers, inspired artists, men of practical experience, or drug-crazed oracles? And what is "truth"? In short, Socrates put the questions asked by intelligent, sensitive, civilized people—the questions that always occur to young people—indeed, many of the questions no doubt formulated at one time or another by you, the reader.

It has been well said that philosophy begins in the conflict of opinions. Each part of this book contains a section of readings dealing with certain contemporary issues, with some of the questions asked and discussed in the public life of America today: Can men be made happy by science? Is anyone ever responsible for his acts and deserving of punishment? How do we distinguish science from pseudoscience? Do we live forever or rot when we are dead? Do we need religion to lead a meaningful life? Should we give creationism equal time with evolution in American school curricula? Are men merely complex machines? Can we have a sound sexual morality? Should society promote greater equality, or should it encourage excellence?

The selections chosen for each contemporary issue clearly conflict with one another. Both affirmative and negative sides of the debate are presented on each issue, and every effort has been made by the editors to find equally powerful and persuasive statements both pro and con.

Yet whatever the issue, as men reflect and by argument are driven back to question their fundamental assumptions, as the protagonists discover they were ignorant of their own ignorance, as they realize they know least about that of which they talk most, then debate and discussion mature into philosophical inquiry. Etymologically, *philosophy* means "love of wisdom." This definition may satisfy the beginning student temporarily. However, more probing queries soon come to mind. What is love? What is wisdom? Does Jean-Paul Sartre really love wisdom? Was William James really wise? Traditionally, philosophy has been surveyed into such general fields as ethics; metaphysics; logic; epistemology; and, more recently, aesthetics or philosophy of art. Library catalogues still divide philosophy in this manner. Yet this approach with its dry and abstract schematism sheds little illumination for the unskilled in philosophy. The editors judge that students will derive the most enlightenment from first encountering philosophy as a congeries of problems or issues invariably met by men when they no longer are content to reflect superficially on human life. As long as men are certain that their fundamental assumptions in morality, politics, religion, art, science, and other cultural enterprises are true and complete, they do not philosophize. If they argue, it is only over matters of detail, over the application to particular cases of commonly accepted principles. In our revolutionary era, no such complacency remains honorable for intelligent and informed people. The Contemporary Issues sections in each part of the book show men being led to question their fundamental assumptions. Grouped with the contemporary issues selections are readings scrutinizing some of the relevant philosophical issues all too often left implicit. One cannot sensibly discuss whether or not religion is necessary to a meaningful life until he has settled for himself the question of whether or not religion is an illusion. How can men be praised or blamed if they are not morally responsible but are complex machines? Is capitalism necessary to preserve our political freedom? Why should we elect car salesmen, country lawyers, chicken farmers, real estate agents, and other such people ignorant of science to the United States Congress if all genuine knowledge comes from science? Faced with questions such as these, one may ignore them and play golf, make money, watch television—in short, act the typical middle-class citizen of the world and be content to be a fatuous, go-getting cipher. Or he may pluck up his courage and think for himself, follow his own reason, and philosophize.

Intellectual independence does not necessitate the repudiation of all tradition. Ample and venerable precedent exists for inaugurating a new enterprise with ten commandments. Here are ten commandments for beginning philosophizers written down by Bertrand Russell, one of the most intellectually independent persons of our day:

1 Do not feel certain of anything.

2 Do not think it worthwhile to produce belief by concealing evidence, for the evidence is sure to come to light.

3 Never try to discourage thinking, for you are sure to succeed.

4 When met with opposition, even if it should be from your husband or your children, endeavour to overcome it by argument and not by authority, for a victory dependent upon authority is unreal and illusory.

5   Have no respect for the authority of others, for there are always contrary authorities to be found.

6   Do not use power to suppress opinions you think pernicious, for if you do the opinions will suppress you.

7   Do not fear to be eccentric in opinion, for every opinion now accepted was once eccentric.

8   Find more pleasure in intelligent dissents than in passive agreement, for, if you value intelligence as you should, the former implies a deeper agreement than the latter.

9   Be scrupulously truthful, even when truth is inconvenient, for it is more inconvenient when you try to conceal it.

10   Do not feel envious of the happiness of those who live in a fool's paradise, for only a fool will think that it is happiness.[2]

---

[2] Bertrand Russel, *The Independent,* June 1965, p. 4. Reprinted by permission of *The Independent.*

What Philosophy Can Be

1. Philosophy: The Guide of Life   C. J. Ducasse

Curt John Ducasse (1881–1969), born in France and educated in the United States, was a distinguished American philosopher and teacher of philosophy. His interests and writings ranged widely from philosophy of religion, metaphysics, and aesthetics to psychical research. He is the author of numerous books, including *Philosophy as a Science: Its Matter and Method; Nature, Mind, and Death;* and *A Critical Examination of the Belief in a Life After Death.*

In *The History of Phi Beta Kappa* by Oscar M. Voorhees we read that *Philosophia Biou Kubernetes*, the Greek phrase that gives the Society its name, was "formed and adopted" by John Heath, a student of Greek classics at the College of William and Mary, on whose initiative the Phi Beta Kappa Society was founded in 1776. This phrase—philosophy, or love of wisdom, the guide of life—and the Latin phrase *Societas Philosophiae*, the initials of which appear on the reverse of the Phi Beta Kappa key, express the five founders' conviction about the right role of philosophy in life.

But although taking philosophy as one's guide through life seemed to John Heath and his fellow students an eminently wise resolve, today the perspective in which educated people view human life is different from that of 1776; and members of Phi Beta Kappa may find themselves challenged to give reasons for adopting philosophy as the guide of life in preference to religion or to science, either of which today enjoys far more general prestige than does philosophy. I propose to consider those reasons here.

Why Not Science as Guide?

At the time of the founding of Phi Beta Kappa any suggestion that man should take science rather than philosophy as his guide in the conduct of his life would have been hardly intelligible. The investigation of puzzling natural phenomena was not commonly thought to be a potential source of counsels for living. The justification, if any, for studying the mysteries of nature was held to lie only in such gratification of idle curiosity as it might yield to the few impractical persons who engaged in that study. The attitude then prevalent towards their research is well exemplified by the reaction that greeted the first observations of electric

From *The Key Reporter*, Vol. XXIII, No. 2 (January 1958). Reprinted with the permission of *The Key Reporter* and Phi Beta Kappa.

current, made about 1786 by Luigi Galvani, then professor of physiology at the University of Bologna.

The story is that his wife was ill with tuberculosis; and her physician having prescribed a broth made with frogs' legs to give her strength, Galvani was getting some ready for cooking one day, sitting on his balcony. As he proceeded he suspended each pair of legs from the balcony's railing by a copper hook; and he noticed that whenever any of the legs so suspended happened to touch the iron uprights, the leg muscles contracted sharply.

This curious little fact, however, had no discernible utility, nor did it fit in with the scientific knowledge possessed in his day. Hence nobody took seriously what he reported. "I am attacked," he complained in 1792, "by two quite opposite sects—the learned and the ignorant. The ones and the others laugh at me and call me the frogs' dancing master. Yet I know that I have discovered one of the forces of nature."

Other reports of facts or theories belying what W. F. G. Swann has called "the common sense of a given epoch" have encountered a similar attitude, which has been a persistent feature of the history of science. Nevertheless science developed rapidly during the nineteenth century and has continued to do so at an even faster pace in the twentieth. The result of this has been, in the words of Sir William Dampier, that "the whole conception of the natural Universe has been changed by the recognition that man, subject to the same physical laws and processes as the world around him, cannot be considered separately from that world, and that scientific methods of observation, induction, deduction and experiment are applicable, not only to the original subject matter of pure science, but to nearly all the many and varied fields of human thought and activity."[1]

Furthermore, the fruits of pure scientific research have in many cases turned out to be applicable to the solution of concrete practical problems; and in civilized countries these practical applications have immeasurably improved the material conditions of human life. That science has put into the hands of man power undreamed of before over the processes of nature, and enabled him to utilize her forces for attainment of his purposes, is today evident to everybody, and accounts for the enormous prestige science now enjoys.

On the other hand, the fact is now becoming all too evident that the ledger of scientific progress has a debit as well as a credit side. The power that scientific knowledge brings has indeed made possible the cure or prevention of many diseases; it has provided new and highly efficient means of production, communication, and transportation; and it has given man all the convenient gadgets on which he is today so dependent. But at the same time it has complicated his life, robbed it in large measure of the joy of craftsmanship, multiplied its needs, and brought it new diseases and ghastly perils. The natural sciences and the might they have brought to man are in themselves wholly neutral as regards values; they lend themselves equally to the efficient implementation of good and of evil purposes.

[1] Sir William Dampier, *A History of Science* (New York, Macmillan, 1936) p. 217.

But whereas in the last hundred years the natural sciences have made more progress than in the preceding thousands, the soul of man, on the contrary, has during that time undergone no great change. Some customs and institutions have altered, but the passions that are the main springs of human conduct have remained much the same. Men are better informed today but probably not much more intelligent than before; their economic standard of living has risen; but when occasion offers, they exhibit a nature hardly less selfish or brutal or greedy than of old. They are not fundamentally much more self-disciplined, honest, kindly, or wise than in earlier ages. Measured in terms of spiritual maturity, the average man today is still a child. And it is in the hands of that child that the natural sciences, almost overnight, have placed powers that in their magnitude and possibilities of evil, no less than of good, are to those man had earlier as dynamite is to the strength of bare hands. Great nations have risen in the past only to fall victim to destructive forces within them. But today it is the whole of life on earth, or even the very earth itself, the continued existence of which is in danger.

Obviously, then, if man is to be saved, what he now needs is not more of the power the natural sciences bring, but more wisdom wherewith to direct the use he makes of the powers he already has.

Why Not Religion as Guide?

For such direction, and for the serenity that obedience to it brings, men have traditionally turned to religion. But to many people nowadays religion no longer carries the authority it did in earlier times.

A number of factors are responsible for this. As a result of efficient means of communication and transportation, men—and especially educated men—are better acquainted than in earlier times with the religions of mankind other than their own. A person with the wider perspective of such acquaintance sees that the dogmas of the other religions are different from, and sometimes irreconcilable with, those of his own; and yet that the needs that turn men to religion are on the whole satisfied by the other religions for their devotees as effectively as they are satisfied for him by his own.

Furthermore, he realizes that if he had been born and brought up in a different part of the world, his religion would almost automatically have been the one that happened to prevail in that particular region. And this thrusts upon him the question whether the location of a man's birthplace determines not merely which religion he *will believe,* but also its *truth or falsity.* And of course merely to ask this question is virtually to answer it, especially in an epoch when so many of the traditional religious teachings about the place of the earth in the universe, the age and history of the earth, and the origin of life and of man, have been conclusively disproved by the knowledge that science has produced in lieu of mere creeds, pious opinions, and crude cosmological or biological fancies handed down by the religious traditions.

In the light of these and similar considerations, the articles of faith of the various religions—of one's own as well as of the others—are seen to be not statements known to be true or false, but essentially *psychological tools:* instruments mankind has automatically devised for performance of certain important social and personal functions. For religious dogmas to influence the conduct, the feelings, and the attitudes of men, they need not be true but need only be firmly *believed.*

Like other tools, moreover, they can be used otherwise than in the beneficent manner that gives them worth. As we know only too well, bigoted men who were ignorant, stupid, arrogant, sadistic or perverse, and who happened to have power over their fellows, have too often interpreted the dogmas of their religion as warranting the wars, persecutions, and senseless cruelties that stain the histories of even the monotheistic, self-styled higher religions. This forces on modern man's attention the fact that the religions, like the sciences, are ambivalent and have a dark side; and hence that the teachings contained in their various sacred books or promulgated by their officials cannot be uncritically assumed to supply ready-made the wise guidance that man so direly needs. Rather, those teachings have to be carefully sifted and the wisdom or folly of each intelligently appraised.

How About Philosophy?

And this brings us back to philosophy. Does it offer a better prospect than either science or religion of furnishing man with the wisdom he needs?

In the popular opinion at least, hardly so. For philosophy is commonly reputed to be nearly the most nebulous and impractical thing there is. Yet if philosophy were really so remote from practical affairs, it would be hard to understand either the execration or the veneration in which various philosophers have at times been held. Why, for instance, should Socrates, Hypatia, and Giordano Bruno have been put to death, Plato sold into slavery, and Campanella imprisoned, for voicing the philosophical opinions they held? On the other side of the picture, why should the same Plato have sometimes been referred to as "the divine Plato," and Kant as "the immortal Kant"? Why have their writings and those of other great philosophers continued to be read and prized through the centuries?

The answer, I believe, lies in the fact that philosophy, despite the seeming idleness of some of its technicalities, really has practical import and indeed in this respect may ultimately outrank most things of more obvious utility.

The nature of the practical value peculiar to philosophy will become evident if we try to gain a clearer conception than is common of what philosophy and philosophical reflection in fact are.

Philosophical reflection is not an activity indulged in only by specialists called philosophers who allegedly live in architectural monstrosities known as ivory towers. Just as each of us at times engages casually in horticulture or medicine or carpentry without special training, so practically all of us on certain occasions spontaneously occupy ourselves with philosophical questions.

We may, for example, read in the newspapers of a child born hopelessly malformed and defective, but who, if operated upon at once, might nonetheless be kept alive. And we may read further that the physician in charge, realizing that the child's life could not be other than a grievous burden to himself, to his parents, and to society, refrained from operating and allowed the child to die. Then, in letters from readers to the editors of newspapers all over the country, controversy rages about whether the physician's action was morally right or morally wrong. And even if we do not ourselves take active part in them, we too form opinions on the question.

In such a controversy the participants do not merely state their moral appraisal of the physician's course. They also give reasons of one kind or another to support the validity of their judgment. And if these reasons are in turn challenged, each participant brings forth considerations he believes adequate to vindicate the validity of his reasons.

The reasons, and the reasons for the reasons, that are thus appealed to as grounds for endorsing or condemning the physician's action, constitute a moral philosophy, or at least a fragment of one. And the mental activity of searching for those reasons, and of then so editing them as to purge them of the inconsistencies or exaggerations or errors that opponents were able to point out, constitute philosophizing, or philosophical reflection.

In this example the issue is a moral one, and the philosophy constructed on the spur of the occasion by a participant is therefore, as far as it goes, a moral philosophy: that is, a theory of the nature of the difference between moral right and wrong, and of the nature of the situations to which appraisal in terms of morality and immorality is congruous. But similar controversies, or indeed doubts within one person's mind, arise about issues of other kinds: about the merits of certain works of art, for example, or about educational issues, or about the sufficiency of the evidence offered as basis for a given assertion, and so on. The fragmentary philosophies similarly improvised on such occasions are then a philosophy of art, a philosophy of education, or a philosophy of knowledge. And there can be no doubt that, on the occasions impelling us to engage in such reflection, a judgment shaped by the conclusions reached in that reflective manner is likely to be wiser than would be one made without it.

Practical problems of the type illustrated induce philosophical reflection automatically and cannot be solved without it if the solution is to be rational, not arbitrary. Let us call them *practical problems of appraisal.* They do not arise from ignorance or misinformation about the objective circumstances of the action or thing appraised. The disagreement concerning the moral rightness or wrongness of the physician's inaction did not arise from a difference of opinion about the possibility of the child's being cured eventually if he had lived. If this was the issue, it was then medical, not philosophical.

A divergence of appraisals is philosophical only if the conflicting judgments are of strictly the same action or thing in the same circumstances. When this is the case, the divergence of appraisals has one of two sources. One is inadequate understanding of the criterion of moral rightness or wrongness, or, as the case may be, of truth or falsity, of justice or injustice, of beauty or ugliness, of wisdom or folly, and so forth. The ordinary ingenuous understanding we all have of the meaning of such predicates is good enough to enable us to apply them without doubt or dispute in stereotyped cases. Hence in such cases problems of the type in view do not arise. If one does arise, it is because the case concerned is not a stereotyped one and therefore requires a more precise, analytical understanding of the meaning of the value-predicate employed, in order to reach a responsible, not arbitrary, appraisal. One needs to know, for example, precisely what constitutes the moral rightness or wrongness of an action.

The other possible source of divergence of appraisals is uncertainty about the congruity of appraising the action in terms of the proposed value-predicate. For example, could the act of rubbing one's chin in ordinary circumstances be, without incongruity, judged either morally right or morally wrong? What characteristics must something have in order that it may appropriately be appraised in moral terms, rather than in, perhaps, aesthetic terms?

Philosophical reflection is the only process by which divergence of appraisal arising from either of these two sources can be responsibly removed. If one engages in philosophical reflection under pressure of immediate need to solve a particular practical problem of appraisal, such reflection will inevitably be hasty and relatively uncritical. But the persons called philosophers make it their life work to reflect on the meaning of the various value-predicates and on the kind of subject that is alone congruously appraisable in terms of each. They attempt to purge such reflection of the narrowness and imprecision that are the unavoidable defects of the extempore philosophical reflection we all undertake as occasion compels. Not only does the philosopher strive to carry on his reflections in a thoroughly methodical manner; he also strives to make them comprehensive rather than particularistic. That is, his business as a philosopher is not to solve himself the many practical problems of appraisal. It is, on the one hand, to clarify, in the two directions described, the various value-concepts that enter into the formulation of the problems; and on the other, to specify the kinds of empirical knowledge that must be obtained in order to discern whether or not a given appraisal is valid in a given case. Actually to obtain that empirical knowledge is not the business of the philosopher; it is the business of the particular person who is confronted with a particular practical problem of appraisal.

Clarification of the meaning of terms, however, whether in general or in the particular case of terms of appraisal, is a semantic task. Consequently the question immediately suggests itself whether philosophical reflection, in undertaking it, is not concerning itself with mere words, and therefore, presumably, with something of no great importance.

The answer is that to speak of "mere words" is much like speaking of "mere dynamite." For although words do not in themselves control the processes of inanimate nature, they do control the thoughts, the feelings, and the acts of men—initiating and shaping them, or inhibiting them. In men's dealings with one another and in the individual's dealings with himself, words are analogous in function and in importance to the insignificant-looking switches that govern the operations of giant machines in industry.

Hence it is of the greatest moment for man to know just where the psychological wires lead from the verbal switches; for the terrible thing about words is that to a great extent they cause and shape the acts of men, whether or not they really fit the things to which men apply them, and whether or not men understand their meaning correctly. Common sayings such as "Give a dog a bad name, and you can hang him," or "Slander on, some of it always sticks," testify to this fact. Among us today, for example, to call a man a Communist is to damage his reputation even if it is not true that he is a Communist, and even if the persons who hear him so called have but the vaguest idea of what communism is. And, similarly, the most potent of the weapons Communists have employed is perversion of the meaning of words: calling "liberation" what is in fact enslavement, for example.

Thus when the words we use do not fit or are ill-understood, the feelings, the beliefs, and the courses of action they nonetheless generate cheat our aims and stultify us. This is especially true when the words concerned are value-predicates, for a man's course is shaped at innumerable points by evaluative statements. Whether he formulates these for himself or accepts them from others ready-made, they determine the basic policies, the tactics, and the strategic decisions of his life. This vast power of language is what gives outstanding practical importance to clear, analytical knowledge of just which things our substantives denote, and just what characters our adjectives predicate of the things to which we apply them.

Love of Wisdom as the Guide of Life

In conclusion let us consider briefly the term "wisdom" and note the light that philosophical analysis of its meaning throws on Phi Beta Kappa's counsel to take philosophy—that is, love of wisdom—as the guide of life.

What exactly, then, is wisdom? It consists in *knowledge of what in given circumstances would on the whole be the best thing for a person with given equipment to do.*

Thus the counsel to make love of wisdom the guide of one's life packs together four distinct recommendations, which may be separately stated.

One is that, when a person attempts to reach a wise decision about a difficult practical problem, he should inform himself as accurately and completely as is practicable about its *objective circumstances.*

Another is that, with similar care, he should take stock of *the powers at his disposal:* on the one hand, of the diverse means he happens to have, any one of which would enable him to achieve a particular end he might decide on; and on the other, of the diverse ends, any one of which he could achieve with the particular stock of means he commands.

The third recommendation is that he should then consider *the various kinds of value*—positive and negative, intrinsic and instrumental—which, for the persons who would be affected, would follow from each of the courses of action open to him in the circumstances of the case, with only the particular powers he has.

And the fourth recommendation is that, when he has thus considered as well as he can all the values at stake, he should then choose the course of action that *on the whole is best,* or *least bad:* the course that, *everything considered,* will probably yield the maximum total positive value, or the minimum total negative value.

Needless to say, this choice will in many cases be anything but easy or confident. And the person who makes it may well come eventually to judge it to have been mistaken. But this will be the judgment of the wiser person he will then have become by learning from his mistakes. At the time a decision has to be made, however, no way exists for any man to make a wiser one than by the procedure just described. For "wisdom"— so much of it as in practice happens to be obtainable by a given person at a given time—*means* what emerges out of that procedure.

Finally, under the shelter of the preceding elucidations I shall venture to state as a sharp choice what I take to be the gist of Phi Beta Kappa's advice to its initiates. And to formulate it I shall borrow the sharp words of the title of a book on a somewhat similar theme, written by an Australian journalist.

That sharp choice, so sharply worded, is *Think—or be damned!*[2]

---

[2] Brian Penton, *Think—or be damned* (Sydney, Angus and Robertson, 1944).

One: Freedom or Determinism

Introduction

As currently discussed, the issue of whether man's behavior is free or determined has been generated by the development of the natural sciences since the sixteenth century. A basic assumption of the evolving sciences was universal causation, i.e., that every event has a cause. Further, it was thought that events occurred in orderly patterns, which could be formulated as causal or natural laws. On the basis of these laws and knowledge of the actual causes at work, accurate predictions would be made. In principle, any event could be predicted; it was only the lack of knowledge of the laws or the present causes that limited prediction. The theory asserting universal causation and total predictability traditionally has been called *determinism.*

For the determinist, human actions are events as predictable as any other type of event. Just as the behavior of water heated to 212 degrees can be predicted, so, in principle, can the behavior of a person given a million dollars. The determinist would admit that, at the moment, the latter sort of prediction cannot be made reliably because we lack the necessary exact laws of human behavior. Someday, however, the social sciences may find such laws, and correct predictions will become possible.

Determinism is rejected by a group of theorists holding a position called *libertarianism.* Although libertarians present a number of specific criticisms of determinism, most of these objections are concerned primarily with what appears to be a consequence of that position. Libertarians contend that if all actions are the result of causes (and those causes of other causes, and so on), then no actions are ones for which anyone can be held morally responsible. The robber sticking up a bank today does so as a result of a series of causes that can be traced back prior to his birth. His behavior results from such factors as his education, a lack of parental love, and the nutritional quality of the food he ate as a child. In turn, these causes flow from the kind of education his parents received, their lack of parental love, and other such elements. How can the robber justifiably be held responsible or blamed for his behavior? He could not help the way his parents treated him nor the manner in which they were educated. For the libertarian, to be considered responsible for an act is to be free to have acted otherwise; but such freedom apparently cannot exist when all human actions are the predictable outcome of various causes. In "Freedom of Choice and Human Responsibility," Corliss Lamont presents a detailed defense of libertarianism. He maintains that we have an immediate, powerful, common-sense intuition that we are free. While such an intuition could be false, it puts the burden of proving that it is so on the determinists. Also, Lamont maintains that determinism must be considered false because if it were true it would imply that all deliberation is illusory since one never can choose. To maintain that all our deliberation never results in any real choice seems, to Lamont, absurd. *Hard determinism,* a major version of determinism, denies, as does libertarianism, that moral responsibility is compatible with universal causation. Unlike libertarians, however, hard determinists often maintain that the knowledge that no one is morally responsible provides the basis for a satisfactory personal life as well as the ground for a more rational and humane system of interpersonal relationships. For them, the realization that man is completely determined produces a liberating cessation of worry about the future (since it is out of one's control) and the fortitude to accept whatever befalls one. In dealing with others, one realizes the irrationality of concern about blame, merit, or retribution. In his article "The Delusion of Free Will," Robert Blatchford presents the hard determinists' position. He argues both that there is no free will and that the traditional notions of responsibility are unacceptable. All human actions are ruled by heredity and environment; and, since we are not responsible for either of these, all blame is unjust. Blatchford argues that if the will were free, prediction on the basis of environment and training would be impossible. But since in many cases we can make very reliable predictions about future behavior, free will cannot be true. Blatchford also doubts that most supporters of free will really believe it. If they did, would they try so hard to secure a good environment for their children? The concern for the child's environment indicates a belief that it is of great importance in molding the man.

Not all philosophers have been willing to accept the libertarian claim that determinism erases moral responsibility. Some, defending *soft determinism,* maintain that people can be morally responsible even though their behavior is determined. One argument soft determinists frequently use holds that a person's behavior is free if it is not the result of any compulsion. If you go to the movies because you wish to and are not pressured or coerced by anyone to do so, then your action ordinarily would be called a free one. Of course your wish is the result of numerous causes swarming in your background. Thus, we have an action that is determined and yet called "free." The soundness of this soft determinist argument depends on the cogency of the analysis of the meaning of "free." W. T. Stace defends soft determinism in his article "The Problem of Free Will."

A number of important issues has arisen as a result of different views regarding determinism. One often-debated issue concerns the control of human behavior. Determinists see enormous possibilities in directing the development of man through the study of the hereditary and environmental factors influencing behavior. Many look forward to the day when the various social sciences will have formulated laws that allow us to produce happier and "better" people. The selections from B. F. Skinner's *Walden Two* give us a famous psychologist's view of an ideal society possibly resulting from a greater knowledge of human conditioning. Skinner argues that through the application of various conditioning and reinforcement techniques, we can produce people who have those psychological characteristics necessary for a productive and viable society. In the selection, he shows how children might be conditioned to have self-control and a large degree of tolerance to annoying situations. It should be kept in mind that Skinner does not desire to manipulate men otherwise free; rather, he wants to change present causal determinants for ones productive of more capable and happy human beings.

Libertarians maintain that precise laws of human behavior will always elude investigators because such behavior, being undetermined, is unpredictable. Other philosophers think human behavior may be controllable someday, but they fear the manner in which such power might be used. In "Ignoble Utopias," Joseph Wood Krutch argues that even if a society like Walden Two were possible, it would be morally unpalatable because such a community would end in a dictatorship capable of manipulating men in any way the rulers desired. He feels that before any techniques are tried, there should first be some agreement on the goals sought. But perhaps more worrisome to Krutch is the conviction that, if conditioning procedures are successful, all human thinking as we have known it will come to an end. Unlike Thomas Huxley, whom he quotes, Krutch is appalled at the prospect that man might be turned into a robot. Skinner, who feels that Krutch is really fearful of new scientific developments, sees no virtue in ignorance. New scientific knowledge can help us better understand man and design a world that satisifes man's needs. Rejection of science would mean the end of our only hope to build a better world.

A second frequently debated problem arising from the conflict between determinists and libertarians involves the proper treatment of criminals. Many determinists argue that any punishment resting on notions of moral blame, retribution, and desert should be replaced by a treatment of criminals that recognizes their lack of responsibility. Thus, such advocates often defend changing the character of society or rehabilitating criminals rather than any sort of traditional punishment. In "An Address Delivered to the Prisoners in the Chicago County Jail," Clarence Darrow maintains that criminals are no more responsible for being in a jail than honest men are for being outside of one. Since certain factors in our environment cause crime, he is convinced crime would be eliminated if the environment were suitably changed. A more equitable distribution of the wealth would, he believes, eliminate men's desire to commit crimes, and so, the need for any jails.

C. S. Lewis, in his article "The Humanitarian Theory of Punishment," asserts that the criminals are responsible for their actions and thus deserve punishment. He opposes both those who favor replacing punishment with rehabilitation and those who would use punishment to influence people's future behavior. He believes that the methods used to rehabilitate criminals can be harsher and more inhuman than traditional penalties, and that the use of punishment merely to influence people's behavior is open to a variety of moral abuses. He champions punishment on the basis of desert because only this position avoids morally unacceptable consequences and preserves the criminal's dignity as a responsible agent.

Hard Determinism

2. The Delusion of Free Will   Robert Blatchford

Robert Blatchford (1851–1943) was an English determinist, agnostic, socialist, and crusading social reformer, whose writings exerted great influence and were translated into many languages.

The free will delusion has been a stumbling block in the way of human thought for thousands of years. Let us try whether common sense and common knowledge cannot remove it.

Free will is a subject of great importance to us in this case; and it is one we must come to with our eyes wide open and our wits wide awake; not because it is very difficult, but because it has been tied and twisted into a tangle of Gordian knots by twenty centuries full of wordy but unsuccessful philosophers.

The free will party claim that man is responsible for his acts, because his will is free to choose between right and wrong.

We reply that the will is not free, and that if it were free man could not know right from wrong until he was taught.

As to the knowledge of good and evil the free will party will claim that conscience is an unerring guide. But I have already proved that conscience does not and cannot tell us what is right and what is wrong; it only reminds us of the lessons we have learnt as to right and wrong.

The "still small voice" is not the voice of God: it is the voice of heredity and environment.

And now to the freedom of the will.

When a man says his will is free, he means that it is free of all control or interference: that it can over-rule heredity and environment.

We reply that the will is ruled by heredity and environment.

The cause of all the confusion on this subject may be shown in a few words.

When the free will party say that man has a free will, they mean that he is free to act as he chooses to act.

There is no need to deny that. *But what causes him to choose?*

That is the pivot upon which the whole discussion turns.

The free will party seem to think of the will as something independent of the man, as something outside him. They seem to think that the will decides without the control of the man's reason.

From *Not Guilty* by Robert Blatchford, Albert and Charles Boni, Inc., 1913. Albert and Charles Boni, Inc.

If that were so, it would not prove the man responsible. "The will" would be responsible, and not the man. It would be as foolish to blame a man for the act of a "free" will, as to blame a horse for the action of its rider.

But I am going to prove to my readers, by appeals to their common sense and common knowledge, that the will is not free; and that it is ruled by heredity and environment.

To begin with, the average man will be against me. He knows that he chooses between two courses every hour, and often every minute, and he thinks his choice is free. But that is a delusion: his choice is not free. He can choose, and does choose. But he can only choose as his heredity and his environment cause him to choose. He never did choose and never will choose except as his heredity and his environment—his temperament and his training—cause him to choose. And his heredity and his environment have fixed his choice before he makes it.

The average man says "I know that I can act as I wish to act." But what causes him to wish?

The free will party say, "We know that a man can and does choose between two acts." But what settles the choice?

There is a cause for every wish, a cause for every choice; and every cause of every wish and choice arises from heredity, or from environment.

For a man acts always from temperament, which is heredity, or from training, which is environment.

And in cases where a man hesitates in his choice between two acts, the hesitation is due to a conflict between his temperament and his training, or, as some would express it, "between his desire and his conscience."

A man is practising at a target with a gun, when a rabbit crosses his line of fire. The man has his eye and his sights on the rabbit, and his finger on the trigger. The man's will is free. If he press the trigger the rabbit will be killed.

Now, how does the man decide whether or not he shall fire? He decides by feeling, and by reason.

He would like to fire, just to make sure that he could hit the mark. He would like to fire, because he would like to have the rabbit for supper. He would like to fire, because there is in him the old, old hunting instinct, to kill.

But the rabbit does not belong to him. He is not sure that he will not get into trouble if he kills it. Perhaps—if he is a very uncommon kind of man—he feels that it would be cruel and cowardly to shoot a helpless rabbit.

Well. The man's will is free. He can fire if he likes: he can let the rabbit go if he likes. How will he decide? On what does his decision depend?

His decision depends upon the relative strength of his desire to kill the rabbit, and of his scruples about cruelty, and the law.

Not only that, but, if we knew the man fairly well, we could guess how his free will would act before it acted. The average sporting Briton would kill the rabbit. But we know that there are men who would on no account shoot any harmless wild creature.

Broadly put, we may say that the sportsman would will to fire, and that the humanitarian would not will to fire.

Now, as both their wills are free, it must be something outside the wills that makes the difference.

Well. The sportsman will kill, because he is a sportsman: the humanitarian will not kill, because he is a humanitarian.

And what makes one man a sportsman and another a humanitarian? Heredity and environment: temperament and training.

One man is merciful, another cruel, by nature; or one is thoughtful and the other thoughtless, by nature. That is a difference of heredity.

One may have been taught all his life that to kill wild things is "sport"; the other may have been taught that it is inhuman and wrong: that is a difference of environment.

Now, the man by nature cruel or thoughtless, who has been trained to think of killing animals as sport, becomes what we call a sportsman, because heredity and environment have made him a sportsman.

The other man's heredity and environment have made him a humanitarian.

The sportsman kills the rabbit, because he is a sportsman, and he is a sportsman because heredity and environment have made him one.

That is to say the "free will" is really controlled by heredity and environment.

Allow me to give a case in point. A man who had never done any fishing was taken out by a fisherman. He liked the sport, and for some months followed it eagerly. But one day an accident brought home to his mind the cruelty of catching fish with a hook, and he instantly laid down his rod, and never fished again.

Before the change he was always eager to go fishing if invited: after the change he could not be persuaded to touch a line. His will was free all the while. How was it that his will to fish changed to his will not to fish? It was the result of environment. He had learnt that fishing was cruel. This knowledge controlled his will.

But, it may be asked, how do you account for a man doing the thing he does not wish to do?

No man ever did a thing he did not wish to do. When there are two wishes the stronger rules.

Let us suppose a case. A young woman gets two letters by the same post; one is an invitation to go with her lover to a concert, the other is a request that she will visit a sick child in the slums. The girl is very fond of music, and is rather afraid of the slums. She wishes to go to the concert, and to be with her lover; she dreads the foul street and the dirty home, and shrinks from the risk of measles and fever. But she goes to the sick child, and she foregoes the concert. Why?

Because her sense of duty is stronger than her self-love.

Now, her sense of duty is partly due to her nature—that is, to her heredity—but it is chiefly due to environment. Like all of us, this girl was born without any kind of knowledge, and with only the rudiments of a conscience. But she has been well taught, and the teaching is part of her environment.

We may say that the girl is free to act as she chooses, but she *does* act as she has been *taught* that she *ought* to act. This teaching, which is part of her environment, controls her will.

We may say that a man is free to act as he chooses. He is free to act as *he* chooses, but *he* will choose as heredity and environment cause *him* to choose. For heredity and environment have made him that which he is.

A man is said to be free to decide between two courses. But really he is only free to decide in accordance with his temperament and training. . . .

Macbeth was ambitious; but he had a conscience. He wanted Duncan's crown; but he shrank from treason and ingratitude. Ambition pulled him one way, honour pulled him the other way. The opposing forces were so evenly balanced that he seemed unable to decide. Was Macbeth free to choose? To what extent was he free? He was so free that he could arrive at no decision, and it was the influence of his wife that turned the scale to crime.

Was Lady Macbeth free to choose? She did not hesitate. Because her ambition was so much stronger than her conscience that she never was in doubt. She chose as her over-powering ambition compelled her to choose.

And most of us in our decisions resemble either Macbeth or his wife. Either our nature is so much stronger than our training, or our training is so much stronger than our nature, that we decide for good or evil as promptly as stream decides to run down hill; or our nature and our training are so nearly balanced that we can hardly decide at all.

In Macbeth's case the contest is quite clear and easy to follow. He was ambitious, and his environment had taught him to regard the crown as a glorious and desirable possession. But environment had also taught him that murder, and treason, and ingratitude were wicked and disgraceful.

Had he never been taught these lessons, or had he been taught that gratitude was folly, that honour was weakness, and murder excusable when it led to power, he would not have hesitated at all. It was his environment that hampered his will. . . .

In all cases the action of the will depends upon the relative strength of two or more motives. The stronger motive decides the will; just as the heavier weight decides the balance of a pair of scales. . . .

How, then, can we believe that free will is outside and superior to heredity and environment? . . .

"What! Cannot a man be honest if he choose?" Yes, if he choose. But that is only another way of saying that he can be honest if his nature and his training lead him to choose honesty.

"What! Cannot I please myself whether I drink or refrain from drinking?" Yes. But that is only to say you will not drink because it pleases *you* to be sober. But it pleases another man to drink, because his desire for drink is strong, or because his self-respect is weak.

And you decide as you decide, and he decides as he decides, because you are *you,* and he is *he;* and heredity and environment made you both that which you are.

And the sober man may fall upon evil days, and may lose his self-respect, or find the burden of his trouble greater than he can bear, and may fly to drink for comfort, or oblivion, and may become a drunkard. Has it not been often so?

And the drunkard may, by some shock, or some disaster, or some passion, or some persuasion, regain his self-respect, and may renounce drink, and lead a sober and useful life. Has it not been often so?

And in both cases the freedom of the will is untouched: it is the change in the environment that lifts the fallen up, and beats the upright down.

We might say that a woman's will is free, and that she could, if she wished, jump off a bridge and drown herself. But she cannot *wish.* She is happy, and loves life, and dreads the cold and crawling river. And yet, by some cruel turn of fortune's wheel, she may become destitute and miserable; so miserable that she hates life and longs for death, and *then* she can jump into the dreadful river and die.

Her will was free at one time as at another. It is the environment that has wrought the change. Once she could not wish to die; now she cannot wish to live.

The apostles of free will believe that all men's wills are free. But a man can only will that which he is able to will. And one man is able to will that which another man is unable to will. To deny this is to deny the commonest and most obvious facts of life. . . .

We all know that we can foretell the action of certain men in certain cases, because we know the men.

We know that under the same conditions Jack Sheppard would steal and Cardinal Manning would not steal. We know that under the same conditions the sailor would flirt with the waitress, and the priest would not; that the drunkard would get drunk, and the abstainer would remain sober. We know that Wellington would refuse a bribe, that Nelson would not run away, that Buonaparte would grasp at power, that Abraham Lincoln would be loyal to his country, that Torquemada would not spare a heretic. Why? If the will is free, how can we be sure, before a test arises, how the will must act?

Simply because we know that heredity and environment have so formed and moulded men and women that under certain circumstances the action of their wills is certain.

Heredity and environment having made a man a thief, he will steal. Heredity and environment having made a man honest, he will not steal.

That is to say, heredity and environment have decided the action of the will, before the time has come for the will to act.

This being so—and we all know that it is so—what becomes of the sovereignty of the will?

Let any man that believes that he can "do as he likes" ask himself *why* he *likes,* and he will see the error of the theory of free will, and will understand why the will is the servant and not the master of the man; for the man is the product of heredity and environment, and these control the will.

As we want to get this subject as clear as we can, let us take one or two familiar examples of the action of the will.

Jones and Robinson meet and have a glass of whisky. Jones asks Robinson to have another. Robinson says, "no thank you, one is enough." Jones says, "all right: have another cigarette." Robinson takes the cigarette. Now, here we have a case where a man refuses a second drink, but takes a second smoke. Is it because he would like another cigarette, but would not like another glass of whisky? No. It is because he knows that it is *safer* not to take another glass of whisky.

How does he know that whisky is dangerous? He has learnt it—from his environment.

"But he *could* have taken another glass if he wished."

But he could not wish to take another, because there was something he wished more strongly—to be safe.

And why did he want to be safe? Because he had learnt—from his environment—that it was unhealthy, unprofitable, and shameful to get drunk. Because he had learnt—from his environment—that it is easier to avoid forming a bad habit than to break a bad habit when formed. Because he valued the good opinion of his neighbors, and also his position and prospects.

These feelings and this knowledge ruled his will, and caused him to refuse the second glass.

But there was no sense of danger, no well-learned lesson of risk to check his will to smoke another cigarette. Heredity and environment did not warn him against that. So, to please his friend, and himself, he accepted.

Now suppose Smith asks Williams to have another glass. Williams takes it, takes several, finally goes home—as he often goes home. Why?

Largely because drinking is a habit with him. And not only does the mind instinctively repeat an action, but, in the case of drink, a physical craving is set up, and the brain is weakened. It is easier to refuse the first glass than the second: easier to refuse the second than the third; and it is very much harder for a man to keep sober who has frequently got drunk.

So, when poor Williams has to make his choice, he has habit against him, he has a physical craving against him, and he has a weakened brain to think with.

"But. Williams could have refused the first glass."

No. Because in his case the desire to drink, or to please a friend, was stronger than his fear of the danger. Or he may not have been so conscious of the danger as Robinson was. He may not have been so well taught, or he may not have been so sensible, or he may not have been so cautious. So that his heredity and environment, his temperament and training, led him to take the drink, as surely as Robinson's heredity and environment led him to refuse it.

And now, it is my turn to ask a question. If the will is "free," if conscience is a sure guide, how is it that the free will and the conscience of Robinson caused him to keep sober, while the free will and the conscience of Williams caused him to get drunk?

Robinson's will was curbed by certain feelings which failed to curb the will of Williams. Because in the case of Williams the feelings were stronger on the other side.

It was the nature and the training of Robinson which made him refuse the second glass, and it was the nature and the training of Williams which made him drink the second glass.

What had free will to do with it?

We are told that *every* man has a free will, and a conscience.

Now, if Williams had been Robinson, that is to say if his heredity and his environment had been exactly like Robinson's, he would have done exactly as Robinson did.

It was because his heredity and environment were not the same that his act was not the same.

Both men had free wills. What made one do what the other refused to do?

Heredity and environment. To reverse their conduct we should have to reverse their heredity and environment. . . .

Two boys work at a hard and disagreeable trade. One leaves it, finds other work, "gets on," is praised for getting on. The other stays at the trade all his life, works hard all his life, is poor all his life, and is respected as an honest and humble working man; that is to say, he is regarded by society as Mr. Dorgan was regarded by Mr. Dooley—"he is a fine man, and I despise him."

What causes these two free wills to will so differently? One boy knew more than the other boy. He "knew better." All knowledge is environment. Both boys had free wills. It was in knowledge they differed: environment!

Those who exalt the power of the will, and belittle the power of environment, belie their words by their deeds.

For they would not send their children amongst bad companions or allow them to read bad books. They would not say the children have free will and therefore have power to take the good and leave the bad.

They know very well that evil environment has power to pervert the will, and that good environment has power to direct it properly.

They know that children may be made good or bad by good or evil training, and that the will follows the training.

That being so, they must also admit that the children of other people may be good or bad by training.

And if a child gets bad training, how can free will save it? Or how can it be blamed for being bad? It never had a chance to be good. That they know this is proved by their carefulness in providing their own children with better environment.

As I have said before, every church, every school, every moral lesson is a proof that preachers and teachers trust to good environment, and not to free will, to make children good.

In this, as in so many other matters, actions speak louder than words.

That, I hope, disentangles the many knots into which thousands of learned men have tied the simple subject of free will; and disposes of the claim that man is responsible because his will is free. But there is one other cause of error, akin to the subject, on which I should like to say a few words.

We often hear it said that a man is to blame for his conduct because "he knows better."

It is true that men do wrong when they know better. Macbeth "knew better" when he murdered Duncan. But it is true, also, that we often think a man "knows better," when he does not know better.

For a man cannot be said to know a thing until he believes it. If I am told that the moon is made of green cheese, it cannot be said that I *know* it to be made of green cheese.

Many moralists seem to confuse the words "to know" with the words "to hear."

Jones reads novels and plays opera music on Sunday. The Puritan says Jones "knows better," when he means that Jones has been told that it is wrong to do those things.

But Jones does not know that it is wrong. He has heard someone say that it is wrong, but does not believe it. Therefore it is not correct to say that he knows it.

And, again, as to that matter of belief. Some moralists hold that it is wicked not to believe certain things, and that men who do not believe those things will be punished.

But a man cannot believe a thing he is told to believe; he can only believe a thing which he *can* believe; and he can only believe that which his own reason tells him is true.

It would be no use asking Sir Roger Ball to believe that the earth is flat. He *could not* believe it.

It is no use asking an agnostic to believe the story of Jonah and the whale. He *could not* believe it. He might pretend to believe it. He might try to believe it. But his reason would not allow him to believe it.

Therefore it is a mistake to say that a man "knows better," when the fact is that he has been told "better" and cannot believe what he has been told.

That is a simple matter, and looks quite trivial; but how much ill-will, how much intolerance, how much violence, persecution, and murder have been caused by the strange idea that a man is wicked because *his* reason *cannot* believe that which to another man's reason [is] quite true.

Free will has no power over a man's belief. A man cannot believe by will, but only by conviction. A man cannot be forced to believe. You may threaten him, wound him, beat him, burn him; and he may be frightened, or angered, or pained; but he cannot *believe,* nor can he be made to believe. Until he is convinced.

Now, truism as it may seem, I think it necessary to say here that a man cannot be convinced by abuse, nor by punishment. He can only be convinced by *reason.*

Yes. If we wish a man to believe a thing, we shall find a few words of reason more powerful than a million curses, or a million bayonets. To burn a man alive for failing to believe that the sun goes round the world is not to convince him. The fire is searching, but it does not seem to him to be relevant to the issue. He never doubted that fire would burn; but prechance his dying eyes may see the sun sinking down into the west, as the world rolls on its axis. He dies in his belief. And knows no "better."

Libertarianism

3. Freedom of Choice and Human Responsibility   Corliss Lamont

Corliss Lamont (1902–) is an American philosopher whose philosophical defense of humanism has been combined with active participation in human affairs. Secretary-Treasurer of the *Journal of Philosophy,* he is also Chairman of the National Emergency Civil Liberties Committee.

It is my thesis that a man who is convinced he possesses freedom of choice or free will has a greater sense of responsibility than a person who thinks that total determinism rules the universe and human life. Determinism in the classic sense means that the flow of history, including all human choices and actions, is completely predetermined from the beginning of time. He who believes that "whatever is, was to be" can try to escape moral responsibility for wrongdoing by claiming that he was compelled to act as he did because it was predestined by the iron laws of cause and effect.

But if free choice truly exists at the moment of choosing, men clearly have full moral responsibility in deciding between two or more genuine alternatives, and the deterministic alibi has no weight. The heart of our discussion, then, lies in the question of whether free choice or universal determinism represents the truth. I shall try to summarize briefly the main reasons that point to the existence of free will.

First, there is the immediate, powerful, common-sense intuition shared by virtually all human beings that freedom of choice is real. This intuition seems as strong to me as the sensation of pleasure or pain; and the attempt of the determinists to explain the intuition away is as artificial as the Christian Scientist claim that pain is not real. The intuition of free choice does not, of course, in itself prove that such freedom exists, but that intuition is so strong that the burden of proof is on the determinists to show that it is based on an illusion.

Second, we can defuse the determinist argument by admitting, and indeed insisting, that a great deal of determinism exists in the world. Determinism in the form of if-then causal laws governs much of the human body's functioning and much of the universe as a whole. We can be glad that the automatic system of breathing, digestion, circulation of the blood, and beating of the heart operate deterministically—until they get out of order. Determinism *versus* free choice is a false issue; what we always have is *relative* determinism and *relative* free choice. Free will is

Reprinted from *Religious Humanism,* Vol. III, No. 3, Summer 1969. This paper was followed by a discussion by Professors Van Meter Ames, Robert Atkins, John Herman Randall, Williard Enteman, James Gould, Milic Capek, and Sterling Lamprecht. A copy of these papers can be obtained from the Fellowship of Religious Humanists, Yellow Springs, Ohio.

ever limited by the past and by the vast range of if-then laws. At the same time, human beings utilize free choice to take advantage of those deterministic laws embodied in science and man-made machines. Most of us drive cars, but it is we and not the autos that decide when and where they are to go. Determinism wisely used and controlled—which is by no means always the case—can make us freer and happier.

Third, determinism is a relative thing, not only because human free choice exists, but also because contingency or chance is an ultimate trait of the cosmos. Contingency is best seen in the intersection of mutually independent event-streams between which there was no previous causal connection. My favorite example here is the collision of the steamship *Titanic* with an iceberg off Newfoundland, in the middle of the night on April 14, 1912. It was a terrible accident, with more than 1,500 persons lost. The drifting of the iceberg down from the north and the steaming of the *Titanic* west from England clearly represented two causal streams independent of each other.

Even if a team of scientific experts had been able, *per impossible,* to trace back the two causal streams and ascertain that the catastrophe had been predestined from the moment the steamship left Southampton, that would not upset my thesis. For the space-time relation of the iceberg and the *Titanic,* as the ship started on its voyage, would have been itself a matter of contingency, since there was no relevant cause to account for that precise relation.

The pervasive presence of contingency in the world is also proved by the fact that all natural laws, as I have observed, take the form of if-then sequences or relations. The *if* factor is obviously conditional and demonstrates the continual coexistence of contingency with determinism. The actuality of contingency negates the idea of total and all-inclusive necessity operating throughout the universe. As regards human choice, contingency ensures that at the outset the alternatives one faces are indeterminate in relation to the act of choosing, which proceeds to make one of them determinate.

My fourth point is that the accepted meaning of *potentiality,* namely, that every object and event in the cosmos possesses plural possibilities of behavior, interaction, and development, knocks out the determinist thesis. From the determinist viewpoint, multiple potentialities are an illusion. If you want to take a vacation trip next summer, you will no doubt think over a number of possibilities before you make a final decision. Determinism logically implies that such deliberation is mere play-acting, because you were destined all the time to choose the trip you did choose. When we relate the causal pattern to potentiality, we find that causation as mediated through free choice can have its appropriate effect in the actualization of any one of various possibilities.

Fifth, the normal processes of human thought are tied in with potentiality as I have just described it, and likewise tend to show that freedom of choice is real. Thinking constantly involves general conceptions, universals, or abstractions under which are classified many varying particulars. In the case that I discussed under my fourth point, "vacation travel" was the general conception and the different places that might be visited were the particulars, the alternatives, the potentialities, among which one could freely choose. Unless there is free choice, the function of human thought in solving problems becomes superfluous and a mask of make-believe.

Sixth, it is clarifying for the problem of free choice to realize that only the present exists, and that it is always some present activity that builds up the past, as a skier leaves a trail behind him in the snow as he weaves down a hill. Everything that exists—the whole vast aggregate of inanimate matter, the swarming profusion of earthly life, man in his every aspect—exists only as an event or events taking place at this instant moment, which is now. The past is dead and gone; it is efficacious only as it is embodied in present structures and activities.

The activity of former presents establishes the foundations upon which the immediate present operates. What happened in the past creates both limitations and potentialities, always conditioning the present. But conditioning in this sense is not the same as determining; and each day sweeps onward under its own momentum, actualizing fresh patterns of existence, maintaining other patterns and destroying still others. Thus a man choosing and acting in the present is not wholly controlled by the past, but is part of the unending forward surge of cosmic power. He is an active, initiating agent, riding the wave of the present, as it were, and deliberating among open alternatives to reach decisions regarding the many different phases of his life.

My seventh point is that the doctrine of universal and eternal determinism is seen to be self-refuting when we work out its full implications in the cases of *reductio ad absurdum* implied. If our choices and actions today were all predestined yesterday, then they were equally predestined yesteryear, at the day of our birth, and at the birth of our solar system and earth some five billion years ago. To take another instance: for determinism, the so-called *irresistible impulse* that the law recognizes in assessing crimes by the insane must hold with equal force for the actions of the sane and virtuous. In the determinist philosophy, the good man has an irresistible impulse to tell the truth, to be kind to animals, and to expose the graft in City Hall.

Eighth, in the novel dialect of determinism many words lose their normal meaning. I refer to such words as *refraining, forbearance, self-restraint,* and *regret.* If determinism turns out to be true, we shall have to scrap a great deal in existing dictionaries and do a vast amount of redefining. What meaning, for example, is to be assigned to *forbearance* when it is determined in advance that you are going to refuse that second Martini cocktail? You can truly forbear only when you refrain from doing something that it is possible for you to do. But under the determinist dispensation it is not possible for you to accept the second cocktail because fate has already dictated your "No." I am not saying that nature necessarily conforms to our linguistic usages, but human language habits that have evolved over aeons of time cannot be neglected in the analysis of free choice and determinism.

Finally, I do not think that the term *moral responsibility* can retain its traditional meaning unless freedom of choice exists. From the viewpoint of ethics, law, and criminal law, it is difficult to understand how a consistent determinist would have a sufficient sense of personal responsibility for the development of decent ethical standards. But the question remains whether there have ever been or can be any consistent determinists or whether free choice runs so deep in human nature as an innate characteristic that, as Jean-Paul Sartre suggests, "We are not free to cease being free."

Soft Determinism

4. The Problem of Free Will　W. T. Stace

Walter Terence Stace (1886–1967) was born in Britain and served in the British Civil Service in Ceylon before coming to the United States to teach at Princeton University in 1932. He has written widely acclaimed books in many areas of philosophy.

[A] great problem which the rise of scientific naturalism has created for the modern mind concerns the foundations of morality. The old religious foundations have largely crumbled away, and it may well be thought that the edifice built upon them by generations of men is in danger of collapse. A total collapse of moral behavior is, as I pointed out before, very unlikely. For a society in which this occurred could not survive. Nevertheless the danger to moral standards inherent in the virtual disappearance of their old religious foundations is not illusory.

I shall first discuss the problem of free will, for it is certain that if there is no free will there can be no morality. Morality is concerned with what men ought and ought not to do. But if a man has no freedom to choose what he will do, if whatever he does is done under compulsion, then it does not make sense to tell him that he ought not to have done what he did and that he ought to do something different. All moral precepts would in such case be meaningless. Also if he acts always under compulsion, how can he be held morally responsible for his actions? How can he, for example, be punished for what he could not help doing?

It is to be observed that those learned professors of philosophy or psychology who deny the existence of free will do so only in their professional moments and in their studies and lecture rooms. For when it comes to doing anything practical, even of the most trivial kind, they invariably behave as if they and others were free. They inquire from you at dinner whether you will choose this dish or that dish. They will ask a child why he told a lie, and will punish him for not having chosen the way of truthfulness. All of which is inconsistent with a disbelief in free will. This should cause us to suspect that the problem is not a real one; and this, I believe, is the case. The dispute is merely verbal, and is due to nothing but a confusion about the meanings of words. It is what is now fashionably called a semantic problem.

How does a verbal dispute arise? Let us consider a case which, although it is absurd in the sense that no one would ever make the mistake which is involved in it, yet illustrates the principle which we shall have to use in the solution of the problem. Suppose that someone believed

Specified excerpts (pp. 248–258) from *Religion and The Modern Mind* by W. T. Stace (J. B. Lippincott Company), Copyright 1952 by W. T. Stace. Reprinted by permission of Harper & Row, Publishers, Inc.

that the word "man" means a certain sort of five-legged animal; in short that "five-legged animal" is the correct *definition* of man. He might then look around the world, and rightly observing that there are no five-legged animals in it, he might proceed to deny the existence of men. This preposterous conclusion would have been reached because he was using an incorrect definition of "man." All you would have to do to show him his mistake would be to give him the correct definition; or at least to show him that his definition was wrong. Both the problem and its solution would, of course, be entirely verbal. The problem of free will, and its solution, I shall maintain, is verbal in exactly the same way. The problem has been created by the fact that learned men, especially philosophers, have assumed an incorrect definition of free will, and then finding that there is nothing in the world which answers to their definition, have denied its existence. As far as logic is concerned, their conclusion is just as absurd as that of the man who denies the existence of men. The only difference is that the mistake in the latter case is obvious and crude, while the mistake which the deniers of free will have made is rather subtle and difficult to detect.

Throughout the modern period, until quite recently, it was assumed, both by the philosophers who denied free will and by those who defended it, that *determinism is inconsistent with free will.* If a man's actions were wholly determined by chains of causes stretching back into the remote past, so that they could be predicted beforehand by a mind which knew all the causes, it was assumed that they could not in that case be free. This implies that a certain definition of actions done from free will was assumed, namely that they are actions *not* wholly determined by causes or predictable beforehand. Let us shorten this by saying that free will was defined as meaning indeterminism. This is the incorrect definition which has led to the denial of free will. As soon as we see what the true definition is we shall find that the question whether the world is deterministic, as Newtonian science implied, or in a measure indeterministic, as current physics teaches, is wholly irrelevant to the problem.

Of course there is a sense in which one can define a word arbitrarily in any way one pleases. But a definition may nevertheless be called correct or incorrect. It is correct if it accords with a *common usage* of the word defined. It is incorrect if it does not. And if you give an incorrect definition, absurd and untrue results are likely to follow. For instance, there is nothing to prevent you from arbitrarily defining a man as a five-legged animal, but this is incorrect in the sense that it does not accord with the ordinary meaning of the word. Also it has the absurd result of leading to a denial of the existence of men. This shows that *common usage is the criterion for deciding whether a definition is correct or not.* And this is the principle which I shall apply to free will. I shall show that indeterminism is not what is meant by the phrase "free will" *as it is commonly used.* And I shall attempt to discover the correct definition by inquiring how the phrase is used in ordinary conversation.

Here are a few samples of how the phrase might be used in ordinary conversation. It will be noticed that they include cases in which the question whether a man acted with free will is asked in order to determine whether he was morally and legally responsible for his acts.

Jones   I once went without food for a week.
Smith   Did you do that of your own free will?
Jones   No. I did it because I was lost in a desert and could find no food.

But suppose that the man who had fasted was Mahatma Gandhi. The conversation might then have gone:

Gandhi   I once fasted for a week.
Smith   Did you do that of your own free will?
Gandhi   Yes. I did it because I wanted to compel the British Government to give India its independence.

Take another case. Suppose that I had stolen some bread, but that I was as truthful as George Washington. Then, if I were charged with the crime in court, some exchange of the following sort might take place:

Judge   Did you steal the bread of your own free will?
Stace   Yes. I stole it because I was hungry.

Or in different circumstances the conversation might run:

Judge   Did you steal of your own free will?
Stace   No. I stole because my employer threatened to beat me if I did not.

At a recent murder trial in Trenton some of the accused had signed confessions, but afterwards asserted that they had done so under police duress. The following exchange might have occurred:

Judge   Did you sign this confession of your own free will?
Prisoner   No. I signed it because the police beat me up.

Now suppose that a philosopher had been a member of the jury. We could imagine this conversation taking place in the jury room.

Foreman of the Jury   The prisoner says he signed the confession because he was beaten, and not of his own free will.
Philosopher   This is quite irrelevant to the case. There is no such thing as free will.
Foreman   Do you mean to say that it makes no difference whether he signed because his conscience made him want to tell the truth or because he was beaten?
Philosopher   None at all. Whether he was caused to sign by a beating or by some desire of his own—the desire to tell the truth,

for example—in either case his signing was causally determined, and therefore in neither case did he act of his own free
will. Since there is no such thing as free will, the question
whether he signed of his own free will ought not to be discussed
by us.

The foreman and the rest of the jury would rightly conclude that
the philosopher must be making some mistake. What sort of mistake
could it be? There is only one possible answer. The philosopher must
be using the phrase "free will" in some peculiar way of his own which
is not the way in which men usually use it when they wish to determine
a question of moral responsibility. That is, he must be using an incorrect
definition of it as implying action not determined by causes.

Suppose a man left his office at noon, and were questioned about it.
Then we might hear this:

Jones Did you go out of your own free will?
Smith Yes. I went out to get my lunch.

But we might hear:

Jones Did you leave your office of your own free will?
Smith No. I was forcibly removed by the police.

We have now collected a number of cases of actions which, in the
ordinary usage of the English language, would be called cases in which
people have acted of their own free will. We should also say in all these
cases that they *chose* to act as they did. We should also say that they could
have acted otherwise, if they had chosen. For instance, Mahatma Gandhi
was not compelled to fast; he chose to do so. He could have eaten if he
had wanted to. When Smith went out to get his lunch, he chose to do
so. He could have stayed and done some more work, if he had wanted
to. We have also collected a number of cases of the opposite kind. They
are cases in which men were not able to exercise their free will. They
had no choice. They were compelled to do as they did. The man in the
desert did not fast of his own free will. He had no choice in the matter.
He was compelled to fast because there was nothing for him to eat. And
so with the other cases. It ought to be quite easy, by an inspection of
these cases, to tell what we ordinarily mean when we say that a man did
or did not exercise free will. We ought therefore to be able to extract
from them the proper definition of the term. Let us put the cases in a
table:

Free Acts	Unfree Acts
Gandhi fasting because he wanted to free India.	The man fasting in the desert because there was no food.
Stealing bread because one is hungry.	Stealing because one's employer threatened to beat one.
Signing a confession because one wanted to tell the truth.	Signing because the police beat one.
Leaving the office because one wanted one's lunch.	Leaving because forcibly removed.

It is obvious that to find the correct definition of free acts we must discover what characteristic is common to all the acts in the left-hand column, and is, at the same time, absent from all the acts in the right-hand column. This characteristic which all free acts have, and which no unfree acts have, will be the defining characteristic of free will.

Is being uncaused, or not being determined by causes, the characteristic of which we are in search? It cannot be, because although it is true that all the acts in the right-hand column have causes, such as the beating by the police or the absence of food in the desert, so also do the acts in the left-hand column. Mr. Gandhi's fasting was caused by his desire to free India, the man leaving his office by his hunger, and so on. Moreover there is no reason to doubt that these causes of the free acts were in turn caused by prior conditions, and that these were again the results of causes, and so on back indefinitely into the past. Any physiologist can tell us the causes of hunger. What caused Mr. Gandhi's tremendously powerful desire to free India is no doubt more difficult to discover. But it must have had causes. Some of them may have lain in peculiarities of his glands or brain, others in his past experiences, others in his heredity, others in his education. Defenders of free will have usually tended to deny such facts. But to do so is plainly a case of special pleading, which is unsupported by any scrap of evidence. The only reasonable view is that all human actions, both those which are freely done and those which are not, are either wholly determined by causes, or at least as much determined as other events in nature. It may be true, as the physicists tell us, that nature is not as deterministic as was once thought. But whatever degree of determinism prevails in the world, human actions appear to be as much determined as anything else. And if this is so, it cannot be the case that what distinguishes actions freely chosen from those which are not free is that the latter are determined by causes while the former are not. Therefore, being uncaused or being undetermined by causes, must be an incorrect definition of free will.

What, then, is the difference between acts which are freely done and those which are not? What is the characteristic which is present to all the acts in the left-hand column and absent from all those in the right-hand column? Is it not obvious that, although both sets of actions have causes, the causes of those in the left-hand column are *of a different kind* from the causes of those in the right-hand column? The free acts are all caused by desires, or motives, or by some sort of internal psychological states of the agent's mind. The unfree acts, on the other hand, are all caused by physical forces or physical conditions, outside the agent. Police arrest means physical force exerted from the outside; the absence of food in the desert is a physical condition of the outside world. We may therefore frame the following rough definitions. *Acts freely done are those whose immediate causes are psychological states in the agent. Acts not freely done are those whose immediate causes are states of affairs external to the agent.*

It is plain that if we define free will in this way, then free will certainly exists, and the philosopher's denial of its existence is seen to be what it is—nonsense. For it is obvious that all those actions of men which we should ordinarily attribute to the exercise of their free will, or of which we should say that they freely chose to do them, are in fact actions which have been caused by their own desires, wishes, thoughts, emotions, impulses, or other psychological states.

In applying our definition we shall find that it usually works well, but that there are some puzzling cases which it does not seem exactly to fit. These puzzles can always be solved by paying careful attention to the ways in which words are used, and remembering that they are not always used consistently. I have space for only one example. Suppose that a thug threatens to shoot you unless you give him your wallet, and suppose that you do so. Do you, in giving him your wallet, do so of your own free will or not? If we apply our definition, we find that you acted freely, since the immediate cause of the action was not an actual outside force but the fear of death, which is a psychological cause. Most people, however, would say that you did not act of your own free will but under compulsion. Does this show that our definition is wrong? I do not think so. Aristotle, who gave a solution of the problem of free will substantially the same as ours (though he did not use the term "free will") admitted that there are what he called "mixed" or borderline cases in which it is difficult to know whether we ought to call the acts free or compelled. In the case under discussion, though no actual force was used, the gun at your forehead so nearly approximated to actual force that we tend to say the case was one of compulsion. It is a borderline case.

Here is what may seem like another kind of puzzle. According to our view an action may be free though it could have been predicted beforehand with certainty. But suppose you told a lie, and it was certain beforehand that you would tell it. How could one then say, "You could have told the truth"? The answer is that it is perfectly true that you could have told the truth *if* you had wanted to. In fact you would have done so, for in that case the causes producing your action, namely your desires, would have been different, and would therefore have produced different effects. It is a delusion that predictability and free will are incompatible. This agrees with common sense. For if, knowing your character, I predict that you will act honorably, no one would say when you do act honorably, that this shows you did not do so of your own free will.

Since free will is a condition of moral responsibility, we must be sure that our theory of free will gives a sufficient basis for it. To be held morally responsible for one's actions means that one may be justly punished or rewarded, blamed or praised, for them. But it is not just to punish a man for what he cannot help doing. How can it be just to punish him for an action which it was certain beforehand that he would do? We have not attempted to decide whether, as a matter of fact, all events, including human actions, are completely determined. For that question is irrelevant to the problem of free will. But if we assume for the purposes of argument that complete determinism is true, but that we are nevertheless free, it may then be asked whether such a deterministic free will is compatible with moral responsibility. For it may seem unjust to punish a man for an action which it could have been predicted with certainty beforehand that he would do.

But that determinism is incompatible with moral responsibility is as much a delusion as that it is incompatible with free will. You do not excuse a man for doing a wrong act because, knowing his character, you felt certain beforehand that he would do it. Nor do you deprive a man of a reward or prize because, knowing his goodness or his capabilities, you felt certain beforehand that he would win it.

Volumes have been written on the justification of punishment. But so far as it affects the question of free will, the essential principles involved are quite simple. The punishment of a man for doing a wrong act is justified, either on the ground that it will correct his own character, or that it will deter other people from doing similar acts. The instrument of punishment has been in the past, and no doubt still is, often unwisely used; so that it may often have done more harm than good. But that is not relevant to our present problem. Punishment, if and when it is justified, is justified only on one or both of the grounds just mentioned. The question then is how, if we assume determinism, punishment can correct character or deter people from evil actions.

Suppose that your child develops a habit of telling lies. You give him a mild beating. Why? Because you believe that his personality is such that the usual motives for telling the truth do not cause him to do so. You therefore supply the missing cause, or motive, in the shape of pain and the fear of future pain if he repeats his untruthful behavior. And you hope that a few treatments of this kind will condition him to the habit of truth-telling, so that he will come to tell the truth without the infliction of pain. You assume that his actions are determined by causes, but that the usual causes of truth-telling do not in him produce their usual effects. You therefore supply him with an artificially injected motive, pain and fear, which you think will in the future cause him to speak truthfully.

The principle is exactly the same where you hope, by punishing one man, to deter others from wrong actions. You believe that the fear of punishment will cause those who might otherwise do evil to do well.

We act on the same principle with non-human, and even with inanimate, things, if they do not behave in the way we think they ought to behave. The rose bushes in the garden produce only small and poor blooms, whereas we want large and rich ones. We supply a cause which will produce large blooms, namely fertilizer. Our automobile does not go properly. We supply a cause which will make it go better, namely oil in the works. The punishment for the man, the fertilizer for the plant, and the oil for the car, are all justified by the same principle and in the same way. The only difference is that different kinds of things require different kinds of causes to make them do what they should. Pain may be the appropriate remedy to apply, in certain cases, to human beings, and oil to the machine. It is, of course, of no use to inject motor oil into the boy or to beat the machine.

Thus we see that moral responsibility is not only consistent with determinism, but requires it. The assumption on which punishment is based is that human behavior is causally determined. If pain could not be a cause of truth-telling there would be no justification at all for punishing lies. If human actions and volitions were uncaused, it would be useless either to punish or reward, or indeed to do anything else to correct people's bad behavior. For nothing that you could do would in any way influence them. Thus moral responsibility would entirely disappear. If there were no determinism of human beings at all, their actions would be completely unpredictable and capricious, and therefore irresponsible. And this is in itself a strong argument against the common view of philosophers that free will means being undetermined by causes.

Contemporary Issues

The Control of Men

5. Walden Two: Selections   B. F. Skinner

Burrhus Frederic Skinner (1904–), professor of psychology at Harvard University, is one of America's most prominent psychologists. He is known both for his defense of behaviorism and his experimentation with modern teaching devices.

The participants of the following discussion are Frazier, the founder of Walden Two; Castle, a philosopher who is skeptical of the society's achievements and purposes; and Professor Burris, the narrator of the discussion, who is trying objectively to evaluate Frazier's new society.

"Each of us," Frazier began, "is engaged in a pitched battle with the rest of mankind."

"A curious premise for a Utopia," said Castle. "Even a pessimist like myself takes a more hopeful view than that."

"You do, you do," said Frazier. "But let's be realistic. Each of us has interests which conflict with the interest of everybody else. That's our original sin, and it can't be helped. Now, 'everybody else' we call 'society.' It's a powerful opponent, and it always wins. Oh, here and there an individual prevails for a while and gets what he wants. Sometimes he storms the culture of a society and changes it slightly to his own advantage. But society wins in the long run, for it has the advantage of numbers and of age. Many prevail against one, and men against a baby. Society attacks early, when the individual is helpless. It enslaves him almost before he has tasted freedom. The 'ologies' will tell you how it's done. Theology calls it building a conscience or developing a spirit of selflessness. Psychology calls it the growth of the super-ego.

"Considering how long society has been at it, you'd expect a better job. But the campaigns have been badly planned and the victory has never been secure. The behavior of the individual has been shaped according to revelations of 'good conduct,' never as the result of experimental study. But why not experiment? The questions are simple enough. What's the best behavior for the individual so far as the group is concerned? And how can the individual be induced to behave in that way? Why not explore these questions in a scientific spirit?

"We could do just that in Walden Two. We had already worked out a code of conduct—subject, of course, to experimental modification. The code would keep things running smoothly if everybody lived up to it. Our job was to see that everybody did. Now, you can't get people to follow a useful code by making them into so many jacks-in-the-box. You can't foresee all future circumstances, and you can't specify adequate future conduct. You don't know what will be required. Instead you have to set up certain behavioral processes which will lead the individual to design his own 'good' conduct when the time comes. We call that sort of thing 'self-control.' But don't be misled, the control always rests in the last analysis in the hands of society.

"One of our Planners, a young man named Simmons, worked with me. It was the first time in history that the matter was approached in an experimental way. Do you question that statement, Mr. Castle?"

"I'm not sure I know what you are talking about," said Castle.

"Then let me go on. Simmons and I began by studying the great works on morals and ethics—Plato, Aristotle, Confucius, the New Testament, the Puritan divines, Machiavelli, Chesterfield, Freud—there were scores of them. We were looking for any and every method of shaping human behavior by imparting techniques of self-control. Some techniques were obvious enough, for they had marked turning points in human history. 'Love your enemies' is an example—a psychological invention for easing the lot of an oppressed people. The severest trial of oppression is the constant rage which one suffers at the thought of the oppressor. What Jesus discovered was how to avoid these inner devastations. His technique was to *practice the opposite emotion.* If a man can succeed in 'loving his enemies' and 'taking no thought for the morrow,' he will no longer be assailed by hatred of the oppressor or rage at the loss of his freedom or possessions. He may not get his freedom or possessions back, but he's less miserable. It's a difficult lesson. It comes late in our program."

"I thought you were opposed to modifying emotions and instincts until the world was ready for it," said Castle. "According to you, the principle of 'love your enemies' should have been suicidal."

"It would have been suicidal, except for an entirely unforseen consequence. Jesus must have been quite astonished at the effect of his discovery. We are only just beginning to understand the power of love because we are just beginning to understand the weakness of force and aggression. But the science of behavior is clear about all that now. Recent discoveries in the analysis of punishment—but I am falling into one digression after another. Let me save my explanation of why the Christian virtues—and I mean merely the Christian techniques of self-control—have not disappeared from the face of the earth, with due recognition of the fact that they suffered a narrow squeak within recent memory.

"When Simmons and I had collected our techniques of control, we had to discover how to teach them. That was more difficult. Current educational practices were of little value, and religious practices scarcely any better. Promising paradise or threatening hell-fire is, we assumed, generally admitted to be unproductive. It is based upon a fundamental fraud which, when discovered, turns the individual against society and nourishes the very thing it tries to stamp out. What Jesus offered in return for loving one's enemies was heaven *on earth,* better known as peace of mind.

"We found a few suggestions worth following in the practices of the clinical psychologist. We undertook to build a tolerance for annoying experiences. The sunshine of midday is extremely painful if you come from a dark room, but take it in easy stages and you can avoid pain altogether. The analogy can be misleading, but in much the same way it's possible to build a tolerance to painful or distasteful stimuli, or to frustration, or to situations which arouse fear, anger or rage. Society and nature throw these annoyances at the individual with no regard for the development of tolerances. Some achieve tolerances, most fail. Where would the science of immunization be if it followed a schedule of accidental dosages?

"Take the principle of 'Get thee behind me, Satan,' for example," Frazier continued. "It's a special case of self-control by altering the environment. Subclass A 3, I believe. We give each child a lollipop which has been dipped in powdered sugar so that a single touch of the tongue can be detected. We tell him he may eat the lollipop later in the day, provided it hasn't already been licked. Since the child is only three or four, it is a fairly diff—"

"Three or four!" Castle exclaimed.

"All our ethical training is completed by the age of six," said Frazier quietly. "A simple principle like putting temptation out of sight would be acquired before four. But at such an early age the problem of not licking the lollipop isn't easy. Now, what would you do, Mr. Castle, in a similar situation?"

"Put the lollipop out of sight as quickly as possible."

"Exactly. I can see you've been well trained. Or perhaps you discovered the principle for yourself. We're in favor of original inquiry wherever possible, but in this case we have a more important goal and we don't hesitate to give verbal help. First of all, the children are urged to examine their own behavior while looking at the lollipops. This helps them to recognize the need for self-control. Then the lollipops are concealed, and the children are asked to notice any gain in happiness or any reduction in tension. Then a strong distraction is arranged—say, an interesting game. Later the children are reminded of the candy and encouraged to examine their reaction. The value of the distraction is generally obvious. Well, need I go on? When the experiment is repeated a day or so later, the children all run with the lollipops to their lockers and do exactly what Mr. Castle would do—a sufficient indication of the success of our training."

"I wish to report an objective observation of my reaction to your story," said Castle, controlling his voice with great precision. "I find myself revolted by this display of sadistic tyranny."

"I don't wish to deny you the exercise of an emotion which you seem to find enjoyable," said Frazier. "So let me go on. Concealing a tempting but forbidden object is a crude solution. For one thing, it's not always feasible. We want a sort of psychological concealment—covering up the candy by paying no attention. In a later experiment the children wear their lollipops like crucifixes for a few hours."

> Instead of the cross, the lollipop,
> About my neck was hung,

said Castle. . . .

"How do you build up a tolerance to an annoying situation?" I said.

"Oh, for example, by having the children 'take' a more and more painful shock, or drink cocoa with less and less sugar in it until a bitter concoction can be savored without a bitter face."

"But jealousy or envy—you can't administer them in graded doses," I said.

"And why not? Remember, we control the social environment, too, at this age. That's why we get our ethical training in early. Take this case. A group of children arrive home after a long walk tired and hungry. They're expecting supper; they find, instead, that it's time for a lesson in self-control: they must stand for five minutes in front of steaming bowls of soup.

"The assignment is accepted like a problem in arithmetic. Any groaning or complaining is a wrong answer. Instead, the children begin at once to work upon themselves to avoid any unhappiness during the delay. One of them may make a joke of it. We encourage a sense of humor as a good way of not taking an annoyance seriously. The joke won't be much, according to adult standards—perhaps the child will simply pretend to empty the bowl of soup into his upturned mouth. Another may start a song with many verses. The rest join in at once, for they've learned that it's a good way to make time pass."

Frazier glanced uneasily at Castle, who was not to be appeased.

"That also strikes you as a form of torture, Mr. Castle?" he asked.

"I'd rather be put on the rack," said Castle.

"Then you have by no means had the thorough training I supposed. You can't imagine how lightly the children take such an experience. It's a rather severe biological frustration, for the children are tired and hungry and they must stand and look at food; but it's passed off as lightly as a five-minute delay at curtain time. We regard it as a fairly elementary test. Much more difficult problems follow."

"I suspected as much," muttered Castle.

"In a later stage we forbid all social devices. No songs, no jokes—merely silence. Each child is forced back upon his own resources—a very important step."

"I should think so," I said. "And how do you know it's successful? You might produce a lot of silently resentful children. It's certainly a dangerous stage."

"It is, and we follow each child carefully. If he hasn't picked up the necessary techniques, we start back a little. A still more advanced stage"—Frazier glanced again at Castle, who stirred uneasily—"brings me to my point. When it's time to sit down to the soup, the children count off—heads and tails. Then a coin is tossed and if it comes up heads, the 'heads' sit down and eat. The 'tails' remain standing for another five minutes."

Castle groaned.

"And you call that envy?" I asked.

"Perhaps not exactly," said Frazier. "At least there's seldom any aggression against the lucky ones. The emotion, if any, is directed against Lady Luck herself, against the toss of the coin. That, in itself, is a lesson worth learning, for it's the only direction in which emotion has a surviving chance to be useful. And resentment toward things in general, while perhaps just as silly as personal aggression, is more easily controlled. Its expression is not socially objectionable." . . .

"May you not inadvertently teach your children some of the very emotions you're trying to eliminate?" I said. "What's the effect, for example, of finding the anticipation of a warm supper suddenly thwarted? Doesn't that eventually lead to feelings of uncertainty, or even anxiety?"

"It might. We had to discover how often our lessons could be safely administered. But all our schedules are worked out experimentally. We watch for undesired consequences just as any scientist watches for disrupting factors in his experiments.

"After all, it's a simple and sensible program," he went on in a tone of appeasement. "We set up a system of gradually increasing annoyances and frustrations against a background of complete serenity. An easy environment is made more and more difficult as the children acquire the capacity to adjust."

"But *why?*" said Castle. "Why these deliberate unpleasantnesses—to put it mildly? I must say I think you and your friend Simmons are really very subtle sadists."

"You've reversed your position, Mr. Castle," said Frazier in a sudden flash of anger with which I rather sympathized. Castle was calling names, and he was also being unaccountably and perhaps intentionally obtuse. "A while ago you accused me of breeding a race of softies," Frazier continued. "Now you object to toughening them up. But what you don't understand is that these potentially unhappy situations are never very annoying. Our schedules make sure of that. You wouldn't understand, however, because you're not so far advanced as our children."

Castle grew black.

"But what do your children get out of it?" he insisted, apparently trying to press some vague advantage in Frazier's anger.

"What do they get out of it!" exclaimed Frazier, his eyes flashing with a sort of helpless contempt. His lips curled and he dropped his head to look at his fingers, which were crushing a few blades of grass.

"They must get happiness and freedom and strength," I said, putting myself in a ridiculous position in attempting to make peace.

"They don't sound happy or free to me, standing in front of bowls of Forbidden Soup," said Castle, answering me parenthetically while continuing to stare at Frazier.

"If I must spell it out," Frazier began with a deep sigh, "what they get is escape from the petty emotions which eat the heart out of the unprepared. They get the satisfaction of pleasant and profitable social relations on a scale almost undreamed of in the world at large. They get immeasurably increased efficiency, because they can stick to a job without suffering the aches and pains which soon beset most of us. They get new horizons, for they are spared the emotions characteristic of frustration and failure. They get—" His eyes searched the branches of the trees. "Is that enough?" he said at last.

"And the community must gain their loyalty," I said, "when they discover the fears and jealousies and diffidences in the world at large."

"I'm glad you put it that way," said Frazier. "You might have said that they must feel superior to the miserable products of our public schools. But we're at pains to keep any feeling of superiority or contempt under control, too. Having suffered most acutely from it myself, I put the subject first on our agenda. We carefully avoid any joy in a personal triumph which means the personal failure of somebody else. We take no pleasure in the sophistical, the disputative, the dialectical." He threw a vicious glance at Castle, "We don't use the motive of domination, because we are always thinking of the whole group. We could motivate a few geniuses that way—it was certainly my own motivation—but we'd sacrifice some of the happiness of everyone else. Triumph over nature and over oneself, yes. But over others, never."

"You've taken the mainspring out of the watch," said Castle flatly.

"That's an experimental question, Mr. Castle, and you have the wrong answer." . . .

"Are your techniques really so very new?" I said hurriedly. "What about the primitive practice of submitting a boy to various tortures before granting him a place among adults? What about the disciplinary techniques of Puritanism? Or of the modern school, for that matter?"

"In one sense you're right," said Frazier. "And I think you've nicely answered Mr. Castle's tender concern for our little ones. The unhappinesses we deliberately impose are far milder than the normal unhappiness from which we offer protection. Even at the height of our ethical training, the unhappiness is ridiculously trivial—to the well-trained child.

"But there's a world of difference in the way we use these annoyances," he continued. "For one thing, we don't punish. We never administer an unpleasantness in the hope of repressing or eliminating undesirable behavior. But there's another difference. In most cultures the child meets up with annoyances and reverses of uncontrolled magnitude. Some are imposed in the name of discipline by persons in authority. Some, like hazings, are condoned though not authorized. Others are merely accidental. No one cares to, or is able to, prevent them.

"We all know what happens. A few hardy children emerge, particularly those who have got their unhappiness in doses that could be swallowed. They become brave men. Others become sadists or masochists of varying degrees of pathology. Not having conquered a painful environment, they become preoccupied with pain and make a devious art of it. Others submit—and hope to inherit the earth. The rest—the cravens, the cowards—live in fear for the rest of their lives. And that's only a single field—the reaction to pain. I could cite a dozen parallel cases. The optimist and the pessimist, the contented and the disgruntled, the loved and the unloved, the ambitious and the discouraged—these are only the extreme products of a miserable system.

"Traditional practices are admittedly better than nothing," Frazier went on. "Spartan or Puritan—no one can question the occasional happy result. But the whole system rests upon the wasteful principle of selection. The English public school of the nineteenth century produced brave men—by setting up almost insurmountable barriers and making the most of the few who came over. But selection isn't education. Its crops of brave men will always be small, and the waste enormous. Like all primitive principles, selection serves in place of education only through a profligate use of material. Multiply extravagantly and select with rigor. It's the philosophy of the 'big litter' as an alternative to good child hygiene.

"In Walden Two we have a different objective. We make every man a brave man. They all come over the barriers. Some require more preparation than others, but they all come over. The traditional use of adversity is to select the strong. We control adversity to build strength. And we do it deliberately, no matter how sadistic Mr. Castle may think us, in order to prepare for adversities which are beyond control. Our children eventually experience the 'heartache and the thousand natural shocks that flesh is heir to.' It would be the cruelest possible practice to protect them as long as possible, especially when we *could* protect them so well."

Frazier held out his hands in an exaggerated gesture of appeal.

"What alternative *had* we?" he said, as if he were in pain. "What else could we do? For four or five years we could provide a life in which no important need would go unsatisfied, a life practically free of anxiety or frustration or annoyance. What would *you* do? Would you let the child enjoy this paradise with no thought for the future—like an idolatrous and pampering mother? Or would you relax control of the environment and let the child meet accidental frustrations? *But what is the virtue of accident?* No, there was only one course open to us. We had to *design* a series of adversities, so that the child would develop the greatest possible self-control. Call it deliberate, if you like, and accuse us of sadism; there was no other course." . . .

"A modern, mechanized, managerial Machiavelli—that is my final estimate of you, Mr. Frazier," he [Castle] said, with the same challenging stare.

"It must be gratifying to know that one has reached a 'final estimate,' " said Frazier.

"An artist in power," Castle continued, "whose greatest art is to conceal art. The silent despot."

"Since we are dealing in 'M's,' why not sum it all up and say 'Mephistophelian'?" said Frazier, curiously reviving my fears of the preceding afternoon.

"I'm willing to do that!" said Castle. "And unless God is very sure of himself, I suspect He's by no means easy about this latest turn in the war of the angels. So far as I can see, you've blocked every path through which man was to struggle upward toward salvation. Intelligence, initiative—you have filled their places with a sort of degraded instinct, engineered compulsion. Walden Two is a marvel of efficient coordination—as efficient as an anthill!"

"Replacing intelligence with instinct—" muttered Frazier: "I had never thought of that. It's an interesting possibility. How's it done?" It was a crude maneuver. The question was a digression, intended to spoil Castle's timing and to direct our attention to practical affairs in which Frazier was more at home.

"The behavior of your members is carefully shaped in advance by a Plan," said Castle, not to be taken in, "and it's shaped to perpetuate that Plan. Intellectually Walden Two is quite as incapable of a spontaneous change of course as the life within a beehive."

"I see what you mean." said Frazier distantly. But he returned to his strategy. "And have you discovered the machinery of my power?"

"I have, indeed. We were looking in the wrong place. There's no *current* contact between you and the members of Walden Two. You threw us off the track very skillfully on that point last night. But you were behaving as a despot when you first laid your plans—when you designed the social structure and drew up the contract between community and member, when you worked out your educational practices and your guarantees against despotism—What a joke! Don't tell me you weren't in control *then!* Burris saw the point. What about your career as organizer? *There* was leadership! And the most damnable leadership in history, because you were setting the stage for the withdrawal of yourself as a personal force, knowing full well that everything that happened would still be your doing. Hundreds—you predicted millions—of unsuspecting souls were to fall within the scope of your ambitious scheme."

Castle was driving his argument home with great excitement, but Frazier was lying in exaggerated relaxation, staring at the ceiling, his hands cupped behind his head.

"Very good, Mr. Castle," he said softly. "I gave you the clue, of course, when we parted last night."

"You did, indeed. And I've wondered why. Were you led into that fatal error by your conceit? Perhaps that's the ultimate answer to your form of despotism. No one could enjoy the power you have seized without wishing to display it from time to time."

"I've admitted neither power nor despotism. But you're quite right in saying that I've exerted an influence and in one sense will continue to exert it forever. I believe you called me a *primum mobile*—not quite correctly, as I found upon looking the term up last night. But I did plan Walden Two—not as an architect plans a building, but as a scientist plans a long-term experiment, uncertain of the conditions he will meet but knowing how he will deal with them when they arise. In a sense, Walden Two is predetermined, but not as the behavior of a beehive is determined. Intelligence, no matter how much it may be shaped and extended by our educational system, will still function as intelligence. It will be used to puzzle out solutions to problems to which a beehive would quickly succumb. What the plan does is to keep intelligence on the right track, for the good of society rather than of the intelligent individual—or for the eventual rather than the immediate good of the individual. It does this by making sure that the individual will not forget his personal stake in the welfare of society."

"But you are forestalling many possibly useful acts of intelligence which aren't encompassed by your plan. You have ruled out points of view which may be more productive. You are implying that T. E. Frazier, looking at the world from the middle of the twentieth century, understands the best course for mankind forever."

"Yes, I suppose I do."

"But that's absurd!"

"Not at all. I don't say I foresee the course man will take a hundred years hence, let alone forever, but I know which he should take now."

"How can you be sure of it? It's certainly not a question you have answered experimentally."

"I think we're in the course of answering it," said Frazier. "But that's beside the point. There's no alternative. We must take that course."

"But that's fantastic. You who are taking it are in a small minority."

Frazier sat up.

"And the majority are in a big quandary," he said. "They're not on the road at all, or they're scrambling back toward their starting point, or sidling from one side of the road to the other like so many crabs. What do you think two world wars have been about? Something as simple as boundaries or trade? Nonsense. The world is trying to adjust to a new conception of man in relation to men."

"Perhaps it's merely trying to adjust to despots whose ideas are incompatible with the real nature of man."

"Mr. Castle," said Frazier very earnestly, "let me ask you a question. I warn you, it will be the most terrifying question of your life. *What would you do if you found yourself in possession of an effective science of behavior?* Suppose you suddenly found it possible to control the behavior of men as you wished. What would you do?"

"That's an assumption?"

"Take it as one if you like. *I* take it as a fact. And apparently you accept it as a fact too. I can hardly be as despotic as you claim unless I hold the key to an extensive practical control."

"What would I do?" said Castle thoughtfully. "I think I would dump your science of behavior in the ocean."

"And deny men all the help you could otherwise give them?"

"And give them the freedom they would otherwise lose forever!"

"How could you give them freedom?"

"By refusing to control them!"

"But you would only be leaving the control in other hands."

"Whose?"

"The charlatan, the demagogue, the salesman, the ward heeler, the bully, the cheat, the educator, the priest—all who are now in possession of the techniques of behavioral engineering."

"A pretty good share of the control would remain in the hands of the individual himself."

"That's an assumption, too, and it's your only hope. It's your only possible chance to avoid the implications of a science of behavior. If man is free, then a technology of behavior is impossible. But I'm asking you to consider the other case."

"Then my answer is that your assumption is contrary to fact and any further consideration idle."

"And your accusations—?"

"—were in terms of intention, not of possible achievement."

Frazier sighed dramatically.

"It's a little late to be proving that a behavioral technology is well advanced. How can you deny it? Many of its methods and techniques are really as old as the hills. Look at their frightful misuse in the hands of the Nazis! And what about the techniques of the psychological clinic?

What about education? Or religion? Or practical politics? Or advertising and salesmanship? Bring them all together and you have a sort of rule-of-thumb technology of vast power. No, Mr. Castle, the science is there for the asking. But its techniques and methods are in the wrong hands—they are used for personal aggrandizement in a competitive world or, in the case of the psychologist and educator, for futilely corrective purposes. My question is, have you the courage to take up and wield the science of behavior for the good of mankind? You answer that you would dump it in the ocean!"

"I'd want to take it out of the hands of the politicians and advertisers and salesmen, too."

"And the psychologists and educators? You see, Mr. Castle, you can't have that kind of cake. The fact is, we not only *can* control human behavior, we *must*. But who's to do it, and what's to be done?"

"So long as a trace of personal freedom survives, I'll stick to my position," said Castle, very much out of countenance.

"Isn't it time we talked about freedom?" I said. "We parted a day or so ago on an agreement to let the question of freedom ring. It's time to answer, don't you think?"

"My answer is simple enough," said Frazier. "I deny that freedom exists at all. I must deny it—or my program would be absurd. You can't have a science about a subject matter which hops capriciously about. Perhaps we can never *prove* that man isn't free; it's an assumption. But the increasing success of a science of behavior makes it more and more plausible."

"On the contrary, a simple personal experience makes it untenable," said Castle. "The experience of freedom. I *know* that I'm free."

"It must be quite consoling," said Frazier.

"And what's more—you do, too," said Castle hotly. "When you deny your own freedom for the sake of playing with a science of behavior, you're acting in plain bad faith. That's the only way I can explain it." He tried to recover himself and shrugged his shoulders. "At least you'll grant that you *feel* free."

"The 'feeling of freedom' should deceive no one," said Frazier. "Give me a concrete case."

"Well, right now," Castle said. He picked up a book of matches. "I'm free to hold or drop these matches."

"You will, of course, do one or the other," said Frazier. "Linguistically or logically there seem to be two possibilities, but I submit that there's only one in fact. The determining forces may be subtle but they are inexorable. I suggest that as an orderly person you will probably hold—ah! you drop them! Well, you see, that's all part of your behavior with respect to me. You couldn't resist the temptation to prove me wrong. It was all lawful. You had no choice. The deciding factor entered rather late, and naturally you couldn't foresee the result when you first held them up. There was no strong likelihood that you would act in either direction, and so you said you were free."

"That's entirely too glib," said Castle. "It's easy to argue lawfulness after the fact. But let's see you predict what I will do in advance. Then I'll agree there's law."

"I didn't say that behavior is always predictable, any more than the weather is always predictable. There are often too many factors to be taken into account. We can't measure them all accurately, and we couldn't perform the mathematical operations needed to make a prediction if we had the measurements. The legality is usually an assumption—but none the less important in judging the issue at hand."

"Take a case where there's no choice, then," said Castle. "Certainly a man in jail isn't free in the sense in which I am free now."

"Good! That's an excellent start. Let us classify the kinds of determiners of human behavior. One class, as you suggest, is physical restraint—handcuffs, iron bars, forcible coercion. These are ways in which we shape human behavior according to our wishes. They're crude, and they sacrifice the affection of the controllee, but they often work. Now, what other ways are there of limiting freedom?"

Frazier had adopted a professorial tone and Castle refused to answer.

"The threat of force would be one," I said.

"Right. And here again we shan't encourage any loyalty on the part of the controllee. He has perhaps a shade more of the feeling of freedom, since he can always 'choose to act and accept the consequences,' but he doesn't feel exactly free. He knows his behavior is being coerced. Now what else?"

I had no answer.

"Force or the threat of force—I see no other possibility," said Castle after a moment.

"Precisely," said Frazier.

"But certainly a large part of my behavior has no connection with force at all. There's my freedom!" said Castle.

"I wasn't agreeing that there was no other possibility—merely that *you* could see no other. Not being a good behaviorist—or a good Christian, for that matter—you have no feeling for a tremendous power of a different sort."

"What's that?"

"I shall have to be technical," said Frazier. "But only for a moment. It's what the science of behavior calls 'reinforcement theory.' The things that can happen to us fall into three classes. To some things we are indifferent. Other things we like—we want them to happen, and we take steps to make them happen again. Still other things we don't like—we don't want them to happen and we take steps to get rid of them or keep them from happening again.

"*Now*," Frazier continued earnestly, "if it's in our power to create any of the situations which a person likes or to remove any situation he doesn't like, we can control his behavior. When he behaves as we want him to behave, we simply create a situation he likes, or remove one he doesn't like. As a result, the probability that he will behave that way again goes up, which is what we want. Technically it's called 'positive reinforcement.'

"The old school made the amazing mistake of supposing that the reverse was true, that by removing a situation a person likes or setting up one he doesn't like—in other words by punishing him—it was possible to *reduce* the probability that he would behave in a given way again. That simply doesn't hold. It has been established beyond question. What is emerging at this critical stage in the evolution of society is a behavioral and cultural technology based on positive reinforcement alone. We are gradually discovering—at an untold cost in human suffering—that in the long run punishment doesn't reduce the probability that an act will occur. We have been so preoccupied with the contrary that we always take 'force' to mean punishment. We don't say we're using force when we send shiploads of food into a starving country, though we're displaying quite as much *power* as if we were sending troops and guns."

"I'm certainly not an advocate of force," said Castle. "But I can't agree that it's not effective."

"It's *temporarily* effective, that's the worst of it. That explains several thousand years of bloodshed. Even nature has been fooled. We 'instinctively' punish a person who doesn't behave as we like—we spank him if he's a child or strike him if he's a man. A nice distinction! The immediate effect of the blow teaches us to strike again. Retribution and revenge are the most natural things on earth. But in the long run the man we strike is no less likely to repeat his act."

"But he won't repeat it if we hit him hard enough," said Castle.

"He'll still *tend* to repeat it. He'll *want* to repeat it. We haven't really altered his potential behavior at all. That's the pity of it. If he doesn't repeat it in our presence, he will in the presence of someone else. Or it will be repeated in the disguise of a neurotic symptom. If we hit hard enough, we clear a little place for ourselves in the wilderness of civilization, but we make the rest of the wilderness still more terrible.

"Now, early forms of government are naturally based on punishment. It's the obvious technique when the physically strong control the weak. But we're in the throes of a great change to positive reinforcement—from a competitive society in which one man's reward is another man's punishment, to a cooperative society in which no one gains at the expense of anyone else.

"The change is slow and painful because the immediate, temporary effect of punishment overshadows the eventual advantage of positive reinforcement. We've all seen countless instances of the temporary effect of force, but clear evidence of the effect of not using force is rare. That's why I insist that Jesus, who was apparently the first to discover the power of refusing to punish, must have hit upon the principle by accident. He certainly had none of the experimental evidence which is available to us today, and I can't conceive that it was possible, no matter what the man's genius, to have discovered the principle from casual observation."

"A touch of revelation, perhaps?" said Castle.

"No, accident. Jesus discovered one principle because it had immediate consequences, and he got another thrown in for good measure."

I began to see light.

"You mean the principle of 'love your enemies'?" I said.

"Exactly! To 'do good to those who despitefully use you' has two unrelated consequences. You gain the peace of mind we talked about the other day. Let the stronger man push you around—at least you avoid the torture of your own rage. *That's* the immediate consequence. What an astonishing discovery it must have been to find that in the long run you could *control the stronger man* in the same way!"

"It's generous of you to give so much credit to your early colleague," said Castle, "but why are we still in the throes of so much misery? Twenty centuries should have been enough for one piece of behavioral engineering."

"The conditions which made the principle difficult to discover made it difficult to teach. The history of the Christian Church doesn't reveal many cases of doing good to one's enemies. To inoffensive heathens, perhaps, but not enemies. One must look outside the field of organized religion to find the principle in practice at all. Church governments are devotees of *power*, both temporal and bogus."

"But what has all this got to do with freedom?" I said hastily.

Frazier took time to reorganize his behavior. He looked steadily toward the window, against which the rain was beating heavily.

"Now that we *know* how positive reinforcement works and why negative doesn't," he said at last, " we can be more deliberate, and hence more successful, in our cultural design. We can achieve a sort of control under which the controlled, though they are following a code much more scrupulously than was ever the case under the old system, nevertheless *feel free*. They are doing what they want to do, not what they are forced to do. That's the source of the tremendous power of positive reinforcement—there's no restraint and no revolt. By a careful cultural design, we control not the final behavior, but the *inclination* to behave—the motives, the desires, the wishes.

"The curious thing is that in that case *the question of freedom never arises*. Mr. Castle was free to drop the matchbook in the sense that nothing was preventing him. If it had been securely bound to his hand he wouldn't have been free. Nor would he have been quite free if I'd covered him with a gun and threatened to shoot him if he let it fall. The question of freedom arises when there is restraint—either physical or psychological.

"But restraint is only one sort of control, and absence of restraint isn't freedom. It's not control that's lacking when one feels 'free,' but the objectionable control of force. Mr. Castle felt free to hold or drop the matches in the sense that he felt no restraint—no threat of punishment in taking either course of action. He neglected to examine his positive reasons for holding or letting go, in spite of the fact that these were more compelling in this instance than any threat of force.

"We have no vocabulary of freedom in dealing with what we want to do," Frazier went on. "The question never arises. When men strike for freedom, they strike against jails and the police, or the threat of them—against oppression. They never strike against forces which make them want to act the way they do. Yet, it seems to be understood that governments will operate only through force or the threat of force, and that all other principles of control will be left to education, religion, and commerce. If this continues to be the case, we may as well give up. A government can never create a free people with the techniques now allotted to it.

"The question is: Can men live in freedom and peace? And the answer is: Yes, if we can build a social structure which will satisfy the needs of everyone and in which everyone will want to observe the supporting code. But so far this has been achieved only in Walden Two. Your ruthless accusations to the contrary, Mr. Castle, this is the freest place on earth. And it is free precisely because we make no use of force or the threat of force. Every bit of our research, from the nursery through the psychological management of our adult membership, is directed toward that end—to exploit every alternative to forcible control. By skillful planning, by a wise choice of techniques we *increase* the feeling of freedom.

"It's not planning which infringes upon freedom, but planning which uses force. A sense of freedom was practically unknown in the planned society of Nazi Germany, because the planners made a fantastic use of force and the threat of force.

"No, Mr. Castle, when a science of behavior has once been achieved, there's no alternative to a planned society. We can't leave mankind to an accidental or biased control. But by using the principle of positive reinforcement—carefully avoiding force or the threat of force—we can preserve a personal sense of freedom."

6. Ignoble Utopias   Joseph Wood Krutch

Joseph Wood Krutch (1893–1970) was a philosopher, essayist, and naturalist. He taught English at Columbia until the early 1950s, when he moved to the Arizona desert. *The Measure of Man* is generally considered his most important philosophical work.

Walden Two is a utopian community created by an experimental psychologist named Frazier who has learned the techniques for controlling thought with precision and who has conditioned his subjects to be happy, obedient and incapable of antisocial behavior. Universal benevolence and large tolerance of individual differences reign—not because it is assumed, as the founders of such utopias generally do assume, that they are natural to all innocent men uncorrupted by society—but because an experimental scientist, having at last mastered the "scientific ability to control men's thoughts with precision," has caused them to think benevolently and tolerantly.

An appeal to reason in contradistinction to passion, habit, or mere custom has been the usual basis of utopias from Plato to Sir Thomas

More and even down to Samuel Butler. Mr. Skinner's is, on the other hand, distinctly modern in that it puts its faith in the conditioned reflex instead, and proposes to perfect mankind by making individual men incapable of anything except habit and prejudice. At Walden Two men behave in a fashion we are accustomed to call "reasonable," not because they reason, but because they do not; because "right responses" are automatic. At the very beginning of the story we are shown a flock of sheep confined to the area reserved for them by a single thread which long ago replaced the electric fence once employed to condition them not to wander. As predicted in official Communist theory, the State—represented here by electricity—has "withered away" and no actual restraint is necessary to control creatures in whom obedience has become automatic. Obviously the assumption is that what will work with sheep will work with men.

Now though men can reason, they are not exclusively reasoning creatures. None, therefore, of the classic utopias could be realized because each is based on the assumption that reason alone can be made to guide human behavior. Moreover—and what is perhaps more important—few people have ever seriously wished to be exclusively rational. The good life which most desire is a life warmed by passions and touched with that ceremonial grace which is impossible without some affectionate loyalty to traditional forms and ceremonies. Many have, nevertheless, been very willing to grant that a little more reason in the conduct of private and public affairs would not be amiss. That is why, as fantasies, the utopias of Plato and Sir Thomas More have seemed interesting, instructive, even inspiring. But who really wants, even in fancy, to be, as Walden Two would make him, more unthinking, more nearly automatic than he now is? Who, even in his imagination, would like to live in a community where, instead of thinking part of the time, one never found it possible to think at all?

Is it not meaningful to say that whereas Plato's Republic and More's Utopia are noble absurdities, Walden Two is an ignoble one; that the first two ask men to be more than human, while the second urges them to be less? When, in the present world, men behave well, that is no doubt sometimes because they are creatures of habit as well as, sometimes, because they are reasonable. But if one proposes to change Man as Professor Skinner and so many other cheerful mechanists propose, is it really so evident that he should be changed in the direction they advocate? Is he something which, in Nietzsche's phrase, "must be surpassed," or is he a creature to whom the best advice one can give is the advice to retreat—away from such reasoned behavior as he may be capable of and toward that automatism of which he is also capable.

Obviously Walden Two represents—glorified, perfected, and curiously modernized—that ideal of a "cloistered virtue" which European man has tended to find not only unsatisfactory as an ideal but almost meaningless in terms of his doubtless conflicting aspirations. Nevertheless it must be admitted that Thomas Henry Huxley, a protomodern, once admitted in an often quoted passage that "if some great power would agree to make me always think what is true and do what is right, on

condition of being turned into a sort of clock and wound up every morning before I got out of bed. I should instantly close with the offer." And
what a Huxley would have agreed to, prospective candidates for admission into Walden Two might also find acceptable.

Frazier himself is compelled to make a significant confession: the
motives which led him to undertake his successful experiment included
a certain desire to exercise power over his fellows. That is not admirable
in itself and is obviously not without its dangers. But he insists that the
danger will disappear with him because those who succeed to his authority
and inherit his techniques will have enjoyed, as he did not, the advantages
of a scientific conditioning process and that therefore such potentially
antisocial impulses as his will no longer exist. In other words, though the
benevolent dictator is a rare phenomenon today, the happy chance which
produced this one will not have to be relied on in the future. Walden
Two will automatically produce the dictators necessary to carry it on.

Nevertheless and even if the skeptical reader will grant for the sake
of argument that automatic virtue represents an ideal completely satisfactory, a multitude of other doubts and fears are likely to arise in his
mind. He will remember of course that Brook Farm and the rest failed
promptly and decisively. Perhaps he will remember also that Russian
communism achieved at least some degree of permanence only by rejecting, more and more completely, everything which in any way parallels
the mildness, the gentleness, and the avoidance of all direct restraints
and pressures which is characteristic of Walden Two; that the makers
of Soviet policy came to denounce and repress even that somewhat paradoxical enthusiasm for the culture of a different world which was as
much encouraged in the earliest days of the experiment as it is at Walden
Two.

Hence, if a Walden Two is possible it obviously has become so only
because—and this is a point which presumably Mr. Skinner himself wishes
to emphasize—it differs in several respects from all superficially similar
projects. Like the Russian experiment it assumes that, for all practical
purposes, man is merely the product of society; but it also assumes a
situation which did not exist when the Communist state was set up:
namely one in which "the scientific ability to control men's thoughts with
precision" has fully matured.

Thus if the man upon whom the experiment is performed is nothing
but the limitlessly plastic product of external processes operating upon
him and is, by definition, incapable of any significant autonomous activity,
he is also, in this case, a creature who has fallen into the hands of an
ideally competent dictator. His desires, tastes, convictions and ideals are
precisely what the experimenter wants to make them. He is the repository
of no potentialities which can ever develop except as they are called forth
by circumstances over which he has no control. Finally, of course, his
happy condition is the result of the fortunate accident which determined
that the "engineer" who created him and, indirectly, will create all of his
progeny, was an experimenter whose own random conditioning happened to produce, not the monster who might just as likely have been

the first to seize the power that science offered, but a genuinely benevolent dictator instead.

A propos this last premise it might, in passing, be remarked as a curious
fact that though scientific method abhors the accidental, the uncontrollable and the unpredicted; though Mr. Skinner's own ideal seems to be
to remove forever any possible future intrusion of it into human affairs;
yet the successful establishment of the first utopia depended ultimately
on the decisive effect of just such an accident as will henceforth be impossible.

Critics of the assumption that technological advance is the true key
to human progress have often urged that new powers are dangerous
rather than beneficial unless the question of how they should be used
is at least opened before the powers become available. With more than
usual anxiety they might contemplate the situation in which we are now
placed if it is true that only chance will answer the question by whom
and in the interest of what "our approaching scientific ability to control
men's thoughts with precision" is to be used. But this is only one of several
desperate questions which the premises of *Walden Two* provoke. Most
of them can also be related to points made by Mr. Skinner in less fanciful
contexts and to one or two of them we may turn in connection with a
more general consideration of problems raised if we are ready to assume
that we actually do stand at the threshold of a world in which men's
thoughts will be controlled scientifically and as a matter of course.

To begin with, we must, of course, abandon the old platitude, "You
can't change human nature," and accept its opposite, "You can change
human nature as much and in whatever direction you wish"—because
"human nature" does not exist in the sense which the phrase implies.
Whatever desires, tastes, preferences, and tendencies have been so general and so persistent as to create the assumption that they are innate
or "natural" must be, as a matter of fact, merely the most ancient and
deeply graven of the conditionings to which the human animal has been
subjected. As Pascal—an odd thinker to be invoked in defense of a mechanistic and completely relativist ethic—once exclaimed in one of those
terrifying speculations of which, no doubt, his own conditioning made
him capable: "They say that habit is Second Nature; but perhaps Nature
is only First Habit."

By eager reformers "You can't change human nature" has often been
denounced as both a counsel of despair and a convenient excuse for lazy
indifference in the face of the world's ills. Yet the fact or alleged fact
which the phrase attempts to state has also its positive aspect. To say that
human nature cannot be changed means that human nature is something
in itself and there is at least the possibility that part of this something is
valuable. If we say that it cannot be changed we are also saying that it
cannot be completely corrupted; that it cannot be transformed into
something which we would not recognize as human at all. This is what
the eighteenth century allowed Pope to say for it, and as long as one
holds the doctrine that the term Nature actually describes some enduring
set of possibilities and values, then some limit is set, not only to human

perfectibility, but also, and more encouragingly, to things which it can become or be made.

But once this view of "Nature" has been dismissed as an illusion and even what appear to be the most persistent of its traits are thought of as merely the result of conditioning, then there is no limit to the extent to which men may become different from what they now are. There is nothing against which it may be assumed that human nature will revolt. Only by a temporarily established convention is any kind of vice a "creature of so frightful mien." Anything can be made to seem "natural." Cruelty, treachery, slander and deceit might come generally to seem not frightful but beautiful. And if it be said that the successful putting into practice of certain recent political philosophies supports the contention of determinists that man may, indeed, be taught to believe precisely this, it must be added that something more is also implied: namely that we must abandon—along with the conviction that human nature cannot be changed—all the hopes expressed in such phrases as "human nature will in the end revolt against" this or that.

Since no human nature capable of revolting against anything is now presumed to exist, then some other experimenter—conditioned perhaps as the son of the commandant of a Nazi labor camp—might decide to develop a race of men who found nothing more delightful than the infliction of suffering, and to establish for them a colony to be called Walden Three. By what standards could the dictator of Walden Two presume to judge that his utopia was any more desirable than its new rival? He could not appeal to God's revealed word; to the inner light of conscience; or to that eighteenth-century stand-by, the voice of Nature. He could say only that the accidents of his previous existence in a world where accident still played its part in determining how an individual should be conditioned had conditioned him to prefer what he would, in full realization of the unjustifiability of the metaphor, call "light rather than darkness." The life in Walden Two appears to him as "good" but the adjective would, of course, have no meaning in relation to anything outside himself.

In the light of such possibilities those who have not yet been molded by either Walden Two or Walden Three will tend to feel that before the "scientific ability to control men's thoughts with precision" has been fully utilized by whoever may seize the limitless power it will confer, we had better take a last look around—if not for that way of escape which may not exist, then at least in order to grasp certain implications and possible consequences as they appear to the minds of men who are still "free"— free at least in the limited sense that they are the product of conditions which were brought about, in part, through the presence of random factors destined to play a smaller and smaller part in determining human personality. That second generation of dictators to whom the dictator of Walden Two expects to pass on the control of affairs will be conditioners who have themselves been conditioned. The circle of cause and effect will have been closed and no man will ever again be anything which his predecessor has not consciously willed him to be.

According to the mechanist's own theories, everything which happened in the universe from its beginning down, at least until yesterday, was the result of chance. The chemical molecule didn't "want" or "plan" to grow more complex until it was a protein; the protein did not plan to become protoplasm; and the amoeba did not plan to become man. As a matter of fact, a theory very popular at the moment explains the fact that life seems to have arisen on our earth but once in all the billions of years of the planet's existence by saying that it could arise only as the result of a combination of circumstances so fantastically improbable that they have never occurred again. Yet though they owe to chance both their very existence and all progress from the protozoan to civilization, they are eager to take a step which would make it forever impossible for the unexpected and the unplanned to erupt again into the scheme which will pass completely under their own control.

No doubt many practical-minded people will object that such speculations as these are a waste of time. After all, they will say, even Walden Two does not exist except in fancy and no one has yet claimed that the "approaching scientific ability to control men's thoughts with precision" has already arrived. Logical dilemmas and metaphysical difficulties are cobwebs which will not entangle those who refuse to take seriously their gossamer threads. We have work to do and practical problems to solve.

But to all such it may be replied that practical problems and the metaphysical forms to which they may be reduced are not so unrelated as they may think, and that the logical extreme sometimes serves to make clear the real nature of a purely practical problem. It is true that no man has yet established a Walden Two or Walden Three, and that neither has any man yet controlled *with precision* men's thoughts. But it is also true that there has been a movement in a direction which suggests Walden Two as an ideal. Moreover, statesmen, educators and publicists have already achieved considerable success in their frankly admitted attempts to use the techniques already developed to control and condition large sections of the public and have increasingly declared their faith in the desirability and practicality of such methods in contradistinction to what used to be called education, on the one hand, and appeals to the enlightened understanding of the public, on the other. Already it has quite seriously and without any conviction of cynicism been proposed that the advertisers' principle, "say a thing often enough and it will be believed," be utilized by those who have what they regard as "correct" or "healthy" or "socially useful" ideas to sell. Every time it is proposed that schools should develop certain attitudes in their pupils or that the government should undertake propaganda along a certain line, the question of the difficult distinction between education in some old-fashioned sense and "conditioning" definitely arises.

Moreover, it is because the techniques of the social scientist and the experimental psychologists do to some extent work that some attempt must be made to understand their implications. By their methods many men may be made to do and think many things. Already in the relatively simple case of education versus "useful conditioning," the difficult distinction ceases to be difficult once a border line has been definitely crossed. Writing to George Washington not long after our particular democracy had been founded, Thomas Jefferson remarked, "It is an axiom in my mind that our liberty can never be safe but in the hands of the people themselves, and that, too, of the people with a certain degree of instruction." What would Jefferson have thought of the suggestion that "a certain degree of instruction" be interpreted to mean "a certain degree of conditioning"? Would he not have pointed out that the distinction between the two is clear and fundamental; that "conditioning" is achieved by methods which by-pass or, as it were, short-circuit those very reasoning faculties which education proposes to cultivate and exercise? And would he not have added that democracy can have no meaning or no function unless it is assumed that these faculties do lie within a realm of freedom where the sanctions of democracy arise?

Thus the whole future of mankind may well depend not only on the question whether man is entirely or only in part the product of conditionings, but also on the extent to which he is treated as though he were. Will we come ultimately to base what we call "education," in and out of schools, on the assumption that conditioning by propaganda as well as other methods is the most effective, even if it is not the only, method of influencing human beings?

To all such questions an answer in pragmatic terms has already been given at least positively enough to make it very pertinent to ask into whose hands the power already being exercised is to fall; to ask who is to decide in what direction the citizen is to be conditioned, and on the bases of what standards of value those decisions are to be made. That is simply the practical aspect of the theoretical question, "Who shall be master of Walden Two?"

In the totalitarian countries, where deterministic theories have been accepted in their most unqualified form and the techniques of control most systematically practiced, the question just posed has been answered in the simplest possible manner, and very much in the same way that it was answered at Walden Two. Power is exercised by those who seized it and, theoretically at least, this seizure was the last event which could "happen" because henceforward human destiny will be in the hands of those who are now in a position to control it. The question whether they ought to have done so and whether it is well for humanity that they did was either always meaningless or soon to become so since all the value judgments made in the future will be made by those who have been conditioned to approve what has happened to them.

One result of all this is that during the transition period while there are still survivors from the age when men's minds had not yet been controlled with precision and a conflict of wills is still possible—*i.e.,* under the conditions prevailing in the totalitarian states as they actually exist— a sharp distinction has to be made between those in possession of the power which they have seized and those who are subject to their manipulations. As a catchword the old term "classless society" may be used, but it is evident that no two classes could be more widely separated than the class of those who decide what shall be done and the class of those who are conditioned and controlled.

Obviously such a situation cannot arise either in Germany, Russia or Walden Two until the seizure of power has actually occurred and the power seized must include not only the classic essential, "the instruments of production," but also those "instruments of thought control" which seem to be assuming a more crucial importance than Marx assigned them.

No less obviously this seizure has not yet been made in the countries still called "democratic." Power may be drifting into the hands of certain groups but most of the members of these groups are not quite so completely committed as the totalitarian leaders were to the theories by which they justified their acts and are therefore not so ready to assume the dictatorship which may possibly be already within their reach. In such countries it is, therefore, still possible to consider certain questions, both practical and metaphysical, which even those still capable of considering them are forbidden to raise publicly in totalitarian states. We can still think—or at least go through those mental motions which were formerly called thinking—about the direction in which our own society seems to be moving, about certain large questions of values and ethics, even about the possibilities that under certain conditions men may not be the automata they are more and more assumed to be and that therefore their thoughts never can be controlled either completely or "with precision." Even more specifically we may ask whether totalitarianism on either the model of Soviet Russia or Walden Two is what we wish for or must inevitably accept.

It has sometimes been said that the totalitarian state is merely what democracy must in time become. Enthusiastically in the one case, reluctantly in the other; the same premises lead to the same methods and the same methods to the same results. What one proclaims definitively as dogma is the same as what the other drifts toward and this distinction is the only one which can be made, no matter where we attempt to draw it. In this view a "people's democracy" is only a "welfare state" which has fully accepted its implications. In theory as well as in practice the difference is always merely in the degree to which the logic of any position has been followed to its ultimate conclusion.

No doubt reality is much less simple. But after this large proviso has been accepted much can be said to support the contention that what we of the democracies toy with and lean toward are the same scientific hypotheses and the same philosophical notions that totalitarians proclaim as truths it is forbidden to question.

Roman Catholic doctrine makes the useful distinction between those beliefs which are *de fide* and those which are no more than *pia sententia*. The one must be accepted without dispute by all who wish to remain within the fold; the other, though part of commonly held opinion, have the weight of no authority behind them. In many cases the distinction between what the Communist state proclaims concerning the real nature of man and the proper methods of dealing with it differs from what many of our own psychologists and sociologists tend to assume only as an article of belief which has been proclaimed *de fide* differs from *pia sententia*. What we may tend to deduce from, say, the Pavlovian experiments does not differ too significantly from what an orthodox Russian scientist would say that these same experiments have proved with ultimate finality.

In what the sociologist previously quoted was pleased to call "today's thinking" man tends to appear very much what the Russian version of Marxist science would make him and those who follow such lines of thought are inevitably led to the same next step. If man is the product of the conditioning to which chance has subjected him, why should we not make him what we would like him to be?

We have, it is said, already effectively asserted our control over nature, animate and inanimate. Technology has already entered its mature phase and biology is entering it. We have mastered the atom; we have also learned how both to breed and to train animals. Since man is part of nature he also should be subject to control and no more should be necessary to make him so than easy extensions of the methods already successfully applied. We boast that we have mastered nature but that mastery can hardly be called complete until human nature is at least as completely under our control as the other phenomena of animate nature have become.

Perhaps the most general aspect of this subtle but inclusive shift of emphasis is revealed in the almost unconscious substitution of one term for another when the characteristics of a good social order are discussed. At the beginning of the democratic movement the watchword was "opportunity." Social and political evils were thought of as impediments to the free development of aspirations and abilities. But because "opportunity" as an ideal implies faith in the autonomous powers of the individual it has given way to others embodied in words which suggest in one way or another, not what men may be permitted to do for themselves, but what with benevolent intentions of course may be done to them.

The most brutally frank of such words is of course "control" but it is used most freely by those who have come frankly to accept a barely disguised totalitarian ideal. In those who wish still to pay lip service at least to some sort of faith in democracy and freedom the preferred words are "education," "adjustment" and, with a closer approach to frankness, "conditioning." But the difference is one of degree, not in the fundamental assumption which is that men should not be left to develop but must have their characters and temperaments, as well as their daily lives, somehow "planned" for them. The most benign aspect of this assumption is revealed in the desire for a "welfare state" which will assure the physical well-being of its citizens. The most sinister aspect is that more fully revealed in the speculations of the most advanced and theoretical social psychologists who have passed on, as the author of *Walden Two* has, to consider how the character, opinions and tastes of the individual may also be "planned" for him.

No doubt many of those who agree with that Dean of the Humanities to whose happy phrase we find ourselves again and again recurring would speak with the customary horror of the frankly totalitarian states which have, to date, achieved the greatest success in controlling men's thoughts with precision. They would carefully avoid such frank terms as "brain washing" which the Communists use to state clearly their intentions. But it is difficult to see what difference there is except the difference between a philosophy which is still tentative and somewhat reluctant to admit its ultimate implications and one which, facing those implications, proceeds confidently to put into practice the techniques which it has found effective. If "adjustment" is not to become "control" and "conditioning" is to shop short of "brain washing," some limits must be set which are not defined or even hinted at in such statements as those made by some psychologists.

Even those of us whose convictions permit us to doubt that men's thoughts will ever be completely controlled with absolute "precision" must realize, nevertheless, that the "scientific ability" to control them to some considerable degree has been growing and that in all probability it will grow still further. The terrifying extent to which many (if not all) the individuals in a group may be made to act and think in ways which we would once have thought inconceivable is already all too evident. Hence the question of how that power, whether it be limited or unlimited, will be used in our own society is of immediate as well as remote importance. It is no longer merely a metaphysical one.

It does no good to say that the democracy to which we assure ourselves we are committed safeguards us against the arbitrary use of that power. To say anything of the sort is merely to beg the question because an essential part of the question has to do with the reasonable doubt whether what we call democracy can survive the maturing techniques for determining in advance what "the voice of the people" will say. "Democracy," as the West defined it and in contradistinction to the new definition which totalitarianism has attempted to formulate, is meaningless except on the assumption that the individual man's thoughts and desires are to some extent uncontrollable and unpredictable. There can be no possible reason for taking a vote if the results can either be determined or even predicted in advance. In a society which assures, rightly or wrongly, that events are predictably determined, elections can be no more than those rituals with only a formal, ceremonial significance which, in Soviet Russia and Nazi Germany, they actually became.

In Walden Two this fact is tacitly recognized. Its founding dictator expects authority to "wither away" at the time of his death if not before, precisely as, in Communist theory, the dictatorship of the party will some day wither. But before withering away has occurred, the whole future history of mankind will have been set in a pattern which can never suffer any fundamental change because it must correspond to the pattern of conditionings which are self-perpetuating once they have been firmly and universally established. It is hard to see how we can accept even pragmatically the convictions and ideals of Walden Two without incurring consequences which correspond in the realm of the actual to the theoretical consequences of its theoretical premises. The question whether our own society is in the process of turning itself into some sort of Walden Two is far from being merely fantastic.

The Responsibility of Criminals

7. An Address Delivered to the Prisoners in the Chicago County Jail   Clarence Darrow

Clarence Seward Darrow (1857–1938) was one of America's outstanding criminal and trial lawyers. Among his famous cases were the Leopold and Loeb murder trial and the Scopes evolution trial in Tennessee. He was an outspoken agnostic and an opponent of traditional penal practices.

If I looked at jails and crimes and prisoners in the way the ordinary person does, I should not speak on this subject to you. The reason I talk to you on the question of crime, its cause and cure, is because I really do not in the least believe in crime. There is no such thing as a crime as the word is generally understood. I do not believe there is any sort of distinction between the real moral condition of the people in and out of jail. One is just as good as the other. The people here can no more help being here than the people outside can avoid being outside. I do not believe that people are in jail because they deserve to be. They are in jail simply because they can not avoid it on account of circumstances which are entirely beyond their control and for which they are in no way responsible.

I suppose a great many people on the outside would say I was doing you harm if they should hear what I say to you this afternoon, but you can not be hurt a great deal anyway, so it will not matter. Good people outside would say that I was really teaching you things that were calculated to injure society, but it's worth while now and then to hear something different from what you ordinarily get from preachers and the like. These will tell you that you should be good and then you will get rich and be happy. Of course we know that people do not get rich by being good, and that is the reason why so many of you people try to get rich some other way, only you do not understand how to do it quite as well as the fellow outside.

There are people who think that everything in this world is an accident. But really there is no such thing as an accident. A great many folks admit that many of the people in jail ought not to be there, and many who are outside ought to be in. I think none of them ought to be here. There ought to be no jails, and if it were not for the fact that the people on the outside are so grasping and heartless in their dealings with the people on the inside, there would be no such institutions as jails.

I do not want you to believe that I think all you people here are

Reprinted from *Crime and Criminals* by Clarence Darrow, published by Charles H. Kerr & Company, 1902.

angels. I do not think that. You are people of all kinds, all of you doing the best you can, and that is evidently not very well—you are people of all kinds and conditions and under all circumstances. In one sense everybody is equally good and equally bad. We all do the best we can under the circumstances. But as to the exact things for which you are sent here, some of you are guilty and some of you are not guilty. Some of you did the particular act because you needed the money. Some of you did it because you are in the habit of doing it, and some of you because you are born to it, and it comes to be as natural as it does, for instance, for me to be good.

Most of you probably have nothing against me, and most of you would treat me the same as any other person would; probably better than some of the people on the outside would treat me, because you think I believe in you and they know I do not believe in them. While you would not have the least thing against me in the world you might pick my pockets. I do not think all of you would, but I think some of you would. You would not have anything against me, but that's your profession, a few of you. Some of the rest of you, if my doors were unlocked, might come in if you saw anything you wanted—not out of any malice to me, but because that is your trade. There is no doubt there are quite a number of people in this jail who would pick my pockets. And still I know this, that when I get outside pretty nearly everybody picks my pocket. There may be some of you who would hold up a man on the street, if you did not happen to have something else to do, and needed the money; but when I want to light my house or my office the gas company holds me up. They charge me one dollar for something that is worth twenty-five cents, and still all these people are good people; they are pillars of society and support the churches, and they are respectable.

When I ride on the street cars, I am held up—I pay five cents for a ride that is worth two and a half cents, simply because a body of men have bribed the city council and the legislature, so that all the rest of us have to pay tribute to them.

If I do not want to fall into the clutches of the gas trust and choose to burn oil instead of gas, then good Mr. Rockefeller holds me up, and he uses a certain portion of his money to build universities and support churches which are engaged in telling us how to be good.

Some of you are here for obtaining property under false pretenses—yet I pick up a great Sunday paper and read the advertisements of a merchant prince—"Shirt waists for 39 cents, marked down from $3.00."

When I read the advertisements in the paper I see they are all lies. When I want to get out and find a place to stand anywhere on the face of the earth, I find that it has all been taken up long ago before I came here, and before you came here, and somebody says, "Get off, swim into the lake, fly into the air; go anywhere, but get off." That is because these people have the police and they have the jails and the judges and the lawyers and the soldiers and all the rest of them to take care of the earth and drive everybody off that comes in their way.

A great many people will tell you that all this is true, but that it does not excuse you. These facts do not excuse some fellow who reaches into my pocket and takes out a five dollar bill; the fact that the gas company bribes the members of the legislature from year to year, and fixes the law, so that all you people are compelled to be "fleeced" whenever you deal with them; the fact that the street car companies and the gas companies have control of the streets and the fact that the landlords own all the earth, they say, has nothing to do with you.

Let us see whether there is any connection between the crimes of the respectable classes and your presence in the jail. Many of you people are in jail because you have really committed burglary. Many of you, because you have stolen something: in the meaning of the law, you have taken some other person's property. Some of you have entered a store and carried off a pair of shoes because you did not have the price. Possibly some of you have committed murder. I can not tell what all of you did. There are a great many people here who have done some of these things who really do not know themselves why they did them. I think I know why you did them—every one of you; you did these things because you were bound to do them. It looked to you at the time as if you had a chance to do them or not, as you saw fit, but still after all you had no choice. There may be people here who had some money in their pockets and who still went out and got some more money in a way society forbids. Now you may not yourselves see exactly why it was you did this thing, but if you look at the question deeply enough and carefully enough you would see that there were circumstances that drove you to do exactly the thing which you did. You could not help it any more than we outside can help taking the positions that we take. The reformers who tell you to be good and you will be happy, and the people on the outside who have property to protect—they think that the only way to do it is by building jails and locking you up in cells on week-days and praying for you Sundays.

I think that all of this has nothing whatever to do with right conduct. I think it is very easily seen what has to do with right conduct. Some so-called criminals—and I will use this word because it is handy, it means nothing to me—I speak of the criminals who get caught as distinguished from the criminals who catch them—some of these so-called criminals are in jail for the first offenses, but nine-tenths of you are in jail because you did not have a good lawyer and of course you did not have a good lawyer because you did not have enough money to pay a good lawyer. There is no very great danger of a rich man going to jail.

Some of you may be here for the first time. If we would open the doors and let you out, and leave the laws as they are to-day, some of you would be back to-morrow. This is about as good a place as you can get anyway. There are many people here who are so in the habit of coming that they would not know where else to go. There are people who are born with the tendency to break into jail every chance they get, and they can not avoid it. You can not figure out your life and see why it was, but still there is a reason for it, and if we were all-wise and knew all the facts we could figure it out.

In the first place, there are a good many more people who go to jail in the winter time than in summer. Why is this? Is it because people are more wicked in winter? No, it is because the coal trust begins to get in its grip in the winter. A few gentlemen take possession of the coal, and unless the people will pay $7 or $8 a ton for something that is worth $3, they will have to freeze. Then there is nothing to do but to break into jail, and so there are many more in jail in the winter than in summer. It costs more for gas in the winter because the nights are longer, and people go to jail to save gas bills. The jails are electric-lighted. You may not know it, but these economic laws are working all the time, whether we know it or do not know it.

There are more people who go to jail in hard times than in good times—few people comparatively go to jail except when they are hard up. They go to jail because they have no other place to go. They may not know why, but it is true all the same. People are not more wicked in hard times. That is not the reason. The fact is true all over the world that in hard times more people go to jail than in good times, and in winter more people go to jail than in summer. Of course it is pretty hard times for people who go to jail at any time. The people who go to jail are almost always poor people—people who have no other place to live first and last. When times are hard then you find large numbers of people who go to jail who would not otherwise be in jail.

Long ago, Mr. Buckle, who was a great philosopher and historian, collected facts and he showed that the number of people who are arrested increased just as the price of food increased. When they put up the price of gas ten cents a thousand I do not know who will go to jail, but I do know that a certain number of people will go. When the meat combine raises the price of beef I do not know who is going to jail, but I know that a large number of people are bound to go. Whenever the Standard Oil Company raises the price of oil, I know that a certain number of girls who are seamstresses, and who work night after night long hours for somebody else, will be compelled to go out on the streets and ply another trade, and I know that Mr. Rockefeller and his associates are responsible and not the poor girls in the jails.

First and last, people are sent to jail because they are poor. Sometimes, as I say, you may not need money at the particular time, but you wish to have thrifty forehanded habits, and do not always wait until you are in absolute want. Some of you people are perhaps plying the trade, the profession, which is called burglary. No man in his right senses will go into a strange house in the dead of night and prowl around with a dark lantern through unfamiliar rooms and take chances of his life if he has plenty of the good things of the world in his own home. You would not take any such chances as that. If a man had clothes in his clothes-press and beefsteak in his pantry, and money in a bank, he would not navigate around nights in houses where he knows nothing about the premises whatever. It always requires experience and education for this profession, and people who fit themselves for it are no more to blame than I am for being a lawyer. A man would not hold up another man on the street if he had plenty of money in his own pocket. He might do it if he had one dollar or two dollars, but he wouldn't if he had as much money as

Mr. Rockefeller has. Mr. Rockefeller has a great deal better hold-up game than that.

The more that is taken from the poor by the rich, who have the chance to take it, the more poor people there are who are compelled to resort to these means for a livelihood. They may not understand it, they may not think so at once, but after all they are driven into that line of employment.

There is a bill before the legislature of this State to punish kidnaping children, with death. We have wise members of the Legislature. They know the gas trust when they see it and they always see it,—they can furnish light enough to be seen, and this Legislature thinks it is going to stop kidnaping children by making a law punishing kidnapers of children, with death. I don't believe in kidnaping children, but the Legislature is all wrong. Kidnaping children is not a crime, it is a profession. It has been developed with the times. It has been developed with our modern industrial conditions. There are many ways of making money—many new ways that our ancestors knew nothing about. Our ancestors knew nothing about a billion dollar trust; and here comes some poor fellow who has no other trade and he discovers the profession of kidnaping children.

This crime is born, not because people are bad; people don't kidnap other people's children because they want the children or because they are devilish, but because they see a chance to get some money out of it. You cannot cure this crime by passing a law punishing by death kidnapers of children. There is one way to cure it. There is one way to cure all these offenses, and that is to give the people a chance to live. There is no other way, and there never was any other way since the world began, and the world is so blind and stupid that it will not see. If every man and woman and child in the world had a chance to make a decent, fair, honest living, there would be no jails, and no lawyers and no courts. There might be some persons here or there with some peculiar formation of their brain, like Rockefeller, who would do these things simply to be doing them; but they would be very, very few, and those should be sent to a hospital and treated, and not sent to jail; and they would entirely disappear in the second generation, or at least in the third generation.

I am not talking pure theory. I will just give you two or three illustrations.

The English people once punished criminals by sending them away. They would load them on a ship and export them to Australia. England was owned by lords and nobles and rich people. They owned the whole earth over there, and the other people had to stay in the streets. They could not get a decent living. They used to take their criminals and send them to Australia—I mean the class of criminals who got caught. When these criminals got over there, and nobody else had come, they had the whole continent to run over, and so they could raise sheep and furnish their own meat, which is easier than stealing it; these criminals then became decent, respectable people because they had a chance to live. They did not commit any crimes. They were just like the English people who sent them there, only better. And in the second generation the descendants of those criminals were as good and respectable a class of people as there were on the face of the earth, and then they began building churches and jails themselves.

A portion of this country was settled in the same way, landing prisoners down on the southern coast; but when they got here and had a whole continent to run over and plenty of chances to make a living, they became respectable citizens, making their own living just like any other citizen in the world; but finally these descendants of the English aristocracy, who sent the people over to Australia, found out they were getting rich, and so they went over to get possession of the earth as they always do, and they organized land syndicates and got control of the land and ores, and then they had just as many criminals in Australia as they did in England. It was not because the world had grown bad; it was because the earth had been taken away from the people.

Some of you people have lived in the country. It's prettier than it is here. And if you have ever lived on a farm you understand that if you put a lot of cattle in a field, when the pasture is short they will jump over the fence; but put them in a good field where there is plenty of pasture, and they will be law-abiding cattle to the end of time. The human animal is just like the rest of the animals, only a little more so. The same thing that governs in the one governs in the other.

Everybody makes his living along the lines of least resistance. A wise man who comes into a country early sees a great undeveloped land. For instance, our rich men twenty-five years ago saw that Chicago was small and knew a lot of people would come here and settle, and they readily saw that if they had all the land around here it would be worth a good deal, so they grabbed the land. You can not be a landlord because somebody has got it all. You must find some other calling. In England and Ireland and Scotland less than five per cent own all the land there is, and the people are bound to stay there on any kind of terms the landlords give. They must live the best they can, so they develop all these various professions—burglary, picking pockets and the like.

Again, people find all sorts of ways of getting rich. These are diseases like everything else. You look at people getting rich, organizing trusts, and making a million dollars, and somebody gets the disease and he starts out. He catches it just as a man catches the mumps or the measles; he is not to blame, it is in the air. You will find men speculating beyond their means, because the mania of money-getting is taking possession of them. It is simply a disease; nothing more, nothing less. You can not avoid catching it; but the fellows who have control of the earth have the advantage of you. See what the law is; when these men get control of things, they make the laws. They do not make the laws to protect anybody; courts are not instruments of justice; when your case gets into court it will make little difference whether you are guilty or innocent; but it's better if you have a smart lawyer. And you can not have a smart lawyer unless you have money. First and last it's a question of money. Those men who own the earth make the laws to protect what they have. They fix up a sort of fence or pen around what they have, and they fix the law so the fellow on the outside can not get in. The laws are really organized for the protection of the men who rule the world. They were never organized or enforced to do justice. We have no system for doing justice, not the slightest in the world.

Let me illustrate: Take the poorest person in this room. If the community had provided a system of doing justice the poorest person in this room would have as good a lawyer as the richest, would he not? When you went into court you would have just as long a trial, and just as fair a trial as the richest person in Chicago. Your case would not be tried in fifteen or twenty minutes, whereas it would take fifteen days to get through with a rich man's case.

Then if you were rich and were beaten, your case would be taken to the Appellate Court. A poor man can not take his case to the Appellate Court; he has not the price; and then to the Supreme Court, and if he were beaten there he might perhaps go to the United States Supreme Court. And he might die of old age before he got into jail. If you are poor, it's a quick job. You are almost known to be guilty, else you would not be there. Why should any one be in the criminal court if he were not guilty? He would not be there if he could be anywhere else. The officials have not time to look after all these cases. The people who are on the outside, who are running banks and building churches and making jails, they have no time to examine 600 or 700 prisoners each year to see whether they are guilty or innocent. If the courts were organized to promote justice the people would elect somebody to defend all these criminals, somebody as smart as the prosecutor—and give him as many detectives and as many assistants to help, and pay as much money to defend you as to prosecute you. We have a very able man for State's Attorney, and he has many assistants, detectives and policemen without end, and judges to hear the cases—everything handy.

Most of all our criminal code consists in offenses against property. People are sent to jail because they have committed a crime against property. It is of very little consequence whether one hundred people more or less go to jail who ought not to go—you must protect property, because in this world property is of more importance than anything else.

How is it done? These people who have property fix it so they can protect what they have. When somebody commits a crime it does not follow that he had done something that is morally wrong. The man on the outside who has committed no crime may have done something. For instance: to take all the coal in the United States and raise the price two dollars or three dollars when there is no need of it, and thus kill thousands of babies and send thousands of people to the poorhouse and tens of thousands to jail, as is done every year in the United States,—this is a greater crime than all the people in our jails ever committed, but the law does not punish it. Why? Because the fellows who control the earth make the laws. If you and I had the making of the laws, the first thing we would do would be to punish the fellow who gets control of the earth. Nature put this coal in the ground for me as well as for them and nature made the prairies up here to raise wheat for me as well as for them, and then the great railroad companies came along and fenced it up.

Most all of the crimes for which we are punished are property crimes.

There are a few personal crimes, like murder—but they are very few. The crimes committed are mostly those against property. If this punishment is right the criminals must have a lot of property. How much money is there in this crowd? And yet you are all here for crimes against property. The people up and down the Lake Shore have not committed crime, still they have so much property they don't know what to do with it. It is perfectly plain why these people have not committed crimes against property; they make the laws and therefore do not need to break them. And in order for you to get some property you are obliged to break the rules of the game. I don't know but what some of you may have had a very nice chance to get rich by carrying the hod for one dollar a day, twelve hours. Instead of taking that nice, easy profession, you are a burglar. If you had been given a chance to be a banker you would rather follow that. Some of you may have had a chance to work as a switchman on a railroad where you know, according to statistics, that you can not live and keep all your limbs more than seven years, and you can get fifty dollars or seventy-five dollars a month for taking your lives in your hands, and instead of taking that lucrative position you choose to be a sneak thief, or something like that. Some of you made that sort of choice. I don't know which I would take if I was reduced to this choice. I have an easier choice.

I will guarantee to take from this jail, or any jail in the world, five hundred men who have been the worst criminals and law-breakers who ever got into jail, and I will go down to our lowest streets and take five hundred of the most abandoned prostitutes, and go out somewhere where there is plenty of land, and will give them a chance to make a living, and they will be as good people as the average in the community.

There is a remedy for the sort of condition we see here. The world never finds it out, or when it does find it out it does not enforce it. You may pass a law punishing every person with death for burglary, and it will make no difference. Men will commit it just the same. In England there was a time when one hundred different offenses were punishable with death, and it made no difference. The English people strangely found out that so fast as they repealed the severe penalties and so fast as they did away with punishing men by death, crime decreased instead of increased; that the smaller the penalty the fewer the crimes.

Hanging men in our county jails does not prevent murder. It makes murderers.

And this has been the history of the world. It's easy to see how to do away with what we call crime. It is not so easy to do it. I will tell you how to do it. It can be done by giving the people a chance to live—by destroying special privileges. So long as big criminals can get the coal fields, so long as the big criminals have control of the city council and get the public streets for street cars and gas rights, this is bound to send thousands of poor people to jail. So long as men are allowed to monopolize all the earth, and compel others to live on such terms as these men see fit to make, then you are bound to get into jail.

The only way in the world to abolish crime and criminals is to abolish the big ones and the little ones together. Make fair conditions of life.

Give men a chance to live. Abolish the right of the private ownership of land, abolish monopoly, make the world partners in production, partners in the good things of life. Nobody would steal if he could get something of his own some easier way. Nobody will commit burglary when he has a house full. No girl will go out on the streets when she has a comfortable place at home. The man who owns a sweatshop or a department store may not be to blame himself for the condition of his girls, but when he pays them five dollars, three dollars, and two dollars a week, I wonder where he thinks they will get the rest of their money to live. The only way to cure these conditions is by equality. There should be no jails. They do not accomplish what they pretend to accomplish. If you would wipe them out, there would be no more criminals than now. They terrorize nobody. They are a blot upon any civilization, and a jail is an evidence of the lack of charity of the people on the outside who make the jails and fill them with the victims of their greed.

8. The Humanitarian Theory of Punishment   C. S. Lewis

Clive Staples Lewis (1898–1963) was professor of Medieval and Renaissance English at Cambridge University from 1954 until his death. He is most famous for his numerous books and essays that defend various aspects of Christianity.

In England we have lately had a controversy about Capital Punishment. I do not know whether a murderer is more likely to repent and make a good end on the gallows a few weeks after his trial or in the prison infirmary thirty years later. I do not know whether the fear of death is an indispensable deterrent. I need not, for the purpose of this article, decide whether it is a morally permissible deterrent. Those are questions which I propose to leave untouched. My subject is not Capital Punishment in particular, but that theory of punishment in general which the controversy showed to be almost universal among my fellow-countrymen. It may be called the Humanitarian Theory. Those who hold it think that it is mild and merciful. In this I believe that they are seriously mistaken. I believe that the "Humanity" which it claims is a dangerous illusion and disguises the possibility of cruelty and injustice without end. I urge a return to the traditional or Retributive theory not solely, nor even primarily, in the interests of society but in the interests of the criminal.

According to the Humanitarian theory, to punish a man because he deserves it, and as much as he deserves, is mere revenge, and, therefore, barbarous and immoral. It is maintained that the only legitimate motives for punishing are the desire to deter others by example or to mend the

From *Res Judicatae,* June 1953. Reprinted with permission of Walter Hooper, Trustee of the C. S. Lewis estate.

criminal. When this theory is combined, as frequently happens, with the belief that all crime is more or less pathological, the idea of mending tails off into that of healing or curing and punishment becomes therapeutic. Thus it appears at first sight that we have passed from the harsh and self-righteous notion of giving the wicked their deserts to the charitable and enlightened one of tending the psychologically sick. What could be more amiable? One little point which is taken for granted in this theory needs, however, to be made explicit. The things done to the criminal, even if they are called cures, will be just as compulsory as they were in the old days when we called them punishments. If a tendency to steal can be cured by psychotherapy, the thief will no doubt be forced to undergo the treatment. Otherwise, society cannot continue.

My contention is that this doctrine, merciful though it appears, really means that each one of us, from the moment he breaks the law, is deprived of the rights of a human being.

The reason is this. The Humanitarian theory removes from Punishment the concept of Desert. But the concept of Desert is the only connecting link between punishment and justice. It is only as deserved or undeserved that a sentence can be just or unjust. I do not here contend that the question "Is it deserved?" is the only one we can reasonably ask about a punishment. We may very properly ask whether it is likely to deter others and to reform the criminal. But neither of these two last questions is a question about justice. There is no sense in talking about a "just deterrent" or a "just cure." We demand of a deterrent not whether it is just but whether it will deter. We demand of a cure not whether it is just but whether it succeeds. Thus when we cease to consider what the criminal deserves and consider only what will cure him or deter others, we have tacitly removed him from the sphere of justice altogether; instead of a person, a subject of rights, we now have a mere object; a patient, a "case."

The distinction will become clearer if we ask who will be qualified to determine sentences when sentences are no longer held to derive their propriety from the criminal's deservings. On the old view the problem of fixing the right sentence was a moral problem. Accordingly, the judge who did it was a person trained in jurisprudence; trained, that is, in a science which deals with rights and duties, and which, in origin at least, was consciously accepting guidance from the Law of Nature, and from Scripture. We must admit that in the actual penal code of most countries at most times these high originals were so much modified by local custom, class interests, and utilitarian concessions, as to be very imperfectly recognizable. But the code was never in principle, and not always in fact, beyond the control of the conscience of the society. And when (say, in Eighteenth Century England) actual punishments conflicted too violently with the moral sense of the community, juries refused to convict and reform was finally brought about. This was possible because, so long as we are thinking in terms of Desert, the propriety of the penal code, being a moral question, is a question on which every man has the right to an opinion, not because he follows this or that profession, but because he is simply a man, a rational animal enjoying the Natural Light. But all this is changed when we drop the concept of Desert. The only two questions we may now ask about a punishment are whether it deters and whether it cures. But these are not questions on which anyone is entitled to have an opinion simply because he is a man. He is not entitled to an opinion even if, in addition to being a man, he should happen also to be a jurist, a Christian, and a moral theologian. For they are not questions about principle but about matter of fact; and for such *cuiquam in sua arte credendum.** Only the expert "penologist" (let barbarous things have barbarous names), in the light of previous experiment, can tell us what is likely to deter; only the psychotherapist can tell us what is likely to cure. It will be in vain for the rest of us, speaking simply as men, to say, "but this punishment is hideously unjust, hideously disproportionate to the criminal's deserts." The experts with perfect logic will reply, "but nobody was talking about deserts. No one was talking about *punishment* in your archaic vindictive sense of the word. Here are the statistics proving that this treatment cures. What is your trouble?

The Humanitarian theory, then, removes sentences from the hands of jurists whom the public conscience is entitled to criticize and places them in the hands of technical experts whose special sciences do not even employ such categories as Rights or Justice. It might be argued that since this transference results from an abandonment of the old idea of punishment, and, therefore, of all vindictive motives, it will be safe to leave our criminals in such hands. I will not pause to comment on the simple minded view of fallen human nature which such a belief implies. Let us rather remember that the "cure" of criminals is to be compulsory; and let us then watch how the theory actually works in the mind of the Humanitarian. The immediate starting point of this article was a letter I read in one of our Leftist weeklies. The author was pleading that a certain sin, now treated by our Laws as a crime, should henceforward be treated as a disease. And he complained that under the present system the offender, after a term in gaol, was simply let out to return to his original environment where he would probably relapse. What he complained of was not the shutting up but the letting out. On his remedial view of punishment the offender should, of course, be detained until he was cured. And of course the official straighteners are the only people who can say when that is. The first result of the Humanitarian theory is, therefore, to substitute for a definite sentence (reflecting to some extent the community's moral judgment on the degree of ill-desert involved) an indefinite sentence terminable only by the word of those experts— and they are not experts in moral theology nor even in the Law of Nature—who inflict it. Which of us, if he stood in the dock, would not prefer to be tried by the old system?

It may be said that by the continued use of the word Punishment and the use of the verb "inflict" I am misrepresenting the Humanitarians. They are not punishing, not inflicting, only healing. But do not let us be deceived by a name. To be taken without consent from my home and

*["Experts must be believed."—Ed.]

friends; to lose my liberty; to undergo all those assaults on my personality which modern psychotherapy knows how to deliver; to be remade after some pattern of "normality" hatched in a Viennese laboratory to which I never professed allegiance; to know that this process will never end until either my captors have succeeded or I grown wise enough to cheat them with apparent success—who cares whether this is called Punishment or not? That it includes most of the elements for which any punishment is feared—shame, exile, bondage and years eaten by the locust—is obvious. Only enormous ill-desert could justify it; but ill-desert is the very conception which the Humanitarian theory has thrown overboard.

If we turn from the curative to the deterrent justification of punishment we shall find the new theory even more alarming. When you punish a man *in terrorem,* make of him an "example" to others, you are admittedly using him as a means to an end; someone else's end. This, in itself, would be a very wicked thing to do. On the classical theory of Punishment it was of course justified on the ground that the man deserved it. That was assumed to be established before any question of "making him an example" arose. You then, as the saying is, killed two birds with one stone; in the process of giving him what he deserved you set an example to others. But take away desert and the whole morality of the punishment disappears. Why, in Heaven's name, am I to be sacrificed to the good of society in this way?—unless, of course, I deserve it.

But that is not the worst. If the justification of exemplary punishment is not to be based on desert but solely on its efficacy as a deterrent, it is not absolutely necessary that the man we punish should even have committed the crime. The deterrent effect demands that the public should draw the moral, "If we do such an act we shall suffer like that man." The punishment of a man actually guilty whom the public think innocent will not have the desired effect; the punishment of a man actually innocent will, provided the public think him guilty. But every modern State has powers which make it easy to fake a trial. When a victim is urgently needed for exemplary purposes and a guilty victim cannot be found, all the purposes of deterrence will be equally served by the punishment (call it "cure" if you prefer) of an innocent victim, provided that the public can be cheated into thinking him guilty. It is no use to ask me why I assume that our rulers will be so wicked. The punishment of an innocent, that is, and undeserving, man is wicked only if we grant the traditional view that righteous punishment means deserved punishment. Once we have abandoned that criterion, all punishments have to be justified, if at all, on other grounds that have nothing to do with desert. Where the punishment of the innocent can be justified on those grounds (and it could in some cases be justified as a deterrent) it will be no less moral than any other punishment. Any distaste for it on the part of a Humanitarian will be merely a hang-over from the Retributive theory.

It is, indeed, important to notice that my argument so far supposes no evil intentions on the part of the Humanitarian and considers only what is involved in the logic of his position. My contention is that good men (not bad men) consistently acting upon that position would act as cruelly and unjustly as the greatest tyrants. They might in some respects act even worse. Of all tyrannies a tyranny sincerely exercised for the good of its victims may be the most oppressive. It may be better to live under robber barons than under omnipotent moral busybodies. The robber baron's cruelty may sometimes sleep, his cupidity may at some point be satiated; but those who torment us for our own good will torment us without end for they do so with the approval of their own conscience. They may be more likely to go to Heaven yet at the same time like-lier to make a Hell of earth. Their very kindness stings with intolerable insult. To be "cured" against one's will and cured of states which we may not regard as disease is to be put on a level with those who have not yet reached the age of reason or those who never will; to be classed with infants, imbeciles, and domestic animals. But to be punished, however severely, because we have deserved it, because we "ought to have known better," is to be treated as a human person made in God's image.

In reality, however, we must face the possibility of bad rulers armed with a Humanitarian theory of punishment. A great many popular blue prints for a Christian society are merely what the Elizabethans called "eggs in moonshine" because they assume that the whole society is Christian or that the Christians are in control. This is not so in most contemporary States. Even if it were, our rulers would still be fallen men, and, therefore, neither very wise nor very good. As it is, they will usually be unbelievers. And since wisdom and virtue are not the only or the commonest qualifications for a place in the government, they will not often be even the best unbelievers. The practical problem of Christian politics is not that of drawing up schemes for a Christian society, but that of living as innocently as we can with unbelieving fellow-subjects under unbelieving rulers who will never be perfectly wise and good and who will sometimes be very wicked and very foolish. And when they are wicked the Humanitarian theory of Punishment will put in their hands a finer instrument of tyranny than wickedness ever had before. For if crime and disease are to be regarded as the same thing, it follows that any state of mind which our masters choose to call "disease" can be treated as crime; and compulsorily cured. It will be vain to plead that states of mind which displease government need not always involve moral turpitude and do not therefore always deserve forfeiture of liberty. For our masters will not be using the concepts of Desert and Punishment but those of disease and cure. We know that one school of psychology already regards religion as a neurosis. When this particular neurosis becomes inconvenient to government what is to hinder government from proceeding to "cure" it? Such "cure" will, of course, be compulsory; but under the Humanitarian theory it will not be called by the shocking name of Persecution. No one will blame us for being Christians, no one will hate us, no one will revile us. The new Nero will approach us with the silky manners of a doctor, and though all will be in fact as compulsory as the *tunica molesta* or Smithfield or Tyburn, all will go on within the unemotional therapeutic sphere where words like "right" and "wrong" or "freedom" and "slavery" are never heard. And thus when the command is given every prominent Christian in the land may vanish overnight into Institutions for the Treatment of the Ideologically Unsound, and it will rest with the expert gaolers to say when (if ever) they are to re-emerge. But it will not be persecution. Even if the treatment is painful, even if it is life-long, even if it is fatal, that will be only a regrettable accident; the intention was purely therapeutic. Even in ordinary medicine there were painful operations and fatal operations; so in this. But because they are "treatment," not punishment, they can be criticized only by fellow-experts and on technical grounds, never by men as men and on grounds of justice.

This is why I think it essential to oppose the Humanitarian theory of Punishment, root and branch, wherever we encounter it. It carries on its front a semblance of Mercy which is wholly false. That is how it can deceive men of good will. The error began, perhaps, with Shelley's statement that the distinction between Mercy and Justice was invented in the courts of tyrants. It sounds noble, and was indeed the error of a noble mind. But the distinction is essential. The older view was that Mercy "tempered" Justice, or (on the highest level of all) that Mercy and Justice had met and kissed. The essential act of Mercy was to pardon; and pardon in its very essence involves the recognition of guilt and ill-desert in the recipient. If crime is only a disease which needs cure, not sin which deserves punishment, it cannot be pardoned. How can you pardon a man for having a gum-boil or a club foot? But the Humanitarian theory wants simply to abolish Justice and substitute Mercy for it. This means that you start being "kind" to people before you have considered their rights, and then force upon them supposed kindnesses which they in fact had a right to refuse, and finally kindnesses which no one but you will recognize as kindnesses and which the recipient will feel as abominable cruelties. You have overshot the mark. Mercy, detached from Justice, grows unmerciful. That is the important paradox. As there are plants which will flourish only in mountain soil, so it appears that Mercy will flower only when it grows in the crannies of the rock of Justice; transplanted to the marshlands of mere Humanitarianism, it becomes a man-eating weed, all the more dangerous because it is still called by the same name as the mountain variety. But we ought long ago to have learned our lesson. We should be too old now to be deceived by those humane pretensions which have served to usher in every cruelty of the revolutionary period in which we live. These are the "precious balms" which will "break our heads."

There is a fine sentence in Bunyan: "It came burning hot into my mind, whatever he said, and however he flattered, when he got me home to his house, he would sell me for a slave." There is a fine couplet, too, in John Ball:

> Be ware ere ye be wo.
> Know your friend from your foe.

One last word. You may ask why I send this to an Australian periodical. The reason is simple and perhaps worth recording; I can get no hearing for it in England.

Suggestions
for Further Reading

Anthologies

Enteman, Willard F. (ed.). *The Problem of Free Will*. New York: Scribners, 1967. A collection of important articles on various aspects of the free will–determinism controversy. Since most of the articles are easily readable, this is a good book for the beginning student to turn to for additional reading.

Hook, Sidney (ed.). *Determinism and Freedom in the Age of Modern Science*. New York: New York U.P., 1958. A collection of twenty-seven articles that analyzes the concepts of determinism and freedom and the significance of these concepts in physics, law, and ethics. Most of the articles will be difficult for the beginning student.

Individual Works

Clemens, Samuel, "What is Man?" in *What is Man? and Other Essays*. New York: Harper, 1917. An interesting and amusing statement of the determinist position by a famous writer.

Cranston, Maurice. *Freedom: A New Analysis*. London: Longmans, 1953. The latter half of this book is a good discussion of the main positions and a defense of libertarianism.

D'Angelo, Edward. *The Problem of Freedom and Determinism*. Columbia, Mo.: U. of Missouri, 1968. A good, clear discussion of the three major positions.

Darrow, Clarence. *Crime: Its Cause and Treatment*. New York: Crowell, 1922. A famous discussion of criminal treatment from the hard determinist viewpoint.

Lamont, Corliss. *Freedom of Choice Affirmed*. New York: Horizon, 1967. A clear statement and defense of libertarianism.

Matson, Floyd W. *The Broken Image*. New York: George Braziller, 1964. A good discussion of how the hard determinist position has affected man's image of himself. There is also an examination of Skinner and other behaviorists in this connection.

O'Connor, D. J. *Free Will*. Garden City, N.Y.: Doubleday, 1971. A careful survey of the main arguments both for and against determinism.

Schopenhauer, Arthur. "Free-Will and Fatalism" in *The Pessimist's Handbook (Parerga und Paralipomena)*. Translated by T. Bailey Saunders, edited by Hazel E. Barnes. Lincoln: U. of Nebraska, 1964. A concise and forceful defense of fatalism. Schopenhauer, a clear stylist, uses many illustrations drawn from everyday human behavior and world literature in this essay intended for the general reading public.

Taylor, Richard. *Metaphysics*. Englewood Cliffs, N.J.: Prentice-Hall, 1974 (2nd ed). Chapter Five contains a clearly written attack on hard and soft determinism and a defense of a version of libertarianism.

Dictionary of the History of Ideas: Studies of Selected Pivotal ideas. Philip P. Weiner, editor-in-chief. New York: Scribners, 1973. Substantial and clearly written essays emphasizing the historical development of topics discussed in this part. Designed to inform the nonspecialist, each essay concludes with a select bibliography.

Encyclopedia of Philosophy. Paul Edwards, editor-in-chief. New York: Macmillan, 1967. The student will find many worthwhile articles on the subject treated in this part, and excellent bibliographies.

Two:
God
and
Religion

Introduction

A question troubling many students is whether they should believe in religion. One reason for their hesitation simply to follow in the paths of their parents in this matter is their conviction that religion has failed to bring about a better world for mankind. Perhaps an even more important reason is that there appears to be no scientific manner by which the basic religious tenets can be established. The desire that one's beliefs be supported by science has its roots in the movement of Western civilization away from a religious view of the world to a scientific one. The great success of science has led many to the view that we should believe only those things that can be established in a proper scientific manner. Further, the advance of science has certainly tended to undermine any simplistic acceptance of religious doctrines and writings. The scientifically trained no longer accept, for example, the biblical accounts of creation and the Garden of Eden as literally true. Thus, it is easy to understand why so many of today's students are dubious about accepting traditional orthodox religion. In the light of modern science it appears to be a remnant of ancient superstition that will one day be completely replaced by a scientific view of the world.

Contemporary religious thinkers generally deplore the tendency to view science and religion as competing views of the world. For them, religion and science are concerned with different issues. Science is concerned to discover the laws that are operative in the physical universe, whereas religion is concerned with issues beyond the scope of science, such as the reason for the existence of the universe, the existence of God, and the purpose of man's life. Since the issues with which religion is concerned are not within the scope of science, it is held to be inappropriate to demand that religious beliefs should be substantiated by scientific facts.

Must religious beliefs be supported by scientific evidence, or is it acceptable to believe without proof? Do the discoveries of modern science show that the views of the major religions are untenable? These are some of the questions that the philosopher seeks to answer about religion. The philosopher's interest in such questions arises out of the fact that religion gives answers to many of man's most fundamental questions about himself and his place in the world. The philosopher wants to know if the answers are true. Thus, in examining religious views, the philosopher is concerned with their accurate assessment rather than their defense or destruction. The readings in this section show that a great diversity of opinion exists among philosophers regarding the truth and value of religion. Some hold that only in a religious framework can a foundation for morality and a meaning to life be found. Others see various religious views as not only false but a great detriment to man's happiness. The student's job is to assess carefully the various positions and arguments to determine which, if any, is sound.

The basic tenet of the major Western religions is that there exists a supernatural being called "God." God is defined as being an all-good, all-knowing, all-powerful creator of the universe. God is viewed as concerned with our affairs rather than being withdrawn and aloof. For the most part, religious believers are convinced that such a God exists without inquiring into the question of scientific or rational proofs for their conviction. Yet many religious theorists believe it important to show, if possible, that the existence of God can be proven or at least shown to be probable on the basis of scientific evidence or other rational arguments. If God's existence could be proven, not only could the skeptics and atheists be converted but many who believe would feel more confident in their belief.

Numerous proofs have been offered for the existence of God. Most are of little interest to philosophers since they are clearly unsound. Typical of these widely used but unsound arguments are the argument from agreement and the argument from Scripture. *The argument from agreement* consists in attempting to show that God exists on the basis of the fact that so many people throughout the world have believed in the existence of God. It is claimed that such a widespread belief cannot be explained on any other basis than the actual existence of God. One problem with arguing in this manner is that it makes the majority opinion the basis of truth; but it is certainly well known that large majorities have been wrong. At one time there was widespread agreement that the earth was flat. Another difficulty with this argument is that the widespread belief in God can perhaps be explained as the result of superstition, wishful thinking, or fear. If so, the belief in God would not indicate his existence but the psychological characteristics or the lack of scientific knowledge of the majority of mankind. *The argument from Scripture* attempts to prove God's existence on the basis of the fact that we have some writings (Old Testament, New Testament, Koran, and so on) that tell of God. These writings are assumed to be inspired by God and therefore reliable. The obvious dificulty with attempting to prove God in this manner is that the events recorded in the writings must be proved to be accurate and such proof seems impossible to get. Those who doubt the existence of God will also be doubtful that the Bible was inspired by God and that the events given there are accurately reported.

In the readings that follow, some of the arguments that philosophers have considered more plausible are presented. The one that will probably be most familiar to the student is the *argument from design.* According to this argument the world is so intricately put together to maintain the existence of various types of life that it must have been designed by an extremely rational being. This argument is presented in a simple, straightforward manner by A. Cressy Morrison, a highly respected American scientist. Morrison argues that life could not possibly exist by chance since the probability of all the necessary factors existing in the proper relationships would be too great. Also, he claims that the fact that nature is so balanced that no species can conquer all the others indicates that some great intelligence planned the world. The soundness of the argument is attacked by Clarence Darrow, who argues that the universe shows no clear order or design. He goes on to say that even if it did, it was apparently not designed for human life since we could easily imagine ways in which the world could have been made to provide a better habitation for human beings.

Another frequently encountered argument, *the argument from religious experience,* is presented by James Bisset Pratt. Pratt maintains that belief in God can be upheld by mystical experiences that supporters of various religions have had. The main problem that he feels stands in the way of acceptance of such experiences as evidence of God is the naturalistic explanation of them given by psychologists. It would seem that if such experiences could be accounted for as the result of unusual psychological states, then they could not be considered as evidence of God's existence. Pratt argues, however, that such psychological interpretations are not necessarily incompatible with a religious interpretation of the same phenomena. The student should consider whether Pratt has shown merely that certain experiences could be given a religious interpretation, or whether he has shown that such experiences must be given a religious interpretation and thus are good evidence of God's existence.

In "The Basis of the Moral Law," C. S. Lewis presents a version of the *moral argument* for God. He maintains that men have a sense of moral obligation, which they feel as a claim coming from outside themselves. No naturalistic account of this sense of obligation in terms of human needs or interests satisfactorily explains it. It can only be explained, Lewis argues, by assuming the existence of a lawgiver outside the universe. The crucial issue in assessing this argument is whether he is correct in denying that the sense of obligation can be given an alternative explanation.

Many of the arguments for the existence of God, including the argument from design, are discussed by Bertrand Russell. Russell maintains that none of the arguments for the existence of God are convincing. Further, he attacks all religions, not just Christianity, on several grounds. Religion, he maintains, is born of fear and a desire to have a protector. We must not give in to such feelings but must learn to stand on our own feet and conquer the world by intelligence. Further, the various organized religions have hindered progress by defending a morality that is not conducive to human happiness. To improve human institutions and allow for moral progress, the morality of the churches must be opposed.

Some philosophers have maintained that not only is God's existence unprovable but that we can show that God does not exist. The main attempt to show that an all-good, all-powerful God does not exist arises from a consideration of the evil that exists in the world. It seems undeniably true that bad or evil things happen. Hurricanes and floods destroy houses and crops, children are born crippled or deformed, and murderers and thieves plague our cities. The question that must be answered is this: Why does a God who has the power to eliminate such evils allow them to occur? If God is indifferent to or powerless to prevent such evils, then he is not the kind of good and all-powerful being that Western religions worship. Many theologians have argued that all of the things we call evils are allowed to occur by God for some good purpose. For this view to be defended, it must be shown that God could not have produced equally good results without this evil or at least with less of it.

The existence of evil and its bearing on God's existence are discussed by B. C. Johnson and John Hick. In "God and the Problem of Evil," Johnson examines the traditional explanations of an all-good God's purpose for allowing evil to exist and concludes that these explanations are inadequate. He argues that a careful assessment of the possible alternatives leads to the conclusion that the existence of an all-good God is unlikely. John Hick rejects the claim that no adequate explanation for the evil in the world is possible. He argues that evil is allowed to exist because God's purpose for man in this world is not to provide him with a carefree, happy existence but to continue the process of "soul-making." To achieve full development, man must experience and learn to overcome the problems that exist in this world.

When confronted with the difficulty of proving the existence of God, many philosophers and theologians fall back on faith as the basis for religious belief. Faith is usually thought of as belief unsupported by evidence. The contention that it is acceptable to believe the claims of religion or any other topic without evidence has not gone unchallenged. In "The Ethics of Belief," W. K. Clifford argues that it is always wrong to believe anything without evidence since such a belief could either produce some harm or lead the holder to accept too readily other unsupported and potentially harmful beliefs. Our beliefs should be determined by an assessment of the evidence and probabilities involved, not by unfounded hopes and wishes. In contrast to this view of the value of faith, William James argues that belief without evidence is sometimes justified. James is careful to point out, however, that such belief is justified only in certain types of situations. He does not want to encourage the holding of unsupported beliefs in every instance where evidence is not available. Ultimately, James believes that to withhold belief on an important matter like religion just because there is insufficient evidence of God's existence would be too cautious. Since withholding belief might cut one off from God's grace, he believes that one should run the risk of error in hopes one's belief may be true. In considering James's position, the student should consider whether it rests on a conception of God as a wrathful being. Would James's argument be correct if God would not punish those who do not believe without evidence? Also, it is interesting to decide if there are any areas outside of religion where one should believe without evidence.

It is frequently claimed that religion is necessary to give life any meaning or purpose. Unless there is a future life, many consider it pointless to live. Not only would there be no goal to strive for but the pains and sorrows endured in this world make life on balance more trouble than it is worth. In his autobiography, *My Confession,* Leo Tolstoy vividly describes how he reached a state of utter despair because he thought that death, which is inevitable and destructive of everyone and everything one loves, makes confronting and overcoming the problems of living pointless. He believed that life was a "stupid joke" and that the courageous and consistent course to end his despair was to commit suicide. He was saved from suicide and acquired a renewed interest in life only when he returned to his faith in God. He was convinced that such faith was the only way to provide life with any significance and value. In "Meaning and Value of Life," Paul Edwards maintains that the claim that earthly life is worthless without some type of future life is based on several mistakes and confusions. One mistake is the adoption of an unjustifiably high standard by which the value of life is judged. A reasonable standard, according to Edwards, would permit earthly life to be deemed worthwhile.

Does God Exist?

9. Seven Reasons Why a Scientist Believes in God
A. Cressy Morrison

A. Cressy Morrison (1884–1951) was an astronomer and was president of the New York Academy of Sciences from 1938 until 1939. He wrote a number of books on scientific topics, as well as *Man Does Not Stand Alone,* from which the following article was condensed.

We are still in the dawn of the scientific age and every increase of light reveals more brightly the handiwork of an intelligent Creator. In the 90 years since Darwin we have made stupendous discoveries; with a spirit of scientific humility and of faith grounded in knowledge we are approaching even nearer to an awareness of God.

For myself, I count seven reasons for my faith:

First: *By unwavering mathematical law we can prove that our universe was designed and executed by a great engineering Intelligence.*

Suppose you put ten pennies, marked from one to ten, into your pocket and give them a good shuffle. Now try to take them out in sequence from one to ten, putting back the coin each time and shaking them all again. Mathematically we know that your chance of first drawing number one is one to ten; of drawing one and two in succession, one to 100; of drawing one, two and three in succession, one in a thousand, and so on; your chance of drawing them all, from number one to number ten in succession, would reach the unbelievable figure of one chance in ten billion.

By the same reasoning, so many exacting conditions are necessary for life on the earth that they could not possibly exist in proper relationship by chance. The earth rotates on its axis one thousand miles an hour; if it turned at one hundred miles an hour, our days and nights would be ten times as long as now, and the hot sun would then burn up our vegetation each long day while in the long night any surviving sprout would freeze.

Again, the sun, source of our life, has a surface temperature of 12,000 degrees Fahrenheit, and our earth is just far enough away so that this "eternal fire" warms us *just enough and not too much!* If the sun gave off only one half its present radiation, we would freeze and if it gave half as much more, we would roast.

The slant of the earth, tilted at an angle of 23 degrees, gives us our seasons; if it had not been so tilted, vapors from the ocean would move north and south, piling up for us continents of ice. If our moon was, say, only 50 thousand miles away instead of its actual distance, our tides would be so enormous that twice a day all continents would be submerged; even the mountains would soon be eroded away. If the crust of the earth had been only ten feet thicker, there would be no oxygen, without which animal life must die. Had the ocean been a few feet deeper, carbon dioxide and oxygen would have been absorbed and no vegetable life could exist. Or if our atmosphere had been much thinner, some of the meteors, now burned in space by the millions every day, would be striking all parts of the earth, setting fires everywhere.

Because of these and a host of other examples, there is not one chance in millions that life on our planet is an accident.

Second: *The resourcefulness of life to accomplish its purpose is a manifestation of all-pervading Intelligence.*

What life itself is, no man has fathomed. It has neither weight nor dimensions; but it does have force; a growing root will crack a rock. Life has conquered water, land and air, mastering the elements, compelling them to dissolve and reform their combinations.

Life, the sculptor, shapes all living things; an artist, it designs every leaf of every tree, and colors every flower. Life is a musician and has taught each bird to sing it love songs, the insects to call each other in the music of their multitudinous sounds. Life is a sublime chemist, giving taste to fruits and spices, and perfume to the rose, changing water and carbonic acid into sugar and wood, and, in so doing, releasing oxygen that animals may have the breath of life.

Behold an almost invisible drop of protoplasm, transparent, jellylike, capable of motion, drawing energy from the sun. This single cell, this transparent mistlike droplet, holds within itself the germ of life, and has the power to distribute this life to every living thing, great and small. The powers of this droplet are greater than our vegetation and animals and people, for all life came from it. Nature did not create life; fire-blistered rocks and a saltless sea could not meet the necessary requirements.

Who, then, has put it here?

Third: *Animal wisdom speaks irresistibly of a good Creator who infused instinct into otherwise helpless little creatures.*

The young salmon spends years at sea, then comes back to his own river, and travels up the very side of the river into which flows the tributary where he was born. What brings him back so precisely? If you transfer him to another tributary he will know at once that he is off his course and he will fight his way down and back to the main stream and then turn up against the current to finish his destiny accurately.

Even more difficult to solve is the mystery of eels. These amazing creatures migrate at maturity from all ponds and rivers everywhere—those from Europe across thousands of miles of ocean—all bound for the same abysmal deeps near Bermuda. There they breed and die. The little ones, with no apparent means of knowing anything except that they are in a wilderness of water, nevertheless start back and find their way not only to the very shore from which their parents came but thence to the rivers, lakes or little ponds—so that each body of water is always populated with eels. No American eel has ever been caught in Europe, no European eel in American waters. Nature has even delayed the maturity of the European eel by a year or more to make up for its longer journey. Where does the directing impulse originate?

A wasp will overpower a grasshopper, dig a hole in the earth, sting the grasshopper in exactly the right place so that he does not die but becomes unconscious and lives on as a form of preserved meat. Then the wasp will lay her eggs handily so that her children when they hatch can nibble without killing the insect on which they feed; to them dead meat would be fatal. The mother then flies away and dies; she never sees her young. Surely the wasp must have done all this right the first time and every time, else there would be no wasps. Such mysterious techniques cannot be explained by adaptation; they were bestowed.

Fourth: *Man has something more than animal instinct—the power of reason.*

No other animal has ever left a record of its ability to count ten, or even to understand the meaning of ten. Where instinct is like a single note of a flute, beautiful but limited, the human brain contains all the notes of all the instruments in the orchestra. No need to belabor this fourth point; thanks to human reason we can contemplate the possibility that we are what we are only because we have received a spark of Universal Intelligence.

Fifth: *Provision of all living is revealed in phenomena which we know today but which Darwin did not know—such as the wonders of genes.*

So unspeakably tiny are these genes that, if all of them responsible for all living people in the world could be put in one place, there would be less than a thimbleful. Yet these ultramicroscopic genes and their companions, the chromosomes, inhabit every living cell and are the absolute keys to all human, animal, and vegetable characteristics. A thimble is a small place in which to put all the individual characteristics of two billions of human beings. However, the facts are beyond question. Well, then—how do genes lock up all the normal heredity of a multitude of ancestors and preserve the psychology of each in such an infinitely small space?

Here evolution really begins—at the cell, the entity which holds and carries the genes. How a few million atoms, locked up as an ultramicroscopic gene, can absolutely rule all life on earth is an example of profound cunning and provision that could emanate only from a Creative Intelligence; no other hypothesis will serve.

Sixth: *By the economy of nature, we are forced to realize that only infinite wisdom could have foreseen and prepared with such astute husbandry.*

Many years ago a species of cactus was planted in Australia as a protective fence. Having no insect enemies in Australia the cactus soon began a prodigious growth; the alarming abundance persisted until the plants covered an area as long and wide as England, crowding inhabitants out of towns and villages, and destroying their farms. Seeking a defense, the entomologists scoured the world; finally they turned up an insect which lived exclusively on cactus, and would eat nothing else. It would breed freely, too; and it had no enemies in Australia. So animal soon conquered vegetable and today the cactus pest has retreated, and with it all but a small protective residue of the insects, enough to hold the cactus in check forever.

Such checks and balances have been universally provided. Why have not fast-breeding insects dominated the earth? Because they have no lungs such as man possesses; they breathe through tubes. But when insects grow large, their tubes do not grow in ratio to the increasing size of the body. Hence there never has been an insect of great size; this limitation on growth has held them all in check. If this physical check had not been provided, man could not exist. Imagine meeting a hornet as big as a lion!

Seventh: *The fact that man can conceive the idea of God is in itself a unique proof.*

The conception of God rises from a divine faculty of man, unshared with the rest of our world—the faculty we call imagination. By its power, man and man alone can find the evidence of things unseen. The vista that power opens up is unbounded; indeed, as man's perfected imagination becomes a spiritual reality, he may discern in all the evidences of design and purpose the great truth that heaven is wherever and whatever; that God is everywhere and in everything but nowhere so close as in our hearts.

It is scientifically as well as imaginatively true, as the Psalmist said: *The heavens declare the glory of God and the firmament showeth His handiwork.*

10. The Delusion of Design and Purpose   Clarence Darrow

Seldom do the believers in mysticism fail to talk about the evidence of purpose and design shown in the universe itself. This idea runs back at least one hundred and five years, to Paley's "Natural Theology." There was a time when this book was a part of the regular course in all schools of higher learning, which then included theology; but the book is now more likely to be found in museums.

Paley points out that if a man travelling over the heath should find a watch and commence examining it he would soon discover in the watch itself abundant evidence of purpose and design. He would observe the wheels that fit into each other and turn the hour hand and the minute hand, the crystal made to fit over the face, etc., etc.

What the hypothetical man would observe and conclude would depend on the man. Most men that we know would think that the watch showed a design to accomplish a certain purpose, and therefore must have had a maker. They would reach that conclusion because they are familiar with tools and their use by man. But, suppose the watch had been picked up by a bushman or some other savage or an ape? None of them would draw an inference, for the article would be new to them. Supposing, instead of a man, a coyote or wolf came upon the watch, turned it over and examined it, would the animal read or sense any design? Most assuredly not. Suppose the civilized man should pick up an unfamiliar object, a stone, or a piece of quartz; he might view it and examine it, but it would never enter his head that it was designed, and yet on close inspection and careful study the stone or quartz is just as marvellous as the watch.

Paley passes from the watch to the human structure and shows how the mouth and teeth are adjusted to prepare the food for man's digestion, and how his stomach is formed to digest it; how the eye and ear were made to carry sensations to the brain, etc. Many of the clergy say the same thing to-day, in spite of the fact that the organs of man were never made for any such purposes. In fact, man never was made. He was evolved from the lowest form of life. His ancestors in the sea slowly threw its jellylike structure around something that nourished it and absorbed it. Slowly through ages of continued development and change and mutations the present man was evolved, and with him the more perfect and adaptable and specialized structure, with which he sees and hears and takes his food, and digests it and assimilates it to his structure. The stomach was not made first, and then food created for its use. The food came first, and certain forms of life slowly developed an organ that would absorb food to be utilized in the process of growth. By degrees, through the survival of the construction most fitted for life, the stomach and digestive apparatus for men and other animals gradually grew and unfolded in endless time.

To discover that certain forms and formations are adjusted for certain action has nothing to do with design. None of these developments are perfect, or anywhere near so. All of them, including the eye, are botchwork that any good mechanic would be ashamed to make. All of them need constant readjustment, are always out of order, and are entirely too complicated for dependable work. They are not made for any purpose; they simply grew out of needs and adaptations; in other words, they happened. Just as God must have happened, if he exists at all.

Turning from Paley and his wornout watch to the universe and the physical world in general, is there any more evidence here? First, the "design and order" sharks ought to tell what they mean by their terms, and how they find out what they think they understand. To say that a certain scheme or process shows order or system, one must have some norm or pattern by which to determine whether the matter concerned shows any design or order. We have a norm, a pattern, and that is the universe itself, from which we fashion our ideas. We have observed this universe and its operation and we call it order. To say that the universe is patterned on order is to say that the universe is patterned on the universe. It can mean nothing else.

The earth revolves around the sun in a long curve not far from a circle. Does that show order? Let us suppose that instead of going in a circle it formed a rectangle. Would this not have been accepted as order?

Suppose it were a triangle, or any other figure. Suppose it took a toothlike course, would that, then, be considered order? As a matter of fact, the earth does not go regularly in the same path around the sun; it is drawn out into the universe with the whole solar system, and never travels the same course twice. The solar system really has an isolated place in space. The sun furnishes light and heat to nine different planets, of which the earth is one of the smallest and most insignificant. The earth has one satellite, the moon. Saturn and Jupiter have eight moons each, and, besides that, Saturn has a ring that looks very beautiful from here, running all around the planet. We do know that all the planets of the solar system, and the sun as well, are made of the same stuff. It is most likely that every moving thing in the universe has the same constituents as the earth. What is the plan that gave Jupiter eight moons, while only one was lavished upon the earth, supposed to be the special masterpiece of the Almighty, and for whose benefit all the hosts of the heavens were made? Jupiter is three hundred and seventeen times the weight of the earth, and it takes four years for it to go around the sun. Perhaps the universe was made for inhabitants that will one day live on Jupiter.

It is senseless to talk about order and system and design in the universe. Sir James Jeans' book published in 1931, "The Stars in Their Course," tells us his theory of the origin of our solar system, which is of more interest to us than the Milky Way. The theory of Jeans, and most of the other astronomers, is that there was a time when all the planets of the solar system were a part of the sun, and that some wandering star in its course across the heavens entered the sphere of the sun and dragged after it the planets and moons that make up the solar system by the power of gravitation. This is the planetismal theory, postulated by Professors Chamberlain and Moulton of the University of Chicago. These mighty chunks of matter drawn from the sun rushed on through space at a terrific speed, and each was caught by gravitation and revolved around the sun. Their distance from the sun depended largely upon their size before gravitation held them in its grasp.

There is nothing in the solar system that could be called design and order. It came from a catastrophe of whose immensity no one could even dream. Religionists have pointed to the ability of an astronomer to fix the time of an eclipse as evidence of system. There are only a few heavenly bodies involved in an eclipse of the sun or moon, from the standpoint of the earth. The motions and positions of all these bodies are well known, and from this the passage of another heavenly planet or the moon between the earth and the sun can be easily determined. It matters not whether the date of an eclipse is far-off or near-by, the method is the same. To an astronomer the computation is as simple as the question propounded to the first-grade pupil: "If John had three apples and James gave him two more, how many apples would John then have?"

We know that gravitation caught the various planets at a certain point as they sped across space, and that these accidents of colliding bodies are very rare; the reason is that regardless of what seems to be the distance between the stars, they are so far apart that it is almost impossible for them ever to meet. To quote from Jeans': "For the most part, each voyage is in splendid isolation, like a ship on the ocean. In a scale model in which the stars are ships, the average ship will be well over a million miles from its neighbor."

Still, catastrophes have occurred and do occur. Our solar system was probably born from one. The moon was thrown from the earth by some pull of gravitation. The heavens are replete with dark planets, and parts of planets, and meteors hurrying through space. Now and then one drops onto the earth, and is preserved in some park or museum; so that in various parts of the world numerous specimens exist. If there was any purpose in the creation of the universe, or any part of it, what was it? Would any mortal dare to guess?

Our solar system is one of the smallest of the endless systems of which we have any knowledge. Our earth is eight thousand miles in diameter. The star, Betelgeuse, is so large that it would fill all the space occupied in the heavens in the whole orbit made by the earth going around the sun. There are many stars known to be much larger than Betelgeuse. The diameter of this sun is thirty-seven thousand times that of our little earth, for which all the universe is supposed to have been made, and whose inhabitants are endowed with everlasting life.

When the telescope is turned toward the heavens we learn another story. Leaving the sparsely settled section of eternity in which we live forever, and going out into the real main universe, we find worlds on worlds, systems upon systems, and nebula after nebula. No one can possibly imagine the dimensions of endless space. The great Nebula M. 31 in Andromeda is so far away from the earth that it takes light nine hundred thousand millions of years to reach our planet. The nebula itself is so vast that it takes fifty thousand years for light to cross it. To make it still more simple I have taken the pains to figure the distance of this nebula from our important planet, called the earth, which boasts of a diameter of eight thousand miles. This nebula is 5,279,126,400,000,000,000 miles away from us, if my computations are right. I would not positively guarantee the correctness of the answer, but I think it is all right, although I did it by hand. I have gone over the figures three times, and got a different result each time, so I think the answer can be pretty well depended upon. I cannot help feeling sorry for the residents of Nebula M. 31 in Andromeda, when I think what a great deprivation they must suffer through living so far away from our glorious planet, which Mark Twain named "the wart," but which theology has placed at the centre of the universe and as the sole concern of gods and men.

What lies beyond Andromeda? No one can answer that question. And still there is every reason to believe that other worlds and systems and nebulae reach out into stellar space, without end. It is obvious that no one can form a conception of the extent of space or the infinite number of suns and planets with which the limitless sky is strewn. No one can vision a beginning or an end. If it were possible for any fertile mind to imagine a conception of the end of space, then we should wonder what lies beyond that limit. We cannot attain the slightest comprehension of the extent of our pigmy solar system, much less any of the greater ones. The planet which is the farthest from our sun is Pluto, one of the smallest in our system. The diameter of Pluto's orbit around the sun is only about 7,360,000,000 miles. This may be taken as the extent of our solar system. This can be compared with the distance to the nebula in Andromeda, which I hesitate to record again, showing the trifling importance of our whole solar system in so much of the universe as we can scan.

When the new telescope is completed and mounted on the top of Mount Wilson, it is hoped that we can produce figures of distance that are real figures.

Among the endless number of stars that whirl in the vastnesses of illimitable space, how many millions of billions of planets are likely to be in existence? How many of these may possibly have as much special and historical importance as the tiny globe to which we so frantically cling? To find that number, go and count the grains of sand on all the coasts of all the waters of the earth, and then think of the catastrophe that would result to the coasts if one grain were shattered or lost.

In spite of the countless numbers of bodies moving about in limitless space, and the distances between them so great that they seldom clash, still they do sometimes clash. What is our solar system in comparison with the great nebula out there in the beginning, or end, or middle stretch of real space? Compared with that part of the heavens the density of the stellar population of our solar system is like the prairies of Kansas compared with the city of New York. Can anything be inferred about the origin or arrangement of all this, so far as man can tell, except that it is the outcome of the merest, wildest chance?

But let us try to clear the cobwebs from our brains, and the dizziness from our stomachs, and come back to earth, as it were. Let us talk of something where we can deal with what at least approaches facts. Does the earth show design, and order, and system, and purpose? Again, it would be well for the designers to tell what the scheme really is. If the plan is so clear as to justify the belief in a master designer, then it must be plain that the believers should be able to give the world some idea of the purpose of it all. Knowing winks and Delphic utterances and cryptic insinuations are not enough. Was the earth ever designed for the home of man? Sir James Jeans, in his admirable book on astronomy, shows us in no uncertain way that it evidently was not; that the human race has made the most of a bad environment and a most unfortunate habitation. Strange that the highpriests of superstition should so convulsively clutch Jeans and Eddington; neither one believes in a future life of the individual; neither one believes in the God of the theologians; neither believes in a special revelation, although Jeans does manage to say that Venus is the planet that the religionists thought was the star that led the camels over the desert to the stable where Jesus was born. Is this science or religion?—this bit of hearsay.

Even had this planet been meant for life, it plainly was not meant for human life. Three-fourths of the surface is covered with water, which would show that if it was ever designed for life it was designed for fishes and not for men. But what about the dry land? Two-thirds of this is not fitted for human beings. Both the polar zones are too cold for the abode of man. The equatorial regions are too hot. Vast deserts are spread out in various sections, and impassable and invincible mountain ranges make human habitation and the production of food impossible over immense areas. The earth is small enough, to begin with; the great seas, the wide useless stretches of land and the hostile climates have shrunk the livable portion almost to the vanishing point, and it is continually shrinking day by day. The human race is here because it is here, and it clings to the soil because there is nowhere else to go.

Even a human being of very limited capacity could think of countless ways in which the earth could be improved as the home of man, and from the earliest time the race has been using all sorts of efforts and resources to make it more suitable for its abode. Admitting that the earth is a fit place for life, and certainly every place in the universe where life exists is fitted for life, then what sort of life was this planet designed to support? There are some millions of different species of animals on this earth, and one-half of these are insects. In numbers, and perhaps in other ways, man is in a great minority. If the land of the earth was made for life, it seems as if it was intended for insect life, which can exist almost anywhere. If no other available place can be found they can live by the million on man, and inside of him. They generally succeed in destroying his life, and, if they have a chance, wind up by eating his body.

Aside from the insects, all sorts of life infest the earth and sea and air. In large portions of the earth man can make no headway against the rank growths of jungles and the teeming millions of animals that are seeking his death. He may escape the larger and most important of these only to be imperilled and probably eaten by the microbes, which seem instinctively to have their own idea of the worth and purpose of man's existence. If it were of any importance, we might view man from the standpoint of the microbe and consider his utility as the microbe's "meal-ticket." Can any one find any reason for claiming that the earth was meant for man, any more than for any other form of life that is spawned from land and sea and air?

But, how well is the earth itself adapted to human life? Even in the best parts of this world, speaking from the standpoint of man, one-fourth of the time it is too cold and another fourth of the seasons it is too hot, leaving little time for the comfort and pleasure of the worthiest product of the universe, or, that small fraction of it that we have some limited knowledge about.

Passing up the manifold difficulties that confront man and his brief life and career upon this mundane sphere, let us look at the world itself. It is a very wobbly place. Every year, upon the surface of this globe, and in the seas that cover such a major part of it, there are ten thousand earthquakes, ranging from light shocks to the total destruction of large areas of territory and the annihilation of great numbers of human lives. Were these, too, designed? Then, there is no such meaning as is usually applied to the word "design." What "design" was there in the earthquake that destroyed Lisbon in 1755? The entire city was blotted out, together with the destruction of thirty thousand to forty thousand human beings.

This earthquake occurred on a Sunday which was also a saint's day, and a large number were killed in a cathedral, which was also destroyed. And yet people talk about design and purpose and order and system as though they knew the meaning of the words.

Let us look at the earth as it exists to-day. It is not the same earth that came into some sort of separate existence millions of years ago. It has not only experienced vast and comparatively sudden changes, like the throwing up of mountain ranges in the cooling and contracting processes, but other changes not so sudden and acute have worked their way through ages of time, and changes are still going on all the time all over the earth. New lands keep rising, others sinking away. Volcanoes are sending out millions of tons of matter each year, new islands are rising above the surface of the sea, while other islands are lowered beneath the waves. Continents are divided by internal forces and the ruthless powers of the sea.

Great Britain was cut off from the mainland not so very long ago, according to geological time. The shores of America and Africa were once connected, as seems evident from looking at the maps, and countless other geological shiftings have happened all over the surface and inside the earth, so that the world was no more made as it is now than was man created as we find him to-day. The destruction of the island of Martinique, the Mont Pelée disaster, the earthquake of San Francisco, are all within the memory of many now living. Active volcanoes are continuously pouring solid matter into the waters and slowly or rapidly building up new land where once was only sea.

The various archipelagoes are instances of this formation of fairly recent times. The Allegheny Mountains were once thirty thousand feet high. The crevices of their rocks have been penetrated by rain, split by frost and ice, pulverized by friction, and every minute are moving off toward the Gulf of Mexico. This range of mountains, which once reached an altitude of thirty thousand feet at the highest point, now has its highest peak but six thousand feet above the sea. These mountains have been worn down day after day, and the Ohio and Tennessee and Mississippi Rivers, carrying off the sediment, are building up the delta on the Louisiana coast. The earth and its seas were never made; they are in constant flux, moved by cold and heat and rain, and with no design or purpose that can be fathomed by the wit of man.

The delta of the Nile has through the long ages been carried down in mud and sand and silt from two thousand miles away and deposited in the open sea; and this is also called design by those who look for things they wish to find.

Nature brings hordes of insects that settle over the land and destroy the farmers' crops. Who are the objects of the glorious design: the farmers who so patiently and laboriously raise the crops or the grasshoppers that devour them? It must be the insects, because the farmers hold prayer meetings and implore their God to kill the bugs, but the pests go on with their deadly work unmolested. Man prates glibly about design, but Nature furnishes not a single example or fact as proof. Perhaps the microbe who bores a hole into the vitals of man and brings him down to his death may believe in a Providence and a design. How else could he live so royally on the vitals of one of the lords of creation?

All that we know is that we were born on this little grain of sand we call the earth. We know that it is one of the smallest bits of matter that floats in the great shoreless sea of space, and we have every reason to believe that it is as inconsequential in every other respect. On board the same craft, sailing the same seas, are all sorts of living things, fighting each other, and us, that each may survive. Most of these specimens are living on the carcasses of the dead. The strongest instinct of most of our crew is to stay here and live. The strongest in intellect and prowess live the longest. Nature, in all her manifestations, is at war with life, and sooner or later will doubtless have her way. No one can give a reason for any or all of the manifestations which we call life. We are like a body of shipwrecked sailors clutching to a raft and desperately engaged in holding on.

Men have built faith from hopes. They have struggled and fought in despair. They have frantically clung to life because of the will to live. The best that we can do is to be kindly and helpful toward our friends and fellow passengers who are clinging to the same speck of dirt while we are drifting side by side to our common doom.

11. Religious Knowledge and Mystical Experience
James Bisset Pratt

James Bisset Pratt (1875–1944) was a prominent American philosopher who wrote widely on the philosophy of religion and metaphysics.

In spite of innumerable differences between the experiences of individual Christians, the general sense of some kind of divine presence . . . is common to a surprisingly large number. For that matter, it is very like the mystical experiences found in some of the non-Christian religions. Naturally it has been differently nurtured and differently expressed in the various religious cultures within which it has arisen. It has had a prominent place in the faith and worship of every Christian generation. In our time it has received, and is receiving, unusual stress. This for two reasons. One is the interest which our time feels in psychology, and the interest which our psychologists have come to feel in religion. The other reason is of a theological sort. As we have seen, various influences have united, during the last half-century, to diminish the prestige of the historical arguments for the existence of God and to reduce almost to the vanishing point the old confidence in the literal inspiration of the Scriptures. As a result the defenders of the Christian belief have evacuated one position after another, and many of them are today concentrating their strength within the fortifications of what they sometimes call the "inner experience."

At the close of the last century the psychologists awoke to the fact that religion was interesting, and began to take the lead in studying it. The first results of this serious work of psychologists upon religion were heartening in the extreme. The theologians were assured by their technical colleagues of the reality and the depth of the religious life. The next step to be taken by the psychologists was not quite so reassuring, namely, the description and analysis of the experience. The third step was frankly disquieting, though inevitable—the attempt, namely, not only to describe but to explain. Once more it seemed that the Ark of the Lord had fallen into the hands of the Philistines. For if the religious experience could be explained, set within the nexus of scientific law, it seemed to be in effect explained away; not indeed denied, but put in a position where it could no longer be used as an empirical argument for the existence of God.

In view of this situation the attempt has been made to take back the religious experience from psychology to theology, so to speak, by insisting that theology is an empirical science and that "God" is as objective a fact as are the objects of the physical sciences. Thus it is said that in the experience of moral regeneration and in the mystics' apprehension of the Divine, God is directly presented as a scientific fact and not merely as a hypothesis for the explanation of other facts. In other words, that the religious experience is an experience of God and that this proposition is neither a philosophical hypothesis nor a matter of faith and hope, but a plain fact of science.

In making up our minds as to the tenability of this view we should first ask ourselves what we mean by a fact of science. As was pointed out in a previous paragraph, a little reflection will show that a scientific fact, as distinguished from a private and individual experience, must have the characteristics of being repeatable and verifiable. The experiences of the isolated individual may be as real as you like, but they cannot possess the social authority of a scientific fact unless they are describable in terms capable of communication to all rational beings and verifiable by all properly equipped observers. The question now is: Can God, even in the vaguest sense, as a Source of Power not identical with our empirical selves, be truly said to be a directly experienced fact in this scientific sense? Is He a verifiable object in the sense of being directly presented to the experience of all normal or standardized and properly equipped observers? For my part, I cannot honestly answer this question in the affirmative. The experience of moral regeneration through religious influence may give us reasons to infer the influence of a Power not ourselves; but God, if reached in this way, would be an inference (as logical as you like, but still an inference, a hypothesis) and not an empirical fact. The mystical experience is on a different footing from moral regeneration, for it purports to be an immediate apprehension of the Divine as a directly felt object. But while it is conceivable that God for the mystic may be no hypothesis but a fact, can we honestly say He is even here a *scientific* fact? I judge we cannot. For a scientific fact, let me repeat, must be verifiable by all standardized observers with suitable training. And very few would maintain that the God of the mystics is verifiable in this fashion; and certainly He is, at all events, very far from having been thus scientifically verified. The man who doubts the existence of x-rays can be put in a position where he can perceive them; but there is no laboratory in which the mystics' God can be exhibited to the nonmystical. Nor is it an answer to assert that the mystics' God is verifiable by anyone with the proper physical make-up; for while this is doubtless true, it really is merely a tautologous assertion to the effect that all mystics can perceive what all mystics can perceive. As much could be said of the hallucinatory objects commonly seen under the influence of nitrous oxide. And as a fact, those most eloquent in their assertions that only a few can apprehend God in the mystic fashion are just the mystics themselves. If not all, at any rate a very large portion of them assert that no amount of training, no amount of effort will enable one to attain to the mystic apprehension. It is like the wind which bloweth where it listeth. What need we any further witness? With mystics and nonmystics agreeing almost universally that God as an object of direct apprehension is not verifiable, it would seem to follow inevitably that God is not a scientific fact and that therefore theology cannot be regarded as an empirical science.

Hence we are back again with the religious experience in the hands of the psychologists, and faced with the question: Has the psychological description and explanation of this experience made it valueless in the attempt to give a spiritual interpretation to the universe? Students of the psychology of religion are often tempted to say that it is valueless; and it is, I think, their scientific duty to point out all that can be said to justify this negative interpretation. To put the psychologist's position in summary fashion, one may maintain that since the religious experience is experience, the interpretation of it belongs solely to psychology; and that the question whether the religious experience proves the existence and presence of God is an empirical and scientific question, and one with which, therefore, not the theologian but only the psychologist is qualified to deal. If now the religious experience can be explained in purely naturalistic fashion, it is said, we are not warranted in looking for any divine explanation or in using it as evidence for the existence of God. Can the religious experience be so explained?

With this problem in mind the psychologist proceeds to an elaborate description and analysis of the religious—and especially of the mystical—consciousness; and he comes to the conclusion that the religious experience is essentially of the same sort as nonreligious experience, having the same character and the same causation. Thus there would seem to be nothing in it to indicate that the mystic or the religious person has come in touch with God in any peculiar sense. It is in content and character on a par with nonreligious experience. What *appears* to be more is a matter not of actual experience but of interpretation. It may be the philosopher can show that all experience points to God, or somehow implies the Absolute; but the psychologist is very doubtful whether the religious or mystical experience implies God any more directly or obviously or in any other way than the most commonplace experience of sense perception.

The psychologist, moreover, has another argument against what I might call the religious interpretation of the religious experience. Not only does psychological analysis show that the religious experience is like other experience in quality; it also shows that its occurrence, its rise, intensity, and decline may be explained by the same general psychological laws that account for the various changes in the nonreligious consciousness. This, to be sure, is not yet fully proved. The situation is complex; many factors, some of them quite obscure, are involved, and no one could seriously claim that all the factors of the religious experience are known. But many of them are known, and it is the necessary hypothesis of psychology that the unknown factors must be of the same general type as the known ones. This position of the psychologist is, in a sense, a matter of faith rather than of demonstration, but it is for him a necessary faith; for unless he makes the postulate that psychological laws can explain all the facts of human psychosis, he would have to give up his claim that psychology is a complete science.

A good deal has been done to substantiate the first of the two arguments referred to above, by which psychology throws a doubt on the significance of mysticism: a large part of religious experience turns out on analysis to be of the same sort as nonreligious experience. Even the more striking phenomena of ecstasy can largely be paralleled by the effects of drugs and of Yoga training. Personally I am not convinced that the peculiar joy of religion, or what Otto calls numinous feeling, is really to be paralleled outside of religion. And so far as I can judge, the central thing in the religious experience—the sense of immediate contact with some being other than, though possibly inclusive of, oneself—is strictly unique. This sense of presence differentiates the religious experience pretty sharply from the various forms of drug ecstasy, and also from the usual results of Yoga. I think it is safe to say that when Yoga brings an intuition of the Absolute as present and directly known, some other factor is at work besides the Yoga methods. In other words, the sort of experience brought about by controllable physical and phychological means lacks the one characteristic that is essential to the religious experience.

It may indeed be argued that what has been added in this experience is easily explained by the rationalizing interpretation of the mystic, on the basis of his already accepted belief in the supernatural. We must distinguish, it is frequently and properly pointed out, between what the mystic actually experiences and his interpretation of it. No one will doubt that he has the sensations which he reports; but interpretation is not the product of psychological introspection but of philosophical theory. It does not grow out of the experience, or at any rate, not out of it alone. As Professor J. M. Moore points out, "our categories and established modes of reaction are present before any particular experience, and condition the form which the experience takes. The relation of experience and interpretation is reciprocal and complex rather than being a simple one-way relation of dependence."[1]

There is much truth in this criticism of mystic pronouncements. When the Salvation Army lassie tells us she has seen Christ, when Suzo asserts that he has communed with the Madonna, when the Hindu Vaishnavite recounts his immediate apprehension of Sri Krishna, very few of us will doubt that rationalistic interpretation has been busy, and that what we are given is not a description of actually experienced fact, but an interpretation of some simpler experience, formulated on the plan of some familiar creed. There is a line, however, beyond which this distinction of immediate sense data and interpretation cannot profitably and truthfully be carried. For the simplest elements of actual adult experience are seldom if ever sensations, but what John Laird significantly calls "sign facts."[2] A pure sensation is something that few of us who have passed infancy any longer experience. Our simplest forms of perceptual activity are drenched with meaning. The immediately given is already significant; it is never a mere sense datum, but a sense datum that means more than it is. And this is as true of the religious man's sense of presence as of any other form of experience. What he tells us of the further nature of the being he experiences is doubtless a matter of interpretation, but his immediate awareness that he is in the presence of an Other is hardly to be analyzed further without altering it into something very different from what it really is. This awareness of an Other, stripped of its creedal interpretation, differs, so the mystic asserts, *toto coelo* from a mere belief. It comes with all the immediacy of sense perception. It has, of course, sensuous elements, as every percept has; but to identify it with any collection of mere sense data is to mutilate it beyond recognition. It is, in short, if we may trust the mystics' introspective description (not their interpretation), a sign fact.

In saying this I have not forgotten Professor Leuba's artificial production of the sense of presence in the laboratory.[3] But is is well to remind ourselves in passing that Professor Leuba did not produce the *religious* sense of presence in his laboratory. His experiments were not dealing with that directly. What his experiments showed was that a sense of presence in general may be induced without anyone actually being present. The subject, that is, may be fooled. In short, like other forms of cognitive experience, the sense of presence may be illusory. But surely we did not need experimental evidence to show us this. Occasionally any of us may be mistaken about the presence of a human fellow. We may suppose ourselves not alone in the room and discover that we are. When in doubt about the matter we put the thing to a test, using various methods to find out. The fact that sometimes we are mistaken does not prove to us that we are always mistaken. Each case must stand on its own merits and be judged by its own evidence. As a fact, the cases of mistake are so small a fraction of the total, and the cases in which we are correct form so

---

[1]J. M. Moore, *Theories of Religious Experience*, p.187.
[2]See John Laird, *A Study of Realism*, chaps. ii, v.
[3]See Leuba, *The Psychology of Religious Mysticism*, pp. 283–286.

large a majority, that in normal human experience this sense of another's presence carries with it a strong a priori probability of its own validity.

Now there is no doubt that the mystic may be mistaken like other people. As Professor James pointed out, his emotion of conviction as to the validity of his experience of presence may be authoritative for him, but it is not for anyone else. It is quite possible that various causes, known or unknown, may have united to delude him. His own certainty is no guarantee of the truth of his assertion. But the fact that he *may be* mistaken does not prove that he *is* mistaken. The fact—if it be a fact—that he is *sometimes* mistaken does not prove that he is *always* mistaken. Here as elsewhere each case must be judged on its merits. Nor can we say that there is so much uncertainty about the cause of this experience that the assertion of the religious man is entirely negligible. The matter is not left as if nothing had happened. Certainly the mystic's evidence is not as good as the ordinary evidence of eye and ear, for we have a means of testing the validity of these instruments of knowledge, and in the vast majority of cases they prove trustworthy. The mystic's assertion does not carry with it the same weight of a priori probability as does the more common conviction that someone we do not see is in the room with us. But the assertion of the mystic is not entirely worthless as evidence. It at least sets us a problem of further investigation; and if such investigation can produce no complete explanation for the mystic's experience, the experience must be set down at least tentatively as having a certain minimal evidential value in favor of the truth of the mystic's assertion. The strength of this evidence will be increased with every demonstration that the religious sense of presence, its joy and its other by-products, are different in quality from the corresponding experiences of the nonreligious life.

The claim to evidential validity on the part of the religious sense of presence is the more difficult wholly to deny because of the immense number of witnesses that might be called upon to give confirmatory testimony. A student of the history of religions can hardly fail to be struck with the ubiquity of this experience. The way it springs up, spontaneously and independently in remotely separated lands, among peoples of unrelated races, in nearly all the ages and in all the religions with which we are acquainted, is at least an impressive fact. Indeed, one might argue that if any evidential value whatever is to be granted the religious experience, one will have to go on and grant it a good deal, because of the cumulative nature of its testimony.

Whether it has any evidential value is, of course, just the question we are discussing. It will be recalled that there are two principal arguments for the naturalistic interpretation of the religious experience. The one based on the similarity between religious and nonreligious experiences we have discussed. The other argument—which indeed is so closely related to the first as to be hardly separable except for purposes of exposition—consists in pointing out that the same psychological laws obtain among religious facts as those which govern the whole mental life of man. In other words, it is the aim of this argument to show that the various experiences of the religious life follow laws of definite and regular sequence, and are therefore susceptible of purely psychological explanation. Since they can be explained psychologically, the argument continues, they need no other explanation, and hence cannot be used as evidence for anything beyond the human mind with its human contents and its human ways of working.

As I have already pointed out, psychology has not yet been fully successful in making out these laws of regular sequence between religious phenomena and various psychophysical conditions; they represent rather a program and ideal than an actual achievement. Much successful work toward this ideal has been done and more may be expected. The psychologist, I think, is justified in making a working hypothesis of this ideal of complete psychological explanation for all mental facts. In a sense it is a necessary hypothesis, for his claim that psychology is at least potentially a science capable of giving complete explanation and prediction depends upon it. Unfortunately many psychologists often forget that this hypothesis is as yet only a hypothesis and is very far indeed from having been empirically verified. The truth is, we cannot as yet explain all the facts of human experience and of mental activity by psychological laws. To assert in the present state of our ignorance that we can because we must—which means because we want to—is not science but dogma and the will to make believe.

It is, however, perfectly conceivable that some day all the activities of the human mind, including the religious experience, will be explicable in psychological fashion; in other words, that we shall be able to show how, say, the mystical experience follows invariably upon certain definable conditions, and that by going through certain psychophysical processes one may induce it. This possibility opens up a rather interesting logical question. For if this situation should ever be reached, how would it, and how should it be interpreted? The interpretation that would be given it by most psychologists is obvious enough: they would say that the religious experience was thereby shown to be, like any other conscious state, producible by certain definite conditions, and therefore no more significant of objective reality than dreams of hypnosis. But there would be an equally obvious interpretation open to the mystics. It will be recalled that in our discussion of the claims of theology to rank as an empirical science, I argued that this was not admissable because the mystic fact is not a scientific fact; and that it is not a scientific fact because it is not verifiable by all normal or standardized human beings—that is to say, not reproducible at will within the field of awareness. But on the hypothesis we have now set up of the future perfecting of psychology, the mystic experience is to be reproducible at will. We can therefore picture the mystics, or their philosophical defenders, turning the tables on the psychologists by saying: you told us our apprehension of the Divine was not a scientific fact because it is not verifiable in the sense of being reproducible. Now, thanks to your kind of researches, it is reproducible and verifiable. Is not our apprehension of the Divine, therefore, a fact, and a scientific fact? Is it not a scientific fact in the same sense as your apprehension of brain cells; and immeasurably more scientific than the physicist's apprehension of the invisible electrons? Instead of interpreting it as you do dreams and illusions, should you not rather, on your own showing, interpret it as you do veridical perception?

The situation is sufficiently bewildering. Plainly it will hardly do to argue: mysticism is illusory because its cognitive states are *not* reproducible; and with the next breath to argue, mysticism is illusory because its cognitive states *are* reproducible. To do that would be to blow hot and cold, to play fast and loose with nature. Either the religious experience is reproducible, given certain conditions, or it is not; and from both these opposites we can hardly draw the same conclusion. If it is incumbent upon us to give the devil his due, surely it is only fair to give the Lord a chance!

How, then, should we construe this rather puzzling situation? A good deal, I think, would depend on the actual details of the actual facts which, by hypothesis, psychology shall one day discover. If, for example, it were found that the religious experience, in all its fullness and with its cognizable quality, could be reproduced by a dose of some newly discovered drug, and that it never arose except under psychophysical conditions which were, in the last analysis, identical with those induced by this drug; it would then follow—that the new-found drug was an excellent means for bringing about the psychophysical conditions requisite for the religious experience! It would prove nothing more; and it would still be open to anyone who wished to do so to assert that these identical psychophysical conditions might be produced by the direct action of God. It is unlikely, however, that many would make such an assertion; and probably not only the psychologists but most of us would agree that the religious experience was a symptom of certain physical conditions but without further objective or cosmic significance. We may, however, picture other results from the scientific investigation of the religious consciousness and its "causes." We may well imagine that psychology might discover that the religious experience followed regularly upon a long process of purifying the heart and concentrating the mind, by proper means, upon the thought of the Divine. Now if this were true, if it were a verifiable scientific fact that the experience of the Divine Presence, the immediate and undoubtable sense of the numinous at hand, sufficiently different from every other sort of experience to be the distinguishable and recognizable, and having the same compelling objectivity that visual and tactual experiences possess—if this form of cognitive consciousness, I say, were found to follow invariably upon a definable process of heart purification and mind concentration, how should we interpret the logic of the situation?

I think it is perfectly plain that there would be two answers. The conscientious psychologist *as psychologist* would say: The religious consciousness is now fully explained in psychological terms. I leave to the philosopher the explanation of the cosmos, but I have shown that no reference to anything supernatural, to anything outside of human nature, is needed to explain the sense of divine presence and its various by-products. It follows regularly upon definable and predictable psycho-physical conditions by laws of regular and invariable sequence. On the other hand, the mystic would say: the direct apprehension of God is now become a verifiable fact. If you doubt my word, put yourself through the long course of mental and spiritual training which the psychologist and I can plan out for you, and you shall see for yourself. If any man will follow the religious life in the light of modern science, he shall know of the doctrine. For it is God who will be working in you, God who will be revealing Himself to you, who can now be *counted on* to reveal Himself to you, through the working of the laws of the human mind which He Himself made. The religious experience is now a scientific fact, and is to be explained by the actual presence of the Divine before the eyes of the soul.

Of these two interpretations which would be correct? By hypothesis all the relevant facts would be in, and further empirical evidence would be unnecessary. The question would be purely a matter of logic. Plainly it would be exceedingly difficult to prove either of the rival interpretations wrong. And I want to suggest that they might *both* be right.

For what, after all, is a psychological explanation? It consists (in logical outline) in tracing laws of regular sequence between the psychosis to be explained and certain definable conditions, either within the psycho-physical mechanism of the subject or within so much of the environment as natural science is able to define, understand, and for experimental purposes, control. Psychological explanation is therefore a form of de-scription and generalization. It does not pretend to point out ultimate or original causes. Psychology is not interested in ultimate or original causes. Its explanation is complete if it has constructed a formula of sequence among scientific, i.e., verifiable facts, and on the basis of this sequence is able without failure to predict the psychosis in question on the appearance of the facts with which the formula connects it. Now there is nothing in the actuality of this kind of an explanation inconsistent with the religious interpretation of the situation. The mystic is not in-terested in denying the validity of the psychologist's explanation, but he is interested in something more. To him explanation means something different from a generalized description of regular sequences. He is in-terested in ultimate and original causes. And provided we are willing to relieve the concept of the Divine from the attribute of arbitrariness, there is nothing to prevent our supposing that the steady action of the Divine upon the soul is the ultimate cause of the religious experience, and that what the psychologist describes is the regular process by which the soul may be exposed to this Divine influence. The white radiance of eternity, we may suppose, steadily beats upon us, but only in certain conditions of body and mind can we become sensitive to its light. If this were so, it would be quite within the province of psychology to describe exactly and completely what these conditions are, and on the basis of them to predict and "explain" the rise of the religious experience. To do so, and to do it without any reference to the ultimate source of the inflowing Light, would be to give a complete and exhaustive psychological explanation. Yet it would be equally true that religious experience was exactly what the religious man insists that it is—an immediate awareness of a Divine Other.

By making these suggestions I do not mean that God is to be taken as filling the gaps which science leaves, nor that He is to be proved by miraculous interventions. As I have said, it is quite likely that all religious experience will some day be found to have its scientific explanation—in the sense I have indicated. The Unity of the World is not destroyed. God must be conceived as existing in and expressing Himself through all reality. Yet owing to the finiteness of our human nature and our very limited and partial insight, it may be true—and I think it is true—that most of us apprehend the universal Divine more readily and clearly in some parts of our experience than in others. To the angel's vision God may be "as full, as perfect, in a hair as hart." Yet so long as man remains a little lower than the angels it is probable that he will realize God more fully and perfectly in the religious experience than anywhere else. My aim in this chapter has been, not to attack science nor to defend a view of supernatural divine interventions, but to show that something may be said for the faith of the religious man that, in what he knows as his most religious moments, it is God with whom he comes in touch. Later on he may learn that he is in touch with God always and everywhere; but it is in the mystic experience that he first and most fully *recognizes* God.

Possibly we can make a little plainer to ourselves the contribution made by mysticism to the religious view of the world if we put to ourselves one further question. Let us suppose that in all the world's history there had been no mystics, and no suggestion in any mind of an immediate apprehension of the Divine. Would not, I ask, a religious view of the world under those circumstances have been much less probable, much harder to believe, than it is today? Would not many people, would not most people, on hearing a religious philosophy propounded, have asked the question: "Why, if there be a Divine, has it never come in touch with any human mind?" In other words, if there be a God, would you not naturally expect mystics?" The facts of mysticism makes the existence of God considerably more probable.

Thus, I believe, a psychological study of the mystical states combined with a philosophical interpretation of the nature of science may make a distinct contribution to the religious view of reality. But if this is to be done, religion, I trust, will make fewer demands of a specific nature than it has been accustomed to make as to the interpretation of the Divine. It will be content to *believe* in God without *defining* Him. More in particular, it will lay less stress than formerly upon the anthropomorphic and excessively personal aspects of the Divine. It will have nothing to say of specific answer to prayer or of Divine interventions. And in place of the dogmatic view of the older theology, it will adopt a more empirical attitude toward the universe, and while less eager to tell who and what God is, it will be more ready to learn.

We come back, then, after our long discussion, to the question: Is the religious experience such as to furnish any relevant empirical evidence on the ultimate religious problems of our time? The answer would seem to be emphatically in the affirmative. A chastened theology may appeal to the facts of the religious life with a certain justifiable confidence. The testimony of the religious consciousness through thirty centuries is not without cosmic significance.

12. The Basis of the Moral Law   C. S. Lewis

I now go back to what I said . . . that there were two odd things about the human race. First, that they were haunted by the idea of a sort of behaviour they ought to practice, what you might call fair play, or decency, or morality, or the Law of Nature. Second, that they did not in fact do so. Now some of you may wonder why I called this odd. It may seem to you the most natural thing in the world. In particular, you may have thought I was rather hard on the human race. After all, you may say, what I call breaking the Law of Right and Wrong or of Nature, only means that people are not perfect. And why on earth should I expect them to be? That would be a good answer if what I was trying to do was to fix the exact amount of blame which is due to us for not behaving as we expect others to behave. But that is not my job at all. I am not concerned at present with blame; I am trying to find out truth. And from that point of view the very idea of something being imperfect, of its not being what it ought to be, has certain consequences.

If you take a thing like a stone or a tree, it is what it is and there seems no sense in saying it ought to have been otherwise. Of course you may say a stone is "the wrong shape" if you want to use it for a rockery, or that a tree is a bad tree because it does not give you as much shade as you expected. But all you mean is that the stone or tree does not happen to be convenient for some purpose of your own. You are not, except as a joke, blaming them for that. You really know, that, given the weather and the soil, the tree could not have been any different. What we, from our point of view call a "bad" tree is obeying the laws of its nature just as much as a "good" one.

Now have you noticed what follows? It follows that what we usually call the laws of nature—the way weather works on a tree for example—may not really be *laws* in the strict sense, but only in a manner of speaking. When you say that falling stones always obey the law of gravitation, is not this much the same as saying that the law only means "what stones always do"? You do not really think that when a stone is let go, it suddenly remembers that it is under orders to fall to the ground. You only mean that, in fact, it does fall. In other words, you cannot be sure that there is anything over and above the facts themselves, any law about what ought to happen, as distinct from what does happen. The laws of nature, as applied to stones or trees, may only mean "what Nature, in fact, does."

But if you turn to the Law of Human Nature, the Law of Decent Behaviour, it is a different matter. That law certainly does not mean "what human beings, in fact, do"; for as I said before, many of them do not obey this law at all, and none of them obey it completely. The law of gravity tells you what stones do if you drop them; but the Law of Human Nature tells you what human beings ought to do and do not. In other words, when you are dealing with humans, something else comes in above and beyond the actual facts. You have the facts (how men do behave) and you also have something else (how they ought to behave). In the rest of the universe there need not be anything but the facts. Electrons and molecules behave in a certain way, and certain results follow, and that may be the whole story. But men behave in a certain way and that is not the whole story, for all the time you know that they ought to behave differently.

Now this is really so peculiar that one is tempted to try to explain it away. For instance, we might try to make out that when you say a man ought not to act as he does, you only mean the same as when you say that a stone is the wrong shape; namely, that what he is doing happens to be inconvenient to you. But that is simply untrue. A man occupying the corner seat in the train because he got there first, and a man who slipped into it while my back was turned and removed my bag, are both equally inconvenient. But I blame the second man and do not blame the first. I am not angry—except perhaps for a moment before I come to my senses—with a man who trips me up by accident; I am angry with a man who tries to trip me up even if he does not succeed. Yet the first has hurt me and the second has not. Sometimes the behaviour which I call bad is not inconvenient to me at all, but the very opposite. In war, each side may find a traitor on the other side very useful. But though they use him and pay him they regard him as human vermin. So you cannot say that what we call decent behaviour in others is simply the behaviour that happens to be useful to us. And as for decent behaviour in ourselves, I suppose it is pretty obvious that it does not mean the behaviour that pays. It means things like being content with thirty shillings when you might have got three pounds, doing school work honestly when it would be easy to cheat, leaving a girl alone when you would like to make love to her, staying in dangerous places when you could go somewhere safer, keeping promises you would rather not keep, and telling the truth even when it makes you look a fool.

Some people say that though decent conduct does not mean what pays each particular person at a particular moment, still, it means what pays the human race as a whole; and that consequently there is no mystery about it. Human beings, after all, have some sense; they see that you cannot have real safety or happiness except in a society where every one plays fair, and it is because they see this that they try to behave decently. Now, of course, it is perfectly true that safety and happiness can only come from individuals, classes, and nations being honest and fair and kind to each other. It is one of the most important truths in the world. But as an explanation of why we feel as we do about Right and Wrong it just misses the point. If we ask: "Why ought I to be unselfish?" and you reply "Because it is good for society," we may then ask, "Why should

I care what's good for society except when it happens to pay *me* person-ally?" and then you will have to say, "Because you ought to be unselfish"—which simply brings us back to where we started. You are saying what is true, but you are not getting any further. If a man asked what was the point of playing football, it would not be much good saying "in order to score goals," for trying to score goals is the game itself, not the reason for the game, and you would really only be saying that football was foot-ball—which is true, but not worth saying. In the same way, if a man asks what is the point of behaving decently, it is no good replying, "in order to benefit society," for trying to benefit society, in other words being unselfish (for "society" after all only means "other people"), is one of the things decent behaviour consists in; all you are really saying is that decent behaviour is decent behaviour. You would have said just as much if you had stopped at the statement, "Men ought to be unselfish."

And that is where I do stop. Men ought to be unselfish, ought to be fair. Not that men are unselfish, nor that they like being unselfish, but that they ought to be. The Moral Law, or Law of Human Nature, is not simply a fact about human behviour in the same way as the Law of Grav-itation is, or may be, simply a fact about how heavy objects behave. On the other hand, it is not a mere fancy, for we cannot get rid of the idea, and most of the things we say and think about men would be reduced to nonsense if we did. And it is not simply a statement about how we should like men to behave for our own convenience; for the behaviour we call bad or unfair is not exactly the same as the behaviour we find inconvenient, and may even be the opposite. Consequently, this Rule of Right and Wrong, or Law of Human Nature, or whatever you call it, must somehow or other be a real thing—a thing that is really there, not made up by ourselves. And yet it is not a fact in the ordinary sense, in the same way as our actual behaviour is a fact. It begins to look as if we shall have to admit that there is more than one kind of reality; that, in this particular case, there is something above and beyond the ordinary facts of men's behaviour, and yet quite definitely real—a real law, which none of us made, but which we find pressing on us.

Let us sum up what we have reached so far. In the case of stones and trees and things of that sort, what we call the Laws of Nature may not be anything except a way of speaking. When you say that nature is governed by certain laws, this may only mean that nature does, in fact, behave in a certain way. The so-called laws may not be anything real—anything above and beyond the actual facts which we observe. But in the case of Man, we saw that this will not do. The Law of Human Nature, or of Right and Wrong, must be something above and beyond the actual facts of human behaviour. In this case, besides the actual facts, you have something else—a real law which we did not invent and which we know we ought to obey.

I now want to consider what this tells us about the universe we live in. Ever since men were able to think, they have been wondering what this universe really is and how it came to be there. And, very roughly, two views have been held. First, there is what is called the materialist view. People who take that view think that matter and space just happen to exist, and always have existed, nobody knows why; and that the matter, behaving in certain fixed ways, has just happened, by a sort of fluke, to produce creatures like ourselves who are able to think. By one chance in a thousand something hit our sun and made it produce our planets; and by another thousandth chance the chemicals necessary for life, and the right temperature, occurred on one of these planets, and so some of the matter on this earth came alive; and then, by a very long series of chances, the living creatures developed into things like us. The other view is the religious view. According to it, what is behind the universe is more like a mind than it is like anything else we know. That is to say, it is conscious, and has purposes, and prefers one thing to another. And on this view it made the universe, partly for purposes we do not know, but partly, at any rate, in order to produce creatures like itself—I mean, like itself to the extent of having minds. Please do not think that one of these views was held a long time ago and that the other has gradually taken its place. Wherever there have been thinking men both views turn up. And note this too. You cannot find out which view is the right one by science in the ordinary sense. Science works by experiments. It watches how things behave. Every scientific statement in the long run, however complicated it looks, really means something like, "I pointed the telescope to such and such a part of the sky at 2:20 A.M. on January 15th and saw so-and-so," or, "I put some of this stuff in a pot and heated it to such-and-such a temperature and it did so-and-so." Do not think I am saying anything against science: I am only saying what its job is. And the more scientific a man is, the more (I believe) he would agree with me that this is the job of science—and a very useful and necessary job it is too. But why anything comes to be there at all, and whether there is anything behind the things science observes—something of a different kind—this is not a scientific question. If there is "Something Behind," then either it will have to remain altogether unknown to men or else make itself known in some different way. The statement that there is any such thing, and the statement that there is no such thing, are neither of them statements that science can make. And real scientists do not usually make them. It is usually the journalists and popular novelists who have picked up a few odds and ends of half-baked science from textbooks who go in for them. After all, it is really a matter of common sense. Supposing science ever became complete so that it knew every single thing in the whole universe. Is it not plain that the questions, "Why is there a universe?" "Why does it go on as it does?" "Has it any meaning?" would remain just as they were?

Now the position would be quite hopeless but for this. There is one thing, and only one, in the whole universe which we know more about than we could learn from external observation. That one thing is Man. We do not merely observe men, we *are* men. In this case we have, so to speak, inside information; we are in the know. And because of that, we know that men find themselves under a moral law, which they did not make, and cannot quite forget even when they try, and which they know they ought to obey. Notice the following point. Anyone studying Man from the outside as we study electricity or cabbages, not knowing our language and consequently not able to get any inside knowledge from us, but merely observing what we did, would never get the slightest evidence that we had this moral law. How could he? for his observations would only show what we did, and the moral law is about what we ought to do. In the same way, if there were anything above or behind the observed facts in the case of stones or the weather, we, by studying them from outside, could never hope to discover it.

The position of the question, then, is like this. We want to know whether the universe simply happens to be what it is for no reason or whether there is a power behind it that makes it what it is. Since that power, if it exists, would be not one of the observed facts but a reality which makes them, no mere observation of the facts can find it. There is only one case in which we can know whether there is anything more, namely our own case. And in that one case we find there is. Or put it the other way round. If there was a controlling power outside the universe, it could not show itself to us as one of the facts inside the universe—no more than the architect of a house could actually be a wall or staircase or fireplace in that house. The only way in which we could expect it to show itself would be inside ourselves as an influence or a command trying to get us to behave in a certain way. And that is just what we do find inside ourselves. Surely this ought to arouse our suspicions? In the only case where you can expect to get an answer, the answer turns out to be Yes; and in the other cases, where you do not get an answer, you see why you do not. Suppose someone asked me, when I see a man in a blue uniform going down the street leaving little paper packets at each house, why I suppose that they contain letters? I should reply, "Because whenever he leaves a similar little packet for me I find it does contain a letter." And if he then objected, "But you've never seen all these letters which you think the other people are getting," I should say, "Of course not, and I shouldn't expect to, because they're not addressed to me. I'm explaining the packets I'm not allowed to open by the ones I am allowed to open." It is the same about this question. The only packet I am allowed to open is Man. When I do, especially when I open that particular man called Myself, I find that I do not exist on my own, that I am under a law; that somebody or something wants me to behave in a certain way. I do not, of course, think that if I could get inside a stone or tree I should find exactly the same thing, just as I do not think all the people in the street get the same letters as I do. I should expect, for instance, to find that the stone had to obey the law of gravity—that whereas the sender of the letters merely tells me to obey the law of my human nature, He compels the stone to obey the laws of its stony nature. But I should expect to find that there was, so to speak, a sender of letters in both cases, a Power behind the facts, a Director, a Guide.

Do not think I am going faster than I really am. I am not yet within a hundred miles of the God of Christian theology. All I have got to is a Something which is directing the universe, and which appears in me as a law urging me to do right and making me feel responsible and uncomfortable when I do wrong. I think we have to assume it is more like a mind than it is like anything else we know—because after all the only other thing we know is matter and you can hardly imagine a bit of matter giving instructions. But, of course, it need not be very like a mind, still less like a person. . . .

13. Why I Am Not a Christian   Bertrand Russell

Bertrand Russell (1872–1970) was one of the most prominent philosophers of the twentieth century. He is the author of numerous books on a wide variety of philosophical and social issues. He is known to the general public for his outspoken stands on religion, marriage, the banning of the nuclear bomb. In 1950 he was awarded the Nobel Prize for Literature.

As your Chairman has told you, the subject about which I am going to speak to you tonight is "Why I Am Not a Christian." Perhaps it would be as well, first of all, to try to make out what one means by the word *Christian*. It is used these days in a very loose sense by a great many people. Some people mean no more by it than a person who attempts to live a good life. In that sense I suppose there would be Christians in all sects and creeds; but I do not think that that is the proper sense of the word, if only because it would imply that all the people who are not Christians—all the Buddhists, Confucians, Mohammedans, and so on— are not trying to live a good life. I do not mean by a Christian any person who tries to live decently according to his lights. I think that you must have a certain amount of definite belief before you have a right to call yourself a Christian. The word does not have quite such a full-blooded meaning now as it had in the times of St. Augustine and St. Thomas Aquinas. In those days, if a man said that he was a Christian it was known what he meant. You accepted a whole collection of creeds which were set out with great precision, and every single syllable of those creeds you believed with the whole strength of your convictions.

What Is a Christian?

Nowadays it is not quite that. We have to be a little more vague in our meaning of Christianity. I think, however, that there are two different items which are quite essential to anybody calling himself a Christian. The first is one of a dogmatic nature—namely, that you must believe in God and immortality. If you do not believe in those two things, I do not think that you can properly call yourself a Christian. Then, further than that, as the name implies, you must have some kind of belief about Christ. The Mohammedans, for instance, also believe in God and in immortality, and yet they would not call themselves Christians. I think you must have at the very lowest the belief that Christ was, if not divine, at least the best and wisest of men. If you are not going to believe that much about Christ, I do not think you have any right to call yourself a Christian. Of course, there is another sense, which you find in *Whitaker's Almanack* and in geography books, where the population of the world is said to be divided into Christians, Mohammedans, Buddhists, fetish worshipers, and so on; and in that sense we are all Christians. The geography books count us all in, but that is a purely geographical sense, which I suppose we can ignore. Therefore I take it that when I tell you why I am not a Christian I have to tell you two different things: first, why I do not believe in God and in immortality; and secondly, why I do not think that Christ was the best and wisest of men, although I grant him a very high degree of moral goodness.

But for the successful efforts of unbelievers in the past, I could not take so elastic a definition of Christianity as that. As I said before, in olden days it had a much more full-blooded sense. For instance, it included the belief in hell. Belief in eternal hell-fire was an essential item of Chrisitian belief until pretty recent times. In this country, as you know, it ceased to be an essential item because of a decision of the Privy Council, and from that decision the Archbishop of Canterbury and the Archbishop of York dissented; but in this country our religion is settled by Act of Parliament, and therefore the Privy Council was able to override their Graces and hell was no longer necessary to a Christian. Consequently I shall not insist that a Christian must believe in hell.

The Existence of God

To come to this question of the existence of God: it is a large and serious question, and if I were to attempt to deal with it in any adequate manner I should have to keep you here until Kingdom Come, so that you will have to excuse me if I deal with it in a somewhat summary fashion. You know, of course, that the Catholic Church has laid it down as a dogma that the existence of God can be proved by the unaided reason. That is a somewhat curious dogma, but it is one of their dogmas. They had to introduce it because at one time the freethinkers adopted the habit of saying that there were such and such arguments which mere reason might urge against the existence of God, but of course they knew as a matter of faith that God did exist. The arguments and the reasons were set out at great length, and the Catholic Church felt that they must stop it. Therefore they laid it down that the existence of God can be proved by the unaided reason and they have had to set up what they considered were arguments to prove it. There are, of course, a number of them, but I shall take only a few.

The First-Cause Argument

Perhaps the simplest and easiest to understand is the argument of the First Cause. (It is maintained that everything we see in this world has a cause, and as you go back in the chain of causes further and further you must come to a First Cause, and to that First Cause you give the name of God.) That argument, I suppose, does not carry very much weight nowadays, because, in the first place, cause is not quite what it used to be. The philosophers and the men of science have got going on cause, and it has not anything like the vitality it used to have; but, apart from that, you can see that the argument that there must be a First Cause is one that cannot have any validity. I may say that when I was a young man and was debating these questions very seriously in my mind, I for a long time accepted the argument of the First Cause, until one day, at the age of eighteen, I read John Stuart Mill's Autobiography, and I there found this sentence: "My father taught me that the question 'Who made me?' cannot be answered, since it immediately suggests the further question 'Who made God?'" That very simple sentence showed me, as I still think, the fallacy in the argument of the First Cause. If everything must have a cause, then God must have a cause. If there can be anything without a cause, it may just as well be the world as God, so that there cannot be any validity in that argument. It is exactly of the same nature as the Hindu's view, that the world rested upon an elephant and the elephant rested upon a tortoise; and when they said, "How about the tortoise?" the Indian said, "Suppose we change the subject." The argument is really no better than that. There is no reason why the world could not have come into being without a cause; nor, on the other hand, is there any reason why it should not have always existed. There is no reason to suppose that the world had a beginning at all. The idea that things must have a beginning is really due to the poverty of our imagination. Therefore, perhaps, I need not waste any more time upon the argument about the First Cause.

The Natural-Law Argument

Then there is a very common argument from natural law. That was a favorite argument all through the eighteenth century, especially under the influence of Sir Isaac Newton and his cosmogony. People observed the planets going around the sun according to the law of gravitation, and they thought that God had given a behest to these planets to move in that particular fashion, and that was why they did so. That was, of course, a convenient and simple explanation that saved them the trouble of looking any further for explanations of the law of gravitation. Nowadays we explain the law of gravitation in a somewhat complicated fashion that Einstein has introduced. I do not propose to give you a lecture on the law of gravitation, as interpreted by Einstein, because that again would take some time; at any rate, you no longer have the sort of natural law that you had in the Newtonian system, where, for some reason that nobody could understand, nature behaved in a uniform fashion. We now find that a great many things we thought were natural laws are really human conventions. You know that even in the remotest depths of stellar space there are still three feet to a yard. That is, no doubt, a very remarkable fact, but you would hardly call it a law of nature. And a great many things that have been regarded as laws of nature are of that kind.

On the other hand, where you can get down to any knowledge of what atoms actually do, you will find they are much less subject to law than people thought, and that the laws at which you arrive are statistical averages of just the sort that would emerge from chance. There is, as we all know, a law that if you throw dice you will get double sixes only about once in thirty-six times, and we do not regard that as evidence that the fall of the dice is regulated by design; on the contrary, if the double sixes came every time we should think that there was design. The laws of nature are of that sort as regards a great many of them. They are statistical averages such as would emerge from the laws of chance; and that makes this whole business of natural law much less impressive than it formerly was. Quite apart from that, which represents the momentary state of science that may change tomorrow, the whole idea that natural laws imply a lawgiver is due to a confusion between natural and human laws. Human laws are behests commanding you to behave a certain way, in which way you may choose to behave, or you may choose not to behave; but natural laws are a description of how things do in fact behave, and being a mere description of what they in fact do, you cannot argue that there must be somebody who told them to do that, because even supposing that there were, you are then faced with the question "Why did God issue just those natural laws and no others?" If you say that he did it simply from his own good pleasure, and without any reason, you then find that there is something which is not subject to law, and so your train of natural law is interrupted. If you say, as more orthodox theologians do, that in all the laws which God issues he had a reason for giving those laws rather than others—the reason, of course, being to create the best universe, although you would never think it to look at it—if there were a reason for the laws which God gave, then God himself was subject to law, and therefore you do not get any advantage by introducing God as an intermediary. You have really a law outside and anterior to the divine edicts, and God does not serve your purpose, because he is not the ultimate lawgiver. In short, this whole argument about natural law no longer has anything like the strength that it used to have. I am traveling on in time in my review of the arguments. The arguments that are used for the existence of God change their character as time goes on. They were at first hard intellectual arguments embodying certain quite definite fallacies. As we come to modern times they become less respectable intellectually and more and more affected by a kind of moralizing vagueness.

The Argument from Design

The next step in this process brings us to the argument from design. You all know the argument from design: everything in the world is made just so that we can manage to live in the world, and if the world was ever so little different, we could not manage to live in it. That is the argument from design. It sometimes takes a rather curious form; for instance, it is argued that rabbits have white tails in order to be easy to shoot. I do not know how rabbits would view that application. It is an easy argument to parody. You all know Voltaire's remark, that obviously the nose was designed to be such as to fit spectacles. That sort of parody has turned out to be not nearly so wide of the mark as it might have seemed in the eighteenth century, because since the time of Darwin we understand much better why living creatures are adapted to their environment. It is not that their environment was made to be suitable to them but that they grew to be suitabe to it, and that is the basis of adaptation. There is no evidence of design about it.

When you come to look into this argument from design, it is a most astonishing thing that people can believe that this world, with all the things that are in it, with all its defects, should be the best that omnipotence and omniscience have been able to produce in millions of years. I really cannot believe it. Do you think that, if you were granted omnipotence and omniscience and millions of years in which to perfect your world, you could produce nothing better than the Ku Klux Klan or the Fascists? Moreover, if you accept the ordinary laws of science, you have to suppose that human life and life in general on this planet will die out in due course: it is a stage in the decay of the solar system; at a certain stage of decay you get the sort of conditions of temperature and so forth which are suitable to protoplasm, and there is life for a short time in the life of the whole solar system. You see in the moon the sort of thing to which the earth is tending—something dead, cold, and lifeless.

I am told that that sort of view is depressing, and people will sometimes tell you that if they believed that, they would not be able to go on living. Do not believe it; it is all nonsense. Nobody really worries much about what is going to happen millions of years hence. Even if they think they are worrying much about that, they are really deceiving themselves. They are worried about something much more mundane, or it may merely be a bad digestion; but nobody is really seriously rendered unhappy by the thought of something that is going to happen to this world millions and millions of years hence. Therefore, although it is of course a gloomy view to suppose that life will die out—at least I suppose we may say so, although sometimes when I contemplate the things that people do with their lives I think it is almost a consolation—it is not such as to render life miserable. It merely makes you turn your attention to other things.

The Moral Arguments for Deity

Now we reach one stage further in what I shall call the intellectual descent that the Theists have made in their argumentations, and we come to what are called the moral arguments for the existence of God. You all know, of course, that there used to be in the old days three intellectual arguments for the existence of God, all of which were disposed of by Immanuel Kant in the *Critique of Pure Reason;* but no sooner had he disposed of those arguments than he invented a new one, a moral argument, and that quite convinced him. He was like many people: in intellectual matters he was skeptical, but in moral matters he believed implicitly in the maxims that he had imbibed at his mother's knee. That illustrates what the psychoanalysts so much emphasize—the immensely stronger hold upon us that our early associations have than those of later times.

Kant, as I say, invented a new moral argument for the existence of God, and that in varying forms was extremely popular during the nineteenth century. It has all sorts of forms. One form is to say that there would be no right or wrong unless God existed. I am not for the moment concerned with whether there is a difference between right and wrong, or whether there is not: that is another question. The point I am concerned with is that, if you are quite sure there is a difference between right and wrong, you are then in this situation: Is that difference due to God's fiat or is it not? If it is due to God's fiat, then for God himself there is no difference between right and wrong, and it is no longer a significant statement to say that God is good. If you are going to say, as theologians do, that God is good, you must then say that right and wrong have some meaning which is independent of God's fiat, because God's fiats are good and not bad independently of the mere fact that he made them. If you are going to say that, you will then have to say that it is not only through God that right and wrong came into being, but that they are in their essence logically anterior to God. You could, of course, if you liked, say that there was a superior deity who gave orders to the God who made this world, or could take up the line that some of the gnostics took up—a line which I often thought was a very plausible one— that as a matter of fact this world that we know was made by the devil at a moment when God was not looking. There is a good deal to be said for that, and I am not concerned to refute it.

The Argument for the Remedying of Injustice

Then there is another very curious form of moral argument, which is this: they say that the existence of God is required in order to bring justice into the world. In the part of this universe that we know there is great injustice, and often the good suffer, and often the wicked prosper, and one hardly knows which of those is the more annoying; but if you are going to have justice in the universe as a whole you have to suppose a future life to redress the balance of life here on earth. So they say that there must be a God, and there must be heaven and hell in order that in the long run there may be justice. That is a very curious argument. If you looked at the matter from a scientific point of view, you would say, "After all, I know only this world. I do not know about the rest of the universe, but so far as one can argue at all on probabilities one would say that probably this world is a fair sample, and if there is injustice here the odds are that there is injustice elsewhere also." Supposing you got a crate of oranges that you opened, and you found all the top layer of oranges bad, you would not argue, "The underneath ones must be good, so as to redress the balance." You would say, "Probably the whole lot is a bad consignment"; and that is really what a scientific person would argue about the universe. He would say, "Here we find in this world a great deal of injustice, and so far as that goes that is a reason for supposing that justice does not rule in the world; and therefore so far as it goes it affords a moral argument against deity and not in favor of one." Of course I know that the sort of intellectual arguments that I have been talking to you about are not what really moves people. What really moves people to believe in God is not any intellectual argument at all. Most people believe in God because they have been taught from early infancy to do it, and that is the main reason.

Then I think that the next most powerful reason is the wish for safety, a sort of feeling that there is a big brother who will look after you. That plays a very profound part in influencing people's desire for a belief in God.

The Character of Christ

I now want to say a few words upon a topic which I often think is not quite sufficiently dealt with by Rationalists, and that is the question whether Christ was the best and the wisest of men. It is generally taken for granted that we should all agree that that was so. I do not myself. I think that there are a good many points upon which I agree with Christ a great deal more than the professing Christians do. I do not know that I could go with Him all the way, but I could go with Him much further than most professing Christians can. You will remember that He said, "Resist not evil: but whosoever shall smite thee on thy right cheek, turn to him the other also." That is not a new precept or a new principle. It was used by Lao-tse and Buddha some 500 or 600 years before Christ, but it is not a principle which as a matter of fact Christians accept. I have no doubt that the present Prime Minister,[1] for instance, is a most sincere Christian, but I should not advise any of you to go and smite him on one cheek. I think you might find that he thought this text was intended in a figurative sense.

Then there is another point which I consider excellent. You will remember that Christ said, "Judge not lest ye be judged." That principle I do not think you would find was popular in the law courts of Christian countries. I have known in my time quite a number of judges who were very earnest Christians, and none of them felt that they were acting contrary to Christian principles in what they did. Then Christ says, "Give to him that asketh of thee, and from him that would borrow of thee turn not thou away." That is a very good principle. Your Chairman has reminded you that we are not here to talk politics, but I cannot help observing that the last general election was fought on the question of how desirable it was to turn away from him that would borrow of thee, so that one must assume that the Liberals and Conservatives of this country are composed of people who do not agree with the teaching of Christ, because they certainly did very emphatically turn away on that occasion.

Then there is one other maxim of Christ which I think has a great deal in it, but I do not find that it is very popular among some of our

[1] Stanley Baldwin.

Christian friends. He says, "If thou wilt be perfect, go and sell that which thou hast, and give to the poor." That is a very excellent maxim, but as I say, it is not much practiced. All these, I think, are good maxims, although they are a little difficult to live up to. I do not profess to live up to them myself; but then, after all, it is not quite the same thing as for a Christian.

Defects in Christ's Teaching

Having granted the excellence of these maxims, I come to certain points in which I do not believe that one can grant either the superlative wisdom or the superlative goodness of Christ as depicted in the Gospels; and here I may say that one is not concerned with the historical question. Historically it is quite doubtful whether Christ ever existed at all, and if He did we do not know anything about Him, so that I am not concerned with the historical question, which is a very difficult one. I am concerned with Christ as He appears in the Gospels, taking the Gospel narrative as it stands, and there one does find some things that do not seem to be very wise. For one thing, He certainly thought that His second coming would occur in clouds of glory before the death of all the people who were living at that time. There are a great many texts that prove that. He says, for instance, "Ye shall not have gone over the cities of Israel till the Son of Man be come." Then He says, "There are some standing here which shall not taste death till the Son of Man comes into His Kingdom"; and there are a lot of places where it is quite clear that He believed that His second coming would happen during the lifetime of many then living. That was the belief of His earlier followers, and it was the basis of a good deal of His moral teaching. When He said, "Take no thought for the morrow," and things of that sort, it was very largely because He thought that the second coming was going to be very soon, and that all ordinary mundane affairs did not count. I have, as a matter of fact, known some Christians who did believe that the second coming was imminent. I knew a person who frightened his congregation terribly by telling them that the second coming was very imminent indeed, but they were much consoled when they found that he was planting trees in his garden. The early Christians did really believe it, and they did abstain from such things as planting trees in their gardens, because they did accept from Christ the belief that the second coming was imminent. In that respect, clearly He was not so wise as some other people have been, and He was certainly not superlatively wise.

The Moral Problem

Then you come to moral questions. There is one very serious defect to my mind in Christ's moral character, and that is that He believed in hell. I do not myself feel that any person who is really profoundly humane can believe in everlasting punishment. Christ certainly as depicted in the Gospels did believe in everlasting punishment, and one does find repeatedly a vindictive fury against those people who would not listen to

His preaching—an attitude which is not uncommon with preachers, but which does somewhat detract from superlative excellence. You do not, for instance, find that attitude in Socrates. You find him quite bland and urbane toward the people who would not listen to him; and it is, to my mind, far more worthy of a sage to take that line than to take the line of indignation. You probably all remember the sort of things that Socrates was saying when he was dying, and the sort of things that he generally did say to people who did not agree with him.

You will find that in the Gospels Christ said, "Ye serpents, ye generation of vipers, how can ye escape the damnation of hell." That was said to people who did not like His preaching. It is not really to my mind quite the best tone, and there are a great many of these things about hell. There is, of course, the familiar text about the sin against the Holy Ghost: "Whosoever speaketh against the Holy Ghost it shall not be forgiven him neither in this World nor in the world to come." That text has caused an unspeakable amount of misery in the world, for all sorts of people have imagined that they have committed the sin against the Holy Ghost, and thought that it would not be forgiven them either in this world or in the world to come. I really do not think that a person with a proper degree of kindliness in his nature would have put fears and terrors of that sort into the world.

Then Christ says, "The Son of Man shall send forth His angels, and they shall gather out of His kingdom all things that offend, and them which do iniquity, and shall cast them into a furnace of fire; there shall be wailing and gnashing of teeth"; and He goes on about the wailing and gnashing of teeth. It comes in one verse after another, and it is quite manifest to the reader that there is a certain pleasure in contemplating wailing and gnashing of teeth, or else it would not occur so often. Then you all, of course, remember about the sheep and the goats; how at the second coming He is going to divide the sheep from the goats, and He is going to say to the goats, "Depart from me, ye cursed, into everlasting fire." He continues, "And these shall go away into everlasting fire." Then He says again, "If thy hand offend thee, cut it off; it is better for thee to enter into life maimed, than having two hands to go into hell, into the fire that never shall be quenched; where the worm dieth not and the fire is not quenched." He repeats that again and again also. I must say that I think all this doctrine, that hell-fire is a punishment for sin, is a doctrine of cruelty. It is a doctrine that put cruelty into the world and gave the world generations of cruel torture: and the Christ of the Gospels, if you could take Him as His chroniclers represent Him, would certainly have to be considered partly responsible for that.

There are other things of less importance. There is the instance of the Gadarene swine, where it certainly was not very kind to the pigs to put the devils into them and make them rush down the hill to the sea. You must remember that He was omnipotent, and He could have made the devils simply go away; but He chose to send them into the pigs. Then there is the curious story of the fig tree, which always rather puzzled me. You remember what happened about the fig tree. "He was hungry; and seeing a fig tree afar off having leaves, He came if haply He might find anything thereon; and when He came to it He found nothing but leaves, for the time of figs was not yet. And Jesus answered and said unto it: 'No man eat fruit of thee hereafter for ever' . . . and Peter . . . saith unto Him: 'Master, behold the fig tree which thou cursedst is withered away.' " This is a very curious story, because it was not the right time of year for figs, and you really could not blame the tree. I cannot myself feel that either in the matter of wisdom or in the matter of virtue Christ stands quite as high as some other people known to history. I think I should put Buddha and Socrates above Him in those respects.

The Emotional Factor

As I said before, I do not think that the real reason why people accept religion has anything to do with argumentation. They accept religion on emotional grounds. One is often told that it is a very wrong thing to attack religion, because religion makes men virtuous. So I am told; I have not noticed it. You know, of course, the parody of that argument in Samuel Butler's book, *Erewhon Revisited*. You will remember that in *Erewhon* there is a certain Higgs who arrives in a remote country, and after spending some time there he escapes from that country in a balloon. Twenty years later he comes back to that country and finds a new religion in which he is worshiped under the name of the "Sun Child," and it is said that he ascended into heaven. He finds that the Feast of the Ascension is about to be celebrated, and he hears Professors Hanky and Panky say to each other that they never set eyes on the man Higgs, and they hope they never will; but they are the high priests of the religion of the Sun Child. He is very indignant, and he comes up to them, and he says, "I am going to expose all this humbug and tell the people of Erewhon that it was only I, the man Higgs, and I went up in a balloon." He was told, "You must not do that, because all the morals of this country are bound round this myth, and if they once know that you did not ascend into heaven they will all become wicked"; and so he is persuaded of that and he goes quietly away.

That is the idea—that we should all be wicked if we did not hold to the Christian religion. It seems to me that the people who have held to it have been for the most part extremely wicked. You find this curious fact, that the more intense has been the religion of any period and the more profound has been the dogmatic belief, the greater has been the cruelty and the worse has been the state of affairs. In the so-called ages of faith, when men really did believe the Christian religion in all its completeness, there was the Inquisition, with its tortures; there were millions of unfortunate women burned as witches; and there was every kind of cruelty practiced upon all sorts of people in the name of religion.

You find as you look around the world that every single bit of progress in humane feeling, every improvement in the criminal law, every step toward the diminution of war, every step toward better treatment of the colored races, or every mitigation of slavery, every moral progress that there has been in the world, has been consistently opposed by the organized churches of the world. I say quite deliberately that the Christian religion, as organized in its churches, has been and still is the principal enemy of moral progress in the world.

How the Churches Have Retarded Progress

You may think that I am going too far when I say that that is still so. I do not think that I am. Take one fact. You will bear with me if I mention it. It is not a pleasant fact, but the churches compel one to mention facts that are not pleasant. Supposing that in this world that we live in today an inexperienced girl is married to a syphilitic man; in that case the Catholic Church says, "This is an indissoluble sacrament. You must endure celibacy or stay together. And if you stay together, you must not use birth control to prevent the birth of syphilitic children." Nobody whose natural sympathies have not been warped by dogma, or whose moral nature was not absolutely dead to all sense of suffering, could maintain that it is right and proper that that state of things should continue.

That is only an example. There are a great many ways in which, at the present moment, the church, by its insistence upon what it chooses to call morality, inflicts upon all sorts of people undeserved and unnecessary suffering. And of course, as we know, it is in its major part an opponent still of progress and of improvement in all the ways that diminish suffering in the world, because it has chosen to label as morality a certain narrow set of rules of conduct which have nothing to do with human happiness; and when you say that this or that ought to be done because it would make for human happiness, they think that has nothing to do with the matter at all. "What has human happiness to do with morals? The object of morals is not to make people happy."

Fear, the Foundation of Religion

Religion is based, I think, primarily and mainly upon fear. It is partly the terror of the unknown and partly, as I have said, the wish to feel that you have a kind of elder brother who will stand by you in all your troubles and disputes. Fear is the basis of the whole thing—fear of the mysterious, fear of defeat, fear of death. Fear is the parent of cruelty, and therefore it is no wonder if cruelty and religion have gone hand in hand. It is because fear is at the basis of those two things. In this world we can now begin a little to understand things, and a little to master them by help of science, which has forced its way step by step against the Christian religion, against the churches, and against the opposition of all the old precepts. Science can help us to get over this craven fear in which mankind has lived for so many generations. Science can teach us, and I think our own hearts can teach us, no longer to look around for imaginary supports, no longer to invent allies in the sky, but rather to look to our own efforts here below to make this world a fit place to live in, instead of the sort of place that the churches in all these centuries have made it.

What We Must Do

We want to stand upon our own feet and look fair and square at the world—its good facts, its bad facts, its beauties, and its ugliness; see the world as it is and be not afraid of it. Conquer the world by intelligence and not merely by being slavishly subdued by the terror that comes from it. The whole conception of God is a conception derived from the ancient Oriental despotisms. It is a conception quite unworthy of free men. When you hear people in church debasing themselves and saying that they are miserable sinners, and all the rest of it, it seems contemptible and not worthy of self-respecting human beings. We ought to stand up and look the world frankly in the face. We ought to make the best we can of the world, and if it is not so good as we wish, after all it will still be better than what these others have made of it in all these ages. A good world needs knowledge, kindliness, and courage; it does not need a regretful hankering after the past or fettering of the free intelligence by the words uttered long ago by ignorant men. It needs a fearless outlook and a free intelligence. It needs hope for the future, not looking back all the time toward a past that is dead, which we trust will be far surpassed by the future that our intelligence can create.

The Problem of Evil

14. God and The Problem of Evil   B. C. Johnson

B. C. Johnson is a pen name for the author who wishes to remain anonymous.

Here is a common situation: a house catches on fire and a six-month-old baby is painfully burned to death. Could we possibly describe as "good" any person who had the power to save this child and yet refused to do so? God undoubtedly has this power and yet in many cases of this sort he has refused to help. Can we call God "good"? Are there adequate excuses for his behavior?

First, it will not do to claim that the baby will go to heaven. It was either necessary for the baby to suffer or it was not. If it was not, then it was wrong to allow it. The child's ascent to heaven does not change this fact. If it was necessary, the fact that the baby will go to heaven does not explain why it was necessary, and we are still left without an excuse for God's inaction.

It is not enough to say that the baby's painful death would in the long run have good results and therefore should have happened, otherwise God would not have permitted it. For if we know this to be true, then we know—just as God knows—that every action successfully performed must in the end be good and therefore the right thing to do, otherwise God would not have allowed it to happen. We could deliberately set houses ablaze to kill innocent people and if successful we would then know we had a duty to do it. A defense of God's goodness which takes as its foundation duties known only after the fact would result in a morality unworthy of the name. Furthermore, this argument does not explain why God allowed the child to burn to death. It merely claims that there is some reason discoverable in the long run. But the belief that such a reason is within our grasp must rest upon the additional belief that God is good. This is just to counter evidence against such a belief by assuming the belief to be true. It is not unlike a lawyer defending his client by claiming that the client is innocent and therefore the evidence against him must be misleading—that proof vindicating the defendant will be found in the long run. No jury of reasonable men and women would accept such a defense and the theist cannot expect a more favorable outcome.

The theist often claims that man has been given free will so that if he accidentally or purposefully causes fires, killing small children, it is his fault alone. Consider a bystander who had nothing to do with starting the fire but who refused to help even though he could have saved the child with no harm to himself. Could such a bystander be called good? Certainly not. If we would not consider a mortal human being good under these circumstances, what grounds could we possibly have for continuing to assert the goodness of an all-powerful God?

The suggestion is sometimes made that it is best for us to face disasters without assistance, otherwise we would become dependent on an outside power for aid. Should we then abolish modern medical care or do away with efficient fire departments? Are we not dependent on their help? Is it not the case that their presence transforms us into soft, dependent creatures? The vast majority are not physicians or firemen. These people help in their capacity as professional outside sources of aid in much the same way that we would expect God to be helpful. Theists refer to aid from firemen and physicians as cases of man helping himself. In reality, it is a tiny minority of men helping a great many. We can become just as dependent on them as we can on God. Now the existence of this kind of outside help is either wrong or right. If it is right, then God should assist those areas of the world which do not have this kind of help. In fact, throughout history, such help has not been available. If aid ought to have been provided, then God should have provided it. On the other hand, if it is wrong to provide this kind of assistance, then we should abolish the aid altogether. But we obviously do not believe it is wrong.

Similar considerations apply to the claim that if God interferes in disasters, he would destroy a considerable amount of moral urgency to make things right. Once again, note that such institutions as modern medicine and fire departments are relatively recent. They function irrespective of whether we as individuals feel any moral urgency to support them. To the extent that they help others, opportunities to feel moral urgency are destroyed because they reduce the number of cases which appeal to us for help. Since we have not always had such institutions, there must have been a time when there was greater moral urgency than there is now. If such a situation is morally desirable, then we should abolish modern medical care and fire departments. If the situation is not morally desirable, then God should have remedied it.

Besides this point, we should note that God is represented as one who tolerates disasters, such as infants burning to death, in order to create moral urgency. It follows that God approves of these disasters as a means to encourage the creation of moral urgency. Furthermore, if there were no such disasters occurring, God would have to see to it that they occur. If it so happened that we lived in a world in which babies never perished in burning houses, God would be morally obliged to take an active hand in setting fire to houses with infants in them. In fact, if the frequency of infant mortality due to fire should happen to fall below a level necessary for the creation of maximum moral urgency in our real world, God would be justified in setting a few fires of his own. This may well be happening right now, for there is no guarantee that the maximum number of infant deaths necessary for moral urgency are occurring.

All of this is of course absurd. If I see an opportunity to create otherwise nonexistent opportunities for moral urgency by burning an infant or two, then I should *not* do so. But if it is good to maximize moral urgency, then I *should* do so. Therefore, it is not good to maximize moral urgency. Plainly we do not in general believe that it is a good thing to maximize moral urgency. The fact that we approve of modern medical care and applaud medical advances is proof enough of this.

The theist may point out that in a world without suffering there would be no occasion for the production of such virtues as courage, sympathy, and the like. This may be true, but the atheist need not demand a world without suffering. He need only claim that there is suffering which is in excess of that needed for the production of various virtues. For example, God's active attempts to save six-month-old infants from fires would not in itself create a world without suffering. But no one could sincerely doubt that it would improve the world.

The two arguments against the previous theistic excuse apply here also. "Moral urgency" and "building virtue" are susceptible to the same criticisms. It is worthwhile to emphasize, however, that we encourage efforts to eliminate evils; we approve of efforts to promote peace, prevent famine, and wipe out disease. In other words, we do value a world with fewer or (if possible) no opportunities for the development of virtue (when "virtue" is understood to mean the reduction of suffering). If we produce such a world for succeeding generations, how will they develop virtues? Without war, disease, and famine, they will not be virtuous. Should we then cease our attempts to wipe out war, disease, and famine? If we do not believe that it is right to cease attempts at improving the world, then by implication we admit that virtue-building is not an excuse for God to permit disasters. For we admit that the development of virtue is no excuse for permitting disasters.

It might be said that God allows innocent people to suffer in order to deflate man's ego so that the latter will not be proud of his apparently deserved good fortune. But this excuse succumbs to the arguments used against the preceding excuses and we need discuss them no further.

Theists may claim that evil is a necessary by-product of the laws of nature and therefore it is irrational for God to interfere every time a disaster happens. Such a state of affairs would alter the whole causal order and we would then find it impossible to predict anything. But the death of a child caused by an electrical fire could have been prevented by a miracle and no one would ever have known. Only a minor alteration in electrical equipment would have been necessary. A very large disaster could have been avoided simply by producing in Hitler a miraculous heart attack—and no one would have known it was a miracle. To argue that continued miraculous intervention by God would be wrong is like insisting that one should never use salt because ingesting five pounds of it would be fatal. No one is requesting that God interfere all of the time. He should, however, intervene to prevent especially horrible disasters. Of course, the question arises: where does one draw the line? Well, certainly the line should be drawn somewhere this side of infants burning to death. To argue that we do not know where the line should be drawn is no excuse for failing to interfere in those instances that would be called clear cases of evil.

It will not do to claim that evil exists as a necessary contrast to good so that we might know what good is. A very small amount of evil, such as a toothache, would allow that. It is not necessary to destroy innocent human beings.

The claim could be made that God has a "higher morality" by which his actions are to be judged. But it is a strange "higher morality" which claims that what we call "bad" is good and what we call "good" is bad. Such a morality can have no meaning to us. It would be like calling black "white" and white "black." In reply the theist may say that God is the wise Father and we are ignorant children. How can we judge God any more than a child is able to judge his parent? It is true that a child may be puzzled by his parents' conduct, but his basis for deciding that their conduct is nevertheless good would be the many instances of good behavior he has observed. Even so, this could be misleading. Hitler, by all accounts, loved animals and children of the proper race; but if Hitler had had a child, this offspring would hardly have been justified in arguing that his father was a good man. At any rate, God's "higher morality," being the opposite of ours, cannot offer any grounds for deciding that he is somehow good.

Perhaps the main problem with the solutions to the problem of evil we have thus far considered is that no matter how convincing they may be in the abstract, they are implausible in certain particular cases. Picture an infant dying in a burning house and then imagine God simply observing from afar. Perhaps God is reciting excuses in his own behalf. As the child succumbs to the smoke and flames, God may be pictured as saying: "Sorry, but if I helped you I would have considerable trouble deflating the ego of your parents. And don't forget I have to keep those laws of nature consistent. And anyway if you weren't dying in that fire, a lot of moral urgency would just go down the drain. Besides, I didn't start this fire, so you can't blame *me*."

It does no good to assert that God may not be all-powerful and thus not able to prevent evil. He can create a universe and yet is conveniently unable to do what the fire department can do—rescue a baby from a burning building. God should at least be as powerful as a man. A man, if he had been at the right place and time, could have killed Hitler. Was this beyond God's abilities? If God knew in 1910 how to produce polio vaccine and if he was able to communicate with somebody, he should have communicated this knowledge. He must be incredibly limited if he could not have managed this modest accomplishment. Such a God if not dead, is the next thing to it. And a person who believes in such a ghost of a God is practically an atheist. To call such a thing a god would be to strain the meaning of the word.

The theist, as usual, may retreat to faith. He may say that he has faith in God's goodness and therefore the Christian Deity's existence has not been disproved. "Faith" is here understood as being much like confidence in a friend's innocence despite the evidence against him. Now in order to have confidence in a friend one must know him well enough to justify faith in his goodness. We cannot have justifiable faith in the supreme goodness of strangers. Moreover, such confidence must come not just from a speaking acquaintance. The friend may continually assure us with his words that he is good but if he does not act like a good person, we would have no reason to trust him. A person who says he has faith in God's goodness is speaking as if he had known God for a long time and during that time had never seen Him do any serious evil. But we know that throughout history God has allowed numerous atrocities to occur. No one can have justifiable faith in the goodness of such a God. This faith would have to be based on a close friendship wherein God was never found to do anything wrong. But a person would have to be blind and deaf to have had such a relationship with God. Suppose a friend of yours had always claimed to be good yet refused to help people when he was in a position to render aid. Could you have justifiable faith in his goodness?

You can of course say that you trust God anyway—that no arguments can undermine your faith. But this is just a statement describing how stubborn you are; it has no bearing whatsoever on the question of God's goodness.

The various excuses theists offer for why God has allowed evil to exist have been demonstrated to be inadequate. However, the conclusive objection to these excuses does not depend on their inadequacy.

First, we should note that every possible excuse making the actual world consistent with the existence of a good God could be used in reverse to make that same world consistent with an evil God. For example, we could say that God is evil and that he allows free will so that we can freely do evil things, which would make us more truly evil than we would be if forced to perform evil acts. Or we could say that natural disasters occur in order to make people more selfish and bitter, for most people tend to have a "me-first" attitude in a disaster (note, for example, stampedes to leave burning buildings). Even though some people achieve virtue from disasters, this outcome is necessary if persons are to react freely to disaster—necessary if the development of moral degeneracy is to continue freely. But, enough; the point is made. Every excuse we could provide to make the world consistent with a good God can be paralleled by an excuse to make the world consistent with an evil God. This is so because the world is a mixture of both good and bad.

Now there are only three possibilities concerning God's moral character. Considering the world as it actually is, we may believe: (a) that God is more likely to be all evil than he is to be all good; (b) that God is less likely to be all evil than he is to be all good; or (c) that God is equally as likely to be all evil as he is to be all good. In case (a) it would be admitted that God is unlikely to be all good. Case (b) cannot be true at all, since—as we have seen—the belief that God is all evil can be justified to precisely the same extent as the belief that God is all good. Case (c) leaves us with no reasonable excuses for a good God to permit evil. The reason is as follows: if an excuse is to be a reasonable excuse, the circumstances it identifies as excusing conditions must be actual. For example, if I run over a pedestrian and my excuse is that the brakes failed because someone tampered with them, then the facts had better bear this out. Otherwise the excuse will not hold. Now if case *(c)* is correct and, given the facts of the actual world, God is as likely to be all evil as he is to be all good, then these facts do not support the excuses which could be made for a good God permitting evil. Consider an analogous example. If my excuse for running over the pedestrian is that my brakes were tampered with, and if the actual facts lead us to believe that it is no more likely that they were tampered with than that they were not, the excuse is no longer reasonable. To make good my excuse, I must show that it is a fact or at least highly probable that my brakes were tampered with—not that it is just a possibility. The same point holds for God. His excuse must not be a possible excuse, but an actual one. But case *(c)*, in maintaining that it is just as likely that God is all evil as that he is all good, rules this out. For if case *(c)* is true, then the facts of the actual world do not make it any more likely that God is all good than that he is all evil. Therefore, they do not make it any more likely that his excuses are good than that they are not. But, as we have seen, good excuses have a higher probability of being true.

Cases *(a)* and *(c)* conclude that it is unlikely that God is all good, and case *(b)* cannot be true. Since these are the only possible cases, there is no escape from the conclusion that it is unlikely that God is all good. Thus the problem of evil triumphs over traditional theism.

15. The Problem of Evil   John Hick

John Hick (1922–) is lecturer in divinity at Cambridge University in England. He is the author of several books on the philosophy of religion.

To many, the most powerful positive objection to belief in God is the fact of evil. Probably for most agnostics it is the appalling depth and extent of human suffering, more than anything else, that makes the idea of a loving Creator seem too implausible and disposes them toward one or another of the various naturalistic theories of religion.

As a challenge to theism, the problem of evil has traditionally been posed in the form of a dilemma: if God is perfectly loving, he must wish to abolish evil; and if he is all-powerful, he must be able to abolish evil. But evil exists; therefore God cannot be both omnipotent and perfectly loving.

Certain solutions, which at once suggest themselves, have to be ruled out so far as the Judaic-Christian faith is concerned.

To say, for example (with contemporary Christian Science), that evil

John Hick, *Philosophy of Religion,* © 1963, pp. 40–46. Reprinted by permission of Prentice-Hall, Inc., Englewood Cliffs, New Jersey.

is an illusion of the human mind, is impossible within a religion based upon the stark realism of the Bible. Its pages faithfully reflect the characteristic mixture of good and evil in human experience. They record every kind of sorrow and suffering, every mode of man's inhumanity to man and of his painfully insecure existence in the world. There is no attempt to regard evil as anything but dark, menacingly ugly, heart-rending, and crushing. In the Christian scriptures, the climax of this history of evil is the crucifixion of Jesus, which is presented not only as a case of utterly unjust suffering, but as the violent and murderous rejection of God's Messiah. There can be no doubt, then, that for biblical faith, evil is unambiguously evil, and stands in direct opposition to God's will.

Again, to solve the problem of evil by means of the theory (sponsored for example, by the Boston "Personalist" School) of a finite deity who does the best he can with a material, intractable and coeternal with himself, is to have abandoned the basic premise of Hebrew-Christian monotheism; for the theory amounts to rejecting belief in the infinity and sovereignty of God.

Indeed, any theory which would avoid the problem of the origin of evil by depicting it as an ultimate constituent of the universe, coordinate with good, has been repudiated in advance by the classic Christian teaching, first developed by Augustine, that evil represents the going wrong of something which in itself is good. Augustine holds firmly to the Hebrew-Christian conviction that the universe is *good*—that is to say, it is the creation of a good God for a good purpose. He completely rejects the ancient prejudice, widespread in his day, that matter is evil. There are, according to Augustine, higher and lower, greater and lesser goods in immense abundance and variety; but everything which has being is good in its own way and degree, except in so far as it may have become spoiled or corrupted. Evil—whether it be an evil will, an instance of pain, or some disorder or decay in nature— has not been set there by God, but represents the distortion of something that is inherently valuable. Whatever exists is, as such, and in its proper place, good: evil is essentially parasitic upon good, being disorder and perversion in a fundamentally good creation. This understanding of evil as something negative means that it is not willed and created by God; but it does not mean (as some have supposed) that evil is unreal and can be disregarded. On the contrary, the first effect of this doctrine is to accentuate even more the question of the origin of evil.

Theodicy,[1] as many modern Christian thinkers see it, is a modest enterprise, negative rather than positive in its conclusions. It does not claim to explain, nor to explain away, every instance of evil in human experience, but only to point to certain considerations which prevent the fact of evil (largely incomprehensible though it remains) from constituting a final and insuperable bar to rational belief in God.

In indicating these considerations it will be useful to follow the tra-

---

[1] The word "theodicy," from the Greek *theos* (God) and *dike* (righteous), means the justification of God's goodness in the face of the fact of evil.

ditional division of the subject. There is the problem of *moral evil* or wickedness: why does an all-good and all-powerful God permit this? And there is the problem of the *non-moral evil* of suffering and pain, both physical and mental: why has an all-good and all-powerful God created a world in which this occurs?

Christian thought has always considered moral evil in its relation to human freedom and responsibility. To be a person is to be a finite center of freedom, a (relatively) free and self-directing agent responsible for one's own decisions. This involves being free to act wrongly as well as to act rightly. The idea of a person who can be infallibly guaranteed always to act rightly is self-contradictory. There can be no guarantee in advance that a genuinely free moral agent will never choose amiss. Consequently, the possibility of wrongdoing or sin is logically inseparable from the creation of finite persons, and to say that God should not have created beings who might sin amounts to saying he should not have created people.

This thesis has been challenged in some recent philosophical discussions of the problem of evil, in which it is claimed that no contradiction is involved in saying that God might have made people who would be genuinely free and who could yet be guaranteed always to act rightly. A quote from one of these discussions follows:

> If there is no logical impossibility in a man's freely choosing the good on one, or on several occasions, there cannot be a logical impossibility in his freely choosing the good on every occasion. God was not, then, faced with a choice between making innocent automata and making beings who, in acting freely, would sometimes go wrong: there was open to him the obviously better possibility of making beings who would act freely but always go right. Clearly, his failure to avail himself of this possibility is inconsistent with his being both omnipotent and wholly good.[2]

A reply to this argument is suggested in another recent contribution to the discussion.[3] If by a free action we mean an action which is not externally compelled but which flows from the nature of the agent as he reacts to the circumstances in which he finds himself, there is, indeed, no contradiction between our being free and our actions being "caused" (by our own nature) and therefore being in principle predictable. There is a contradiction, however, in saying that God is the cause of our acting as we do but that we are free beings in relation to God. There is, in other words, a contradiction in saying that God has made us so that we shall of necessity act in a certain way, and that we are genuinely independent persons in relation to him. If all our thoughts and actions are divinely predestined, however free and morally responsible we may seem to be to ourselves, we cannot be free and morally responsible in the sight of God, but must instead be his helpless puppets. Such "freedom" is like that of a patient acting out a series of post-hypnotic suggestions: he appears, even to himself, to be free, but his volitions have actually been

---

[2] J. L. Mackie, "Evil and Omnipotence." *Mind* (April 1955), 209.
[3] Flew, in *New Essays in Philosophical Theology*.

pre-determined by another will, that of the hypnotist, in relation to whom the patient is not a free agent.

A different objector might raise the question of whether or not we deny God's omnipotence if we admit that he is unable to create persons who are free from the risks inherent in personal freedom. The answer that has always been given is that to create such beings is logically impossible. It is no limitation upon God's power that he cannot accomplish the logically impossible, since there is nothing here to accomplish, but only a meaningless conjunction of words—in this case "person who is not a person." God is able to create beings of any and every conceivable kind; but creatures who lack moral freedom, however superior they might be to human beings in other respects, would not be what we mean by persons. They would constitute a different form of life which God might have brought into existence instead of persons. When we ask why God did not create such beings in place of persons, the traditional answer is that only persons could, in any meaningful sense, become "children of God," capable of entering into a personal relationship with their Creator by a free and uncompelled response to his love.

When we turn from the possibility of moral evil as a correlate of man's personal freedom to its actuality, we face something which must remain inexplicable even when it can be seen to be possible. For we can never provide a complete causal explanation of a free act; if we could, it would not be a free act. The origin of moral evil lies forever concealed within the mystery of human freedom.

The necessary connection between moral freedom and the possibility, now actualized, of sin throws light upon a great deal of the suffering which afflicts mankind. For an enormous amount of human pain arises either from the inhumanity or the culpable incompetence of mankind. This includes such major scourges as poverty, oppression and persecution, war, and all the injustice, indignity, and inequity which occur even in the most advanced societies. These evils are manifestations of human sin. Even disease is fostered to an extent, the limits of which have not yet been determined by psychosomatic medicine, by moral and emotional factors seated both in the individual and in his social environment. To the extent that all of these evils stem from human failures and wrong decisions, their possibility is inherent in the creation of free persons inhabiting a world which presents them with real choices which are followed by real consequences.

We may now turn more directly to the problem of suffering. Even though the major bulk of actual human pain is traceable to man's misused freedom as a sole or part cause, there remain other sources of pain which are entirely independent of the human will, for example, earthquake, hurricane, storm, flood, drought, and blight. In practice it is often impossible to trace a boundary between the suffering which results from human wickedness and folly and that which falls upon mankind from without. Both kinds of suffering are inextricably mingled together in human experience. For our present purpose, however, it is important to note that the latter category does exist and that it seems to be built into the very structure of our world. In response to it, theodicy, if it is wisely conducted, follows a negative path. It is not possible to show positively that each item of human pain serves the divine purpose of good; but, on the other hand, it does seem possible to show that the divine purpose as it is understood in Judaism and Christianity could not be forwarded in a world which was designed as a permanent hedonistic paradise.

An essential premise of this argument concerns the divine purpose in creating the world. The skeptic's assumption is that man is to be viewed as a completed creation and that God's purpose in making the world was to provide a suitable dwelling-place for this fully-formed creature. Since God is good and loving, the environment which he has created for human life to inhabit is naturally as pleasant and comfortable as possible. The problem is essentially similar to that of a man who builds a cage for some pet animal. Since our world, in fact, contains sources of hardship, inconvenience, and danger of innumerable kinds, the conclusion follows that this world cannot have been created by a perfectly benevolent and all-powerful deity.

Christianity, however, has never supposed that God's purpose in the creation of the world was to construct a paradise whose inhabitants would experience a maximum of pleasure and a minimum of pain. The world is seen, instead, as a place of "soul-making" in which free beings, grappling with the tasks and challenges of their existence in a common environment, may become "children of God" and "heirs of eternal life." A way of thinking theologically of God's continuing creative purpose for man was suggested by some of the early Hellenistic Fathers of the Christian Church, especially Irenaeus. Following hints from St. Paul, Irenaeus taught that man has been made as a person in the image of God but has not yet been brought as a free and responsible agent into the finite likeness of God, which is revealed in Christ. Our world, with all its rough edges, is the sphere in which this second and harder stage of the creative process is taking place.

This conception of the world (whether or not set in Irenaeus' theological framework) can be supported by the method of negative theodicy. Suppose, contrary to fact, that this world were a paradise from which all possibility of pain and suffering were excluded. The consequences would be very far-reaching. For example, no one could ever injure anyone else; the murderer's knife would turn to paper or his bullets to thin air; the bank safe, robbed of a million dollars, would miraculously become filled with another million dollars (without this device, on however large a scale, proving inflationary); fraud, deceit, conspiracy, and treason would somehow always leave the fabric of society undamaged. Again, no one would ever be injured by accident: the mountain-climber, steeplejack, or playing child falling from a height would float unharmed to the ground; the reckless driver would never meet with disaster. There would be no need to work, since no harm could result from avoiding work; there would be no call to be concerned for others in time of need or danger, for in such a world there could be no real needs or dangers.

To make possible this continual series of individual adjustments, nature would have to work by "special providences" instead of running according to general laws which men must learn to respect on penalty of pain or death. The laws of nature would have to be extremely flexible: sometimes gravity would operate, sometimes not; sometimes an object would be hard and solid, sometimes soft. There could be no sciences, for there would be no enduring world structure to investigate. In eliminating the problems and hardships of an objective environment, with its own laws, life would become like a dream in which, delightfully but aimlessly, we would float and drift at ease.

One can at least begin to imagine such a world. It is evident that our present ethical concepts would have no meaning in it. If, for example, the notion of harming someone is an essential element in the concept of a wrong action, in our hedonistic paradise there could be no wrong actions—nor any right actions in distinction from wrong. Courage and fortitude would have no point in an environment in which there is, by definition, no danger of difficulty. Generosity, kindness, the *agape* aspect of love, prudence, unselfishness, and all other ethical notions which presuppose life in a stable environment, could not even be formed. Consequently, such a world, however well it might promote pleasure, would be very ill adapted for the development of the moral qualities of human personality. In relation to this purpose it would be the worst of all possible worlds.

It would seem, then, that an environment intended to make possible the growth in free beings of the finest characteristics of personal life, must have a good deal in common with our present world. It must operate according to general and dependable laws; and it must involve real dangers, difficulties, problems, obstacles, and possibilities of pain, failure, sorrow, frustration, and defeat. If it did not contain the particular trials and perils which—subtracting man's own very considerable contribution—our world contains, it would have to contain others instead.

To realize this is not, by any means, to be in possession of a detailed theodicy. It is to understand that this world, with all its "heartaches and the thousand natural shocks that flesh is heir to," an environment so manifestly not designed for the maximization of human pleasure and the minimization of human pain, may be rather well adapted to the quite different purpose of "soul-making."

Contemporary Issues

Should We Believe in God Without Evidence?

16. The Ethics of Belief   W. K. Clifford

William Kingdon Clifford (1845–1879) was a prominent English mathematician and philosopher who made important contributions to the theory of knowledge and the philosophy of science.

A shipowner was about to send to sea an emigrant ship. He knew that she was old, and not over-well built at the first; that she had seen many seas and climes, and often had needed repairs. Doubts had been suggested to him that possibly she was not seaworthy. These doubts preyed upon his mind and made him unhappy; he thought that perhaps he ought to have her thoroughly overhauled and refitted, even though this should put him to great expense. Before the ship sailed, however, he succeeded in overcoming these melancholy reflections. He said to himself that she had gone safely through so many voyages and weathered so many storms that it was idle to suppose she would not come safely home from this trip also. He would put his trust in Providence, which could hardly fail to protect all these unhappy families that were leaving their fatherland to seek for better times elsewhere. He would dismiss from his mind all ungenerous suspicions about the honesty of builders and contractors. In such ways he acquired a sincere and comfortable conviction that his vessel was thoroughly safe and seaworthy; he watched her departure with a light heart, and benevolent wishes for the success of the exiles in their strange new home that was to be; and he got his insurance money when she went down in midocean and told no tales.

What shall we say of him? Surely this, that he was verily guilty of the death of those men. It is admitted that he did sincerely believe in the soundness of his ship; but the sincerity of his conviction can in no wise help him, because *he had no right to believe on such evidence as was before him*. He had acquired his belief not by honestly earning it in patient investigation, but by stifling his doubts. And although in the end he may have felt so sure about it that he could not think otherwise, yet inasmuch as he had knowingly and willingly worked himself into that frame of mind, he must be held responsible for it.

Let us alter the case a little, and suppose that the ship was not unsound after all; that she made her voyage safely, and many others after it. Will that diminish the guilt of her owner? Not one jot. When an action is once done, it is right or wrong forever; no accidental failure of its good or evil fruits can possibly alter that. The man would not have been innocent, he would only have been not found out. The question of right or wrong has to do with the origin of his belief, not the matter of it; not

Reprinted from *Lectures and Essays* by William K. Clifford, Macmillan & Co., London, 1879.

what it was, but how he got it; not whether it turned out to be true or false, but whether he had a right to believe on such evidence as was before him.

There was once an island in which some of the inhabitants professed a religion teaching neither the doctrine of original sin nor that of eternal punishment. A suspicion got abroad that the professors of this religion had made use of unfair means to get their doctrines taught to children. They were accused of wresting the laws of their country in such a way as to remove children from the care of their natural and legal guardians; and even of stealing them away and keeping them concealed from their friends and relations. A certain number of men formed themselves into a society for the purpose of agitating the public about this matter. They published grave accusations against individual citizens of the highest position and character, and did all in their power to injure those citizens in the exercise of their professions. So great was the noise they made, that a Commission was appointed to investigate the facts; but after the Commission had carefully inquired into all the evidence that could be got, it appeared that the accused were innocent. Not only had they been accused on insufficient evidence, but the evidence of their innocence was such as the agitators might easily have obtained, if they had attempted a fair inquiry. After these disclosures the inhabitants of that country looked upon the members of the agitating society, not only as persons whose judgment was to be distrusted, but also as no longer to be counted honorable men. For although they had sincerely and conscientiously believed in the charges they had made, *yet they had no right to believe on such evidence as was before them*. Their sincere convictions, instead of being honestly earned by patient inquiring, were stolen by listening to the voice of prejudice and passion.

Let us vary this case also, and suppose, other things remaining as before, that a still more accurate investigation proved the accused to have been really guilty. Would this make any difference in the guilt of the accusers? Clearly not; the question is not whether their belief was true or false, but whether they entertained it on wrong grounds. They would no doubt say, "Now you see that we were right after all; next time perhaps you will believe us." And they might be believed, but they would not thereby become honorable men. They would not be innocent, they would only be not found out. Every one of them, if he chose to examine himself *in foro conscientiae*, would know that he had acquired and nourished a belief, when he had no right to believe on such evidence as was before him; and therein he would know that he had done a wrong thing.

It may be said, however, that in both of these supposed cases it is not the belief which is judged to be wrong, but the action following upon it. The shipowner might say, "I am perfectly certain that my ship is sound, but still I feel it my duty to have her examined, before trusting the lives of so many people to her." And it might be said to the agitator, "However convinced you were of the justice of your cause and the truth of your convictions, you ought not to have made public attack upon any man's character until you had examined the evidence on both sides with the utmost patience and care."

In the first place, let us admit that, so far as it goes, this view of the case is right and necessary; right, because even when a man's belief is so fixed that he cannot think otherwise, he still has a choice in regard to the action suggested by it, and so cannot escape the duty of investigating on the ground of the strength of his convictions; and necessary, because those who are not yet capable of controlling their feelings and thoughts must have a plain rule dealing with overt acts.

But this being premised as necessary, it becomes clear that it is not sufficient, and that our previous judgment is required to supplement it. For it is not possible so to sever the belief from the action it suggests as to condemn the one without condemning the other. No man holding a strong belief on one side of a question, or even wishing to hold a belief on one side, can investigate it with such fairness and completeness as if he were really in doubt and unbiased; so that the existence of a belief not founded on fair inquiry unfits a man for the performance of this necessary duty.

Nor is that truly a belief at all which has not some influence upon the actions of him who holds it. He who truly believes that which prompts him to an action has looked upon the action to lust after it, he has committed it already in his heart. If a belief is not realized immediately in open deeds, it is stored up for the guidance of the future. It goes to make a part of that aggregate of beliefs which is the link between sensation and action at every moment of all our lives, and which is so organized and compacted together that no part of it can be isolated from the rest, but every new addition modifies the structure of the whole. No real belief, however trifling and fragmentary it may seem, is ever truly insignificant; it prepares us to receive more of its like, confirms those which resembled it before, and weakens others; and so gradually it lays a stealthy train in our inmost thoughts, which may some day explode into overt action, and leave its stamp upon our character forever.

And no one man's belief is in any case a private matter which concerns himself alone. Our lives are guided by that general conception of the course of things which has been created by society for social purposes. Our words, our phrases, our forms and processes and modes of thought, are common property, fashioned and perfected from age to age; an heirloom which every succeeding generation inherits as a precious deposit and a sacred trust to be handed on to the next one, not unchanged but enlarged and purified, with some clear marks of its proper handiwork. Into this, for good or ill, is woven every belief of every man who has speech of his fellows. An awful privilege, and an awful responsibility, that we should help to create the world in which posterity will live.

In the two supposed cases which have been considered, it has been judged wrong to believe on insufficient evidence, or to nourish belief by suppressing doubts and avoiding investigation. The reason of this judgment is not far to seek; it is that in both these cases the belief held by one man was of great importance to other men. But for as much as no belief held by one man, however seemingly trivial the belief, and however obscure the believer, is ever actually insignificant or without its effect on the fate of mankind, we have no choice but to extend our judgment to all cases of belief whatever. Belief, that sacred faculty which prompts the decisions of our will, and knits into harmonious working all the compacted energies of our being, is ours not for ourselves but for humanity. It is rightly used on truths which have been established by long experience and waiting toil, and which have stood in the fierce light of free and fearless questioning. Then it helps to bind men together, and to strengthen and direct their common action. It is desecrated when given to unproved and unquestioned statements, for the solace and private pleasure of the believer; to add a tinsel splendor to the plain straight road of our life and display a bright mirage beyond it; or even to drown the common sorrows of our kind by a self-deception which allows them not only to cast down, but also to degrade us. Whoso would deserve well of his fellows in this matter will guard the purity of his belief with a very fanaticism of jealous care, lest at any time it should rest on an unworthy object, and catch a stain which can never be wiped away.

It is not only the leader of men, statesman, philosopher, or poet, that owes this bounden duty to mankind. Every rustic who delivers in the village alehouse his slow, infrequent sentences, may help to kill or keep alive the fatal superstitions which clog his race. Every hard-worked wife of an artisan may transmit to her children beliefs which shall knit society together, or rend it in pieces. No simplicity of mind, no obscurity of station, can escape the universal duty of questioning all that we believe.

It is true that this duty is a hard one, and the doubt which comes out of it is often a very bitter thing. It leaves us bare and powerless where we thought that we were safe and strong. To know all about anything is to know how to deal with it under all circumstances. We feel much happier and more secure when we think we know precisely what to do, no matter what happens, than when we have lost our way and do not know where to turn. And if we have supposed ourselves to know all about anything, and to be capable of doing what is fit in regard to it, we naturally do not like to find that we are really ignorant and powerless, that we have to begin again at the beginning, and try to learn what the thing is and how it is to be dealt with—if indeed anything can be learned about it. It is the sense of power attached to a sense of knowledge that makes men desirous of believing, and afraid of doubting.

This sense of power is the highest and best of pleasures when the belief on which it is founded is true belief, and has been fairly earned by investigation. For then we may justly feel that it is common property, and holds good for others as well as for ourselves. Then we may be glad, not that *I* have learned secrets by which I am safer and stronger, but that *we men* have got mastery over more of the world; and we shall be strong, not for ourselves, but in the name of Man and in his strength. But if the belief has been accepted on insufficient evidence, the pleasure is a stolen one. Not only does it deceive ourselves by giving us a sense of power which we do not really possess, but it is sinful, because it is stolen in defiance of our duty to mankind. That duty is to guard ourselves from such beliefs as from a pestilence, which may shortly master our own body and then spread to the rest of the town. What would be thought of one who, for the sake of a sweet fruit, should deliberately run the risk of bringing a plague upon his family and his neighbors?

And, as in other such cases, it is not the risk only which has to be considered; for a bad action is always bad at the time when it is done, no matter what happens afterwards. Every time we let ourselves believe for unworthy reasons, we weaken our powers of self-control, of doubting, of judicially and fairly weighing evidence. We all suffer severely enough from the maintenance and support of false beliefs and the fatally wrong actions which they lead to, and the evil born when one such belief is entertained is great and wide. But a greater and wider evil arises when the credulous character is maintained and supported, when a habit of believing for unworthy reasons is fostered and made permanent. If I steal money from any person, there may be no harm done by the mere transfer of possession; he may not feel the loss, or it may prevent him from using the money badly. But I cannot help doing this great wrong towards Man, that I make myself dishonest. What hurts society is not that it should lose its property, but that it should become a den of thieves; for then it must cease to be society. This is why we ought not to do evil that good may come; for at any rate this great evil has come, that we have done evil and are made wicked thereby. In like manner, if I let myself believe anything on insufficient evidence, there may be no great harm done by the mere belief; it may be true after all, or I may never have occasion to exhibit it in outward acts. But I cannot help doing this great wrong toward Man, that I make myself credulous. The danger to society is not merely that it should believe wrong things, though that is great enough; but that it should become credulous, and lose the habit of testing things and inquiring into them; for then it must sink back into savagery.

The harm which is done by credulity in a man is not confined to the fostering of a credulous character in others, and consequent support of false beliefs. Habitual want of care about what I believe leads to habitual want of care in others about the truth of what is told to me. Men speak the truth to one another when each reveres the truth in his own mind and in the other's mind; but how shall my friend revere the truth in my mind when I myself am careless about it, when I believe things because I want to believe them, and because they are comforting and pleasant? Will he not learn to cry, "Peace," to me, when there is no peace? By such a course I shall surround myself with a thick atmosphere of falsehood and fraud, and in that I must live. It may matter little to me, in my cloud-castle of sweet illusions and darling lies; but it matters much to Man that I have made my neighbors ready to deceive. The credulous man is father to the liar and the cheat; he lives in the bosom of this his family, and it is no marvel if he should become even as they are. So closely are our duties knit together, that whoso shall keep the whole law, and yet offend in one point, he is guilty of all.

To sum up; it is wrong always, everywhere, and for anyone, to believe anything upon insufficient evidence.

If a man, holding a belief which he was taught in childhood or persuaded of afterwards, keeps down and pushes away any doubts which arise about it in his mind, purposely avoids the reading of books and the company of men that call in question or discuss it, and regards as impious those questions which cannot easily be asked without disturbing it—the life of that man is one long sin against mankind.

If this judgment seems harsh when applied to those simple souls who have never known better, who have been brought up from the cradle with a horror of doubt, and taught that their eternal welfare depends on what they believe, then it leads to the very serious question. Who hath made Israel to sin? . . .

Inquiry into the evidence of a doctrine is not to be made once for all, and then taken as finally settled. It is never lawful to stifle a doubt; for either it can be honestly answered by means of the inquiry already made, or else it proves that the inquiry was not complete.

"But," says one, "I am a busy man; I have no time for the long course of study which would be necessary to make me in any degree a competent judge of certain questions, or even able to understand the nature of the arguments." Then he should have no time to believe. . . .

17. The Will to Believe   William James

William James (1842–1910) is considered one of America's greatest philosophers. He attended Harvard Medical School and later taught anatomy and physiology at Harvard. Later his interests were primarily in the fields of psychology and philosophy. He is considered one of the main developers of pragmatism.

. . . I have long defended to my own students the lawfulness of voluntarily adopted faith; but as soon as they have got well imbued with the logical spirit, they have as a rule refused to admit my contention to be lawful philosophically, even though in point of fact they were personally all the time chock-full of some faith or other themselves. I am all the while, however, so profoundly convinced that my own position is correct, that your invitation has seemed to me a good occasion to make my statements more clear. Perhaps your minds will be more open than those with which I have hitherto had to deal. I will be as little technical as I can, though I must begin by setting up some technical distinctions that will help us in the end.

Let us give the name of *hypothesis* to anything that may be proposed to our belief; and just as the electricians speak of live and dead wires, let us speak of any hypothesis as either *live* or *dead*. A live hypothesis is one which appeals as a real possibility to him to whom it is proposed. If I ask you to believe in the Mahdi, the notion makes no electric connection

Reprinted from *The Will to Believe and Other Essays in Popular Philosophy* by William James. Published by Longmans, Green (New York, 1896).

with your nature—it refuses to scintillate with any credibility at all. As an hypothesis it is completely dead. To an Arab, however (even if he be not one of the Mahdi's followers), the hypothesis is among the mind's possibilities: it is alive. This shows that deadness and liveness in an hypothesis are not intrinsic properties, but relations to the individual thinker. They are measured by his willingness to act. The maximum of liveness in an hypothesis means willingness to act irrevocably. Practically, that means belief; but there is some believing tendency wherever there is willingness to act at all.

Next, let us call the decision between two hypotheses an *option*. Options may be of several kinds. They may be—1, *living* or *dead;* 2, *forced* or *avoidable;* 3, *momentous* or *trivial;* and for our purposes we may call an option a *genuine* option when it is of the forced, living, and momentous kind.

1. A living option is one in which both hypotheses are live ones. If I say to you: "Be a theosophist or be a Mohammedan," it is probably a dead option, because for you neither hypothesis is likely to be alive. But if I say: "Be an agnostic or be a Christian," it is otherwise: trained as you are, each hypothesis makes some appeal, however small, to your belief.

2. Next, if I say to you: "Choose between going out with your umbrella or without it," I do not offer you a genuine opinion, for it is not forced. You can easily avoid it by not going out at all. Similarly, if I say, "Either love me or hate me," "Either call my theory true or call it false," your option is avoidable. You may remain indifferent to me, neither loving nor hating, and you may decline to offer any judgment as to my theory. But if I say, "Either accept this truth or go without it," I put on you a forced option, for there is no standing place outside of the alternative. Every dilemma based on a complete logical disjunction, with no possibility of not choosing, is an option of this forced kind.

3. Finally, if I were Dr. Nansen and proposed to you to join my North Pole expedition, your option would be momentous; for this would probably be your only similar opportunity, and your choice now would either exclude you from the North Pole sort of immortality altogether or put at least the chance of it into your hands. He who refuses to embrace a unique opportunity loses the prize as surely as if he tried and failed. *Per contra,* the option is trivial when the opportunity is not unique, when the stake is insignificant, or when the decision is reversible if it later prove unwise. Such trivial options abound in the scientific life. A chemist finds an hypothesis live enough to spend a year in its verification: he believes in it to that extent. But if his experiments prove inconclusive either way, he is quit for his loss of time, no vital harm being done.

It will facilitate our discussion if we keep all these distinctions well in mind. . . .

The thesis I defend is, briefly stated, this: *Our passional nature not only lawfully may, but must, decide an option between propositions, whenever it is a genuine option that cannot by its nature be decided on intellectual grounds; for to say, under such circumstances, "Do not decide, but leave the question open," is itself a passional decision,—just like deciding yes or no,—and is attended with the same risk of losing the truth. . . .*

Wherever the option between losing truth and gaining it is not momentous, we can throw the chance of *gaining truth* away, and at any rate save ourselves from any chance of *believing falsehood*, by not making up our minds at all till objective evidence has come. In scientific questions, this is almost always the case; and even in human affairs in general, the need of acting is seldom so urgent that a false belief to act on is better than no belief at all. Law courts, indeed, have to decide on the best evidence attainable for the moment, because a judge's duty is to make law as well as to ascertain it, and (as a learned judge once said to me) few cases are worth spending much time over: the great thing is to have them decided on *any* acceptable principle, and got out of the way. But in our dealings with objective nature we obviously are recorders, not makers, of the truth; and decisions for the mere sake of deciding promptly and getting on to the next business would be wholly out of place. Throughout the breadth of physical nature facts are what they are quite independently of us, and seldom is there any such hurry about them that the risks of being duped by believing a premature theory need be faced. The questions here are always trivial options, the hypotheses are hardly living (at any rate not living for us spectators), the choice between believing truth or falsehood is seldom forced. The attitude of sceptical balance is therefore the absolutely wise one if we would escape mistakes. What difference, indeed, does it make to most of us whether we have or have not a theory of the Röntgen rays, whether we believe or not in mind-stuff, or have a conviction about the causality of conscious states? It makes no difference. Such options are not forced on us. On every account it is better not to make them, but still keep weighing reasons *pro et contra* with an indifferent hand.

I speak, of course, here of the purely judging mind. For purposes of discovery such indifferences is to be less highly recommended, and science would be far less advanced than she is if the passionate desires of individuals to get their own faiths confirmed had been kept out of the game. . . . On the other hand, if you want an absolute duffer in an investigation, you must, after all, take the man who has no interest whatever in its results: he is the warranted incapable, the positive fool. The most useful investigator, because the most sensitive observer, is always he whose eager interest in one side of the question is balanced by an equally keen nervousness lest he become deceived. Science has organized this nervousness into a regular *technique*, her so-called method of verification; and she has fallen so deeply in love with the method that one may even say she has ceased to care for truth by itself at all. It is only truth as technically verified that interests here. The truth of truths might come in merely affirmative form, and she would decline to touch it. Such truth as that, she might repeat with Clifford, would be stolen in defiance of her duty to mankind. Human passions, however, are stronger than technical rules. "Le coeur a ses raisons," as Pascal says, "que la raison ne connaît pas";* and however indifferent to all but the bare rules of the game the umpire, the abstract intellect, may be, the concrete players who

*[The heart has its reasons that reason does not know.—Ed.]

furnish him the materials to judge of are usually, each one of them, in love with some pet 'live hypothesis' of his own. Let us agree, however, that wherever there is no forced option, the dispassionately judicial intellect with no pet hypothesis, saving us, as it does, from dupery at any rate, ought to be our ideal.

The question next arises: Are there not somewhere forced options in our speculative questions, and can we (as men who may be interested at least as much in positively gaining truth as in merely escaping dupery) always wait with impunity till the coercive evidence shall have arrived? It seems *a priori* improbable that the truth should be so nicely adjusted to our needs and powers as that. In the great boarding-house of nature, the cakes and the butter and the syrup seldom come out so even and leave the plates so clean. Indeed, we should view them with scientific suspicion if they did.

Moral questions immediately present themselves as questions whose solution cannot wait for sensible proof. A moral question is a question not of what sensibly exists, but of what is good, or would be good if it did exist. Science can tell us what exists; but to compare the *worths*, both of what exists and of what does not exist, we must consult not science, but what Pascal calls our heart. Science herself consults her heart when she lays it down that the infinite ascertainment of fact and correction of false belief are the supreme goods for man. Challenge the statement, and science can only repeat it oracularly, or else prove it by showing that such ascertainment and correction bring man all sorts of other goods which man's heart in turn declares. The question of having moral beliefs at all or not having them is decided by our will. Are our moral preferences true or false, or are they only odd biological phenomena, making things good or bad for *us*, but in themselves indifferent? How can your pure intellect decide? If your heart does not *want* a world of moral reality, your head will assuredly never make you believe in one. Mephistophelian scepticism, indeed, will satisfy the head's play-instincts much better than any rigorous idealism can. Some men (even at the student age) are so naturally cool-hearted that the moralistic hypothesis never has for them any pungent life, and in their supercilious presence the hot young moralist always feels strangely ill at ease. The appearance of knowingness is on their side, of *naïveté* and gullibility on his. Yet, in the inarticulate heart of him, he clings to it that he is not a dupe, and that there is a realm in which (as Emerson says) all their wit and intellectual superiority is no better than the cunning of a fox. Moral scepticism can no more be refuted or proved by logic than intellectual scepticism can. When we stick to it that there *is* truth (be it of either kind), we do so with our whole nature, and resolve to stand or fall by the results. The sceptic with his whole nature adopts the doubting attitude; but which of us is the wiser, Omniscience only knows.

Turn now from these wide questions of good to a certain class of questions of fact, questions concerning personal relations, states of mind between one man and another. *Do you like me or not?*—for example. Whether you do or not depends, in countless instances, on whether I meet you half-way, am willing to assume that you must like me, and show you trust and expectation. The previous faith on my part in your liking's existence is in such cases what makes your liking come. But if I stand aloof, and refuse to budge an inch until I have objective evidence, until you shall have done something apt, as the absolutists say, *ad extorquendum assensum meum,* ten to one your liking never comes. How many women's hearts are vanquished by the mere sanguine insistence of some man that they *must* love him! he will not consent to the hypothesis that they cannot. The desire for a certain kind of truth here brings about that special truth's existence; and so it is in innumerable cases of other sorts. Who gains promotions, boons, appointments, but the man in whose life they are seen to play the part of live hypotheses, who discounts them, sacrifices other things for their sake before they have come, and takes risks for them in advance? His faith acts on the powers above him as a claim, and creates its own verification.

A social organism of any sort whatever, large or small, is what it is because each member proceeds to his own duty with a trust that the other members will simultaneously do theirs. Wherever a desired result is achieved by the co-operation of many independent persons, its existence as a fact is a pure consequence of the precursive faith in one another of those immediately concerned. A government, an army, a commercial system, a ship, a college, an athletic team, all exist on this condition, without which not only is nothing achieved, but nothing is even attempted. A whole train of passengers (individually brave enough) will be looted by a few highwaymen, simply because the latter can count on one another, while each passenger fears that if he makes a movement of resistance, he will be shot before any one else backs him up. If we believed that the whole car-full would rise at once with us, we should each severally rise, and train-robbing would never even be attempted. There are, then, cases where a fact cannot come at all unless a preliminary faith exists in its coming. *And where faith in a fact can help create the fact,* that would be an insane logic which should say that faith running ahead of scientific evidence is the 'lowest kind of immorality' into which a thinking being can fall. Yet such is the logic by which our scientific absolutists pretend to regulate our lives!

In truths dependent on our personal action, then, faith based on desire is certainly a lawful and possibly an indispensable thing.

But now, it will be said, these are all childish human cases, and have nothing to do with great cosmical matters, like the question of religious faith. Let us then pass on to that. Religions differ so much in their accidents that in discussing the religious question we must make it very generic and broad. What then do we now mean by the religious hypothesis? Science says things are; morality says some things are better than other things; and religion says essentially two things.

First, she says that the best things are the more eternal things, the overlapping things, the things in the universe that throw the last stone, so to speak, and say the final word. "Perfection is eternal,"—this phrase of Charles Secrétan seems a good way of putting his first affirmation of religion, an affirmation which obviously cannot yet be verified scientifically at all.

The second affirmation of religion is that we are better off even now if we believe her first affirmation to be true.

Now, let us consider what the logical elements of this situation are *in case the religious hypothesis in both its branches be really true.* (Of course, we must admit that possibility at the outset. If we are to discuss the question at all, it must involve a living option. If for any of you religion be a hypothesis that cannot, by any living possibility be true, then you need go no farther. I speak to the 'saving remnant' alone.) So proceeding, we see, first, that religion offers itself as a *momentous* option. We are supposed to gain, even now, by our belief, and to lose by our nonbelief, a certain vital good. Secondly, religion is a *forced* option, so far as that good goes. We cannot escape the issue by remaining sceptical and waiting for more light, because, although we do avoid error in that way *if religion be untrue,* we lose the good, *if it be true,* just as certainly as if we positively chose to disbelieve. It is as if a man should hesitate indefinitely to ask a certain woman to marry him because he was not perfectly sure that she would prove an angel after he brought her home. Would he not cut himself off from that particular angel-possibility as decisively as if he went and married some one else? Scepticism, then, is not avoidance of option; it is option of a certain particular kind of risk. *Better risk loss of truth than chance of error,*—that is your faith-vetoer's exact position. He is actively playing his stake as much as the believer is; he is backing the field against the religious hypothesis, just as the believer is backing the religious hypothesis against the field. To preach scepticism to us as a duty until 'sufficient evidence' for religion be found, is tantamount therefore to telling us, when in presence of the religious hypothesis, that to yield to our fear of its being error is wiser and better than to yield to our hope that it may be true. It is not intellect against all passions, then; it is only intellect with one passion laying down its law. And by what, forsooth, is the supreme wisdom of this passion warranted? Dupery for dupery, what proof is there that dupery through hope is so much worse than dupery through fear? I, for one, can see no proof; and I simply refuse obedience to the scientist's command to imitate his kind of option, in a case where my own stake is important enough to give me the right to choose my own form of risk. If religion be true and the evidence for it be still insufficient, I do not wish, by putting your extinguisher upon my nature (which feels to me as if it had after all some business in this matter), to forfeit my sole chance in life of getting upon the winning side,—that chance depending, of course, on my willingness to run the risk of acting as if my passional need of taking the world religiously might be prophetic and right.

All this is on the supposition that it really may be prophetic and right, and that, even to us who are discussing the matter, religion is a live hypothesis which may be true. Now, to most of us religion comes in a still further way that makes a veto on our active faith even more illogical. The more perfect and more eternal aspect of the universe is represented in our religions as having personal form. The universe is no longer a mere *It* to us, but a *Thou,* if we are religious; and any relation that may be possible from person to person might be possible here. For instance, although in one sense we are passive portions of the universe, in another we show a curious autonomy, as if we were small active centres on our own account. We feel, too, as if the appeal of religion to us were made to our own active good-will, as if evidence might be forever withheld from us unless we met the hypothesis half-way. To take a trivial illustration: just as a man who in a company of gentlemen made no advances, asked a warrant for every concession, and believed no one's word without proof, would cut himself off by such churlishness from all the social rewards that a more trusting spirit would earn,—so here, one who should shut himself up in snarling logicality and try to make the gods extort his recognition willy-nilly, or not get it at all, might cut himself off forever from his only opportunity of making the gods' acquaintance. This feeling, forced on us we know not whence, that by obstinately believing that there are gods (although not to do so would be so easy both for our logic and our life) we are doing the universe the deepest service we can, seems part of the living essence of the religious hypothesis. If the hypothesis *were* true in all its parts, including this one, then pure intellectualism, with its veto on our making willing advances, would be an absurdity; and some participation of our sympathetic nature would be logically required. I, therefore, for one, cannot see my way to accepting the agnostic rules for truth-seeking, or wilfully agree to keep my willing nature out of the game. I cannot do so for this plain reason, that *a rule of thinking which would absolutely prevent me from acknowledging certain kinds of truth if those kinds of truth were really there, would be an irrational rule.* That for me is the long and short of the formal logic of the situation, no matter what the kinds of truth might materially be.

I confess I do not see how this logic can be escaped. But sad experience makes me fear that some of you may still shrink from radically saying with me, *in abstracto*, that we have the right to believe at our own risk any hypothesis that is live enough to tempt our will. I suspect, however, that if this is so, it is because you have got away from the abstract logical point of view altogether, and are thinking (perhaps without realizing it) of some particular religious hypothesis which for you is dead. The freedom to 'believe what we will' you apply to the case of some patent superstition; and the faith you think of is the faith defined by the schoolboy when he said, "Faith is when you believe something that you know ain't true." I can only repeat that this is misapprehension. *In concreto*, the freedom to believe can only cover living options which the intellect of the individual cannot by itself resolve; and living options never seem absurdities to him who has them to consider. When I look at the religious question as it really puts itself to concrete men, and when I think of all the possibilities which both practically and theoretically it involves, then this command that we shall put a stopper on our heart, instincts, and courage, and *wait*—acting of course meanwhile more or less as if religion were *not* true—till doomsday, or till such time as our intellect and senses working together may have raked in evidence enough,—this command, I say, seems to me the queerest idol ever manufactured in the philosophic cave. Were we scholastic absolutists, there might be more excuse. If we had an infallible intellect with its objective certitudes, we might feel ourselves disloyal to such a perfect organ of knowledge in not trusting to it exclusively, in not waiting for its releasing word. But if we are empiricists, if we believe that no bell in us tolls to let us know for certain when truth is in our grasp, then it seems a piece of idle fantasticality to preach so solemnly our duty of waiting for the bell. Indeed we *may* wait if we will,— I hope you do not think that I am denying that—but if we do so, we do so at our peril as much as if we believed. In either case we *act,* taking our life in our hands. No one of us ought to issue vetoes to the other, nor should we bandy words of abuse. We ought, on the contrary, delicately and profoundly to respect one another's mental freedom: then only shall we bring about the intellectual republic: then only shall we have that spirit of inner tolerance without which all our outer tolerance is soulless, and which is empiricism's glory; then only shall we live and let live, in speculative as well as in practical things. . . .

Is Religion Necessary to Give Meaning to Life?

18. My Confession   Leo Tolstoy

Leo Tolstoy (1828–1910), author of such famous novels as *War and Peace* and *Anna Karenina,* was an important social and moral reformer in his native Russia.

IV

My life came to a standstill. I could breathe, eat, drink, and sleep, and could not help breathing, eating, drinking, and sleeping; but there was no life, because there were no desires the gratification of which I might find reasonable. If I wished for anything, I knew in advance that, whether I gratified my desire or not, nothing would come of it. If a fairy had come and had offered to carry out my wish, I should not have known what to say. If in moments of intoxication I had, not wishes, but habits of former desires, I knew in sober moments that that was a deception, that there was nothing to wish for. I could not even wish to find out the truth, because I guessed what it consisted in. The truth was that life was meaningless. It was as though I had just been living and walking along, and had come to an abyss, where I saw clearly that there was nothing ahead but perdition. And it was impossible to stop and go back, and impossible to shut my eyes, in order that I might not see that there was nothing ahead but suffering and imminent death,—complete annihilation.

What happened to me was that I, a healthy, happy man, felt that I could not go on living,—an insurmountable force drew me on to find release from life. I cannot say that I *wanted* to kill myself.

The force which drew me away from life was stronger, fuller, more general than wishing. It was a force like the former striving after life, only in an inverse sense. I tended with all my strength away from life. The thought of suicide came as naturally to me as had come before the ideas of improving life. That thought was so seductive that I had to use cunning against myself, lest I should rashly execute it. I did not want to be in a hurry, because I wanted to use every effort to disentangle myself: if I should not succeed in disentangling myself, there would always be time for that. And at such times I, a happy man, hid a rope from myself so that I should not hang myself on a cross-beam between two safes in my room, where I was by myself in the evening, while taking off my clothes, and did not go out hunting with a gun, in order not to be tempted by an easy way of doing away with myself. I did not know myself what it was I wanted: I was afraid of life, strove to get away from it, and, at the same time, expected something from it.

All that happened with me when I was on every side surrounded by what is considered to be complete happiness. I had a good, loving, and beloved wife, good children, and a large estate, which grew and increased without any labour on my part. I was respected by my neighbours and friends, more than ever before, was praised by strangers, and, without any self-deception, could consider my name famous. With all that, I was not deranged or mentally unsound,—on the contrary, I was in full command of my mental and physical powers, such as I had rarely met with in people of my age: physically I could work in a field, mowing, without falling behind a peasant; mentally I could work from eight to ten hours in succession, without experiencing any consequences from the strain. And while in such condition I arrived at the conclusion that I could not live, and, fearing death, I had to use cunning against myself, in order that I might not take my life.

This mental condition expressed itself to me in this form: my life is a stupid, mean trick played on me by somebody. Although I did not recognize that "somebody" as having created me, the form of the conception that some one had played a mean, stupid trick on me by bringing me into the world was the most natural one that presented itself to me.

Involuntarily I imagined that there, somewhere, there was somebody who was now having fun as he looked down upon me and saw me, who had lived for thirty or forty years, learning, developing, growing in body and mind, now that I had become strengthened in mind and had reached that summit of life from which it lay all before me, standing as a complete fool on that summit and seeing clearly that there was nothing in life and never would be. And that was fun to him—

But whether there was or was not that somebody who made fun of me, did not make it easier for me. I could not ascribe any sensible meaning to a single act, or to my whole life. I was only surprised that I had not understood that from the start. All that had long ago been known to everybody. Sooner or later there would come diseases and death (they had come already) to my dear ones and to me, and there would be nothing left but stench and worms. All my affairs, no matter what they might be, would sooner or later be forgotten, and I myself should not exist. So why should I worry about all these things? How could a man fail to see that and live,—that was surprising! A person could live only so long as he was drunk; but the moment he sobered up, he could not help seeing that all that was only a deception, and a stupid deception at that! Really, there was nothing funny and ingenious about it, but only something cruel and stupid.

Long ago has been told the Eastern story about the traveller who in the steppe is overtaken by an infuriated beast. Trying to save himself from the animal, the traveller jumps into a waterless well, but at its bottom he sees a dragon who opens his jaws in order to swallow him. And the unfortunate man does not dare climb out, lest he perish from the infuriated beast, and does not dare jump down to the bottom of the well, lest he be devoured by the dragon, and so clutches the twig of a wild bush growing in a cleft of the well and holds on to it. His hands grow weak and he feels that soon he shall have to surrender to the peril which awaits him at either side; but he still holds on and sees two mice, one white, the other black, in even measure making a circle around the main trunk of the bush to which he is clinging, and nibbling at it on all sides. Now, at any moment, the bush will break and tear off, and he will fall into the dragon's jaws. The traveller sees that and knows that he will inevitably perish; but while he is still clinging, he sees some drops of honey hanging on the leaves of the bush, and so reaches out for them with his tongue and licks the leaves. Just so I hold on to the branch of life, knowing that the dragon of death is waiting inevitably for me, ready to tear me to pieces, and I cannot understand why I have fallen on such suffering. And I try to lick that honey which used to give me pleasure; but now it no longer gives me joy, and the white and the black mouse day and night nibble at the branch to which I am holding on. I clearly see the dragon and the mice, and am unable to turn my glance away from them. That is not a fable, but a veritable, indisputable, comprehensible truth.

The former deception of the pleasures of life, which stifled the terror of the dragon, no longer deceives me. No matter how much one should say to me. "You cannot understand the meaning of life, do not think, live!" I am unable to do so, because I have been doing it too long before. Now I cannot help seeing day and night, which run and lead me up to death. I see that alone, because that alone is the truth. Everything else is a lie.

The two drops of honey that have longest turned my eyes away from the cruel truth, the love of family and of authorship, which I have called an art, are no longer sweet to me.

"My family—" I said to myself, "but my family, my wife and children, they are also human beings. They are in precisely the same condition that I am in: they must either live in the lie or see the terrible truth. Why should they live? Why should I love them, why guard, raise, and watch them? Is it for the same despair which is in me, or for fullness of perception? Since I love them, I cannot conceal truth from them,—every step in cognition leads them up to this truth. And the truth is death."

"Art, poetry?" For a long time, under the influence of the success of human praise, I tried to persuade myself that that was a thing which could be done, even though death should come and destroy everything, my deeds, as well as my memory of them; but soon I came to see that that too, was a deception. It was clear to me that art was an adornment of life, a decoy of life. But life lost all its attractiveness for me. How, then, could I entrap others? So long as I did not live my own life, and a strange life bore me on its waves; so long as I believed that life had some sense, although I was not able to express it,—the reflections of life of every description in poetry and in the arts afforded me pleasure, and I was delighted to look at life through this little mirror of art; but when I began to look for the meaning of life, when I experienced the necessity of living myself, that little mirror became either useless, superfluous, and ridiculous, or painful to me. I could no longer console myself with what I saw in the mirror, namely, that my situation was stupid and desperate. It was all right for me to rejoice so long as I believed in the depth of my soul that life had some sense. At that time the play of lights—of the comical, the tragical, the touching, the beautiful, the terrible in life— afforded me amusement. But when I knew that life was meaningless and terrible, the play in the little mirror could no longer amuse me. No sweetness of honey could be sweet to me, when I saw the dragon and the mice that were nibbling down my support.

That was not all. If I had simply comprehended that life had no meaning, I might have known that calmly,—I might have known that that was my fate. But I could not be soothed by that. If I had been like a man living in a forest from which he knew there was no way out, I might have lived: but I was like a man who had lost his way in the forest, who was overcome by terror because he had lost his way, who kept tossing about in his desire to come out on the road, knowing that every step got him only more entangled, and who could not help tossing.

That was terrible. And, in order to free myself from that terror, I wanted to kill myself. I experienced terror before what was awaiting me,—I knew that that terror was more terrible than the situation itself, but I could not patiently wait for the end. No matter how convincing the reflection was that it was the same whether a vessel in the heart should break or something should burst, and all should be ended, I could not wait patiently for the end. The terror of the darkness was too great, and I wanted as quickly as possible to free myself from it by means of a noose or a bullet. It was this feeling that more than anything else drew me on toward suicide. . . .

VII

Having found no elucidation in science, I began to look for it in life, hoping to find it in the men who surrounded me. I began to observe the people such as I, to see how they lived about me and what attitude they assumed to the question that had brought me to the point of despair.

This is what I found in people who were in the same position as myself through their education and manner of life.

I found that for people of my circle there were four ways out from the terrible condition in which we all are.

The first way out is through ignorance. It consists in not knowing, not understanding that life is evil and meaningless. People of this category—mostly women or very young or very dull persons—have not yet come to understand that question of life which presented itself to Schopenhauer, Solomon, and Buddha. They see neither the dragon that awaits them, nor the mice that are nibbling at the roots of the bushes to which they are holding on, and continue to lick the honey. But they lick the honey only till a certain time: something will direct their attention to the dragon and the mice, and there will be an end to their licking. From them I can learn nothing,—it is impossible to stop knowing what you know.

The second way out is through Epicureanism. It consists in this, that, knowing the hopelessness of life, one should in the meantime enjoy such good as there is, without looking either at the dragon or the mice, but licking the honey in the best manner possible, especially if there is a lot of it in one spot. Solomon expresses this way out like this:

"Go thy way, eat thy bread with joy, and drink thy wine. Live joyfully with the wife whom thou lovest all the days of the life of thy vanity, which he hath given thee under the sun, all the days of thy vanity; for that is thy portion in this life, and in thy labour which thou takest under the sun. Whatsoever thy hand findeth to do, do it with thy might; for there is no work, nor device, nor knowledge, nor wisdom, in the grave, whither thou goest."

Thus the majority of the people of our circle support the possibility of life in themselves. The conditions in which they are give them more good than evil, and their moral dullness makes it possible for them to forget that the advantage of their situation is a casual one; that not everybody can have a thousand wives and palaces, like Solomon; that to every man with a thousand wives there are a thousand men without wives, and for every palace there are a thousand people who built it in the sweat of their brows; and that the accident which has made me Solomon to-day, will tomorrow make me a slave of Solomon. The dullness of the imagination of these people makes it possible for them to forget that which gave no rest to Buddha,—the inevitableness of sickness, old age, and death, which sooner or later will destroy all those pleasures.

Thus think and feel the majority of men of our time and our manner of life. The fact that some of these people assert that the dullness of their comprehension and imagination is philosophy, which they call positive, in my opinion does not take them out of the category of those who, in order not to see the question, lick the honey. Such people I could not imitate: as I did not possess their dullness of comprehension, I could not artificially reproduce it in myself. Just like any live man, I could not tear my eyes away from the mice and the dragon, having once seen them.

The third way out is through force and energy. It consists in this, that, having comprehended that life is evil and meaningless, one should set out to destroy it. Thus now and then act strong, consistent people. Having comprehended all the stupidity of the joke which has been played upon them, and seeing that the good of the dead is better than that of the living, and that it is better not to be at all, they go and carry this out and at once put an end to that stupid joke, so long as there are means for it: a noose about the neck, the water, a knife to pierce the heart with, railway trains. The number of people of our circle who do so is growing larger and larger. These people commit the act generally at the best period of life, when the mental powers are in full bloom and few habits have been acquired that lower human reason.

I saw that that was the worthiest way out, and I wanted to act in that way.

The fourth way out is through weakness. It consists in this, that, comprehending the evil and the meaninglessness of life, one continues to drag it out, knowing in advance that nothing can come of it. People of this calibre know that death is better than life, but, not having the strength to act reasonably, to make an end to the deception, and to kill themselves, they seem to be waiting for something. This is the way of weakness, for if I know that which is better, which is in my power, why not abandon myself to that which is better? I belonged to that category.

Thus people of my calibre have four ways of saving themselves from the terrible contradiction. No matter how much I strained my mental attention, I saw no other way out but those four. The one way out was not to understand that life was meaningless, vanity, and an evil, and that it was better not to live. I could not help knowing it and, having once learned it, I could not shut my eyes to it. The second way out was to make use of life such as it is, without thinking of the future. I could not do that either. Like Sakya-Muni, I could not go out hunting, when I knew that there was old age, suffering, death. My imagination was too vivid. Besides, I could not enjoy the accident of the moment, which for a twinkling threw enjoyment in my path. The third way out was, having come to see that life was an evil and a foolishness, to make an end of it and kill myself. I comprehended that, but for some reason did not kill myself. The fourth way out was to live in the condition of Solomon, of Schopenhauer,—to know that life was a stupid joke played on me, and yet to live, wash and dress myself, dine, speak, and even write books. That was repulsive and painful for me, but still I persisted in that situation. . . .

XII

I remember, it was early in spring, I was by myself in the forest, listening to the sounds of the woods. I listened and thought all the time of one and the same thing that had formed the subject of my thoughts for the last three years. I was again searching after God.

"All right, there is no God," I said to myself, "there is not such a being as would be, not my concept, but reality, just like my whole life,— there is no such being. And nothing, no miracles, can prove him to me, because the miracles would be my concept, and an irrational one at that.

"But my idea about God, about the one I am searching after?" I asked myself. "Where did that idea come from?" And with this thought the joyous waves of life again rose in me. Everything about me revived, received a meaning; but my joy did not last long,—the mind continued its work.

"The concept of God is not God," I said to myself. "A concept is what takes place within me; the concept of God is what I can evoke or can not evoke in myself. It is not that which I am searching after. I am trying to find that without which life could not be." And again everything began to die around me and within me, and I wanted again to kill myself.

Then I looked at myself, at what was going on within me, and I recalled those deaths and revivals which had taken place within me hundreds of times. I remembered that I lived only when I believed in God. As it had been before, so it was even now: I needed only to know about God, and I lived; I needed to forget and not believe in him, and I died.

What, then are these revivals and deaths? Certainly I do not live when I lose my faith in the existence of God; I should have killed myself long ago, if I had not had the dim hope of finding him. "So what else am I looking for?" a voice called out within me. "Here he is. He is that without which one cannot live. To know God and live is one and the same thing. God is life.

"Live searching after God, and then there will be no life without God." And stronger than ever all was lighted up within me and about me, and that light no longer abandoned me.

Thus I was saved from suicide. When and how this transformation took place in me I could not say. Just as imperceptibly and by degrees as my force of life had waned, and I had arrived at the impossibility of living, at the arrest of life, at the necessity of suicide, just so by degrees and imperceptibly did that force of life return to me. Strange to say, the force of life which returned to me was not a new, but the same old force which had drawn me on in the first period of my life.

I returned in everything to the most remote, the childish and the youthful. I returned to the belief in that will which had produced me and which wanted something of me; I returned to this, that the chief and only purpose of my life was to be better, that is, to live more in accord with that will; I returned to this, that the expression of this will I could find in that which all humanity had worked out for its guidance in the vanishing past, that is, I returned to the faith in God, in moral perfection, and in the tradition which had handed down the meaning of life. There was only this difference, that formerly it had been assumed unconsciously, while now I knew that I could not live without it.

This is what seemed to have happened with me: I do not remember when I was put in a boat, was pushed off from some unknown shore, had pointed out to me the direction toward another shore, had a pair of oars given into my inexperienced hands, and was left alone. I plied my oars as well as I could, and moved on; but the farther I rowed toward the middle, the swifter did the current become which bore me away from my goal, and the more frequently did I come across oarsmen like myself, who were carried away by the current, others submitted to it. The farther I rowed, the more did I look down the current, whither all those boats were carried, and forget the direction which had been pointed out to me. In the middle of the current, in the crush of the boats and ships which bore me down, I lost my direction completely and threw down the oars. On every side of me sailing vessels and rowboats were borne down the current with merriment and rejoicing, and the people in them assured me and each other that there could not even be any other direction, and I believed them and went down the stream with them. I was carried away, so far away, that I heard the noise of the rapids where I should be wrecked, and saw boats that had already been wrecked there. I regained my senses. For a long time I could not understand what had happened with me. I saw before me nothing but ruin toward which I was rushing and of which I was afraid; nowhere did I see any salvation, and I did not know what to do; but, on looking back, I saw an endless number of boats that without cessation stubbornly crossed the current, and I thought of the shore, the oars, and the direction, and began to make my way back, up the current and toward the shore.

That shore was God, the direction was tradition, the oars were the freedom given me to row toward the shore,—to unite myself with God. Thus the force of life was renewed in me, and I began to live once more.

19. Meaning and Value of Life   Paul Edwards

Paul Edwards (1923–) is professor of philosophy at City University of New York. He is editor-in-chief of the *Encyclopedia of Philosophy* and the author of many important books and scholarly articles on a variety of philosophical topics.

To the questions "Is human life ever worthwhile?" and "Does (or can) human life have any meaning?" many religious thinkers have offered affirmative answers with the proviso that these answers would not be justified unless two of the basic propositions of most Western religions were true—that human life is part of a divinely ordained cosmic scheme and that after death at least some human beings will be rewarded with eternal bliss. Thus, commenting on Bertrand Russell's statement that not only must each individual human life come to an end but that life in general will eventually die out, C. H. D. Clark contrasts this "doctrine of despair" with the beauty of the Christian scheme. "If we are asked to believe that all our striving is without final consequence," then "life is meaningless and it scarcely matters how we live if all will end in the dust of death." According to Christianity, on the other hand, "each action has vital significance." Clark assures us that "God's grand design is life

This material is excerpted in part from the article "The Meaning and Value of Life" by Paul Edwards. Reprinted with permission of the publisher from *Encyclopedia of Philosophy*, Paul Edwards, Editor in Chief, Volume 4. Copyright © 1967 by Macmillan, Inc.

eternal for those who walk in the steps of Christ. Here is the one grand incentive to good living. . . . As life is seen to have purpose and meaning, men find release from despair and the fear of death" (*Christianity and Bertrand Russell,* p. 30). In a similar vein, the Jewish existentialist Emil Fackenheim claims that "whatever meaning life acquires" is derived from the encounter between God and man. The meaning thus conferred upon human life "cannot be understood in terms of some finite human purpose, supposedly more ultimate than the meeting itself. For what could be more ultimate than the Presence of God?" It is true that God is not always "near," but "times of Divine farness" are by no means devoid of meaning. "Times of Divine nearness do not light up themselves alone. Their meaning extends over all of life." There is a "dialectic between Divine nearness and Divine farness," and it points to "an eschatological future in which it is overcome" ("Judaism and the Meaning of Life").

Among unbelievers not a few maintain that life can be worthwhile and have meaning in some humanly important sense even if the religious world view is rejected. Others, however, agree with the religious theorists that our two questions must be given negative answers if there is no God and if death means personal annihilation. Having rejected the claims of religion, they therefore conclude that life is not worthwhile and that it is devoid of meaning. These writers, to whom we shall refer here as "pessimists," do not present their judgments as being merely expressions of certain moods or feelings but as conclusions that are in some sense objectively warranted. They offer reasons for their conclusions and imply that anybody reaching a contradictory conclusion is mistaken or irrational. Most pessimists do not make any clear separation between the statements that life is not worthwhile and that life is without meaning. They usually speak of the "futility" or the "vanity" of life, and presumably they mean by this both that life is not worth living and that it has no meaning. For the time being we, too, shall treat these statements as if they were equivalent. However, later we shall see that in certain contexts it becomes important to distinguish between them.

Our main concern in this article will be to appraise pessimism as just defined. We shall not discuss either the question whether life is part of a divinely ordained plan or the question whether we survive our bodily death. Our question will be whether the pessimistic conclusions are justified if belief in God and immortality are rejected. . . .

Strengths of the Pessimist Position

Is it possible for somebody who shares the pessimists' rejection of religion to reach different conclusions without being plainly irrational? Whatever reply may be possible, any intelligent and realistic person would surely have to concede that there is much truth in the pessimists' claims. That few people achieve real and lasting happiness, that the joys of life (where there are any) pass away much too soon, that totally unpredictable events frequently upset the best intentions and wreck the noblest plans— this and much more along the same lines is surely undeniable. Although one should not dogmatize that there will be no significant improvements in the future, the fate of past revolutions, undertaken to rid man of some of his apparently avoidable suffering, does not inspire great hope. The thought of death, too, even in those who are not so overwhelmed by it as Tolstoy, can be quite unendurable. Moreover, to many who have reflected on the implications of physical theory it seems plain that because of the constant increase of entropy in the universe all life anywhere will eventually die out. Forebodings of this kind moved Bertrand Russell to write his famous essay "A Free Man's Worship," in which he concluded that "all the labors of the ages, all the devotion, all the inspiration, all the noonday brightness of human genius, are destined to extinction in the vast death of the solar system, and the whole temple of man's achievement must inevitably be buried beneath the debris of a universe in ruins." Similarly, Wilhelm Ostwald observed that "in the longest run the sum of all human endeavor has no recognizable significance." Although it is disputed whether physical theory really has such gloomy implications, it would perhaps be wisest to assume that the position endorsed by Russell and Ostwald is well-founded.

Comparative Value Judgments about Life and Death

Granting the strong points in the pessimists' claims, it is still possible to detect certain confusions and dubious inferences in their arguments. To begin with, there is a very obvious inconsistency in the way writers like Darrow and Tolstoy arrive at the conclusion that death is better than life. They begin by telling us that death is something terrible because it terminates the possibility of any of the experiences we value. From this they infer that nothing is really worth doing and that death is better than life. Ignoring for the moment the claim that in view of our inevitable death nothing is "worth doing," there very plainly seems to be an inconsistency in first judging death to be such a horrible evil and in asserting later on that death is better than life. Why was death originally judged to be an evil? Surely because it is the termination of life. And if something, y, is bad because it is the termination of something, x, this can be so only if x is good or has postiive value. If x were not good, the termination of x would not be bad. One cannot consistently have it both ways.

To this it may be answered that life did have positive value prior to one's realization of death but that once a person has become aware of the inevitability of his destruction life becomes unbearable and that this is the real issue. This point of view is well expressed in the following exchange between Cassius and Brutus in Shakespeare's *Julius Caesar* (III.i. 102–105):

> *Cassius:*   Why he that cuts off twenty years of life
>   Cuts off so many years of fearing death.
> *Brutus:*   Grant that, and then is death a benefit:
>   So are we Caesar's friends that have abridged His time of fearing death.

There is a very simple reply to this argument. Granting that some people after once realizing their doom cannot banish the thought of it from their minds, so much so that it interferes with all their other activities, this is neither inevitable nor at all common. It is, on the contrary, in the opinion of all except some existentialists, morbid and pathological. The realization that one will die does not in the case of most people prevent them from engaging in activities which they regard as valuable or from enjoying the things they used to enjoy. To be told that one is not living "authentically" if one does not brood about death day and night is simply to be insulted gratuitously. A person who knows that his talents are not as great as he would wish or that he is not as handsome as he would have liked to be is not usually judged to live "inauthentically," but on the contrary to be sensible if he does not constantly brood about his limitations and shortcomings and uses whatever talents he does possess to maximum advantage.

There is another and more basic objection to the claim that death is better than life. This objection applies equally to the claim that while death is better than life it would be better still not to have been born in the first place and to the judgment that life is better than death. It should be remembered that we are here concerned with such pronouncements when they are intended not merely as the expression of certain moods but as statements which are in some sense true or objectively warranted. It may be argued that a value comparison—any judgment to the effect that *A* is better or worse than *B* or as good as *B*—makes sense only if *both A* and *B* are, in the relevant respect, in principle open to inspection. If somebody says, for example, that Elizabeth Taylor is a better actress than Betty Grable, this seems quite intelligent. Or, again, if it is said that life for the Jews is better in the United States than it was in Germany under the Nazis, this also seems readily intelligible. In such cases the terms of the comparison are observable or at any rate describable. These conditions are fulfilled in some cases when value comparisons are made between life and death, but they are not fulfilled in the kind of case with which Tolstoy and the pessimists are concerned. If the conception of an afterlife is intelligible, then it would make sense for a believer or for somebody who has not made up his mind to say such things as "Death cannot be worse than this life" or "I wonder if it will be any better for me after I am dead." Achilles, in the *Iliad,* was not making a senseless comparison when he exclaimed that he would rather act

> . . . as a serf of another.
> A man of little possessions, with scanty means of subsistence,
> Than rule as a ghostly monarch the ghosts of all the departed.

Again, the survivors can meaningfully say about a deceased individual "It is better (for the world) that he is dead" or the opposite. For the person himself, however, if there is no afterlife, death is not a possible object of observation or experience, and statements by him that his own life is better than, as good as, or worse than his own death, unless they are intended to be no more than expressions of certain wishes or moods, must be dismissed as senseless. At first sight the contention that in the circumstances under discussion value comparisons between life and death are senseless may seem implausible because of the widespread tendency to think of death as a shadowy kind of life—as sleep, rest, or some kind of home-coming. Such "descriptions" may be admirable as poetry or consolation, but taken literally they are simply false.

Irrelevance of the Distant Future

These considerations do not, however, carry us very far. They do not show either that life is worth living or that it "has meaning." Before tackling these problems directly, something should perhaps be said about the curious and totally arbitrary preference of the future to the present, to which writers like Tolstoy and Darrow are committed without realizing it. Darrow implies that life would not be "futile" if it were not an endless cycle of the same kind of activities and if instead it were like a journey toward a destination. Tolstoy clearly implies that life would be worthwhile, that some of our actions at least would have a "reasonable meaning," if the present life were followed by eternal bliss. Presumably, what would make life no longer futile as far as Darrow is concerned is some feature of the destination, not merely the fact that it is a destination; and what would make life worthwhile in Tolstoy's opinion is not merely the eternity of the next life but the "bliss" which it would confer—eternal misery and torture would hardly do. About the bliss in the next life, if there is such a next life, Tolstoy shows no inclination to ask "What for?" or "So what?" But if bliss in the next life is not in need of any further justification, why should any bliss that there might be in the present life need justification?

The Logic of Value Judgments

Many of the pessimists appear to be confused about the logic of value judgments. It makes sense for a person to ask about something "Is it really worthwhile?" or "Is it really worth the trouble?" if he does not regard it as intrinsically valuable or if he is weighing it against another good with which it may be in conflict. It does not make sense to ask such a question about something he regards as valuable in its own right and where there is no conflict with the attainment of any other good. (This observation, it should be noted, is quite independent of what view one takes of the logical status of intrinsic value judgments.) A person driving to the beach on a crowded Sunday, may, upon finally getting there, reflect on whether the trip was really worthwhile. Or, after undertaking a series of medical treatments, somebody may ask whether it was worth the time and the money involved. Such questions make sense because the discomforts of a car ride and the time and money spent on medical treatments are not usually judged to be valuable for their own sake. Again, a woman who has given up a career as a physician in order to raise a family may ask herself whether it was worthwhile, and in this case the question would make sense not because she regards the raising of a family as no more than a means, but because she is weighing it against another good. However, if somebody is very happy, for any number of reasons— because he is in love, because he won the Nobel prize, because his child recovered from a serious illness—and if this happiness does not prevent him from doing or experiencing anything else he regards as valuable, it would not occur to him to ask "Is it worthwhile?" Indeed, this question would be incomprehensible to him, just as Tolstoy himself would presumably not have known what to make of the question had it been raised about the bliss in the hereafter.

It is worth recalling here that we live not in the distant future but in the present and also, in a sense, in the relatively near future. To bring the subject down to earth, let us consider some everyday occurrences: A man with a toothache goes to a dentist, and the dentist helps him so that the toothache disappears. A man is falsely accused of a crime and is faced with the possibility of a severe sentence as well as with the loss of his reputation; with the help of a devoted attorney his innocence is established, and he is acquitted. It is true that a hundred years later all of the participants in these events will be dead and none of them will *then* be able to enjoy the fruits of any of the efforts involved. But this most emphatically does not imply that the dentist's efforts were not worthwhile or that the attorney's work was not worth doing. To bring in considerations of what will or will not happen in the remote future is, in such and many other though certainly not in all human situations, totally irrelevant. Not only is the finality of death irrelevant here; equally irrelevant are the facts, if they are facts, that life is an endless cycle of the same kind of activities and that the history of the universe is not a drama with a happy ending.

This is, incidentally, also the answer to religious apologists like C. H. D. Clark who maintain that all striving is pointless if it is "without final consequence" and that "it scarcely matters how we live if all will end in the dust of death." Striving is not pointless if it achieves what it is intended to achieve even if it is without *final* consequence, and it matters a great deal how we live if we have certain standards and goals, although we cannot avoid "the dust of death."

The Vanished Past

In asserting the worthlessness of life Schopenhauer remarked that "what has been exists as little as what has never been" and that "something of great importance now past is inferior to something of little importance now present." Several comments are in order here. To begin with, if Schopenhauer is right, it must work both ways: if only the present counts, then past sorrows no less than past pleasures do not "count." Furthermore, the question whether "something of great importance now past is inferior to something of little importance now present" is not, as Schopenhauer supposed, a straightforward question of fact but rather one of valuation, and different answers, none of which can be said to be mistaken, will be given by different people according to their circumstances and interests. Viktor Frankl, the founder of "logotherapy," has compared the pessimist to a man who observes, with fear and sadness, how his wall calendar grows thinner and thinner as he removes a sheet from it every day. The kind of person whom Frankl admires, on the other hand, "files each successive leaf neatly away with its predecessors" and reflects "with pride and joy" on all the richness represented by the leaves removed from the calendar. Such a person will not in old age envy the young. 'No, thank you,' he will think. 'Instead of possibilities, I have realities in my past' " *(Man's Search for Meaning,* pp. 192–193). This passage is quoted not because it contains any great wisdom but because it illustrates that we are concerned here not with judgments of fact but with value judgments and that Schopenhauer's is not the only one that is possible. Nevertheless, his remarks are, perhaps, a healthy antidote to the cheap consolation and the attempts to cover up deep and inevitable misery that are the stock in trade of a great deal of popular psychology. Although Schopenhauer's judgments about the inferior value of the past cannot be treated as objectively true propositions, they express only too well what a great many human beings are bound to feel on certain occasions. To a man dying of cancer it is small consolation to reflect that there was a time when he was happy and flourishing; and while there are undoubtedly some old people who do not envy the young, it may be suspected that more often the kind of talk advocated by the prophets of positive thinking is a mask for envy and a defense against exceedingly painful feelings of regret and helplessness in the face of aging and death and the now unalterable past. . . .

Is Human Life Ever Worthwhile?

Let us now turn to the question of whether life is ever worth living. This also appears to be denied by the pessimists when they speak of the vanity or the futility of human life. We shall see that in a sense it cannot be established that the pessimists are "mistaken," but it is also quite easy to show that in at least two senses which seem to be of importance to many people, human lives frequently are worth living. To this end, let us consider under what circumstances a person is likely to raise the question "Is my life (still) worthwhile?" and what is liable to provoke somebody into making a statement like "My life has ceased to be worth living." We saw in an earlier section that when we say of certain acts, such as the efforts of a dentist or a lawyer, that they were worthwhile we are claiming that they achieved certain goals. Something similar seems to be involved when we say that a person's life is (still) worthwhile or worth living. We seem to be making two assertions: first, that the person has some goals (other than merely to be dead or to have his pains eased) which do not seem to him to be trivial and, second, that there is some genuine possibility that he will attain these goals. These observations are confirmed by various systematic studies of people who contemplated suicide, of others who unsuccessfully attempted suicide, and of situations in which people did commit suicide. When the subjects of these studies declared that their lives were no longer worth living they generally meant either that there was nothing left in their lives about which they seriously cared or that there was no real likelihood of attaining any of the goals that mattered to them. It should be noted that in this sense an individual may well be mistaken in his assertion that his life is or is not worthwhile any longer: he may, for example, mistake a temporary indisposition for a more permanent loss of interest, or, more likely, he may falsely estimate his chances of achieving the ends he wishes to attain.

Different Senses of "Worthwhile".   According to the account given so far, one is saying much the same thing in declaring a life to be worthwhile and in asserting that it has meaning in the "terrestrial" sense of the word. There is, however, an interesting difference. When we say that a person's life has meaning (in the terrestrial sense) we are not committed to the claim that the goal or goals to which he is devoted have any positive value. (This is a slight oversimplification, assuming greater uniformity in the use of "meaning of life" than actually exists, but it will not seriously affect any of the controversial issues discussed here.) The question "As long as his life was dedicated to the spread of communism it has meaning to *him*, but was it really meaningful?" seems to be senseless. We are inclined to say, "If his life had meaning to him, then it had meaning—that's all there is to it." We are not inclined (or we are much less inclined) to say something of this kind when we speak of the worth of a person's life. We might say—for example, of someone like Eichmann—"While he was carrying out the extermination program, his life *seemed* worthwhile to him, but since his goal was so horrible, his life *was not* worthwhile." One might perhaps distinguish between a "subjective" and an "objective" sense of "worthwhile." In the subjective sense, saying that a person's life is worthwhile simply means that he is attached to some goals which he does not consider trivial and that these goals are attainable for him. In declaring that somebody's life is worthwhile in the objective sense, one is saying that he is attached to certain goals which are both attainable and of positive value.

It may be held that unless one accepts some kind of rationalist or intuitionist view of fundamental value judgments one would have to conclude that in the objective sense of "worthwhile" no human life (and indeed no human action) could ever be shown to be worthwhile. There is no need to enter here into a discussion of any controversial questions about the logical status of fundamental value judgments. But it may be pointed out that somebody who favors a subjectivist or emotivist account can quite consistently allow for the distinction between ends that only seem to have positive value and those that really do. To mention just one way in which this could be done: one may distinguish between ends that would be approved by rational and sympathetic human beings and those that do not carry such an endorsement. One may then argue that when we condemn such a life as Eichmann's as not being worthwhile we mean not that the ends to which he devoted himself possess some non-natural characteristic of badness but that no rational or sympathetic person would approve of them.

The Pessimists' Special Standards

The unexciting conclusion of this discussion is that some human lives are at certain times not worthwhile in either of the two senses we have distinguished, that some are worthwhile in the subjective but not in the objective sense, some in the objective but not in the subjective sense, and some are worthwhile in both senses. The unexcitingness of this conclusion is not a reason for rejecting it, but some readers may question whether it meets the challenge of the pessimists. The pessimist, it may be countered, surely does not deny the plain fact that human beings are on occasions attached to goals which do not seem to them trivial, and it is also not essential to his position to deny (and most pessimists do not in fact deny) that these goals are sometimes attainable. The pessimist may even allow that in a superficial ("immediate") sense the goals which people try to achieve are of positive value, but he would add that because our lives are not followed by eternal bliss they are not "really" or "ultimately" worthwhile. If this is so, then the situation may be characterized by saying that the ordinary man and the pessimist do not mean the same by "worthwhile," or that they do mean the same in that both use it as a positive value expression but that their standards are different: the standards of the pessimist are very much more demanding than those of most ordinary people.

Anybody who agrees that death is final will have to concede that the pessimist is not mistaken in his contention that judged by *his* standards, life is never worthwhile. However, the pessimist is mistaken if he concludes, as frequently happens, that life is not worthwhile by ordinary standards because it is not worthwhile by his standards. Furthermore, setting aside the objection mentioned earlier (that there is something arbitrary about maintaining that eternal bliss makes life worthwhile but not allowing this role to bliss in the present life), one may justifiably ask why one should abandon ordinary standards in favor of those of the pessimist. Ordinarily, when somebody changes standards (for example, when a school raises or lowers its standards of admission) such a change can be supported by reasons. But how can the pessimist justify his special standards? It should be pointed out here that our ordinary standards do something for us which the pessimist's standards do not: they guide our choices, and as long as we live we can hardly help making choices. It is true that in one type of situation the pessimist's standards also afford guidance—namely, in deciding whether to go on living. It is notorious, however, that whether or not they are, by their own standards, rational in this, most pessimists do not commit suicide. They are then faced with much the same choices as other people. In these situations their own demanding standards are of no use, and in fact they avail themselves of the ordinary standards. Schopenhauer, for example, believed that if he had hidden his antireligious views he would have had no difficulty in obtaining an academic appointment and other worldly honors. He may have been mistaken in this belief, but in any event his actions indicate that he regarded intellectual honesty as worthwhile in a sense in which worldly honors were not. Again, when Darrow had the choice between continuing as counsel for the Chicago and North Western Railway and taking on the defense of Eugene V. Debs and his harassed and persecuted American Railway Union, he did not hesitate to choose the latter, apparently regarding it as worthwhile to go to the assistance of the suppressed and not worthwhile to aid the suppressor. In other words, although no human action is worthwhile, some human actions and presumably some human lives are less unworthwhile than others.

Suggestions
for Further Reading

Anthologies

Brody, Baruch A. *Readings in the Philosophy of Religion.* Englewood Cliffs, N.J.: Prentice-Hall, 1974. A comprehensive collection emphasizing contemporary essays in the recent, analytical tradition.

Flew, Anthony, and Macintyre, Alasdair (eds.). *New Essays in Philosophical Theology.* London: SCM Press, 1955. A collection of important writings on various aspects of the philosophy of religion. Many of these articles will be difficult for the beginning student.

Hick, John (ed.). *The Existence of God.* New York: Macmillan, 1964. A good collection of classical and contemporary writings on the major arguments for the existence of God.

Kaufmann, Walter (ed.). *Religion from Tolstoy to Camus.* New York: Harper, 1961. A collection of some of the most important writings on the philosophy of religion.

Pike, Nelson (ed.). *God and Evil.* Englewood Cliffs, N.J.: Prentice-Hall, 1964. A collection of opposing views and arguments about the problem of evil. There is a good bibliography for the student who wishes to read further on this topic.

Sanders, Steven, and David R. Cheney (eds.). *The Meaning of Life.* Englewood Cliffs, N.J.: Prentice-Hall, 1980. A collection of significant writings on the meaning and value of life.

Yandell, Keith E. *God, Man, and Religion.* New York: McGraw-Hill, 1973. A collection of essays that deals with areas of primary concern to contemporary philosophers and theologians.

Individual Works

Collins, John. *God in Modern Philosophy.* Chicago: Regnery, 1959. A survey of many of the major issues in the philosophy of religion from a Catholic point of view.

Du No üy, Lecompte. *Human Destiny.* New York: Longmans, 1947. A version of the argument from design. Du No üy argues that the facts of biology cannot be adequately explained unless the existence of a Designer is accepted.

Hick, John. *Philosophy of Religion.* Englewood Cliffs, N.J.: Prentice-Hall, 1965. An excellent brief introduction to the philosophy of religion. The student will find this a valuable guide in organizing the issues raised by the readings in his text.

Hume, David. *Dialogues on Natural Religion,* edited by Norman Kemp Smith. Indianapolis: Bobbs, 1947. A classic discussion of the argument from design. The beginning student will find this difficult but very rewarding.

Matson, Wallace I. *The Existence of God.* Ithaca, N.Y.: Cornell U.P., 1965. An excellent, detailed analysis of the major arguments for the existence of God.

Paley, William. *Natural Theology: Selections,* edited by Frederick Ferré. Indianapolis: Bobbs, 1963. The classic statement of the argument from design.

Purtill, Richard L. *Thinking About Religion.* Englewood Cliffs, N.J.: Prentice-Hall, 1978. A clear, entertainingly written introduction to the main issues in the philosophy of religion.

Scriven, Michael. *Primary Philosophy.* New York: McGraw-Hill, 1966. Chapter Four presents an interesting and detailed defense of atheism.

Smith, George H. *Atheism: The Case Against God.* Buffalo, N.Y.: Prometheus, 1979. A recent analysis and defense of atheism.

Warren, Thomas B., and Wallace I. Matson. *The Warren-Matson Debate on the Existence of God.* Jonesboro, Ark.: National Christian Press, 1978. This debate is especially noteworthy because of Matson's provocative arguments and emotionally moving appeals for tolerance.

Dictionary of the History of Ideas: Studies of Selected Pivotal Ideas. Philip P. Weiner, editor-in-chief. New York: Scribners, 1973. Substantial and clearly written essays emphasizing the historical development of topics discussed in this part. Designed to inform the nonspecialist, each essay concludes with a select bibliography.

Encyclopedia of Philosophy. Paul Edwards, editor-in-chief. New York: Macmillan, 1967. The beginning student will find many worthwhile articles on the subjects treated in this part and excellent bibliographies.

Three: Morality and Society

Introduction

Just about everyone seeks to distinguish right behavior from wrong and to determine what is worthwhile in life. In our society we frequently encounter discussions about the morality of the death penalty, the decline in current moral values, and the injustice done to minority groups. Also, at times, we are faced with personal moral decisions: Should we lie to get out of an unpleasant situation? Should we fight in a war if we think it unjust? Should we cheat on our income tax if we are sure we will not get caught? It is these kinds of questions that produce philosophical speculations about the basis of morality and the good life.

Although the philosopher is concerned with the kinds of moral problems we face in daily life, he believes that his primary concern should be given to a number of very basic problems that must be answered before it is possible to give a reasoned answer to any other moral issues. *Ethics* is that branch of philosophy that is concerned with finding answers to these basic problems. Some of the problems most often discussed in the study of ethics are: Is there a basis for deciding whether any act is right? How can we prove or disprove that there is such a basis? What kinds of things are most worth attaining? When does a person deserve to be praised or blamed? In answering these kinds of questions, the philosopher does not merely give his opinion or list a variety of opinions on the subject but rather attempts to find reasons that will show that a certain answer is correct. The student, if he is to get much out of the readings, must pay close attention to reasons that are offered and attempt to decide which philosopher, if any, has proven his case.

Many students approach ethics with the belief that there is little to be gained from the investigation because they believe that moral standards or principles are merely products of the society in which one lives. They believe that the moral views of people in other societies, no matter how much they differ from one's own, are correct for the people in those societies. Such a view is called *relativism.*

Two kinds of relativism, sociological and ethical, must be distinguished and defined before the topic can be clearly discussed. *Sociological relativism* is the name given to the factual claim that societies sometimes have different ultimate principles. An ultimate principle is one that is used as a basis for defending all other moral judgments and principles. It seems evident that societies do have different moral principles regarding a variety of matters such as marriage, raising the young, and the treatment of women. The crucial point, however, is whether societies that obviously differ in their moral practices also differ on their view of the correct ultimate principle. The observed differences may not indicate differences in ultimate principles but merely the necessity of different behavior to satisfy the same principle. For example, a society with insufficient food to feed everyone might kill the elderly when they are no longer productive in order to save the young. A society with abundant means to care for the elderly would probably consider killing them abhorrent. Yet if the latter society were suddenly to find its means reduced to that of the former, it mght well consider the killing of the elderly as a necessity because, like the first society, it too wants to ensure survival of the group.

The belief in sociological relativism has been of great significance because for many it justifies ethical relativism. *Ethical relativism* is the view that there are different but equally correct ultimate principles. This position is opposed to that of *ethical absolutism,* a theory that holds that there is only one correct ultimate principle or set of principles. The conflict between the ethical absolutist and relativist is of crucial importance. If the relativist is right, it would be necessary to give up the criticism of other societies, and possibly each individual's ultimate moral principles, although one still could criticize the application of these principles.

W. T. Stace presents the arguments for and against both ethical relativism and absolutism. He shows that sociological relativism, even if true, would not require a belief in ethical relativism, for the absolutist could claim that those ultimate moral principles contrary to the "true" one were merely mistaken. Further, Stace argues that the consequences of ethical relativism are unacceptable and that absolutism, despite the difficulty of establishing the correct moral principle, is preferable.

Philosophers have presented a number of theories concerning the correct ultimate moral principles. Three of the most prominent views are *egoism, utilitarianism,* and *formalism.* The main tenet of *egoism* is that self-interest is the only proper standard of conduct. Egoists deny that they ever have a moral duty to sacrifice their own interests for the interests of others. Egoists may frequently act generously or charitably, but this is only because they find such acts to be in their own long-term interests. Many egoists defend their position by claiming that everyone is motivated solely by self-interest, and, thus, it would be pointless to urge people to act in a nonegoistic manner. Ayn Rand presents an original and provocative version of egoism. She maintains that each person should have his own happiness as his highest moral purpose. To achieve this happiness, any moral theory requiring altruism and renunciation of personal desires must be rejected. For Rand, the usual appeals for self-sacrifice and the love of others are actually appeals for the sacrifice of one's reason, integrity, and potential as a human being.

Utilitarianism is a moral theory that holds that right acts are acts producing the greatest happiness. In deciding which acts are right, a utilitarian considers the consequences of all the acts open to him and performs the one that would produce the best consequences for everybody concerned. Although many would agree that this is generally a proper procedure, sometimes there is dissatisfaction with some kinds of acts that might turn out to be right on this basis. For example, if it would produce the best results for all concerned, then it would be right to lie, steal, and even murder. Jeremy Bentham presents a clear statement of the utilitarian position and attempts to work out some of the details required for its implementation. He maintains that in assessing the consequences of various possible acts, we should be concerned with the amounts of pleasure and pain produced and perform only those acts resulting in the most pleasure or the least pain. Bentham believed that the only thing ultimately worthwhile in life is pleasure. Such a view that the good is pleasure is called *hedonism*. The student should realize, however, that a utilitarian need not be a hedonist. He could believe that many things besides pleasure, such as intellectual growth, beauty, and integrity, are worthwhile and that these should be considered in assessing possible actions.

Unlike egoists and utilitarians, some moral theorists maintain that the rightness or wrongness of actions is not determined by the consequences produced by the actions. Such a view is called *formalism* in ethical theory. The kinds of ultimate principles that formalists have held have varied widely. One formalist principle that has had great appeal is the golden rule, "Do unto others as you would have others do unto you." R. M. MacIver defends this rule as the only one that can bring agreement out of the conflicting moral viewpoints because it lays down a procedure to follow in determining proper behavior rather than stating final goals and values. A problem for the student in considering MacIver's view is to decide on what basis the golden rule is being defended. Is MacIver appealing to the utility of accepting it or is there some other basis of appeal?

An issue much debated at present is what obligation, if any, people in affluent countries have to the poor throughout the world. The practical significance of this issue increases steadily as the world's population outstrips food and other resources. In "Lifeboat Ethics: The Case Against Helping the Poor," Garrett Hardin argues that so long as there is no world government to institute rational control of the world's resources, each nation should protect its citizens against encroachments on their resources by others. Unbridled altruism by countries with surpluses will lead to eventual worldwide disaster. In "Famine, Affluence, and Morality," Peter Singer takes a quite different stand on helping the world's poor. He contends that, on utilitarian grounds, sacrifices are required insofar as they produce more total good than harm. Thus, people in affluent countries may be required to give up most of their luxuries to help the poor. The reader must decide whether there are reasons, other than egoistic ones, for refusing to lower our own standard of living to help the needy in other countries.

An issue much debated at present is the morality of abortion. Opinions on this issue range from the extreme liberal view that women should be free to end unwanted pregnancies by abortion at any time to the extreme conservative view that all abortions are wrong since they involve killing an innocent person. Necessary for appreciating and assessing the various views on abortion are a variety of metaphysical and moral issues: Is the fetus a human being? If so, when does it become one? Is it ever morally justified intentionally to kill one innocent person to save another? Should fetuses have the same rights as children? The two readings on this issue deal with these fundamental questions. In "An Almost Absolute Value in History," John T. Noonan contends that a fetus should be considered a human being at the moment of conception because at that time the genetic code which determines human potentialities is acquired. Noonan examines and rejects other proposed criteria for determining when a fetus should be considered human. If every fetus possesses full human rights, then abortion involves the taking of a human life. So, for Noonan, abortion would only be justified in those rare instances when the rights of others outweighed the fetus's right to life. In "A Defense of Abortion," Judith Jarvis Thomson argues that even if a fetus is a human being from the moment of conception, abortion is still morally permissible in many cases. She contends that women, having the right to use their bodies as they choose, need not allow a fetus to use it. Although a fetus needs a mother's body, its use of it must depend on the mother's good will.

Are Ethical Values Relative?

20. Ethical Relativism   W. T. Stace

Any ethical position which denies that there is a single moral standard which is equally applicable to all men at all times may fairly be called a species of ethical relativity. There is not, the relativist asserts, merely one moral law, one code, one standard. There are many moral laws, codes, standards. What morality ordains in one place or age may be quite different from what morality ordains in another place or age. The moral code of Chinamen is quite different from that of Europeans, that of African savages quite different from both. Any morality, therefore, is relative to the age, the place, and the circumstances in which it is found. It is in no sense absolute.

This does not mean merely—as one might at first sight be inclined to suppose—that the very same kind of action which is *thought* right in one country and period may be *thought* wrong in another. This would be a mere platitude, the truth of which everyone would have to admit. Even the absolutist would admit this—would even wish to emphasize it— since he is well aware that different people have different sets of moral ideas, and his whole point is that some of these sets of ideas are false. What the relativist means to assert is, not this platitude, but that the very same kind of action which *is* right in one country and period may *be* wrong in another. And this, far from being a platitude, is a very startling assertion.

It is very important to grasp thoroughly the difference between the two ideas. For there is reason to think that many minds tend to find ethical relativity attractive because they fail to keep them clearly apart. It is so very obvious that moral ideas differ from country to country and from age to age. And it is so very easy, if you are mentally lazy, to suppose that to say this means the same as to say that no universal moral standard exists,—or in other words that it implies ethical relativity. We fail to see that the word "standard" is used in two different senses. It is perfectly true that, in one sense, there are many variable moral standards. We speak of judging a man by the standard of his time. And this implies that different times have different standards. And this, of course, is quite true. But when the word "standard" is used in this sense it means simply the set of moral ideas current during the period in question. It means what people *think* right, whether as a matter of fact it *is* right or not. On the other hand when the absolutist asserts that there exists a single universal moral "standard," he is not using the word in this sense at all. He means by "standard" what *is* right as distinct from what people merely think right. His point is that although what people think right varies in different countries and periods, yet what actually is right is everywhere and always the same. And it follows that when the ethical relativist disputes the position of the absolutist and denies that any universal moral standard exists he too means by "standard" what actually is right. But it is exceedingly easy, if we are not careful, to slip loosely from using the word in the first sense to using it in the second sense; and to suppose that the variability of moral beliefs is the same thing as the variability of what really is moral. And unless we keep the two senses of the word "standard" distinct, we are likely to think the creed of ethical relativity much more plausible than it actually is.

The genuine relativist, then, does not merely mean that Chinamen may think right what Frenchmen think wrong. He means that what *is* wrong for the Frenchman may *be* right for the Chinaman. And if one enquires how, in those circumstances, one is to know what actually is right in China or in France, the answer comes quite glibly. What is right in China is the same as what people think right in China; and what is right in France is the same as what people think right in France. So that, if you want to know what is moral in any particular country or age all you have to do is to ascertain what are the moral ideas current in that age or country. Those ideas are, *for that age or country*, right. Thus what is morally right is identified with what is thought to be morally right, and the distinction which we made above between these two is simply denied. To put the same thing in another way, it is denied that there can be or ought to be any distinction between the two senses of the word "standard." There is only one kind of standard of right and wrong, namely, the moral ideas current in any particular age or country.

Moral right *means* what people think morally right. It has no other meaning. What Frenchmen think right is, therefore, right *for Frenchmen.* And evidently one must conclude—though I am not aware that relativists are anxious to draw one's attention to such unsavoury but yet absolutely necessary conclusions from their creed—that cannibalism is right for people who believe in it, that human sacrifice is right for those races which practice it, and that burning widows alive was right for Hindus until the British stepped in and compelled the Hindus to behave immorally by allowing their widows to remain alive.

When it is said that, according to the ethical relativist, what is thought right in any social group is right for that group, one must be careful not to misinterpret this. The relativist does not, of course, mean that there actually is an objective moral standard in France and a different objective standard in England, and that French and British opinions respectively give us correct information about these different standards. His point is rather that there are no objectively true moral standards at all. There is no single universal objective standard. Nor are there a variety of local objective standards. All standards are subjective. People's subjective feelings about morality are the only standards which exist.

To sum up. The ethical relativist consistently denies, it would seem, whatever the ethical absolutist asserts. For the absolutist there is a single universal moral standard. For the relativist there is no such standard. There are only local, ephemeral, and variable standards. For the absolutist there are two senses of the word "standard." Standards in the sense of sets of current moral ideas are relative and changeable. But the standard in the sense of what is actually morally right is absolute and unchanging. For the relativist no such distinction can be made. There is only one meaning of the word standard, namely, that which refers to local and variable sets of moral ideas. Or if it is insisted that the word must be allowed two meanings, then the relativist will say that there is at any rate no actual example of a standard in the absolute sense, and that the word as thus used is an empty name to which nothing in reality corresponds; so that the distinction between the two meanings becomes empty and useless. Finally—though this is merely saying the same thing in another way—the absolutist makes a distinction between what actually is right and what is thought right. The relativist rejects this distinction and iden- tifies what is moral with what is thought by certain human beings or groups of human beings. . . .

I shall now proceed to consider, first, the main arguments which can be urged in favour of ethical relativity; and secondly, the arguments which can be urged against it. . . . The first is that which relies upon the actual varieties of moral "standards" found in the world. It was easy enough to believe in a single absolute morality in older times when there was no anthropology, when all humanity was divided clearly into two groups, Christian peoples and the "heathen." Christian peoples knew and possessed the one true morality. The rest were savages whose moral ideas could be ignored. But all this is changed. Greater knowledge has brought greater tolerance. We can no longer exalt our own morality as alone true, while dismissing all other moralities as false or inferior. The investigations of anthropologists have shown that there exist side by side in the world a bewildering variety of moral codes. On this topic endless volumes have been written, masses of evidence piled up. Anthropologists have ransacked the Melanesian Islands, the jungles of New Guinea, the steppes of Siberia, the deserts of Australia, the forests of central Africa, and have brought back with them countless examples of weird, extrav- agant, and fantastic "moral" customs with which to confound us. We learn that all kinds of horrible practices are, in this, that, or the other place, regarded as essential to virtue. We find that there is nothing, or next to nothing, which has always and everywhere been regarded as morally good by all men. Where then is our universal morality? Can we, in face of all this evidence, deny that it is nothing but an empty dream?

This argument, taken by itself, is a very weak one. It relies upon a single set of facts—the variable moral customs of the world. But this variability of moral ideas is admitted by both parties to the dispute, and is capable of ready explanation upon the hypothesis of either party. The relativist says that the facts are to be explained by the non-existence of any absolute moral standard. The absolutist says that they are to be ex- plained by human ignorance of what the absolute moral standard is. And he can truly point out that men have differed widely in their opinions about all manner of topics including the subject-matters of the physical sciences—just as much as they differ about morals. And if the various different opinions which men have held about the shape of the earth do not prove that it has no one real shape, neither do the various opinions which they have held about morality prove that there is no one true morality.

Thus the facts can be explained equally plausibly on either hypothesis. There is nothing in the facts themselves which compels us to prefer the relativistic hypothesis to that of the absolutist. And therefore the argument fails to prove the relativist conclusion. If that conclusion is to be established, it must be by means of other considerations.

This is the essential point. But I will add some supplementary remarks. The work of the anthropologists, upon which ethical relativists seem to rely so heavily, has as a matter of fact added absolutely nothing *in principle* to what has always been known about the variability of moral ideas. Educated people have known all along that the Greeks tolerated sodomy, which in modern times has been regarded in some countries as an abominable crime; that the Hindus thought it a sacred duty to burn their widows; that trickery, now thought despicable, was once believed to be a virtue; that terrible torture was thought by our own ancestors only a few centuries ago to be a justifiable weapon of justice; that it was only yesterday that western peoples came to believe that slavery is immoral. Even the ancients knew very well that moral customs and ideas vary—witness the writings of Herodotus. Thus the principle of the variability of moral ideas was well understood long before modern anthropology was ever heard of. Anthropology has added nothing to the knowledge of this principle except a mass of new and extreme examples of it drawn from very remote sources. But to multiply examples of a principle already well known and universally admitted adds nothing to the argument which is built upon that principle. The discoveries of the anthropologists have no doubt been of the highest importance in their own sphere. But in my considered opinion they have thrown no new light upon the special problems of the moral philosopher.

Although the multiplication of examples has no logical bearing on the argument, it does have an immense *psychological* effect upon people's minds. These masses of anthropological learning are impressive. They are propounded in the sacred name of "science." If they are quoted in support of ethical relativity—as they often are—people *think* that they must prove something important. They bewilder and over-awe the simple-minded, batter down their resistance, make them ready to receive humbly the doctrine of ethical relativity from those who have acquired a reputation by their immense learning and their claims to be "scientific." Perhaps this is why so much ado is made by ethical relativists regarding the anthropological evidence. But we must refuse to be impressed. We must discount all this mass of evidence about the extraordinary moral customs of remote peoples. Once we have admitted—as everyone who is instructed must have admitted these last two thousand years without any anthropology at all—the principle that moral ideas vary, all this new evidence adds nothing to the argument. And the argument itself proves nothing for the reasons already given. . . .

The second argument in favour of ethical relativity is also a very strong one. And it does not suffer from the disadvantage that it is dependent upon the acceptance of any particular philosophy such as radical empiricism. It makes its appeal to considerations of a quite general character. It consists in alleging that no one has ever been able to discover upon what foundation an absolute morality could rest, or from what source a universally binding moral code could derive its authority.

If, for example, it is an absolute and unalterable moral rule that all men ought to be unselfish, from whence does this *command* issue? For a command it certainly is, phrase it how you please. There is no difference in meaning between the sentence "You ought to be unselfish" and the sentence "Be unselfish." Now a command implies a commander. An obligation implies some authority which obliges. Who is the commander, what this authority? Thus the vastly difficult question is raised of *the basis of moral obligation.* Now the argument of the relativist would be that it is impossible to find any basis for a universally binding moral law; but that it is quite easy to discover a basis for morality if moral codes are admitted to be variable, ephemeral, and relative to time, place, and circumstance.

In this book I am assuming that it is no longer possible to solve this difficulty by saying naively that the universal moral law is based upon the uniform commands of God to all men. There will be many, no doubt, who will dispute this. But I am not writing for them. I am writing for those who feel the necessity of finding for morality a basis independent of particular religious dogmas. And I shall therefore make no attempt to argue the matter.

The problem which the absolutist has to face, then, is this. The religious basis of the one absolute morality having disappeared, can there be found for it any other, any secular, basis? If not, then it would seem that we cannot any longer believe in absolutism. We shall have to fall back upon belief in a variety of perhaps mutually inconsistent moral codes operating over restricted areas and limited periods. No one of these will be better, or more true, than any other. Each will be good and true for those living in those areas and periods. We shall have to fall back, in a word, on ethical relativity.

For there is no great difficulty in discovering the foundations of morality, or rather of moralities, if we adopt the relativistic hypothesis. Even if we cannot be quite certain *precisely* what these foundations are—and relativists themselves are not entirely agreed about them—we can at least see in a general way the *sort* of foundations they must have. We can see that the question on this basis is not in principle impossible of answer—although the details may be obscure; while, if we adopt the absolutist hypothesis—so the argument runs—no kind of answer is conceivable at all. . . .

This argument is undoubtedly very strong. It *is* absolutely essential to solve the problem of the basis of moral obligation if we are to believe in any kind of moral standards other than those provided by mere custom or by irrational emotions. It is idle to talk about a universal morality unless we can point to the source of its authority—or at least to do so is to indulge in a faith which is without rational ground. To cherish a blind faith in morality may be, for the average man whose business is primarily to live aright and not to theorize, sufficient. Perhaps it is his wisest course. But it will not do for the philosopher. His function, or at least one of his functions, is precisely to discover the rational grounds of our everyday beliefs—if they have any. Philosophically and intellectually, then, we cannot accept belief in a universally binding morality unless we can discover upon what foundation its obligatory character rests.

But in spite of the strength of the argument thus posed in favour of ethical relativity, it is not impregnable. For it leaves open one loop-hole. It is always possible that some theory, not yet examined, may provide a basis for a universal moral obligation. The argument rests upon the negative proposition that *there is no theory which can provide a basis for a universal morality.* But it is notoriously difficult to prove a negative. How can you prove that there are no green swans? All you can show is that none have been found so far. And then it is always possible that one will be found tomorrow. . . .

It is time that we turned our attention from the case in favour of ethical relativity to the case against it. Now the case against it consists, to a very large extent, in urging that, if taken seriously and pressed to its logical conclusion, ethical relativity can only end in destroying the conception of morality altogether, in undermining its practical efficacy, in rendering meaningless many almost universally accepted truths about human affairs, in robbing human beings of any incentive to strive for a better world, in taking the life-blood out of every ideal and every aspiration which has ever ennobled the life of man. . . .

First of all, then, ethical relativity, in asserting that the moral standards of particular social groups are the only standards which exist, renders meaningless all propositions which attempt to compare these standards with one another in respect to their moral worth. And this is a very serious matter indeed. We are accustomed to think that the moral ideas of one nation or social group may be "higher" or "lower" than those of another. We believe, for example, that Christian ethical ideals are nobler than those of the savage races of central Africa. Probably most of us would think that the Chinese moral standards are higher than those of the inhabitants of New Guinea. In short we habitually compare one civilization with another and judge the sets of ethical ideas to be found in them to be some better, some worse. The fact that such judgments are very difficult to make with any justice, and that they are frequently made on very superficial and prejudiced grounds, has no bearing on the question now at issue. The question is whether such judgments have any *meaning.* We habitually assume that they have.

But on the basis of ethical relativity they can have none whatever. For the relativist must hold that there is no *common* standard which can be applied to the various civilizations judged. Any such comparison of moral standards implies the existence of some superior standard which is applicable to both. And the existence of any such standard is precisely what the relativist denies. According to him the Christian standard is applicable only to Christians, the Chinese standard only to Chinese, the New Guinea standard only to the inhabitants of New Guinea.

What is true of comparisons between the moral standards of different races will also be true of comparisons between those of different ages. It is not unusual to ask such questions as whether the standard of our own day is superior to that which existed among our ancestors five hundred years ago. And when we remember that our ancestors employed slaves, practiced barbaric physical tortures, and burnt people alive, we may be inclined to think that it is. At any rate we assume that the question is one which has meaning and is capable of rational discussion. But if the ethical relativist is right, whatever we assert on this subject must be totally meaningless. For here again there is no common standard which could form the basis of any such judgments.

This in its turn implies that the whole notion of moral *progress* is a sheer delusion. Progress means an advance from lower to higher, from worse to better. But on the basis of ethical relativity it has no meaning to say that the standards of this age are better (or worse) than those of a previous age. For there is no common standard by which both can be measured. Thus it is nonsense to say that the morality of the New Testament is higher than that of the Old. And Jesus Christ, if he imagined that he was introducing into the world a higher ethical standard than existed before his time, was merely deluded. . . .

I come now to a second point. Up to the present I have allowed it to be taken tacitly for granted that, though judgments comparing different races and ages in respect of the worth of their moral codes are impossible for the ethical relativist, yet judgments of comparison between individuals living within the same social group would be quite possible. For individuals living within the same social group would presumably be subject to the same moral code, that of their group, and this would therefore constitute, as between these individuals, a common standard by which they could both be measured. We have not here, as we had in the other case, the difficulty of the absence of any common standard of comparison. It should therefore be possible for the ethical relativist to say quite meaningfully that President Lincoln was a better man than some criminal or moral imbecile of his own time and country, or that Jesus was a better man than Judas Iscariot.

But is even this minimum of moral judgment really possible on relativist grounds? It seems to me that it is not. For when once the whole of humanity is abandoned as the area covered by a single moral standard, what smaller areas are to be adopted as the *loci* of different standards? Where are we to draw the lines of demarcation? We can split up humanity, perhaps,—though the procedure will be very arbitrary—into races, races into nations, nations into tribes, tribes into families, families into individuals. Where are we going to draw the moral boundaries? Does the *locus* of a particular moral standard reside in a race, a nation, a tribe, a family, or an individual? Perhaps the blessed phrase "social group" will be dragged in to save the situation. Each such group, we shall be told, has its own moral code which is, for it, right. But what *is* a group? Can any one define it or give its boundaries? This is the seat of that ambiguity in the theory of ethical relativity to which reference was made on an earlier page.

The difficulty is not, as might be thought, merely an academic difficulty of logical definition. If that were all, I should not press the point. But the ambiguity has practical consequences which are disastrous for morality. No one is likely to say that moral codes are confined within the arbitrary limits of the geographical divisions of countries. Nor are the notions of race, nation, or political state likely to help us. To bring out the essentially practical character of the difficulty let us put it in the form of concrete questions. Does the American nation constitute a "group" having a single moral standard? Or does the standard of what I ought to do change continuously as I cross the continent in a railway train? Do different States of the Union have different moral codes? Perhaps every town and village has its own peculiar standard. This may at first sight seem reasonable enough. "In Rome do as Rome does" may seem as good a rule in morals as it is in etiquette. But can we stop there? Within the village are numerous cliques each having its own set of ideas. Why should not each of these claim to be bound only by its own special and peculiar moral standards? And if it comes to that, why should not the gangsters of Chicago claim to constitute a group having its own morality, so that its murders and debaucheries must be viewed as "right" by the only standard which can legitimately be applied to it? And if it be answered that the nation will not tolerate this, that may be so. But this is to put the foundation of right simply in the superior force of the majority. In that case whoever is stronger will be right, however monstrous his ideas and actions. And if we cannot deny to any set of people the right to have its own morality, is it not clear that, in the end, we cannot even deny this right to the individual? Every individual man and woman can put up, on this view, an irrefutable claim to be judged by no standard except his or her own.

If these arguments are valid, the ethical relativist cannot really maintain that there is anywhere to be found a moral standard binding upon anybody against his will. And he cannot maintain that, even within the social group, there is a common standard as between individuals. And if that is so, then even judgments to the effect that one man is morally better than another become meaningless. All moral valuation thus vanishes. There is nothing to prevent each man from being a rule unto himself. The result will be moral chaos and the collapse of all effective standards. . . .

But even if we assume that the difficulty about defining moral groups has been surmounted, a further difficulty presents itself. Suppose that we have now definitely decided what are the exact boundaries of the social group within which a moral standard is to be operative. And we will assume—as is invariably done by relativists themselves—that this group is to be some actually existing social community such as a tribe or nation. How are we to know, even then, what actually *is* the moral standard within that group? How is anyone to know? How is even a member of the group to know? For there are certain to be within the group—at least this will be true among advanced peoples—wide differences of opinion as to what is right, what wrong. Whose opinion, then, is to be taken as representing *the* moral standard of the group? Either we must take the opinion of the majority within the group, or the opinion of some minority. If we rely upon the ideas of the majority, the results will be disastrous. Wherever there is found among a people a small band of select spirits, or perhaps one man, working for the establishment of higher and nobler ideals than those commonly accepted by the group, we shall be compelled to hold that, for that people at that time, the majority are right, and that the reformers are wrong and are preaching what is immoral. We shall have to maintain, for example, that Jesus was preaching immoral doctrines to the Jews. Moral goodness will have to be equated always with the mediocre and sometimes with the definitely base and ignoble. If on the other hand we said that the moral standard of the group is to be identified with the moral opinions of some minority, then what minority is this to be? We cannot answer that it is to be the minority composed of the best and most enlightened individuals of the group. This would involve us in a palpably vicious circle. For by what standard are these individuals to be judged the best and the most enlightened? There is no principle by which we could select the right minority. And therefore we should have to consider every minority as good as every other. And this means that we should have no logical right whatever to resist the claim of the gangsters of Chicago—if such a claim were made—that their practices represent the highest standards of American morality. It means in the end that every individual is to be bound by no standard save his own.

The ethical relativists are great empiricists. *What* is the actually moral standard of any group can only be discovered, they tell us, by an examination on the ground of the moral opinions and customs of that group. But will they tell us how they propose to decide, when they get to the ground, which of the many moral opinions they are sure to find there is *the* right one in that group? To some extent they will be able to do this for the Melanesian Islanders—from whom apparently all lessons in the nature of morality are in future to be taken. But it is certain that they cannot do it for advanced peoples whose members have learnt to think for themselves and to entertain among themselves a wide variety of opinions. They cannot do it unless they accept the calamitous view that the ethical opinion of the majority is always right. We are left therefore once more with the conclusion that, even within a particular social group, anybody's moral opinion is as good as anybody else's, and that every man is entitled to be judged by his own standards.

Finally, not only is ethical relativity disastrous in its consequences for moral theory. It cannot be doubted that it must tend to be equally disastrous in its impact upon practical conduct. If men come really to believe that one moral standard is as good as another, they will conclude that their own moral standard has nothing special to recommend it. They might as well then slip down to some lower and easier standard. It is true that, for a time, it may be possible to hold one view in theory and to act practically upon another. But ideas, even philosophical ideas, are not so ineffectual that they can remain for ever idle in the upper chambers of the intellect. In the end they seep down to the level of practice. They get themselves acted on.

How Should We Behave?

21. Value Yourself Ayn Rand

Ayn Rand (1908–1982) is best known as the author of such widely read novels as *The Fountainhead* and *Atlas Shrugged*. She has also written several books on social and political issues in which she defends individualism and egoism.

". . . Yes, this *is* an age of moral crisis. Yes, you *are* bearing punishment for your evil. But it is not man who is now on trial and it is not human nature that will take the blame. It is your moral code that's through, this time. Your moral code has reached its climax, the blind alley at the end of its course. And if you wish to go on living, what you now need is not to *return* to morality—you who have never known any—but to *discover* it.

"You have heard no concepts of morality but the mystical or the social. You have been taught that morality is a code of behavior imposed on you by whim, the whim of a supernatural power or the whim of society, to serve God's purpose or your neighbor's welfare, to please an authority beyond the grave or else next door—but not to serve *your* life or pleasure. Your pleasure, you have been taught, is to be found in immorality, your interests would best be served by evil, and any moral code must be designed not *for* you, but *against* you, not to further your life, but to drain it.

"For centuries, the battle of morality was fought between those who claimed that your life belongs to God and those who claimed that it belongs to your neighbors—between those who preached that the good is self-sacrifice for the sake of ghosts in heaven and those who preached that the good is self-sacrifice for the sake of incompetents on earth. And no one came to say that your life belongs to you and that the good is to live it.

"Both sides agreed that morality demands the surrender of your self-interest and of your mind, that the moral and the practical are opposites, that morality is not the province of reason, but the province of faith and force. Both sides agreed that no rational morality is possible, that there is no right or wrong in reason—that in reason there's no reason to be moral.

"Whatever else they fought about, it was against man's mind that all your moralists have stood united. It was man's mind that all their schemes and systems were intended to despoil and destroy. Now choose to perish or to learn that the anti-mind is the anti-life.

From *Atlas Shrugged* by Ayn Rand. Published by Random House, Inc. Reprinted by permission of the executor of the Estate of Ayn Rand.

"Man's mind is his basic tool of survival. Life is given to him, survival is not. His body is given to him, its sustenance is not. His mind is given to him, its content is not. To remain alive, he must act, and before he can act he must know the nature and purpose of his action. He cannot obtain his food without a knowledge of food and of the way to obtain it. He cannot dig a ditch—or build a cyclotron—without a knowledge of his aim and of the means to achieve it. To remain alive, he must think.

"But to think is an act of choice. The key to what you so recklessly call 'human nature,' the open secret you live with, yet dread to name, is the fact that *man is a being of volitional consciousness.* Reason does not work automatically; thinking is not a mechanical process; the connections of logic are not made by instinct. The function of your stomach, lungs or heart is automatic; the function of your mind is not. In any hour and issue of your life, you are free to think or to evade that effort. But you are not free to escape from your nature, from the fact that *reason* is your means of survival—so that for *you,* who are a human being, the question 'to be or not to be' is the question 'to think or not to think.'

"A being of volitional consciousness has no automatic course of behavior. He needs a code of values to guide his actions. 'Value' is that which one acts to gain and keep, 'virtue' is the action by which one gains and keeps it. 'Value' presupposes an answer to the question: of value to whom and for what? 'Value' presupposes a standard, a purpose and the necessity of action in the face of an alternative. Where there are no alternatives, no values are possible.

"There is only one fundamental alternative in the universe: existence or non-existence—and it pertains to a single class of entities: to living organisms. The existence of inanimate matter is unconditional, the existence of life is not: it depends on a specific course of action. Matter is indestructible, it changes its forms, but it cannot cease to exist. It is only a living organism that faces a constant alternative: the issue of life or death. Life is a process of self-sustaining and self-generated action. If an organism fails in that action, it dies; its chemical elements remain, but its life goes out of existence. It is only the concept of 'Life' that makes the concept of 'Value' possible. It is only to a living entity that things can be good or evil.

"A plant must feed itself in order to live; the sunlight, the water, the chemicals it needs are the values its nature has set it to pursue; its life is the standard of value directing its actions. But a plant has no choice of action; there are alternatives in the conditions it encounters, but there is no alternative in its function: it acts automatically to further its life, it cannot act for its own destruction.

"An animal is equipped for sustaining its life; its senses provide it with an automatic code of action, an automatic knowledge of what is good for it or evil. It has no power to extend its knowledge or to evade it. In conditions where its knowledge proves inadequate, it dies. But so long as it lives, it acts on its knowledge, with automatic safety and no power of choice, it is unable to ignore its own good, unable to decide to choose the evil and act as its own destroyer.

"Man has no automatic code of survival. His particular distinction from all other living species is the necessity to act in the face of alternatives by means of *volitional choice*. He has no automatic knowledge of what is good for him or evil, what values his life depends on, what course of action it requires. Are you prattling about an instinct of self-preservation? An *instinct* of self-preservation is precisely what man does not possess. An 'instinct' is an unerring and automatic form of knowledge. A desire is not an instinct. A desire to live does not give you the knowledge required for living. And even man's desire to live is not automatic: your secret evil today is that *that* is the desire you do not hold. Your fear of death is not a love for life and will not give you the knowledge needed to keep it. Man must obtain his knowledge and choose his actions by a process of thinking, which nature will not force him to perform. Man has the power to act as his own destroyer—and that is the way he has acted through most of his history.

"A living entity that regarded its means of survival as evil, would not survive. A plant that struggled to mangle its roots, a bird that fought to break its wings would not remain for long in the existence they affronted. But the history of man has been a struggle to deny and to destroy his mind.

"Man has been called a rational being, but rationality is a matter of choice—and the alternative his nature offers him is: rational being or suicidal animal. Man has to be man—by choice; he has to hold his life as a value—by choice; he has to learn to sustain it—by choice; he has to discover the values it requires and practice his virtues—by choice.

"A code of values accepted by choice is a code of morality.

"Whoever you are, you who are hearing me now, I am speaking to whatever living remnant is left uncorrupted within you, to the remnant of the human, to your *mind*, and I say: There *is* a morality of reason, a morality proper to man, and *Man's Life* is its standard of value.

"All that which is proper to the life of a rational being is the good; all that which destroys it is the evil.

"Man's life, as required by his nature, is not the life of a mindless brute, of a looting thug or a mooching mystic, but the life of a thinking being—not life by means of force or fraud, but life by means of achievement—not survival at any price, since there's only one price that pays for man's survival: reason.

"Man's life is the *standard* of morality, but your own life is its *purpose*. If existence on earth is your goal, you must choose your actions and values by the standard of that which is proper to man—for the purpose of preserving, fulfilling and enjoying the irreplaceable value which is your life.

"Since life requires a specific course of action, any other course will destroy it. A being who does not hold his own life as the motive and goal of his actions, is acting on the motive and standard of *death*. Such a being is a metaphysical monstrosity, struggling to oppose, negate and contradict the fact of his own existence, running blindly amuck on a trail of destruction, capable of nothing but pain.

"Happiness is the successful state of life, pain is an agent of death. Happiness is that state of unconsciousness which proceeds from the achievement of one's values. A morality that dares to tell you to find happiness in the renunciation of your happiness—to value the failure of your values—is an insolent negation of morality. A doctrine that gives you, as an ideal, the role of a sacrificial animal seeking slaughter on the altars of others, is giving you *death* as your standard. By the grace of reality and the nature of life, man—every man—is an end in himself, he exists for his own sake, and the achievement of his own happiness is his highest moral purpose.

"But neither life nor happiness can be achieved by the pursuit of irrational whims. Just as man is free to attempt to survive in any random manner, but will perish unless he lives as his nature requires, so he is free to seek his happiness in any mindless fraud, but the torture of frustration is all he will find, unless he seeks the happiness proper to man. The purpose of morality is to teach you, not to suffer and die, but to enjoy yourself and live.

"Sweep aside those parasites of subsidized classrooms, who live on the profits of the mind of others and proclaim that man needs no morality, no values, no code of behavior. They, who pose as scientists and claim that man is only an animal, do not grant him inclusion in the law of existence they have granted to the lowest of insects. They recognize that every living species has a way of survival demanded by its nature, they do not claim that a fish can live out of water or that a dog can live without its sense of smell—but man, they claim, the most complex of beings, man can survive in any way whatever, man has no identity, no nature, and there's no practical reason why he cannot live with his means of survival destroyed, with his mind throttled and placed at the disposal of any orders *they* might care to issue.

"Sweep aside those hatred-eaten mystics, who pose as friends of humanity and preach that the highest virtue man can practice is to hold his own life as of no value. Do they tell you that the purpose of morality is to curb man's instinct of self-preservation? It is for the purpose of self-preservation that man needs a code of morality. The only man who desires to be moral is the man who desires to live.

"No, you do not have to live; it is your basic act of choice; but if you choose to live, you must live as a man—by the work and the judgment of your mind.

"No, you do not have to live as a man: it is an act of moral choice. But you cannot live as anything else—and the alternative is that state of living death which you now see within you and around you, the state of a thing unfit for existence, no longer human and less than animal, a thing that knows nothing but pain and drags itself through its span of years in the agony of unthinking self-destruction.

"No, you do not have to think; it is an act of moral choice. But someone had to think to keep you alive; if you choose to default, you default on existence and you pass the deficit to some moral man, expecting him to sacrifice his good for the sake of letting you survive by your evil. . . .

"This much is true: the most *selfish* of all things is the independent mind that recognizes no authority higher than its own and no value higher than its judgment of truth. You are asked to sacrifice your intellectual integrity, your logic, your reason, your standard of truth—in favor of becoming a prostitute whose standard is the greatest good for the greatest number.

"If you search your code for guidance, for an answer to the question: 'What *is* the good?'—the only answer you will find is '*The good of others.*' The good is whatever others wish, whatever you feel they feel they wish, or whatever you feel they ought to feel. 'The good of others' is a magic formula that transforms anything into gold, a formula to be recited as a guarantee of moral glory and as a fumigator for any action, even the slaughter of a continent. Your standard of virtue is not an object, not an act, nor a principle, but an *intention.* You need no proof, no reasons, no success, you need not achieve *in fact* the good of others—all you need to know is that your motive was the good of others, *not* your own. Your only definition of the good is a negation: the good is the 'non-good for me.'

"Your code—which boasts that it upholds eternal, absolute, objective moral values and scorns the conditional, the relative and the subjective— your code hands out, as its version of the absolute, the following rule of moral conduct: If *you* wish it, it's evil; if others wish it, it's good; if the motive of your action is *your* welfare, don't do it; if the motive is the welfare of others, then anything goes.

"As this double-jointed, double-standard morality splits you in half, so it splits mankind into two enemy camps: one is *you,* the other is all the rest of humanity. *You* are the only outcast who has no right to wish or live. *You* are the only servant, the rest are the masters, *you* are the only giver, the rest are the takers, *you* are the eternal debtor, the rest are the creditors never to be paid off. You must not question their right to your sacrifice, or the nature of their wishes and their needs: their right is conferred upon them by a negative, by the fact that they are 'non-you.'

"For those of you who might ask questions, your code provides a consolation prize and booby-trap: it is for your own happiness, it says, that you must serve the happiness of others, the only way to achieve your joy is to give it up to others, the only way to achieve your prosperity is to surrender your wealth to others, the only way to protect your life is to protect all men except yourself—and if you find no joy in this procedure, it is your own fault and the proof of your evil; if you were good, you would find your happiness in providing a banquet for others, and your dignity in existing on such crumbs as *they* might care to toss you.

"You who have no standard of self-esteem, accept the guilt and dare not ask the questions. But you know the unadmitted answer, refusing to acknowledge what you see, what hidden premise moves your world. You know it, not in honest statement, but as a dark uneasiness within you, while you flounder between guiltily cheating and grudgingly practicing a principle too vicious to name.

"I, who do not accept the unearned, neither in values nor in *guilt,* am here to ask the questions you evaded. Why is it moral to serve the happiness of others, but not your own? If enjoyment is a value, why is it moral when experienced by others, but immoral when experienced by you? If the sensation of eating a cake is a value, why is it an immoral indulgence in your stomach, but a moral goal for you to achieve in the stomach of others? Why is it immoral for you to desire, but moral for others to do so? Why is it immoral to produce a value and keep it, but moral to give it away? And if it is not moral for you to keep a value, why is it moral for others to accept it? If you are selfless and virtuous when you give it, are they not selfish and vicious when they take it? Does virtue consist of serving vice? Is the moral purpose of those who are good, self-immolation for the sake of those who are evil? . . .

"Under a morality of sacrifice, the first value you sacrifice is morality; the next is self-esteem. When need is the standard, every man is both victim and parasite. As a victim, he must labor to fill the needs of others, leaving himself in the position of a parasite whose needs must be filled by others. He cannot approach his fellow men except in one of two disgraceful roles: he is both a beggar and a sucker.

"You fear the man who has a dollar less than you, that dollar is rightfully his, he makes you feel like a moral defrauder. You hate the man who has a dollar more than you, that dollar is rightfully yours, he makes you feel that you are morally defrauded. The man below is a source of your guilt, the man above is a source of your frustration. You do not know what to surrender or demand, when to give and when to grab, what pleasure in life is rightfully yours and what debt is still unpaid to others—you struggle to evade, as 'theory,' the knowledge that by the moral standard you've accepted you are guilty every moment of your life, there is no mouthful of food you swallow that is not *needed* by someone somewhere on earth—and you give up the problem in blind resentment, you conclude that moral perfection is not to be achieved *or desired*, that you will muddle through by snatching as snatch can and by avoiding the eyes of the young, of those who look at you as if self-esteem were possible and they expected you to have it. Guilt is all that you retain within your soul—and so does every other man, as he goes past, avoiding *your* eyes. Do you wonder why your morality has not achieved brotherhood on earth or the good will of man to man?

"The justification of sacrifice, that your morality propounds, is more corrupt than the corruption it purports to justify. The motive of your sacrifice, it tells you, should be *love*—the love you ought to feel for every man. A morality that professes the belief that the values of the spirit are more precious than matter, a morality that teaches you to scorn a whore who gives her body indiscriminately to all men—this same morality demands that you surrender your soul to promiscuous love for all comers.

"As there can be no causeless wealth, so there can be no causeless love or any sort of causeless emotion. An emotion is a response to a fact of reality, an estimate dictated by your standards. To love is to *value*. The man who tells you that it is possible to value without values, to love those whom you appraise as worthless, is the man who tells you that it is possible to grow rich by consuming without producing and that paper money is as valuable as gold.

"Observe that he does not expect you to feel a causeless fear. When his kind get into power, they are expert at contriving means of terror, at giving you ample cause to feel the fear by which they desire to rule you. But when it comes to love, the highest of emotions, you permit them to shriek at you accusingly that you are a moral delinquent if you're incapable of feeling causeless love. When a man feels fear without reason, you call him to the attention of a psychiatrist; you are not so careful to protect the meaning, the nature and the dignity of love.

"Love is the expression of one's values, the greatest reward you can earn for the moral qualities you have achieved in your character and person, the emotional price paid by one man for the joy he receives from the virtues of another. Your morality demands that you divorce your love from values and hand it down to any vagrant, not as response to his worth, but as response to his *need*, not as reward, but as alms, not as a payment for virtues, but as a blank check on vices. Your morality tells you that the purpose of love is to set you free of the bonds of morality, that love is superior to moral judgment, that true love transcends, forgives and survives every manner of evil in its object, and the greater the love the greater the depravity it permits to the loved. To love a man for his virtues is paltry and human, it tells you; to love him for his flaws is divine. To love those who are worthy of it is self-interest; to love the unworthy is sacrifice. You owe your love to those who don't deserve it, and the less they deserve it, the more love you owe them—the more loathsome the object, the nobler your love—the more unfastidious your love, the greater your virtue—and if you can bring your soul to the state of a dump heap that welcomes anything on equal terms, if you can cease to value moral values, you have achieved the state of moral perfection.

"Such is your morality of sacrifice and such are the twin ideals it offers: to refashion the life of your body in the image of a human stock-yards, and the life of your spirit in the image of a dump. . . .

"Since childhood, you have been hiding the guilty secret that you feel no desire to be moral, no desire to seek self-immolation, that you dread and hate your code, but dare not say it even to yourself, that you're devoid of those moral 'instincts' which others profess to feel. The less you felt, the louder you proclaimed your selfless love and servitude to others, in dread of ever letting them discover your own self, the self that you betrayed, the self that you kept in concealment, like a skeleton in the closet of your body. And they, who were at once your dupes and your deceivers, they listened and voiced their loud approval, in dread of ever letting you discover that they were harboring the same unspoken secret. Existence among you is a giant pretense, an act you all perform for one another, each feeling that he is the only guilty freak, each placing his moral authority in the unknowable known only to others, each faking the reality he feels they expect him to fake, none having the courage to break the vicious circle.

"No matter what dishonorable compromise you've made with your impracticable creed, no matter what miserable balance, half-cynicism, half-superstition, you now manage to maintain, you still preserve the root, the lethal tenet: the belief that the moral and the practical are op-posites. Since childhood, you have been running from the terror of a choice you have never dared fully to identify: If the *practical*, whatever you must practice to exist, whatever works, succeeds, achieves your purpose, whatever brings you food and joy, whatever profits you is evil—and if the good, the moral is the *impractical,* whatever fails, destroys, frustrates, whatever injures you and brings you loss or pain—then your choice is to be moral or to live.

"The sole result of that murderous doctrine was to remove morality from life. You grew up to believe that moral laws bear no relation to the job of living, except as an impediment and threat, that man's existence is an amoral jungle where anything goes and anything works. And in that fog of switching definitions which descends upon a frozen mind, you have forgotten that the evils damned by your creed were the virtues required for living, and you have come to believe that actual evils are the *practical* means of existence. Forgetting that the impractical 'good' was self-sacrifice, you believe that self-esteem is impractical; forgetting that the practical 'evil' was production, you believe that robbery is practical. . . .

"Accept the fact that the achievement of your happiness is the only *moral* purpose of your life, and that *happiness*—not pain or mindless self-indulgence—is the proof of your moral integrity, since it is the proof and the result of your loyalty to the achievement of your values. Happiness was the responsibility you dreaded, it required the kind of rational discipline you did not value yourself enough to assume—and the anxious staleness of your days is the monument to your evasion of the knowledge that there is no moral substitute for happiness, that there is no more despicable coward than the man who deserted the battle for his joy, fearing to assert his right to existence, lacking the courage and the loyalty to life of a bird or a flower reaching for the sun. Discard the protective rags of that vice which you called a virtue: humility—learn to value yourself, which means: to fight for your happiness—and when you learn that *pride* is the sum of all virtues, you will learn to live like a man.

"As a basic step of self-esteem, learn to treat as the mark of a cannibal any man's *demand* for your help. To demand it is to claim that your life is *his* property—and loathsome as such claim might be, there's something still more loathsome: your agreement. Do you ask if it's ever proper to help another man? No—if he claims it as his right or as a moral duty that you owe him. Yes—if such is your own desire based on your own selfish pleasure in the value of his person and his struggle.

22. Utilitarianism   Jeremy Bentham

Jeremy Bentham (1748–1832), the English philosopher and political theorist, developed the utilitarian theory as a basis for political and legal reform.

From Jeremy Bentham, *An Introduction to the Principles of Morals and Legislation.* First published in 1789.

Of the Principle of Utility

I. Nature has placed mankind under the governance of two sovereign masters, *pain* and *pleasure*. It is for them alone to point out what we ought to do, as well as to determine what we shall do. On the one hand the standard of right and wrong, on the other the chain of causes and effects are fastened to their throne. They govern us in all we do, in all we say, in all we think: every effort we can make to throw off our subjection, will serve but to demonstrate and confirm it. In words a man may pretend to abjure their empire: but in reality he will remain subject to it all the while. The *principle of utility* recognises this subjection, and assumes it for the foundation of that system, the object of which is to tear the fabric of felicity by the hands of reason and of law. Systems which attempt to question it, deal in sounds instead of sense in caprice instead of reason, in darkness instead of light.

But enough of metaphor and declamation: it is not by such means that moral science is to be improved.

II. The principle of utility is the foundation of the present work: it will be proper therefore at the outset to give an explicit and determinate account of what is meant by it. By the principle of utility is meant that principle which approves or disapproves of every action whatsoever, according to the tendency which it appears to have to augment or diminish the happiness of the party whose interest is in question: or, what is the same thing in other words, to promote or to oppose that happiness. I say of every action whatsoever; and therefore not only of every action of a private individual, but of every measure of government.

III. By utility is meant that property in any object, whereby it tends to produce benefit, advantage, pleasure, good, or happiness (all this in the present case comes to the same thing) or (what comes again to the same thing) to prevent the happening of mischief, pain, evil, or unhappiness to the party whose interest is considered: if that party be the community in general, then the happiness of the community: if a particular individual, then the happiness of that individual.

IV. The interest of the community is one of the most general expressions that can occur in the phraseology of morals: no wonder that the meaning of it is often lost. When it has a meaning, it is this. The community is a fictitious *body*, composed of the individual persons who are considered as constituting as it were its *members*. The interest of the community then is, what?—the sum of the interests of the several members who compose it.

V. It is in vain to talk of the interest of the community, without understanding what is the interest of the individual. A thing is said to promote the interest, or to be *for* the interest, of an individual, when it tends to add to the sum total of his pleasures: or, what comes to the same thing, to diminish the sum total of his pains.

VI. An action then may be said to be comfortable to the principle of utility, or, for shortness sake, to utility (meaning with respect to the community at large), when the tendency it has to augment the happiness of the community is greater than any it has to diminish it.

VII. A measure of government (which is but a particular kind of action, performed by a particular person or persons) may be said to be conformable to or dictated by the principle of utility, when in like manner the tendency which it has to augment the happiness of the community is greater than any which it has to diminish it.

VIII. When an action, or in particular a measure of government is supposed by a man to be conformable to the principle of utility, it may be convenient, for the purposes of discourse, to imagine a kind of law or dictate, called a law or dictate of utility: and to speak of the action in question, as being conformable to such law or dictate.

IX. A man may be said to be a partisan of the principle of utility, when the approbation or disapprobation he annexes to any action, or to any measure, is determined by and proportioned to the tendency which he conceives it to have to augment or to diminish the happiness of the community: or in other words, to its conformity or unconformity to the laws or dictates of utility.

X. Of an action that is conformable to the principle of utility one may always say either that it is one that ought to be done, or at least that it is not one that ought not to be done. One may say also, that it is right it should be done; at least that it is not wrong it should be done: that it is a right action; at least that it is not a wrong action. When thus interpreted, the words *ought*, and *right* and *wrong*, and others of that stamp, have a meaning: when otherwise, they have none.

XI. Has the rectitude of this principle been ever formally contested? It should seem that it had, by those who have not known what they have been meaning. Is it susceptible of any direct proof? it should seem not: for that which is used to prove everything else, cannot itself be proved: a chain of proofs must have their commencement somewhere. To give such proof is as impossible as it is needless.

XII. Not that there is or ever has been that human creature breathing, however stupid or perverse, who has not on many, perhaps on most occasions of his life, deferred to it. By the natural constitution of the human frame, on most occasions of their lives men in general embrace this principle, without thinking of it: if not for the ordering of their own actions, yet for the trying of their own actions, as well as of those of other men. There have been, at the same time, not many, perhaps, even of the most intelligent, who have been disposed to embrace it purely and without reserve. There are even few who have not taken some occasion or other to quarrel with it, either on account of their not understanding always how to apply it, or on account of some prejudice or other which they were afraid to examine into, or could not bear to part with. For such is the stuff that man is made of: in principle and in practice, in a right track and in a wrong one, the rarest of all human qualities is consistency.

XIII. When a man attempts to combat the principle of utility, it is with reasons drawn, without his being aware of it, from that very principle itself. His arguments, if they prove any thing, prove not that the principle is *wrong*, but that, according to the applications he supposes to be made of it, it is *misapplied*. Is it possible for a man to move the earth? Yes, but he must first find out another earth to stand upon.

Of Principles Adverse to That of Utility

I. If the principle of utility be a right principle to be governed by, and that in all cases, it follows from what has been just observed, that whatever principle differs from it in any case must necessarily be a wrong one. To prove any other principle, therefore, to be a wrong one, there needs no more than just to show it to be what it is, a principle of which the dictates are in some point or other different from those of the principle of utility: to state it is to confute it.

II. A principle may be different from that of utility in two ways: 1. By being constantly opposed to it: this is the case with a principle which may be termed the principle of *asceticism*. 2. By being sometimes opposed to it, and sometimes not, as it may happen: this is the case with another, which may be termed the principle of *sympathy* and *antipathy*.

III. By the principle of asceticism I mean that principle, which, like the principle of utility, approves or disapproves of any action, according to the tendency which it appears to have to augment or diminish the happiness of the party whose interest is in question; but in an inverse manner: approving of actions in as far as they tend to diminish his happiness; disapproving of them in as far as they tend to augment it.

IV. It is evident that any one who reprobates any the least particle of pleasure, as such, from whatever source derived, is *pro tanto* a partisan of the principle of asceticism. It is only upon that principle, and not from the principle of utility, that the most abominable pleasure which the vilest of malefactors ever reaped from his crime would be to be reprobated, if it stood alone. The case is, that it never does stand alone; but is necessarily followed by such a quality of pain (or, what comes to the same thing, such a chance for a certain quantity of pain) that the pleasure in comparison of it, is as nothing: and this is the true and sole, but perfectly sufficient, reason for making it a ground for punishment. . . .

X. The principle of utility is capable of being consistently pursued; and it is but tautology to say, that the more consistently it is pursued, the better it must ever be for humankind. The principle of asceticism never was, nor ever can be, consistently pursued by any living creature. Let but one tenth part of the inhabitants of this earth pursue it consistently, and in a day's time they will have turned it into a hell.

XI. Among principles adverse to that of utility, that which at this day seems to have most influence in matters of government, is what may be called the principle of sympathy and antipathy. By the principle of sympathy and antipathy, I mean that principle which approves or disapproves of certain actions, not on account of their tending to augment the happiness, nor yet on account of their tending to diminish the happiness of the party whose interest is in question, but merely because a man finds himself disposed to approve or disapprove of them: holding up that approbation or disapprobation as a sufficient reason for itself, and disclaiming the necessity of looking out for any extrinsic ground. Thus far in the general department of morals: and in the particular department of politics, measuring out the quantum (as well as determining the ground) of punishment, by the degree of the disapprobation.

XII. It is manifest, that this is rather a principle in name than in reality: it is not a positive principle of itself, so much as a term employed to signify the negation of all principle. What one expects to find in a principle is something that points out some external consideration, as a means of warranting and guiding the internal sentiments of approbation and disapprobation: this expectation is but ill fulfilled by a proposition, which does neither more nor less than hold up each of those sentiments as a ground and standard for itself.

XIII. In looking over the catalogue of human actions (says a partisan of this principle) in order to determine which of them are to be marked with the seal of disapprobation, you need but to take counsel of your own feelings: whatever you find in yourself a propensity to condemn, is wrong for that very reason. For the same reason it is also meet for punishment: in what proportion it is adverse to utility, or whether it be adverse to utility at all, is a matter that makes no difference. In that same *proportion* also is it meet for punishment: if you hate much, punish much: if you hate little, punish little: punish as you hate. If you hate not at all, punish not at all; the fine feelings of the soul are not to be overborne and tyrannized by the harsh and rugged dictates of political utility. . . .

XV. It is manifest, that the dictates of this principle will frequently coincide with those of utility, though perhaps without intending any such thing. Probably more frequently than not: and hence it is that the business of penal justice is carried on upon that tolerable sort of footing upon which we see it carried on in common at this day. For what more natural or more general ground of hatred to a practice can there be, than the mischievousness of such practice? What all men are exposed to suffer by, all men will be disposed to hate. It is far yet, however, from being a constant ground: for when a man suffers, it is not always that he knows what it is he suffers by. A man may suffer grievously, for instance, by a new tax, without being able to trace up the cause of his sufferings to the injustice of some neighbour, who has eluded the payment of an old one.

XVI. The principle of sympathy and antipathy is most apt to err on the side of severity. It is for applying punishment in many cases which deserve none: in many cases which deserve some, it is for applying more than they deserve. There is no incident imaginable, be it ever so trivial, and so remote from mischief, from which this principle may not extract a ground of punishment. Any difference in taste: any difference in opinion: upon one subject as well as upon another. No disagreement so trifling which perseverance and altercation will not render serious. Each becomes in the other's eyes an enemy, and, if laws permit, a criminal. This is one of the circumstances by which the human race is distinguished (not much indeed to its advantage) from the brute creation. . . .

XIX. There are two things which are very apt to be confounded, but which it imports us carefully to distinguish:—the motive or cause, which, by operating on the mind of an individual, is productive of any act: and the ground or reason which warrants a legislator, or other bystander, in regarding that act with an eye of approbation. When the act happens, in the particular instance in question, to be productive of effects which we approve of, much more if we happen to observe that the same motive may frequently be productive, in other instances, of the like effects, we are apt to transfer our approbation to the motive itself, and to assume, as the just ground for the approbation we bestow on the act, the circumstance of its originating from that motive. It is in this way that the sentiment of antipathy has often been considered as a just ground of action. Antipathy, for instance, in such or such a case, is the cause of an action which is attended with good effects: but this does not make it a right ground of action in that case, any more than in any other. Still farther. Not only the effects are good, but the agent sees beforehand that they will be so. This may make the action indeed a perfectly right action: but it does not make antipathy a right ground of action. For the same sentiment of antipathy, if implicitly deferred to, may be, and very frequently is, productive of the very worst effects. Antipathy, therefore, can never be a right ground of action. No more, therefore, can resentment, which, as will be seen more particularly hereafter, is but a modification of antipathy. The only right ground of action, that can possibly subsist, is, after all, the consideration of utility, which, if it is a right principle of action, and of approbation, in any one case, is so in every other. Other principles in abundance, that is, other motives, may be the reasons why such and such an act *has* been done: that is, the reasons or causes of its being done: but it is this alone that can be the reason why it might or ought to have been done. Antipathy or resentment requires always to be regulated, to prevent its doing mischief: to be regulated by what? always by the principle of utility. The principle of utility neither requires nor admits of any other regulator than itself.

Value of a Lot of Pleasure or Pain, How to Be Measured

I. Pleasures then, and the avoidance of pains, are the *ends* which the legislator has in view: it behooves him therefore to understand their *value*. Pleasures and pains are the *instruments* he has to work with: it behooves him therefore to understand their force, which is again, in other words, their value.

II. To a person considered *by himself*, the value of a pleasure or pain considered *by itself*, will be greater or less, according to the four following circumstances:

1. Its *intensity*.
2. Its *duration*.
3. Its *certainty* or *uncertainty*.
4. Its *propinquity* or *remoteness*.

III. These are the circumstances which are to be considered in estimating a pleasure or a pain considered each of them by itself. But when the value of any pleasure or pain is considered for the purpose of estimating the tendency of any *act* by which it is produced, there are two other circumstances to be taken into the account; these are,

5. Its *fecundity*, or the chance it has of being followed by sensations of the *same* kind: that is, pleasures, if it be a pleasure: pains, if it be a pain.
6. Its *purity*, or the chance it has of *not* being followed by sensations

of the *opposite* kind: that is, pains, if it be a pleasure: pleasures, if it be a pain.

These two last, however, are in strictness scarcely to be deemed properties of the pleasure or the pain itself; they are not, therefore, in strictness to be taken into the account of the value of that pleasure or that pain. They are in strictness to be deemed properties only of the act, or other event, by which such pleasure or pain has been produced; and accordingly are only to be taken into the account of the tendency of such act or such event.

IV. To a *number* of persons, with reference to each of whom the value of a pleasure or a pain is considered, it will be greater or less, according to seven circumstances: to wit, the six preceding ones; *viz.*

1. Its *intensity*.
2. Its *duration*.
3. Its *certainty* or *uncertainty*.
4. Its *propinquity* or *remoteness*.
5. Its *fecundity*.
6. Its *purity*.

And one other; to wit:

7. Its *extent*, that is, the number of persons to whom it *extends;* or (in other words) who are affected by it.

V. To take an exact account then of the general tendency of any act, by which the interests of a community are affected, proceed as follows. Begin with any one person of those whose interests seem most immediately to be affected by it: and take an account.

1. Of the value of each distinguishable *pleasure* which appears to be produced by it in the *first* instance.

2. Of the value of each *pain* which appears to be produced by it in the *first* instance.

3. Of the value of each pleasure which appears to be produced by it *after* the first. This constitutes the *fecundity* of the first *pleasure* and the *impurity* of the first *pain*.

4. Of the value of each *pain* which appears to be produced by it after the first. This constitutes the *fecundity* of the first *pain*, and the *impurity* of the first pleasure.

5. Sum up all the values of all the *pleasures* on the one side, and those of all the pains on the other. The balance, if it be on the side of pleasure, will give the *good* tendency of the act upon the whole, with respect to the interests of that *individual* person: if on the side of pain, the *bad* tendency of it upon the whole.

6. Take an account of the *number* of persons whose interests appear to be concerned; and repeat the above process with respect to each. *Sum up* the numbers expressive of the degrees of *good* tendency, which the act has, with respect to each individual, in regard to whom the tendency of it is *good* upon the whole: do this again with respect to each individual,

in regard to whom the tendency of it is *good* upon the whole: do this again with respect to each individual, in regard to whom the tendency of it is *bad* upon the whole. Take the *balance;* which, if on the side of *pleasure,* will give the general *good tendency* of the act, with respect to the total number or community of individuals concerned; if on the side of pain, the general *evil tendency,* with respect to the same community.

VI. It is not to be expected that this process should be strictly pursued previously to every moral judgment, or to every legislative or judicial operation. It may, however, be always kept in view: and as near as the process actually pursued on these occasions approaches to it, so near will such process approach to the character of an exact one.

VII. The same process is alike applicable to pleasure and pain, in whatever shape they appear: and by whatever denomination they are distinguished: to pleasure, whether it be called *good* (which is properly the cause or instrument of pleasure) or *profit* (which is distant pleasure, or the cause or instrument of distant pleasure), or *convenience,* or *advantage, benefit, emolument, happiness,* and so forth: to pain, whether it be called *evil* (which corresponds to *good*), or *mischief,* or *inconvenience,* or *disadvantage,* or *loss,* or *unhappiness,* and so forth.

VIII. Nor is this a novel and unwarranted, any more than it is a useless theory. In all this there is nothing but what the practice of mankind, wheresoever they have a clear view of their own interest, is perfectly comfortable to. An article of property, an estate in land, for instance, is valuable, on what account? On account of the pleasures of all kinds which it enables a man to produce, and what comes to the same thing the pains of all kinds which it enables him to avert. But the value of such an article of property is universally understood to rise or fall according to the length or shortness of the time which a man has in it: the certainty or uncertainty of its coming into possession: and the nearness or remoteness of the time at which, if at all, it is to come into possession. As to the *intensity* of the pleasures which a man may derive from it, this is never thought of, because it depends upon the use which each particular person may come to make of it; which cannot be estimated till the particular pleasures he may come to derive from it, or the particular pains he may come to exclude by means of it, are brought to view. For the same reason, neither does he think of the *fecundity* or *purity* of those pleasures.

Thus much for pleasure and pain, happiness and unhappiness, in *general.*

23. The Deep Beauty of the Golden Rule   R. M. MacIver

Robert M. MacIver (1882–1970) was a prominent sociologist and political theorist who had a strong interest in a number of philosophical issues.

"The Deep Beauty of the Golden Rule" (pp 39–47) by R. M. MacIver from *Moral Principles of Action* edited by Ruth Nanda Anshen. Copyright 1952 by Harper & Row, Publishers, Inc. Reprinted by permission of the publisher.

The subject that learned men call ethics is a wasteland on the philosophical map. Thousands of books have been written on this matter, learned books and popular books, books that argue and books that exhort. Most of them are empty and nearly all are vain. Some claim that pleasure is *the* good; some prefer the elusive and more enticing name of happiness; others reject such principles and speak of equally elusive goals such as self-fulfillment. Others claim that *the* good is to be found in looking away from the self, in devotion to the whole—which whole? in the service of God—whose God?—even in the service of the State— who prescribes the service? Here indeed, if anywhere, after listening to the many words of many apostles, one goes out by the same door as one went in.

The reason is simple. You say: "This is the way you should behave." But I say: "No, that is not the way." You say: "This is right." But I say: "No, that is wrong, and this is right." You appeal to experience. I appeal to experience against you. You appeal to authority: it is not mine. What is left? If you are strong, you can punish me for behaving my way. But does that prove anything except that you are stronger than I? Does it prove the absurd dogma that might makes right? Is the slavemaster right because he owns the whip, or Torquemada because he can send his heretics to the flames?

From this impasse no system of ethical rules has been able to deliver itself. How can ethics lay down final principles of behavior that are not your values against mine, your group's values against my group's?

Which, by the way, does not mean that your rules are any less valid for you because they are not valid for me. Only a person of shallow nature and autocratic leanings would draw that conclusion. For the sake of your integrity you must hold to your own values, no matter how much others reject them. Without *your* values you are nothing. True, you should search them and test them and learn by *your* experience and gain wisdom where you can. Your values are your guides through life but you need to use your own eyes. If I have different guides I shall go another way. So far as we diverge, values are relative as between you and me. But your values cannot be relative for you or mine for me.

That is not here the issue. It is that the relativity of values between you and me, between your group and my group, your sect and my sect, makes futile nearly all learned disquisitions about the first principles of ethics.

By ethics I mean the philosophy of how men should behave in their relations to one another. I am talking about philosophy, not about religion. When you have a creed, you can derive from it principles of ethics. Philosophy cannot begin with a creed, but only with reasoning about the nature of things. It cannot therefore presume that the values of other men are less to be regarded than the values of the proponent. If it does, it is not philosophy but dogma, dogma that is the enemy of philosophy, the kind of dogma that has been the source of endless tyranny and repression.

Can it be a philosophy worth the name that makes a universal of your values and thus rules mine out of existence, where they differ from yours?

How can reasoning decide between my values and yours? Values do not claim truth in any scientific sense; instead they claim validity, rightness. They do not declare what is so but what *should* be so. I cling to my values, you to yours. Your values, some of them, do not hold for me; some of them may be repulsive to me; some of them may threaten me. What then? To what court of reason shall we appeal? To what court that you and I both accept is there any appeal?

The lack of any court is the final *fact* about final values. It is a fundamental fact. It is a terrifying fact. It is also a strangely challenging fact. It gives man his lonely autonomy, his true responsibility. If he has anything that partakes of the quality of a God it comes from this fact. Man has more than the choice to obey or disobey. If he accepts authority he also chooses the authority he accepts. He is responsible not only to others but, more deeply, to himself.

Does all this mean that a universal ethical principle, applicable alike to me and you, even where our values diverge, is impossible? That there is no rule to go by, based on reason itself, in this world of irreconcilable valuations?

There is no rule that can prescribe both my values and yours or decide between them. There is one universal rule, and one only, that can be laid down, on ethical grounds—that is, apart from the creeds of particular religions and apart from the ways of the tribe that falsely and arrogantly universalize themselves.

Do to others as you would have others do to you. This is the only rule that stands by itself in the light of its own reason, the only rule that can stand by itself in the naked, warring universe, in the face of the contending values of men and groups.

What makes it so? Let us first observe that the universal herein laid down is one of procedure. It prescribes a mode of behaving, not a goal of action. On the level of goals, of *final* values, there is irreconcilable conflict. One rule prescribes humility, another pride; one prescribes abstinence, another commends the flesh-pots; and so forth through endless variations. All of us wish that *our* principle could be universal; most of us believe that it *should* be, that our *ought* ought to be all men's *ought*, but since we differ there can be on this level, no possible agreement.

When we want to make our ethical principle prevail we try to persuade others, to "convert" them. Some may freely respond, if their deeper values are near enough to ours. Others will certainly resist and some will seek to persuade us in turn—why shouldn't they? Then we can go no further except by resort to force and fraud. We can, if we are strong, dominate some and we can bribe others. We compromise our own values in doing so and we do not in the end succeed; even if we were masters of the whole world we could never succeed in making our principle universal. We could only make it falsely tyrannous.

So if we look for a principle in the name of which we can appeal to all men, one to which their reason can respond in spite of their differences, we must follow another road. When we try to make our values prevail over those cherished by others, we attack their values, their dynamic of behavior, their living will. If we go far enough we assault their very being. For the will is simply valuation in action. Now the deep beauty of the golden rule is that instead of attacking the will that is in other men, it offers their will a new dimension. "Do as you *would* have others . . ." As *you* would will others to do. It bids you expand your vision, see yourself in new relationships. It bids you transcend your insulation, see yourself in the place of others, see others in your place. It bids you test your values or at least your way of pursuing them. If you would disapprove that another should treat you as you treat him, the situations being reversed is not that a sign that, by the standard of your own values, you are mistreating him?

This principle obviously makes for a vastly greater harmony in the social scheme. At the same time it is the only universal of ethics that does not take sides with or contend with contending values. It contains no dogma. It bids everyone follow his own rule, as it would apply *apart* from the accident of his particular fortunes. It bids him enlarge his own rule, as it would apply whether he is up or whether he is down. It is an accident that you are up and I am down. In another situation you would be down and I would be up. That accident has nothing to do with my *final* values or with yours. You have numbers and force on your side. In another situation I would have the numbers and the force. All situations of power are temporary and precarious. Imagine then the situations reversed and that you had a more wonderful power than is at the command of the most powerful, the power to make the more powerful act toward you as you would want him to act. If power is your dream, then dream of a yet greater power—and act out the spirit of your dream.

But the conclusive argument is not in the terms of power. It goes far deeper, down to the great truth that power so often ignores and that so often in the end destroys it, the truth that when you maltreat others you detach yourself from them, from the understanding of them, from the understanding of yourself. You insulate yourself, you narrow your own values, you cut yourself off from that which you and they have in common. And this commonness is more enduring and more satisfying than what you possess in insulation. You separate yourself, and for all your power you weaken yourself. Which is why power and fear are such close companions.

This is the reason why the evil you do to another, you do also, in the end, to yourself. While if you and he refrain from doing evil, one to another—not to speak of the yet happier consequences of doing positive good—this reciprocity of restraint from evil will redound to the good of both.

That makes a much longer story and we shall not here enter upon it. Our sole concern is to show that the golden rule is the *only* ethical principle, as already defined, that can have clear right of way everywhere in the kind of world we have inherited. It is the only principle that allows every man to follow his own intrinsic values while nevertheless it transforms the chaos of warring codes into a reasonably well-ordered universe.

Let us explain the last statement. What are a man's intrinsic values? Beyond his mere self-seeking every human being needs, and must find, some attachment to a larger purpose. These attachments, in themselves and apart from the way he pursues them, are his intrinsic values. For some men they are centered in the family, the clan, the "class," the community, the nation, the "race." It is the warfare of their group-attachments that creates the deadliest disturbances of modern society. For some men the focus of attachment is found in the greater "cause," the faith, the creed, the way of life. The conflict of these attachments also unlooses many evils on society and at some historical stages has brought about great devastation.

The greatest evils inflicted by man on man over the face of the earth are wrought not by the self-seekers, the pleasure lovers, or the merely amoral, but by the fervent devotees of ethical principles, those who are bound body and soul to some larger purpose, the nation, the "race," the "masses," the "brethren" whoever they may be. The faith they invoke, whatever it may be, is not large enough when it sets a frontier between the members and the non-members, the believers and the non-believers. In the heat of devotion to that larger but exclusive purpose there is bred the fanaticism that corrodes and finally destroys all that links man to the common humanity. In the name of the cause, they will torture and starve and trample under foot millions on millions of their fellowmen. In its name they will cultivate the blackest treachery. And if their methods fail, as fail in the end they must, they will be ready, as was Hitler, to destroy their own cause or their own people, the chosen ones, rather than accept the reality their blinded purpose denied.

How then can we say that the golden rule does not disqualify the intrinsic values of such people—even of people like Hitler or, say, Torquemada? In the name of his values Torquemada burned at the stake many persons who differed from their fellows mainly by being more courageous, honest, and faithful to their faith. What then were Torquemada's values? He was a servant of the Church and the Church was presumptively a servant of Jesus Christ. It was not the intrinsic values of his creed that moved him and his masters to reject the Christian golden rule. Let us concede they had some kind of devotion to religion. It was the distorted, fanatical way in which they pursued the dimmed values they cherished, it was not the values themselves, to which their inhumanity can be charged.

Let us take the case of Hitler. Apart from his passion for Germany, or the German "folk," he would have been of no account, for evil or for good. That passion of itself, that in his view intrinsic value, might have inspired great constructive service instead of destruction. It was the method he used, and not the values he sought to promote thereby, that led to ruin, his blind trust in the efficacy of ruthless might. Belonging to a "folk" that had been reduced in defeat from strength to humiliation, fed on false notions of history and responsive to grotesque fallacies about a "master race," he conceived the resurgence of Germany in the distorted light of his vindictive imagination. Had Hitler been a member of some small "folk," no more numerous, say, than the population of his native Austria, he might have cherished the same values with no less passion, but his aspirations would have taken a different form and would never have expressed themselves in horror and tragedy.

The golden rule says nothing against Hitler's mystic adoration of the German "race," against any man's intrinsic values. By "intrinsic values" we signify the goals, beyond mere self-seeking, that animate a human being. If your group, your nation, your "race," your church, is for you a primary attachment, continue to cherish it—give it all you have, if you are so minded. But do not use means that are repugnant to the standards according to which you would have others conduct themselves to you and your values. If your nation were a small one, would you not seethe with indignation if some large neighbor destroyed its independence? Where, then, is your personal integrity if, belonging instead to the large nation, you act to destroy the independence of a small one? You falsify your own values, in the longer run you do them injury, when you pursue them in ways that cannot abide the test of the golden rule.

It follows that while this first principle attacks no intrinsic values, no primary attachments of men to goods that reach beyond themselves, it nevertheless purifies every attachment, every creed, of its accidents, its irrelevancies, its excesses, its false reliance on power. It saves every human value from the corruption that comes from the arrogance of detachment and exclusiveness, from the shell of the kind of absolutism that imprisons its vitality.

At this point a word of caution is in order. The golden rule does not solve for us our ethical problems but offers only a way of approach. It does not prescribe our treatment of others but only the spirit in which we should treat them. It has no simple mechanical application and often enough is hard to apply—what general principle is not? It certainly does not bid us treat others as others *want* us to treat them—that would be an absurdity. The convicted criminal wants the judge to set him free. If the judge acts in the spirit of the golden rule, within the limits of the discretion permitted him as judge, he might instead reason somewhat as follows: "How would I feel the judge ought to treat *me* were I in this man's place? What could I—the man I am and yet somehow standing where this criminal stands—properly ask the judge to do for me, to me? In this spirit I shall assess his guilt and his punishment. In this spirit I shall give full consideration to the conditions under which he acted. I shall try to understand *him*, to do what I properly can for him, while at the same time I fulfill my judicial duty in protecting society against the dangers that arise if criminals such as he go free."

"Do to others as you would have others do to you." The disease to which all values are subject is the growth of a hard insulation. "I am right: I have the truth. If you differ from me, you are a heretic, you are in error. *Therefore* while you must allow me every liberty when you are in power I need not, in truth I ought not to, show any similar consideration for you." The barb of falsehood has already begun to vitiate the cherished value. While *you* are in power I advocate the equal rights of all creeds: when *I* am in power, I reject any such claim as ridiculous. This is the position taken by various brands of totalitarianism, and the communists in particular have made it a favorite technique in the process of gaining power, clamoring for rights they will use to destroy the rights of those who grant them. Religious groups have followed the same line. Roman Catholics, Calvinists, Lutherans, Presbyterians, and others have on occasion vociferously advocated religious liberty where they were in the minority, often to curb it where in turn they became dominant.

This gross inconsistency on the part of religious groups was flagrantly displayed in earlier centuries, but examples are still not infrequent. Here is one. *La Civilita Catholicâ,* a Jesuit organ published in Rome, has come out as follows:

"The Roman Catholic Church, convinced, through its divine prerogatives, of being the only true church, must demand the right to freedom for herself alone, because such a right can only be possessed by truth, never by error. As to other religions, the church will certainly never draw the sword, but she will require that by legitimate means they shall not be allowed to propagate false doctrine. Consequently, in a state where the majority of the people are Catholic, the Church will require that legal existence be denied to error. . . . In some countries, Catholics will be obliged to ask full religious freedom for all, resigned at being forced to cohabilitate where they alone should rightly be allowed to live. . . . The Church cannot blush for her own want of tolerance, as she asserts it in principle and applies it in practice."[1]

Since this statement has the merit of honesty it well illustrates the fundamental lack of rationality that lies behind all such violations of the golden rule. The argument runs: "Roman Catholics know they possess the truth; *therefore* they should not permit others to propagate error." By parity of reasoning why should not Protestants say—and indeed they have often said it—"We know we possess the truth; therefore we should not tolerate the errors of Roman Catholics." Why then should not atheists say: "We know we possess the truth; therefore we should not tolerate the errors of dogmatic religion."

No matter what we believe, we are equally convinced that *we* are right. We have to be. That is what belief means, and we must all believe something. The Roman Catholic Church is entitled to declare that all other religious groups are sunk in error. But what follows? That other groups have not the right to believe they are right? That you have the right to repress them while they have no right to repress you? That they should concede to you what you should not concede to them? Such reasoning is mere childishness. Beyond it lies the greater foolishness that truth is advanced by the forceful suppression of those who believe differently from you. Beyond that lies the pernicious distortion of meanings which claims that liberty is only "the liberty to do right"—the "liberty" for me to do what *you* think is right. This perversion of the meaning of liberty has been the delight of all totalitarians. And it might be well to reflect that it was the radical Rousseau who first introduced the doctrine that men could be "forced to be free."

How much do they have truth who think they must guard it within the fortress of their own might? How little that guarding has availed in the past! How often it has kept truth outside while superstition grew moldy within! How often has the false alliance of belief and force led

---

[1] Quoted in the *Christian Century* (June 1948).

to civil dissension and the futile ruin of war! But if history means nothing to those who call themselves "Christian" and still claim exclusive civil rights for their particular faith, at least they might blush before this word of one they call their Master: "All things therefore whatsoever ye would that men should do unto you, even so do ye also unto them; for this is the law and the prophets."

Contemporary Issues

Are We Obligated to Help Everyone?

24. Lifeboat Ethics: The Case Against Helping the Poor
Garrett Hardin

Garrett Hardin (1915–   ) is professor of human ecology at the University of California, Santa Barbara. His books and articles on population control and other social issues have been widely read.

Environmentalists use the metaphor of the earth as a "spaceship" in trying to persuade countries, industries, and people to stop wasting and polluting our natural resources. Since we all share life on this planet, they argue, no single person or institution has the right to destroy, waste, or use more than a fair share of its resources.

But does everyone on earth have an equal right to an equal share of its resources? The spaceship metaphor can be dangerous when used by misguided idealists to justify suicidal policies for sharing our resources through uncontrolled immigration and foreign aid. In their enthusiastic but unrealistic generosity, they confuse the ethics of a spaceship with those of a lifeboat.

A true spaceship would have to be under the control of a captain, since no ship could possibly survive if its course were determined by committee. Spaceship Earth certainly has no captain; the United Nations is merely a toothless tiger, with little power to enforce any policy upon its bickering members.

If we divide the world crudely into rich nations, two thirds of them are desperately poor, and only one third comparatively rich, with the United States the wealthiest of all. Metaphorically each rich nation can be seen as a lifeboat full of comparatively rich people. In the ocean outside each lifeboat swim the poor of the world, who would like to get in, or at least to share some of the wealth. What should the lifeboat passengers do?

First, we must recognize the limited capacity of any lifeboat. For example, a nation's land has a limited capacity to support a population, and, as the current energy crisis has shown us, in some ways we have already exceeded the carrying capacity of our land.

Adrift in a Moral Sea

So here we sit, say fifty people in our lifeboat. To be generous, let us assume it has room for ten more, making a total capacity of sixty. Suppose the fifty of us in the lifeboat see 100 others swimming in the water outside, begging for admission to our boat or for handouts. We have several options: we may be tempted to try to live by the Christian ideal of being "our brother's keeper," or by the Marxist ideal of "to each according to his needs." Since the needs of all in the water are the same, and since they can all be seen as "our brothers," we could take them all into our boat, making a total of 150 in a boat designed for sixty. The boat swamps, everyone drowns. Complete justice, complete catastrophe.

Since the boat has an unused excess capacity of ten more passengers, we could admit just ten more to it. But which ten do we let in? How do we choose? Do we pick the best ten, the neediest ten, "first come, first served"? And what do we say to the ninety we exclude? If we do let an extra ten into our lifeboat, we will have lost our "safety factor," an engineering principle of critical importance. For example, if we don't leave room for excess capacity as a safety factor in our country's agriculture, a new plant disease or a bad change in the weather could have disastrous consequences.

Suppose we decide to preserve our small safety factor and admit no more to the lifeboat. Our survival is then possible, although we shall have to be constantly on guard against boarding parties.

While this last solution clearly offers the only means of our survival, it is morally abhorrent to many people. Some say they feel guilty about their good luck. My reply is simple: "Get out and yield your place to others." This may solve the problem of the guilt-ridden person's conscience, but it does not change the ethics of the lifeboat. The needy person to whom the guilt-ridden person yields his place will not himself feel guilty about his good luck. If he did, he would not climb aboard. The net result of conscience-stricken people giving up their unjustly held seats is the elimination of that sort of conscience from the lifeboat.

This is the basic metaphor within which we must work out our solutions. Let us now enrich the image, step by step, with substantive additions from the real world, a world that must solve real and pressing problems of overpopulation and hunger.

The harsh ethics of the lifeboat become even harsher when we consider the reproductive differences between the rich nations and the poor nations. The people inside the lifeboats are doubling in numbers every eighty-seven years; those swimming around outside are doubling, on the average, every thirty-five years, more than twice as fast as the rich. And since the world's resources are dwindling, the difference in prosperity between the rich and the poor can only increase.

As of 1973, the U.S. had a population of 210 million people, who were increasing by 0.8 per cent per year. Outside our lifeboat, let us imagine another 210 million people (say the combined populations of Colombia, Ecuador, Venezuela, Morocco, Pakistan, Thailand, and the

Philippines), who are increasing at a rate of 3.3 percent per year. Put differently, the doubling time for this aggregate population is twenty-one years, compared to eighty-seven years for the U.S.

Multiplying the Rich and the Poor

Now suppose the U.S. agreed to pool its resources with those seven countries, with everyone receiving an equal share. Initially the ratio of Americans to non-Americans in this model would be one-to-one. But consider what the ratio would be after eighty-seven years, by which time the Americans would have doubled to a population of 420 million. By then, doubling every twenty-one years, the other group would have swollen to 3.54 billion. Each American would have to share the available resources with more than eight people.

But, one could argue, this discussion assumes that current population trends will continue, and they may not. Quite so. Most likely the rate of population increase will decline much faster in the U.S. than it will in the other countries, and there does not seem to be much we can do about it. In sharing with "each according to his needs," we must recognize that needs are determined by population size, which is determined by the rate of reproduction, which at present is regarded as a sovereign right of every nation, poor or not. This being so, the philanthropic load created by the sharing ethic of the spaceship can only increase.

The Tragedy of the Commons

The fundamental error of spaceship ethics, and the sharing it requires, is that it leads to what I call "the tragedy of the commons." Under a system of private property, the men who own property recognize their responsibility to care for it, for if they don't they will eventually suffer. A farmer, for instance, will allow no more cattle in a pasture than its carrying capacity justifies. If he overloads it, erosion sets in, weeds take over, and he loses the use of the pasture.

If a pasture becomes a commons open to all, the right of each to use it may not be matched by a corresponding responsibility to protect it. Asking everyone to use it with discretion will hardly do, for the considerate herdsman who refrains from overloading the commons suffers more than a selfish one who says his needs are greater. If everyone would restrain himself, all would be well; but it takes only one less than everyone to ruin a system of voluntary restraint. In a crowded world of less-than-perfect human beings, mutual ruin is inevitable if there are no controls. This is the tragedy of the commons.

One of the major tasks of education today should be the creation of such an acute awareness of the dangers of the commons that people will recognize its many varieties. For example, the air and water have become polluted because they are treated as commons. Further growth in the population, or per-capita conversion of natural resources into pollutants, will only make the problem worse. The same holds true for the fish of the oceans. Fishing fleets have nearly disappeared in many parts of the world: technological improvements in the art of fishing are hastening the day of complete ruin. Only the replacement of the system of the commons with a responsible system of control will save the land, air, water, and oceanic fisheries.

The World Food Bank

In recent years there has been a push to create a new commons called a World Food Bank, an international depository of food reserves to which nations would contribute according to their abilities and from which they would draw according to their needs. This humanitarian proposal has received support from many liberal international groups, and from such prominent citizens as Margaret Mead, U.N. Secretary General Kurt Waldheim, and Senators Edward Kennedy and George McGovern.

A world food bank appeals powerfully to our humanitarian impulses. But before we rush ahead with such a plan, let us recognize where the greatest political push comes from, lest we be disillusioned later. Our experience with the Food for Peace program, or Public Law 480, gives us the answer. This program moved billions of dollars worth of U.S. surplus grain to food-short, population-long countries during the past two decades. But when P.L. 480 first became law, a headline in the business magazine *Forbes* revealed the real power behind it: "Feeding the World's Hungry Millions: How It Will Mean Billions for U.S. Business."

And indeed it did. In the years 1960 to 1970, U.S. taxpayers spent a total of $7.9 billion on the Food for Peace program. Between 1948 and 1970, they also paid an additional $50 billion for other economic-aid programs, some of which went for food and food-producing machinery and technology. Though all U.S. taxpayers were forced to contribute to the cost of P.L. 480, certain special-interest groups gained handsomely under the program. Farmers did not have to contribute the grain; the Government, or rather the taxpayers, bought it from them at full market prices. The increased demand raised prices of farm products generally. The manufacturers of farm machinery, fertilizers, and pesticides benefited by the farmers' extra efforts to grow more food. Grain elevators profited from storing the surplus until it could be shipped. Railroads made money hauling it to ports, and shipping lines profited from carrying it overseas. The implementation of P.L. 480 required the creation of a vast Government bureaucracy, which then acquired its own vested interest in continuing the program regardless of its merits.

Extracting Dollars

Those who proposed and defended the Food for Peace program in public rarely mentioned its importance to any of these special interests. The public emphasis was always on its humanitarian effects. The combination of silent selfish interests and highly vocal humanitarian apologists made a powerful and successful lobby for extracting money from taxpayers. We can expect the same lobby to push now for the creation of a World Food Bank.

However great the potential benefit to selfish interests, it should not be a decisive argument against a truly humanitarian program. We must ask if such a program would actually do more good than harm, not only momentarily but also in the long run. Those who propose the food bank usually refer to a current "emergency" or "crisis" in terms of world food supply. But what is an emergency? Although they may be infrequent and sudden, everyone knows that emergencies will occur from time to time. A well-run family, company, organization, or country prepares for the likelihood of accidents and emergencies. It expects them, it budgets for them, it saves for them.

Learning the Hard Way

What happens if some organizations or countries budget for accidents and others do not? If each country is solely responsible for its own well-being, poorly managed ones will suffer. But they can learn from experience. They may mend their ways, and learn to budget for infrequent but certain emergencies. For example, the weather varies from year to year, and periodic crop failures are certain. A wise and competent government saves out of the production of the good years in anticipation of bad years to come. Joseph taught this policy to Pharaoh in Egypt more than 2,000 years ago. Yet the great majority of the governments in the world today do not follow such a policy. They lack either the wisdom or the competence, or both. Should those nations that do manage to put something aside be forced to come to the rescue each time an emergency occurs among the poor nations?

"But it isn't their fault!" some kindhearted liberals argue. "How can we blame the poor people who are caught in an emergency? Why must they suffer for the sins of their governments?" The concept of blame is simply not relevant here. The real question is, what are the operational consequences of establishing a world food bank? If it is open to every country every time a need develops, slovenly rulers will not be motivated to take Joseph's advice. Someone will always come to their aid. Some countries will deposit food in the world food bank, and others will withdraw it. There will be almost no overlap. As a result of such solutions to food shortage emergencies, the poor countries will not learn to mend their ways, and will suffer progressively greater emergencies as their populations grow.

Population Control the Crude Way

On the average, poor countries undergo a 2.5 per cent increase in population each year; rich countries, about 0.8 per cent. Only rich countries have anything in the way of food reserves set aside, and even they do not have as much as they should. Poor countries have none. If poor countries received no food from the outside, the rate of their population growth would be periodically checked by crop failures and famines. But if they can always draw on a world food bank in time of need, their population can continue to grow unchecked, and so will their "need" for aid. In the short run, a world food bank may diminish that need, but in the long run it actually increases the need without limit.

Without some system of worldwide food sharing, the proportion of people in the rich and poor nations might eventually stabilize. The over-populated poor countries would decrease in numbers, while the rich countries that had room for more people would increase. But with a well-meaning system of sharing, such as a world food bank, the growth differential between the rich and the poor countries will not only persist, it will increase. Because of the higher rate of population growth in the poor countries of the world, 88 percent of today's children are born poor, and only 12 percent rich. Year by year the ratio becomes worse, as the fast-reproducing poor outnumber the slow-reproducing rich.

A world food bank is thus a commons in disguise. People will have more motivation to draw from it than to add to any common store. The less provident and less able will multiply at the expense of the abler and more provident, bringing eventual ruin upon all who share in the commons. Besides, any system of "sharing" that amounts to foreign aid from the rich nations to the poor nations will carry the taint of charity, which will contribute little to the world peace so devoutly desired by those who support the idea of a world food bank.

As past U.S. foreign-aid programs have amply and depressingly demonstrated, international charity frequently inspires mistrust and antagonism rather than gratitude on the part of the recipient nation.

Chinese Fish and Miracle Rice

The modern approach to foreign aid stresses the export of technology and advice, rather than money and food. As an ancient Chinese proverb goes: "Give a man a fish and he will eat for a day; teach him how to fish and he will eat for the rest of his days." Acting on this advice, the Rockefeller and Ford Foundations have financed a number of programs for improving agriculture in the hungry nations. Known as the "Green Revolution," these programs have led to the development of "miracle rice" and "miracle wheat," new strains that offer bigger harvests and greater resistance to crop damage. Norman Borlaug, the Nobel Prize-winning agonomist who, supported by the Rockefeller Foundation, developed "miracle wheat," is one of the most prominent advocates of a world food bank.

Whether or not the Green Revolution can increase food production as much as its champions claim is a debatable but possibly irrelevant point. Those who support this well-intended humanitarian effort should first consider some of the fundamentals of human ecology. Ironically, one man who did was the late Alan Gregg, a vice president of the Rockefeller Foundation. Two decades ago he expressed strong doubts about the wisdom of such attempts to increase food production. He likened the growth and spread of humanity over the surface of the earth to the spread of cancer in the human body, remarking that "cancerous growths demand food; but, as far as I know, they have never been cured by getting it."

Overloading the Environment

Every human born constitutes a draft on all aspects of the environment: food, air, water, forests, beaches, wildlife, scenery, and solitude. Food can, perhaps, be significantly increased to meet a growing demand. But what about clean beaches, unspoiled forests, and solitude? If we satisfy a growing population's need for food, we necessarily decrease its per capita supply of the other resources needed by men.

India, for example, now has a population of 600 million, which increases by 15 million each year. This population already puts a huge load on a relatively improverished environment. The country's forests are now only a small fraction of what they were three centuries ago, and floods and erosion continually destroy the insufficient farmland that remains. Every one of the 15 million new lives added to India's population puts an additional burden on the environment, and increases the economic and social costs of crowding. However humanitarian our intent, every Indian life saved through medical or nutritional assistance from abroad diminishes the quality of life for those who remain, and for subsequent generations. If rich countries make it possible, through foreign aid, for 600 million Indians to swell to 1.2 billion in a mere twenty-eight years, as their current growth rate threatens, will future generations of Indians thank us for hastening the destruction of their environment? Will our good intentions be sufficient excuse for the consequences of our actions?

My final example of a commons in action is one for which the public has the least desire for rational discussion—immigration. Anyone who publicly questions the wisdom of current U.S. immigration policy is promptly charged with bigotry, prejudice, ethnocentrism, chauvinism, isolationism, or selfishness. Rather than encounter such accusations, one would rather talk about other matters, leaving immigration policy to wallow in the crosscurrents of special interests that take no account of the good of the whole, or the interests of posterity.

Perhaps we still feel guilty about things we said in the past. Two generations ago the popular press frequently referred to Dagos, Wops, Polacks, Chinks, and Krauts, in articles about how America was being "overrun" by foreigners of supposedly inferior genetic stock. But because the implied inferiority of foreigners was used then as justification for keeping them out, people now assume that restrictive policies could only be based on such misguided notions. There are other grounds.

A Nation of Immigrants

Just consider the numbers involved. Our Government acknowledges a net inflow of 400,000 immigrants a year. While we have no hard data on the extent of illegal entries, educated guesses put the figure at about 600,000 a year. Since the natural increase (excess of births over deaths) of the resident population now runs about 1.7 million per year, the yearly gain from immigration amounts to at least 19 per cent of the total annual increase, and may be as much as 37 per cent if we include the estimate for illegal immigrants. Considering the growing use of birth-control devices, the potential effect of educational campaigns by such organizations as Planned Parenthood Federation of America and Zero Population Growth, and the influence of inflation and the housing shortage, the fertility rate of American women may decline so much that immigration could account for all the yearly increase in population. Should we not at least ask if that is what we want?

For the sake of those who worry about whether the "quality" of the average immigrant compares favorably with the quality of the average resident, let us assume that immigrants and native-born citizens are of exactly equal quality, however one defines that term. We will focus here only on quantity; and since our conclusions will depend on nothing else, all charges of bigotry and chauvinism become irrelevant.

Immigration vs. Food Supply

World food banks *move food to the people*, hastening the exhaustion of the environment of the poor countries. Unrestricted immigration, on the other hand, *moves people to the food*, thus speeding up the destruction of the environment of the rich countries. We can easily understand why poor people should want to make this latter transfer, but why should rich hosts encourage it?

As in the case of foreign-aid programs, immigration receives support from selfish interests and humanitarian impulses. The primary selfish interest in unimpeded immigration is the desire of employers for cheap labor, particularly in industries and trades that offer degrading work: In the past, one wave of foreigners after another was brought into the U.S. to work at wretched jobs for wretched wages. In recent years the Cubans, Puerto Ricans, and Mexicans have had this dubious honor. The interests of the employers of cheap labor mesh well with the guilty silence of the country's liberal intelligentsia. White Anglo-Saxon Protestants are particularly reluctant to call for a closing of the doors to immigration, for fear of being called bigots.

But not all countries have such reluctant leadership. Most educated Hawaiians, for example, are keenly aware of the limits of their environment, particularly in terms of population growth. There is only so much room on the islands, and the islanders know it. To Hawaiians, immigrants from the other forty-nine states present as great a threat as those from other nations. At a recent meeting of Hawaiian government officials in Honolulu, I had the ironic delight of hearing a speaker, who like most of his audience was of Japanese ancestry, ask how the country might practically and constitutionally close its doors to further immigration. One member of the audience countered: "How can we shut the doors now? We have many friends and relatives in Japan that we'd like to bring here some day so that they can enjoy Hawaii too." The Japanese-American speaker smiled sympathetically and answered: "Yes, but we have children now, and someday we'll have grandchildren too. We can bring more people here from Japan only by giving away some of the land that we hope to pass on to our grandchildren some day. What right do we have to do that?"

At this point, I can hear U.S. liberals asking: "How can you justify slamming the door once you're inside? You say that immigrants should be kept out. But aren't we all immigrants, or the descendants of immigrants? If we insist on staying, must we not admit all others?" Our craving for intellectual order leads us to seek and prefer symmetrical rules and morals: a single rule for me and everybody else; the same rule yesterday, today, and tomorrow. Justice, we feel, should not change with time and place.

We Americans of non-Indian ancestry can look upon ourselves as the descendants of thieves who are guilty morally, if not legally, of stealing this land from its Indian owners. Should we then give back the land to the now living American descendants of those Indians? However morally or logically sound this proposal may be, I, for one, am unwilling to live by it and I know no one else who is. Besides, the logical consequence would be absurd. Suppose that, intoxicated with a sense of pure justice, we should decide to turn our land over to the Indians. Since all our wealth has also been derived from the land, wouldn't we be morally obliged to give that back to the Indians too?

Pure Justice vs. Reality

Clearly, the concept of pure justice produces an infinite regression to absurdity. Centuries ago, wise men invented statutes of limitations to justify the rejection of such pure justice, in the interest of preventing continual disorder. The law zealously defends property rights, but only relatively recent property rights. Drawing a line after an arbitrary time has elapsed may be unjust, but the alternatives are worse.

We are all the descendants of thieves, and the world's resources are inequitably distributed. But we must begin the journey to tomorrow from the point where we are today. We cannot remake the past. We cannot safely divide the wealth equitably among all peoples so long as people reproduce at different rates. To do so would guarantee that our grandchildren, and everyone else's grandchildren, would have only a ruined world to inhabit.

To be generous with one's own possessions is quite different from being generous with those of posterity. We should call this point to the attention of those who, from a commendable love of justice and equality, would institute a system of the commons, either in the form of a world food bank, or of unrestricted immigration. We must convince them, if we wish to save at least some parts of the world from environmental ruin.

Without a true world government to control reproduction and the use of available resources, the sharing ethic of the spaceship is impossible. For the foreseeable future, our survival demands that we govern our actions by the ethics of a lifeboat, harsh though they may be. Posterity will be satisfied with nothing less.

25. Famine, Affluence, and Morality   Peter Singer

Peter Singer, (1946–) who teaches philosophy in Australia, has written books and articles on a variety of moral issues. His defense of the rights of animals has received much attention.

As I write this, in November 1971, people are dying in East Bengal from lack of food, shelter, and medical care. The suffering and death that are occurring there now are not inevitable, not unavoidable in any fatalistic sense of the term. Constant poverty, a cyclone, and a civil war have turned at least nine million people into destitute refugees; nevertheless, it is not beyond the capacity of the richer nations to give enough assistance to reduce any further suffering to very small proportions. The decisions and actions of human beings can prevent this kind of suffering. Unfortunately, human beings have not made the necessary decisions. At the individual level, people have, with very few exceptions, not responded to the situation in any significant way. Generally speaking, people have not given large sums to relief funds; they have not written to their parliamentary representatives demanding increased government assistance; they have not demonstrated in the streets, held symbolic fasts, or done anything else directed toward providing the refugees with the means to satisfy their essential needs. At the government level, no government has given the sort of massive aid that would enable the refugees to survive for more than a few days. Britain, for instance, has given rather more than most countries. It has, to date, given £14,750,000. For comparative purposes, Britain's share of the nonrecoverable development costs of the Anglo-French Concorde project is already in excess of £275,000,000, and on present estimates will reach £440,000,000. The implication is that the British government values a supersonic transport more than thirty times as highly as it values the lives of the nine million refugees. Australia is another country which, on a per capita basis, is well up in the "aid to Bengal" table. Australia's aid, however, amounts to less than one-twelfth of the cost of Sydney's new opera house. The total amount given, from all sources, now stands at about £65,000,000. The estimated cost of keeping the refugees alive for one year is £464,000,000. Most of the refugees have now been in the camps for more than six months. The World Bank has said that India needs a minimum of £300,000,000 in assistance from other countries before the end of the year. It seems obvious that assistance on this scale will not be forthcoming. India will be forced to choose between letting the refugees starve or diverting funds from her own development program, which will mean that more of her own people will starve in the future.[1]

Peter Singer, "Famine, Affluence, and Morality," *Philosophy & Public Affairs* 1, no. 3 (Spring 1972). Copyright © 1972 by Princeton University Press. Reprinted by permission of Princeton University Press.

[1] There was also a third possibility: that India would go to war to enable the refugees to return to their lands. Since I wrote this paper, India has taken this way out. The situation is no longer that described above, but this does not affect my argument, as the next paragraph indicates.

These are the essential facts about the present situation in Bengal. So far as it concerns us here, there is nothing unique about this situation except its magnitude. The Bengal emergency is just the latest and most acute of a series of major emergencies in various parts of the world, arising both from natural and from man-made causes. There are also many parts of the world in which people die from malnutrition and lack of food independent of any special emergency. I take Bengal as my example only because it is the present concern, and because the size of the problem has ensured that it has been given adequate publicity. Neither individuals nor governments can claim to be unaware of what is happening there.

What are the moral implications of a situation like this? In what follows, I shall argue that the way people in relatively affluent countries react to a situation like that in Bengal cannot be justified; indeed, the whole way we look at moral issues—our moral conceptual scheme—needs to be altered, and with it, the way of life that has come to be taken for granted in our society.

In arguing for this conclusion I will not, of course, claim to be morally neutral. I shall, however, try to argue for the moral position that I take, so that anyone who accepts certain assumptions, to be made explicit, will, I hope, accept my conclusion.

I begin with the assumption that suffering and death from lack of food, shelter, and medical care are bad. I think most people will agree about this, although one may reach the same view by different routes. I shall not argue for this view. People can hold all sorts of eccentric positions, and perhaps from some of them it would not follow that death by starvation is in itself bad. It is difficult, perhaps impossible, to refute such positions, and so for brevity I will henceforth take this assumption as accepted. Those who disagree need read no further.

My next point is this: if it is in our power to prevent something bad from happening, without thereby sacrificing anything of comparable moral importance, we ought, morally, to do it. By "without sacrificing anything of comparable moral importance" I mean without causing anything else comparably bad to happen, or doing something that is wrong in itself, or failing to promote some moral good, comparable in significance to the bad thing that we can prevent. This principle seems almost as uncontroversial as the last one. It requires us only to prevent what is bad, and not to promote what is good, and it requires this of us only when we can do it without sacrificing anything that is, from the moral point of view, comparably important. I could even, as far as the application of my argument to the Bengal emergency is concerned, qualify the point so as to make it: if it is in our power to prevent something very bad from happening, without thereby sacrificing anything morally significant, we ought, morally, to do it. An application of this principle would be as follows: if I am walking past a shallow pond and see a child drowning in it, I ought to wade in and pull the child out. This will mean getting my clothes muddy, but this is insignificant, while the death of the child would presumably be a very bad thing.

The uncontroversial appearance of the principle just stated is deceptive. If it were acted upon, even in its qualified form, our lives, our society, and our world would be fundamentally changed. For the principle takes, firstly, no account of proximity or distance. It makes no moral difference whether the person I can help is a neighbor's child ten yards from me or a Bengali whose name I shall never know, ten thousand miles away. Secondly, the principle makes no distinction between cases in which I am the only person who could possibly do anything and cases in which I am just one among millions in the same position.

I do not think I need to say much in defense of the refusal to take proximity and distance into account. The fact that a person is physically near to us, so that we have personal contact with him, may make it more likely that we *shall* assist him, but this does not show that we *ought* to help him rather than another who happens to be further away. If we accept any principle of impartiality, universalizability, equality, or whatever, we cannot discriminate against someone merely because he is far away from us (or we are far away from him). Admittedly, it is possible that we are in a better position to judge what needs to be done to help a person near to us than one far away, and perhaps also to provide the assistance we judge to be necessary. If this were the case, it would be a reason for helping those near to us first. This may once have been a justification for being more concerned with the poor in one's town than with famine victims in India. Unfortunately for those who like to keep their moral responsibilities limited, instant communication and swift transportation have changed the situation. From the moral point of view, the development of the world into a "global village" has made an important, though still unrecognized, difference to our moral situation. Expert observers and supervisors, sent out by famine relief organizations or permanently stationed in famine-prone areas, can direct our aid to a refugee in Bengal almost as effectively as we could get it to someone in our own block. There would seem, therefore, to be no possible justification for discriminating on geographical grounds.

There may be a greater need to defend the second implication of my principle—that the fact that there are millions of other people in the same position, in respect to the Bengali refugees, as I am, does not make the situation significantly different from a situation in which I am the only person who can prevent something very bad from occurring. Again, of course, I admit that there is a psychological difference between the cases; one feels less guilty about doing nothing if one can point to others, similarly placed, who have also done nothing. Yet this can make no real difference to our moral obligations.[2] Should I consider that I am less obliged to pull the drowning child out of the pond if on looking around

---

[2] In view of the special sense philosophers often give to the terms, I should say that I use "obligation" simply as the abstract noun derived from "ought," so that "I have an obligation to" means no more, and no less, than "I ought to." This usage is in accordance with the definition of "ought" given by the *Shorter Oxford English Dictionary:* "The general verb to express duty or obligation." I do not think any issue of substance hangs on the way the term is used: sentences in which I use "obligation" could all be rewritten, although somewhat clumsily, as sentences in which a clause containing "ought" replaces the term "obligation."

I see other people, no further away than I am, who have also noticed the child but are doing nothing? One has only to ask this question to see the absurdity of the view that numbers lessen obligation. It is a view that is an ideal excuse for inactivity; unfortunately most of the major evils—poverty, overpopulation, pollution—are problems in which everyone is almost equally involved.

The view that numbers do make a difference can be made plausible if stated in this way: if everyone in circumstances like mine gave £5 to the Bengal Relief Fund, there would be enough to provide food, shelter, and medical care for the refugees; there is no reason why I should give more than anyone else in the same circumstances as I am; therefore I have no obligation to give more than £5. Each premise in this argument is true, and the argument looks sound. It may convince us, unless we notice that it is based on a hypothetical premise, although the conclusion is not stated hypothetically. The argument would be sound if the conclusion were: if everyone in circumstances like mine were to give £5, I would have no obligation to give more than £5. If the conclusion were so stated, however, it would be obvious that the argument has no bearing on a situation in which it is not the case that everyone else gives £5. This, of course, is the actual situation. It is more or less certain that not everyone in circumstances like mine will give £5. So there will not be enough to provide the needed food, shelter, and medical care. Therefore by giving more than £5 I will prevent more suffering than I would if I gave just £5.

It might be thought that this argument has an absurd consequence. Since the situation appears to be that very few people are likely to give substantial amounts, it follows that I and everyone else in similar circumstances ought to give as much as possible, that is, at least up to the point at which by giving more one would begin to cause serious suffering for oneself and one's dependents—perhaps even beyond this point to the point of marginal utility, at which by giving more one would cause oneself and one's dependents as much suffering as one would prevent in Bengal. If everyone does this, however, there will be more than can be used for the benefit of the refugees, and some of the sacrifice will have been unnecessary. Thus, if everyone does what he ought to do, the result will not be as good as it would be if everyone did a little less than he ought to do, or if only some do all that they ought to do.

The paradox here arises only if we assume that the actions in question—sending money to the relief funds—are performed more or less simultaneously, and are also unexpected. For if it is to be expected that everyone is going to contribute something, then clearly each is not obliged to give as much as he would have been obliged to had others not been giving too. And if everyone is not acting more or less simultaneously, then those giving later will know how much more is needed, and will have no obligation to give more than is necessary to reach this amount. To say this is not to deny the principle that people in the same circumstances have the same obligations, but to point out that the fact that others have given, or may be expected to give, is a relevant circumstance: those giving after it has become known that many others are giving and those giving before are not in the same circumstances. So the seemingly absurd consequence of the principle I have put forward can occur only if people are in error about the actual circumstances—that is, if they think they are giving when others are not, but in fact they are giving when others are. The result of everyone doing what he really ought to do cannot be worse than the result of everyone doing less than he ought to do, although the result of everyone doing what he reasonably believes he ought to do could be.

If my argument so far has been sound, neither our distance from a preventable evil nor the number of other people who, in respect to that evil, are in the same situation as we are, lessens our obligation to mitigate or prevent that evil. I shall therefore take as established the principle I asserted earlier. As I have already said, I need to assert it only in its qualified form: if it is in our power to prevent something very bad from happening, without thereby sacrificing anything else morally significant, we ought, morally, to do it.

The outcome of this argument is that our traditional moral categories are upset. The traditional distinction between duty and charity cannot be drawn, or at least, not in the place we normally draw it. Giving money to the Bengal Relief Fund is regarded as an act of charity in our society. The bodies which collect money are known as "charities." These organizations see themselves in this way—if you send them a check, you will be thanked for your "generosity." Because giving money is regarded as an act of charity, it is not thought that there is anything wrong with not giving. The charitable man may be praised, but the man who is not charitable is not condemned. People do not feel in any way ashamed or guilty about spending money on new clothes or a new car instead of giving it to famine relief. (Indeed, the alternative does not occur to them.) This way of looking at the matter cannot be justified. When we buy new clothes not to keep ourselves warm but to look "well-dressed" we are not providing for any important need. We would not be sacrificing anything significant if we were to continue to wear our old clothes, and give the money to famine relief. By doing so, we would be preventing another person from starving. It follows from what I have said earlier that we ought to give money away, rather than spend it on clothes which we do not need to keep us warm. To do so is not charitable, or generous. Nor is it the kind of act which philosophers and theologians have called "supererogatory"—an act which it would be good to do, but not wrong not to do. On the contrary, we ought to give the money away, and it is wrong not to do so.

I am not maintaining that there are no acts which are charitable, or that there are no acts which it would be good to do but not wrong not to do. It may be possible to redraw the distinction between duty and charity in some other place. All I am arguing here is that the present way of drawing the distinction, which makes it an act of charity for a man, living at the level of affluence which most people in the "developed nations" enjoy, to give money to save someone else from starvation, cannot be supported. It is beyond the scope of my argument to consider whether the distinction should be redrawn or abolished altogether. There would be many other possible ways of drawing the distinction—for instance, one might decide that it is good to make other people as happy as possible, but not wrong not to do so.

Despite the limited nature of the revision in our moral conceptual scheme which I am proposing, the revision would, given the extent of both affluence and famine in the world today, have radical implications. These implications may lead to further objections, distinct from those I have already considered. I shall discuss two of these.

One objection to the position I have taken might be simply that it is too drastic a revision of our moral scheme. People do not ordinarily judge in the way I have suggested they should. Most people reserve their moral condemnation for those who violate some moral norm, such as the norm against taking another person's property. They do not condemn those who indulge in luxury instead of giving to famine relief. But given that I did not set out to present a morally neutral description of the way people make moral judgments, the way people do in fact judge has nothing to do with the validity of my conclusion. My conclusion follows from the principle which I advanced earlier, and unless that principle is rejected, or the arguments shown to be unsound, I think the conclusion must stand, however strange it appears.

It might, nevertheless, be interesting to consider why our society, and most other societies, do judge differently from the way I have suggested they should. In a well-known article, J. O. Urmson suggests that the imperatives of duty, which tell us what we must do, as distinct from what it would be good to do but not wrong not to do, function so as to prohibit behavior that is intolerable if men are to live together in society.[3] This may explain the origin and continued existence of the present division between acts of duty and acts of charity. Moral attitudes are shaped by the needs of society, and no doubt society needs people who will observe the rules that make social existence tolerable. From the point of view of a particular society, it is essential to prevent violations of norms against killing, stealing, and so on. It is quite inessential, however, to help people outside one's own society.

If this is an explanation of our common distinction between duty and supererogation, however, it is not a justification of it. The moral point of view requires us to look beyond the interests of our own society. Previously, as I have already mentioned, this may hardly have been feasible, but it is quite feasible now. From the moral point of view, the prevention of the starvation of millions of people outside our society must be considered at least as pressing as the upholding of property norms within our society.

It has been argued by some writers, among them Sidgwick and Urmson, that we need to have a basic moral code which is not too far beyond the capacities of the ordinary man, for otherwise there will be a general breakdown of compliance with the moral code. Crudely stated, this argument suggests that if we tell people that they ought to refrain from

---

[3]J. O. Urmson, "Saints and Heroes," in *Essays in Moral Philosophy*, ed. Abraham I. Melden (Seattle: University of Washington Press 1958), p. 214. For a related but significantly different view see also Henry Sidgwick, *The Methods of Ethics*, 7th edn. (London: Dover Press, 1907), pp. 220–21, 492–93.

murder and give everything they do not really need to famine relief, they will do neither, whereas if we tell them that they ought to refrain from murder and that it is good to give to famine relief but not wrong not to do so, they will at least refrain from murder. The issue here is: Where should we draw the line between conduct that is required and conduct that is good although not required, so as to get the best possible result? This would seem to be an empirical question, although a very difficult one. One objection to the Sidgwick-Urmson line of argument is that it takes insufficient account of the effect that moral standards can have on the decisions we make. Given a society in which a wealthy man who gives 5 per cent of his income to famine relief is regarded as most generous, it is not surprising that a proposal that we all ought to give away half our incomes will be thought to be absurdly unrealistic. In a society which held that no man should have more than enough while others have less than they need, such a proposal might seem narrow-minded. What it is possible for a man to do and what he is likely to do are both, I think, very greatly influenced by what people around him are doing and expecting him to do. In any case, the possibility that by spreading the idea that we ought to be doing very much more than we are to relieve famine we shall bring about a general breakdown of moral behavior seems remote. If the stakes are an end to widespread starvation, it is worth the risk. Finally, it should be emphasized that these considerations are relevant only to the issue of what we should require from others, and not to what we ourselves ought to do.

The second objection to my attack on the present distinction between duty and charity is one which has from time to time been made against utilitarianism. It follows from some forms of utilitarian theory that we all ought, morally, to be working full time to increase the balance of happiness over misery. The position I have taken here would not lead to this conclusion in all circumstances, for if there were no bad occurrences that we could prevent without sacrificing something of comparable moral importance, my argument would have no application. Given the present conditions in many parts of the world, however, it does follow from my argument that we ought, morally, to be working full time to relieve great suffering of the sort that occurs as a result of famine or other disasters. Of course, mitigating circumstances can be adduced—for instance, that if we wear ourselves out through overwork, we shall be less effective than we would otherwise have been. Nevertheless, when all considerations of this sort have been taken into account, the conclusion remains: we ought to be preventing as much suffering as we can without sacrificing something else of comparable moral importance. This conclusion is one which we may be reluctant to face. I cannot see, though, why it should be regarded as a criticism of the position for which I have argued, rather than a criticism of our ordinary standards of behavior. Since most people are self-interested to some degree, very few of us are likely to do everything that we ought to do. It would, however, hardly be honest to take this as evidence that it is not the case that we ought to do it.

It may still be thought that my conclusions are so wildly out of line with what everyone else thinks and has always thought that there must be something wrong with the argument somewhere. In order to show that my conclusions, while certainly contrary to contemporary Western moral standards, would not have seemed so extraordinary at other times and in other places, I would like to quote a passage from a writer not normally thought of as a way-out radical, Thomas Aquinas.

> Now, according to the natural order instituted by divine providence, material goods are provided for the satisfaction of human needs. Therefore the division and appropriation of property, which proceeds from human law, must not hinder the satisfaction of man's necessity from such goods. Equally, whatever a man has in superabundance is owed, of natural right, to the poor for their sustenance. So Ambrosius says, and it is also to be found in the *Decretum Gratiani:* "The bread which you withhold belongs to the hungry; the clothing you shut away, to the naked; and the money you bury in the earth is the redemption and freedom of the penniless."[4]

I now want to consider a number of points, more practical than philosophical, which are relevant to the application of the moral conclusion we have reached. These points challenge not the idea that we ought to be doing all we can to prevent starvation, but the idea that giving away a great deal of money is the best means to this end.

It is sometimes said that overseas aid should be a government responsibility, and that therefore one ought not to give to privately run charities. Giving privately, it is said, allows the government and the non-contributing members of society to escape their responsibilities.

This argument seems to assume that the more people there are who give to privately organized famine relief funds, the less likely it is that the government will take over full responsibility for such aid. This assumption is unsupported, and does not strike me as at all plausible. The opposite view—that if no one gives voluntarily, a government will assume that its citizens are uninterested in famine relief and would not wish to be forced into giving aid—seems more plausible. In any case, unless there were a definite probability that by refusing to give one would be helping to bring about massive government assistance, people who do refuse to make voluntary contributions are refusing to prevent a certain amount of suffering without being able to point to any tangible beneficial consequence of their refusal. So the onus of showing how their refusal will bring about government action is on those who refuse to give.

I do not, of course, want to dispute the contention that governments of affluent nations should be giving many times the amount of genuine, no-strings-attached aid that they are giving now. I agree, too, that giving privately is not enough, and that we ought to be campaigning actively for entirely new standards for both public and private contributions to famine relief. Indeed I would sympathize with someone who thought that campaigning was more important than giving oneself, although I doubt whether preaching what one does not practice would be very effective. Unfortunately, for many people the idea that "it's the government's responsibility" is a reason for not giving which does not appear to entail any political action either.

---

[4] *Summa Theologica*, II–II, Question 66, Article 7, in *Aquinas, Selected Political Writings*, ed. A. P. d'Entreves, trans. J. G. Dawson (Oxford: Basil Blackwell, 1948), p. 171.

Another, more serious, reason for not giving to famine relief funds is that until there is effective population control, relieving famine merely postpones starvation. If we save the Bengal refugees now, others, perhaps the children of these refugees, will face starvation in a few years time. In support of this, one may cite the now well-known facts about the population explosion and the relatively limited scope for expanded production.

This point, like the previous one, is an argument against relieving suffering that is happening now, because of a belief about what might happen in the future; it is unlike the previous point in that very good evidence can be adduced in support of this belief about the future. I will not go into the evidence here. I accept that the earth cannot support indefinitely a population rising at the present rate. This certainly poses a problem for anyone who thinks it important to prevent famine. Again, however, one could accept the argument without drawing the conclusion that it absolves one from any obligation to do anything to prevent famine. The conclusion that should be drawn is that the best means of preventing famine, in the long run, is population control. It would then follow from the position reached earlier that one ought to be doing all one can to promote population control (unless one held that all forms of population control were wrong in themselves, or would have significantly bad consequences). Since there are organizations working specifically for population control, one would then support them rather than more orthodox methods of preventing famine.

A third point raised by the conclusion reached earlier relates to the question of just how much we all ought to be giving away. One possibility, which has already been mentioned, is that we ought to give until we reach the level of marginal utility—that is, the level at which, by giving more, I would cause as much suffering to myself or my dependents as I would relieve by my gift. This would mean, of course, that one would reduce oneself to very near the material circumstances of a Bengali refugee. It will be recalled that earlier I put forward both a strong and a moderate version of the principle of preventing bad occurrences. The strong version, which required us to prevent bad things from happening unless in doing so we would be sacrificing something of comparable moral significance, does seem to require reducing ourselves to the level of marginal utility. I should also say that the strong version seems to me to be the correct one. I proposed the more moderate version—that we should prevent bad occurrences unless, to do so, we had to sacrifice something morally significant—only in order to show that even on this surely undeniable principle a great change in our way of life is required. On the more moderate principle, it may not follow that we ought to reduce ourselves to the level of marginal utility, for one might hold that to reduce oneself and one's family to this level is to cause something significantly bad to happen. Whether this is so I shall not discuss, since, as I have said, I can see no good reason for holding the moderate version of the principle rather than the strong version. Even if we accepted the principle only in its moderate form, however, it should be clear that we would have to give away enough to ensure that the consumer society, dependent as it is on people spending on trivia rather than giving to famine relief, would slow down and perhaps disappear entirely. There are several reasons why this would be desirable in itself. The value and necessity of economic growth are now being questioned not only by conservationists, but by economists as well.[5] There is no doubt, too, that the consumer society has had a distorting effect on the goals and purposes of its members. Yet looking at the matter purely from the point of view of overseas aid, there must be a limit to the extent to which we should deliberately slow down our economy; for it might be the case that if we gave away, say, 40 per cent of our Gross National Product, we would slow down the economy so much that in absolute terms we would be giving less than if we gave 25 per cent of the much larger GNP that we would have if we limited our contribution to this smaller percentage.

I mention this only as an indication of the sort of factor that one would have to take into account in working out an ideal. Since Western societies generally consider one per cent of the GNP an acceptable level for overseas aid, the matter is entirely academic. Nor does it affect the question of how much an individual should give in a society in which very few are giving substantial amounts.

It is sometimes said, though less often now than it used to be, that philosophers have no special role to play in public affairs, since most public issues depend primarily on an assessment of facts. On questions of fact, it is said, philosophers as such have no special expertise, and so it has been possible to engage in philosophy without committing oneself to any position on major public issues. No doubt there are some issues of social policy and foreign policy about which it can truly be said that a really expert assessment of the facts is required before taking sides or acting, but the issue of famine is surely not one of these. The facts about the existence of suffering are beyond dispute. Nor, I think, is it disputed that we can do something about it, either through orthodox methods of famine relief or through population control or both. This is therefore an issue on which philosophers are competent to take a position. The issue is one which faces everyone who has more money than he needs to support himself and his dependents, or who is in a position to take some sort of political action. These categories must include practically every teacher and student of philosophy in the universities of the Western world. If philosophy is to deal with matters that are relevant to both teachers and students, this is an issue that philosophers should discuss.

Discussion, though, is not enough. What is the point of relating philosophy to public (and personal) affairs if we do not take our conclusions seriously? In this instance, taking our conclusion seriously means acting upon it. The philosopher will not find it any easier than anyone else to alter his attitudes and way of life to the extent that, if I am right, is involved in doing everything that we ought to be doing. At the very least, though, one can make a start. The philosopher who does so will have to sacrifice

[5] See, for instance, John Kenneth Galbraith, *The New Industrial State* (Boston: Houghton Mifflin, 1967); and E. J. Mishan, *The Costs of Economic Growth* (New York: Praeger, 1967).

some of the benefits of the consumer society, but he can find compensation in the satisfaction of a way of life in which theory and practice, if not yet in harmony, are at least coming together.

The Morality of Abortion

26. An Almost Absolute Value in History   John T. Noonan, Jr.

John T. Noonan, Jr. (1926–) is professor of law at the University of Southern California Law School. He is the author and editor of many books on social and legal issues.

The most fundamental question involved in the long history of thought on abortion is: How do you determine the humanity of a being? To phrase the question that way is to put in comprehensive humanistic terms what the theologians either dealt with as an explicitly theological question under the heading of "ensoulment" or dealt with implicitly in their treatment of abortion. The Christian position as it originated did not depend on a narrow theological or philosophical concept. It had no relation to theories of infant baptism.[1] It appealed to no special theory of instantaneous ensoulment. It took the world's view on ensoulment as that view changed from Aristotle to Zacchia. There was, indeed, theological influence affecting the theory of ensoulment, finally adopted, and, of course, ensoulment itself was a theological concept, so that the position was always explained in theological terms. But the theological notion of ensoulment could easily be translated into humanistic language by substituting "human" for "rational soul"; the problem of knowing when a man is a man is common to theology and humanism.

If one steps outside the specific categories used by the theologians, the answer they gave can be analyzed as a refusal to discriminate among human beings on the basis of their varying potentialities. Once conceived, the being was recognized as man because he had man's potential. The criterion for humanity, thus, was simple and all-embracing: if you are conceived by human parents, you are human.

Reprinted by permission of the publishers, from The Morality of Abortion: Legal and Historical Perspectives, John T. Noonan, Jr., ed., Cambridge, Mass.: Harvard University Press, (c) 1970 by the President and Fellows of Harvard College.

[1] According to Glanville Williams (*The Sanctity of Human Life supra* n. 169, at 193), "The historical reason for the Catholic objection to abortion is the same as for the Christian Church's historical opposition to infanticide: the horror of bringing about the death of an unbaptized child." This statement is made without any citation of evidence. As has been seen, desire to administer baptism could, in the Middle Ages, even be urged as a reason for procuring an abortion. It is highly regrettable that the American Law Institute was apparently misled by Williams' account and repeated after him the same baseless statement. See Americna Law Institute, *Model Penal Code: Tentative Draft No. 9* (1959), p. 148, n. 12.

The strength of this position may be tested by a review of some of the other distinctions offered in the contemporary controversy over legalizing abortion. Perhaps the most popular distinction is in terms of viability. Before an age of so many months, the fetus is not viable, that is, it cannot be removed from the mother's womb and live apart from her. To that extent, the life of the fetus is absolutely dependent on the life of the mother. This dependence is made the basis of denying recognition to its humanity.

There are difficulties with this distinction. One is that the perfection of artificial incubation may make the fetus viable at any time: it may be removed and artificially sustained. Experiments with animals already show that such a procedure is possible. This hypothetical extreme case relates to an actual difficulty: there is considerable elasticity to the idea of viability. Mere length of life is not an exact measure. The viability of the fetus depends on the extent of its anatomical and functional development. The weight and length of the fetus are better guides to the state of its development than age, but weight and length vary. Moreover, different racial groups have different ages at which their fetuses are viable. Some evidence, for example, suggests that Negro fetuses mature more quickly than white fetuses. If viability is the norm, the standard would vary with race and with many individual circumstances.

The most important objection to this approach is that dependence is not ended by viability. The fetus is still absolutely dependent on someone's care in order to continue existence; indeed a child of one or three or even five years of age is absolutely dependent on another's care for existence; uncared for, the older fetus or the younger child will die as surely as the early fetus detached from the mother. The unsubstantial lessening in dependence at viability does not seem to signify any special acquisition of humanity.

A second distinction has been attempted in terms of experience. A being who has had experience, has lived and suffered, who possesses memories, is more human than one who has not. Humanity depends on formation by experience. The fetus is thus "unformed" in the most basic human sense.

This distinction is not serviceable for the embryo which is already experiencing and reacting. The embryo is responsive to touch after eight weeks and at least at that point is experiencing. At an earlier stage the zygote is certainly alive and responding to its environment. The distinction may also be challenged by the rare case where aphasia has erased adult memory: has it erased humanity? More fundamentally, this distinction leaves even the older fetus or the younger child to be treated as an unformed inhuman thing. Finally, it is not clear why experience as such confers humanity. It could be argued that certain central experiences such as loving or learning are necessary to make a man human. But then human beings who have failed to love or to learn might be excluded from the class called man.

A third distinction is made by appeal to the sentiments of adults. If a fetus dies, the grief of the parents is not the grief they would have for a living child. The fetus is an unnamed "it" till birth, and is not perceived as personality until at least the fourth month of existence when movements in the womb manifest a vigorous presence demanding joyful recognition by the parents.

Yet feeling is notoriously an unsure guide to the humanity of others. Many groups of humans have had difficulty in feeling that persons of another tongue, color, religion, sex, are as human as they. Apart from reactions to alien groups, we mourn the loss of a ten-year-old boy more than the loss of his one-day-old brother or his 90-year-old grandfather. The difference felt and the grief expressed vary with the potentialities extinguished, or the experience wiped out; they do not seem to point to any substantial difference in the humanity of baby, boy, or grandfather.

Distinctions are also made in terms of sensation by the parents. The embryo is felt within the womb only after about the fourth month. The embryo is seen only at birth. What can be neither seen nor felt is different from what is tangible. If the fetus cannot be seen or touched at all, it cannot be perceived as man.

Yet experience shows that sight is even more untrustworthy than feeling in determining humanity. By sight, color became an appropriate index for saying who was a man, and the evil of racial discrimination was given foundation. Nor can touch provide the test; a being confined by sickness, "out of touch" with others, does not thereby seem to lose his humanity. To the extent that touch still has appeal as a criterion, it appears to be a survival of the old English idea of "quickening"—a possible mistranslation of the Latin *animatus* used in the canon law. To that extent touch as a criterion seems to be dependent on the Aristotelian notion of ensoulment, and to fall when this notion is discarded.

Finally, a distinction is sought in social visibility. The fetus is not socially perceived as human. It cannot communicate with others. Thus, both subjectively and objectively, it is not a member of society. As moral rules are rules for the behavior of members of society to each other, they cannot be made for behavior toward what is not yet a member. Excluded from the society of men, the fetus is excluded from the humanity of men.[2]

By force of the argument from the consequences, this distinction is to be rejected. It is more subtle than that founded on an appeal to physical sensation, but it is equally dangerous in its implications. If humanity depends on social recognition, individuals or whole groups may be dehumanized by being denied any status in their society. Such a fate is fictionally portrayed in *1984* and has actually been the lot of many men in many societies. In the Roman empire, for example, condemnation to slavery meant the practical denial of most human rights; in the Chinese Communist world, landlords have been classified as enemies of the people and so treated as nonpersons by the state. Humanity does not depend

---

[2] . . . Thomas Aquinas gave an analogous reason against baptizing a fetus in the womb: "As long as it exists in the womb of the mother, it cannot be subject to the operation of the ministers of the Church as it is not known to men" (*In sententias Petri Lombardi* 4.6 1.1.2).

on social recognition, though often the failure of society to recognize the prisoner, the alien, the heterodox as human has led to the destruction of human beings. Anyone conceived by a man and a woman is human. Recognition of this condition by society follows a real event in the objective order, however imperfect and halting the recognition. Any attempt to limit humanity to exclude some group runs the risk of furnishing authority and precedent for excluding other groups in the name of the consciousness or perception of the controlling group in the society.

A philosopher may reject the appeal to the humanity of the fetus because he views "humanity" as a secular view of the soul and because he doubts the existence of anything real and objective which can be identified as humanity. One answer to such a philosopher is to ask how he reasons about moral questions without supposing that there is a sense in which he and the others of whom he speaks are human. Whatever group is taken as the society which determines who may be killed is thereby taken as human. A second answer is to ask if he does not believe that there is a right and wrong way of deciding moral questions. If there is such a difference, experience may be appealed to: to decide who is human on the basis of the sentiment of a given society has led to consequences which rational men would characterize as monstrous.

The rejection of the attempted distinctions based on viability and visibility, experience and feeling, may be buttressed by the following considerations: Moral judgments often rest on distinctions, but if the distinctions are not to appear arbitrary *fiat*, they should relate to some real difference in probabilities. There is a kind of continuity in all life, but the earlier stages of the elements of human life possess tiny probabilities of development. Consider for example, the spermatozoa in any normal ejaculate: There are about 200,000,000 in any single ejaculate, of which one has a chance of developing into a zygote. Consider the oocytes which may become ova: there are 100,000 to 1,000,000 oocytes in a female infant, of which a maximum of 390 are ovulated. But once spermatozoon and ovum meet and the conceptus is formed, such studies as have been made show that roughly in only 20 percent of the cases will spontaneous abortion occur. In other words, the chances are about 4 out of 5 that this new being will develop. At this stage in the life of the being there is a sharp shift in probabilities, an immense jump in potentialities. To make a distinction between the rights of spermatozoa and the rights of the fertilized ovum is to respond to an enormous shift in possibilities. For about twenty days after conception the egg may split to form twins or combine with another egg to form a chimera, but the probability of either event happening is very small.

It may be asked, What does a change in biological probabilities have to do with establishing humanity? The argument from probabilities is not aimed at establishing humanity but at establishing an objective discontinuity which may be taken into account in moral discourse. As life itself is a matter of probabilities, as most moral reasoning is an estimate of probabilities, so it seems in accord with the structure of reality and the nature of moral thought to found a moral judgment on the change in probabilities at conception. The appeal to probabilities is the most commonsensical of arguments, to a greater or smaller degree all of us base our actions on probabilities, and in morals, as in law, prudence and negligence are often measured by the account one has taken of the probabilities. If the chance is 200,000,000 to 1 that the movement in the bushes into which you shoot is a man's, I doubt if many persons would hold you careless in shooting; but if the chances are 4 out of 5 that the movement is a human being's, few would acquit you of blame. Would the argument be different if only one out of ten children conceived came to term? Of course this argument would be different. This argument is an appeal to probabilities that actually exist, not to any and all state of affairs which may be imagined.

The probabilities as they do exist do not show the humanity of the embryo in the sense of a demonstration in logic any more than the probabilities of the movement in the bush being a man demonstrate beyond all doubt that the being is a man. The appeal is a "buttressing" consideration, showing the plausibility of the standard adopted. The argument focuses on the decisional factor in any moral judgment and assumes that part of the business of a moralist is drawing lines. One evidence of the nonarbitrary character of the line drawn is the difference of probabilities on either side of it. If a spermatozoon is destroyed, one destroys a being which had a chance of far less than 1 in 200 million of developing into a reasoning being, possessed of the genetic code, a heart and other organs, and capable of pain. If a fetus is destroyed, one destroys a being already possessed of the genetic code, organs, and sensitivity to pain, and one which had an 80 percent chance of developing further into a baby outside the womb who, in time, would reason.

The positive argument for conception as the decisive moment of humanization is that at conception the new being receives the genetic code. It is this genetic information which determines his characteristics, which is the biological carrier of the possibility of human wisdom, which makes him a self-evolving being. A being with a human genetic code is man.

This review of current controversy over the humanity of the fetus emphasizes what a fundamental question the theologians resolved in asserting the inviolability of the fetus. To regard the fetus as possessed of equal rights with other humans was not, however, to decide every case where abortion might be employed. It did decide the case where the argument was that the fetus should be aborted for its own good. To say a being was human was to say it had a destiny to decide for itself which could not be taken from it by another man's decision. But human beings with equal rights often come in conflict with each other, and some decision must be made as whose claims are to prevail. Cases of conflict involving the fetus are different only in two respects: the total inability of the fetus to speak for itself and the fact that the right of the fetus regularly at stake is the right to life itself.

The approach taken by the theologians to these conflicts was articulated in terms of "direct" and "indirect." Again, to look at what they were doing from outside their categories, they may be said to have been drawing lines or "balancing values." "Direct" and "indirect" are spatial metaphors; "line-drawing" is another. "To weigh" or "to balance" values is a metaphor of a more complicated mathematical sort hinting at the process which goes on in moral judgments. All the metaphors suggest that, in the moral judgments made, comparisons were necessary, that no value completely controlled. The principle of double effect was no doctrine fallen from heaven, but a method of analysis appropriate where two relative values were being compared. In Catholic moral theology, as it developed, life even of the innocent was not taken as an absolute. Judgments on acts affecting life issued from a process of weighing. In the weighing, the fetus was always given a value greater than zero, always a value separate and independent from its parents. This valuation was crucial and fundamental in all Christian thought on the subject and marked it off from any approach which considered that only the parents' interests needed to be considered.

Even with the fetus weighed as human, one interest could be weighed as equal or superior: that of the mother in her own life. The casuists between 1450 and 1895 were willing to weigh this interest as superior. Since 1895, that interest was given decisive weight only in the two special cases of the cancerous uterus and the ectopic pregnancy. In both of these cases the fetus itself had little chance of survival even if the abortion were not performed. As the balance was once struck in favor of the mother whenever her life was endangered, it could be so struck again. The balance reached between 1895 and 1930 attempted prudentially and pastorally to forestall a multitude of exceptions for interests less than life.

The perception of the humanity of the fetus and the weighing of fetal rights against other human rights constituted the work of the moral analysts. But what spirit animated their abstract judgments? For the Christian community it was the injunction of Scripture to love your neighbor as yourself. The fetus as human was a neighbor; his life had parity with one's own. The commandment gave life to what otherwise would have been only rational calculation.

The commandment could be put in humanistic as well as theological terms: Do not injure your fellow man without reason. In these terms, once the humanity of the fetus is perceived, abortion is never right except in self-defense. When life must be taken to save life, reason alone cannot say that a mother must prefer a child's life to her own. With this exception, now of great rarity, abortion violates the rational humanist tenet of the equality of human lives.

For Christians the commandment to love had received a special imprint in that the exemplar proposed of love was the love of the Lord for his disciples. In the light given by this example, self-sacrifice carried to the point of death seemed in the extreme situations not without meaning. In the less extreme cases, preference for one's own interests to the life of another seemed to express cruelty or selfishness irreconcilable with the demands of love.

27. A Defense of Abortion[1]   Judith Jarvis Thomson

Judith Jarvis Thomson, professor of philosophy at Massachusetts Institute of Technology, is coeditor of an anthology entitled *Ethics* and the author of numerous articles that have appeared in philosophical journals both here and abroad.

Most opposition to abortion relies on the premise that the fetus is a human being, a person, from the moment of conception. The premise is argued for, but, as I think, not well. Take, for example, the most common argument. We are asked to notice that the development of a human being from conception through birth into childhood is continuous; then it is said that to draw a line, to choose a point in this development and say "before this point the thing is not a person, after this point it is a person" is to make an arbitrary choice, a choice for which in the nature of things no good reason can be given. It is concluded that the fetus is, or anyway that we had better say it is, a person from the moment of conception. But this conclusion does not follow. Similar things might be said about the development of an acorn into an oak tree, and it does not follow that acorns are oak trees, or that we had better say they are. Arguments of this form are sometimes called "slippery slope arguments"— the phrase is perhaps self-explanatory—and it is dismaying that opponents of abortion rely on them so heavily and uncritically.

I am inclined to agree, however, that the prospects for "drawing a line" in the development of the fetus look dim. I am inclined to think also that we shall probably have to agree that the fetus has already become a human person well before birth. Indeed, it comes as a surprise when one first learns how early in its life it begins to acquire human characteristics. By the tenth week, for example, it already has a face, arms and legs, fingers and toes; it has internal organs, and brain activity is detectable.[2] On the other hand, I think that the premise is false, that the fetus is not a person from the moment of conception. A newly fertilized ovum, a newly implanted clump of cells, is no more a person than an acorn is an oak tree. But I shall not discuss any of this. For it seems to me to be of great interest to ask what happens if, for the sake of argument, we allow the premise. How, precisely, are we supposed to get from there to the conclusion that abortion is morally impermissible? Opponents of abortion commonly spend most of their time establishing that the fetus

"A Defense of Abortion," by Judith Jarvis Thomson. *Philosophy and Public Affairs*, vol. 1, no. 1 (Fall 1971) Copyright © 1971 by Princeton University Press, pp. 47–66. Reprinted by permission of Princeton University Press.

[1] I am very much indebted to James Thomson for discussion, criticism, and many helpful suggestions.

[2] Daniel Callahan, *Abortion: Law, Choice and Morality* (New York, 1970), p. 373. This book gives a fascinating survey of the available information on abortion. The Jewish tradition is surveyed in David M. Feldman, *Birth Control in Jewish Law* (New York, 1968), Part 5, the Catholic tradition in John T. Noonan, Jr., "An Almost Absolute Value in History," in *The Morality of Abortion,* ed. John T. Noonan, Jr. (Cambridge, Mass., 1970).

is a person, and hardly any time explaining the step from there to the impermissibility of abortion. Perhaps they think the step too simple and obvious to require much comment. Or perhaps instead they are simply being economical in argument. Many of those who defend abortion rely on the premise that the fetus is not a person, but only a bit of tissue that will become a person at birth; and why pay out more arguments than you have to? Whatever the explanation, I suggest that the step they take is neither easy nor obvious, that it calls for closer examination than it is commonly given, and that when we do give it this closer examination we shall feel inclined to reject it.

I propose, then, that we grant that the fetus is a person from the moment of conception. How does the argument go from here? Something like this, I take it. Every person has a right to life. So the fetus has a right to life. No doubt the mother has a right to decide what shall happen in and to her body; everyone would grant that. But surely a person's right to life is stronger and more stringent than the mother's right to decide what happens in and to her body, and so outweighs it. So the fetus may not be killed: an abortion may not be performed.

It sounds plausible. But now let me ask you to imagine this. You wake up in the morning and find yourself back to back in bed with an unconscious violinist. A famous unconscious violinist. He has been found to have a fatal kidney ailment, and the Society of Music Lovers has canvassed all the available medical records and found that you alone have the right blood type to help. They have therefore kidnapped you, and last night the violinist's circulatory system was plugged into yours, so that your kidneys can be used to extract poisons from his blood as well as your own. The director of the hospital now tells you, "Look, we're sorry the Society of Music Lovers did this to you—we would never have permitted it if we had known. But still, they did it, and the violinist now is plugged into you. To unplug you would be to kill him. But never mind, it's only for nine months. By then he will have recovered from his ailment, and can safely be unplugged from you." Is it morally incumbent on you to accede to this situation? No doubt it would be very nice of you if you did, a great kindness. But do you *have* to accede to it? What if it were not nine months, but nine years? Or longer still? What if the director of the hospital says, "Tough luck, I agree, but you've now got to stay in bed, with the violinist plugged into you, for the rest of your life. Because remember this. All persons have a right to life, and violinists are persons. Granted you have a right to decide what happens in and to your body, but a person's right to life outweighs your right to decide what happens in and to your body. So you cannot ever be unplugged from him." I imagine you would regard this as outrageous, which suggests that something really is wrong with that plausible-sounding argument I mentioned a moment ago.

In this case, of course, you were kidnapped; you didn't volunteer for the operation that plugged the violinist into your kidneys. Can those who oppose abortion on the ground I mentioned make an exception for a pregnancy due to rape? Certainly. They can say that persons have a right to life only if they didn't come into existence because of rape; or they can say that all persons have a right to life, but that some have less of a right to life than others, in particular, that those who came into existence because of rape have less. But these statements have a rather unpleasant sound. Surely the question of whether you have a right to life at all, or how much of it you have, shouldn't turn on the question of whether or not you are the product of a rape. And in fact the people who oppose abortion on the ground I mentioned do not make this distinction, and hence do not make an exception in case of rape.

Nor do they make an exception for a case in which the mother has to spend the nine months of her pregnancy in bed. They would agree that would be a great pity, and hard on the mother; but all the same, all persons have a right to life, the fetus is a person, and so on. I suspect, in fact, that they would not make an exception for a case in which, miraculously enough, the pregnancy went on for nine years, or even the rest of the mother's life.

Some won't even make an exception for a case in which continuation of the pregnancy is likely to shorten the mother's life; they regard abortion as impermissible even to save the mother's life. Such cases are nowadays very rare, and many opponents of abortion do not accept this extreme view. All the same, it is a good place to begin: a number of points of interest come out in respect to it.

1. Let us call the view that abortion is impermissible even to save the mother's life "the extreme view." I want to suggest first that it does not issue from the argument I mentioned earlier without the addition of some fairly powerful premises. Suppose a woman has become pregnant, and now learns that she has a cardiac condition such that she will die if she carries the baby to term. What may be done for her? The fetus, being a person, has a right to life, but as the mother is a person too, so has she a right to life. Presumably they have an equal right to life. How is it supposed to come out that an abortion may not be performed? If mother and child have an equal right to life, shouldn't we perhaps flip a coin? Or should we add to the mother's right to life her right to decide what happens in and to her body, which everybody seems to be ready to grant—the sum of her rights now outweighing the fetus' right to life?

The most familiar argument here is the following. We are told that performing the abortion would be directly killing[3] the child, whereas doing nothing would not be killing the mother, but only letting her die. Moreover, in killing the child, one would be killing an innocent person, for the child has committed no crime, and is not aiming at his mother's death. And then there are a variety of ways in which this might be continued. (1) But as directly killing an innocent person is always and absolutely impermissible, an abortion may not be performed. Or, (2) as directly killing an innocent person is murder, and murder is always and

---

[3] The term "direct" in the arguments I refer to is a technical one. Roughly, what is meant by "direct killing" is either killing as an end in itself, or killing as a means to some end, for example, the end of saving someone else's life. See note 6, below, for an example of its use.

absolutely impermissible, an abortion may not be performed.[4] Or, (3) as one's duty to refrain from directly killing an innocent person is more stringent than one's duty to keep a person from dying, an abortion may not be performed. Or, (4) if one's only options are directly killing an innocent person or letting a person die, one must prefer letting the person die, and thus an abortion may not be performed.[5]

Some people seem to have thought that these are not further premises which must be added if the conclusion is to be reached, but that they follow from the very fact that an innocent person has a right to life.[6] But this seems to me to be a mistake, and perhaps the simplest way to show this is to bring out that while we must certainly grant that innocent persons have a right to life, the theses in (1) through (4) are all false. Take (2), for example. If directly killing an innocent person is murder, and thus is impermissible, then the mother's directly killing the innocent person inside her is murder, and thus is impermissible. But it cannot seriously be thought to be murder if the mother performs an abortion on herself to save her life. It cannot seriously be said that she *must* refrain, that she *must* sit passively by and wait for her death. Let us look again at the case of you and the violinist. There you are, in bed with the violinist, and the director of the hospital says to you, "It's all most distressing, and I deeply sympathize, but you see this is putting an additional strain on your kidneys, and you'll be dead within the month. But you *have* to stay where you are all the same. Because unplugging you would be directly killing an innocent violinist, and that's murder, and that's impermissible." If anything in the world is true, it is that you do not commit murder, you do not do what is impermissible, if you reach around to your back and unplug yourself from the violinist to save your life.

The main focus of attention in writings on abortion has been on what a third party may or may not do in answer to a request from a woman for an abortion. This is in a way understandable. Things being as they are, there isn't much a woman can surely do to abort herself. So the question asked is what a third party may do, and what the mother may do, if it is mentioned at all, is deduced, almost as an afterthought, from

---

[4] Cf. *Encyclical Letter of Pope Pius XI on Christian Marriage*, St. Paul Editions (Boston, n.d.), p. 32: "however much we may pity the mother whose health and even life is gravely imperiled in the performance of the duty allotted to her by nature, nevertheless what could ever be a sufficient reason for excusing in any way the direct murder of the innocent? This is precisely what we are dealing with here." Noonan (*The Morality of Abortion*, p. 43) reads this as follows: "What cause can ever avail to excuse in any way the direct killing of the innocent? For it is a question of that."

[5] The thesis in (4) is in an interesting way weaker than those in (1), (2), and (3): they rule out abortion even in cases in which both mother *and* child will die if the abortion is not performed. By contrast, one who held the view expressed in (4) could consistently say that one needn't prefer letting two persons die to killing one.

[6] Cf. the following passage from Pius XII, *Address to the Italian Catholic Society of Midwives*: "The baby in the maternal breast has the right to life immediately from God.—Hence there is no man, no human authority, no science, no medical, eugenic, social, economic or moral 'indication' which can establish or grant a valid juridical ground for a direct deliberate disposition of an innocent human life, that is a disposition which looks to its destruction either as an end or as a means to another end perhaps in itself not illicit.— The baby, still not born, is a man in the same degree and for the same reason as the mother" (quoted in Noonan, *The Morality of Abortion*, p. 45).

what it is concluded that third parties may do. But it seems to me that to treat the matter in this way is to refuse to grant to the mother that very status of person which is so firmly insisted on for the fetus. For we cannot simply read off what a person may do from what a third party may do. Suppose you find yourself trapped in a tiny house with a growing child. I mean a very tiny house, and a rapidly growing child—you are already up against the wall of the house and in a few minutes you'll be crushed to death. The child on the other hand won't be crushed to death; if nothing is done to stop him from growing he'll be hurt, but in the end he'll simply burst open the house and walk out a free man. Now I could well understand it if a bystander were to say, "There's nothing we can do for you. We cannot choose between your life and his, we cannot be the ones to decide who is to live, we cannot intervene." But it cannot be concluded that you too can do nothing, that you cannot attack it to save your life. However innocent the child may be, you do not have to wait passively while it crushes you to death. Perhaps a pregnant woman is vaguely felt to have the status of house, to which we don't allow the right of self-defense. But if the woman houses the child, it should be remembered that she is a person who houses it.

I should perhaps stop to say explicitly that I am not claiming that people have a right to do anything whatever to save their lives. I think, rather, that there are drastic limits to the right of self-defense. If someone threatens you with death unless you torture someone else to death, I think you have not the right, even to save your life, to do so. But the case under consideration here is very different. In our case there are only two people involved, one whose life is threatened, and one who threatens it. Both are innocent; the one who is threatened is not threatened because of any fault, the one who threatens does not threaten because of any fault. For this reason we may feel that we bystanders cannot intervene. But the person threatened can.

In sum, a woman surely can defend her life against the threat to it posed by the unborn child, even if doing so involves its death. And this shows not merely that the theses in (1) through (4) are false; it shows also that the extreme view of abortion is false, and so we need not canvass any other possible ways of arriving at it from the argument I mentioned at the outset.

2. The extreme view could of course be weakened to say that while abortion is permissible to save the mother's life, it may not be performed by a third party, but only by the mother herself. But this cannot be right either. For what we have to keep in mind is that the mother and the unborn child are not like two tenants in a small house which has, by an unfortunate mistake, been rented to both; the mother *owns* the house. The fact that she does adds to the offensiveness of deducing that the mother can do nothing from the supposition that third parties can do nothing. But it does more than this: it casts a bright light on the supposition that third parties can do nothing. Certainly it lets us see that a third party who says "I cannot choose between you" is fooling himself if he thinks this is impartiality. If Jones has found and fastened on a certain coat, which he needs to keep him from freezing, but which Smith

also needs to keep him from freezing, then it is not impartiality that says "I cannot choose between you" when Smith owns the coat. Women have said again and again "This body is *my* body!" and they have reason to feel angry, reason to feel that it has been like shouting into the wind. Smith, after all, is hardly likely to bless us if we say to him, "Of course it's your coat, anybody would grant that it is. But no one may choose between you and Jones who is to have it."

We should really ask what it is that says "no one may choose" in the face of the fact that the body that houses the child is the mother's body. It may be simply a failure to appreciate this fact. But it may be something more interesting, namely the sense that one has a right to refuse to lay hands on people, even where it would be just and fair to do so, even where justice seems to require that somebody do so. Thus justice might call for somebody to get Smith's coat back from Jones, and yet you have a right to refuse to be the one to lay hands on Jones, a right to refuse to do physical violence to him. This, I think, must be granted. But then what should be said is not "no one may choose," but only "*I* cannot choose," and indeed not even this, but "*I* will not *act*," leaving it open that somebody else can or should, and in particular that anyone in a position of authority, with the job of securing people's rights, both can and should. So this is no difficulty. I have not been arguing that any given third party must accede to the mother's request that he perform an abortion to save her life, but only that he may.

I suppose that in some views of human life the mother's body is only on loan to her, the loan not being one which gives her any prior claim to it. One who held this view might well think it impartiality to say "I cannot choose." But I shall simply ignore this possibility. My own view is that if a human being has any just, prior claim to anything at all, he has a just, prior claim to his own body. And perhaps this needn't be argued for here anyway, since, as I mentioned, the arguments against abortion we are looking at do grant that the woman has a right to decide what happens in and to her body.

But although they do grant it, I have tried to show that they do not take seriously what is done in granting it. I suggest the same thing will reappear even more clearly when we turn away from cases in which the mother's life is at stake, and attend, as I propose we now do, to the vastly more common cases in which a woman wants an abortion for some less weighty reason than preserving her own life.

3. Where the mother's life is not at stake, the argument I mentioned at the outset seems to have a much stronger pull. "Everyone has a right to life, so the unborn person has a right to life." And isn't the child's right to life weightier than anything other than the mother's own right to life, which she might put forward as ground for an abortion?

This argument treats the right to life as if it were unproblematic. It is not, and this seems to me to be precisely the source of the mistake.

For we should now, at long last, ask what it comes to, to have a right to life. In some views having a right to life includes having a right to be given at least the bare minimum one needs for continued life. But suppose that what in fact *is* the bare minimum a man needs for continued life is something he has no right at all to be given? If I am sick unto death, and the only thing that will save my life is the touch of Henry Fonda's cool hand on my fevered brow, then all the same, I have no right to be given the touch of Henry Fonda's cool hand on my fevered brow. It would be frightfully nice of him to fly in from the West Coast to provide it. It would be less nice, though no doubt well meant, if my friends flew out to the West Coast and carried Henry Fonda back with them. But I have no right at all against anybody that he should do this for me. Or again, to return to the story I told earlier, the fact that for continued life that violinist needs the continued use of your kidneys does not establish that he has a right to be given the continued use of your kidneys. He certainly has no right against you that *you* should give him continued use of your kidneys. For nobody has any right to use your kidneys unless you give him such a right; and nobody has the right against you that you shall give him this right—if you do allow him to go on using your kidneys, this is a kindness on your part, and not something he can claim from you as his due. Nor has he any right against anybody else that *they* should give him continued use of your kidneys. Certainly he had no right against the Society of Music Lovers that they should plug him into you in the first place. And if you now start to unplug yourself, having learned that you will otherwise have to spend nine years in bed with him, there is nobody in the world who must try to prevent you, in order to see to it that he is given something he has a right to be given.

Some people are rather stricter about the right to life. In their view, it does not include the right to be given anything, but amounts to, and only to, the right not to be killed by anybody. But here a related difficulty arises. If everybody is to refrain from killing that violinist, then everybody must refrain from doing a great many different sorts of things. Everybody must refrain from slitting his throat, everybody must refrain from shooting him—and everybody must refrain from unplugging you from him. But does he have a right against everybody that they shall refrain from unplugging you from him? To refrain from doing this is to allow him to continue to use your kidneys. It could be argued that he has a right against us that *we* should allow him to continue to use your kidneys. That is, while he had no right against us that we should give him the use of your kidneys, it might be argued that he anyway has a right against us that we shall not now intervene and deprive him of the use of your kidneys. I shall come back to third-party interventions later. But certainly the violinist has no right against you that *you* shall allow him to continue to use your kidneys. As I said, if you do allow him to use them, it is a kindness on your part, and not something you owe him.

The difficulty I point to here is not peculiar to the right to life. It reappears in connection with all the other natural rights; and it is something which an adequate account of rights must deal with. For present purposes it is enough just to draw attention to it. But I would stress that I am not arguing that people do not have a right to life—quite to the contrary, it seems to me that the primary control we must place on the acceptability of an account of rights is that it should turn out in that account to be a truth that all persons have a right to life. I am arguing only that having a right to life does not guarantee having either a right to be given the use of or a right to be allowed continued use of another person's body—even if one needs it for life itself. So the right to life will not serve the opponents of abortion in the very simple and clear way in which they seem to have thought it would.

4. There is another way to bring out the difficulty. In the most ordinary sort of case, to deprive someone of what he has a right to is to treat him unjustly. Suppose a boy and his small brother are jointly given a box of chocolates for Christmas. If the older boy takes the box and refuses to give his brother any of the chocolates, he is unjust to him, for the brother has been given a right to half of them. But suppose that, having learned that otherwise it means nine years in bed with that violinist, you unplug yourself from him. You surely are not being unjust to him, for you gave him no right to use your kidneys, and no one else can have given him any such right. But we have to notice that in unplugging yourself, you are killing him; and violinists, like everybody else, have a right to life, and thus in the view we were considering just now, the right not to be killed. So here you do what he supposedly has a right you shall not do, but you do not act unjustly to him in doing it.

The emendation which may be made at this point is this: the right to life consists not in the right not to be killed, but rather in the right not to be killed unjustly. This runs a risk of circularity, but never mind: it would enable us to square the fact that the violinist has a right to life with the fact that you do not act unjustly toward him in unplugging yourself, thereby killing him. For if you do not kill him unjustly, you do not violate his right to life, and so it is no wonder you do him no injustice.

But if this emendation is accepted, the gap in the argument against abortion stares us plainly in the face: it is by no means enough to show that the fetus is a person, and to remind us that all persons have a right to life—we need to be shown also that killing the fetus violates its right to life, i.e., that abortion is unjust killing. And is it?

I suppose we may take it as a datum that in a case of pregnancy due to rape the mother has not given the unborn person a right to the use of her body for food and shelter. Indeed, in what pregnancy could it be supposed that the mother has given the unborn person such a right? It is not as if there were unborn persons drifting about the world, to whom a woman who wants a child says "I invite you in."

But it might be argued that there are other ways one can have acquired a right to the use of another person's body than by having been invited to use it by that person. Suppose a woman voluntarily indulges in intercourse, knowing of the chance it will issue in pregnancy, and then she does become pregnant; is she not in part responsible for the presence, in fact the very existence, of the unborn person inside her? No doubt she did not invite it in. But doesn't her partial responsibility for its being there itself give it a right to the use of her body?[7] If so, then her aborting it would be more like the boy's taking away the chocolates, and less like your unplugging yourself from the violinist—doing so would be depriving it of what it does have a right to, and thus would be doing it an injustice.

[7] The need for a discussion of this argument was brought home to me by members of the Society for Ethical and Legal Philosophy, to whom this paper was originally presented.

And then, too, it might be asked whether or not she can kill it even to save her own life: If she voluntarily called it into existence, how can she now kill it, even in self-defense?

The first thing to be said about this is that it is something new. Opponents of abortion have been so concerned to make out the independence of the fetus, in order to establish that it has a right to life, just as its mother does, that they have tended to overlook the possible support they might gain from making out that the fetus is *dependent* on the mother, in order to establish that she has a special kind of responsibility for it, a responsibility that gives it rights against her which are not possessed by any independent person—such as an ailing violinist who is a stranger to her.

On the other hand, this argument would give the unborn person a right to its mother's body only if her pregnancy resulted from a voluntary act, undertaken in full knowledge of the chance a pregnancy might result from it. It would leave out entirely the unborn person whose existence is due to rape. Pending the availability of some further argument, then, we would be left with the conclusion that unborn persons whose existence is due to rape have no right to the use of their mother's bodies, and thus that aborting them is not depriving them of anything they have a right to and hence is not unjust killing.

And we should also notice that it is not at all plain that this argument really does go even as far as it purports to. For there are cases and cases, and the details make a difference. If the room is stuffy, and I therefore open a window to air it, and a burglar climbs in, it would be absurd to say, "Ah, now he can stay, she's given him a right to the use of her house— for she is partially responsible for his presence there, having voluntarily done what enabled him to get in, in full knowledge that there are such things as burglars, and that burglars burgle." It would be still more absurd to say this if I had had bars installed outside my windows, precisely to prevent burglars from getting in, and a burglar got in only because of a defect in the bars. It remains equally absurd if we imagine it is not a burglar who climbs in, but an innocent person who blunders or falls in. Again, suppose it were like this: people-seeds drift about in the air like pollen, and if you open your windows, one may drift in and take root in your carpets or upholstery. You don't want children, so you fix up your windows with fine mesh screens, the very best you can buy. As can happen, however, and on very, very rare occasions does happen, one of the screens is defective; and a seed drifts in and takes root. Does the person-plant who now develops have a right to the use of your house? Surely not—despite the fact that you voluntarily opened your windows, you knowingly kept carpets and upholstered furniture, and you knew that screens were sometimes defective. Someone may argue that you are responsible for its rooting, that it does have a right to your house, because after all you *could* have lived out your life with bare floors and furniture, or with sealed windows and doors. But this won't do—for by the same token anyone can avoid a pregnancy due to rape by having a hysterectomy, or anyway by never leaving home without a (reliable!) army.

It seems to me that the argument we are looking at can establish at most that there are *some* cases in which the unborn person has a right to the use of its mother's body, and therefore *some* cases in which abortion is unjust killing. There is room for much discussion and argument as to precisely which, if any. But I think we should sidestep this issue and leave it open, for at any rate the argument certainly does not establish that all abortion is unjust killing.

5. There is room for yet another argument here, however. We surely must all grant that there may be cases in which it would be morally indecent to detach a person from your body at the cost of his life. Suppose you learn that what the violinist needs is not nine years of your life, but only one hour; all you need do to save his life is to spend one hour in that bed with him. Suppose also that letting him use your kidneys for that one hour would not affect your health in the slightest. Admittedly you were kidnapped. Admittedly you did not give anyone permission to plug him into you. Nevertheless it seems to me plain you *ought* to allow him to use your kidneys for that hour—it would be indecent to refuse.

Again, suppose pregnancy lasted only an hour, and constituted no threat to life or health. And suppose that a woman becomes pregnant as a result of rape. Admittedly she did not voluntarily do anything to bring about the existence of a child. Admittedly she did nothing at all which would give the unborn person a right to the use of her body. All the same it might well be said, as in the newly emended violinist story, that she *ought* to allow it to remain for that hour—that it would be indecent of her to refuse.

Now some people are inclined to use the term "right" in such a way that it follows from the fact that you ought to allow a person to use your body for the hour he needs, that he has a right to use your body for the hour he needs, even though he has not been given that right by any person or act. They may say that it follows also that if you refuse, you act unjustly toward him. This use of the term is perhaps so common that it cannot be called wrong; nevertheless it seems to me to be an unfortunate loosening of what we would do better to keep a tight rein on. Suppose that box of chocolates I mentioned earlier had not been given to both boys jointly, but was given only to the older boy. There he sits, stolidly eating his way through the box, his small brother watching enviously. Here we are likely to say "You ought not to be so mean. You ought to give your brother some of those chocolates." My own view is that it just does not follow from the truth of this that the brother has any right to any of the chocolates. If the boy refuses to give his brother any, he is greedy, stingy, callous—but not unjust. I suppose that the people I have in mind will say it does follow that the brother has a right to some of the chocolates, and thus that the boy does not unjustly if he refuses to give his brother any. But the effect of saying this is to obscure what we should keep distinct, namely the difference between the boy's refusal in this case and the boy's refusal in the earlier case, in which the box was given to both boys jointly, and in which the small brother thus had what was from any point of view clear title to half.

A further objection to so using the term "right" that from the fact that A ought to do a thing for B, it follows that B has a right against A that A do it for him, is that it is going to make the question of whether or not a man has a right to a thing turn on how easy it is to provide him with it; and this seems not merely unfortunate, but morally unacceptable. Take the case of Henry Fonda again. I said earlier that I had no right to the touch of his cool hand on my fevered brow, even though I needed it to save my life. I said it would be frightfully nice of him to fly in from the West Coast to provide me with it, but that I had no right against him that he should do so. But suppose he isn't on the West Coast. Suppose he has only to walk across the room, place a hand briefly on my brow— and lo, my life is saved. Then surely he ought to do it, it would be indecent to refuse. Is it to be said "Ah, well, it follows that in this case she has a right to the touch of his hand on her brow, and so it would be an injustice in him to refuse"? So that I have a right to it when it is easy for him to provide it, though no right when it's hard? It's rather a shocking idea that anyone's rights should fade away and disappear as it gets harder and harder to accord them to him.

So my own view is that even though you ought to let the violinist use your kidneys for the one hour he needs, we should not conclude that he has a right to do so—we should say that if you refuse, you are, like the boy who owns all the chocolates and will give none away, self-centered and callous, indecent in fact, but not unjust. And similarly, that even supposing a case in which a woman pregnant due to rape ought to allow the unborn person to use her body for the hour he needs, we should not conclude that he has a right to do so; we should conclude that she is self-centered, callous, indecent, but not unjust, if she refuses. The complaints are no less grave; they are just different. However, there is no need to insist on this point. If anyone does wish to deduce "he has a right" from "you ought," then all the same he must surely grant that there are cases in which it is not morally required of you that you allow that violinist to use your kidneys, and in which he does not have a right to use them, and in which you do not do him an injustice if you refuse. And so also for mother and unborn child. Except in such cases as the unborn person has a right to demand it—and we were leaving open the possibility that there may be such cases—nobody is morally *required* to make large sacrifices, of health, of all other interests and concerns, of all other duties and commitments, for nine years, or even for nine months, in order to keep another person alive.

6. We have in fact to distinguish between two kinds of Samaritan: the Good Samaritan and what we might call the Minimally Decent Samaritan. The story of the Good Samaritan, you will remember, goes like this:

> A certain man went down from Jerusalem to Jericho, and fell among thieves, which stripped him of his raiment, and wounded him, and departed, leaving him half dead.
> And by chance there came down a certain priest that way; and when he saw him, he passed by on the other side.
> And likewise a Levite, when he was at the place, came and looked on him, and passed by on the other side.
> But a certain Samaritan, as he journeyed, came where he was; and when he saw him he had compassion on him.
> And went to him, and bound up his wounds, pouring in oil and wine,

and set him on his own beast, and brought him to an inn, and took care
of him.
And on the morrow, when he departed, he took out two pence, and gave
them to the host, and said unto him, "Take care of him; and whatsoever
thou spendest more, when I come again, I will repay thee."

(Luke 10:30–35)

The Good Samaritan went out of his way, at some cost to himself, to
help one in need of it. We are not told what the options were, that is,
whether or not the priest and the Levite could have helped by doing
less than the Good Samaritan did, but assuming they could have, then
the fact they did nothing at all shows they were not even Minimally Decent
Samaritans, not because they were not Samaritans, but because they were
not even minimally decent.

These things are a matter of degree, of course, but there is a difference, and it comes out perhaps most clearly in the story of Kitty Genovese, who, as you will remember, was murdered while thirty-eight people
watched or listened, and did nothing at all to help her. A Good Samaritan
would have rushed out to give direct assistance against the murderer.
Or perhaps we had better allow that it would have been a Splendid Samaritan who did this, on the ground that it would have involved a risk
of death for himself. But the thirty-eight not only did not do this, they
did not even trouble to pick up a phone to call the police. Minimally
Decent Samaritanism would call for doing at least that, and their not
having done it was monstrous.

After telling the story of the Good Samaritan, Jesus said "Go, and
do thou likewise." Perhaps he meant that we are morally required to act
as the Good Samaritan did. Perhaps he was urging people to do more
than is morally required of them. At all events it seems plain that it was
not morally required of any of the thirty-eight that he rush out to give
direct assistance at the risk of his own life, and that it is not morally
required of anyone that he give long stretches of his life—nine years or
nine months—to sustaining the life of a person who has no special right
(we were leaving open the possibility of this) to demand it.

Indeed, with one rather striking class of exceptions, no one in any
country in the world is *legally* required to do anywhere near as much as
this for anyone else. The class of exceptions is obvious. My main concern
here is not the state of the law in respect to abortion, but it is worth
drawing attention to the fact that in no state in this country is any man
compelled by law to be even a Minimally Decent Samaritan to any person;
there is no law under which charges could be brought against the thirty-
eight who stood by while Kitty Genovese died. By contrast, in most states
in this country women are compelled by law to be not merely Minimally
Decent Samaritans, but Good Samaritans to unborn persons inside them.
This doesn't by itself settle anything one way or the other, because it
may well be argued that there should be laws in this country—as there
are in many European countries—compelling at least Minimally Decent
Samaritanism.[8] But it does show that there is a gross injustice in the

---

[8] For a discussion of the difficulties involved, and a survey of the European experience
with such laws, see *The Good Samaritan and the Law,* ed. James M. Ratcliffe (New York,
1966).

existing state of the law. And it shows also that the groups currently working against liberalization of abortion laws, in fact working toward having it declared unconstitutional for a state to permit abortion, had better start working for the adoption of Good Samaritan laws generally, or earn the charge that they are acting in bad faith.

I should think, myself, that Minimally Decent Samaritan laws would be one thing, Good Samaritan laws quite another, and in fact highly improper. But we are not here concerned with the law. What we should ask is not whether anybody should be compelled by law to be a Good Samaritan, but whether we must accede to a situation in which somebody is being compelled—by nature, perhaps—to be a Good Samaritan. We have, in other words, to look now at third-party interventions. I have been arguing that no person is morally required to make large sacrifices to sustain the life of another who has no right to demand them, and this even where the sacrifices do not include life itself: we are not morally required to be Good Samaritans or anyway Very Good Samaritans to one another. But what if a man cannot extricate himself from such a situation? What if he appeals to us to extricate him? It seems to me plain that there are cases in which we can, cases in which a Good Samaritan would extricate him. There you are, you were kidnapped, and nine years in bed with that violinist lie ahead of you. You have your own life to lead. You are sorry, but you simply cannot see giving up so much of your life to the sustaining of his. You cannot extricate yourself, and ask us to do so. I should have thought that—in light of his having no right to the use of your body—it was obvious that we do not have to accede to your being forced to give up so much. We can do what you ask. There is no injustice to the violinist in our doing so.

7. Following the lead of the opponents of abortion, I have throughout been speaking of the fetus merely as a person, and what I have been asking is whether or not the argument we began with, which proceeds only from the fetus being a person, really does establish its conclusion. I have argued that it does not.

But of course there are arguments and arguments, and it may be said that I have simply fastened on the wrong one. It may be said that what is important is not merely the fact that the fetus is a person, but that it is a person for whom the woman has a special kind of responsibility issuing from the fact that she is its mother. And it might be argued that all my analogies are therefore irrelevant—for you do not have that special kind of responsibility for that violinist, Henry Fonda does not have that special kind of responsibility for me. And our attention might be drawn to the fact that men and women both *are* compelled by law to provide support for their children.

I have in effect dealt (briefly) with this argument in section 4 above; but a (still briefer) recapitulation now may be in order. Surely we do not have any such "special responsibility" for a person unless we have assumed it, explicitly or implicitly. If a set of parents do not try to prevent pregnancy, do not obtain an abortion, and then at the time of birth of the child do not put it out for adoption, but rather take it home with them, then they have assumed responsibility for it, they have given it rights, and they cannot *now* withdraw support from it at the cost of its life because they now find it difficult to go on providing for it. But if they have taken all reasonable precautions against having a child, they do not simply by virtue of their biological relationship to the child who comes into existence have a special responsibility for it. They may wish to assume responsibility for it, or they may not wish to. And I am suggesting that if assuming responsibility for it would require large sacrifices, then they may refuse. A Good Samaritan would not refuse—or anyway, a Splendid Samaritan, if the sacrifices that had to be made were enormous. But then so would a Good Samaritan assume responsibility for that violinist; so would Henry Fonda, if he is a Good Samaritan, fly in from the West Coast and assume responsibility for me.

8. My argument will be found unsatisfactory on two counts by many of those who want to regard abortion as morally permissible. First, while I do argue that abortion is not impermissible, I do not argue that it is always permissible. There may well be cases in which carrying the child to term requires only minimally Decent Samaritanism of the mother, and this is a standard we must not fall below. I am inclined to think it a merit of my account precisely that it does *not* give a general yes or a general no. It allows for and supports our sense that, for example, a sick and desperately frightened fourteen-year-old schoolgirl, pregnant due to rape, may *of course* choose abortion, and that any law which rules this out is an insane law. And it also allows for and supports our sense that in other cases resort to abortion is even positively indecent. It would be indecent in the woman to request an abortion, and indecent in a doctor to perform it, if she is in her seventh month, and wants the abortion just to avoid the nuisance of postponing a trip abroad. The very fact that the arguments I have been drawing attention to treat all cases of abortion, or even all cases of abortion in which the mother's life is not at stake, as morally on a par ought to have made them suspect at the outset.

Secondly, while I am arguing for the permissibility of abortion in some cases, I am not arguing for the right to secure the death of the unborn child. It is easy to confuse these two things in that up to a certain point in the life of the fetus it is not able to survive outside the mother's body; hence removing it from her body guarantees its death. But they are importantly different. I have argued that you are not morally required to spend nine months in bed, sustaining the life of that violinist; but to say this is by no means to say that if, when you unplug yourself, there is a miracle and he survives, you then have a right to turn round and slit his throat. You may detach yourself even if this costs him his life; you have no right to be guaranteed his death, by some other means, if unplugging yourself does not kill him. There are some people who will feel dissatisfied by this feature of my argument. A woman may be utterly devastated by the thought of a child, a bit of herself, put out for adoption and never seen or heard of again. She may therefore want not merely that the child be detached from her, but more, that it die. Some opponents of abortion are inclined to regard this as beneath contempt—thereby showing insensitivity to what is surely a powerful source of despair. All the same, I agree that the desire for the child's death is not one which anybody may gratify, should it turn out to be possible to detach the child alive.

At this place, however, it should be remembered that we have only been pretending throughout that the fetus is a human being from the moment of conception. A very early abortion is surely not the killing of a person, and so is not dealt with by anything I have said here.

Suggestions
for Further Reading

Anthologies

Feinberg, Joel (ed.). *The Problem of Abortion.* Belmont, Calif.: Wadsworth, 1973. A collection of some of the best contemporary philosophical essays on the abortion controversy.

Rachels, James (ed.). *Moral Problems.* 2nd ed. New York: Harper, 1975. Recent essays on such currently discussed moral issues as sex, abortion, punishment, and death.

Regan, Tom (ed.). *Matters of Life and Death.* New York: Random House, 1980. A collection of original essays on a variety of moral issues.

Singer, Marcus (ed.). *Morals and Values.* New York: Scribner, 1977. A good collection of readings on the main problems of ethical theory.

Taylor, Paul (ed.). *Problems of Moral Philosophy.* Belmont, Calif.: Wadsworth, 1978. A good anthology of important writings on a wide range of ethical problems.

Wasserstrom, Richard (ed.). *Today's Moral Problems.* New York: Macmillan, 1979. Recent essays on a variety of moral issues.

Individual Works

Barnes, Hazel E. *An Existentialist Ethics.* New York: Knopf, 1967. A clear presentation of an existentialist approach to ethics, as well as a consideration and rejection of a number of other contemporary ethical views.

Binkley, Luther. *Contemporary Ethical Theories.* New York: Citadel, 1961. A clear discussion of the twentieth-century analytic philosophers' approach to ethics.

Brandt, William. *Ethical Theory,* Englewood Cliffs, N.J.: Prentice-Hall, 1959. This is an excellent but somewhat difficult introduction to ethical theory. There are excellent bibliographies on almost all major topics in ethical theory.

Fletcher, Joseph. *Situation Ethics: The New Morality.* Philadelphia: Westminster, 1966. A contemporary Christian view of ethics, which stresses love as the basis for decision-making in ethics.

Frankena, William. *Ethics.* Englewood Cliffs, N.J.: Prentice-Hall, 1963. Provides a clear, concise statement of the major ethical problems and positions.

Hospers, John. *Human Conduct.* New York: Harcourt, 1982. An excellent, clearly written textbook, which is highly recommended for the beginning student.

Mill, John Stuart. *Utilitarianism,* Indianapolis: Bobbs, 1957. A classic statement of the utilitarian position, which differs from Bentham's version in several important ways.

Olson, Robert G. *The Morality of Self-interest.* New York: Harcourt, 1965. An interesting defense of a version of egoism.

Rand, Ayn. *The Virtue of Selfishness.* New York: Signet, 1964. An interesting, but at times confusing, defense of egoism by a popular novelist and an intellectual leader of the libertarian movement.

Russell, Bertrand. *Human Society in Ethics and Politics.* New York: Simon & Schuster, 1952. A clearly written analysis of a variety of ethical issues by a great modern philosopher.

Smart, J. J. C., and Bernard Williams. *Utilitarianism: For and Against.* London: Cambridge U.P., 1973. Smart gives a detailed description and defense of utilitarianism, and Williams offers a variety of criticisms.

Dictionary of the History of Ideas: Studies of Selected Pivotal Ideas. Philip P. Weiner, editor-in-chief. New York: Scribners, 1973. Substantial and clearly written essays emphasizing the historical development of topics discussed in this part. Designed to inform the nonspecialist, each essay concludes with a select bibliography.

Encyclopedia of Philosophy. Paul Edwards, editor-in-chief. New York: Macmillan, 1967. The student will find many worthwhile articles on the subject treated in this part, and excellent bibliographies.

Four:
State
and
Society

Introduction

Consider these two situations. It is April 14, late in the evening. Completing your federal income tax form, you discover to your dismay that you owe an additional tax of two hundred dollars to the U.S. government. After triple-checking your return, you sigh and write out a personal check in the amount required. For it is either pay or be fined or perhaps be clapped into jail. Nothing voluntary here. You are being coerced by other human beings; if you do not comply, you will suffer. Muttering, you trudge to the mailbox located on the next block. Returning to your home, a man you've never seen before points a revolver at you and demands that you give him all of your money. Nothing voluntary here, either. Choking down your anger, you give the robber the fifty dollars in your wallet. The story ends somewhat happily. You reach home safe but poorer.

Do these two situations differ in any significant way? Or are they the same except for incidental details? Both involve financial loss and coercion that you would prefer to avoid. Is the government nothing more than a robber on a more ambitious scale? Is the robber really an individual entrepreneur heroically defying a company monopoly? Of course, many would hold that the two situations are not comparable at all. The federal income tax is legitimate, legal, justifiable, whereas robbery is criminal, illegal, unjustifiable. The income tax constitutes a self-assessment; through your elected representatives you've consented to it. You have not consented to be robbed. As a result of the Sixteenth Amendment, the federal income tax is constitutional. Armed robbery is unconstitutional. Certainly armed robbery is undemocratic. The federal income tax possesses a political philosophy to give it rational support; armed robbery remains innocent of any political philosophy justifying it.

The field of political philosophy offers a rich and varied landscape of problems, methods of analysis, and solutions. This section focuses on one problem; Can the democratic state be justified rationally? Can its superiority to other forms of government be shown on rational grounds? All governments, whether allegedly democratic or not, claim to be legitimate. That is to say, they assert that they not only have the allegiance of those subject to their authority but that they also deserve loyalty. Democratic governments are no exception to this generalization. The government of the United States claims not only that its citizens must support it by paying taxes and, if necessary, must protect and defend it by fighting and dying in war; it further holds that American citizens ought to be ready and willing to make these sacrifices. If any individual American citizen or group of American citizens refuse to obey the government, then those in authority not only can use the police power to compel obedience but are justified in doing so.

A legitimate government maintains that its physical authority ultimately rests on moral authority. Governments justify their existence and policies by appealing to a political philosophy. Democratic governments claim to be promoting the political philosophy of democracy. Defending the cause of the Union at Gettysburg, Lincoln did not rest that defense on the threat of force; he declared that the nation was "conceived in liberty and dedicated to the proposition that all men are created equal." A political philosophy, whatever else it may comprise, consists of propositions claiming to be true and consistent with one another. And governments, particularly when their authority is seriously and sharply questioned, picture themselves implementing some political philosophy. Therefore, the political philosophy of democracy is not to be identified with familiar democratic practices such as universal suffrage, the two-party system, political conventions, a president and a congress, specific legislation, and so on; these actual governmental forms and exercises presumably are the most effective means so far devised for translating the abstract propositions of democratic political philosophy into concrete reality. A democratic government is supposed to be democratic political philosophy in action.

Of course, the political philosophy of democracy includes many more propositions than merely one or two basic ones such as that all men are created equal. Any serious political philosophy turns out to be more complex than that in the sense of being composed of a large number of propositions. Incidentally, this fact accounts for the inconsistency, which often exists unnoticed in the crowd, among some of the propositions. However, let us concentrate on the proposition that all men are created equal for the moment in order to facilitate the task of briefly sketching what a philosopher in his professional capacity does when he scrutinizes a political philosophy. Democratic politicians seek to implement the political philosophy of democracy, espouse principles, and renew people's dedication to those tenets. The philosopher works along different lines. He seeks to articulate each and every proposition constituting the political philosophy of democracy and to state them as free from ambiguity, vagueness, and emotional connotations as possible. What does the proposition "All men are created equal" mean? Is this the best statement of the proposition? Each word in the statement of the proposition can be found in the dictionary and the words are combined in a grammatically correct way. Does "created" imply some conception of a divine creation of man so that democratic political philosophy would have to include certain theological statements about God and the origin of man? Certainly some proponents of democracy have argued that democracy rests on supernatural and revealed religion, that it really is God's will. Some critics of democracy also have agreed with the religious defenders of democracy that it has a divine basis, that democracy is Christian ethics translated into a secular vocabulary. However, these critics have gone on to argue that the soundness and even the sense of Christian ethics is inextricably bound up with acceptance of the whole Christian faith. But in terms of the scientific outlook of the present, the Christian faith changes from truth to myth and so democracy along with it becomes no more than a dream, no matter how appealing. In reply, religious exponents of democracy have contended that the warranted conclusion to draw is that if democracy is to survive and prosper, everyone should "get religion." Our religiously pluralistic society has encouraged defenders of this religious basis of democracy to enlarge that basis beyond Christianity to embrace other religions and, even further, just to embrace religion in general. Further, how is the proposition that each individual is of unique worth to be rendered consistent with the principle that all men are created equal? What is meant by "equality"? Equal talents? Equal incomes? Equality before the law? Equality of opportunity? That every adult citizen who is not obviously insane or retarded can fulfill competently the duties of any elective office? Does "equality" mean all of these, some of these, or none of these? Finally, granted clarity and agreement on the meaning of the proposition "All men are created equal," is the proposition true or false? At least what evidence, were it to be found, would be accepted as falsifying the proposition? Is "All men are created equal" an empirical generalization such as "Water freezes at 32 degrees F"? If it is, then producing one human being created unequal would prove the generalization false. Or is the proposition "All men are created equal" prescriptive, rather than descriptive? Instead of asserting some state of affairs, is the proposition simply the expression of a desire: I, or we, wish that all men were created equal? But, then, if it were prescriptive, the proposition "All men are created equal" would be neither true nor false. A wish is neither true nor false.

The aim in this introduction is not to answer these questions but to suggest the distinctive character of the philosophic approach to political thought, an enterprise consisting in the combination of clarification of concepts, determination of logical consistency, formulation and assessment of criteria of truth and falsity, and the ultimate weighing of the truth claims of the principles appealed to to justify political action. Political philosophy is distinct from day-to-day political debate and descriptive accounts of actual political behavior, although the latter may influence political philosophy and vice versa. Some political philosophies are so comprehensive they range from offering shrewd practical advice on how to be a successful tyrant or win a revolution to envisioning a total form or way of life covering all aspects of individual and collective human life; from how to win elections or seize control of the state to doctrines about the nature of human nature, the direction of history, and the nature of reality; from maneuvers to metaphysics. Certainly, in terms of speculative boldness and development, political philosophy extends beyond what social scientists would consider genuinely scientific theorizing. This bulging over the boundaries of the strictly scientific often has enhanced the power of political philosophies to elicit an active devotion from millions, which at times is religious in both intensity and endurance. From Plato to Karl Popper, influencing the actions of men has been one of the main goals of political philosophers.

For a moment let us return to the cases of paying one's taxes and being robbed. The federal income tax is constitutional and the law of the land, and so presumably it represents the will of a majority of American citizens. Yet there are Americans who do not want, do not consent, to pay income taxes any more than they do to being robbed. What rationally persuasive grounds can be found in democratic political philosophy why a dissenting minority should abide by the will of a majority and not seek to do everything possible to successfully evade it? Does a majority vote really reflect the will of a majority of the citizens? Convincing answers to these questions are not as easy to find as one might first suppose. Laws are devised and passed by elected representatives and not by a direct vote of the people. Representatives in government are cultivated constantly by skillful lobbyists representing not the people in general but powerful, wealthy special interest groups. Before laws can be voted on by a legislature as a whole, they must be reported out of a legislative committee composed only of a small number of legislators. As a result of the seniority system in the U.S. Congress, the powerful chairmanships of these committees often are held by representatives who are reelected many times by a small minority of the American people in districts and states where the candidate faces no significant political opposition. The cost of campaigning for high national office has grown to the point where only wealthy individuals or those who have put themselves heavily in debt to wealthy individuals, corporations, unions, and other groups can afford it. The president of the United States, ostensibly representing all of the American people, is not elected directly by the people. Provided he has the necessary number of electoral votes, a candidate can become president of the United States even though he does not gain a majority of the popular vote. Furthermore, a majority of the eligible voters often do not even vote. Finally, few candidates for public office are elected unanimously; voters cast ballots against them by voting for opponents or by abstaining from voting entirely. That is to say, at any given time a considerable number of Americans are opposed to those governing them and do not consider their elected rulers to be representing their will at all.

However, let us suppose that the machinery of democratic government functioned perfectly and infallibly registered the will of the people. Is what the majority believes to be true or good always so? At one time a majority of Europeans believed the earth to be flat. A few generations ago a majority of Americans believed that slavery was right and just. Of course, by sheer overwhelming weight of numbers, a majority could force a dissenting minority to go along with its wishes, however much the minority might disagree silently. But all this would prove is the superior might of the majority, not its superior knowledge or virtue. If a dissenting minority should submit to a majority merely because decision, however arrived at, is better than indecisive drifting, a dictator securely in power could supply the decisiveness in a less inconstant manner than could a vague, shifting majority confused by conflicting propaganda. The quality of a majority decision is the resultant of the quality of the individuals who compose the majority; for example, a majority composed of stupid people would be more likely to reach foolish decisions than wise ones. Such a majority of poor quality might accidentally produce some wise decisions; nevertheless, fortuitous wisdom hardly seems a very persuasive reason for always accepting the will of the majority. Should not the vote of an intelligent, informed, responsible, civic-minded person count two, three, or more times the vote of some lout who must be dragged out of a saloon on election day and lured to the polls to vote with the promise of a free drink afterwards? Perhaps individuals should earn the privilege of the vote by first making some worthwhile contribution to society or only on the condition that they be self-supporting or have I.Q.s over 80. It has been argued that those who possess more property and more capital hold a greater stake in the fate of the country because they have more to lose than those who possess less, and that therefore, these wealthier people should determine government policy. Those with little or nothing to lose are likely to act selfishly, rashly, and irresponsibly. Wealthy officeholders would be immune to bribes since they don't need more money, already having more than enough.

A rational justification of democracy would be impossible without weighing the merits of alternative forms of government. Everyone is familiar with the *mot* to the effect that democracy is the worst form of government except for all the other forms of government that have been tried. Yet the claimed superior worth of democracy hardly goes uncontested. The political philosophy of communism, now subscribed to by millions of people, views American democracy as a sham doomed to disappear in the future. The political philosophy of anarchism opposes American democracy because it sees all government as inherently evil.

These foregoing remarks are not intended to settle the issue of the merits of democracy; they are intended to point up the fact that it is a real, vital issue.

John Dewey long has been recognized as one of the foremost philosophical defenders of democracy. Throughout an unusually long, productive life, Dewey sought to reinterpret nineteenth-century American democracy in a way that would be consonant with the scientific–industrial society of the twentieth century. He envisions democracy as a total way of life and not merely as a form of government. For Dewey, democracy is the complete realization of what it means to be a community. The political practices associated with democracy are the "best means" so far invented for achieving the "participation of every mature human being in the formation of the values that regulate the living of men together." Dewey sees this "formation" of values as a never-finished, ongoing process, rather than as the discovery of some eternal, absolute system of values. The spirit of democracy is a liberal one, a spirit that ceaselessly criticizes its first principles. Such criticism does not weaken society, as both reactionary and radical dogmatists contend; it strengthens democracy. Hence, the basic freedom in a democracy must be freedom of mind, an essential condition for the flourishing of the liberal spirit.

Dewey appeals to the nature of human nature to justify democracy. No one is wise or good enough to rule others without their consent. The Plato of the *Re-*

public is wrong; no one can be *made* wise or good enough. There is no expertise of ruling and consequently no experts at the task to whom we should submit ourselves totally. The main reason for this irremediable lack of experts at
ruling is that no ruler or set of rulers can ever know enough to justify their absolute authority. As Dewey puts it, only the person who wears the shoe best
knows where it pinches. And he must be able to make the rulers pay attention
to his pain. A democratic form of government, however imperfect it may be, has
been more effective in accomplishing this securing of the attention of rulers and
getting them to act to remove the pain than has any king or dictatorship, whether exercised by the proletariat or by some other group or individual. Unless rulers can be checked and brought to heel by the ruled, the former, no matter how
well intentioned, invariably will oppress the latter. And all oppression is evil. This
restraint of the few by the many is the *leitmotiv* of any democratic society. The
less gifted, the layman, always must be able to control the more gifted, the expert, or else sooner or later the latter will ride roughshod over the former. This
is a hard saying for many academics and other intellectuals, all too many of
whom have willingly served "benevolent" despots while dreaming in their sleep
of being such despots.

Dewey finds this democratic subordination of the rulers to the ruled, whether in
government or any other social institution, very imperfectly realized in any existing society. For him democracy is a faith, an ideal. A faith, an ideal can only be
assessed by discovering what consequences flow from acting on it. And we
cannot discover those consequences except by acting. To use an illustration
Dewey does not employ, the merits of Woodrow Wilson's ideal of a League of
Nations could not be rationally justified by abstract speculation alone but only
by trying to put it into practice. Did the failure of the actual League of Nations
prove Wilson's ideal a fatuous one? No, the Wilsonian faith was reincarnated in
the United Nations, whose ultimate fate has not yet been decided. And the nature of the decision depends on what we do now and in the future. Similarly, the
merit of any individual cannot be assessed by any principle such as family,
race, religion, or other criterion antecedent to what he does and its consequences. Democratic equality must not be confused with equality of abilities; it
is equality of opportunity, opportunity for each individual to show what he *can*
do. Ideals, individuals, institutions, and philosophies must be tested by their results, not by their origins or some fixed nature ascribed to them. Therefore, the
only adequate test of democracy would be the fuller practice of democracy. The
cure for the ills of democracy is more democracy. Many of our social institutions
developed before the advent of modern democracy and so reflect the undemocratic habits of an authoritarian past. Education is the key to the success of democracy; modern education must be so designed as to nurture democratic habits in the young. For the anarchists are wrong in contending all government to
be evil; group life, particularly in our complex society, necessitates planning, organization—that is, government of some form. The issue is not whether there
shall be government or no government but rather what kind of government will

elicit from each member of the community whatever of value he has to contribute through his voluntary participation.

The American critic of ideas H. L. Mencken has been particularly critical of the democratic idea. Mencken also was a journalist who reported on nearly every national political convention of the first half of the twentieth century and possessed an intimate knowledge of American politics and politicians. Mencken believed that most defenders of democracy viewed the workings of democratic government through an idealistic haze and so did not see them as they actually were but as the defenders wanted them to be. Mencken sees democratic politics as a "mere battle of rival rogues" to get into office and then to stay in office. Without exception, all politicians are frauds, the worst being the reformers who try to disguise their fraudulence with moral pretense. No politician could ever fully tell what he honestly believes and hope to get elected. Democracy demands its leaders be dishonest. Democracy does not promote human dignity; it destroys it as surely as any authoritarian regime, indeed more surely, by steady moral erosion rather than by violent suppression.

To Mencken, the political philosophy of democracy rests on false premises. The common man is not the repository of some special wisdom; on the contrary, he is incurably stupid and incompetent, dominated by the emotion of fear, above all the fear of ideas. He does not yearn for liberty; he dreads it. What he wants is security, a cowlike contentment. A small minority composed of unusual people like Dewey desire intellectual freedom; Dewey, in Mencken's view, succumbs to the common error of supposing that most men want what he wants. No wonder liberals again and again are surprised and outraged when they fall victim to periodic witch hunts. If the liberals were realistic, they would expect this in a democracy. They then would see that more democracy would not cure the ills of democracy but would instead utterly destroy the liberty they cherish so highly. The common man does not want equality of opportunity, which would give the superior man the opportunity to develop his superiority and thereby triumph over his inferiors. The common man does not want to be "underprivileged"; he longs for the advantage over his betters, not equality with them. The unmistakable sign of the inferiority of the common man is his preoccupation with morality. Hence, in a democracy where the common man rules, every issue becomes a moral issue. Morality is the chief weapon in the arsenal of the weak, inferior man in his struggle with his natural superiors, whom he seeks to enfeeble by poisoning them with bad conscience. Those who feel threatened or incapable of mastering their environment gabble most about "justice" and their "sacred rights." John D. Rockefeller, Sr., amassing a gigantic fortune by ruthlessly destroying his business competitors while teaching Sunday school every week, symbolizes the dream of the common man come true. America has generated an aristocracy; but, alas, it has turned out to be merely common after all—a fearful, selfish, hypocritical plutocracy.

According to Mencken's criticism, not only is the political philosophy of democracy dependent on false propositions but it also promotes meretricious values. It exalts dunderheads, cowards, cads; it persecutes intelligent, honest, courageous men who will not lie and who cannot be bought. The communists are correct in seeing human history as a protracted struggle but interpret it too narrowly as a war of economic classes. In reality, this long civil war within humanity is broader and more fundamental than economics; it is the conflict between a superior minority struggling to grow and progress against the repeated efforts of an inferior and envious majority to hold it back. The political philosophy of democracy amounts to nothing more than the war propaganda of that reactionary majority. And the war? It is the forays of those denied admittance to gain entrance to an exclusive club. When at last they succeed, they fail. For when all can belong, the club has lost its exclusivity and membership loses all value. Meanwhile, the original members have formed another exclusive club now ripe for attack. And so the self-defeating war goes on, thrilling, sometimes hilarious, always cruel.

Corliss Lamont, while agreeing with Mencken's description of the actual functioning of contemporary democracy, refuses to confine himself to pathology; he offers a cure. That treatment is the voluntary adoption of socialism. Government and politics in reality are economics in action. Democracy has been corrupted by capitalism; indeed, democracy and capitalism are incompatible. Lamont agrees with Dewey that as a social philosophy democracy is the practical attempt to realize the humanistic ideal of the happiness, freedom, and progress of *all* humanity. However, capitalism by its very nature works to thwart the realization of this egalitarian ideal. However altruistic some individual capitalists may be, as an economic system capitalism appeals to human greed by lavishing on a fortunate few enormous wealth far exceeding what their efforts deserve, at the morally intolerable cost of the ruthless exploitation of the majority, thereby generating a ceaseless war of the poor against the rich. Economic recession, mass unemployment, waste, and war are, Lamont claims, inherent in the capitalistic system; capitalism may ameliorate them but cannot cure them. When palliative measures (i.e., the welfare state) no longer suffice, capitalism tears off the sentimental mask of democracy and civil rights to expose the ugly visage of fascism—"capitalism in the nude," as Lamont phrases it.

In Lamont's description, democratic socialism seeks to realize the humanitarian ideal of democracy throughout the world, not only politically, but economically and culturally, by means of overall socialist planning combined with public ownership of the main means of production and distribution. Lamont is convinced that socialism would so transform human motivation that people would "find their welfare and happiness in working for the general good instead of always putting their economic welfare first, as in capitalist theory." Lamont denies the charge that socialism is hopelessly utopian by pointing to its success in elevating the Soviet Union to the status of a world power in spite of capitalist attempts to destroy it. Lamont denies that socialism necessarily means political tyranny, attributing the lack of political democracy and civil liberties in the Soviet Union and China to their backward and authoritarian past, the effects of revolution and civil war, and the need to defend themselves against capitalist hostility. He argues that countries with established traditions of political democracy and civil liberties, such as the United States and Great Britain, can adopt socialism voluntarily and preserve those traditions as living realities.

According to the Libertarian political philosophy of John Hospers, the state itself is the villain, the chief cause of our social woes. He sharply distinguishes the state from society, seeing the former as a robber and the latter as his victim. Realistically viewed, government in essence amounts to legalized, organized plunder over a particular territory. The old joke that when the legislature is in session no one's property and life are safe really is one of the grim truths we try to laugh away rather than face squarely. Beneath the pious rhetoric, politics is a war among competing interest groups for control of the coercive apparatus of the state for the purpose of imposing the victor's will on all the rest. Democratic states are no exception to this indictment. The democratic politician is a cynical Robin Hood, seeking to remain in office forever by robbing A to give to B in return for B's vote and then robbing B to give to A in return for A's vote. The politician always promises freedom, peace, and prosperity and always delivers dictatorship, war, and poverty. The state and society are not only distinguishable from one another; they mortally conflict with one another.

The state is a brigand hostile to liberty because it is coercive rather than voluntary. According to Hospers, any sound political philosophy will recognize the right of a citizen to sever connection with the state because it views the state as an agency that may voluntarily be employed or not employed by individual members of society. Any political philosophy that ignores or rejects such a right rests political authority on an immoral basis because it enslaves man to the state by forbidding him to support it or withdraw from it as he sees fit.

Although Hospers claims that he is "not necessarily" an anarchist and that he certainly does not advocate the violent overthrow of all constituted forms and institutions of society and government if they are not replaced by any other system of order, he clearly is in favor of voluntary association as the most satisfactory means of organizing society. He frankly declares that he prefers anarchism—in the sense that society consists only of voluntary associations—to the "fascist type" of state now regnant in the United States and in many other countries. Americans may believe fatuously that they enjoy a free society; in reality the state already possesses a "life-and-death stranglehold" over American society. Progressives yesterday feared Americans were becoming the feudal serfs of corporate capital; Americans today have become the feudal serfs of the corporate state.

In "The Future of Capitalism" Milton Friedman contends that political freedom depends on the capitalistic free enterprise system, which is "free" in the sense that it allows individuals to set up enterprises only so long as voluntary methods of inducing individuals to cooperate are used. Government, however, ultimately relies on coercion, not on voluntary choice. We may buy or not buy from General Motors; if we refuse to pay taxes the government will fine us, sell our property to pay the taxes, or even jail us. Friedman attempts to show by specific examples that Americans have lost considerable economic freedom, and therefore political freedom as well, as the result of the growth of government. He judges the two greatest threats to private enterprise to be intellectuals who want freedom of speech for themselves but not for others and businessmen who oppose government regulation yet clamor for government subsidies. Friedman argues that it is possible to halt the growth of government and its obstruction of the beneficent operation of the free enterprise system.

Sidney Hook defends the American welfare state, variously called the "New Deal," the "Fair Deal," and the "Great Society," as a successful alternative to socialism and *laissez-faire* capitalism. Unlike the former, the welfare state does not oppose the profit motive and is experimental rather than doctrinaire. Unlike the latter, the welfare state is committed to state intervention to provide economic security and equality of opportunity for all Americans. The welfare state is not committed to public ownership of all the main means of production and distribution, nor is it opposed to the state doing what individuals and groups are unable or unwilling to do for themselves. It views the state not as a savior or an enemy, but as a power to be used democratically on a piecemeal basis. Hook argues that the welfare state's lack of a coherent philosophy is outweighed by the virtues of improvisation. He argues that the welfare state is indispensable to a strong, growing economy and an effective national defense. He sees our only real choice as one between the welfare state and the " 'ill-fare' state."

A recurring area of controversy in democratic countries concerns the relation that should exist between law and morality. Should there be laws that require people to act in the way that the majority of society thinks moral, or should the laws deal only with certain very important matters, such as the protection of rights and the defense of one's person against physical harm? Should there be laws that prevent storeowners from opening on Sunday or laws against the possession of pornographic literature? Many people, perhaps a majority, think that suicide and sexual intercourse outside of marriage are immoral. Should there be laws against them?

Sir Patrick Devlin, a prominent English judge, considers this problem in the light of a recommendation by a government committee to eliminate any laws against homosexuality among consenting adults. He believes that such a change in the law would weaken public morality and thereby add to those pressures that could lead to the disintegration of the society. For him, "the suppression of vice is as much the law's business as the suppression of subversive activities." H. L. A. Hart opposes this view. Although he agrees that a stable society needs some moral cohesion, he doubts that every moral matter is of equal importance to society. Surely society will not disintegrate if some activities of which it disapproves are left open to the individual. Hart fears that Sir Patrick Devlin's approach to the problem might result in giving legal sanction to the public's moral whims no matter how irrational they may be.

Democracy

28. A Defense of Democracy   John Dewey

John Dewey (1859–1952) wrote systematic treatises on subjects in all major fields of philosophy and earned a worldwide reputation as one of America's greatest philosophers.

. . . Democracy is much broader than a special political form, a method of conducting government, of making laws and carrying on governmental administration by means of popular suffrage and elected officers. It is that, of course. But it is something broader and deeper than that. The political and governmental phase of democracy is a means, the best means so far found, for realizing ends that lie in the wide domain of human relationships and the development of human personality. It is, as we often say, though perhaps without appreciating all that is involved in the saying, a way of life, social and individual. The key-note of democracy as a way of life may be expressed, it seems to me, as the necessity for the participation of every mature human being in formation of the values that regulate the living of men together: which is necessary from the standpoint of both the general social welfare and the full development of human beings as individuals.

Universal suffrage, recurring elections, responsibility of those who are in political power to the voters, and the other factors of democratic government are means that have been found expedient for realizing democracy as the truly human way of living. They are not a final end and a final value. They are to be judged on the basis of their contribution to the end. It is a form of idolatry to erect means into the end which they serve. Democratic political forms are simply the best means that human wit has devised up to a special time in history. But they rest back upon the idea that no man or limited set of men is wise enough or good enough to rule others without their consent; the positive meaning of this statement is that all those who are affected by social institutions must have a share in producing and managing them. The two facts that each one is influenced in what he does and enjoys and in what he becomes by the institutions under which he lives, and that therefore he shall have,

From "Democracy and Educational Administration," *School and Society,* Vol. 45, No. 1162, April 3, 1937. Reprinted by permission of USA TODAY, successor to SCHOOL AND SOCIETY.

in a democracy, a voice in shaping them, are the passive and active sides of the same fact.

The development of political democracy came about through substitution of the method of mutual consultation and voluntary agreement for the method of subordination of the many to the few enforced from above. Social arrangements which involve fixed subordination are maintained by coercion. The coercion need not be physical. There have existed, for short periods, benevolent despotisms. But coercion of some sort there has been; perhaps economic, certainly psychological and moral. The very fact of exclusion from participation is a subtle form of suppression. It gives individuals no opportunity to reflect and decide upon what is good for them. Others who are supposed to be wiser and who in any case have more power decide the question for them and also decide the methods and means by which subjects may arrive at the enjoyment of what is good for them. This form of coercion and suppression is more subtle and more effective than is overt intimidation and restraint. When it is habitual and embodied in social institutions, it seems the normal and natural state of affairs. The mass usually become unaware that they have a claim to a development of their own powers. Their experience is so restricted that they are not conscious of restriction. It is part of the democratic conception that they as individuals are not the only sufferers, but that the whole social body is deprived of the potential resources that should be at its service. The individuals of the submerged mass may not be very wise. But there is one thing they are wiser about than anybody else can be, and that is where the shoe pinches, the troubles they suffer from.

The foundation of democracy is faith in the capacities of human nature; faith in human intelligence and in the power of pooled and co-operative experience. It is not belief that these things are complete but that if given a show they will grow and be able to generate progressively the knowledge and wisdom needed to guide collective action. Every autocratic and authoritarian scheme of social action rests on a belief that the needed intelligence is confined to a superior few, who because of inherent natural gifts are endowed with the ability and the right to control the conduct of others; laying down principles and rules and directing the ways in which they are carried out. It would be foolish to deny that much can be said for this point of view. It is that which controlled human relations in social groups for much the greater part of human history. The democratic faith has emerged very, very recently in the history of mankind. Even where democracies now exist, men's minds and feelings are still permeated with ideas about leadership imposed from above, ideas that developed in the long early history of mankind. After democratic political institutions were nominally established, beliefs and ways of looking at life and of acting that originated when men and women were externally controlled and subjected to arbitrary power, persisted in the family, the church, business and the school, and experience shows that as long as they persist there, political democracy is not secure.

Belief in equality is an element of the democratic credo. It is not, however, belief in equality of natural endowments. Those who proclaimed the idea of equality did not suppose they were enunciating a psychological doctrine, but a legal and political one. All individuals are entitled to equality of treatment by law and in its administration. Each one is affected equally in quality if not in quantity by the institutions under which he lives and has an equal right to express his judgment, although the weight of his judgment may not be equal in amount when it enters into the pooled result to that of others. In short, each one is equally an individual and entitled to equal opportunity of development of his own capacities, be they large or small in range. Moreover, each has needs of his own, as significant to him as those of others are to them. The very fact of natural and psychological inequality is all the more reason for establishment by law of equality of opportunity, since otherwise the former becomes a means of oppression of the less gifted.

While what we call intelligence be distributed in unequal amounts, it is the democratic faith that it is sufficiently general so that each individual has something to contribute, whose value can be assessed only as enters into the final pooled intelligence constituted by the contributions of all. Every authoritarian scheme, on the contrary, assumes that its value may be assessed by some *prior* principle, if not of family and birth or race and color or possession of material wealth, then by the position and rank a person occupies in the existing social scheme. The democratic faith in equality is the faith that each individual shall have the chance and opportunity to contribute whatever he is capable of contributing and that the value of his contribution be decided by its place and function in the organized total of similar contributions, not on the basis of prior status of any kind whatever.

I have emphasized in what precedes the importance of the effective release of intelligence in connection with personal experience in the democratic way of living. I have done so purposely because democracy is so often and so naturally associated in our minds with freedom of *action,* forgetting the importance of freed intelligence which is necessary to direct and to warrant freedom of action. Unless freedom of individual action has intelligence and informed conviction back of it, its manifestation is almost sure to result in confusion and disorder. The democratic idea of freedom is not the right of each individual to *do* as he pleases, even if it be qualified by adding "provided he does not interfere with the same freedom on the part of others." While the idea is not always, not often enough, expressed in words, the basic freedom is that of freedom of *mind* and of whatever degree of freedom of action and experience is necessary to produce freedom of intelligence. The modes of freedom guaranteed in the Bill of Rights are all of this nature: Freedom of belief and conscience, of expression of opinion, of assembly for discussion and conference, of the press as an organ of communication. They are guaranteed because without them individuals are not free to develop and society is deprived of what they might contribute.

. . . There is some kind of government, of control, wherever affairs that concern a number of persons who act together are engaged in. It is a superficial view that holds government is located in Washington and Albany. There is government in the family, in business, in the church, in every social group. There are regulations, due to custom if not to enactment, that settle how individuals in a group act in connection with one another.

It is a disputed question of theory and practice just how far a democratic political government should go in control of the conditions of action within special groups. At the present time, for example, there are those who think the federal and state governments leave too much freedom of independent action to industrial and financial groups, and there are others who think the government is going altogether too far at the present time. I do not need to discuss this phase of the problem, much less to try to settle it. But it must be pointed out that if the methods of regulation and administration in vogue in the conduct of secondary social groups are non-democratic, whether directly or indirectly or both, there is bound to be an unfavorable reaction back into the habits of feeling, thought and action of citizenship in the broadest sense of that word. The way in which any organized social interest is controlled necessarily plays an important part in forming the dispositions and tastes, the attitudes, interests, purposes and desires, of those engaged in carrying on the activities of the group. For illustration, I do not need to do more than point to the moral, emotional and intellectual effect upon both employers and laborers of the existing industrial system. Just what the effects specifically are is a matter about which we know very little. But I suppose that every one who reflects upon the subject admits that it is impossible that the ways in which activities are carried on for the greater part of the waking hours of the day, and the way in which the share of individuals are involved in the management of affairs in such a matter as gaining a livelihood and attaining material and social security, can not but be a highly important factor in shaping personal dispositions; in short, forming character and intelligence.

In the broad and final sense all institutions are educational in the sense that they operate to form the attitudes, dispositions, abilities and disabilities that constitute a concrete personality. The principle applies with special force to the school. For it is the main business of the family and the school to influence directly the formation and growth of attitudes and dispositions, emotional, intellectual and moral. Whether this educative process is carried on in a predominantly democratic or non-democratic way becomes, therefore, a question of transcendent importance not only for education itself but for its final effect upon all the interests and activities of a society that is committed to the democratic way of life. . . .

There are certain corollaries which clarify the meaning of the issue. Absence of participation tends to produce lack of interest and concern on the part of those shut out. The result is a corresponding lack of effective responsibility. Automatically and unconsciously, if not consciously, the feeling develops, "This is none of our affair; it is the business of those at the top; let that particular set of Georges do what needs to be done." The countries in which autocratic government prevails are just those in which there is least public spirit and the greatest indifference to matters of general as distinct from personal concern. . . . Where there is little power, there is correspondingly little sense of positive responsibility. It is enough to do what one is told to do sufficiently well to escape flagrant unfavorable notice. About larger matters, a spirit of passivity is engendered. . . .

It still is also true that incapacity to assume the responsibilities involved in having a voice in shaping policies is bred and increased by conditions in which that responsibility is denied. I suppose there has never been an autocrat, big or little, who did not justify his conduct on the ground of the unfitness of his subjects to take part in government. . . . But as was said earlier, habitual exclusion has the effect of reducing a sense of responsibility for what is done and its consequences. What the argument for democracy implies is that the best way to produce initiative and constructive power is to exercise it. Power, as well as interest, comes by use and practice. . . .

The fundamental beliefs and practices of democracy are now challenged as they never have been before. In some nations they are more than challenged. They are ruthlessly and systematically destroyed. Everywhere there are waves of criticism and doubt as to whether democracy can meet pressing problems of order and security. The causes for the destruction of political democracy in countries where it was nominally established are complex. But of one thing I think we may be sure. Wherever it has fallen it was too exclusively political in nature. It had not become part of the bone and blood of the people in daily conduct of its life. Democratic forms were limited to Parliament, elections and combats between parties. What is happening proves conclusively, I think, that unless democratic habits of thought and action are part of the fiber of a people, political democracy is insecure. It can not stand in isolation. It must be buttressed by the presence of democratic methods in all social relationships. The relations that exist in educational institutions are second only in importance in this respect to those which exist in industry and business, perhaps not even to them.

I recur then to the idea that the particular question discussed is one phase of a wide and deep problem. I can think of nothing so important in this country at present as a rethinking of the whole problem of democracy and its implications. Neither the rethinking nor the action it should produce can be brought into being in a day or year. The democratic idea itself demands that the thinking and activity proceed cooperatively. . . .

Individualism

29. The Disease of Democracy H. L. Mencken

Henry Louis Mencken (1880–1956), journalist, literary critic, essayist, philologist, and editor, primarily thought of himself as a critic of ideas, particularly those ideas his fellow Americans considered so obviously true that they needed no critical examination. His *The Philosophy of Friedrich Nietzsche,* published in 1908, was one of the first intelligent and sympathetic books on the thought of the German philosopher to appear in the United States.

. . . Whether it be called a constitutional monarchy, as in England, or a representative republic, as in France, or a pure democracy, as in some of the cantons of Switzerland, it is always essentially the same. There is, first, the mob, theoretically and in fact the ultimate judge of all ideas and the source of all power. There is, second, the camorra of self-seeking minorities, each seeking to inflame, delude and victimize it. The political process thus becomes a mere battle of rival rogues. But the mob remains quite free to decide between them. It may even, under the hand of God, decide for a minority that happens, by some miracle, to be relatively honest and enlightened. If, in common practice, it sticks to the thieves, it is only because their words are words it understands and their ideas are ideas it cherishes. It has the power to throw them off at will, and even at whim, and it also has the means.

A great deal of paper and ink has been wasted discussing the difference between representative government and direct democracy. The theme is a favourite one with university pundits, and also engages and enchants the stall-fed Rousseaus who arise intermittently in the cow States, and occasionally penetrate to Governors' mansions and the United States Senate. It is generally held that representative government, as practically encountered in the world, is full of defects, some of them amounting to organic disease. Not only does it take the initiative in lawmaking out of the hands of the plain people, and leave them only the function of referees; it also raises certain obvious obstacles to their free exercise of that function. Scattered as they are, and unorganized save in huge, unworkable groups, they are unable, it is argued, to formulate their virtuous desires quickly and clearly, or to bring to the resolution of vexed questions the full potency of their native sagacity. Worse, they find it difficult to enforce their decisions, even when they have decided. Every Liberal knows this sad story and has shed tears telling it. The remedy he offers almost always consists of a resort to what he calls a pure democracy. That is to say he proposes to set up the recall, the initiative and referendum, or something else of the sort, and so convert the representative into a mere clerk or messenger. The final determination of all important public questions, he argues, ought to be in the hands of the voters themselves. They alone can muster enough wisdom for the business, and they alone are without guile. The cure for the evils of democracy is more democracy.

All this, of course, is simply rhetoric. Every time anything of the kind is tried it fails ingloriously. Nor is there any evidence that it has ever succeeded elsewhere, to-day or in the past. . . .

The truth is that the difference between representative democracy and direct democracy is a great deal less marked than political sentimentalists assume. Under both forms the sovereign mob must employ agents to execute its will, and in either case the agents may have ideas of their own, based upon interests of their own, and the means at hand to do and get what they will. Moreover, their very position gives them a power of influencing the electors that is far above that of any ordinary citizen: they become politicians *ex officio,* and usually end by selling such influence as remains after they have used all they need for their own ends. Worse, both forms of democracy encounter the difficulty that the generality of citizens, no matter how assiduously they may be instructed, remain congenitally unable to comprehend many of the problems before them, or to consider all of those they do comprehend in an unbiased and intelligent manner. Thus it is often impossible to ascertain their views in advance of action, or even, in many cases, to determine their conclusions *post hoc*. The voters gathered in a typical New England town-meeting were all ardent amateurs of theology, and hence quite competent, in theory, to decide the theological questions that principally engaged them: nevertheless, history shows that they were led facilely by professional theologians, most of them quacks with something to sell. In the same way, the great masses of Americans of to-day, though they are theoretically competent to decide all the larger matters of national policy, and have certain immutable principles, of almost religious authority, to guide them, actually look for leading to professional politicians, who are influenced in turn by small but competent and determined minorities, with special knowledge and special interests. It was thus that the plain people were shoved into the late war, and it is thus that they will be shoved into the next one. They were, in overwhelming majority, against going in, and if they had had any sense and resolution they would have stayed out. But these things they lacked. . . .

There is the art of the demagogue, and there is the art of what may be called, by a shot-gun marriage of Latin and Greek, the demaslave. They are complementary, and both of them are degrading to their practitioners. The demagogue is one who preaches doctrines he knows to be untrue to men he knows to be idiots. The demaslave is one who listens to what these idiots have to say and then pretends that he believes it himself. Every man who seeks elective office under democracy has to be either the one thing or the other and most men have to be both. The whole process is one of false pretences and ignoble concealments. No educated man stating plainly the elementary notions that every educated man holds about the matters that principally concern government, could be elected to office in a democratic state, save perhaps by a miracle. His frankness would arouse fears, and those fears would run against him; it is his business to arouse fears that will run in favour of him. Worse, he must not only consider the weaknesses of the mob, but also the prejudices of the minorities that prey upon it. Some of these minorities have developed a highly efficient technique of intimidation. They not only know how to arouse the fears of the mob; they also know how to awaken its envy, its dislike of privilege, its hatred of its betters. How formidable they may become is shown by the example of the Anti-Saloon League in the United States—a minority body in the strictest sense, however skillful its mustering of popular support, for it nowhere includes a majority of the voters among its subscribing members, and its leaders are nowhere chosen by democratic methods. And how such minorities may intimidate the whole class of place-seeking politicians has been demonstrated brilliantly and obscenely by the same corrupt and unconscionable organization. It has filled all the law-making bodies of the nation with men who have got into office by submitting cravenly to its dictation, and it has filled thousands of administrative posts, and not a few judicial posts, with vermin of the same sort.

Such men, indeed, enjoy vast advantages under democracy. The mob, insensitive to their dishonour, is edified and exhilarated by their success. The competition they offer to men of a decenter habit is too powerful to be met, so they tend, gradually, to monopolize all the public offices. Out of the muck of their swinishness the typical American law-maker emerges. He is a man who has lied and dissembled, and a man who has crawled. He knows the taste of boot-polish. He has suffered kicks in the tonneau of his pantaloons. He has taken orders from his superiors in knavery and he has wooed and flattered his inferiors in sense. His public life is an endless series of evasions and false pretences. He is willing to embrace any issue, however idiotic, that will get him votes, and he is willing to sacrifice any principle, however sound, that will lose them for him. I do not describe the democratic politician at his inordinate worst; I describe him as he is encountered in the full sunshine of normalcy. He may be, on the one hand, a cross-roads idler striving to get into the State Legislature by grace of the local mortgage-sharks and evangelical clergy, or he may be, on the other, the President of the United States. It is almost an axiom that no man may make a career in politics in the Republic without stooping to such ignobility: it is as necessary as a loud voice. Now and then, to be sure, a man of sounder self-respect may make a beginning, but he seldom gets very far. Those who survive are nearly all tarred, soon or late, with the same stick. They are men who, at some time or other, have compromised with their honour, either by swallowing their convictions or by whooping for what they believe to be untrue. They are in the position of the chorus girl who, in order to get her humble job, has had to admit the manager to her person. And the old birds among them, like chorus girls of long experience come to regard the business resignedly and even complacently. It is the price that a man who loves the clapper-clawing of the vulgar must pay for it under the democratic system. He becomes a coward and a trimmer *ex-officio*. Where his dignity was in the days of his innocence there is now only a vacuum in the wastes of his subconscious. Vanity remains to him, but not pride. . . .

To sum up: the essential objection to feudalism (the perfect antithesis to democracy) was that it imposed degrading acts and attitudes upon the vassal; the essential objection to democracy is that, with few exceptions, it imposes degrading acts and attitudes upon the men responsible for the welfare and dignity of the state. The former was compelled to do homage to his suzerain, who was very apt to be a brute and an ignoramus. The latter are compelled to do homage to their constituents, who in overwhelming majority are certain to be both.

Democracy and Liberty

The Will to Peace.   Whenever the liberties of *Homo vulgaris* are invaded and made a mock of in a gross and contemptuous manner, as happened, for example, in the United States during the reign of Wilson, Palmer, Burleson and company, there are always observers who marvel that he bears the outrage with so little murmuring. Such observers only display their unfamiliarity with the elements of democratic science. The truth is that the common man's love of liberty, like his love of sense, justice and truth, is almost wholly imaginary. As I have argued, he is not actually happy when free; he is uncomfortable, a bit alarmed, and intolerably lonely. He longs for the warm, reassuring smell of the herd, and is willing to take the herdsman with it. Liberty is not a thing for such as he. He cannot enjoy it rationally himself, and he can think of it in others only as something to be taken away from them. It is, when it becomes a reality, the exclusive possession of a small and disreputable minority of men, like knowledge, courage and honour. A special sort of man is needed to understand it, nay, to stand it—and he is inevitably an outlaw in democratic societies. The average man doesn't want to be free. He simply wants to be safe.

Nietzsche, with his usual clarity of vision, saw the point clearly. Liberty, he used to say, was something that, to the general, was too cold to be borne. Nevertheless, he apparently believed that there was an unnatural, drug-store sort of yearning for it in *all* men, and so he changed Schopenhauer's will-to-live into a will-to-power, *i.e.*, a will-to-free-function. Here he went too far, and in the wrong direction: he should have made it, on the lower levels, a will-to-peace. What the common man longs for in this world, before and above all his other longings, is the simplest and most ignominious sort of peace—the peace of a trusty in a well-managed penitentiary. He is willing to sacrifice everything else to it. He puts it above his dignity and he puts it above his pride. Above all, he puts it above his liberty. The fact, perhaps, explains his veneration for policemen, in all the forms they take—his belief that there is a mysterious sanctity in law, however absurd it may be in fact. A policeman is a charlatan who offers, in return for obedience, to protect him *(a)* from his superiors, *(b)* from his equals, and *(c)* from himself. This last service, under democracy, is commonly the most esteemed of them all. In the United States, at least theoretically, it is the only thing that keeps ice-wagon drivers, Y.M.C.A. secretaries, insurance collectors and other such human camels from smoking opium, ruining themselves in the night clubs, and going to Palm Beach with Follies girls. It is a democratic invention.

Here, though the common man is deceived, he starts from a sound premise: to wit, that liberty is something too hot for his hands—or, as Nietzsche puts it, too cold for his spine. Worse, he sees in it something that is a weapon against him in the hands of his enemy, the man of superior kidney. Be true to your nature, and follow its teachings: this Emersonian counsel, it must be manifest, offers an embarrassing support to every variety of the *droit de seigneur*. The history of democracy is a history of efforts to force successive minorities to be *un*true to their nature. Democracy, in fact, stands in greater peril of the free spirit than any sort of despotism ever heard of. The despot, at least, is always safe in one respect: his own belief in himself cannot be shaken. But democracies may be demoralized and run amok, and so they are in vast dread of heresy, as a Sunday-school superintendent is in dread of scarlet women, light wines and beer, and the unreadable works of Charles Darwin. It would be unimaginable for a democracy to submit serenely to such gross dissents as Frederick the Great not only permitted, but even encouraged. Once the mob is on the loose, there is no holding it. So the subversive minority must be reduced to impotence; the heretic must be put down.

If, as they say, one of the main purposes of all civilized government is to preserve and augment the liberty of the individual, then surely democracy accomplishes it less efficiently than any other form. Is the individual worth thinking of at all? Then the superior individual is worth more thought than his inferiors. But it is precisely the superior individual who is the chief victim of the democratic process. It not only tries to regulate his acts; it also tries to delimit his thoughts; it is constantly inventing new forms of the old crime of imagining the King's death. The Roman *lex de majestate* was put upon the books, not by an emperor, nor even by a consul, but by Saturninus, a tribune of the people. Its aim was to protect the state against aristocrats, *i.e.*, against free spirits, each holding himself answerable only to his own notions. The aim of democracy is to break all such free spirits to the common harness. It tries to iron them out, to pump them dry of self-respect, to make docile John Does of them. The measure of its success is the extent to which such men are brought down, and made common. The measure of civilization is the extent to which they resist and survive. Thus the only sort of liberty that is real under democracy is the liberty of the have-nots to destroy the liberty of the haves. . . .

For all I know, democracy may be a self-limiting disease, as civilization itself seems to be. There are obvious paradoxes in its philosophy, and some of them have a suicidal smack. It offers John Doe a means to rise above his place beside Richard Roe, and then, by making Roe his equal, it takes away the chief usufructs of the rising. I here attempt no pretty logical gymnastics: the history of democratic states is a history of disingenuous efforts to get rid of the second half of that dilemma. There is not only the natural yearning of Doe to use and enjoy the superiority that he has won; there is also the natural tendency of Roe, as an inferior man, to acknowledge it. Democracy, in fact, is always inventing class distinctions, despite its theoretical abhorrence of them. The baron has departed, but in his place stand the grand goblin, the supreme worthy archon, the sovereign grand commander. Democratic man, as I have remarked, is quite unable to think of himself as a free individual; he must belong to a group, or shake with fear and loneliness—and the group, of course, must have its leaders. It would be hard to find a country in which such brummagem serene highnesses are revered with more passionate devotion than they get in the United States. The distinction that goes with mere office runs far ahead of the distinction that goes with actual achievement. A Harding is regarded as genuinely superior to a Halsted, no doubt because his doings are better understood. But there is a form of human striving that is understood by democratic man even better than Harding's, and that is the striving for money. Thus the plutocracy, in a democratic state, tends to take the place of the missing aristocracy, and even to be mistaken for it. It is, of course, something quite different. It lacks all the essential characters of a true aristocracy: a clean tradition, culture, public spirit, honesty, honour, courage—above all, courage. It stands under no bond of obligation to the state; it has no public duty; it is transient and lacks a goal. Its most puissant dignitaries of to-day came out of the mob only yesterday—and from the mob they bring all its peculiar ignobilities. As practically encountered, the plutocracy stands quite as far from the *honnête homme* as it stands from the Holy Saints. Its main character is its incurable timorousness; it is for ever grasping at the straws held out by demagogues. Half a dozen gabby Jewish youths, meeting in a back room to plan a revolution—in other words, half a dozen kittens preparing to upset the Matterhorn—are enough to scare it half to death. Its dreams are of banshees, hobgoblins, bugaboos. The honest, untroubled snores of a Percy or a Hohenstaufen are quite beyond it.

The plutocracy, as I say, is comprehensible to the mob because its aspirations are essentially those of inferior men: it is not by accident that Christianity, a mob religion, paves heaven with gold and precious stones, *i.e.*, with money. There are, of course, reactions against this ignoble ideal among men of more civilized tastes, even in democratic states, and sometimes they arouse the mob to a transient distrust of certain of the plutocratic pretensions. But that distrust seldom arises above mere envy, and the polemic which engenders it is seldom sound in logic or impeccable in motive. What it lacks is aristocratic disinterestedness, born of aristocratic security. There is no body of opinion behind it that is, in the strictest sense, a free opinion. Its chief exponents, by some divine irony, are pedagogues of one sort or another—which is to say, men chiefly marked by their haunting fear of losing their jobs. Living under such terrors, with the plutocracy policing them harshly on one side and the mob congenitally suspicious of them on the other, it is no wonder that their revolt usually peters out in metaphysics, and that they tend to abandon it as their families grow up, and the costs of heresy become prohibitive. The pedagogue, in the long run, shows the virtues of the Congressman, the newspaper editorial writer or the butler, not those of the aristocrat. When, by any chance, he persists in contumacy beyond thirty, it is only too commonly a sign, not that he is heroic, but simply that he is pathological. So with most of his brethren of the Utopian Fife and Drum Corps, whether they issue out of his own seminary or out of the wilderness. They are fanatics; not statesmen. Thus politics, under democracy, resolves itself into impossible alternatives. Whatever the label on the parties, or the war cries issuing from the demagogues who lead them, the practical choice is between the plutocracy on the one side and a rabble of preposterous impossibilists on the other. One must either follow the New York *Times*, or one must be prepared to swallow Bryan and the Bolsheviki. It is a pity that this is so. For what democracy needs most of all is a party that will separate the good that is in it theoretically from the evils that beset it practically, and then try to erect that good into a workable system. What it needs beyond everything is a party of liberty. It produces, true enough, occasional libertarians, just as despotism produces occasionally regicides, but it treats them in the same drum-head way. It will never have a party of them until it invents and installs a genuine aristocracy, to breed them and secure them.

Last Words.   I have alluded somewhat vaguely to the merits of democracy. One of them is quite obvious: it is, perhaps, the most charming form of government ever devised by man. The reason is not far to seek. It is based upon propositions that are palpably not true—and what is not true, as everyone knows, is always immensely more fascinating and satisfying to the vast majority of men than what is true. Truth has a harshness that alarms them, and an air of finality that collides with their incurable romanticism. They turn, in all the great emergencies of life, to the ancient promises, transparently false but immensely comforting, and of all those ancient promises there is none more comforting than the one to the effect that the lowly shall inherit the earth. It is at the bottom of the dominant religious system of the modern world, and it is at the bottom of the dominant political system. The latter, which is democracy, gives it an even higher credit and authority than the former, which is Christianity. More, democracy gives it a certain appearance of objective and demonstrable truth. The mob man, functioning as citizen, gets a feeling that he is really important to the world—that he is genuinely running things. Out of his maudlin herding after rogues and mountebanks there comes to him a sense of vast and mysterious power—which is what makes archbishops, police sergeants, the grand goblins of the Ku Klux and other such magnificoes happy. And out of it there comes, too, a conviction that he is somehow wise, that his views are taken seriously by his betters—which is what makes United States Senators, fortunetellers and Young Intellectuals happy. Finally, there comes out of it a glowing consciousness of a high duty triumphantly done—which is what makes hangmen and husbands happy.

All these forms of happiness, of course, are illusory. They don't last. The democrat, leaping into the air to flap his wings and praise God, is for ever coming down with a thump. The seeds of his disaster, as I have shown, lie in his own stupidity: he can never get rid of the naive delusion—so beautifully Christian!—that happiness is something to be got by taking it away from the other fellow. But there are seeds, too, in the very nature of things: a promise, after all, is only a promise, even when it is supported by divine revelation, and the chances against its fulfillment may be put into a depressing mathematical formula. Here the irony that lies under all human aspiration shows itself: the quest for happiness, as always, brings only *un*happiness in the end. But saying that is merely saying that the true charm of democracy is not for the democrat but for the spectator. That spectator, it seems to me, is favoured with a show of the first cut and calibre. Try to imagine anything more heroically absurd! What grotesque false pretences! What a parade of obvious imbecilities! What a welter of fraud! But is fraud unamusing? Then I retire forthwith as a psychologist. The fraud of democracy, I contend, is more amusing than any other—more amusing even, and by miles, than the fraud of religion. Go into your praying-chamber and give sober thought to any of the more characteristic democratic inventions: say, Law Enforcement.

Or to any of the typical democratic prophets: say, the late Archangel Bryan. If you don't come out paled and palsied by mirth then you will not laugh on the Last Day itself, when Presbyterians step out of the grave like chicks from the egg, and wings blossom from their scapulae, and they leap into interstellar space with roars of joy.

I have spoken hitherto of the possibility that democracy may be a self-limiting disease, like measles. It is, perhaps, something more: it is self-devouring. One cannot observe it objectively without being impressed by its curious distrust of itself—its apparently ineradicable tendency to abandon its whole philosophy at the first sign of strain. I need not point to what happens invariably in democratic states when the national safety is menaced. All the great tribunes of democracy, on such occasions, convert themselves, by a process as simple as taking a deep breath, into despots of an almost fabulous ferocity. Lincoln, Roosevelt and Wilson come instantly to mind: Jackson and Cleveland are in the background, waiting to be recalled. Nor is this process confined to times of alarm and terror: it is going on day in and day out. Democracy always seems bent upon killing the thing it theoretically loves. I have rehearsed some of its operations against liberty, the very cornerstone of its political metaphysic. It not only wars upon the thing itself; it even wars upon mere academic advocacy of it. I offer the spectacle of Americans jailed for reading the Bill of Rights as perhaps the most gaudily humorous ever witnessed in the modern world. Try to imagine monarchy jailing subjects for maintaining the divine right of Kings! Or Christianity damning a believer for arguing that Jesus Christ was the Son of God! This last, perhaps, has been done: anything is possible in that direction. But under democracy the remotest and most fantastic possibility is a commonplace of every day. All the axioms resolve themselves into thundering paradoxes, many amounting to downright contradictions in terms. The mob is competent to rule the rest of us—but it must be rigorously policed itself. There is a government, not of men, but of laws—but men are set upon benches to decide finally what the law is and may be. The highest function of the citizen is to serve the state—but the first assumption that meets him, when he essays to discharge it, is an assumption of his disingenuousness and dishonour. Is that assumption commonly sound? Then the farce only grows the more glorious.

I confess, for my part, that it greatly delights me. I enjoy democracy immensely. It is incomparably idiotic, and hence incomparably amusing. Does it exalt dunderheads, cowards, trimmers, frauds, cads? Then the pain of seeing them go up is balanced and obliterated by the joy of seeing them come down. Is it inordinately wasteful, extravagant, dishonest? Then so is every other form of government: all alike are enemies to laborious and virtuous men. Is rascality at the very heart of it? Well, we have borne that rascality since 1776, and continue to survive. In the long run, it may turn out that rascality is necessary to human government, and even to civilization itself—that civilization, at bottom, is nothing but a colossal swindle. I do not know: I report only that when the suckers are running well the spectacle is infinitely exhilarating. But I am, it may be, a somewhat malicious man: my sympathies, when it comes to suckers, tend to be coy. What I can't make out is how any man can believe in democracy who feels for and with them, and is pained when they are debauched and made a show of. How can any man be a democrat who is sincerely a democrat?

Socialism

30. Why I Believe in Socialism   Corliss Lamont

I became a convinced believer in socialism as the best way out for America and the world almost twenty years ago, about 1931 or 1932. Since that time, the rise of fascism, the undoubted economic success of socialism in the Soviet Union, the coming of the Second World War, the defeat of international fascism and the postwar developments of 1945–49 in America, Europe and Asia have all deepened and strengthened my socialist convictions.

Unquestionably, the Great Depression that started in 1929 was the immediate stimulus that caused me to become skeptical of the capitalist system and to explore systematically the possibilities of the socialist alternative. My upbringing in a prominent capitalist and banking family certainly had not instilled in me any initial bias in favor of socialism. But my parents early made me see that consideration for others was a high ethical value and gave me a liberal slant on many questions; the Phillips Exeter Academy imbued in me a strong feeling for the American tradition of democracy and equality of opportunity; and Harvard and Columbia taught me that reliance on reason is the best method of solving human problems. In my late twenties I developed an affirmative humanist philosophy of life that holds as its chief ethical goal the happiness, freedom and progress of all humanity—irrespective of nation, race and social origin—upon this earth, where it has its only existence. If we are really serious about achieving this end, I think that intelligence then leads us to work for a planned and democratic socialism on a world scale.

My own path to socialism, therefore, was that of analysis through reason, combined with belief in a humanist ethics and a deep attachment to democracy in its broadest sense. However, half-baked Freudians and capitalist critics who use amateur psychoanalysis as a political weapon are always claiming that well-to-do radicals like myself must be primarily impelled by personal neuroses. We have either a publicity complex, an Oedipus complex, a martyr complex, a romantic-revolt complex or a special complex due to neglect or abuse as a child. Yet, relatively few of those who have come over to socialism from the capitalist class seem to have been afflicted with psychological complexes; indeed, most of those who have severe psychoses or suffer nervous breakdowns or commit suicide are members of the bourgeoisie who are faithful to the capitalist system but who cannot stand the gruelling strains it imposes, or their own nightmares of Reds and Russians under every bed.

Apologists for the status quo cannot, of course, admit for a moment that intelligence supports the socialist case, and so they resort to fantastic fables to discredit those who use their brains and go Left. At the same time, these capitalist apologists have been so blinded by the long-cultivated myth that the profit motive and brute selfishness are the main driving force in men that they consider it dangerously abnormal for people to be motivated by the vision of a just and generous social order and by the desire to serve mankind or the working class.

I like the old phrase "public service." Many honest liberals and conservatives have tried hard to serve the public interest, and I am not implying that only radicals are public-spirited. What I am saying is that the ideal of public service in this era ought to bring more and more people over to the cause of socialism.

Another charge with which I have had to contend is that I am insincere because, while proclaiming the goal of a socialist society, I do not at once reduce my standard of living to that of the most poverty-stricken group in the United States. Many years ago I had an encounter with that picturesque blusterer, former general, banker and Vice-President, Charles G. Dawes, who leapt up from an excellent Sunday dinner at the home of the late Dwight W. Morrow, and paced around the table chewing angrily on his pipe, charging that I had no right to believe in socialism until I gave away my last penny. I reminded the Christian multimillionaire that it was not Marx but Jesus who had advised selling all one's goods and giving the proceeds to the poor. Mr. Morrow, a brilliant and sensitive person, remarked that I still seemed to enjoy heartily the fine facilities of my father's country estate on the Palisades. To this I replied that I liked my parents very much and that I would continue to visit them whether they lived in a palace or a hovel.

The point is that there are far more significant things to do for socialism than to make dramatic gestures such as giving away all one's money or breaking off family relations. It takes all kinds of people from many different walks of life to create a successful radical movement. Workers for socialism like myself do not pretend to be either angels or martyrs; it is our unfriendly critics who concoct that myth and then accuse us of hypocrisy because we do not live up to it. It would be folly for us, as for anyone else in capitalist America, to attempt to act *now* as if full-fledged socialism already existed here. And we cannot help feeling that it is more important for us to be effective on behalf of the socialist goal than to satisfy the preconceived whims and malicious criticisms of upper-class folk who are dedicated to the eternal preservation of capitalism.

I have said enough to indicate that in the particular environment in which I grew up and with which I still have many close connections there were plenty of pressures against my becoming a socialist. I first gave some attention to the merits of socialism when I was a senior at Harvard in 1924. And although at that time I fought, unsuccessfully, for the right of a student organization to invite Eugene V. Debs to speak at the Harvard Union, I personally rejected socialism as undesirable and impracticable. That some years later I reversed my opinion was primarily attributable, I believe, to a more profound study of economics and to a better grasp of the method of reason, which, when most accurate, conforms to modern science's method of experimentation and verification.

My capitalist friends are always accusing me of being biased, but in truth I overcame the antisocialist biases natural to my upbringing and have resisted the unremitting pressures to return to the fold of the capitalist faithful. While emotions have their proper and important place in the life of a radical, as in the life of everyone else, I am convinced that the deciding factor in winning me to socialism was not some sort of emotional urge or reaction, but the voice of reason. Ultimately, the socialist case rests on the mind's objective consideration of the relevant facts and theories. And I find at least eight good reasons why the socialist solution is the best answer to our pressing contemporary social-economic problems in the United States and the world at large.

First, while capitalism has enormously increased the productive capacities of mankind, especially through the development of science and the machine, it has not been able, and never will be able, to overcome the fundamental difficulties and contradictions that beset it. Reforms within the structure of the capitalist system can result in genuine amelioration, but I do not think that they can resolve its major dilemmas of recurring overproduction, economic depression and mass unemployment. The basic cause of these phenomena is that in an economy in which profit is both the chief regulator of business and the main motive of businessmen, the capitalists strive to make as much money as they can and to reinvest the greater part in expanding their profit-yielding enterprises. The result is that the capacity to produce grows much faster than the ability to consume, as determined by the people's purchasing power; and it happens again and again that the disproportion can be "solved" only by a costly crisis and depression. The crisis of overproduction is at the same time a crisis of underconsumption; both are the reflection of the accumulation of wealth at one end of the social scale and of poverty at the other.

Various superficial devices, such as fancy currency schemes and share-the-wealth measures, have been suggested or tried as the cure for this central contradiction of capitalism. The most common and substantial remedy attempted has been government spending on public works, as under the New Deal, or on armaments and Marshall Plans, as under the present Administration. Needless to say, war and war preparation constitute a cure that is worse than the disease, and experience shows that so long as capitalism exists, no program of large-scale public works will be permitted to transcend the character of a temporary emergency program, to be discarded as soon as the economy shows signs of returning to prosperity.

Second, there is the tremendous waste inherent in the capitalist system and its wanton exploitation of men and natural resources. In the United States the drive for big, quick profits has brought about the irredeemable spoilage of billions of dollars worth of oil and gas, coal and timber; and reckless deforestation has led to chronic floods, life-devouring dust bowls, and the ruination of huge tracts of fertile land. Throughout the capitalist world, money-minded businessmen, without regard for the consequences to future generations, have been speedily exhausting the natural abundance of our good earth, creating a situation aptly described as *Our Plundered Planet,* to cite the title of a recent book by Mr. Fairfield Osborn. Also, consider the untold loss of wealth through millions upon millions of men and machines standing idle in depression after depression since the Industrial Revolution; through the deprivation of potential production in "normal" times owing to the competitive, chaotic, unplanned nature of capitalism; and above all, through the colossal squandering of human beings and goods in capitalist-caused wars.

My third point is that a planned socialist society, operating for use instead of profit, can put an end to most of the economic waste that occurs under capitalism and prevent the tragic paradox of poverty amid potential plenty. Socialism does not automatically solve all economic problems, but it will do away with the general crises and mass unemployment so characteristic of the capitalist era. And it will unlock to the fullest extent the economic potentialities of the machine age with its scientific techniques. Because it has no fear of overproduction and technological unemployment, a socialist economy heartily welcomes new industrial inventions and labor-saving devices. Today we all know that in the industrially developed nations there is enough goods-producing machinery to ensure a high standard of living for all of the people in such countries. In the United States, an intelligently run economy such as socialism proposes could promptly guarantee to every American family an annual return of goods and services equivalent in value to more than $5,000.

Fourth, it seems to me that if we follow through the logical implications of the idea of public planning, which has been gaining more and more weight in present-day society, we arrive at the key concept of overall *socialist planning* functioning in conjunction with *public ownership of the main means of production and distribution.* Socialist planning for abundance, democratically administered throughout, permanently overcomes the contradictions of capitalism. The government planning organizations, with control over output, prices, wages, hours of work and currency, are able to keep the purchasing power of the population in close equilibrium with the total production of goods. Under capitalism, countless fine individual intelligences and abilities continually work against one another and cancel one another out. Socialist planning would release and coordinate these frustrated intelligences and abilities, bringing into action a great community mind operating on behalf of the common good and embodying the life of reason in social-economic affairs.

Fifth, I see in the very considerable achievements of the Soviet Union a concrete example of what socialism and socialist planning can do. From an economically backward, chiefly agricultural, 70 percent illiterate country under the Tsars, the Soviet Five-Year Plans have transformed Russia into a dynamic, forward-moving economy with highly developed industry and collectivized agriculture. At the same time the people of the USSR have become 90 percent literate, well educated by twentieth-century standards and excellently trained in modern machine techniques. During the Nazi invasion and four years of all-out warfare, the planned economy of the USSR made an impressive showing, utterly refuting foreign observers who had predicted its speedy collapse. Although American and British Lend-Lease was extremely helpful, the Soviet factories themselves turned out more than 90 percent of the guns, airplanes and tanks that swept Hitler back all the way to Berlin; and the Soviets had the trained manpower to handle efficiently the most up-to-date and complicated engines of war. In its supreme test Soviet socialism worked most successfully.

Since the end of World War II in 1945, a new Soviet Five-Year Plan has been performing a Herculean job of economic reconstruction, and the general standard of living is resuming the advance which was interrupted by the fascist onslaught. The Soviet Union is certainly no Utopia and it still has many defects. It has, for example, shown a definite lag in respect to political democracy and civil liberties, despite forging ahead of any other country in the realm of racial democracy and equality. As a radical who has long been sympathetic to Soviet accomplishments, I think we should guard against being uncritical of Soviet Russia; we must frankly criticize that country for its shortcomings and learn from its mistakes. Other nations that are making progress towards socialism also have much to teach us.

I believe, sixth, that socialism not only lays the basis for a rational and just economic system but also gives promise of bringing about a far-reaching cultural revolution. By creating an economy of abundance, socialist planning is able to multiply the production of cultural goods such as books, school and college buildings, radio sets, musical instruments, theatres and the like. It greatly increases the number of teachers and pays them decent salaries. By replacing production for profit with production for use, socialism ends the capitalist method of judging artistic and cultural products primarily in terms of the money they may make and fosters their evaluation in terms of true merit. The socialist economic system together with socialist teaching effects a transformation in human motives, coordinating the altruistic and egoistic impulses so that people find their welfare and happiness in working for the general good instead of always putting their economic self-interest first, as in capitalist theory. This aspect of socialism entails a far higher ethical philosophy than that of capitalism and one that is decidedly more in harmony with the most enlightened social ideals of Christianity.

My seventh point on the advantages of socialism is perhaps the most important of all because it deals with the elimination of international war—the most terrible scourge that has ever afflicted mankind and so dangerous today, in light of the new weapons of the atom bomb and germ warfare, that it could set back for centuries all civilization, socialist and capitalist. My thesis is that, while economics is not the whole story, economic dilemmas and drives are the primary causes of war and that in our modern era the capitalist system itself has been responsible for almost all international conflict, notably the two world wars of the twentieth century. Imperialist rivalries between the European capitalist powers brought on World War I. Capitalism in its last, most brutal stage—fascism, as exemplified in Germany, Italy and Japan—started World War II, aided by the Munich appeasers. It attacked both the Western democracies and the Soviet Union, a nation that had made every effort to preserve peace through a genuine system of collective security.

A socialist society cuts away the economic roots of war. Public ownership of the instrumentalities of production means that no individuals or groups can make money from manufacturing armaments. Central planning, by establishing a coordinated economy at home, makes it unnecessary for a socialist country to extricate itself from domestic economic troubles through military adventures abroad, or by striving desperately to get rid of surplus goods on the foreign market. As it unfolds internationally, socialism puts a finish once and for all to the fierce struggle, with the whole earth as the arena, among the capitalist imperialisms, to survive and expand at the expense of one another and of exploited colonial peoples. It brings into being the essential economic conditions for permanent peace and for that enduring fraternity of peoples that has always been one of its highest aims. When the socialist principle has gained enough strength throughout the world, we can be confident that the United Nations will be a success.

Eighth and finally, I am convinced that socialism offers the best way of fulfilling the promise of modern democracy, both in America and elsewhere, and of preventing the resurgence of fascism. Since fascism is simply capitalism stripped of all democratic pretenses and other unessentials—capitalism in the nude, as it were—the danger of fascism remains as long as the capitalist system is with us. A socialist society builds the necessary foundations of a broad and lasting democracy by establishing a stable economy and giving to the workers and the masses of the people the economic and cultural prerequisites for their democratic liberties. And it insists on extending full democratic rights to all racial groups and to the approximately one-half of the population that is female.

Furthermore, I am of the opinion that in countries like the United States and Great Britain, which have long and strong traditions of political democracy and civil liberties, we can accomplish the transition to socialism through peaceful and democratic procedures. In nations like Russia and China, however, where under the old regimes democratic institutions were extremely weak or practically nonexistent, violent revolution was in all probability the only way out. So far as the United States is concerned, in order to smooth the path to socialism and maintain our constitutional guarantees for everyone, I am in favor of the government's buying out the capitalists when it receives the voters' mandate to socialize the natural resources, the factories, the banks, transportation and communication facilities, and so on. This would be in accordance with that section of the Bill of Rights which reads: ". . . nor shall private property be taken for public use without just compensation." America is wealthy enough to adopt this procedure, and it would go far in staving off counterrevolutionary violence on the part of the capitalist class.

With the coming of Hitler to power in 1933 and the onset of World War II in 1939, American radicals naturally became largely preoccupied with stopping fascism as the best method of furthering socialism. Since the end of the war we have continued to concentrate on immediate problems of both a domestic and international character. The day has arrived, I think, to renew our direct educational and political work on behalf of a socialist America, while in no way neglecting day-to-day problems. Capitalism has failed America and mankind, and the most fundamental need of our country is to institute a socialist economy. The various types of socialists in the United States have too long been on the defensive; now is the time to militantly take the offensive in order to make American socialism a reality.

Anarchism

31. The Nature of the State   John Hospers

John Hospers (1918–) is professor of philosophy in the University of Southern California School of Philosophy at Los Angeles and editor of the *Pacific Philosophical Quarterly*. In 1972 he was the Libertarian Party's candidate for President of the United States. Had he won, Professor Hospers would have become the second philosopher to have been elected president; the first was Thomas Jefferson.

. . . Most academicians, somewhat isolated from the marketplace which ultimately pays their salaries, still appear to think of the State as a benevolent agent which may have gone wrong in this way or that, but still to be trusted and admired (and in any case, used by them). My own attitude toward the State, based on its workings and the experience of myself and many others with its representatives, is very different.

It is difficult to communicate briefly an attitude toward the State which took many years of reading and reflection to develop. I shall begin with the thesis of Franz Oppenheimer's book *The State* (1908). There are, he said, two ways of obtaining the things one needs and wants: the first method is production and exchange—to produce something out of nature's raw materials or transform them into a product (or service) desired by others, and to take the surplus of one's own production of one thing and exchange it for another kind of surplus from the production of others. This method of survival, production and exchange, he called the *economic* means. But there is also a second means: not to produce anything at all but to seize by force the things that others have produced—the method of plunder. This he called the *political* means.

Not everyone, of course, can use the second means, since one cannot seize from others something they have not already created or produced. But some people can and do, siphoning off the fruits of other people's labor for themselves. In the end, the supply is destroyed if this means is used too extensively, since it does not add to but rather subtracts from the totality of production: the more that is used up by the predator, the more must be created by others to replenish the supply. And of course

From *The Personalist*, Vol. 59, No. 4 (October 1978). Reprinted with permission of the author.

the systematic plunder of the goods that someone has produced considerably reduces his motivation for producing any more.

Now the State, said Oppenheimer, is *the organization of the political means*. It is the systematic use of the predatory process over a given territory. Crimes committed by individuals, e.g. murder and theft, are sporadic and uncertain in their outcome: the victims may resist and even win. But the State provides a legal, orderly, systematic channel for the seizure of the fruits of other men's labor, and through the use of force it renders secure the parasitic caste in society.

> The classic paradigm was a conquering tribe pausing in its time-honored method of looting and murdering a conquered tribe, to realize that the time-span of plunder would be longer and more secure, and the situation more pleasant, if the conquered tribe were allowed to live and produce, with the conquerors settling among them as the rulers exacting a steady annual tribute. One method of the birth of a State may be illustrated as follows: in the hills of southern Ruritania, a bandit group manages to obtain physical control over the territory, and finally the bandit chieftain proclaims himself "King of the sovereign and independent government of South Ruritania"; and, if he and his men have the force to maintain this rule for a while, lo and behold! a new State has joined the "family of nations," and the former bandit leaders have been transformed into the lawful nobility of the realm.[1]

The State cannot keep the process of extortion going indefinitely unless it also confers some benefits (people might sooner or later revolt). One such benefit is protection—protection against other tribes, and protection against aggressors within the tribe. The State seldom manages this efficiently (what *does* it do efficiently?)—e.g. it protects only heads of state, and with everyone else it punishes (if at all) only after the aggression has been committed. And of course it increases its levy on all citizens to pay for this protection. But the State well knows that people also desire other benefits, specifically economic benefits. And these the State endeavors to supply, if for no other reason than to keep them peaceful, and, in the case of a democracy, to win their votes.

But this presents a problem, for the State has no resources of its own with which to confer these benefits. It can give to one person only by first seizing it from another; if one person gets something for nothing, another must get nothing for something. But the citizen-voter's attention is so centered on the attractiveness of the things being promised that he forgets that the politician making the promises doesn't have any of these things to give—and that he will have none of them after he gets into office; he will seize the earnings of one special interest group and distribute those earnings to another such group (minus the government's 40% handling fee, of course). And thus

> . . . the promisees continue to give their votes to the candidate making the biggest promises. One candidate promises to get sufficient federal

---

[1] Murray Rothbard, *Egalitarianism and Other Essays* (New York: Laissez Faire Press, 1973), p. 37. See also the opening pages of Richard Taylor, *Freedom, Anarchy and the Law* (Prentice-Hall, 1973).

funds for urban transportation to maintain the artificially low-priced subway ride in New York City. Another promises sufficient funds to guarantee Kansas wheat farmers more income for less wheat than the open market gives. Both candidates win. They meet in the cloak room on Capitol Hill, confess their sins to each other, and each one pledges to help the other deliver on his promise.

As the farmer collects the higher price for his wheat and the New Yorker enjoys his subsidized subway ride, each of them takes pride in the fine representative he has in Washington. As the farmer and the subway rider see it, each representative has just demonstrated that free servants are available, and that the honest citizen can get something for nothing if he will vote for the right candidate. The New Yorker fails to see that his own taxes have been increased in order to pay the Kansas farmer to cut down on his wheat production so the farmer can get a higher price for what he sells; so the New Yorker will have to pay a higher price for his bread. In like manner, the farmer doesn't seem to realize that his taxes have been increased in order to subsidize the urban transportation system, so the city dweller can enjoy a higher standard of living while lowering his own level of production; so the farmer will have the dubious privilege of paying higher prices for the tools and machinery he has to buy. The farmer and the subway rider are expropriating each other's productive capacity and paying a handsome royalty to an unruly bureaucracy for the privilege of doing it. In the marketplace that would be called plundering. In the political arena it is known as social progress.[2]

Particularly profitable for the State is the "discovery" of scapegoats, those whose earnings it can systematically loot, and gain public approval for doing so through an incessant barrage of propaganda against them. Such scapegoats are not difficult to find: any person who wishes to be independent of the State; anyone who is a "self-made man," and most of all anyone who has produced and marketed something and attained wealth. Those who have not succeeded in open competition tend to envy those who have, and the State fans this envy.[3] Thus the majority of the population actually come to applaud the State for taking it away from those who have been more successful than they. Like those that killed the goose that laid the golden egg, they do not see ahead to the time when there will be no more eggs forthcoming. There will be little incentive to produce if years of effort are confiscated by the State, and many people who were employed before will now find themselves without work. The general standard of living of course will decline—most citizens do not see the inevitability of this, and some politicians do but don't mind, preferring to have a subservient and poverty-stricken population. In some States the process goes so far that the State itself becomes the sole owner of land, the sole employer of everyone (*e.g.,* the Soviet Union); determining the profession and salary of every worker; and anyone who tries to save anything for himself, or earn anything other than through the State, is subject to interrogation, torture, and death by shooting or exile to the Gulag. Yet so successful, often, is the propaganda of the

[2] Bertel Sparks, "How Many Servants Can You Afford?" *The Freeman*, October 1976, p. 593.
[3] See Helmut Schoeck, *Envy.*

State on its own behalf, that even with this ultimate control over the life of every citizen, some people applaud the State as their protector and security ("the sanction of the victim"). As if the State could supply security, instead of (as it does) taking away from its subjects that much chance of ever taking steps to achieve their own security! But the process continues:

> As the competition for votes increases, each candidate finds it necessary to broaden his base. He must make more promises to more people. As these promises are fulfilled, more and more people find it advantageous to lower their own level of production so they can qualify for larger appropriations from the public till. Direct payments to farmers for producing less is an example of this. So are rent subsidies and food stamps for the lower income groups . . . [And] some of the less skilled members of society learn that it is more profitable to them to cease production altogether and rely upon the relief rolls for everything. . . . [Increasingly] the expectations of some special interest group have not been met, and the government is called upon to supply the shortage. That is to say, the government is called upon to supply some "free" services. Unfortunately, the government has nothing to give any special group except what it expropriates through taxation or otherwise from some other group.
>
> The contest becomes a contest between producers and non-producers, with the government aligned on the side of the non-producers. This result has nothing to do with whether government officials are honest or dishonest, wise or stupid. They are mere agents administering a system which the citizens, acting in their capacity as voters, have demanded. It is a system that includes in its own mechanism the seeds of its own destruction. The marginal producer, whether he is a laborer or a manager, cannot avoid seeing the advantages of allowing himself to fall below the survival line, cease his contributions to those who are still further below, and qualify for a claim upon his government, and through his government upon more successful competitors, for his own support. And each individual or business enterprise that takes that step will automatically draw the producer who is only slightly higher on the economic scale just a little closer to that same survival line. Eventually all are pulled below it and are faced with the necessity of beginning over again without any prosperous neighbors upon whom they can call for help, and without any backlog of capital they can use as a starting point.[4]

And thus does the State, once it goes into the business of conferring economic benefits, cause a state of splendidly equalized destitution for everyone. The State itself rises from the ashes more powerful than ever: with every economic crisis a new emergency is declared, giving the State more power with the full approval of the majority of its citizens ("only for the duration of the emergency"—whose end is never in sight), until it ends up in total control of everything and everyone—which of course is just what the State wanted all along. But by that time it is too late for anyone to object.

The full story is far too long even to outline here. I shall mention only a few chapter headings in the saga of The State:

1. *Taxation.* It can usually be relied upon to increase until the point of total collapse ("take till there's nothing left to be taken").

[4] *Bertel Sparks, op. cit.,* pp. 593–5.

2. *Inflation.* Even high taxation is not enough to pay for what the politicians have promised the voters, so the State increases the money supply to meet the deficit. This of course decreases the value of each dollar saved, and ultimately destroys savings, penalizes thrift, wrecks incentive, bankrupts business enterprises and creates huge unemployment. But this is only the beginning:

3. *Dictatorship.* As prices rise out of sight, demand for price controls increases. Price controls create shortages (men cannot continue to produce at a loss). Shortages create strikes, hunger riots, civil commotion as the shortages spread. From this arises a Caesar, to "take a firm hand" and "restore law and order." The economy is now totally controlled from the center (with all the inefficiency and waste that this implies), and each individual, including his wages and conditions of work (and what he may work at), is thoroughly regimented. Liberty has now been lost. Most of this scenario is probably inevitable for the U.S. in the next two decades.[5]

Other chapter headings along the way would include: (4) Depressions. The State, through its interventionist policies, is solely responsible for economic depressions.[6] (5) Poverty. The State is the cause of most of the poverty that there is in this country. If you want to eliminate poverty, eliminate State intervention in the marketplace.[7]—There are others, but the point is aptly summarized by Rose Wilder Lane, commenting on the slogan "Government should do for people what people can not do for themselves":

> Would persons who adopt such resolutions (and say the same thing again and again, all the time, everywhere) put that idea in realistic terms and say, "Government should do nothing but compel other persons, by force, to do what those persons do not want to do?" Because, obviously, if those other persons *want* to do it, they *will* do it, if it can possibly be done; so it will be done, if it can be—if they're simply let alone.
>
> "The people" have in fact done everything that *is* done; they built the houses and roads and railroads and telephones and planes, they organized the oil companies, the banks, the postal services, the schools—what didn't "the people" do? What happens is that, after they do it, the Government *takes* it. The government takes the roads, the postal service, the systems of communications, the banks, the markets, the stock exchange, insurance companies, schools, building trades, telegraphs and telephones, *after* "the people" have done all these things for themselves.[8]

Small children are prolific with their spending proposals because their eyes are on the goodies to be attained, and they do not see the labor, the cost, the hardship and deprivation which their spending schemes

---

[5] See Irwin Schiff, *The Biggest Con* (Arlington House, j1976), C. V. Myers, *The Coming Deflation* (Arlington House, 1976). Clarence B. Carson, *The War on the Poor* (Arlington House, 1970), and others.

[6] See, for example, Lionel Robbins, *The Great Depression,* and Murray Rothbard, *The Great Depression.*

[7] See, e.g., Clarence B. Carson, *The War on the Poor,* and Shirley Scheibla, *Poverty Is Where the Money Is.*

[8] Rose Wilder Lane, in Roger L. MacBride (ed.), *The Lady and the Tycoon* (Caxton Press, 1973), pp. 332–3.

would entail. Social planners are as a whole in the same category; they see the end but not the means.

These views have often been accused of being un-humanitarian. (Though President Ford is also among the big spenders—what else would you call a hundred billion dollar deficit in one year? which is more than all the profits of all American corporations put together—he occasionally vetoes a particularly virulent piece of legislation, and is accused of being un-humanitarian.) What is humanitarian about seizing other people's earnings and using them for purposes which *you* think they should be used for? While others think of the "great social gains" to be achieved (which will not occur anyway, since the State employees waste most of it—what poverty has been ended by poverty programs?), I think of the corner shopkeeper, already forced to the wall by confiscatory taxation, government inflation, and endless government regulation, trying to keep his head above water, and the effect of one government scheme after another to spend his money—what will be the effect of all this on him and others like him? Much more humanitarian are the words of the great French economist Frederic Bastiat, written in 1848:

> How is legal plunder to be identified? Quite simply. See if the law takes from some persons what belongs to them, and gives it to other persons to whom it does not belong. See if the law benefits one citizen at the expense of another by doing what the citizen himself cannot do without committing a crime.[9]

The State, implemented by all the channels of communications which it controls, will use all its powers to resist such advice; and every economic incentive (and threat of deprivation) at its command will be used as well. But this in no way alters the fact that

> ... The State is no proper agency for social welfare, and never will be, for exactly the same reason that an ivory paperknife is nothing to shave with. The interests of society and of the State do not coincide; any pretense that they can be made to coincide is sheer nonsense. Society gets on best when people are most happy and contented, which they are when freest to do as they please and what they please; hence society's interest is in having as little government as possible, and in keeping it as decentralized as possible. The State, on the other hand, is administered by job-holders; hence its interest is in having as much government as possible. It is hard to imagine two sets of interests more directly opposed than these.[10]

Those who ignore these remarks, and seek to use the coercive power of the State to impose their ideas of welfare or utopia on others, must bear a heavy moral burden—the burden of the suffering they impose (however inadvertently) on others by their actions, of the incalculable loss in human well-being.

According to Rawls, man's primary social goods are "rights and liberties, opportunities and powers, income and wealth."[11] But some of these, when put into practice, would negate others. Rawls advocates (to

---

[9] Frederick Bastiat, *The Law* (Foundation for Economic Education edition, p. 21).
[10] Albert Jay Nock, *Cogitations*, p. 40.
[11] John Rawls, *A Theory of Justice* (Harvard University Press, 1971), p. 91.

take one example among many) government ownership of the means of production (though not necessarily all of them). This entails not only the inefficiency and waste and corruption that regularly characterize enterprises handled by the State, from the post office on down (or up?), but the huge bureaucracy required to administer it, which always seeks to increase its own numbers and power, and over which the citizen has no direct control.[12] When one spells out the full implications of all of this, very little is left of liberty; and the ostensible reason for placing such things in the hands of government—"so that everyone can have it"—ends up as its very opposite, "there's nothing left to distribute." Any resemblance between Rawls' theory and justice is strictly coincidental.

Dr. Burrill,* like most of his colleagues, considers some ends so important that he would use the coercive apparatus of the State to enforce his ideals on everyone. He concludes that the marketplace is in need of improvement through State intervention (presumably along the lines of his own ideals), and that we need "a general justification of the entrepreneurial system as it stands." As it stands! As if there were anything left of the entrepreneurial system in this country but a mangled hulk, with a few crumbs thrown out by omnipotent government to produce and make money so that the State could confiscate it! As if this country still had a live and functioning "entrepreneurial system" instead of what we have now, a fascist-type State in which the State has a life-and-death stranglehold on every industry, every trade, every farm, every enterprise that exists! Is this battered ruin to be "improved" by still further interventions by the State? And what justifies one person in imposing *his* ideals on *everyone* through the coercive machinery of the State?[13]

It matters little whether Oppenheimer's account of the origins of the State is correct. (It surely is in most cases, but there are very significant differences in the case of the origin of the U.S.A.) It matters much more what the State is doing *now*. Whether the State was conceived and born in sin is less important than whether it is involved in sin now. And there is little doubt that, whatever its origin, sinning is currently its principal activity.

In a remarkably prescient letter to one H. S. Randall of New York, the British historian Thomas Macaulay wrote (May 23, 1857):

> The day will come when . . . a multitude of people will choose the legislature. Is it possible to doubt what sort of legislature will be chosen? On the one side is a statesman preaching patience, respect for rights, strict observance of the public faith. On the other is the demagogue ranting about the tyranny of capitalism . . . Which of the Candidates is likely to

---

[12] For many examples of this, in the context of American history, see William Wooldridge, *Uncle Sam the Monopoly Man* (Arlington House, 1970).

*[Donald R. Burrill, "Distributive Justice and the Minimal State: A Response to Blackstone," *The Personalist*, Vol. 59, No. 4 (October, 1978)—Ed.]

[13] See John Hospers, *Libertarianism* (Nash, 1971); also Robert Nozick, *Anarchy, State, and Utopia* (Basic Books, 1975); Frederic Bastiat, *The Law;* Henry Hazlitt, *Economics in One Lesson* (Harper 1946); Ludwig von Mises' books *Socialism; Bureaucracy;* and *Omnipotent Government* (all Yale University Press).

be preferred. . . .? I seriously apprehend that you will, in some season of adversity, do things which will prevent prosperity from returning: that you will act like some people in a year of scarcity: devour all the seed corn and thus make next year a year, not of scarcity but of absolute failure. There will be, I fear, spoliation. This spoliation wil increase distress. The distress will produce fresh spoliation. There is nothing to stay you. Your Constitution is all sail and no anchor. When Society has entered on this downward progress, either civilization or liberty must perish. Either some Caesar or Napoleon will seize the reins of government with a strong hand, or your Republic will be as fearfully plundered and laid waste by barbarians in the twentieth century as the Roman Empire in the fifth: with this difference, that the Huns and Vandals who ravaged the Roman Empire came from without, and that your Huns and Vandals will have been engendered within your country, by your own institutions.[14]

The State, says Robert Paul Wolff in his *In Defense of Anarchism*, wields great *power* over us—but whence derives its *authority* (the moral right to wield that power)? In a telling exposition of the distinction, he finds no basis for any such authority; nor does he succeed in solving this problem in the later (more pragmatic) sections of the book. (Even if a contract theory would help—and as Hume cogently argued, it wouldn't—there was in fact no such contract. Unlike other organizations such as churches and clubs, no one contracted to be ruled by the State.)

In all existing States, some individuals (through their representatives) get hold of the State apparatus to enforce their ideas of a good society on others, including those who find it useless, repellent, or immoral. A would like to impose his plan on B and C (they would be pawns on *his* chessboard); B would impose his plan on A and C; and so on. But, observed Bastiat,

> . . . by what right does the law force me to conform to the social plan of Mr. A or Mr. B or Mr. C? If the law has a moral right to do this, why does it not, then, force these gentlemen to submit to *my* plans? Is it logical to suppose that nature has not given *me* sufficient imagination to dream up a utopia also? Should the law choose one fantasy among many, and put the organized force of government at its service only?[15]

Am I then committed to anarchism? Not necessarily, though as it has been worked out in detail by numerous writers, with provisions for a system of private defense and courts, I consider it greatly preferable to the leviathan we have today.[16] One of the greatest and least appreciated of political philosophers, Herbert Spencer, was not an anarchist.[17] He set forth "The Law of Equal Freedom": "Each man should be free to

[14]For similar predictions, see Alexis de Toqueville, *Democracy in America*, 1840.

[15]Bastiat, *The Law*, p. 71.

[16]See, for example, Morris and Linda Tannehill, *The Market for Liberty;* 1970; David Friedman, *The Machinery of Freedom* (Anchor Doubleday, 1973); Leonard Krimerman and Lewis Perry (ed.), *Patterns of Anarchy* (Anchor Doubleday, 1966); Lysander Spooner, *The Constitution of No Authority;* James J. Martin (ed.), *Men against the State* (De Kalb, Ill.: Adrian Allen Associates, 1953); also Chapter 11 of J. Hospers, *Libertarianism* (Nash, 1971).

[17]See his monumental work, *The Man versus the State* (1884; reprinted by Caxton Press, 1940).

act as he chooses, provided he trenches not on the equal freedom of each other man to act as he chooses." Then he attempted to resolve the "problem of political authority" as follows, in the chapter "The Right to Ignore the State" (omitted from most subsequent editions) of his book *Social Statics:*

> . . . we can not choose but admit the right of the citizen to adopt a condition of *voluntary outlawry.* If every man has freedom to do all that he wills, provided he infringes not on the equal freedom of any others, then he is free to *drop connection with the State*—to relinquish its protection and to refuse paying toward its support. It is self-evident that in so behaving he in no way trenches upon the liberty of others, for his position is a passive one, and while passive he cannot become an aggressor . . . He cannot be compelled to continue one of a political corporation without a breach of the moral law, seeing that citizenship involves payment of taxes; and the taking away of a man's property against his will is an infringement of his rights. *Government being simply an agent employed in common by a number of individuals to secure to them certain advantages, the very nature of the connection implies that it is for each to say whether he will employ such an agent or not.* If any one of them determines to ignore this mutual-safety confederation, nothing can be said except that he loses all claim to its good offices and exposes himself to the danger of maltreatment—a thing he is quite at liberty to do if he likes. He cannot be coerced into political combination without breach of the Law of Equal Freedom; he *can* withdraw from it without committing any such breach, and he has therefore a right so to withdraw.[18]

These words of Spencer seem to me to contain the core of any political philosophy worthy of the name. No other provides sufficiently for voluntary consent and human liberty (or as Wolff says, autonomy), not to mention such other human values as individuality, enduring prosperity, creative opportunity, and peace.

[18]Herbert Spencer, *Social Statics,* 1845, p. 185. Italics mine.

Contemporary Issues

Political Freedom and Capitalism

32. The Future of Capitalism   Milton Friedman

Milton Friedman (1912–   ) is Paul Snowden Russell Distinguished Service Professor of Economics at the University of Chicago. He received the Nobel Prize in economics in 1976. He is a columnist for *Newsweek* and also is a contributing editor of that magazine. He combines the technical sophistication of the scholarly economist with the ability to communicate effectively with the general public and politicians. President Reagan called his book *Free to Choose,* coauthored with his wife, a "superb book."

My subject is "The Future of Capitalism." When I speak of the future of capitalism I mean the future of competitive capitalism—a free enterprise capitalism. In a certain sense, every major society is capitalistic. Russia has a great deal of capital but the capital is under the control of governmental officials who are supposedly acting as the agents of the state. That turns capitalism (state capitalism) into a wholly different system than a system under which capital is controlled by individuals in their private capacity as owners and operators of industry. What I want to speak about tonight is the future of private enterprise—of competitive capitalism.

The future of private enterprise capitalism is also the future of a free society. There is no possibility of having a politically free society unless the major part of its economic resources are operated under a capitalistic private enterprise system.

The Trend Toward Collectivism

The real question therefore is the future of human freedom. The question that I want to talk about is whether or not we are going to complete the movement that has been going on for the past forty or fifty years, away from a free society and toward a collectivist society. Are we going to continue down that path until we have followed Chile by losing our political freedom and coming under the thumb of an all-powerful government? Or are we going to be able to halt that trend, perhaps even reverse it, and establish a greater degree of freedom?

One thing is clear, we cannot continue along the lines that we have been moving. In 1928, less than fifty years ago, government at all levels—federal, state, and local—spent less than 10 percent of the national income. Two-thirds of that was at the state and local level. Federal spending amounted to less than 3 percent of the national income. Today, total government spending at all levels amounts to 40 percent of the national income, and two-thirds of that is at the federal level. So federal government spending has moved in less than fifty years from 3 percent to over

From *Vital Speeches of the Day,* Vol. XXXXIII, No. 11 (March 15, 1977). Reprinted with permission of *Vital Speeches of the Day.*

25 percent—total government spending from 10 percent to 40 percent. Now, I guarantee you one thing. In the next fifty years government spending cannot move from 40 percent of the national income to 160 percent. (Legislatures have tried to legislate that the value of π shall be exactly three and a seventh but they cannot repeal the laws of arithmetic!)

We cannot continue on this path. The question is, will we keep trying to continue on this path until we have lost our freedom and turned our lives over to an all-powerful government in Washington, or will we stop?

In judging this possibility, it's worth talking a little bit about where we are and how we got here—about the present and the past. Let me say at the outset that with all the problems I am going to talk about, this still remains a predominantly free society. There is no great country in the world (there are some small enclaves, but no great country) that offers as much freedom to the individual as the United States does. But having said that we ought also to recognize how far we have gone away from the ideal of freedom and the extent to which our lives are restricted by governmental enactments.

In talking about freedom it is important at the outset to distinguish two different meanings on the economic level, of the concept of free enterprise, for there is no term which is more misused or misunderstood. The one meaning that is often attached to free enterprise is the meaning that enterprises shall be free to do what they want. That is not the meaning that has historically been attached to free enterprise. What we really mean by free enterprise is the freedom of individuals to set up enterprises. It is the freedom of an individual to engage in an activity so long as he uses only voluntary methods of getting other individuals to co-operate with him. If you want to see how far we have moved from the basic concept of free enterprise, you can consider how free anyone is to set up an enterprise. You are *not* free to establish a bank or to go into the taxicab business unless you can get a certificate of convenience and necessity from the local, state, or federal authorities. You cannot become a lawyer or a physician or a plumber or a mortician (and you can name many other cases) unless you can get a license from the government to engage in that activity. You cannot go into the business of delivering the mail or providing electricity or of providing telephone service unless you get a permit from the government to do so. You cannot raise funds on the capital market and get other people to lend you money unless you go through the S.E.C. and fill out the 400 pages of forms that they require. To take the latest restriction on freedom, you cannot any longer engage in voluntary deals with others or make bets with other people about the future prices of commodities unless you get the approval of the government.

Rising Taxation

Another example of the extent to which we have moved away from a free society is the 40 percent of our earnings, on the average, which is co-opted by the government. Each and every one of us works from the first of January to late in April or May, in order to pay governmental expenses, before we can start to work for our own expenses.

If you want to look at it still another way, the government owns 48 percent of every corporation in the United States. We talk about ourselves as a free enterprise society. Yet in terms of the fundamental question of who owns the means of production, in the corporate sector we are 48 percent socialistic because the corporate tax is 48 percent. What does it mean if I own 1 percent of a corporation? It means I am entitled to 1 percent of the profits and 1 percent of the losses. Well, the federal government shares 48 percent of your profits and 48 percent of your losses (if you have some previous profits to offset those losses against).

Once when I was in Yugoslavia some years ago I calculated that the difference in the degree of socialism in the United States and in Communist Yugoslavia was exactly 18 percentage points, because the U. S. Government took 48 percent of the profits of every corporation and the Yugoslav government took 66 percent of the profits of every corporation. And of course, those numbers grossly understate the role of the government because of its effect in regulating business in areas other than taxation.

Let me give you another example of the extent to which we have lost freedom. About a year or so ago, I had a debate in Washington with that great saint of the United States consumer, Ralph Nader. I planted a question on him, because I knew what the answer would be and I wanted to extract the answer. The question I took up was the question of state laws requiring people who ride motorcycles to wear motorcycle helmets. Now I believe in many ways that law is the best litmus paper I know to distinguish true believers in individualism from people who do not believe in individualism, because this is the case in which the man riding the motorcycle is risking only his own life. He may be a fool to drive that motorcycle without a helmet. But part of freedom and liberty is the freedom to be a fool! So I expressed the view that the state laws which make it compulsory for people who are riding motorcycles to wear helmets were against individual freedom and against the principles of a free society. I asked Ralph Nader for his opinion and he gave the answer I expected. He said, "Well, that's all very well for a different society. But you must realize that today, if a motorcyclist driving down the road without a helmet splashes himself on the pavement, a government-subsidized ambulance will come to pick him up, they will take him to a government-subsidized hospital, he will be buried in a government-subsidized cemetery, and his wife and children will be supported by government-subsidized welfare. Therefore we can't let him!" What he was saying was that every single one of us bears on our back a stamp that says, "Property of the U.S. Government. Do not fold, bend, or mutilate."

That is essentially the fundamental principle that animates the Ralph Naders of our time—the people who want the power to be in government. You see it everywhere. You see it in a law which was passed a few years ago which requires the Treasury Department to report to the Congress a category called "Tax Expenditures." Tax Expenditures are taxes which are not collected from you because of various deductions permitted by the law (such as interest or excess depreciation). The principle is that you are, after all, the property of the U. S. Government. You work for the U.S. Government, and the U.S. Government lets you keep a little of what you earn in order to be sure that they'll keep you working hard for them. But the rest of it is the property of the U.S. Government. And if the U.S. Government allows you to deduct something from your taxes, it's providing for the expenditure. It's not a right that you have to keep it in. It's theirs!

Other Freedoms Denied

We have gone very far indeed along the road to losing freedom. But you may say that I am talking only about economic matters, about whether you can enter a profession or an occupation. What about political freedom? What about the freedom of speech? How many businessmen have you heard in the past ten years who have been willing to stand up on some public rostrum and take issue with governmental policies? I have heard many a businessman get up and express general sentiments in favor of free enterprise and of competition. I have heard very few get up and criticize particular measures taken by government. And I don't blame them. They would be fools to do it! Because any businessman who has the nerve to do that has to look over one shoulder and see what the I.R.S. is going to do to his books the next day. And he has to look over the other shoulder to see whether the Justice Department is going to launch an anti-trust suit. And then he has to find two or three more shoulders to see what the F.T.C. is going to do. You can take any other three letters of the alphabet and you have to ask what they are going to do to you. In fact, a businessman today does not have effective freedom of speech.

But businessmen don't matter since they're only material business people. What about those people for whom we are really concerned—the intellectuals?

I asked my colleagues, suppose I take a professor from a medical school whose research and training is largely being financed by the National Institutes of Health. Do you suppose he wouldn't think three times before he gives a speech against socialized medicine? Suppose I take one of my colleagues in economics who has been supported by a grant from the National Science Foundation. I personally happen to think there is no justification for the National Science Foundation. (As it happens, I have never received a grant from them though I might have. It isn't that they have turned me down; I haven't asked them!) But nonetheless, do you suppose my colleagues would not be inhibited in speaking out? In fact, I have often said about the only people who have any real freedom of speech left are people who are in the fortunate position of myself—tenured professors at major private universities on the verge of retirement!

Freedom of the Press

Let me give you an even more chilling story about freedom of the press. The other day I got a clipping from an English paper from a friend of mine, indicating that the *London Times* had been prevented from publishing on one day because the unions, who have controlled the press, refused to publish it because the issue carried a story that was critical of the policies of unions. Do you mean to say that there aren't American newspapers which would hesitate very much before printing stories and articles that would be regarded as antagonistic by the trade unions on which they depend to produce their papers?

So there is no way of separating economic freedom from political freedom. If you don't have economic freedom, you don't have political freedom. The only way you can have the one is to have the other.

The Nineteenth Century

So much for the present, what about the past? The closest approach to free enterprise we have ever had in the United States was in the 19th Century. Yet you and your children will hear over and over again in their schools and in their classes the myths that that was a terrible period when the robber barons were grinding the poor miserable people under their heels. That's a myth constructed out of whole cloth. The plain fact is that never in human history has there been a period when the ordinary man improved his condition and benefited his life as much as he did during that period of the 19th Century when we had the closest approach to free enterprise that we have ever had. Most of us in this room, I venture to say, are beneficiaries of that period. I speak of myself. My parents came to this country in the 1890's. Like millions of others they came with empty hands. They were able to find a place in this country, to build a life for themselves and to provide a basis on which their children and their children's children could have a better life. There is no saga in history remotely comparable to the saga of the United States during that era, welcoming millions and millions of people from all over the world and enabling them to find a place for themselves and to improve their lives. And it was possible only because there was an essentially free society.

If the laws and regulations that today hamstring industry and commerce had been in effect in the 19th Century our standard of living today would be below that of the 19th Century. It would have been impossible to have absorbed the millions of people who came to this country.

Why Regimentation?

What produced the shift? Why did we move from a situation in which we had an essentially free society to a situation of increasing regimentation by government? In my opinion, the fundamental cause of most government intervention is an unholy coalition between well-meaning people seeking to do good on the one hand, and special interests (meaning you and me) on the other, taking advantage of those activities for our own purposes.

The great movement toward government has not come about as a result of people with evil intentions trying to do evil. The great growth of government has come about because of good people trying to do good.

But the method by which they have tried to do good has been basically flawed. They have tried to do good with other people's money. Doing good with other people's money has two basic flaws. In the first place, you never spend anybody else's money as carefully as you spend your own. So a large fraction of that money is inevitably wasted. In the second place, and equally important, you cannot do good with other people's money unless you first get the money away from them. So that force— sending a policeman to take the money from somebody's pocket—is fundamentally at the basis of the philosophy of the welfare state. That is why the attempt by good people to do good has led to disastrous results. It was this movement toward welfare statism that produced the phenomenon in Chile which ended the Allende regime. It is this tendency to try to do good with other people's money that has brought Great Britain—once the greatest nation of the earth, the nation which is the source of our traditions and our values and our beliefs in a free society— to the edge of catastrophe. It will be touch and go whether over the next five years Great Britain will be able to maintain a free society or relapse into collectivism.

When you start on the road to do good with other people's money, it is easy at first. You've got a lot of people to pay taxes and a small number of people with whom you are trying to do good. But the later stages become harder and harder. As the number of people on the receiving end grows, you end up in the position where you are taxing 50 percent of the people to help 50 percent of the people. Or, really, 100 percent of the people to distribute benefits to 100 percent! The *reductio ad absurdum* of this policy is a proposal to send out a rain of $50.00 checks to all and sundry in the next few months.

The Future

Where do we go from here? People may say, "You can't turn the clock back. How can you go back?" But the thing that always amuses me about that argument is that the people who make it and who accuse me or my colleagues of trying to turn the clock back to the 19th Century, are themselves busily at work trying to turn the clock back to the 17th Century.

Adam Smith, two hundred years ago, in 1776, wrote *The Wealth of Nations*. It was an attack on the government controls of his time—on mercantilism, on tariffs, on restrictions, on governmental monopoly. But those are exactly the results which the present-day reformers are seeking to achieve.

In any event, that's a foolish question. The real question is not whether you are turning the clock back or forward, but whether you are doing the right thing? Do you mean to say you should never learn from your mistakes?

Some people argue that technological changes require big government and you can no longer talk in the terms of the 19th Century when the government only absorbed 3 percent of the national income. You have to have big government because of these technological changes. That's nonsense from beginning to end. Some technological changes no doubt require the government to engage in activities different from those in which it engaged before. But other technological changes *reduce* the need for government. The improvements in communication and transportation have greatly reduced the possibility of local monopoly which requires government intervention to protect the consumers. Moreover, if you look at the record, the great growth of government has not been in the areas dictated by technological change. The great growth of government has been to take money from some people and to give it to others. The only way technology has entered into that is by providing the computers which make it possible to do so.

Other people will say how can you talk about stopping this trend? What about big business? Is it really any different whether automobiles are made by General Motors, which is an enormous bureaucratic enterprise employing thousands of people, or whether they are made by an agency of the United States Government, which is another bureaucratic enterprise?

The answer to that is very simple. It does make all the difference in the world, because there is a fundamental difference between the two. There is no way in which General Motors can get a dollar from you unless you agree to give it to them. That's a voluntary exchange. They can only get money from you by providing you with something you value more than the money you give them. If they try to force something on you that you don't want, ask Mr. Henry Ford what happened when they tried to introduce the Edsel. On the other hand the government can get money from you without your consent. They can send policemen to take it out of your pocket. General Motors doesn't have that power. And that is all the difference in the world. It is the difference between a society in which exchange is voluntary and a society in which exchange is not voluntary. It's the reason why the government, when it is in the saddle, produces poor quality at high cost, while industry, when it's in the saddle, produces quality at low cost. The one has to satisfy its customers and the other does not.

Two Possible Scenarios

Where shall we go from here? There are two possible scenarios. The one (and I very much fear it's the more likely) is that we will continue in the direction in which we have been going, with gradual increases in the scope of government and government control. If we do continue in that direction, two results are inevitable. One result is financial crisis and the other is a loss of freedom.

The example of England is a frightening example to contemplate. England has been moving in this direction. We're about twenty years behind England in this motion. But England was moving in this direction earlier than we were moving and has moved much farther. The effects are patent and clear. But at least when England moved in this direction and thus lost its power politically and internationally, the United States was there to take over the defense of the free world. But I ask you, when the United States follows that direction, who is going to take over from us? That's one scenario, and I very much fear it's the more likely one.

The other scenario is that we will, in fact, halt this trend—that we will call a halt to the apparently increasing growth of government, set a limit and hold it back.

There are many favorable signs from this point of view. I may say that the greatest reason for hope, in my opinion, is the inefficiency of government. Many people complain about government waste. I welcome it. I welcome it for two reasons. In the first place, efficiency is not a desirable thing if somebody is doing a bad thing. A great teacher of mine, a mathematical economist, once wrote an article on the teaching of statistics. He said, "Pedagogical ability is a vice rather than a virtue if it is devoted to teaching error." That's a fundamental principle. Government is doing things that we don't want it to do, so the more money it wastes the better.

In the second place, waste brings home to the public at large the fact that government is not an efficient and effective instrument for achieving its objectives. One of the great causes for hope is a growing disillusionment around the country with the idea that government is the all-wise, all-powerful big brother who can solve every problem that comes along, that if only you throw enough money at a problem it will be resolved.

Several years ago John Kenneth Galbraith wrote an article in which he said that New York City had no problem that could not be solved by an increase in government spending in New York. Well, since that time, the budget in the city of New York has more than doubled and so have the problems of New York. The one is cause and the other effect. The government has spent more but that meant that the people have less to spend. Since the government spends money less efficiently than individuals spend their own money, as government spending has gone up the problems have gotten worse. My main point is that this inefficiency, this waste, brings home to the public at large the undesirability of governmental intervention. I believe that a major source of hope is in the wide-spread rise in the tide of feeling that government is not the appropriate way to solve our problems.

There are also many unfavorable signs. It's far easier to enact laws than to repeal them. Every special interest including you and me, has great resistance to giving up its special privileges. I remember when Gerald Ford became President and he called a summit conference to do something about the problems of inflation. I sat at that summit conference and heard representatives of one group after another go to the podium—a representative of business, a representative of the farmers, a representative of labor, you name the group—they all went to the podium and they all said the same thing. They said, "Of course, we recognize that in order to stop inflation, we must cut down government spending. And I tell you the way to cut down government spending is to spend more on me." That was the universal refrain.

Many people say that one of the causes for hope is the rising recognition by the business community that business enterprise is a threat to the free enterprise system. I wish I could believe that, but I do not.

You must recognize the facts. Business corporations in general are not a defense of free enterprise. On the contrary, they are one of the chief sources of danger.

The two greatest enemies of free enterprise in the United States, in my opinion, have been on the one hand, my fellow intellectuals, and on the other hand, the business corporations of this country. They are enemies for opposite reasons. Every one of my fellow intellectuals believes in freedom for himself. He wants free speech. He wants free research. I ask him, "Isn't this a terrible waste that a dozen people are studying the same problem? Oughtn't we to have a central planning committee to decide what research projects various individuals are to undertake?" He'll look at me as if I'm crazy, and he'll say, "What do you mean? Don't you understand about the value of academic freedom and freedom of research and duplication?" But when it comes to business he says, "Oh, that's wasteful competition. That's duplication over there! We must have a central planning board to make those things intelligent, sensible!"

So every intellectual is in favor of freedom for himself and against freedom for anybody else. The businessman and the business enterprises are very different. Every businessman and every business enterprise is in favor of freedom for everybody else, but when it comes to himself, that's a different question. We have to have that tariff to protect us against competition from abroad. We have to have that special provision in the tax code. We have to have that subsidy. Businessmen are in favor of freedom for everybody else but not for themselves.

There are many notable exceptions. There are many business leaders who have been extremely farsighted in their understanding of the problem and will come to the defense of a free enterprise system. But for the business community in general, the tendency is to take out advertisements, such as U.S. Steel Company taking out full-page ads to advertise the virtues of free enterprise, but then to plead before Congress for an import quota on steel from Japan. The only result of that is for everybody who is fair-minded to say, "What a bunch of hypocrites!" And they're right.

Now don't misunderstand me. I don't blame business enterprise. I don't blame U.S. Steel for seeking to get those special privileges. The managers of U.S. Steel have an obligation to their stockholders, and they would be false to that obligation if they did not try to take advantage of the opportunities to get assistance. I don't blame them. I blame the rest of us for letting them get away with it. We must recognize what the real problem is and recognize that that is not a source of strength.

Faith in the Future

Where are we going to end up? I do not know. I know that depends upon a great many things.

I am reminded of a story which will illustrate what we may need. It has to do with a young and attractive nun who was driving a car down a super highway and ran out of gas. She remembered that a mile back there had been a gas station. She got out of her car, hiked up her habit, and walked back to the gas station. When she got to the station, she found that there was only one young man in attendance there. He said he'd love to help her but he could't leave the gas station because he was the only one there. He said he would try to find a container in which he could give her some gas. He hunted around the gas station and couldn't find a decent container. The only thing he could find was a little baby's potty that had been left there. So he filled the baby potty with gasoline and he gave it to the nun. She took the baby potty and walked the mile down the road to her car. She got to her car and opened the gas tank and started to pour it in. Just at that moment, a great big Cadillac came barreling down the road at eighty miles an hour. The driver was looking out and couldn't believe what he was seeing. So he jammed on his brakes, stopped, backed up, opened the window and looked out and said, "Sister, I only wish I had such faith!" . . .

33. "Welfare State"—A Debate That Isn't   Sidney Hook

Sidney Hook (1902–   ) is professor emeritus of philosophy at New York University. He now is senior research fellow at the Hoover Institution for the Study of War, Revolution and Peace, Stanford, California. Once a student of the American philosopher, John Dewey, Hook has devoted a long and productive career to the defense and development of Dewey's philosophy, not only when applied to traditional philosophic problems, but above all in what he considers to be its fruition as a distinctively American version of democratic socialism.

". . . the achievements of the welfare state are many. . . ."

The phrase "the welfare state" is one of the most frequently heard battle cries in the American political arena. Since both major parties are committed to some governmental intervention in the economy, they are not as far apart on the issue as they might appear. But in the coming weeks,* as Congress prepares to reassemble and a new administration to take office, we can expect to hear increasingly intense debate about "the welfare state" and what it means.

It is not easy to say exactly what the welfare state is, for it has been developing slowly for almost a century. To be sure, the preamble to the United State Constitution states that one of its aims is "to promote the general welfare." But this is hardly a sufficient clue to the meaning of the welfare state. Everyone is for "the general welfare"; but there is no such unanimity about the welfare state, which many people consider to be decidedly opposed to the general welfare.

The phrase is most widely used to describe the social policies adopted

*[This article appeared on November 27, 1960—Ed.]

by the New Deal and Fair Deal in this country and by the Labor party in England when it came to power in 1945. These policies have not been abandoned but have been continued, albeit with diminishing energy, by liberal Republican and Conservative successors to the Democratic and Labor parties.

The unanimity with which these policies have been followed, in fact, is very impressive. It indicates that no matter what any political group says about the welfare state it will have little or no bearing on what it does. If the welfare state is identified with what the New Deal in the United States and Labor in England have done, then it is as certain as anything can be in human affairs that the direction seems irreversible, for it would be political suicide for the Republicans here or the Tories in England to oppose it.

But if there is agreement on the actual measures taken, there is little agreement on the reasons for these measures, and still less on the social philosophy from which these reasons are derived. The social philosophy behind the welfare state is vague and inchoate. Some of its partisans deny that there is any social philosophy behind it at all. Nonetheless, man is a reason-giving animal even when he doesn't act reasonably.

The basic outlook or commitment of the welfare state is more or less adequately expressed in the complex proposition that it is the responsibility of the government to adopt measures that tend to produce and sustain full employment and, in its absence, to offer some insurance against unemployment; to coordinate policies to strengthen the economy; to provide economic security for the ill, the aged and dependent; to establish minimum standards of compensation and working conditions which are a function of the productive capacity of the country and of our conception of a decent and civilized mode of existence; to protect and ensure the health of its citizens against the hazards of accident and disease; to encourage all local efforts to extend and improve the quality and the quantity of education; and to foster, wherever private enterprise fails, the social, economic and educational conditions that make for equality of opportunity.

In fairness to those who say they oppose the philosophy of the welfare state, it should be acknowledged at once that they are not opposed to these ideal ends. They are opposed only to the state's attempt to realize them, and thus transform itself into a service agency.

They contend that the chief function of the state is to keep peace and order and to lay down the legal rules of the road within which men may freely pursue their own aims. They insist that the methods used by the state must never interfere with the operations of the market economy or free enterprise system.

Those who criticize the welfare state seek to prove, in an attempt to discredit, that it has an unsavory genealogy which can be traced to the traditions and practices of Prussian absolutism tempered by a paternalistic concern for the well-being of its subjects. But whatever may have been the case on the European continent, this is extremely far-fetched in relation to the welfare measures introduced in England and the United States. The influence of Dickens and Bentham was much more profound than that of Bismarck and "the socialists of the chair," as the professorial socialists in German universities were called, in altering British attitudes toward the victims of the industrial revolution and the aged inmates of poorhouses.

In our own country, it was not a theory but a condition of acute distress, resulting from the great depression, which resulted in the complex of state actions that define the New Deal. Even before that, precedents had been established, contested by no one, for state aid to needy businessmen, not only by preferential tariffs but through the establishment of the Reconstruction Finance Corporation. At no time, however, were the needs of businessmen as acute as the sufferings of impoverished farmers and workers and those dependent upon them, after the economic crisis of the early thirties.

The legislation that sought to provide for economic security in its various forms was not planned. It did not flow from any doctrinaire theory. Unlike socialism, it showed no hostility to the profit motive. On the contrary, it appealed to the profit motive and avoided the name of socialism like the very plague. It was undertaken as an ad hoc measure to meet a temporary emergency—but few things are more lasting than the "temporary."

What explains the wide popular support enjoyed by the philosophy behind the welfare state? No simple answer can be found. To begin with, we must list a vague yet real sense of solidarity with our fellows and a desire to mitigate the suffering of those not responsible for their own plight.

These sentiments are nurtured by the age-old religious feeling that "we are all members one of another" and that but for the grace of God, or nature or chance, we might be in the shoes of those less fortunate than ourselves.

Support for the welfare state, however, is not derived merely from sentiment. Anybody who takes seriously the ideal of "equality of opportunity" finds himself committed to programs of social change through legislation which will restore equality of opportunity where it is missing or instate it where it has been absent.

Absolute equality of opportunity, of course, is impossible. Nonetheless, it is clear that children of unemployed or widowed parents or those who live in poverty-stricken, depressed areas have not the same opportunity for a good life as those who are brought up in homes which know no serious privation. Nor can those who suffer from disease and poor health, which could be alleviated by proper medical care, enjoy the same opportunities as those who are medically well provided for.

To some, "equality of opportunity" is limited merely to the formal equality of treatment under a given law. They say that just as traffic rules, enforced by an incorruptible police force, show no favor to big cars or small ones in their use of the road, so the laws of the nation provide equal opportunity for the rich and the poor.

Those who accept the philosophy of the welfare state are quick to point out that in most matters the pains and penalties of the law fall with completely different weight on individuals in different social conditions.

Something more than mere formal equality before the law is necessary.

There is much opposition to the state's exchanging its traditional role of umpire or judge for the role of a service institution for those in distress. This opposition flows from three sources, ethical, psychological and administrative.

The chief ethical objection to the welfare state is that it has no right to play Santa Claus or Lady Bountiful to the underprivileged at the expense of those who have worked diligently to achieve their property and position. After all, it is said, someone must pay for all the benefits bestowed by the welfare state. If it were a matter of voluntary philanthropy, as in the past, no one could reasonably object. But when the state in its official capacity steps in to relieve distress, its philanthropy is really a form of coercion; it robs Peter by taxation to pay Paul—and before long every Tom, Dick and Harry turns to it for relief.

One group wants "just prices," another "just wages," a third "decent housing," a fourth "adequate terms of leisure." The burden of gratifying these demands falls upon the most productive groups in society who are, in effect, punished for their gumption and success.

The second objection to the welfare state is psychological. It is maintained that the normal springs of action, especially initiative and ambition and desire for independence, are gradually eroded by the unearned beneficence of the welfare state.

People come to expect things to be done for them instead of bestirring themselves. The spirit of the pioneer becomes anachronistic. The hard worker becomes suspect as the bosses' tool to increase the pace and output of production. Joy of work and the instinct of workmanship are replaced by the fine arts of boondoggling and featherbedding. The outstretched hand becomes the symbol of the welfare state, "I have a right" its whining motto, and a forward look to the next paid holiday, its sustaining faith.

The third argument against the welfare state is administrative. Government becomes too big and too bureaucratic. Economic life becomes burdened with legal forms and red tape, and subject to multiple decrees of special bureaus whose provisions are derived not from equitable principles of law but from the bureaucratic sense of discretion or fitness. Bureaucracies grow in size by Parkinson's well-known law. A whole new class comes into existence with a vested interest in the social problems that originally induced the state to intervene.

What do the advocates of the welfare state reply to this indictment? First, as to the ethical argument. They point out that the lives of members of a community are so intertwined, the services and obligations of one generation to another so difficult to separate, that it is impossible to establish an exact equation between the services rendered to society by any group and the payments received from it.

The same principle that justifies taxing a bachelor for the education of his neighbor's children, and taxing those without cars for the upkeep of roads they do not use, justifies taxing the entire community in order to moderate the poverty and want of the underprivileged, the needy and the indigent.

Carlyle declared long ago that the sickness of any group in a society is a threat to the health of every group. The poor or underprivileged may suffer more from disease and ignorance and delinquencies than those who are better off. But in the long run, everyone suffers to some extent. No one can seriously contend that large-scale unemployment or the genteel poverty which is a continuous function of inflation are matters for which individuals are personally responsible. Welfare measures may be interpreted, therefore, as a socialization of risk in which the community through taxation collects the premiums and distributes the benefits to those who are unlucky.

There are, to be sure, certain obvious abuses—social security benefits sometimes go to those who do not really need them, unemployment insurance to those who have nest eggs, and certain public services to those who can privately afford them. Gross abuses can be remedied, but any attempt to apply a means test to distinguish between the deserving and undeserving would cost more to enforce than the impartial application of a rule to all.

In addition, there is always something humiliating in having to prove one's need, even when it exists. The bread of charity has a bitter taste which it loses when it is distributed as the legitimate benefits of social insurance.

The psychological argument against the welfare state has more weight because everyone, including the recipients of state aid, agree that self-help is preferable to dependence upon the government. But there is no convincing psychological evidence that most human beings would settle for state aid alone if opportunities existed enabling them to achieve more. Men have always reacted positively to the incentives of higher status and greater rewards. The desire to surpass others is at least as strong as the desire to equal them. There need be no fear, therefore, that mankind necessarily will be leveled to the same plane of privation and mediocrity.

State aid is not incompatible with private and group initiative. For example, I live for part of the year in a rural area where it was unprofitable for private power companies to serve the inhabitants. Because it was sparsely settled, it was impossible for the farmers themselves to raise sufficient capital to electrify the region. With the aid of low-interest loans from the Rural Electrification Administration, a local cooperative finally managed to do the job. The results raised the cultural and economic level of the entire community, and other areas and industries outside the region also benefited greatly.

State aid to cooperative groups and to individuals has stimulated a vast amount of initiative in housing. Sometimes local conditions of scarcity, overcrowding and sanitation make it imperative for municipalities to underwrite public housing. The human costs of waiting for the market to remedy the situation come too high. Slums are more likely to breed a spirit of dependence and defeatism than of lawful enterprise or initiative.

Nor, finally, can it be gainsaid that the welfare state of necessity must be more bureaucratic, since its services are not self-administered. But bureaucracy is a scare word. Large-scale private enterprises have bureaucracies, too. It is the size of an enterprise, not whether it is public or private, that determines the growth of managerial personnel. Those who want to check its growth, and subject it to additional judicial and administrative controls, can succeed only by adding to the number of state officials.

The incontestable fact is that despite, if not because of, the welfare state and its bureaucracy, the nation is today at once both more prosperous and less driven by class conflict than at any previous time. Further, whatever may have been the case when the shibboleth, "That state is best which governs least," was current, today the people do not fear the state as an instrument of oppression.

The state is no longer "they" as opposed to "us." Instead of viewing it as the orthodox Marxists did—as "the ruling class"—or as the robber barons did—as a means of looting the public domain—the farmers and workers and businessmen, the professions, the white-and blue-collar workers, the young and the aged, the veterans and the armed services see the state as a power to be used.

Out of the struggle for its use arise not only compromises between groups but concessions in order to win allies. When the electorate becomes aroused, which unfortunately is not often enough, the consumer is usually the gainer.

The welfare state is neither creeping socialism nor moribund capitalism. It has no coherent philosophy because its policy is one of improvisation to meet evils rather than one of enlightened planning to prevent them. Its wisdom, such as it is, is always ex post facto, which is better than doing nothing about social evils in the hope they will disappear of themselves. But it can safely go much further in anticipating needs on a national and international scale and in planning for them.

It is a profound error, therefore, to pass judgment on the virtues and defects of the welfare state as a whole. What one must appraise are specific proposals that the state do this or that on the ground that the welfare of the community and the preservation of its strategic political freedom require that it be done.

Some things are worth doing but not necessarily by the state. If no individuals or groups are willing or able to do what is worth doing, then the possibility should be seriously entertained that the state do it. Such questions cannot be decided merely on the basis of general allegiance or opposition to the welfare state.

If the state is to be our servant and not our master, a certain skepticism toward state power will always be in order because as the founders of the American republic realized, the state is always run by men, and men are not angels. But so long as those who rule are responsible to those whom they govern and to whom they must return for a renewal of their mandates, we need not fear delegation of power to the state in this complex world—a delegation which, in many areas, is inescapable in any case. If such delegation results in usurpation of power, it will not be the fruit of the welfare state but of the intelligence—or rather, lack of it—of its citizens.

To date, the achievements of the welfare state are many and it can claim credit for the relative material prosperity of our times as compared with many periods of the past. But in a world that requires more and more foresight, more coordination to keep the economy on an even keel and help develop the economies of underdeveloped countries, more planning to avoid the dangers of war and the loss of freedom, the scope of the welfare state may well be extended. Today, its only alternative is the "ill-fare" state.

Even those who condemn the welfare state will, in the very interests of national security, have to continue it and carry the policies of intelligent coordination into more fields of our economy. The resources of freedom cannot be mobilized, whether in peace or in the defense of peace, without a newer and better and bigger "New Deal" irrespective of what we call it.

The Enforcement of Morals

34. Morals and the Criminal Law   Sir Patrick Devlin

Sir Patrick Arthur Devlin (1905–   ), a former Lord Justice of Appeal and Lord of Appeal in Ordinary and now High Steward of Cambridge University, England, has produced writings in the philosophy of law and punishment that have stimulated discussion on the part of philosophers.

. . . What is the connexion between crime and sin and to what extent, if at all, should the criminal law of England concern itself with the enforcement of morals and punish sin or immorality as such?

The statements of principle in the Wolfenden Report provide an admirable and modern starting-point for such an inquiry. . . .

Early in the Report the Committee put forward:

> Our own formulation of the function of the criminal law so far as it concerns the subjects of this enquiry. In this field, its function, as we see it, is to preserve public order and decency, to protect the citizen from what is offensive or injurious, and to provide sufficient safeguards against exploitation and corruption of others, particularly those who are specially vulnerable because they are young, weak in body or mind, inexperienced, or in a state of special physical, official or economic dependence.
>
> It is not, in our view, the function of the law to intervene in the private lives of citizens, or to seek to enforce any particular pattern of behaviour, further than is necessary to carry out the purposes we have outlined.

The Committee preface their most important recommendation

> that homosexual behaviour between consenting adults in private should no longer be a criminal offence, [by stating the argument] which we believe to be decisive, namely, the importance which society and the law ought to give to individual freedom of choice and action in matters of private

morality. Unless a deliberate attempt is to be made by society, acting through the agency of the law, to equate the sphere of crime with that of sin, there must remain a realm of private morality and immorality which is, in brief and crude terms, not the law's business. To say this is not to condone or encourage private immorality.

Similar statements of principle are set out in the chapters of the Report which deal with prostitution. No case can be sustained, the Report says, for attempting to make prostitution itself illegal. The Committee refer to the general reasons already given and add: 'We are agreed that private immorality should not be the concern of the criminal law except in the special circumstances therein mentioned.' They quote with approval the report of the Street Offences Committee, which says: 'As a general proposition it will be universally accepted that the law is not concerned with private morals or with ethical sanctions. It will be observed that the emphasis is on *private* immorality. By this is meant immorality which is not offensive or injurious to the public in the ways defined or described in the first passage which I quoted. In other words, no act of immorality should be made a criminal offence unless it is accompanied by some other feature such as indecency, corruption, or exploitation. This is clearly brought out in relation to prostitution: 'It is not the duty of the law to concern itself with immorality as such . . . it should confine itself to those activities which offend against public order and decency or expose the ordinary citizen to what is offensive or injurious.' . . .

If this view is sound, it means that the criminal law cannot justify any of its provisions by reference to the moral law. It cannot say, for example, that murder and theft are prohibited because they are immoral or sinful. The State must justify in some other way the punishments which it imposes on wrongdoers and a function for the criminal law independent of morals must be found. This is not difficult to do. The smooth functioning of society and the preservation of order require that a number of activities should be regulated. The rules that are made for that purpose and are enforced by the criminal law are often designed simply to achieve uniformity and convenience and rarely involve any choice between good and evil. Rules that impose a speed limit or prevent obstruction on the highway have nothing to do with morals. Since so much of the criminal law is composed of rules of this sort, why bring morals into it at all? Why not define the function of the criminal law in simple terms as the preservation of order and decency and the protection of the lives and property of citizens, and elaborate those terms in relation to any particular subject in the way in which it is done in the Wolfenden Report? The criminal law in carrying out these objects will undoubtedly overlap the moral law. Crimes of violence are morally wrong and they are also offences against good order; therefore they offend against both laws. But this is simply because the two laws in pursuit of different objectives happen to cover the same area. Such is the argument . . . .

I think it is clear that the criminal law as we know it is based upon moral principle. In a number of crimes its function is simply to enforce a moral principle and nothing else. The law, both criminal and civil, claims to be able to speak about morality and immorality generally. Where does it get its authority to do this and how does it settle the moral principles which it enforces? Undoubtedly, as a matter of history, it derived both from Christian teaching. But I think that the strict logician is right when he says that the law can no longer rely on doctrines in which citizens are entitled to disbelieve. It is necessary therefore to look for some other source.

In jurisprudence, as I have said, everything is thrown open to discussion and, in the belief that they cover the whole field, I have framed three interrogatories addressed to myself to answer:

1. Has society the right to pass judgment at all on matters of morals? Ought there, in other words, to be a public morality, or are morals always a matter for private judgment?
2. If society has the right to pass judgment, has it also the right to use the weapon of the law to enforce it?
3. If so, ought it to use that weapon in all cases or only in some; and if only in some, on what principles should it distinguish?

I shall begin with the first interrogatory and consider what is meant by the right of society to pass a moral judgment, that is, a judgment about what is good and what is evil. The fact that a majority of people may disapprove of a practice does not of itself make it a matter for society as a whole. Nine men out of ten may disapprove of what the tenth man is doing and still say that it is not their business. There is a case for a collective judgment (as distinct from a large number of individual opinions which sensible people may even refrain from pronouncing at all if it is upon somebody else's private affairs) only if society is affected. Without a collective judgment there can be no case at all for intervention. Let me take as an illustration the Englishman's attitude to religion as it is now and as it has been in the past. His attitude now is that a man's religion is his private affair; he may think of another man's religion that it is right or wrong, true or untrue, but not that it is good or bad. In earlier times that was not so; a man was denied the right to practice what was thought of as heresy, and heresy was thought of as destructive of society.

The language used in the passages I have quoted from the Wolfenden Report suggests the view that there ought not to be a collective judgment about immorality *per se*. Is this what is meant by 'private morality' and 'individual freedom of choice and action'? Some people sincerely believe that homosexuality is neither immoral nor unnatural. Is the 'freedom of choice and action' that is offered to the individual, freedom to decide for himself what is moral or immoral, society remaining neutral; or is it freedom to be immoral if he wants to be? The language of the Report may be open to question, but the conclusions at which the Committee arrive answer this question unambiguously. If society is not prepared to say that homosexuality is morally wrong, there would be no basis for a law protecting youth from 'corruption' or punishing a man for living on the 'immoral' earnings of a homosexual prostitute, as the Report recommends. This attitude the Committee makes even clearer when they come to deal with prostitution. In truth, the Report takes it for granted that there is in existence a public morality which condemns homosexuality and prostitution. What the Report seems to mean by private morality might perhaps be better described as private behaviour in matters of morals.

This view—that there is such a thing as public morality—can also be justified by *a priori* argument. What makes a society of any sort is community of ideas, not only political ideas but also ideas about the way its members should behave and govern their lives; these latter ideas are its morals. Every society has a moral structure as well as a political one: or rather, since that might suggest two independent systems, I should say that the structure of every society is made up both of politics and morals. Take, for example, the institution of marriage. Whether a man should be allowed to take more than one wife is something about which every society has to make up its mind one way or the other. In England we believe in the Christian idea of marriage and therefore adopt monogamy as a moral principle. Consequently the Christian institution of marriage has become the basis of family life and so part of the structure of our society. It is there not because it is Christian. It has got there because it is Christian, but it remains there because it is built into the house in which we live and could not be removed without bringing it down. The great majority of those who live in this country accept it because it is the Christian idea of marriage and for them the only true one. But a non-Christian is bound by it, not because it is part of Christianity but because, rightly or wrongly, it has been adopted by the society in which he lives. It would be useless for him to stage a debate designed to prove that polygamy was theologically more correct and socially preferable; if he wants to live in the house, he must accept it as built in the way in which it is.

We see this more clearly if we think of ideas or institutions that are purely political. Society cannot tolerate rebellion; it will not allow argument about the rightness of the cause. Historians a century later may say that the rebels were right and the Government was wrong and a percipient and conscientious subject of the State may think so at the time. But it is not a matter which can be left to individual judgment.

The institution of marriage is a good example for my purpose because it bridges the division, if there is one, between politics and morals. Marriage is part of the structure of our society and it is also the basis of a moral code which condemns fornication and adultery. The institution of marriage would be gravely threatened if individual judgments were permitted about the morality of adultery; on these points there must be a public morality. But public morality is not to be confined to those moral principles which support institutions such as marriage. People do not think of monogamy as something which has to be supported because our society has chosen to organize itself upon it; they think of it as something that is good in itself and offering a good way of life and that it is for that reason that our society has adopted it. I return to the statement that I have already made, that society means a community of ideas; without shared ideas on politics, morals, and ethics no society can exist. Each one of us has ideas about what is good and what is evil; they cannot be kept private from the society in which we live. If men and women try to create a society in which there is no fundamental agreement about good and evil they will fail; if, having based it on common agreement, the agreement goes, the society will disintegrate. For society is not something that is kept together physically; it is held by the invisible bonds of common thought. If the bonds were too far relaxed the members would drift apart. A common morality is part of the bondage. The bondage is part of the price of society; and mankind, which needs society, must pay its price. . . .

You may think that I have taken far too long in contending that there is such a thing as public morality, a proposition which most people would readily accept, and may have left myself too little time to discuss the next question which to many minds may cause greater difficulty: to what extent should society use the law to enforce its moral judgments? But I believe that the answer to the first question determines the way in which the second should be approached and may indeed very nearly dictate the answer to the second question. If society has no right to make judgments on morals, the law must find some special justification for entering the field of morality: if homosexuality and prostitution are not in themselves wrong, then the onus is very clearly on the law-giver who wants to frame a law against certain aspects of them to justify the exceptional treatment. But if society has the right to make a judgment and has it on the basis that a recognized morality is as necessary to society as, say, a recognized government, then society may use the law to preserve morality in the same way as it uses it to safeguard anything else that is essential to its existence. If therefore the first proposition is securely established with all its implications, society has a prima facie right to legislate against immorality as such.

The Wolfenden Report, notwithstanding that it seems to admit the right of society to condemn homosexuality and prostitution as immoral, requires special circumstances to be shown to justify the intervention of the law. I think that this is wrong in principle and that any attempt to approach my second interrogatory on these lines is bound to break down. I think that the attempt by the Committee does break down and that this is shown by the fact that it has to define or describe its special circumstances so widely that they can be supported only if it is accepted that the law *is* concerned with immorality as such.

The widest of the special circumstances are described as the provision of "sufficient safeguards against exploitation and corruption of others, particularly those who are specially vulnerable because they are young, weak in body or mind, inexperienced, or in a state of special physical, official or economic dependence.' The corruption of youth is a well-recognized ground for intervention by the State and for the purpose of any legislation the young can easily be defined. But if similar protection were to be extended to every other citizen, there would be no limit to the reach of the law. The 'corruption and exploitation of others' is so wide that it could be used to cover any sort of immorality which involves, as most do, the co-operation of another person. Even if the phrase is

taken as limited to the categories that are particularized as 'specially vulnerable,' it is so elastic as to be practically no restriction. This is not merely
a matter of words. For if the words used are stretched almost beyond
breaking-point, they still are not wide enough to cover the recommendations which the Committee makes about prostitution.

Prostitution is not in itself illegal and the Committee does not think
that it ought to be made so. If prostitution is private immorality and not
the law's business, what concern has the law with the ponce or the broth-
elkeeper or the householder who permits habitual prostitution? The Report recommends that the laws which make these activities criminal offences should be maintained or strengthened and brings them (so far as
it goes into principle; with regard to brothels it says simply that the law
rightly frowns on them) under the head of exploitation. There may be
cases of exploitation in this trade, as there are or used to be in many
others, but in general a ponce exploits a prostitute no more than an
impressario exploits an actress. The Report finds that 'the great majority
of prostitutes are women whose psychological makeup is such that they
choose this life because they find in it a style of living which is to them
easier, freer and more profitable than would be provided by any other
occupation. . . . In the main the association between prostitute and ponce
is voluntary and operates to mutual advantage.' The Committee would
agree that this could not be called exploitation in the ordinary sense.
They say: 'It is in our view an over-simplification to think that those who
live on the earnings of prostitution are exploiting the prostitute as such.
What they are really exploiting is the whole complex of the relationship
between prostitute and customer; they are, in effect, exploiting the human weaknesses which cause the customer to seek the prostitute and the
prostitute to meet the demand.'

All sexual immorality involves the exploitation of human weaknesses.
The prostitute exploits the lust of her customers and the customer the
moral weakness of the prostitute. If the exploitation of human weaknesses
is considered to create a special circumstance, there is virtually no field
of morality which can be defined in such a way as to exclude the law.

I think, therefore, that it is not possible to set theoretical limits to the
power of the State to legislate against immorality. It is not possible to
settle in advance exceptions to the general rule or to define inflexibly
areas of morality into which the law is in no circumstances to be allowed
to enter. Society is entitled by means of its laws to protect itself from
dangers, whether from within or without. Here again I think that the
political parallel is legitimate. The law of treason is directed against aiding
the king's enemies and against sedition from within. The justification
for this is that established government is necessary for the existence of
society and therefore its safety against violent overthrow must be secured.
But an established morality is as necessary as good government to the
welfare of society. Societies disintegrate from within more frequently
than they are broken up by external pressures. There is disintegration
when no common morality is observed and history shows that the loosening of moral bonds is often the first stage of disintegration, so that
society is justified in taking the same steps to preserve its moral code as

it does to preserve its government and other essential institutions. The suppression of vice is as much the law's business as the suppression of subversive activities; it is no more possible to define a sphere of private morality than it is to define one of private subversive activity. It is wrong to talk of private morality or of the law not being concerned with immorality as such or to try to set rigid bounds to the part which the law may play in the suppression of vice. There are no theoretical limits to the power of the State to legislate against treason and sedition, and likewise I think there can be no theoretical limits to legislation against immorality. You may argue that if a man's sins affect only himself it cannot be the concern of society. If he chooses to get drunk every night in the privacy of his own home, is any one except himself the worse for it? But suppose a quarter or a half of the population got drunk every night, what sort of society would it be? You cannot set a theoretical limit to the number of people who can get drunk before society is entitled to legislate against drunkenness. The same may be said of gambling. The Royal Commission on Betting, Lotteries, and Gaming took as their test the character of the citizen as a member of society. They said: 'Our concern with the ethical significance of gambling is confined to the effect which it may have on the character of the gambler as a member of society. If we were convinced that whatever the degree of gambling this effect must be harmful we should be inclined to think that it was the duty of the state to restrict gambling to the greatest extent practicable.'

In what circumstances the State should exercise its power is the third of the interrogatories I have framed. But before I get to it I must raise a point which might have been brought up in any one of the three. How are the moral judgments of society to be ascertained? By leaving it until now, I can ask it in the more limited form that is now sufficient for my purpose. How is the law-maker to ascertain the moral judgments of society? It is surely not enough that they should be reached by the opinion of the majority; it would be too much to require the individual assent of every citizen. English law has evolved and regularly uses a standard which does not depend on the counting of heads. It is that of the reasonable man. He is not to be confused with the rational man. He is not expected to reason about anything and his judgment may be largely a matter of feeling. It is the viewpoint of the man in the street—or to use an archaism familiar to all lawyers—the man in the Clapham omnibus. He might also be called the right-minded man. For my purpose I should like to call him the man in the jury box, for the moral judgment of society must be something about which any twelve men or women drawn at random might after discussion be expected to be unanimous. This was the standard the judges applied in the days before Parliament was as active as it is now and when they laid down rules of public policy. They did not think of themselves as making law but simply as stating principles which every rightminded person would accept as valid. It is what Pollock called 'practical morality,' which is based not on theological or philosophical foundations but 'in the mass of continuous experience half-consciously or unconsciously accumulated and embodied in the morality of common sense.' He called it also 'a certain way of thinking on questions of morality which we expect to find in a reasonable civilized man or a reasonable Englishman, taken at random.'

Immorality then, for the purpose of the law, is what every right-minded person is presumed to consider to be immoral. Any immorality is capable of affecting society injuriously and in effect to a greater or lesser extent it usually does; this is what gives the law its *locus standi*. It cannot be shut out. But—and this brings me to the third question—the individual has a *locus standi* too; he cannot be expected to surrender to the judgment of society the whole conduct of his life. It is the old and familiar question of striking a balance between the rights and interests of society and those of the individual. This is something which the law is constantly doing in matters large and small. To take a very down-to-earth example, let me consider the right of the individual whose house adjoins the highway to have access to it; that means in these days the right to have vehicles stationary in the highway, sometimes for a considerable time if there is a lot of loading or unloading. There are many cases in which the courts have had to balance the private right of access against the public right to use the highway without obstruction. It cannot be done by carving up the highway into public and private areas. It is done by recognizing that each have rights over the whole; that if each were to exercise their rights to the full, they would come into conflict; and therefore that the rights of each must be curtailed so as to ensure as far as possible that the essential needs of each are safeguarded.

I do not think that one can talk sensibly of a public and private morality any more than one can of a public or private highway. Morality is a sphere in which there is a public interest and a private interest, often in conflict, and the problem is to reconcile the two. This does not mean that it is impossible to put forward any general statements about how in our society the balance ought to be struck. Such statements cannot of their nature be rigid or precise; they would not be designed to circumscribe the operation of the law-making power but to guide those who have to apply it. While every decision which a court of law makes when it balances the public against the private interest is an *ad hoc* decision, the cases contain statements of principle to which the court should have regard when it reaches its decision. In the same way it is possible to make general statements of principle to which the court should have regard when it reaches its decision. In the same way it is possible to make general statements of principle which it may be thought the legislature should bear in mind when it is considering the enactment of laws enforcing morals.

I believe that most people would agree upon the chief of these elastic principles. There must be toleration of the maximum individual freedom that is consistent with the integrity of society. It cannot be said that this is a principle that runs all through the criminal law. Much of the criminal law that is regulatory in character—the part of it that deals with *malum prohibitum* rather than *malum in se*—is based upon the opposite principle, that is, that the choice of the individual must give way to the convenience of the many. But in all matters of conscience the principle I have stated is generally held to prevail. It is not confined to thought and speech; it

extends to action, as is shown by the recognition of the right to conscientious objection in war-time; this example shows also that conscience
will be respected even in times of national danger. The principle appears
to me to be peculiarly appropriate to all questions of morals. Nothing
should be punished by the law that does not lie beyond the limits of
tolerance. It is not nearly enough to say that a majority dislike a practice;
there must be a real feeling of reprobation. Those who are dissatisfied
with the present law on homosexuality often say that the opponents of
reform are swayed simply by disgust. If that were so it would be wrong,
but I do not think one can ignore disgust if it is deeply felt and not
manufactured. Its presence is a good indication that the bounds of toleration are being reached. Not everything is to be tolerated. No society
can do without intolerance, indignation, and disgust; they are the forces
behind the moral law, and indeed it can be argued that if they or something like them are not present, the feelings of society cannot be weighty
enough to deprive the individual of freedom of choice. I suppose that
there is hardly anyone nowadays who would not be disgusted by the
thought of deliberate cruelty to animals. No one proposes to relegate
that or any other form of sadism to the realm of private morality or to
allow it to be practised in public or in private. It would be possible no
doubt to point out that until a comparatively short while ago nobody
thought very much of cruelty to animals and also that pity and kindliness
and the unwillingness to inflict pain are virtues more generally esteemed
now than they have ever been in the past. But matters of this sort are
not determined by rational argument. Every moral judgment, unless it
claims a divine source, is simply a feeling that no right-minded man could
behave in any other way without admitting that he was doing wrong. It
is the power of a common sense and not the power of reason that is
behind the judgments of society. But before a society can put a practice
beyond the limits of tolerance there must be a deliberate judgment that
the practice is injurious to society. There is, for example, a general
abhorrence of homosexuality. We should ask ourselves in the first instance whether, looking at it calmly and dispassionately, we regard it as
a vice so abominable that its mere presence is an offence. If that is the
genuine feeling of the society in which we live, I do not see how society
can be denied the right to eradicate it. Our feeling may not be so intense
as that. We may feel about it that, if confined, it is tolerable, but that if
it spread it might be gravely injurious; it is in this way that most societies
look upon fornication, seeing it as a natural weakness which must be
kept within bounds but which cannot be rooted out. It becomes then a
question of balance, the danger to society in one scale and the extent of
the restriction in the other. On this sort of point the value of an investigation by such a body as the Wolfenden Committee and of its conclusions is manifest.

The limits of tolerance shift. This is supplementary to what I have
been saying but of sufficient importance in itself to deserve statement
as a separate principle which law-makers have to bear in mind. I suppose
that moral standards do not shift; so far as they come from divine revelation they do not, and I am willing to assume that the moral judgments
made by a society always remain good for that society. But the extent

to which society will tolerate—I mean tolerate, not approve—departures from moral standards varies from generation to generation. It may be that over-all tolerance is always increasing. The pressure of the human mind, always seeking greater freedom of thought, is outwards against the bonds of society forcing their gradual relaxation. It may be that history is a tale of contraction and expansion and that all developed societies are on their way to dissolution. I must not speak of things I do not know; and anyway as a practical matter no society is willing to make provision for its own decay. I return therefore to the simple and observable fact that in matters of morals the limits of tolerance shift. Laws, especially those which are based on morals, are less easily moved. It follows as another good working principle that in any new matter of morals the law should be slow to act. By the next generation the swell of indignation may have abated and the law be left without the strong backing which it needs. But it is then difficult to alter the law without giving the impression that moral judgment is being weakened. This is now one of the factors that is strongly militating against any alteration to the law on homosexuality.

A third elastic principle must be advanced more tentatively. It is that as far as possible privacy should be respected. This is not an idea that has ever been made explicit in the criminal law. Acts or words done or said in public or private are all brought within its scope without distinction in principle. But there goes with this a strong reluctance on the part of judges and legislators to sanction invasions of privacy in the detection of crime. The police have no more right to trespass than the ordinary citizen has; there is no general right of search; to this extent an Englishman's home is still his castle. The Government is extremely careful in the exercise even of those powers which it claims to be undisputed. Telephone tapping and interference with the mails afford a good illustration of this. A Committee of three Privy Councillors who recently inquired into these activities found that the Home Secretary and his predecessors had already formulated strict rules governing the exercise of these powers and the Committee were able to recommend that they should be continued to be exercised substantially on the same terms. But they reported that the power was 'regarded with general disfavour.'

This indicates a general sentiment that the right of privacy is something to be put in the balance against the enforcement of the law. Ought the same sort of consideration to play any part in the formation of the law? Clearly only in a very limited number of cases. When the help of the law is invoked by an injured citizen, privacy must be irrelevant; the individual cannot ask that his right to privacy should be measured against injury criminally done to another. But when all who are involved in the deed are consenting parties and the injury is done to morals, the public interest in the moral order can be balanced against the claims of privacy. The restriction on police powers of investigation goes further than the affording of a parallel; it means that the detection of crime committed in private and when there is no complaint is bound to be rather haphazard and this is an additional reason for moderation. These considerations do not justify the exclusion of all private immorality from the scope of the law. I think that, as I have already suggested, the test of 'private behaviour' should be substituted for 'private morality' and the influence of the factor should be reduced from that of a definite limitation to that of a matter to be taken into account. Since the gravity of the crime is also a proper consideration, a distinction might well be made in the case of homosexuality between the lesser acts of indecency and the full offence, which on the principles of the Wolfenden Report it would be illogical to do.

The last and the biggest thing to be remembered is that the law is concerned with the minimum and not with the maximum; there is much in the Sermon on the Mount that would be out of place in the Ten Commandments. We all recognize the gap between the moral law and the law of the land. No man is worth much who regulates his conduct with the sole object of escaping punishment, and every worthy society sets for its members standards which are above those of the law. We recognize the existence of such higher standards when we use expressions such as 'moral obligation' and 'morally bound.' The distinction was well put in the judgment of African elders in a family dispute: 'We have power to make you divide the crops, for this is our law, and we will see this is done. But we have not power to make you behave like an upright man.'

It can only be because this point is so obvious that it is so frequently ignored. Discussion among law-makers, both professional and amateur, is too often limited to what is right or wrong and good or bad for society. There is a failure to keep separate the two questions I have earlier posed—the question of society's right to pass a moral judgment and the question of whether the arm of the law should be used to enforce the judgment. The criminal law is not a statement of how people ought to behave; it is a statement of what will happen to them if they do not behave; good citizens are not expected to come within reach of it or to set their sights by it, and every enactment should be framed accordingly.

The arm of the law is an instrument to be used by society, and the decision about what particular cases it should be used in is essentially a practical one. Since it is an instrument, it is wise before deciding to use it to have regard to the tools with which it can be fitted and to the machinery which operates it. Its tools are fines, imprisonment, or lesser forms of supervision (such as Borstal and probation) and—not to be ignored—the degradation that often follows upon the publication of the crime. Are any of these suited to the job of dealing with sexual immorality? The fact that there is so much immorality which has never been brought within the law shows that there can be no general rule. It is a matter for decision in each case; but in the case of homosexuality the Wolfenden Report rightly has regard to the views of those who are experienced in dealing with this sort of crime and to those of the clergy who are the natural guardians of public morals.

The machinery which sets the criminal law in motion ends with the verdict and the sentence; and a verdict is given either by magistrates or by a jury. As a general rule, whenever a crime is sufficiently serious to justify a maximum punishment of more than three months, the accused has the right to the verdict of a jury. The result is that magistrates administer mostly what I have called the regulatory part of the law. They deal extensively with drunkenness, gambling, and prostitution, which are matters of morals or close to them, but not with any of the graver moral offences. They are more responsive than juries to the ideas of the legislature; it may not be accidental that the Wolfenden Report, in recommending increased penalties for solicitation, did not go above the limit of three months. Juries tend to dilute the decrees of Parliament with their own ideas of what should be punishable. Their province of course is fact and not law, and I do not mean that they often deliberately disregard the law. But if they think it is too stringent, they sometimes take a very merciful view of the facts. Let me take one example out of many that could be given. It is an offence to have carnal knowledge of a girl under the age of sixteen years. Consent on her part is no defence; if she did not consent, it would of course amount to rape. The law makes special provision for the situation when a boy and girl are near in age. If a man under twenty-four can prove that he had reasonable cause to believe that the girl was over the age of sixteen years, he has a good defence. The law regards the offence as sufficiently serious to make it one that is triable only by a judge at assizes. 'Reasonable cause' means not merely that the boy honestly believed that the girl was over sixteen but also that he must have had reasonable grounds for his belief. In theory it ought not to be an easy defence to make out but in fact it is extremely rare for anyone who advances it to be convicted. The fact is that the girl is often as much to blame as the boy. The object of the law, as judges repeatedly tell juries, is to protect young girls against themselves; but juries are not impressed.

The part that the jury plays in the enforcement of the criminal law, the fact that no grave offence against morals is punishable without their verdict, these are of great importance in relation to the statements of principle that I have been making. They turn what might otherwise be pure exhortation to the legislature into something like rules that the lawmakers cannot safely ignore. The man in the jury box is not just an expression; he is an active reality. It will not in the long run work to make laws about morality that are not acceptable to him.

This then is how I believe my third interrogatory should be answered—not by the formulation of hard and fast rules, but by a judgment in each case taking into account the sort of factors I have been mentioning. The line that divides the criminal law from the moral is not determinable by the application of any clear-cut principle. It is like a line that divides land and sea, a coastline of irregularities and indentations. There are gaps and promontories, such as adultery and fornication, which the law has for centuries left substantially untouched. Adultery of the sort that breaks up marriage seems to me to be just as harmful to the social fabric as homosexuality or bigamy. The only ground for putting it outside the criminal law is that a law which made it a crime would be too difficult to enforce; it is too generally regarded as a human weakness not suitably punished by imprisonment. All that the law can do with fornication is to act against its worst manifestations; there is a general abhorrence of the commercialization of vice, and that sentiment gives strength to the law against brothels and immoral earnings. There is no logic to be found in this. The boundary between the criminal law and the moral law is fixed by balancing in the case of each particular crime the pros and cons of legal enforcement in accordance with the sort of considerations I have been outlining. The fact that adultery, fornication, and lesbianism are untouched by the criminal law does not prove that homosexuality ought not to be touched. The error of jurisprudence in the Wolfenden Report is caused by the search for some single principle to explain the division between crime and sin. The Report finds it in the principle that the criminal law exists for the protection of individuals; on this principle fornication in private between consenting adults is outside the law and thus it becomes logically indefensible to bring homosexuality between consenting adults in private within it. But the true principle is that the law exists for the protection of society. It does not discharge its function by protecting the individual from injury, annoyance, corruption, and exploitation; the law must protect also the institutions and the community of ideas, political and moral, without which people cannot live together. Society cannot ignore the morality of the individual any more than it can his loyalty; it flourishes on both and without either it dies. . . .

Society cannot live without morals. Its morals are those standards of conduct which the reasonable man approves. A rational man, who is also a good man, may have other standards. If he has no standards at all he is not a good man and need not be further considered. If he has standards, they may be very different; he may, for example, not disapprove of homosexuality or abortion. In that case he will not share in the common morality; but that should not make him deny that it is a social necessity. A rebel may be rational in thinking that he is right but he is irrational if he thinks that society can leave him free to rebel. . . .

35. Immorality and Treason   H. L. A. Hart

Herbert Lionel Adolphus Hart (1907–   ) spent some time as a lawyer in London and then returned to Oxford University where, in 1952, he became professor of jurisprudence. The impact of Hart's writings has been felt widely in contemporary philosophy of law.

The Wolfenden Committee on Homosexual Offences and Prostitution recommended by a majority of 12 to 1 that homosexual behaviour between consenting adults in private should no longer be a criminal offence. One of the Committee's principal grounds for this recommendation was expressed in its report in this way: 'There must remain a realm of private morality and immorality which in brief and crude terms is not the law's business.' I shall call this the liberal point of view: for it is a

Reprinted from *The Listener*, July 30, 1959, by permission of the author.

special application of those wider principles of liberal thought which John Stuart Mill formulated in his essay on Liberty. Mill's most famous words, less cautious perhaps than the Wolfenden Committee's, were:

> The only purpose for which power can be rightfully exercised over any member of a civilized community against his will is to prevent harm to others. His own good, either physical or moral, is not a sufficient warrant. He cannot rightfully be compelled to do or forbear . . . because in the opinion of others to do so would be wise or even right.

Repudiation of the Liberal Point of View

The liberal point of view has often been attacked, both before and after Mill. I shall discuss here the repudiation of it made by Sir Patrick Devlin, in his recent lecture, which has now been published. This contains an original and interesting argument designed to show that *'prima facie* society has the right to legislate against immorality as such' and that the Wolfenden Committee were mistaken in thinking that there is an area of private immorality which is not the law's business. Sir Patrick's case is a general one, not confined to sexual immorality, and he does not say whether or not he is opposed to the Wolfenden Committee's recommendation on homosexual behaviour. Instead he gives us a hypothetical principle by which to judge this issue. He says: 'If it is the genuine feeling of our society that homosexuality is a vice so abominable that its mere presence is an offence, society has the right to eradicate it by the use of the criminal law.

The publication by Sir Patrick of this lecture is in itself an interesting event. It is many years since a distinguished English lawyer delivered himself of general reasoned views about the relationship of morality to the criminal law. The last to do so with comparable skill and clarity was, I think, the great Victorian judge James Fitzjames Stephen. It is worth observing that Stephen, like Sir Patrick, repudiated the liberal point of view. Indeed his gloomy but impressive book *Liberty, Equality, Fraternity* was a direct reply to Mill's essay *On Liberty.* The most remarkable feature of Sir Patrick's lecture is his view of the nature of morality—the morality which the criminal law may enforce. Most previous thinkers who have repudiated the liberal point of view have done so because they thought that morality consisted either of divine commands or of rational principles of human conduct discoverable by human reason. Since morality for them had this elevated divine or rational status as the law of God or reason, it seemed obvious that the state should enforce it, and that the function of human law should not be merely to provide men with the opportunity for leading a good life, but actually to see that they led it. Sir Patrick does not rest his repudiation of the liberal point of view on these religious or rationalist conceptions. Indeed much that he writes reads like an abjuration of the notion that reasoning or thinking has much to do with morality. English popular morality has no doubt its historical connection with the Christian religion: 'That,' says Sir Patrick, 'is how it got there.' But it does not owe its present status or social significance to religion any more than to reason.

What, then, is it? According to Sir Patrick it is primarily a matter of feeling. 'Every moral judgment,' he says, 'is a feeling that no right-minded man could act in any other way without admitting that he was doing wrong.' Who then must feel this way if we are to have what Sir Patrick calls a public morality? He tells us that it is 'the man in the street.' 'the man in the jury box,' or (to use the phrase so familiar to English lawyers) 'the man on the Clapham omnibus.' For the moral judgments of society so far as the law is concerned are to be ascertained by the standards of the reasonable man, and he is not to be confused with the rational man. Indeed, Sir Patrick says 'he is not expected to reason about anything and his judgment may be largely a matter of feeling.'

Intolerance, Indignation, and Disgust

But what precisely are the relevant feelings, the feelings which may justify use of the criminal law? Here the argument becomes a little complex. Widespread dislike of a practice is not enough. There must, says Sir Patrick, be 'a real feeling of reprobation.' Disgust is not enough either. What is crucial is a combination of intolerance, indignation, and disgust. These three are the forces behind the moral law, without which it is not 'weighty enough to deprive the individual of freedom of choice.' Hence there is, in Sir Patrick's outlook, a crucial difference between the mere adverse moral judgment of society and one which is inspired by feeling raised to the concert pitch of intolerance, indignation, and disgust.

This distinction is novel and also very important. For on it depends the weight to be given to the fact that when morality is enforced individual liberty is necessarily cut down. Though Sir Patrick's abstract formulation of his views on this point is hard to follow, his examples make his position fairly clear. We can see it best in the contrasting things he says about fornication and homosexuality. In regard to fornication, public feeling in most societies is not now of the concert-pitch intensity. We may feel that it is tolerable if confined: only its spread might be gravely injurious. In such cases the question whether individual liberty should be restricted is for Sir Patrick a question of balance between the danger to society in the one scale, and the restriction of the individual in the other. But if, as may be the case with homosexuality, public feeling is up to concert pitch, if it expresses a 'deliberate judgment' that a practice as such is injurious to society, if there is 'a genuine feeling that it is a vice so abominable that its mere presence is an offence,' then it is beyond the limits of tolerance, and society may eradicate it. In this case, it seems, no further balancing of the claims of individual liberty is to be done, though as a matter of prudence the legislator should remember that the popular limits of tolerance may shift: the concert-pitch feeling may subside. This may produce a dilemma for the law; for the law may then be left without the full moral backing that it needs, yet it cannot be altered without giving the impression that the moral judgment is being weakened.

A Shared Morality

If this is what morality is—a compound of indignation, intolerance, and disgust—we may well ask what justification there is for taking it, and turning it as such, into criminal law with all the misery which criminal punishment entails. Here Sir Patrick's answer is very clear and simple. A collection of individuals is not a society; what makes them into a society is among other things a shared or public morality. This is as necessary to its existence as an organized government. So society may use the law to preserve its morality like anything else essential to it. 'The suppression of vice is as much the law's business as the suppression of subversive activities.' The liberal point of view which denies this is guilty of 'an error in jurisprudence': for it is no more possible to define an area of private morality than an area of private subversive activity. There can be no 'theoretical limits' to legislation against immorality just as there are no such limits to the power of the state to legislate against treason and sedition.

Surely all this, ingenious as it is, is misleading. Mill's formulation of the liberal point of view may well be too simple. The grounds for interfering with human liberty are more various than the single criterion of 'harm to others' suggests: cruelty to animals or organizing prostitution for gain do not, as Mill himself saw, fall easily under the description of harm to others. Conversely, even where there is harm to others in the most literal sense, there may well be other principles limiting the extent to which he often stresses between theoretical and practical limits. But with criteria, not a single criterion, determining when human liberty may be restricted. Perhaps this is what Sir Patrick means by a curious distinction which he often stresses between theoretical and practical limits. But with all its simplicities the liberal point of view is a better guide than Sir Patrick to clear thought on the proper relation of morality to the criminal law: for it stresses what he obscures—namely, the points at which thought is needed before we turn popular morality into criminal law.

Society and Moral Opinion

No doubt we would all agree that a consensus of moral opinion on certain matters is essential if society is to be worth living in. Laws against murder, theft, and much else would be of little use if they were not supported by a widely diffused conviction that what these laws forbid is also immoral. So much is obvious. But it does not follow that everything to which the moral vetoes of accepted morality attach is of equal importance to society; nor is there the slightest reason for thinking of morality as a seamless web: one which will fall to pieces carrying society with it, unless all its emphatic vetoes are enforced by law. Surely even in the face of the moral feeling that is up to concert pitch—the trio of intolerance, indignation, and disgust—we must pause to think. We must ask a question at two different levels which Sir Patrick never clearly enough identifies or separates. First, we must ask whether a practice which offends moral feeling is harmful, independently of its repercussion on the general moral code. Secondly, what about repercussion on the moral code? Is it really true that failure to translate this item of general morality into criminal law will jeopardize the whole fabric of morality and so of society?

We cannot escape thinking about these two different questions merely by repeating to ourselves the vague nostrum: 'This is part of public morality and public morality must be preserved if society is to exist.' Sometimes Sir Patrick seems to admit this, for he says in words which both Mill and the Wolfenden Report might have used, that there must be the maximum respect for individual liberty consistent with the integrity of society. Yet this, as his contrasting examples of fornication and homosexuality show, turns out to mean only that the immorality which the law may punish must be generally felt to be intolerable. This plainly is no adequate substitute for a reasoned estimate of the damage to the fabric of society likely to ensue if it is not suppressed.

Nothing perhaps shows more clearly the inadequacy of Sir Patrick's approach to this problem than his comparison between the suppression of sexual immorality and the suppression of treason or subversive activity. Private subversive activity is, of course, a contradiction in terms because 'subversion' means over-throwing government, which is a public thing. But it is grotesque, even where moral feeling against homosexuality is up to concert pitch, to think of the homosexual behaviour of two adults in private as in any way like treason or sedition either in intention or effect. We can make it *seem* like treason only if we assume that deviation from a general moral code is bound to affect that code, and to lead not merely to its modification but to its destruction. The analogy could begin to be plausible only if it was clear that offending against this item of morality was likely to jeopardize the whole structure. But we have ample evidence for believing that people will not abandon morality, will not think any better of murder, cruelty and dishonesty, merely because some private sexual practice which they abominate is not punished by the law.

Because this is so the analogy with treason is absurd. Of course 'No man is an island': what one man does in private, if it is known, may affect others in many different ways. Indeed it may be that deviation from general sexual morality by those whose lives, like the lives of many homosexuals, are noble ones and in all other ways exemplary will lead to what Sir Patrick calls the shifting of the limits of tolerance. But if this has any analogy in the sphere of government it is not the overthrow of ordered government, but a peaceful change in its form. So we may listen to the promptings of common sense and of logic, and say that though there could not logically be a sphere of private treason there is a sphere of private morality and immorality.

Sir Patrick's doctrine is also open to a wider, perhaps a deeper, criticism. In his reaction against a rationalist morality and his stress on feeling, he has I think thrown out the baby and kept the bath water; and the bath water may turn out to be very dirty indeed. When Sir Patrick's lecture was first delivered *The Times* greeted it with these words: 'There is a moving and welcome humility in the conception that society should not be asked to give its reason for refusing to tolerate what in its heart it feels intolerable.' This drew from a correspondent in Cambridge the retort: 'I am afraid that we are less humble than we used to be. We once burnt old women because, without giving our reasons, we felt in our hearts that witchcraft was intolerable.'

This retort is a bitter one, yet its bitterness is salutary. We are not, I suppose, likely, in England, to take again to the burning of old women for witchcraft or to punishing people for associating with those of a different race or colour, or to punishing people again for adultery. Yet if these things were viewed with intolerance, indignation, and disgust, as the second of them still is in some countries, it seems that on Sir Patrick's principles no rational criticism could be opposed to the claim that they should be punished by law. We could only pray, in his words, that the limits of tolerance might shift.

Curious Logic

It is impossible to see what curious logic has led Sir Patrick to this result. For him a practice is immoral if the thought of it makes the man on the Clapham omnibus sick. So be it. Still, why should we not summon all the resources of our reason, sympathetic understanding, as well as critical intelligence, and insist that before general moral feeling is turned into criminal law it is submitted to scrutiny of a different kind from Sir Patrick's? Surely, the legislator should ask whether the general morality is based on ignorance, superstition, or misunderstanding; whether there is a false conception that those who practise what it condemns are in other ways dangerous or hostile to society; and whether the misery to many parties, the blackmail and the other evil consequences of criminal punishment, especially for sexual offences, are well understood. It is surely extraordinary that among the things which Sir Patrick says are to be considered before we legislate against immorality these appear nowhere; not even as 'practical considerations,' let alone 'theoretical limits.' To any theory which, like this one, asserts that the criminal law may be used on the vague ground that the preservation of morality is essential to society and yet omits to stress the need for critical scrutiny, our reply should be: 'Morality, what crimes may be committed in thy name!'

As Mill saw, and de Tocqueville showed in detail long ago in his critical but sympathetic study of democracy, it is fatally easy to confuse the democratic principle that power should be in the hands of the majority with the utterly different claim that the majority, with power in their hands, need respect no limits. Certainly there is a special risk in a democracy that the majority may dictate how all should live. This is the risk we run, and should gladly run; for it is the price of all that is so good in democratic rule. But loyalty to democratic principles does not require us to maximize this risk: yet this is what we shall do if we mount the man in the street on the top of the Clapham omnibus and tell him that if only he feels sick enough about what other people do in private to demand its suppression by law no theoretical criticism can be made of his demand.

Suggestions
for Further Reading

Anthologies

Beck, Robert N. *Perspectives in Social Philosophy: Readings in Philosophic Sources of Social Thought.* New York: Holt, 1967. This book contains generous selections from the writings of classical and contemporary political philosophers. There are sections devoted to existentialism and analytic philosophy.

Cranston, Maurice (ed.). *Western Political Philosophers: A Background Book.* New York: Capricorn, 1967. A series of concise and lucid essays by contemporary philosophers and political scientists on Plato, Aristotle, Aquinas, Machiavelli, Hobbes, Locke, Rousseau, Burke, Hegel, Marx, and Mill. The beginning student, particularly, will find this book helpful.

Graham, Keith (ed.). *Contemporary Political Philosophy: Radical Studies.* New York: Cambridge U. P., 1982. This recent collection of original and sophisticated essays by young British philosophers discusses such topics as human nature and political beliefs, liberty and equality, individual rights and socialism, and other topics treated by the readings in this section.

Quinton, Anthony (ed.). *Political Philosophy.* New York: Oxford U.P., 1967. A judicious collection of recent influential writings on various issues in the area of political philosophy.

Somerville, John, and Ronald E. Santoni (eds.). *Social and Political Philosophy: Readings from Plato to Gandhi.* New York: Doubleday, Anchor, 1963. Extensive selections (in some instances the unabridged work) from some of the most famous and influential writings in social and political thought by philosophers and political leaders.

Individual Works

Beck, Robert N. *Handbook in Social Philosophy,* New York: Macmillan, 1979. An examination of such topics as state power and authority, political obligation, and the ideal of justice in terms of various contemporary philosophical perspectives.

Deininger, Whitaker T. *Problems in Social and Political Thought: A Philosophical Introduction.* New York: Macmillan, 1965. An expository text focusing on the contributions of both classical and contemporary philosophers. Designed for the beginning student.

De Tocqueville, Alexis. *Democracy in America.* Edited and abridged by Richard D. Heffner. New York: New American Library, a Mentor Book, 1956. Although written over a hundred years ago, this work remains one of the most perceptive studies of American democracy. With the passage of time, it seems to grow more, not less, pertinent.

Dewey, John. *Freedom and Culture.* New York: Capricorn, 1963.

——. *Individualism: Old and New.* New York: Capricorn, 1962.

——. *Liberalism and Social Action.* New York: Capricorn, 1963.

——. *The Public and Its Problems.* Chicago: Alan Swallow, 1957. The major works on social and political philosophy by the great American philosopher of liberal democracy.

Frankel, Charles. *The Democratic Prospect.* New York: Harper, Harper Colophon Book, 1964. A contemporary defense of democracy by an American philosopher.

Friedman, Milton, and Rose Friedman. *Free to Choose: A Personal Statement.* New York: Harcourt, 1980. The concrete implications of the authors' private-enterprise philosophy are spelled out in terms of proposed policies on taxation, financing education, and other topical issues.

Hook, Sidney. *Social Myths and Democracy.* New preface by the author. New York: Harper, Harper Torchbooks, 1966. A vigorous, clear, and critical examination of various political philosophies, with particular emphasis on Marxism and democracy by a former student of John Dewey and an able defender of his philosophy.

Hospers, John. *Human Conduct.* 2nd ed. New York: Harcourt, 1982. This lucid expository text written for readers with no previous acquaintance with the philosophic literature on problems of ethics devotes a final chapter to morality and the state, containing detailed discussions of many of the topics of this section.

——. *Libertarianism.* New York: Laissez Faire Books, 1971. A book designed to inform voters about Libertarian political philosophy by applying its principles to current public issues.

Macpherson, Crawford B. *The Life and Times of Liberal Democracy.* New York: Oxford U.P., 1977. A brief, clear attempt to set forth the essence of liberal democracy as now conceived.

Mencken, H. L. *Minority Report: H. L. Mencken's Notebooks.* New York: Knopf, 1956. This book consists of memoranda Mencken jotted down over many years. Yet these seemingly disconnected notes, often witty and biting, express a coherent and fundamental criticism of the American democratic scheme of things.

Nozick, Robert. *Anarchy, State, and Utopia.* New York: Basic Books, 1974. Nozick's conception of the minimal State, or the "nightwatchman" State with the primary function of protection rather than redistribution of wealth, has provoked much discussion.

Raphael, D. D. *Problems of Political Philosophy.* London: Pall Mall, 1970. A recent, clearly written introduction for the beginning student.

Rawls, John. *A Theory of Justice.* Cambridge: Belknap Press of Harvard U.P., 1971. An outstanding systematic work in social and political philosophy by an American philosopher. It already has provoked a great deal of discussion. Recommended for the more advanced student.

Reitman, Jeffrey H. *In Defense of Political Philosophy.* New York: Harper, Harper Torchbooks, 1972. The book vigorously argues against R. P. Wolff's *In Defense of Anarchism* (see Wolff, *In Defense of Anarchism*) and for majoritarian democracy.

Spencer, Herbert. *The Man Versus the State.* Edited by Donald Macrae. Baltimore: Penguin, 1969. As the result of the growing conviction that governments have become too strong for the preservation of men's liberties, the writings of the great nineteenth-century champion of *laissez-faire* individualism against an inherently oppressive state have sparked renewed interest.

Taylor, Richard. *Freedom, Anarchy, and the Law: An Introduction to Political Philosophy.* Englewood Cliffs, N.J.: Prentice-Hall, 1973. Beginning and advanced students will find this lucid work stimulating and a pleasure to read.

Wolff, Robert Paul. *In Defense of Anarchism.* New York: Harper, Harper Torchbooks, 1970. This iconoclastic work by an American philosopher has provoked much discussion. (See Reitman, *In Defense of Political Philosophy.*)

Dictionary of the History of Ideas: Studies of Selected Pivotal Ideas. Philip P. Wiener, editor-in-chief. New York: Scribners, 1973. Substantial and clearly written essays emphasizing the historical development of topics discussed in this part. Designed to inform the nonspecialist, each essay concludes with a select bibliography.

Encyclopedia of Philosophy. Paul Edwards, editor-in-chief. New York: Macmillan, 1967. The beginning student will find many worthwhile articles on the subjects treated in this part and excellent bibliographies.

Philosophy and Public Affairs. Princeton, N.J.: Princeton U.P.A. quarterly journal. Philosophers and philosophically inclined writers from various disciplines bring their methods to bear on problems that concern everyone interested in social and political issues.

Five:
Mind
and
Body

Introduction

In Karel Čapek's well-known play *R.U.R.* (Rossum's Universal Robots), scientists have learned to manufacture robots capable of doing all the manual and intellectual activities humans perform. Humans consider the robots to be lacking a soul since they are nothing more than a machine produced by a complex physical process, and they use the robots in any way that serves man's needs. The robots, whose manufacture resulted from a new method of organizing matter, look and act very much like humans except that they lack emotions and feelings, which were purposely omitted to increase productivity. Since the robot's insensitivity to pain often leads to accidents, a scientist at Rossum's robot factory experiments with changes in their formula to give them human emotions. His experiments succeed; but the new, sensitive robots consider themselves man's equal and, frustrated by their inferior status, rebel and destroy man.

This play raises the question of whether the robots, though only complex machines, differ significantly from the men who created them. The answers to this question can have important effects on man's view of himself and his place in the world. One traditional religious view of man, which gives him special importance, is that he alone, because he possesses an immaterial soul, was made in the image of God. But if man can be shown to be nothing more than a complex machine, this view of his special status must be given up. The doctrine that man is spiritual as well as physical has been thought to be of crucial importance for other reasons. The claim that man is immortal is based on his supposed possession of a soul that can continue in existence after the body's destruction. Some philosophers have argued that since a physical world would be controlled by invariable laws, the doctrine of free will can be maintained only if man has a spiritual aspect, and only if man possesses free will can he be morally responsible. In light of such implications, the philosopher is concerned to determine if man really is more than a complex physical object.

The problem of the nature of man, whether he is wholly physical or not, is called the mind-body problem. One prominent view of reality—*materialism*—holds that man, as is every other object in the universe, is totally a physical being. The universe is considered to consist of the motion of particles of matter in a void or space. Any claim that man has a soul or mind is regarded as a myth. The fact that man can do such things as talk and reason is attributed to his highly developed nervous system and brain. Death occurs when the body ceases to function. Any continuation of life after death is not the disembodied personal immortality defended by various religions, but the continued existence of the molecules that make up the body. This metaphysical materialism should not be confused with a popular use of the term *materialism* to refer to those who have no high ethical aims and who are primarily concerned with acquiring worldly goods and pleasures.

Opposed to the materialist view of those who believe that man is more than a material body; he also has a nonmaterial mind or soul. The idea of a person's being more than his body arose for a number of reasons. One possible reason is that primitive man could not comprehend why some bodies were alive and others dead when they apparently had the same physical parts. They endowed the living body with an invisible spirit or soul, which the dead body lacked. The idea of a soul that apparently left the body at the time of death became the foundation for the belief in immortality, i.e., the continued existence of the soul after death.

In speculation about the soul, present-day philosophers generally equate it with the mind, which they claim is that part of us that thinks and has images and sensations. These philosophers posit a nonmaterial mind because, for one reason, the various images and thoughts we have do not have any size, weight, or location and so cannot be material. Further, it is often claimed that a mind is necessary to explain purposive behavior. Purposive behavior is behavior that is determined by one's apprehension of and desire for some future goal, in contrast to behavior determined by prior physical causes. Philosophers who hold that man has both a physical body and a nonphysical mind are *dualists*.

The most generally held form of dualism and the form that is perhaps closest to our ordinary conception of man is *interactionism*. The interactionists maintain that both mind and body can causally affect each other. Thus, events in the mind can produce bodily behavior, and bodily events can produce mental occurrences. An example of events in the mind causing bodily events would be a thought of a girl friend causing one to pick up the phone and call her. An example of a physical event causing a mental event would be a case where stubbing one's toe produces a sensation of pain.

Many philosophers have thought the interactionist view unsatisfactory. The major difficulty is that there seems to be no good explanation of how a mental event, such as a thought, can cause physical behavior. We ordinarily think of causation in terms of one physical event producing another. A simple example would be a moving billiard ball's hitting a second ball and moving it. But how can a thought produce movement in a person's body? And where does the mind act on the body to cause it to move? One might be inclined to say that the mind affects some portion of the brain, but physiologists have found no place where the brain seems to be stimulated by any invisible cause. Similarly, how can the body produce sensations or images in the mind, which is nonphysical?

Confronted with such difficulties, some philosophers who believe that mental phenomena cannot be reduced to physical ones have given up interactionism in favor of *epiphenomenalism*. This view holds that physical events can cause mental events, but that occurrences in the mind are not able to cause any physical events. Rather than interaction, we have a one-way causal relation: from the body to the mind. This view, too, has had its share of critics. This view, like interactionism, needs to explain how a physical event in the body can cause an event to take place in the mind. Another problem is that paradoxical results follow from this theory. One such result is that all thoughts and reasoning are totally without significance in the determination of our behavior. It is certainly hard to believe that the world would be exactly as it is today even though none of men's thoughts about democracy, religion, and morality had ever occurred.

An ingenious theory that asserts the existence of minds but avoids the problems of the various dualist theories is *idealism*. Idealists affirm the existence of minds along with perceptions and feelings but deny the existence of any material objects existing apart from minds. Those objects that we ordinarily consider to exist in an external world are, in fact, nothing but appearances in minds. Although the idealist view of the world as consisting solely of disembodied minds and their contents seems very odd, it should not be dismissed without a careful assessment. Perhaps the most serious difficulty confronting the idealist is that of providing an explanation of the cause of our perceptions. If there is nothing independent of our minds causing our perceptions of such objects as tables and chairs, why do we perceive them at all?

In the first group of readings that follow, several of these positions are defended. In "Materialism," Hugh Elliot presents a detailed defense of the materialistic view of man and the world. He maintains that the main principles of materialism are the uniformity of law, the denial of teleology, and the denial of any form of existence other than those envisaged by physics and chemistry. He attempts to answer some of the major difficulties that materialists face, especially the nature of images and the apparent existence of purposive behavior. In defending the interactionist position, C. E. M. Joad argues that the materialist cannot adequately explain purposive behavior or the way in which meaning is apprehended. He conceives of the mind as an active, creative force, which carries on activities that could not be conceived as resulting from the function of the brain. In opposition to the materialist view, Joad maintains that a perfect knowledge of a person's brain would fail to tell us what he was thinking since different thoughts could result in the same brain state. In "Sense Without Matter," A. A. Luce rejects materialism by denying that we have any knowledge of matter or any need to postulate its existence. The sensations we have cannot, however, exist alone; and, so, we must postulate the existence of minds.

Although the development of robots has long been a subject for science-fiction stories and plays, such as *R.U.R.*, it is becoming a subject of increasing interest to philosophers and scientists as a result of the recent development of computers. Some theorists maintain that computers will eventually be developed to the point where they can perform all of the rational processes of human beings. And with the development of computerized robots, we would have a machine that could do everything a human being can do. In fact, it is argued, such a machine would be a human being, and a human being would have been shown to be nothing more than a machine. But is it possible to develop a machine that can perform all of the "mental" feats of a human being? And if such a machine could be developed, would it still lack something that humans possess? If we produce a machine that can do everything a human being can do, then have we shown that humans are really nothing more than physical objects?

In discussing whether machines can think, Christopher Evans analyses Alan Turing's famous test for machine intelligence. The test, which places a computer and a human behind opaque screens, is designed to prove whether the responses of a computer can be distinguished from those of a human. Turing claimed that computers must be deemed as capable as humans of thought and intelligence if those taking the test cannot determine what is behind each screen. Along with exploring the value of the Turing test, Evans criticizes numerous objections to the possibility of machine intelligence. In contrast to Evans, Morton Hunt contends that certain features of human thought and emotion cannot be duplicated by machines. One such feature is self-awareness, which affects our perspective and reasoning and opens up the possibility of unpredictable responses. Another such feature is the presence in humans of desires and the ability to set goals on the basis of those desires. Thus, although computers will be able to perform many tasks better than humans, other tasks, according to Hunt, will forever be beyond their capabilities.

A major issue that arises from a discussion of the mind-body problem is that of immortality. Continued existence after physical death would require that man have a nonphysical part that can survive without the body. The acceptance of dualism is not, however, by itself sufficient to show that there actually is immortality. It is certainly possible that the mind ceases to function when the body does. So, to have rational grounds for the belief in immortality, one would not only have to show that one has a mind or soul but also that there is evidence that such continued existence occurs.

In "Immortality," Durant Drake examines a variety of arguments both for and against the belief in personal immortality and concludes that there is no evidence to support this belief and serious weaknesses with attempts to defend it. Although Drake does not deny that immortality is possible, he contends that belief in its existence is unnecessary for a happy and moral earthly life. Although Ducasse agrees with Drake that immortality has not been proven, he examines in his paper "Is Life After Death Possible?" the kind of evidence that would suffice to prove its reality. He argues that some kinds of psychic phenomena, if shown to exist, would establish the truth of immortality. Ducasse contends that many of the attempts to show that immortality is false or an impossibility stem from the assumption that materialism is true. Rejection of that assumption at least opens the way for belief in immortality.

Materialism

36. Materialism Hugh Elliot

Hugh Elliot (1881–1930), editor of the Annual Register, England, was a champion of modern science and materialism, and a student and biographer of Herbert Spencer, the famous nineteenth-century philosopher of evolution.

. . . The main purpose of the present work is to defend the doctrine of materialism. . . .

The outlines of this system are not new; the main features of it, indeed, have been admittedly associated with scientific progress for centuries past. An age of science is necessarily an age of materialism; ours is a scientific age, and it may be said with truth that we are all materialists now. The main principles which I shall endeavor to emphasize are three.

1. The uniformity of law. In early times events appeared to be entirely hazardous and unaccountable, and they still seem so, if we confine attention purely to the passing moment. But as science advances, there is disclosed a uniformity in the procedure of Nature. When the conditions at any one moment are precisely identical with those which prevailed at some previous moment, the results flowing from them will also be identical. It is found, for instance, that a body of given mass attracts some other body of given mass at a given distance with a force of a certain strength. It is found that when the masses, distances, and other conditions are precisely repeated, the attraction between the bodies is always exactly the same. It is found, further, that when the distance between the bodies is increased the force of their attraction is diminished in a fixed proportion, and this again is found to hold true at all distances at which they may be placed. The force of their attraction again varies in a different but still constant proportion to their masses. And hence results the law of gravitation, by which the force of attraction can be precisely estimated from a knowledge of the masses and distances between any two bodies whatever. A uniformity is established which remains absolute within the experience of Man, and to an equivalent extent the haphazard appearance of events is found to be only an appearance. Innumerable other laws of a similar character are gradually discovered, establishing a sort of nexus between every kind of event. If oxygen and hydrogen in the proportion by weight of eight to one are mixed together, and an electric spark is passed through them, water is formed; and on every occasion where precisely the same conditions are realized precisely the

From *Modern Science and Materialism* by Hugh Elliot. Published by Longman's, Green and Company, Ltd., 1919.

same result ensues. This truth is the basis of the experimental method. If from similar conditions it were possible that dissimilar results should follow on various occasions, then experiments would be useless for advancing knowledge. . . .

2. The denial of teleology. Scientific materialism warmly denies that there exists any such thing as purpose in the Universe, or that events have any ulterior motive or goal to which they are striving. It asserts that all events are due to the interaction of matter and motion acting by blind necessity in accordance with those invariable sequences to which we have given the name of laws. This is an important bond of connection between the materialism of the ancient Greeks and that of modern science. Among all peoples not highly cultivated there reigns a passionate conviction, not only that the Universe as a whole is working out some pre-determined purpose, but that every individual part of it subserves some special need in the fulfillment of this purpose. Needless to say, the purpose has always been regarded as associated with human welfare. The Universe, down to its smallest parts, is regarded by primitive superstition as existing for the special benefit of man. To such extreme lengths has this view been carried that even Bernardin de Saint-Pierre, who only died last century, argued that the reason why melons are ribbed is that they may be eaten more easily by families. . . .

When it is alleged that the Universe is purposive, it is assumed that humanity is intimately connected with the purpose. Without that assumption, none but the most transcendental of philosophers would have any interest in maintaining teleology. As the anthropocentric doctrine falls, therefore, the doctrine of teleology must fall with it. This, at all events, is the position taken up by scientific, as indeed by all materialism; it is the position that I hope I shall have little difficulty in defending in the following pages. Nevertheless, however obvious its truth, we must recognize that it involves a profound alteration in the existing mental point of view of the majority of mankind; for most men have as yet not shaken off the habit, which all men necessarily start from, that they themselves, or their family, nation or kind, are in fact, as in appearance, the very centre of the cosmos.

3. The denial of any form of existence other than those envisaged by physics and chemistry, that is to say, other than existences that have some kind of palpable material characteristics and qualities. It is here that modern materialism begins to part company with ancient materialism, and it is here that I expect the main criticisms of opponents to be directed. The modern doctrine stands in direct opposition to a belief in any of those existences that are vaguely classed as "spiritual." To this category belong not only ghosts, gods, souls, *et hoc genus omne*, for these have long been rejected from the beliefs of most advanced thinkers. The time has now come to include also in the condemned list that further imaginary entity which we call "mind," "consciousness," etc., together with its various subspecies of intellect, will, feeling, etc., in so far as they are supposed to be independent or different from material existences or processes.

. . . It seems to the ordinary observer that nothing can be more remotely and widely separated than some so-called "act of consciousness" and a material object. An act of consciousness or mental process is a thing of which we are immediately and indubitably aware; so much I admit. But that it differs in any sort of way from a material process, that is to say, from the ordinary transformations of matter and energy, is a belief which I very strenuously deny. . . .

The proposition which I here desire to advance is that every event occurring in the Universe, including those events known as mental processes, and all kinds of human action or conduct, are expressible purely in terms of matter and motion. If we assume in the primeval nebula of the solar system no other elementary factors beyond those of matter and energy or motion, we can theoretically, as above remarked, deduce the existing Universe, including mind, consciousness, etc., without the introduction of any new factor whatsoever. The existing Universe and all things and events therein may be theoretically expressed in terms of matter and energy, undergoing continuous redistribution in accordance with the ordinary laws of physics and chemistry. If all manifestations within our experience can be thus expressed, as has for long been believed by men of science, what need is there for the introduction of any new entity of spiritual character, called mind? It has no part to play; it is impotent in causation. . . . Now there is an ancient logical precept which retains a large validity: *entia non sunt multiplicanda praeter necessitatem.* It is sometimes referred to as William of Occam's razor, which cuts off and rejects from our theories all factors or entities which are superfluous in guiding us to an explanation. "Mind" as a separate entity is just such a superfluity. I will not deny—indeed I cordially affirm—that it is a direct datum of experience; but there is no direct datum of experience to the effect that it is anything different from certain cerebral processes. . . .

The materialism which I shall advocate, therefore, is centred round three salient points: the uniformity of law, the exclusion of purpose, and the assertion of monism; that is to say, that there exists no kind of spiritual substance or entity of a different nature from that of which matter is composed.

The first of these propositions, otherwise called the Law of Universal Causation, affirms that nothing happens without a cause, and that the same causes under the same conditions always produce the same effects. In order to gain a true comprehension of this law, we have to define what we mean by "cause" and "effect," and what is the nature of the nexus between them. The conception of the Universe from which we start is that of a great system of matter and motion undergoing redistribution according to fixed sequences, which in the terminology of science are called laws. The matter is constantly undergoing transformation from one of its forms into another, and the energy is redistributed and transformed in a corresponding manner. From this primary conception alone, we are able to derive a precise definition of what is meant by cause, a problem which is almost insuperable from any other standpoint. . . . If we regard an event as a momentary phase in the redistribution of matter and motion, then the cause of the event is found in the immediately preceding state of distribution of that same matter and motion. Let us ask, for instance, what is the cause of the sudden appearance of a new fixed star in the heavens. Supposing that there were previously two extinct suns moving rapidly towards each other and coming into collision, we should be making a statement of events which would be recognized as a possibly true "cause." The second event, or "effect," is represented exclusively in terms of matter and motion by the idea of two coalesced and volatilized bodies giving rise to vast quantities of heat and light. And the cause is given merely by stating the previous distribution of that matter and energy which is concerned in the production of the event. The *matter* concerned in the event consisted of two solid bodies at a rapidly diminishing distance from one another. The *energy* consisted of half the product of their momentum and velocity. By the collision the matter contained in the solid bodies underwent that redistribution involved in passing into a gaseous state, with the decomposition of many of its molecules, that is to say, with a rearrangement or redistribution of its atoms. The energy of motion previously contained in the solid bodies underwent at the same time a transformation into heat and light. The sudden light, therefore, is explained, or derives its cause, merely by furnishing a statement of the previous distribution of the matter and energy concerned in its production. . . .

And this leads me to the second problem which I have here to deal with, the problem of teleology. I have hitherto endeavored to represent the notion of cause and effect in purely materialistic terms, to the exclusion of all metaphysical transcendentalism; to state the relation of cause and effect in terms of the redistribution of matter and motion. I now have to perform the same task for the conception of purpose, and more particularly of human purpose, in order to show how purposiveness may be translated into purely materialistic and mechanical terms; that is to say, how it, too, may be expressed as a phase of the normal process of redistribution of matter and motion under fixed and invariable laws.

At the outset of this inquiry, we have to notice that the word purpose is involved in the same vagueness of significance that attends almost all words used in popular speech. In general a word in popular use has to be defined and limited to some precise meaning before it is fit for employment in a philosophical discussion. In the present case the word is commonly employed in at least two meanings, which differ greatly from each other; and this duality of meaning leads to a duality in the derivative conceptions of "teleology," "finalism," "end," etc., which has not infrequently given rise to confusion and error. The two significations may be roughly grouped as intelligent purposiveness and unintelligent purposiveness, and the reduction of each of these to mechanistic terms involves two different lines of analysis. I shall deal first with unintelligent purposiveness.

In this case, the word is usually applied to a certain kind of organic reactions that bear an obvious relation to the requirements of the reacting organism. An *Amoeba* in the water throws out pseudopodia at random in all directions. When one of these pseudopodia comes into contact with some substance suitable for food, the protoplasm streams round and encloses the particle, which is thus incorporated in the body of the *Amoeba* and there digested. The reaction is purposive in the sense that a somewhat complicated series of movements is carried out, which leads to the preservation of the active organism.

In just the same way, when we ascend the animal scale, the sea-anemone spreads its tentacles at large under the surface of the water. On contact with any substance suitable for food the tentacles contract around the substance and draw it into the interior of the sea-anemone. This action is similarly purposive in that it procures the continued existence of the animal. In all animals the common movements and reactions are predominantly of this purposive type. If an object suddenly appears close to our eyes, we involuntarily close them for an instant, and this reaction is obviously purposive, as directed towards the protection of the eyes.

All these instinctive actions are purposive in character, yet equally without doubt, they are all of the nature of reflex action, working blindly and inevitably to their conclusion. On contact with the tentacle of a sea-anemone, the stimulus thus applied to that tentacle sets up by entirely mechanical procedure organic processes which necessarily result in the observed contractions. Similarly, in the case of the human being, the sudden appearance of a near object causes an impulse to be conveyed down the optic nerve, which immediately and mechanically propagates its effect to the efferent nerves which lead to the muscles that close the eyelids. The same kind of reaction is characteristic of the functions in plants. The turning of flowers towards the light, and all the processes of absorption, transpiration, etc., are, on the one hand, subservient to the life and prosperity of the plant, while, on the other hand, they are blind mechanical reactions to stimuli.

Seeing that a single action may thus be at the same time both purposive and mechanical, it is plain that there can be no antithesis between the two; but that the difference between purposive and blind mechanism arises simply from our point of view, and not from any difference of objective character. Purposive reactions are not different from mechanical reactions, but they *are* mechanical reactions of a certain kind. Not all mechanical reactions are purposive, but all purposive reactions are mechanical; and it remains to determine *what* mechanical actions may be correctly described as purposive, and what are simply blind and meaningless. . . .

I now come to the second class of activities to which the name of purpose is applied, that is to say, cases of activity which bear reference to an end consciously and intelligently foreseen, such as the acts inspired by the conscious will in human beings. These activities are commonly regarded as being in a higher degree teleological than the unintelligent reactions hitherto considered; and in many uses of the word "purpose," reference is intended exclusively to these intelligent anticipations of future events, and to the activities carried out in consequence of such anticipations. In this sense purpose is allied to will, and purposive actions are more or less synonymous with voluntary actions. . . .

We are now in a position to appreciate the true meaning of those acts which are described as intelligently purposive. Being deliberate and reasoned activities, they are as far as possible removed from the simple type of reflex action in which response follows immediately on external stimulus. They belong to the category in which the immediate stimulus is in the brain itself, and is to be regarded as consisting of rearrangements of the matter and energy contained in the nervous substance of the brain. The brain during consciousness can never be still, and its unceasing activities supply the stimulus, not only for purposive, but for all actions of an intellectual character. Now this permanent cerebral activity can be divided into a number of different types, known psychologically by such names as memory, imagination, reason, etc. Although nervous physiology has not yet advanced far enough to enable us to say what are the different kinds of material processes in the brain corresponding to these psychical processes, yet there is no doubt that the psychical distinction is based upon some actual distinction in the corresponding activities occurring in the brain. Among these cerebral processes is that which is known psychologically as a desire for some external object or event, a visualization of some external phenomenon as an end or purpose to be attained. This desire may then act upon efferent nerves and give rise to the activities which we know as purposive. The essence of a purposive action, and the standard by which it is distinguished from other kinds of actions, is that the "end" to which the action leads was previously represented in the brain of the agent, and composes the stimulus of action. The compound stimulus arises, as I have said, from the composition of large numbers of elementary stimuli previously received. It consists psychologically of a faint representation of the sensation which would be vividly presented by the realization of some outward occurrence. And when this faint representation actually functions as a stimulus which innervates the muscles whose contraction brings about the external occurrence represented, we have what is called an action of intelligent purpose. . . .

Intelligent purpose, like unintelligent purpose, is then only a name given to a particular kind of incident in the midst of the eternal redistribution of matter and motion under blind mechanical laws. It is in perfect harmony with that materialistic scheme; it can be stated in terms of the purest mechanism. As the matter and motion undergo their invariable and unalterable redistribution, we naturally find ourselves more interested in some phases of it than in others; and in one class of evolving events we are so interested and we have such frequent occasion to refer to them, that we denominate them by a special name—the name of purposive. By this name we designate the majority of those redistributions which issue from the little whirlpools of matter and energy called organisms, and those factors in particular by which the immediate continuance of such whirlpools is ensured.

I have now dealt with the law of universal causation, and with the doctrine of teleology. It remains only to say a few words about the third pillar of materialism—the assertion of monism, that is, that there are not two kinds of fundamental existence, material and spiritual, but one kind only. . . . For simplifying the discussion, it will be as well at once to dismiss from consideration all those kinds of spiritual entities imagined by religious believers. The Victorian writers said on this subject nearly all that could be said, and interest now attaches only to those problems of matter and spirit which they left unsolved. I shall, therefore, confine myself to an attempt to reduce the last stronghold of dualism; to ascertain the relation between mind and body; to show that mental manifestations and bodily manifestations are not two different things, as generally supposed, but one and the same thing appearing under different aspects. I shall not attempt to deal with any of the so-called "non-material" existences with the exception of mind; for if mind can be identified with matter, all other kinds of non-material entities must lapse, even those described by religious systems. . . .

We reached the conclusion in a previous chapter that the bodily organism is a complex machine. We found that all its processes and activities are attributable to physico-chemical forces, identical with those which are recognized in the inorganic realm. We learnt that there is no "vital force" or other spiritual interference with the normal physical sequences. If, then, there be a mind, it is reduced to the function of inertly and uselessly accompanying the activities of certain neural elements. This is the doctrine of epiphenomenalism, and it is the last word possible to one who accepts the duality of mind and matter. It is a theory which on the face of it is devoid of verisimilitude. What can be the use of such a shadowy and inefficient entity? What parallel can be found in Nature for the existence of so gratuitous a superfluity? Moreover, what mechanism, conceivable or inconceivable, could cause it thus to shadow neural processes, which *ex hypothesi* do not produce it? If one such mental state is the cause of the next, how does it happen that it causes the one which is necessary to accompany the actual neural process at the moment? Epiphenomenalism involves us in a pre-established harmony that is profoundly opposed to the scientific spirit of the twentieth century. The problem, however, is not one that need be discussed on the grounds of *a priori* probability. It is a theory that may be rigidly refuted, and to that task I now turn.

It is a part of the doctrine of epiphenomenalism that a man would to all external appearance be precisely the same whether he was possessed of his epiphenomenal mind or not. Conduct, action, expression, would not in the slightest extent be affected were he completely devoid of mind and consciousness; for all these things depend upon material sequences alone. Men are puppets or automata, and we have no further grounds for supposing them to have minds than the fact that we know we have a mind ourselves, and the argument by analogy from ourselves to them. But arguments from analogy are notoriously insecure, and it seems, therefore, to be quite within the bounds of possibility to the epiphenomenalist that some or all other men may be mindless syntheses of matter. . . .

Now let us assume that such a man actually exists, or, if you prefer, let us assume that physical chemistry has advanced to such a pitch that a man may be synthetized in the laboratory, starting from the elements, carbon, nitrogen, etc., of which protoplasm is composed. Let us assume in any case a "synthetic man" without a mind, yet indistinguishable by the epiphenomenalist hypothesis from another man identically constituted materially but having a mind. Ask the synthetic man whether he has a mind. What will he say? Inevitably he will say yes. For he must say the same thing as the man, identically made, who *has* a mind. Otherwise the same question would set up different responses in the nervous systems of the two, and that is by hypothesis impossible. The sound of the words "have you a mind?" entering the ears of the synthetic man sets up highly complex cerebral associations (which we call grasping their meaning): these associations will, after a short time, culminate in nervous currents to the tongue, lips and larnyx, which will be moved in such a way as to produce an audible and intelligent answer. Now this answer must be the same in the case of the man who has a mind as in the case of the mindless man, since their nervous systems are the same. If there was a different vocal response to an identical aural stimulus, then there must in one of them have been some external interference with the physico-chemical sequences. Mind must have broken through the chain of physical causality, and that is contrary to hypothesis.

What can the epiphenomenalist say? That the mindless man is a liar, to say he has a mind? That will not do, for if the two men are objectively identical one cannot be a liar, and the other not; one engaged in deceit, while the other speaks the truth. The epiphenomenalist is thrown back, therefore, on the assumption that the mindless man has made a mistake; that he thinks he has a mind, but really has not one; that his nervous constitution is such as to impel him to the conviction that he has a mind when he really has not, to lead him to talk upon psychical phenomena and their differences from matter, and in general to behave exactly as if he knew all about mind and matter, had considered the subject of their relationship, etc.

The example shows, furthermore, that the condition of "knowing one has a mind" is a condition which can be stated and accounted for in rigidly materialistic terms. When the epiphenomenalist himself asserts that he has a mind, the movements of his vocal cords by which he makes that pronouncement are by his own theory led up to by a chain of purely material sequences. He would make just the same pronouncement if he had no mind at all. His claim to possess a mind, therefore, is wholly irrelevent to the real question whether he actually has a mind or not. The events that make him say he has a mind are not the actual possession of a mind, but those cerebral processes which, in epiphenomenalist language, are said to underlie states of consciousness. It is the cerebral processes alone which make him speak, and his utterance, his belief in a mind, furnish testimony alone to the existence of those cerebral processes. Were the mind truly able to compel a belief and an announcement of its own existence, it could only be by breaking through the chain of material bodily sequences, and this is a vitalistic supposition that is ruled out by physiology. The belief in the possession of a mind is a cerebral condition, due, not to the actual possession of a mind, but to definite pre-existing cerebral conditions on the same material plane.

I do not see how epiphenomenalism could be much more effectively refuted. Yet it is the only respectable dualistic theory that is compatible with physiological mechanism. Let me recapitulate for a moment the facts, now before us, upon which we have to establish a theory of the relationship of mind and body.

Physiology has shown that bodily activity of every kind is a product

of purely material sequences, into the course of which there is no ir-
ruption of any spiritualistic factor. On the dualistic theory, that doctrine
is excessively difficult to understand. You move your arm by an act of
will, or what seems to be a non-material cause, and yet it is conclusively
established that the movement of the arm is due to definite material
changes occurring in the brain, and caused by the fixed laws of physics
and chemistry in the most determinist fashion. Now, anchoring ourselves
firmly to that fact, we are confronted with the problem of where to put
the mind. For every mental state there is some corresponding cerebral
state; the one appears to be the exact counterpart of the other down to
the smallest discoverable particular. Now on the dualistic assumption,
there is only one possible hypothesis, namely, that of epiphenomenalism.
Or, rather, it is incorrect to call it an hypothesis; for *if* there are two
things, mind and body, epiphenomenalism is no more than a statement
of the facts established by physiology and psychology. Dualistic physiologists, therefore, are practically forced to accept it. Yet, as I have
shown, it is utterly untenable when properly thought out.

We are faced, therefore, by two possible alternatives: (1) to abandon
mechanism, (2) to abandon dualism. Now mechanism is a physiological
theory which is proved. We must hold fast to it therefore at any expense
to our metaphysical preconceptions. The only remaining alternative,
then, is the abandonment of dualism. . . .

When once we have got over the shock which monism carries to those
accustomed to think in dualistic terms, we find that the great majority
of the difficulties of metaphysics fall away. By an act of will I raise my
arm. The plain man insists that his will did it; the physiologist knows
that it was physico-chemical processes in the brain. The dilemma is at
once overcome when the philosopher points out that the will *is* the physico-chemical processes, and that they both mean the same thing. . . . The
difficulty of the epiphenomenalist is also solved. He says he has a mind.
What makes him say so is not a transcendental "knowledge of having
mind," but a certain cerebral state. When we have affirmed the absolute
identity of that knowledge with that cerebral state, all difficulties vanish.
The mind is the sum-total of cerebral conditions. He says he has a mind;
it is the existence of the cerebral conditions which cause him to say so.
He says he has mind because he has cerebral conditions, and his remark
is true and intelligible only on the one hypothesis that the mind *is* the
cerebral conditions. . . .

Monism resolves the great biological difficulty as to the origin of consciousness. The biological conclusions as to the origin of life are to the
effect that living and organic matter was developed by evolution from
non-living and inorganic matter. The evolution of Man from unicellular
parentage is a fact. There is little or no reason to doubt that his unicellular
ancestor was evolved just as gradually from inorganic matter. Now, says
the dualist, we know that the man has a mind. It follows, therefore, either
that inorganic matter has a psychical accompaniment, or else that, in the
course of evolution, there was a sudden leap: mind was suddenly intruded
at some period of Man's past history. Neither of these hypotheses is easy
to entertain, or perhaps even practicable to conceive. The doctrine of

monism, with its assertion that there are not two ultimate things, but one, causes the difficulty to vanish; for there is then no necessity to introduce a new entity at any period of an organism's evolution. According to our theory, a conscious state is a specific neural functioning. If there is no discontinuity in the evolution of nervous elements from inorganic matter, there is then no discontinuity in the evolution of consciousness.

Interactionism

37. The Mind as Distinct from the Body   C. E. M. Joad

Cyril Edwin Mitchinson Joad (1891–1953) was a prolific English author, whose books and articles and speeches on philosophy exerted broad public appeal in his lifetime.

The issue between those who endeavor to interpret mind action in terms of body action, and those who contend for the unique, distinct, and in some sense independent status of mind, is not capable of definite settlement. . . . The most that can be done is to suggest certain objections that can be and have been brought against the materialist position, . . . and at the same time to indicate a number of independent considerations which seem to demand a different kind of approach to psychology, and a different interpretation of its problems. This interpretation, to put it briefly, insists that a living organism is something over and above the matter of which its body is composed; that it is, in short, an expression of a principal of life, and that life is a force, stream, entity, spirit, call it what you will, that cannot be described or accounted for in material terms; that in human beings this principal of life expresses itself at the level of what is called mind, that this mind is distinct from both body and brain, and, so far from being a mere register of bodily occurrences, is able, acting on its own volition, to produce such occurrences, and that no account of mind action which is given in terms of brain action, gland activity or bodily responses to external stimuli can, therefore, be completely satisfactory. This is the view which in some form or other is held by those who find a materialist explanation of psychology unsatisfactory, and in this chapter we shall be concerned with the reasons for it.

Biological Considerations

Purposiveness.   Some of these reasons, and perhaps the most important, are derived in part from regions which lie outside the scope of psychology proper; they belong to biology, and are based on a consideration of the characteristics which all living beings are found to possess in common. With regard to one of these "alleged" characteristics of living organisms it is necessary to say a few words, since it constitutes a starting point for the method of interpretation with which we shall be concerned in this chapter. The characteristic in question is that to which we give the name of purposiveness, and because of this characteristic it is said

From *How Our Minds Work* by C. E. M. Joad. Published by Philosophical Library. Reprinted by permission of the publishers.

that any attempt to interpret the behaviour of living creatures in terms of material response to stimuli must inevitably break down. Purposiveness implies the capacity to be influenced by and to work for a purpose; this in its turn involves the apprehension, whether conscious or unconscious, of some object which lies in the future and which the purpose seeks to achieve; it therefore necessitates the existence of a mind. If, therefore, purposiveness is a true characteristic of living creatures, then we have established a good starting point for our "mental" approach to psychology.

What, therefore, is meant by saying that living creatures are purposive? Primarily, that in addition to those of their movements which may be interpreted as responses to existing situations, they also act in a way which seems to point to the existence of a spontaneous impulse or need to bring about some other situation which does not yet exist. This impulse or need is sometimes known as a conation; a good instance of the sort of thing that is meant is the impulse we feel to maintain the species by obtaining food or seeking a mate. The impulse is chiefly manifested in the efforts a living organism will make to overcome any obstacle which impedes the fulfillment of its instinctive need. It will try first one way of dealing with it and then another, as if it were impelled by some overmastering force which drove it forward to the accomplishment of a particular purpose. Thus the salmon, proceeding up stream, leaping over rocks and breasting the current in order to deposit her spawn in a particular place, is acting in a way which it is difficult to explain in terms of a response to external stimuli. An organism again will seek to preserve the trend of natural growth and development by which alone the purpose of existence will be fulfilled; in its endeavour to reach and to maintain what we may call its natural state or condition, it is capable, if need arises, of changing or modifying its bodily structure. If you take the hydroid plant Antennularia and remove it from the flat surface to which it is accustomed to adhere, it will begin to proliferate long wavy roots or fibers in the effort to find something solid to grip, while everybody has heard of the crab's habit of growing a new leg in place of one that has been knocked off.

Activity of this kind seems difficult to explain on materialist lines as the response to a stimulus; it appears rather to be due to the presence of a living, creative impulse to develop in the face of any obstacle in a certain way. That a living organism works as a machine works, by reacting in the appropriate way to the appropriate stimulus, is admitted; all that is contended is that it acts in other ways as well, that these other activities depend not only upon the quality of stimulus received, but upon the intensity of the creature's conative impulse, and that the existence of the impulse is only explicable on the assumption that the creature is animated by the need to fulfill a purpose.

Foresight and Expectation.   When we apply this conclusion to human psychology, we are immediately struck by the fact that the individual not only exhibits in common with other organisms this characteristic of purposive behaviour, but is in many cases conscious of the nature of the purpose which inspires his behaviour. The man who studies in order to pass an examination is not only impelled by a push from behind; he is drawn forward by a pull from in front. This pull from in front can only become operative if he can be credited with the capacity to conceive the desirability of a certain state of affairs—namely, the passing of the examination, which does not yet exist; he shows, in other words, foresight and expectation. It is activities of this kind which seem most insistently to involve the assumption of a mind to do the foreseeing and expecting. In other words, the capacity to be influenced by events which lie in the future seems inexplicable on the stimulus-response basis; the *thought* of what does not exist may be allowed to influence the mind, but it is difficult to see how the non-existent can stimulate the body. . . .

The Apprehension of Meaning

An important fact about our mental life is that we are capable of appreciating meaning. A statement of fact written on a piece of paper is, so far as its material content is concerned, merely a number of black marks inscribed on a white background. Considered, then, as a collection of visual, physical stimuli, it is comparatively unimportant; what is important is the meaning which is attached to these marks. If they inform us, for example, that we have received a legacy of ten thousand pounds it is not the black marks on the white background but the meaning they convey that effects a disturbance in our emotional life, sufficiently profound to keep us awake all night. Now the meaning of the marks is obviously not a physical stimulus; it is something immaterial. How, then, is its effect to be explained in terms of bodily responses to physical stimuli, which the mind merely registers? Let us take one or two further examples in order to present the difficulty in a concrete form.

Let us suppose that I am a geometrician and am thinking about the properties of a triangle. As I do not wish at this point to enter into the vexed question of whether *some* physical stimulus is or is not necessary to initiate every chain of reasoning, we will assume that in this case there was a physical stimulus—it may have been a chance remark about Euclid, or the appearance of a red triangular road signpost while I am driving a car—a stimulus which we will call X, which prompted me to embark upon the train of speculations about the triangle. My reasoning proceeds until I arrive at a conclusion, which takes the form of a geometrical proposition expressed in a formula. I carry this formula in my head for a number of days and presently write it down. In due course I write a book, setting forth my formula and giving an account of the reasoning which led me to it. The book is read and understood by A. Presently it is translated into French, and is read and understood by B. Later still I deliver a lecture on the subject which is heard and understood by C. As A, B, and C have each of them understood my formula and the reasoning upon which it is based, we may say that the reasoning process has had for them the same meaning throughout. If it had not, they would not all have reached the same conclusion and understood the same thing by it. Yet in each of the four cases the sensory stimulus was different; for myself it was X, for A it was a number of black marks on a white background, for B a number of different black marks on a white background, and for C a number of vibrations in the atmosphere impinging upon his eardrums. It seems incredible that all these different stimuli should have been able to produce a consciousness of the same meaning, if our respective reactions to them were confined to physical responses (which must in each case have been different) which were subsequently reflected in our minds by a process of mental registration of the different responses. The stimuli being different, the intervention of something possessed of the capacity to grasp the *common* element among these physically different entities alone seems able to account for the facts, but the common element is the meaning, which is immaterial and can be grasped, therefore, only by a mind.

Let us take another example instanced by Professor McDougall:

A man receives a telegram which says "Your son is dead." The visual physical stimulus here is, as before, a collection of black marks on an orange field. The reaction experienced in terms of his bodily behaviour may take the form of a complete cessation of all those symptoms usually associated with life—that is to say, he may faint. When he recovers consciousness his thoughts and actions throughout the whole of the remainder of his life may be completely changed. Now that all these complicated reactions are not constituted by and do not even spring from a response to the *physical* stimulus, may be seen by comparing the reactions of an acquaintance who reads the telegram, and so subjects himself to the same stimulus. Moreover, the omission of a single letter, converting the telegram into "Our son is dead." would cause none of the reactions just described, but might result at most in the writing of a polite letter of condolence.

The independence of the bodily reactions of the physical stimuli actually presented is in these cases very marked, and, unless we are to introduce conceptions such as the intellectual apprehension of the *meaning* of the marks, it seems impossible to explain their effect. Yet such a conception again involves the active intervention of mind.

Synthesizing Power of Mind.   This conclusion is reinforced by what we may call the synthesizing power of mind. Synthesizing means putting together, and one of the most remarkable powers that we possess is that of taking a number of isolated sensations and forming them into a whole. We shall have occasion to return to this point at greater length in connection with our account of sensation in the next chapter. For the present we will content ourselves with giving one or two examples of mental synthesis.

Let us consider for a moment the case of aesthetic appreciation. The notes of a symphony considered separately consist merely of vibrations in the atmosphere. Each note may, when sounded in isolation produce a pleasant sensation, and as one note is struck after another we get a sequence of pleasant sensations. But although this is a sufficient description of the symphony considered as a collection of material events, and of our reactions to these events considered merely in terms of sensations, it is quite clear that we normally think of a symphony as being something more than this. We think of it in fact as a whole, and it is as a whole that it gives what is called aesthetic pleasure. Now in thinking of the symphony in this way our mind is going beyond the mere sequence of pleasant sensations which its individual notes produce, and putting them together into some sort of pattern. If the notes were arranged in a different order, although the actual vibrations which impinged upon our sense would be the same, the pleasurable aesthetic effect would be destroyed.

It seems to follow that our pleasure in a symphony cannot be wholly accounted for, although it may depend upon our physical responses to the stimuli of the individual notes; in order to obtain aesthetic pleasure we must somehow be able to perceive it as more than the sum total of the individual notes—that is, as a whole pattern or arrangement. The pleasure ceases when the *wholeness* of the object perceived is destroyed, as it is, for example, by the transportation of certain notes. We may compare the difference between the physical sensations which are our responses to the visual stimuli of the colours and canvas of which a picture is composed, with our synthesized perception of a picture as a work of art.

We must conclude, then, that we possess the power of realizing external objects not merely as collections of physical stimuli, which of course they are, but as wholes in which the actual sensory elements are combined to form a single object of a higher order. This faculty of combining or putting together seems to involve the existence not only of a mind, but of a mind of an active, creative type which is able to go out beyond the raw material afforded by our bodily sensations, and to apprehend ideal objects as wholes which are more than the collection of physical events which compose their constituent parts.

Summary of Argument

The conclusion to which the arguments of this chapter appear to point is that, in addition to the body and brain, the composition of the living organism includes an immaterial element which we call mind; that this element, although it is in very close association with the brain, is more than a mere glow or halo surrounding the cerebral structure, the function of which is confined to reflecting the events occurring in that structure; that, on the contrary, it is in some sense independent of the brain, and in virtue of its independence is able in part to direct and control the material constituents of the body, using them to carry out its purpose in relation to the external world of objects, much as a driver will make use of the mechanism of his motorcar. Mind so conceived is an active, dynamic, synthesizing force; it goes out beyond the sensations provided by external stimuli and arranges them into patterns, and it seems to be capable on occasion of acting without the provocation of bodily stimuli to set it in motion. It is, in other words, creative, that is, it carries on activities which even the greatest conceivable extension of our physiological knowledge would not enable us to infer from observing the brain. How, then. are we to conceive of the relationship of the mind to the brain?

An actor in a play of Shakespeare not only speaks words, but makes gestures, so that if you were completely deaf you would still be able to infer something of what the play was about from seeing the gestures. It is obvious, however, that there is much more in the play than the pantomime of the players. There are, for example, the words, the characters, the plot, and the poetry. Now to use a simile of the philosopher Bergson, the brain is the organ of pantomime. If you were to observe a man's brain you would know just as much of his thoughts as found vent in gestures. You would know, in other words, all that his thoughts imply in the way of actions or the beginnings of actions,[1] but the thoughts themselves would escape you just as the words and meaning of the play would escape the deaf spectator. This is what is meant by saying that the mind overflows the brain. If our knowledge of both psychology and physiology were perfect, we should be able to describe the movements of the brain without observing it, provided we had complete understanding of a man's state of mind; but we should not from the most minute and thorough inspection of the brain be able to tell what the man was thinking, since just as one gesture of the actor may stand for many different thoughts, so one state of the brain may represent any one of a host of states of mind.

---

[1] Among the beginnings of actions may be mentioned those movements of the larynx which are involved in talking.

Idealism

38. Sense Without Matter   A. A. Luce

Arthur Aston Luce (1882–1940), professor of metaphysics at Trinity College, Dublin, was the author of many books and articles on immaterialism and the philosophy of George Berkeley.

According to the ancient theory of sense-perception, founded on Aristotle's teaching, there are two factors to be distinguished in every case of sense-perception: (1) the sensible qualities or appearances, i.e. the sense-data actually perceived by sense; and (2) the material substance, itself unperceived and unperceivable, that supports the qualities or appearances. In this account of things matter is essential to sense-perception, but is just what we do not perceive; that is why I call it a *residuum*. In so far as there is a theory of matter, this is it. Matter, when taken precisely and positively and apart from its appearances, is to be regarded as spread like a carpet, an unqualitied carpet, under all the outward and obvious aspects of the things of sense. More technically, matter is the substrate, *per se* unperceived and unperceivable, that "supports" sensible qualities, like red and rough and loud, qualities *per se* unsubstantial; matter substantiates them, and let them "materialise." Both factors are, they say, necessary to real existence and sense-perception. Sensible qualities are, they say, flimsy, transient and variable; matter gives them solidity and permanence and invariability. Matter, they say, is all in the dark night, and but for the sensible qualities that reveal it we should know nothing at all about it. Our external world, luminous and solid, is thus the product of these two factors, sensible quality and matter. Every external thing, or body, is the product of the same two factors. The shoe, the ship, the piece of sealing-wax, each is twofold, like a nut. Each has shell and kernel. The shell is the red, the brown, the hard, the soft, the sound, the smell, the taste and whatever else in it is actually sensed or to be sensed; the rest of it is kernel, substance, substrate, matter, which, as matter, is utterly unperceivable.

There it is in its naked simplicity, in its shameless obscurity—this old Greek guess, the theory of matter or material substance. Hammered for centuries into the heads of uncomprehending youth, conned and repeated by rote by learned and unlearned alike, it has entered into the public mind, as did the flatness of the earth; and both superstitions die hard. The theory is venerated, not understood; it is indeed unintelligible, and it is venerated all the more on that account. It is venerated for its comparative antiquity; it is valued more as a blanket than as a carpet; it solves no problems; it gives no support, but it removes certain difficulties out of sight. It holds up an ideal of permanence in the flux of things in

Reprinted with permission of Thomas Nelson & Sons Limited from *Sense Without Matter* (1954) by A. A. Luce. The book has been reprinted in the United States by Greenwood Press.

a changing world; it contains the welcome suggestion of a hidden hand and of an absolute standard behind the scenes, and it offers these things without making any demand on man's moral and spiritual nature. But is it true? No, it is not true. Does it shed light? No, it sheds no light. It is redolent of the *a priori* and the abstract. I doubt if it ever aimed at truth, as the realist understands that term. I doubt if it was ever intended to provide a true-to-fact account of what actually happens when a man sees and touches. It tries to ease certain difficulties in the theories of perception and of change; but it obscures other problems, and removes them out of sight; it makes darkness visible; it sheds no light. . . .

I am indeed asking, "Does matter exist?" And I answer; "No"; but I am also asking a deeper, constructive question, viz.: "What precisely do I see and touch?" If we know precisely what we see and touch and otherwise sense, the question about matter settles itself automatically. We are studying sense-perception in order to find out precisely what man perceives by sense. Matter has always been the intellectual refuge of scepticism and half-knowledge. The materialist distrusts his senses, depreciates their position and rejects their evidence. He holds that sense without matter does not make sense. That contention goes far and cuts deep, and warps a man's attitude, not only to things of spirit, but to reality all along the line. The materialist holds that without matter the sensible could not exist as a *thing*, could not cause, and would be indistinguishable from dream. . . .

I open my eyes and see. What precisely do I see? I stretch out my hand and touch. What precisely do I touch? What precisely do we see and touch, when we see and touch? That is our question. We have many names in ordinary life for the myriad things we see and touch—shoes, ships, sealing-wax, apples, pears and plums; those names are precise enough for action, but they are not precise enough for thought; thought is concerned with common features and resemblances, more than with differences and distinctions. Now, when I see ships and shoes and apples and so forth, what precisely do I see that is common to all those sights? I see colours and shades of colour, light and its modes, illuminated points and lines and surfaces. Those are the things I actually see, and I call them inclusively visual data; they are the elemental objects of the sense of sight. And when I touch shoes and ships and apples and so forth, what precisely do I touch that is common to all those touches? I touch hard, soft, solid, fluid, resistant, yielding, and (in the wider sense of "touch") hot, cold, warm and tepid. Those are the things I actually touch, and I call them inclusively tactual data; they are the elemental objects of the sense of touch. . . .

The theory of matter, as we have seen, requires us to hold that in every instance of sense-perception there are two factors to be recognised and distinguised, viz. the actual object of sense, the sense-data actually perceived by eye or ear or hand or other sense organ, and the material substance, itself unperceived and unperceivable, that supports the sense-data. The case against the theory is, in outline, that the theory postulates an intolerable division, based on an improbable guess. It is not a theory reasonably distinguishing homogeneous parts in a thing, like shell and kernel, pea and pod. It is a theory requiring us to break up the one homogeneous thing into two heterogeneous and inconsistent parts, and, incidentally, to pin our faith to the existence of material substance, for which there is not the slightest evidence from fact.

Let us take an instance, and see how the theory of matter works out. See yonder mahogany table. Its colour is brown, in the main, though it is veined and grained in lighter colours. Its touch is hard and smooth. It has a smell and a taste and a sound; but I hardly ever need to bother about them; for I know the table ordinarily by its colours and by the cut and shape of its lines of light and its shading, and if I am in doubt I can handle it, and feel it and lift it up. It is a sensible table. It is a sensible table through and through. I can bore holes in it, can plane away its surfaces, can burn it with fire and reduce it to ashes; and I shall never come on anything in it that is not an actual or possible object of sense; it is composed entirely of sense-data and *sensibilia*. Now the theory of matter brings in totally different considerations; it asks me to believe that all these sense-data and *sensibilia* do not constitute the real table. I am asked to believe that beneath the table I see and touch stands another table, a supporting table, a table of a totally different nature that cannot be seen or touched or sensed in any other way, a table to be taken on trust, and yet a highly important table, because it is the real, invariable, material table, while the table I see and touch is only apparent, variable, inconstant and volatile. The visible-tangible, sensible table has colour and hardness and the other qualities by which things of sense are known and distinguished. The real table has none of these.

What an impossible duality! Yonder mahogany table proves to be two tables. It is a sensible table, and it is a material table. If I take the theory seriously, and go through with it, I am bound to believe the same of everything else around me; wherever I look, I am condemned to see double, and to grope my way through life with divided aim and reduced efficiency.

No rational account of the coexistence of the two tables has ever been given, nor could be given. Some say that the "real table" is the *cause* of the apparent table, but how the cause works is a mystery. Some say that the "real table" is the original, and the apparent table a copy; but what would be the use of a copy that is totally unlike its original? And who, or what, does the copying, and how? The two tables are left there, juxtaposed, unrelated and unexplained. They are not two aspects of the one thing; they are not two parts of the one thing; they have nothing in common; they are not comparable; they could not stem from the one stock; they are heterogeneous; they are at opposite poles of thought; they differ as light from darkness; if the one is, the other is not. No mixing of the two is possible; they cannot be constituents of the one thing; for they are contradictories; if the table is really coloured, then it is not matter; if the table is really matter, then it is not coloured. The supposition of two heterogeneous bodies in the one thing of sense is self-contradictory, destroying the unity of the thing. . . .

Then consider the question of evidence. What evidence is there for the existence of matter? What evidence is there for non-sensible matter?

Why should I believe in the matter of materialism? Set aside the mis-understanding that confuses matter with the sensible; set aside the prej-udice that would identity with matter the chemical atom, or the subatomic objects of nuclear physics; set aside the legend of the constant sum-total of energy from which all springs and to which all returns; set aside mere tradition and voice of uninformed authority. And what philosophical evidence is there for the matter of materialism? There is no evidence at all. Writers on matter appeal to prejudice and ignorance in favour of matter; they assume and take it for granted that everyone accepts the existence of matter; they never attempt to prove its existence directly. There is no direct evidence to be had. They try to establish it indirectly. There could not be an external *thing*, they say, unless there were matter; unless there were matter, they say, there would be no cause of change in the external world, nor any test for true and false. . . .

I have examined the typical case of seeing and touching, and have shown that there is no place for matter there. I have examined the normal perceptual situation, and have shown that it contains no evidence for matter, and that the forcible intrusion of matter destroys the unity of the thing perceived and of the world of sense. The onus of proof is on the materialist, and the immaterialist can fairly challenge him to produce his evidence. If there is matter, produce it. If there is evidence for matter, produce it. Neither matter, nor valid evidence for matter, has ever yet been produced.

The nearest approach to evidence for matter proves on careful study to be bad evidence. It is not evidence for matter; it is evidence for spirit *spoilt*. I refer to the notion of *support*. The strength of materialism (and its ultimate weakness) is its exploitation of the sub-rational feeling that somehow the pillars of the house rest on matter. People turn to matter for support; they are dimly aware of the need for support; but if they analysed that need, they would look for the support elsewhere.

Sense-data need support, and from the time of Aristotle to the present day men have claimed that matter supplies the desired support. But could matter, if it existed, supply the kind of support that sense-data need? Literal support is not in question. Sense-data do not need literal support, and if they did need it, matter *ex hypothesi* could not supply it. In the literal sense sense-data are *given* supported; they are supported by other sense-data. The table supports the books; the books rest on it; without it they would fall. I can see and feel the books and the table in effective contact. That support is visible and tangible. Literal support means sen-sible support, which is just what matter *e vi termini* could not give; for matter cannot be seen or touched or otherwise sensed. The legs of the table support the table; the floor supports both; the earth supports the floor; in all such cases support and things supported are homogeneous; both are *sensibilia*. Matter is not a *sensibile*. Matter and sense are heter-ogeneous *ex hypothesi*, and therefore matter, if there were such a thing, could not literally support sense-data.

Sense-data cannot stand alone. Like letters of the alphabet or figures or any other symbols they need the support of mind or spirit. By their very mould and nature they are not absolute, but are relative to mind or spirit. An alphabet *in vacuo* would be nonsense. The footprint in the sand implies one to leave the imprint, and the same *understood* implies one to understand it. To "understand" is to stand under and support, as the taking mind stands under and supports the work of the making mind. The materialist's quest of matter as an absolute object of perception, distinct from sense-data, is wrong-headed in principle; he leaves out of the account his own mind. His mind supports his object, as the reader's understanding mind supports the meaning of the printed page, and takes out of it what the writer's mind put into it. Sense-data are not mind or modes of mind; they do not think or will or plan or purpose; but they are from mind and for the mind, and they imply mind and cannot be understood apart from mind. That is why they cannot stand alone; that is why they require support; that is why they require *that sort* of support that only mind or spirit can give. To look to matter for such support would be absurd; for matter is defined as that which is not mind or spirit. Matter cannot support the objects of our senses in theory or practice, literally or metaphorically, and to look to matter for support is to lean on a broken reed.

Let me clinch the argument with an appeal to observable fact in a concrete case. If matter is, I ask, *where* is it? If matter is, it is in things, and in all external things, and the type of external thing selected is neither here nor there. I will choose a homely, explorable thing that we can know through and through, a mutton chop. If matter is, it is in this mutton chop. I ask, where? Where is it in this mutton chop? Where could it be? Take away from this given chop all its sense-data, including its obtainable sense-data. Take away those of the outside and those of the inside, those of the meat and the bone, those of the fat and the lean, be it cooked or uncooked. Take away all that we do sense and all that we might sense, and what is left? There are its visual data, its browns and reds and blacks and whites, and all the other colours and hues of its surface and potential surfaces and centre. There are its tactual data, its rough and smooth, hard and soft, resistant and yielding, solid and fluid, and those varied palpables that admit my knife or hinder its easy passage. It has auditory data; its fat and lean and bone make different sounds when struck by knives and forks. Many smells and savours go to its composing, raw or cooked. Air and moisture link it to its sensible context, and show as steam and vapour under heat. The chop has sensible shapes that may concern artists and even geometricians; it has sensible contents and sensible forms that are specially the concern of chemist and physicist; they are no less sensible and no less real than those contents and forms that are of importance to the butcher and the housewife and the cook. Take them all away in thought. Take away all the *sensa* and the *sensibilia* of this mutton chop, and what is left? Nothing! Nothing is left. In taking away its *sensa* and *sensibilia* you have taken away all the mutton chop, and nothing is left, and its matter is nowhere. Its matter, other than its sense-data, is nothing at all, nothing but a little heap of powdered sentiment, nothing but the ghost of the conventional thing, nothing but the sceptic's question-mark. . . .

Is matter wanted as a cause? Are sense-data or sensible qualities (call them what you wish) effects of matter? Are the immediate objects of our senses caused by matter? Are sense-data so lacking in causal power that material substance must be postulated and assumed? Is material substance the power behind the scenes, the secret spring of causal action? . . .

Is matter wanted as a cause? Several questions are here combined. What is meant by "cause"? Can sense-data cause? Can they make changes begin to be? If they can, is there any need for matter? If they cannot, how can matter help? If sense-data are passive, how could material substance activate them, and confer on them the power of the cause?

These questions answer themselves in the light of the foregoing analysis of "cause." The term "cause" is ambiguous. In one sense, sense-data can cause, in the other sense, not. Sense-data are not spirits; they cannot make changes begin to be; they cannot directly alter the course of events; for they are passive; but indirectly they give rise to effects; they are signs of what is coming; men read those signs and act on them and make changes begin to be. The sign works through the mind that reads it and understands it and acts on it, just as the works of Shakespeare work through minds that read them and understand them and act on them. The passive sign gives rise indirectly to changes it does not produce. In that respect, and in that respect only, the passive objects of sense around us are causes. In strict speech they are not causes, but are like causes, and not unnaturally, but wrongly, they become credited with the power of making changes begin to be. For practical purposes it is enough for us to know that smoke and fire are almost invariably found together. When we see the smoke we expect the fire, and we are on our guard and take precautions. That is the full extent of the causal connection. The smoke is a passive sign of what is coming; it involves you and me in action, but does not act itself. The black smoke is there, and it will soon burst into a red flame unless I extinguish it. That is the only sense in which the black smoke is the cause of the red flame. The smoke does not make the fire begin to be. The smoke is not the true cause of the fire. The smoke is but the customary antecedent; when we see or smell it, we expect its consequent. The two are indissolubly connected in our minds because they are very frequently associated in nature. The association is there in nature, as in the mind; sometimes we see the smoke before the fire, sometimes the fire before the smoke. Hence it matters little which we call *cause*, and which we call *effect*; they are two parts of the one process; all we need to know is that the two events are causally connected in the sense that the one makes us expect the other. It is no truer that the fire is the cause of the smoke than that the smoke is the cause of the fire. Both propositions are on the one level as regards truth and falsity. In respect of significance or cue-causation, both events are indifferently causes and effects. In respect of efficient or true causation, neither is cause, neither is effect of the other.

Then comes the question about matter. Sense-data *per se* are passive; they may be viewed as acting indirectly through their significance for minds. Does matter enter into the cause? Is material substance the hidden hand behind the scenes? No; matter has nothing to say to causation in either sense of the term. *Ex hypothesi* matter has no significance for mind, and has not the power of the cause. Matter could not cause, nor enable sense-data to do so. There is no room for matter in the causal relation. All that matter does is to mystify, and people are too ready to be mystified. They see that the objects of sense cannot truly cause, and yet that some cause of change is required; and instead of thinking the problem out along the lines sketched above, they jump at the hypothesis of material substance. It shelves the problem and puts it out of sight; it is a facile solution that saves men the trouble of thinking. They say to themselves, "Matter is something we know not what; it acts we know not how." And so all issues in mystery.

Putting aside mystery and mystification, we see that what calls for explanation is some sensible event, some event in the world of sense. We *see* the water rise, and the litmus-paper change colour; we feel the wax soft and then still softer. A sensible change has occurred, and as rational sentients we are bound to ask, "What did it? What caused this change in the world of sense?" To reply, "The material substance of moon or wax or acid did it," or "Material substance in general did it," may give some mystic satisfaction to mystic minds; but such replies have no ex-planatory value; they shed no light on the problem. Man wants to know causes, and needs to know causes, in order to have some control over events. If he cannot shape the course of events, he must shape his be-havior to suit the events. He needs to be able to move muscle and limb at the right time and to push and pull the things of sense in immediate contact with his body. To do so to the best advantage man needs a certain attitude to things; he needs confidence in the universe; he needs to be able to trust the course and composition of the universe, its order and regularity, its wisdom and its goodness. Man is spirit and sense. To form and guide his experience man needs a knowledge of spiritual causes and sensible effects. Matter comes under neither category; *ex hypothesi* matter is neither spiritual nor sensible; therefore it can contribute nothing to a knowledge of causes; it cannot be seen or touched, and therefore it cannot tell me when or how to push and pull the things I see and touch around me. Even if matter existed and possessed some occult power of altering sensible things and effecting visible and tangible changes, we never could *know* that this matter effected that change; we never could connect cause and its effect; we should be none the wiser for the existence of matter; we should have nothing to build on, no foundation for experience or for future action. We never could *know* that this invisible was the cause of that visible change, or that that intangible was the cause of this tangible change. In a word, if matter were a cause, we should never have the evidence of sense as to the cause of a sensible effect. Matter would be of no practical use with regard to knowledge of causes, and it would make no practical difference in life and experience. The invention of matter and its intrusion into the causal relation is purely psychological. It gives some sort of relief to the feelings; it cannot be too easily disproved, and it asks nothing of our moral and spiritual nature.

We men originate changes, and we know that we do so. We push; we pull; we strive, purpose and endeavour; we produce effects, often at

second-hand, and working with the effects of another's will, but we produce effects, and we recognise the effects as effects of our causal power.
We are true causes; we are true causes that endure; therefore we are
substantial causes; we are substances that cause. We understand spiritual
causation from within, to some extent at least, and it is the only true
causation that we understand at all; and we know it by the effort involved.
In prospect or retrospect I know what it is to climb a ladder. I connect
causally myself at the foot of it and myself at the top; causal effort is
required. I can look at fire and wax without any similar sense of effort;
I can keep on looking. I can watch the wax soften and melt on the hearth-
stone. I have no sense of effort; it is a smooth, expected transition; it is
a relation between two events or states; it is the relation of simple series
in time, the relation of before and after, completely devoid of any suggestion of true causality. To mount a five-foot ladder and climb down
again involves an effort of mind and body. If I am hoisted up five feet
and let down again, no effort by me is involved. In the former case I
cause the rise and the fall; in the latter case, not. Effort marks the difference; that feeling of effort, be it muscular, mental or mixed, is the
index of finite, causal power. Causal power belongs to the *anima*, to the
finite *anima* or spirit, and it does not belong to the inanimate.

How then to account for the opposite view? Why do people make
the mistake, I will not say of imagining causation where there is none,
but of crediting the inanimate thing or event with the power of the cause?
Why do they attribute causal power to the sun and moon instead of to
the Power that moves them? Several answers might be given; one deserves
special mention here, and that is sympathy or empathy. It may be a relic
of the old notions, classed as animist or hylozoist, or it may be a very
natural result of our real oneness with the things around us. We do feel
with them, and for them and in them. We do project ourselves into them,
as little Alice projects herself into her doll. When Homer makes the river
fight, or Wordsworth sets his daffodils a-dancing, they are projecting
their own efforts into the external world, and thereby enlivening their
themes and winning their readers' sympathies. There lies one great
source of the supposed inanimate second cause. There is no such cause,
but we invent it. We invent it empathetically. As do the poets and the
other masters of language, we project into a passive object splinters and
sparks of our own activity. We throw forward into the inanimate thing
the effort we should make and the action we should take, if we were it.
Smoke follows fire, often, always. It is cause and effect, we say. We see
the fire, and we expect the smoke, or we smell the smoke and we go
looking for the fire. These inanimate, passive things, easily moved, are
cues for the action; they are *like* causes; they make us think causally. But
that is not enough for all of us; for we are sympathetic, imaginative creatures. We are not content with cue causes; we are not content with sequences; we are not content with the observed fact that where there is
smoke there is fire. We proceed to embellish and embroider the fact by
reading ourselves into the situation; we mentally puff a lighted cigar,
and there is the smoke; empathetically we say that the fire produces the
smoke, and we vaguely view the tongues of flame puffing forth the

smoke. The embroidery and embellishment are not true to fact; but they are part of the art of using rich, imaginative language. If taken literally, they misrepresent the primary facts of our sentient existence.

Causal matter is a parallel development. The causal sensible has been developed empathetically from the passive, inanimate thing of sense; and the supposed causal powers of matter have by a similar process of self-projection been embroidered upon the original hypothesis of the passive substrate. Aristotle distinguished the material cause from the efficient cause. His efficient cause was what I have termed the true cause; his material cause was like my cue cause. His efficient cause got things done, and made changes begin to be; his material cause was the inactive *sine qua non* of the doing. The function of Aristotelian matter was to support, and not to act. Aristotelian matter was passive; it was a limiting concept, almost a negation; it was not a thing, nor a quality, nor a quantity; for it had to consist of sensible things and sensible qualities and sensible quantities; it was potentiality and possibility, just short of nothing. Later philosophers referred to matter as "a dead, inactive lump." An object so slight and negative and ineffective might well have been lost to sight altogether, and very naturally there has long been an oscillation between the two poles of thought about matter. Some understand it as active, some as passive. Some adhere to the original notion of it as passive substrate, visualising it as a carpet spread under the things of sense, or as a prop supporting them. Others have gone over to the active theory, making matter the secret source of change in the world of sense, the "hidden hand" behind sensible phenomena.

The modern trends of chemistry and physics have furthered the tendency to regard matter as an active cause. Many people today, I fancy, identify matter vaguely with atomic energy or with the rapid movement of the tiny parts and particles of elements. In olden days Jove's thunderbolt was the secret weapon of the gods; today atomic energy has taken its place as the power behind the scenes. The bomb that controls the policies of nations controls the trend of thought, and in popular imagination appears as proof positive of active matter. Gunpowder and high explosives, when they were first invented, affected popular thought in a similar way. No new factors bearing on the issue for intellect have come to light in our day. No new proof of a non-sensible substrate of the world of sense has been discovered. The bomb is nothing new by way of proof of matter; only the horror, the suddenness and the vast scale of the consequent destruction have reinforced whatever argument is there. The fact is that electrons, neutrons and the other scientific objects and working concepts of today are no nearer possessing the power of the true cause than were acids, alkalis, phlogiston and gravity; but they are more remote from the macroscopic, and in consequence they strike the imagination more forcibly than did the objects and concepts of the older sciences. The bomb may be designed, constructed and described by various concepts and symbols, but such concepts and symbols do not alter the fact that the bomb itself is sensible through and through. In whole and part and particle it can be seen and touched and heard; it contains and releases and conveys motions that can be seen and touched and heard. Atomic energy, however subtle its constitution, however penetrating its results, belongs entirely to the province of sense; its only causality is that of significance, the causality of the sign or cue cause. The bomb, live, exploding, or exploded, is a multiple sign of sights and sounds and feelings that go with and after it; pity and fear and panic movements of escape are aroused in us by the sight or thought of it, and naturally we project into it those incipient movements that we begin, not it. Our sympathies are strongly aroused. "I have a pain in your chest," wrote Madame de Sevigné to her daughter. We feel in the bomb what we might feel in ourselves, and thus we credit it with those efforts and activities that are really our own. Empathy accounts for our *mis*-takes, but does not alter the facts of existence. Empathy cannot transmute passive into active, or make a cue cause into a true cause. The bomb is no true cause; for it is entirely an effect; finite spirits have made it, using and misusing the effects of Will Infinite.

The causal argument for the existence of matter has thus been examined and refuted. I will recapitulate before I leave it. The causal argument owes its cogency to the assumption that colours and touches and all the other objects we actually perceive by sense cannot cause the changes we observe in the world of sense. That assumption is true in one sense of the term "cause," and false in another. It is true that colours and other such objects are passive things, unable to initiate motion or make the smallest change begin to be. But that rule would apply equally to matter, if matter existed; for it is only another way of saying that spirits alone are truly active, and matter, being by definition non-spiritual, would necessarily be ruled out as cause. If, on the other hand, is meant by "cause" merely the inoperative, antecedent sign, created and conserved by cosmic power, in that sense colours and similar objects are causes; for sentients can read their meaning, can grasp their significance, and can act accordingly. To postulate matter as causal sign would be doubly absurd. If you have a perfectly good and adequate sensible sign, there is no need for the material sign, or room for it. And secondly, matter *ex hypothesi* cannot be seen or touched or otherwise perceived by sense, and therefore it could not act as a sign for sentient beings. In sum, no argument for the existence of matter can validly be drawn from the concept of cause or the facts of causation.

Contemporary Issues

Are Men Machines?

39. Can a Machine Think?   Christopher Evans

Christopher Evans (1931–1979) was an experimental psychologist and computer scientist. He wrote several books on various aspects of psychology.

In the early years of the Second World War when the British began, in ultra-secret, to put together their effort to crack German codes, they set out to recruit a team of the brightest minds available in mathematics and the then rather novel field of electronic engineering. Recruiting the electronic whizzes was easy, as many of them were to be found engrossed in the fascinating problem of radio location of aircraft—or radar as it later came to be called. Finding mathematicians with the right kind of obsessive brilliance to make a contribution in the strange field of cryptography was another matter. In the end they adopted the ingenious strategy of searching through lists of young mathematicians who were also top-flight chess players. As a result of a nation-wide trawl an amazing collection of characters were billeted together in the country-house surroundings of Bletchley Park, and three of the most remarkable were Irving John Good, Donald Michie, and Alan Turing. . . .

If contemporary accounts of what the workers at Bletchley were talking about in their few moments of spare time can be relied on, many of them were a bit over-optimistic if anything. Both Good and Michie believed that the use of electronic computers such as Colossus* would result in major advances in mathematics in the immediate post-war era and Turing was of the same opinion. All three (and one or two of their colleagues) were also confident that it would not be long before machines were exhibiting intelligence, including problem-solving abilities, and that their role as simple number-crunchers was only one phase in their evolution. Although the exact substance of their conversations, carried long into the night when they were waiting for the test results of the first creaky Colossus prototypes, has softened with the passage of time, it is known the topic of machine intelligence loomed very large. They discussed, with a *frissom* of excitement and unease, the peculiar ramifications of the subject they were pioneering and about which the rest of the world knew (and still knows) so little. Could there ever be a machine which was able to solve problems that no human could solve? Could a computer ever beat a human at chess? Lastly, could a machine *think*?

Of all the questions that can be asked about computers none has such an eerie ring. Allow a machine intelligence perhaps, the ability to control other machines, repair itself, help us solve problems, compute numbers a millionfold quicker than any human; allow it to fly airplanes, drive

*[An early computer that was first used in 1943.—Ed.]

cars, superintend our medical records and even, possibly, give advice to politicians. Somehow you can see how a machine might come to do all these things. But that it could be made to perform that apparently exclusively human operation known as *thinking* is something else, and something which is offensive, alien and threatening. Only in the most *outré* forms of science fiction, stretching back to Mary Shelley's masterpiece *Frankenstein,* is the topic touched on, and always with a sense of great uncertainty about the enigmatic nature of the problem area.

Good, Michie and their companions were content to work the ideas through in their spare moments. But Turing—older, a touch more serious and less cavalier—set out to consider things in depth. In particular, he addressed himself to the critical question: Can, or could, a machine think? The way he set out to do this three decades ago and long before any other scientists had considered it so cogently, is of lasting interest. The main thesis was published in the philosophical journal *Mind* in 1952. Logically unassailable, when read impartially it serves to break down any barriers of uncertainty which surround this and parallel questions. Despite its classic status the work is seldom read outside the fields of computer science and philosophy, but now that events in the computer science and in the field of artificial intelligence are beginning to move with the rapidity and momentum which the Bletchley scientists knew they ultimately would, the time has come for Turing's paper to achieve a wider public.

Soon after the war ended and the Colossus project folded, Turing joined the National Physical Laboratory in Teddington and began to work with a gifted team on the design of what was to become the world's most powerful computer, ACE. Later he moved to Manchester, where, spurred by the pioneers Kilburn, Hartree, Williams and Newman, a vigorous effort was being applied to develop another powerful electronic machine. It was a heady, hard-driving time, comparable to the state of events now prevailing in microprocessors, when anyone with special knowledge rushes along under immense pressure, ever conscious of the feeling that whoever is second in the race may as well not have entered it at all. As a result, Turing found less time than he would have hoped to follow up his private hobbies, particularly his ideas on computer game-playing—checkers, chess and the ancient game of Go—which he saw was an important sub-set of machine intelligence.

Games like chess are unarguably intellectual pursuits, and yet, unlike certain other intellectual exercises, such as writing poetry or discussing the inconsistent football of the hometown team, they have easily describable rules of operation. The task, therefore, would seem to be simply a matter of writing a computer program which "knew" these rules and which could follow them when faced with moves offered by a human player. Turing made very little headway as it happens, and the first chess-playing programs which were scratched together in the late '40s and early '50s were quite awful—so much so that there was a strong feeling that this kind of project was not worth pursuing, since the game of chess as played by an "expert" involves some special intellectual skill which could never be specified in machine terms.

Turing found this ready dismissal of the computer's potential to be both interesting and suggestive. If people were unwilling to accept the idea of a machine which could play games, how would they feel about one which exhibited "intelligence," or one which could "think?" In the course of discussions with friends, Turing found that a good part of the problem was that people were universally unsure of their definitions. What exactly did one mean when one used the word "thought"? What processes were actually in action when "thinking" took place? If a machine was created which *could* think, how would one set about testing it? The last question, Turing surmised, was the key one, and with a wonderful surge of imagination spotted a way to answer it, proposing what has in computer circles come to be known as "The Turing Test for Thinking Machines." In the next [section], we will examine the test, see how workable it is, and also try to assess how close computers have come, and will come, to passing it.

When Turing asked people whether they believed that a computer could think, he found almost universal rejection of the idea—just as I did when I carried out a similar survey almost thirty years later. The objections I received were similar to those that Turing documented in his paper "Computing Machinery and Intelligence,"* and I will summarize them here, adding my own comments and trying to meet the various objections as they occur.

First there is the Theological Objection. This was more common in Turing's time than it is now, but it still crops up occasionally. It can be summed up as follows: "Man is a creation of God, and has been given a soul and the power of conscious thought. Machines are not spiritual beings, have no soul and thus must be incapable of thought." As Turing pointed out, this seems to place an unwarranted restriction on God. Why shouldn't he give machines souls and allow them to think if he wanted to? On one level I suppose it is irrefutable: if someone chooses to define thinking as something that *only* Man can do and that *only* God can bestow, then that is the end of the matter. Even then the force of the argument does seem to depend upon a confusion between "thought" and "spirituality," upon the old Cartesian dichotomy of the ghost in the machine. The ghost presumably does the thinking while the machine is merely the vehicle which carries the ghost around.

Then there is the Shock/Horror Objection, which Turing called the "Heads in the Sand Objection." Both phrases will do though I prefer my own. When the subject of machine thought is first broached, a common reaction goes something like this: "What a horrible idea! How could any scientist work on such a monstrous development? I hope to goodness that the field of artificial intelligence doesn't advance a step further if its end-product is a thinking machine!" The attitude is not very logical—and it is not really an argument why it *could* not happen, but rather the expression of a heartfelt wish that it never will!

The Extra-sensory Preception Objection was the one that impressed

---

*[Published in *Mind*, Vol. LIX (October, 1950).—Ed.]

Turing most, and impresses me least. *If* there were such a thing as extra-sensory perception and *if* it were in some way a function of human brains, then it could well also be an important constituent of thought. By this token, in the absence of any evidence proving that computers are telepathic, we would have to assume that they could never be capable of thinking in its fullest sense. The same argument applies to any other "psychic" or spiritual component of human psychology. I cannot take this objection seriously because there seems to me to be no evidence which carries any scientific weight that extra-sensory perception does exist. The situation was different in Turing's time, when the world-renowned parapsychology laboratory at Duke University in North Carolina, under Dr. J. B. Rhine, was generating an enormous amount of material supposedly offering evidence for telepathy and precognition. This is not the place to go into the long, and by no means conclusive, arguments about the declining status of parapsychology, but it is certainly true that as far as most scientists are concerned, what once looked like a rather good case for the existence of telepathy, etc., now seems to be an extremely thin one. But even if ESP *is* shown to be a genuine phenomenon, it is, in my own view, something to do with the transmission of information from a source point to a receiver and ought therefore to be quite easy to reproduce in a machine. After all, machines can communicate by radio already, which is, effectively, ESP and is a far better method of long-distance communication than that possessed by any biological system.

The Personal Consciousness Objection is, superficially, a rather potent argument which comes up in various guises. Turing noticed it expressed particularly cogently in a report, in the *British Medical Journal* in 1949, on the Lister Oration for that year, which was entitled "The Mind of Mechanical Man." It was given by a distinguished medical scientist, Professor G. Jefferson. A short quote from the Oration will suffice:

> Not until a machine can write a sonnet or compose a concerto *because of thoughts and emotions felt*, and not by the chance fall of symbols, could we agree that machine equals brain—that is, not only write it but *know that it had written it*. No mechanism could feel (and not merely artificially signal, an easy contrivance) pleasure at its successes, grief when its valves fuse, be warmed by flattery, be made miserable by its mistakes, be charmed by sex, be angry or depressed when it cannot get what it wants.

The italics, which are mine, highlight what I believe to be the fundamental objection: the output of the machine is more or less irrelevant, no matter how impressive it is. Even if it wrote a sonnet—and a very good one—it would not mean much unless it had written it as the result of "thoughts and emotions felt," and it would also have to "know that it had written it." This could be a useful "final definition" of one aspect of human thought—but how would you establish whether or not the sonnet was written with "emotions"? Asking the computer would not help for, as Professor Jefferson realized, there would be no guarantee that it was not simply *declaring* that it had felt emotions. He is really propounding the extreme solipsist position and should, therefore, apply the same rules to humans. Extreme solipsism is logically irrefutable ("I am the only real thing; all else is illusion") but it is so unhelpful a view of the universe that most people choose to ignore it and decide that when people say they are thinking or feeling they may as well believe them. In other words, Professor Jefferson's objection could be over-ridden if you *became* the computer and experienced its thoughts (if any)—only then could you really *know*. His objection is worth discussing in some depth because it is so commonly heard in one form or another, and because it sets us up in part for Turing's resolution of the machine-thought problem, which we will come to later.

The Unpredictability Objection argues that computers are created by humans according to sets of rules and operate according to carefully scripted programs which themselves are sets of rules. So if you wanted to, you could work out exactly what a computer was going to do at any particular time. It is, in principle, totally predictable. *If* you have all the facts available you *can* predict a computer's behavior because it follows rules, whereas there is no way in which you could hope to do the same with a human *because he is not behaving according to a set of immutable rules.* Thus there is an essential difference between computers and humans, so (the argument gets rather weak here) thinking, because it is unpredictable and does not blindly follow rules, must be an essentially human ability.

There are two comments: firstly, computers are becoming so complex that it is doubtful their behavior could be predicted even if everything was known about them—computer programmers and engineers have found that one of the striking characteristics of present-day systems is that they constantly spring surprises. The second point follows naturally: humans are *already* in that super-complex state and the reason that we cannot predict what they do is *not* because they have no ground rules but because (a) we don't know what the rules are, and (b) even if we did know them they would still be too complicated to handle. At best, the unpredictability argument is thin, but it is often raised. People frequently remark that there is always "the element of surprise" in a human. I have no doubt that this is just because *any* very complex system is bound to be surprising. A variant of the argument is that humans are capable of error whereas the "perfect" computer is not. That may well be true, which suggests that machines are superior to humans, for there seems to be little point in having any information-processing system, biological or electronic, that makes errors in processing. It would be possible to build a random element into computers to make them unpredictable from time to time, but it would be a peculiarly pointless exercise.

The "See How Stupid They Are" Objection will not need much introduction. At one level it is expressed in jokes about computers that generate ridiculous bank statements or electricity bills; at another and subtler level, it is a fair appraisal of the computer's stupendous weaknesses in comparison with Man. "How could you possibly imagine that such backward, limited things could ever reach the point where they could be said to think?" The answer, as we have already pointed out, is that they may be dumb now but they have advanced at a pretty dramatic rate and show every sign of continuing to do so. Their present limitations may be valid when arguing whether they could be said to be capable of thinking *now* or in the *very* near future, but it has no relevance to whether they would be capable of thinking at some later date.

The "Ah But It Can't Do That" Objection is an eternally regressing argument which, for a quarter of a century, computer scientists have been listening to, partially refuting, and then having to listen to all over again. It runs: "Oh yes, you obviously make a computer do so and so— you have just demonstrated that, but of course you will never be able to make it do such and such." The such and such may be anything you name—once it was play a good game of chess, have a storage capacity greater than the human memory, read human hand-writing or understand human speech. Now that these "Ah buts" have (quite swiftly) been overcome, one is faced by a new range: beat the world human chess champion, operate on parallel as opposed to serial processing, perform medical diagnosis better than a doctor, translate satisfactorily from one language to another, help solve its own software problems, etc. When these challenges are met, no doubt it will have to design a complete city from scratch, invent a game more interesting than chess, admire a pretty girl/handsome man, work out the unified field theory, enjoy bacon and eggs, and so on. I cannot think of anything more silly than developing a computer which could enjoy bacon and eggs, but there is nothing to suggest that, provided enough time and money was invested, one could not pull off such a surrealistic venture. On the other hand, it might be *most* useful to have computers design safe, optimally cheap buildings. Even more ambitious (and perhaps comparable to the bacon and egg project but more worthwhile) would be to set a system to tackle the problem of the relationship between gravity and light, and my own guess is that before the conclusion of the long-term future (before the start of the twenty-first century), computers will be hard at work on these problems and will be having great success.

The "It Is Not Biological" Objection may seem like another version of the theological objection—only living things could have the capacity for thought, so non-biological systems could not possibly think. But there is a subtle edge that requires a bit more explanation. It is a characteristic of most modern computers that they are discrete state machines, which is to say that they are digital and operate in a series of discrete steps— on/off. Now the biological central nervous system may not be so obviously digital, though there is evidence that the neurone, the basic unit of communication, acts in an on/off, all or nothing way. But if it turned out that it were *not*, and operated on some more elaborate strategy, then it is conceivable that "thought" might only be manifest in things which had switching systems of this more elaborate kind. Put it another way: it might be possible to build digital computers which were immensely intelligent, but no matter how intelligent they became they would never be able to *think*. The argument cannot be refuted at the moment, but even so there is no shred of evidence to suppose that only non-digital systems can think. There may be other facets of living things that make them unique from the point of view of their capacity to generate thought, but none that we can identify, or even guess at. This objection therefore is not a valid one at present, though in the event of some new biological discovery, it may become so.

The Mathematical Objection is one of the most intriguing of the ten objections, and is the one most frequently encountered in discussions with academics. It is based on a fascinating exercise in mathematical logic propounded by the Hungarian, Kurt Gödel. To put it rather superficially, Gödel's theorem shows that within any sufficiently powerful logical system (which could be a computer operating according to clearly defined rules), statements can be formulated which can neither be proved nor disproved *within the system*. In his famous 1936 paper, Alan Turing restructured Gödel's theorem so that it could apply specifically to machines. This effectively states that no matter how powerful a computer is, there are bound to be certain tasks that it cannot tackle on its own. In other words, you could not build a computer which could solve *every* problem no matter how well it is programmed; or, if you wanted to carry the thing to the realms of fancy, no computer (or any other digital system) could end up being God.

Gödel's theorem, and its later refinements by Alonzo Church, Bertrand Russell and others, is interesting to mathematicians, not so much because it assumes an implicit limitation to mathematics itself, but the theorem has been used, incorrectly, by critics of machine intelligence to "prove" that computers could never reach the same intellectual level as Man. The weakness of the position is that it is based on the assumption that the human brain is not a formal logical system. But such evidence as we have suggests very strongly that it is and will, therefore, be bound by the same Gödel-limitations as are machines. There is also a tweak in the tail. While the theorem admittedly states that no system *on its own* can completely tackle its own problems—"understand itself"—it does *not* imply that the areas of mystery could not be tackled by some other system. No individual human brain could solve its own problems or fully "know itself," but with the assistance of other brains these deficiencies might be corrected. Equally, and significantly, problem areas associated with complex computer systems could be solved totally and absolutely by other computer systems, provided that *they* were clever enough.

The last of the ten arguments against the concept of a thinking machine has become known as Lady Lovelace's Objection. . . . Lady Lovelace's Objection is, I suppose, the most commonly-expressed criticism of the idea of computers with intellects paralleling, or exceeding, Man's. . . . In its modern form this comes up as, "A Computer cannot do anything that you have not programmed it to." The objection is so fundamental and so widely accepted that it needs detailed discussion.

In the most absolute and literal sense, this statement is perhaps perfectly correct and applies to any machine or computer that has been made or that could be made. According to the rules of the universe that we live in, nothing can take place without a prior cause; a computer will not spring into action without something powering it and guiding it on its way. In the case of the various tasks that a computer performs, the "cause"—to stretch the use of the word rather—is the program or sets of programs that control these tasks. Much the same applies to a brain: it, too, must come equipped with sets of programs which cause it to run through its repertoire of tasks. This might seem to support Lady Lovelace, at least to the extent that machines "need" a human to set them up, but it would also seem to invalidate the argument that this constitutes an essential difference between computers and people. But is there not still a crucial difference between brains and computers? No matter how sophisticated computers are, must there not always have been a human being to *write* its programs? Surely the same does not have to be said for humans?

To tackle this we need to remember that all brains, human included, are equipped at birth with a comprehensive collection of programs which are common to all members of a species and which are known as instincts. These control respiration, gastric absorption, cardiac activity, and, at a behavioral level, such reflexes as sucking, eyeblink, grasping and so on. There may also be programs which "cause" the young animal to explore its environment, exercise its muscles, play and so on. Where do these come from? Well, they are acquired over an immensely long-winded trial-and-error process through the course of evolution. We might call them permanent software ("firmware" is the phrase used sometimes by computer scientists) and they correspond to the suites of programs which every computer has when it leaves the factory, and which are to do with its basic running, maintenance, and so on.

In addition to this, all biological computers come equipped with a bank of what might best be described as raw programs. No one has the faintest idea whether they are neurological, biochemical, electrical or what—all we know is that they *must* exist. They start being laid down the moment the creature begins to interact with the world around it. In the course of time they build up into a colossal suite of software which ultimately enables us to talk, write, walk, read, enjoy bacon and eggs, appreciate music, think, feel, write books, or come up with mathematical ideas. These programs are useful only to the owner of that particular brain, vanish with his death and are quite separate from the "firmware."

If this seems too trivial a description of the magnificent field of human learning and achievement, it is only because anything appears trivial when you reduce it to its bare components: a fabulous sculpture to a quintillion highly similar electrons and protons, a microprocessor to a million impurities buried in a wafer of sand, the human brain into a collection of neurones, blood cells and chemical elements. What is not trivial is the endlessly devious, indescribably profound way in which these elements are structured to make up the whole. The real difference between the brain and most existing computers is that in the former, data acquisition and the initial writing and later modification of the program is done by a mechanism within the brain itself, while in the latter, the software is prepared outside and passed to the computer in its completed state. But I did use the word "most." In recent years increasing emphasis has been placed on the development of "adaptive" programs—software which can be modified and revised on the basis of the program's interaction with the environment. In simple terms these could be looked upon as "programs which learn for themselves," and they will, in due course, become an important feature of many powerful computer systems.

At this point the sceptic still has a few weapons in his armoury. The first is generally put in the form of the statement. "Ah, but even when computers *can* update their own software and acquire new programs for themselves, they will still only be doing this because of Man's ingenuity. Man may no longer actually write the programs, but had he not invested the idea of the self-adaptive program in the first place none of this could have happened." This is perfectly true but has little to do with whether or not computers could think, or perform any other intellectual exercise. It could place computers eternally in our debt, and we may be able to enjoy a smug sense of pride at having created them, but it offers no real restriction on their development.

The sceptic may also argue that no matter how clever or how intelligent you make computers, they will never be able to perform a creative task. Everything they do will inevitably spring from something they have been taught, have experienced or is the subject of some pre-existing program. There are two points being made here. One is that computers could never have an original or creative thought. The other is that the seeds of everything they do, no matter how intelligent, lie in their existing software. To take the second point first: again one is forced to say that the same comment applies to humans. Unless the argument is that some of Man's thoughts or ideas come from genuine inspiration—a message from God, angels, or the spirits of the departed—no one can dispute that all aspects of our intelligence evolve from preexisting programs and the background experiences of life. This evolution may be enormously complex and its progress might be impossible to track, but any intellectual flowerings arise from the seeds of experience planted in the fertile substrate of the brain.

There still remains the point about creativity, and it is one that is full of pitfalls. Before making any assumptions about creativity being an *exclusive* attribute of Man, the concept has to be defined. It is not enough to say "write a poem," "paint a picture" or "discuss philosophical ideas," because it is easy enough to program computers to do all these things. The fact that their poems, paintings and philosophical ramblings are pretty mediocre is beside the point: it would be just as unfair to ask them to write, say, a sonnet of Shakespearian calibre or a painting of da Vinci quality and fail them for lack of creativity as it would be to give the same task to the man in the street. Beware too of repeating the old saying, "Ah, but you have to program them to paint, play chess and so on," for the same is unquestionably true of people. Try handing a twelve-month-old baby a pot of paint or a chessboard if you have any doubts about the need for some measure of learning and experience.

Obviously a crisper definition of creativity is required, and here is one that is almost universally acceptable: If a person demonstrates a skill which has never been demonstrated before and which was not specifically taught to him by someone else, or in the intellectual domain provides an *entirely novel* solution to a problem—a solution which was not known to any other human being—then they can be said to have done something original or had an original or creative thought. There may be other forms of creativity of course, but this would undeniably be an example of it in action. There is plenty of evidence that humans are creative by this standard and the history of science is littered with "original" ideas which humans have generated. Clearly, until a computer also provides such evidence, Lady Lovelace's Objection still holds, at least in one of its forms.

But alas for the sceptics. This particular barrier has been overthrown by computers on a number of occasions in the past few years. A well-publicized one was the solution, by a computer, of the venerable "four colour problem." This has some mathematical importance, and can best be expressed by thinking of a two-dimensional map featuring a large number of territories, say the counties of England or the states of the USA. Supposing you want to give each territory a colour, what is the minimum number of colours you need to employ to ensure that no two territories of the same colour adjoin each other?

After fiddling around with maps and crayons, you will find that the number seems to come out at four, and no one has ever been able to find a configuration where five colours are required, or where you can always get away with three. Empirically, therefore, four is the answer—hence the name of the problem. But if you attempt to demonstrate this mathematically and *prove* that four colours will do for any conceivable map, you will get nowhere. For decades mathematicians have wrestled with this elusive problem, and from time to time have come up with a "proof" which in the end turns out to be incomplete or fallacious. But the mathematical world was rocked when in 1977 the problem was handed over to a computer, which attacked it with stupendous frontal assault, sifting through huge combinations of possibilities and eventually demonstrating, to every mathematician's satisfaction, that four colours would do the trick. Actually, although this is spectacular testimony to the computer's creative powers, it is not really the most cogent example, for its technique was block-busting rather than heuristic (problem solving by testing hypotheses). It was like solving a chess problem by working out every possible combination of moves, rather than by concentrating on likely areas and experimenting with them. A better, and much earlier, demonstration of computer originality came from a program which was set to generate some totally new proofs in Euclidean geometry. The computer produced a completely novel proof of the well-known theorem which shows that the base angles of an isosceles triangle are equal, by flipping the triangles through 180 degrees and declaring them to be congruent. Quite apart from the fact that it had not before been known to Man, it showed such originality that one famous mathematician remarked, "If any of my students had done that, I would have marked him down as a budding genius."

And so Lady Lovelace's long-lasting objection can be overruled. We have shown that computers can be intelligent, and that they can even be creative—but we have not yet proved that they can, or ever could, *think*.

Now, what do we mean by the word "think"?

Towards the Ultra-Intelligent Machine

The most common objections raised to the notion of thinking machines are based on misunderstandings of fairly simple issues, or on semantic confusions of one kind or another. We are still left with the problem of defining the verb "to think," and in this chapter we will attempt to deal with this, or at least to discuss one particular and very compelling way of dealing with it. From this position we shall find ourselves drifting inevitably into a consideration of the problem of creating thinking machines, and in particular to the eerie concept of the Ultra-Intelligent Machine.

Most people believe that they know what they mean when they talk about "thinking" and have no difficulty identifying it when it is going on in their own heads. We are prepared to believe other human beings think because we have experience of it ourselves and accept that it is a common property of the human race. But we cannot make the same assumption about machines, and would be sceptical if one of them told us, no matter how persuasively, that it too was thinking. But sooner or later a machine will make just such a declaration and the question then will be, how do we decide whether to believe it or not?

When Turing tackled the machine-thought issue, he proposed a characteristically brilliant solution which, while not entirely free from flaws, is nevertheless the best that has yet been put forward. The key to it all, he pointed out, is to ask what the signs and signals are that humans give out, from which we infer that *they* are thinking. It is clearly a matter of *what kind of conversation we can have with them,* and has nothing to do with what kind of face they have and what kind of clothes they wear. Unfortunately physical appearances automatically set up prejudices in our minds, and if we were having a spirited conversation with a micro-processor we might be very sceptical about its capacity for thought, simply because it did not look like any thinking thing we had seen in the past. But we *would* be interested in what it had to say and thus Turing invented his experiment or test.

Put a human—the judge or tester—in a room where there are two computer terminals, one connected to a computer, the other to a person. The judge, of course, does not know which terminal is connected to which, but can type into either terminal and receive typed messages back on them. Now the judge's job is to decide, by carrying out conversations with the entities on the end of the respective terminals, *which is which.* If the computer is very stupid, it will immediately be revealed as such and the human will have no difficulty identifying it. If it is bright, he may find that he can carry on quite a good conversation with it, though he may ultimately spot that it must be the computer. If it is exceptionally bright and has a wide range of knowledge, he may find it impossible to say whether it is the computer he is talking to or the person. In this case, Turing argues, the computer will have passed the test and could for all practical purposes be said to be a thinking machine.

The argument has a simple but compelling force; if the intellectual exchange we achieve with a machine is indistinguishable from that we have with a being we *know* to be thinking, then we are, to all intents and purposes, communicating with another thinking being. This, by the way, does not imply that the personal experience, state of consciousness, level of awareness or whatever, of the entity is going to be the same as that experienced by a human when he or she thinks, so the test is not for these particular qualities. They are not, in any case, the parameters which concern the observer.

At first the Turing Test may seem a surprising way of looking at the problem, but it is an extremely sensible way of approaching it. The question now arises; is any computer at present in existence capable of passing the test?—And if not, how long is it likely to be before one comes along? From time to time one laboratory or another claims that a computer has had at least a pretty good stab at it. Scientists using the big computer conferencing systems (each scientist has a terminal in his office and is connected to his colleagues via the computer, which acts as host and general message-sorter) often find it difficult to be sure, for a brief period of time at least, whether they are talking to the computer or to one of their colleagues. On one celebrated occasion at MIT, two scientists had been chatting via the network when one of them left the scene without telling the other, who carried on a cheery conversation with the computer under the assumption that he was talking to his friend. I have had the same spooky experience when chatting with computers which I have programmed myself, and often find their answers curiously perceptive and unpredictable.

To give another interesting example: in the remarkable match played in Toronto in August 1978 between the International Chess Master, David Levy, and the then computer chess champion of the world, Northwestern University's "Chess 4.7," the computer made a number of moves of an uncannily "human" nature. The effect was so powerful that Levy subsequently told me that he found it difficult to believe that he was not facing an outstanding human opponent. Few chess buffs who looked at the move-by-move transcripts of the match were, without prior knowledge, able to tell which had been made by the computer and which by the flesh-and-blood chess master. David Levy himself suggested that Chess 4.7 had effectively passed the Turing Test.

It would be nice to believe that I had been present on such an historic occasion, but this did not constitute a proper "pass." In the test as Turing formulated it, the judge is allowed to converse with either of his two mystery entities on any topic that he chooses, and he may use any conversational trick he wants. Furthermore he can continue the inquisition for as long as he wants, always seeking some clue that will force the computer to reveal itself. Both the computer and the human can lie if they want to in their attempts to fool the tester, so the answers to questions like "Are you the computer?" or "Do you watch much television?" will not give much away. Obviously any computer with a chance in hell of passing the test will have to have a pretty substantial bank of software at its disposal and not just be extremely bright in one area. Chess 4.7 for example might look as though it was thinking if it was questioned about chess, or, better still, invited to play the game, but switch the area of discourse to human anatomy, politics or good restaurants and it would be shown up as a dunderhead.

As things stand at present, computers have quite a way to go before they jump the hurdle so cleverly laid out for them by Turing. But this should not be taken as providing unmitigated comfort for those who resist the notion of advanced machine intelligence. It should now be clear that the difference, in intellectual terms, between a human being and a computer is one of degree and not of kind.

Turing himself says in his *Mind* paper that he feels computers will have passed the test before the turn of the century, and there is little doubt that he would dearly have liked to live long enough to be around on the splendiferous occasion when "machine thinking" first occurred.

40. What the Human Mind Can Do That the Computer Can't
Morton Hunt

Morton Hunt (1920–   ) is a well-known author. He has published books on a variety of social issues.

Like creative acts, there are a number of important mental phenomena that have not yet been simulated by any computer program and, many cognitive scientists believe, probably never will be. Surprisingly, most of these are everyday aspects of our mental lives that we take for granted and that seem as natural and uncomplicated to us as eating and sleeping.

The first is that obvious, seemingly simple, but largely ineluctable phenomenon, consciousness. To philosophers through the centuries, and to psychologists of recent decades, this concept has proven as elusive as a drop of mercury under one's finger, but the only question we need ask ourselves here is: Can a machine be conscious? Let's say the current is on, the machine has a program stored in it, you address it from a terminal and, in response, it goes through various steps of solving a problem in very much the way a human being would. Now ask yourself: Was it conscious of its cognitive processes as you were of yours? The question answers itself: There is no reason to suppose so. Nothing built into any existing program that I have heard of is meant to, or does, as far as one can tell, yield a state corresponding to consciousness.

Much of our own thinking, to be sure, takes place outside of consciousness, but the results of these processes become conscious, and each of us *experiences* those conscious thoughts: we know them to be taking place in our own minds. We not only think, but perceive ourselves thinking. Artificial intelligence has no analog to this. As Donald Norman put it—and he was only one of many cognitive scientists who made similar remarks to me—"We don't have any programs today that are self-aware or that even begin to approach consciousness such as human beings have. I see this as a critical difference between human intelligence and artificial intelligence. The human mind is aware of itself as an identity, it can introspect, it can examine its own ideas and react to them—not just with thoughts about them but with emotions. We can't begin to simulate consciousness on a computer, and perhaps never will."

Not everyone would agree that consciousness may forever remain impossible to simulate, but what is clear is that it cannot be simulated at present—and for one very good reason: it remains the least understood and most puzzling of psychological phenomena. I am aware of my own thoughts, to be sure, but what is this "I?" How do I distinguish the "I" from the identity of other people or the rest of the world? Surely it is not a matter of the borders of my physical being, for in the dark, or blindfolded and bound, or even cut off by spinal anesthesia from all feeling, I would know myself: the borders are those of thought, not body. Actually, the question "What is this 'I'?" rarely concerns us, for we experience our own identity as a self-evident reality. But that ineluctable sense of I-ness does not exist in any computer; there is no evidence that any computer program has ever realized that it is itself, running in a particular machine, and not a similar program, running on another machine somewhere else.

Cognitive science does offer at least a rudimentary explanation of consciousness: it is thought to be the product of our internalizing the real world in our minds in symbolic form. We perceive not only the real world but also our own mental representation of it; the experience of the difference between the two results in self-awareness. We recognize that there is not only a real world but a simulacrum of it within us; therefore there must be an *us: cogito ergo sum,* yet again. The thought that we have thoughts is the crucial one that becomes consciousness; it is what Douglas Hofstadter, in *Gödel, Escher, Bach,* calls a "strange loop" of the mind, an interaction between different levels, a self-reinforcing resonance. "The self," he says, "comes into being at the moment it has the power to reflect itself." We contemplate our thoughts, but the awareness of doing so is itself a thought, and the foundation of consciousness.

Perhaps the key factor is that consciousness develops in us as a result of our cognitive history. As we have seen, the infant gradually becomes capable of thinking about external objects by means of mental images and symbols stored in memory. The newborn does not seem to be aware of the boundaries between itself and the rest of the world, but it perceives them more and more distinctly as its internal image of the world builds up. Consciousness emerges as a product of the child's mental development. The computer, in contrast, though it may acquire an ever-larger store of information, has no such sense or experience of its own history. Nor does it recognize that what is in its memory is a representation of something outside. To the computer, what is in its system is what *is:* it does not contemplate its thoughts as thoughts, but as the only reality. How could it, then, be aware of itself as an individual?

Some AI enthusiasts do, however, argue that if a program examines its own problem-solving behavior and modifies it to improve it, as HACKER does, this is the equivalent of consciousness; so says Pamela McCorduck in *Machines Who Think.* John McCarthy of Stanford University, one of America's leading computer scientists, goes even further:

he says it is possible to ascribe beliefs, free will, consciousness, and wants to a machine. In his view, even as simple a machine as a thermostat can be said to have beliefs (presumably the thermostat "believes" that the optimum temperature is the one it is set for). But such talk is either metaphorical or, more likely, anthropomorphic; it reads into the machine what the human observer feels, much as primitive people attribute rage to the volcano and prudence to the ant. There is no reason to suppose HACKER or a thermostat experience anything like awareness of the self; they merely respond to certain incoming stimuli with mechanical reactions. HACKER, to be sure, does register corrections in its program for future use, but so does a vine, growing around an obstruction. It seems most unlikely that anywhere within HACKER some small voice says, "I made an error, but I'm correcting it and I'll do better next time."

What difference does it make? If a machine can respond to its own errors and correct them, what does it matter that it isn't aware of doing so?

It matters a lot. Awareness of self is the essence of what being alive means to us. If, through some accident, you remained able to talk and reason but could not realize that you were doing so, would you not be as dead, from your own viewpoint, as if your brain had been destroyed?

More than that, with awareness of self we become conscious of the alternatives in our thoughts; we become conscious of our choices, and of our ability to will the things we choose to do. Choice and will are difficult to account for within a scientific psychology, since it views existence as a continuum in which no phenomenon occurs uncaused. If no event is, itself, a first cause, but is the product of antecedent forces, then the experience of choice and of will must be illusory; the acts of choosing and of willing, though they seem to be within our power, must be products of all that has happened to us in the past and is happening at the moment.

And yet when we are conscious of our own alternatives, that self-awareness is another level of causality—a set of influences in addition to those of the past and present. We are not automata, weighing all the pros and cons of any matter and inevitably acting in accord with our calculations. In mathematical decision theory, the totally rational human being does just that and always selects the most advantageous option; so does a well-designed computer program. But in reality we are aware of our own decision making, and that awareness in itself brings other forces to bear upon the decision—emotional responses to the situation, loyalties, moral values, a sense of our own identity—and these resonances, these loops of thought, affect the outcome.

A simple example: you are annoyed by something a friend has said or done, you fume about it, you imagine a conversation in which the two of you argue about it, you prepare your crushing remarks—and suddenly perceive all this as from a distance; in perspective, you see yourself as an outsider might see you, question your own thoughts and feelings, alter them, and, as a result, accept the friend's behavior and dismiss your anger, or, perhaps, call the friend and talk the matter over amicably.

Another example: like every writer I know, when I am writing a first draft I rattle away at the typewriter, setting down words; but once I see them I think, That isn't quite right—that's not exactly what I mean, and tinker and revise and rewrite until the words are right. But it wasn't that the first words didn't say what I meant; rather, in seeing my thoughts, I had thoughts about them; the strange loop yielded something like freedom—the freedom to make a different choice among my thoughts. If the experiences of choice and will are not what they seem to be, they nonetheless reflect real processes that produce results different from those that would come about without them.

In any case, there is no doubt that we do not experience our thought processes as automatic but as within our control . . .

But what does "want" mean? Can a machine want? In a sense; if its program calls for it to assign different weights to various subgoals and goals it will proceed to choose that option which its program reckons to have the greatest numerical value. All very neat and simple. Human beings are far less neat and far more complicated. We often desire things but lack the motivation to pursue them; conversely, we are sometimes so strongly motivated by beliefs, values, and emotions that we pursue a particular goal with a devotion far beyond what any realistic evaluation would warrant.

Of all the components in human motivation, the one least likely ever to be simulated by a computer is our capacity to find things interesting. It is a mystifying phenomenon. Why do we find any matter interesting? What makes us want to know about, or understand, something—especially something that has no practical value for us, such as the age of the universe or when human beings first appeared on earth? Why do we want to know if there is life elsewhere in the cosmos, if its replies to our messages could not arrive back here for centuries? Why did Pythagoras feel so powerfully impelled to prove his celebrated theorem?

This tendency in us, some cognitive scientists believe, is an intrinsic characteristic of our nervous system. We are driven to think certain thoughts, and to pursue certain goals, by an inherent neurological restlessness, a need to do something with the thoughts in our minds and with the world they represent. The computer, in contrast, is a passive system: its goals and the strength of its drive to reach them are those given it by its designer. Left to itself, it will sit inert, awaiting further orders. We will not; we look for new goals, and, to reach them, are forced to solve problems we did not have before; we do not let well enough alone.

Why don't we? Call it restlessness, call it curiosity, or perhaps, like the historian Huizinga, call it playfulness. Other animals play, but with us playfulness becomes cognitive: we play with our ideas, and afterward with the real-world counterparts of those ideas. How would you simulate that on a machine? Allen Newell and a few other AI researchers say there is no reaon why a program could not be designed to be curious and to create new goals for itself, but they are a small minority; most cognitive scientists think otherwise. Yet even if a machine could be programmed to cast about in some way for new goals and new problems, it would do so because it had been programmed to; it wouldn't do so because it wanted to. It wouldn't give a damn.

And that would be bound to affect the kinds of new problems it chose to tackle and the strength of its motivation to solve them. Maybe the biggest difference between artificial and human intelligence is just that simple: we care about the things we choose to do. Solving a new problem, discovering some new fact, visiting a new place, reading a new book, all make us feel good; that's why we do them. But how would one make a computer feel good? Some AI people have built rewards into their programs: if the machine makes right decisions, its program is automatically altered to strengthen that kind of response, and so it learns. Theoretically, a program could be rewarded if it did something new and different, so that its tendency would be not to maintain itself, unchanged, but to keep changing. But would it *want* to do so or *like* doing so? And lacking that, would there be any meaning to its changes? Perhaps computer-written music and poetry have been unimpressive because the computer itself was neither pleased nor displeased by its own product, as every creative artist is. Without that test, it wasn't able to tell whether it had created a work of genius or a piece of trash. And it didn't care.

We, on the other hand, care—and care most of all about those thoughts which express moral values. Each of us is not just an information processor but the product of a particular culture and its belief system. We perceive the world through the special focus of the values we have learned from parents, schools, books, and peers. Those values become a part of our decision-making processes; in making many of our choices, we weight the alternatives in accordance with our moral, religious, and political beliefs.

This aspect of human thinking can be, and has been, simulated on the machine, as we saw earlier, in the form of the simulations of political decision making created by Jaime Carbonell and his colleagues when he was at Yale (he is now at Carnegie-Mellon). POLITICS has simulated the reasoning of either a conservative or a liberal considering what the United States should do if, for instance, Russia were to build nuclear submarines. Both as conservative and as liberal, POLITICS flawlessly came to conclusions consonant with the assumptions it was programmed to draw upon. Carbonell's purpose was to test his theoretical model of the way in which ideology affects the decision-making process; he did not suggest that POLITICS could be developed into a machine that could do our political thinking for us. But his work does have two important implications for this discussion of what the human mind can do that the computer can't do.

First, even though POLITICS can simulate archetypal conservative or liberal political reasoning, it does so in a wholly predictable way; it produces decisions Carbonell could foresee because they are based entirely on the terms and conditions he had put into it. But that is not the way human beings think. Within any party or ideological group, there is a wide range of variations in how individuals interpret the tenets of that ideology. There are always mavericks, dissenters, and innovators, without whom every party, every church, and every culture would atrophy and die.

Second, within any given ideological group, some people have the emotional maturity, the richness of human experience, and the soundness of judgment to use its tenets wisely; others do not, and use them foolishly. This is not to say that wise persons will reach the same conclusions everywhere; I would not want the wisest judge in Russia, India, or Iran to hear a civil liberties case in which I was accused of slandering the state. But if it is true that within any culture, its ethical system has internal validity, some of its people will interpret those beliefs wisely, others foolishly, and the majority somewhere in between. Moral wisdom is not so much the product of a special method of reasoning as of an ability to harmonize moral beliefs with fundamental individual and societal needs. I do not see how artificial intelligence can simulate that.

Will artificial intelligence, then, ever outstrip human intelligence? Yes, astronomically—in certain ways; and clearly it is already doing so. But in other ways it does not now match our powers, much less exceed them, and seems unlikely to do so soon. And in still other ways it seems incapable of simulating human intellectual functioning at all.

For until it acquires perceptual systems as sophisticated as our own, it will not be able to learn directly from the environment. But the development of such systems is bound to prove more difficult, by many orders of magnitude, than the creation of a living cell—a feat not now imaginable—and lacking such perceptual systems, the machine will remain dependent on the human being for its information.

But that is the least of it. Until artificial intelligence can duplicate human mental development from birth onward; until it can absorb the intricacies and subleties of cultural values; until it can acquire consciousness of self; until it becomes capable of playfulness and curiosity; until it can create new goals for itself, unplanned and uninstigated by any human programmer; until it is motivated not by goals alone but by some restless compulsion to be doing and exploring; until it can care about, and be pleased or annoyed by, its own thoughts; until it can make wise moral judgments—until all these conditions exist, the computer, it seems to me, will not match or even palely imitate the most valuable aspects of human thinking.

There is no doubt that the computer has already transformed our lives, and will continue to do so. But its chief influence will continue to be its utility as a tool. Supercalculators have radically changed, and will continue to change, all human institutions that require reckoning. Artificial intelligence will reconstruct many areas of problem solving—everything from the practice of medicine to literary and historical research and the investigation of the cosmos—and in so doing will change our ways of thinking as profoundly as did the invention of writing. Tools have powerful effects on the thinking of those who use them (the plow radically altered humankind's view of itself and of the world around it), but tools of the mind have the most powerful effects of all. Still, they are our tools, we their users.

But is it not possible that the computer will take over, outthink us, make our decisions for us, become our ruler? Not unless we assign it the power to make our decisions. Joseph Weizenbaum, in *Computer Power and Human Reason,* passionately argues that the computer represents a major danger to humanity not because it can forcibly take over but because we are heedlessly allowing it to make decisions for us in areas where we alone ought to make them. He sees the problem as a moral one rather than a struggle between human and machine: we ought not let the computer function as a psychotherapist, ought not rely on it to tell us whether to bomb civilian enemy targets or only military ones, ought not have it function as a judge in court.

Of course we ought not, but is there any real danger that we will? I hope not; I think not. The computer does not set its own goals: we do, and we human beings are jealous of our own powers. We have often delegated them to some leader—a human being, like ourselves, but one we took to be a greater person than we. Or we have asked some god (who often looks like us, enlarged) to make our decisions for us. But would we ever delegate our intellectual responsibilities to a machine that we ourselves created? I doubt it. Though human beings have often enough been fools, I find it hard to believe that we would ever be foolish enough to think our machines wiser than we; at least, not as long as we are aware of, and proud of, the human difference.

Do We Survive Death?

41. Immortality   Durant Drake

Durant Drake (1878–1933) was a well-known American philosopher and a professor at Vassar College for many years. He was the author of many books and scholarly articles on a variety of philosophical topics.

What Considerations Make Against the Belief?

(1) It takes no critical acumen to perceive the *prima facie* case against immortality. In all our experience a man's conscious life is bound up with the fortunes of his body. We see men stunned by a blow, we see their minds enfeebled by bodily injury, we see their bodies killed and with that their mental life apparently ended. Consciousness seems to be dependent upon the body's supply of food, air, and sleep, and its safety from harm. To suppose that when the bodily mechanism stops entirely, consciousness, which has been so subject to its influence, gains a new lease of life on its own account, has always been difficult for reflective persons. And this explains, no doubt, the pale and impotent existence which the ancients almost universally attributed to the dead.

(2) The rise of modern physiological psychology, showing us, as it does, the intimate correlation of mind and brain, increases the difficulties of faith. We have discovered that thinking tires the brain; or, to put it the other way, the fatigue of brain-cells retards and inhibits thinking. The loss of memory, weakening of the will, increase in petulance of old age go hand in hand with a degeneration of brain-tissue. Certain kinds of consciousness are bound up with specific parts of the brain; when a certain portion of the brain is diseased or injured, the mind is affected in a definite manner. Whatever may be the relation between brain and consciousness, the study of the close parallelism between their activities makes it harder to resist the conviction that the disintegration of the one involves the disintegration of the other.

(3) Moreover, it is difficult to conceive what conscious life can be *like*, without a physical body, with its sense organs and organs of expression. If we cut out of our consciousness the visual, auditory, tactile, motor, and other bodily produced images, what have we left? Very little if anything. Yet how could we have visual experiences without eyes, or touch-experiences without hands? And, setting aside the questions what sort of consciousness we could have, and how we could communicate with our friends, what would they *mean* to us apart from their bodies? Take away the *look* of your dear one, her facial expression, the light in her eyes, the sound of her voice, the grace of her movements, the touch of her hand, what have you remaining to attract and interest you?

(4) Modern psychology has no longer any use for the concept of "soul." But if there is a "soul," a something inhabiting the body as a tenant, and separable from it at death, where does it abide, how does it get into the body, *when* does it get into the body, when does it leave the body, and how? Do portions of the parents' souls separate themselves, join together with the joining of the germ plasms at conception, to form a new immortal soul? If so, does it remain immortal if the incipient fœtus is ejected from the woman's body, if miscarriage takes place, or the child is still-born? Or does a new soul come somewhence at the moment of birth, and enter the child when it first breathes? The more clearly we realize the continuity of the physical processes of conception, pregnancy, and birth, the more difficult it becomes to know where to interpolate a soul.

(5) A similar continuity is seen to pervade the course of evolution, whereby man has emerged from a brute ancestry. If man is immortal, must not his brute ancestors have been immortal, and their descendants in the diverging, non-human lines? A rather disagreeable alternative seems to be offered. On the one hand, you may say that at a certain point in his ascent, man acquired immortality. If so, there was a time, in the slow evolution of the human type, when parents who, like all their ancestors, were doomed to die, gave birth to a child who was blessed with an immortal future. By what miracle was this momentous change effected? It seems unfair to the generations preceding. On the other hand, if you postulate no such moment of acquisition of an immortal soul, you must grant immortality to all the animals—and then perhaps to the plants too, for the vegetable and animal kingdoms merge gradually one into the other, just as brutehood grew insensibly into manhood. Many

animals are, indeed, more intelligent and more affectionate than human babies, or underwitted men, idiots, and—doubtless—primitive savages; one would like to imagine one's pet dog immortal. But when it comes to tigers and snakes and mosquitoes and bedbugs and cholera microbes, our imagination halts!

(6) Where is the heaven to which souls go at death? It was easy enough for the ancients to picture a heavenly region up above the dome of the sky, easy enough for the evangelist to think of Jesus as having ascended into heaven and sitting there on the right hand of God. But we have long since learned the naiveté of that primitive world-view. We can no longer believe, with Dante, in an island in the Western sea, to which Ulysses could sail, where the mountain of purgatory reaches up to paradise. Nor can we believe that sulphur springs and volcanic steam bubble up from a hades under the earth where departed souls groan in torment. The stellar universe, as we scan it with our telescopes, offers indeed unlimited ports to which we may conceive of ourselves as going; but there seems something grotesque about the fancy of our winging our way to Sirius or the Pleiades. And whatever heaven may lie beyond the stars, millions of millions of miles away, we cannot easily feel so sure of it as the pre-Copernicans did of their paradise of God just above the ninth sphere.

All these skeptical reflections give us, however, nothing but a series of difficulties in the way of belief. They may be met by the reminder that we naturally cannot conceive our future life, because we have no experience thereof. We see only one side of the veil; and all we know is that the departed no longer figure in our earthly existence. In the nature of the case, we cannot disprove immortality; nor does the lack of evidence, in this case, constitute a presumption against it, since, if a future life is a reality, there is no reason to suppose that it is such as to be in contact with, and revealed to, this present life. The relation of mind to brain may be conceived in such a way as to make them separable; and it is easy to formulate answers to the other objections, which, if they have no positive evidence to support them, have equally no evidence against them. We may turn then with open minds to consider the leading arguments for the belief in immortality.

What Are the Leading Arguments for the Belief?

(1) The older Christian preaching based its argument for immortality upon the supposedly indubitable fact of the resurrection of Christ. But a critical study of the Gospel narratives has long since shown them to be late, confused, mutually contradictory, and in many respects obviously legendary; more than that, they are at odds with the earliest Christian preaching, as vouched for in the letters of Paul. Paul and the apostles undoubtedly believed themselves to have had revelations of the risen Lord; and that these were genuine revelations we may well believe. But just what their experiences were we shall never know; and that they were mistaken in taking them for revelations of the risen Christ must be admitted to be possible. In any case, that the Messiah, a unique figure with

a unique mission, should have risen from the dead does not prove that ordinary men can do so. Christ's own words on the matter, and those of Paul and the other early Christian writers, are so sharply at variance with our modern conception of the future life that we cannot use them to support our own faith except by reading into them a meaning foreign to their original intention. For the future life anticipated by Christ, and all of his immediate predecessors, contemporaries, and followers, was a life on earth, with a renovated Jerusalem for its capital, to be preceded by the great Judgment Day, and inaugurated within that generation. Our modern hopes have grown so far away from that naïve conception that the faith of Christ in God and that of the disciples in Christ can hardly serve us as more than a stimulus to an equally daring though necessarily different and less tangible faith.

(2) Another Biblical support for faith, still often used, is Paul's analogy of the seed.[1] Briefly, the idea is this: as a seed seems to die when buried in the ground, but really gives birth to a new life, so may the human body, when dead and buried, pass into a new form of life. When read in the vague and sounding periods of the King James Bible, Paul's rhetoric easily wins assent from the unthinking. But a moment's thought suffices to show how empty it is. There is really no analogy between the buried seed and the buried body; the one, still living, and finding itself in an environment favorable to its growth, proceeds to develop into a plant; the other, which is really dead, disintegrates and returns to dust. The greater life that develops, by physical laws, out of the living seed is still a physical life, continuous with that which preceded; the new life postulated to succeed that of the human body is a non-physical life, invisible, intangible, utterly out of relation to the physical world, in which the germination of the seed is a natural and intelligible event. Moreover, at best, the plant produced from a seed is a different plant from that which bore the seed; there is no analogy here that points toward immortality of the individual. Every tree and herb dies in its time; it is only its descendants that survive. The human body has similarly its seed, buried in the mother's womb as the plant's seed is buried in the earth, there to give rise to a new life, which, however, has no continuity of memory or purpose with the parent life. This is the true analogy of the plant seed; there is an indefinitely continued life of the germ plasm, transmitted from body to body. But this is not personal immortality; the individual is only a transient by-product, surviving long enough to hand on the life force to its descendants.

(3) Perhaps the belief in immortality is oftenest held today as a corollary of the belief in God. Since God is good, it is felt, he cannot be so cruel as to deny us our deepest longing, to live on and to have our dear ones live. But the argument is over hasty. If God is not omnipotent, we cannot be sure that he can secure immortality for us. If he is omnipotent, we might suppose that he would deny us immortality; but in view of the fact that we are denied so much that we should have supposed, *a priori*, that a good God would give us, we cannot be sure that he will not deny

---

[1] Cor. 15:35–44.

us this too. Many evils exist, in spite of God's existence; why not death too? If we were ignorant of the actual fact we might argue with equal cogency that since God is good, he could not be so cruel as to send suffering into the world, pain that crushes, agony that kills. Surely the parallelism of the two arguments should show that both are inconclusive. The fact is, we know as little about God's nature and power as we do about our own future; our trust in a personal Ruler of the universe, who is to triumph over evil, is as much a venture of faith as our trust in our own immortality, and cannot be used to prove it.

(4) Another argument that figures prominently in current discussions is that which declares that we have an "instinct" or "instinctive longing" for immortality, and that instincts do not exist unless there are objects that can gratify them. In a moderate degree this is true. We have an instinctive wish to live, and we do have an object which can gratify it to some extent—we have some life. But few instinctive longings are gratified to the extent that we could wish; the instinctive longing for love, for power, for pleasure and freedom from pain—which of our longings is more than in slight measure fulfilled? Why may it not be so with our longing for life—we get some, but not nearly so much as we might desire. It is easy to see (to turn from dialectic to history) that those individuals that had some desire to live would be the only ones that would survive the long struggle for existence; this is the actual cause of the presence in us of the desire to live—this very transient earthly life called it forth, not necessarily any heavenly life beckoning from above.

(5) Certain scientific and philosophical speculations have frequently been invoked. The doctrines of the Conservation of Energy and the Persistence of Matter are held to show that nothing can possibly perish; when wood is burned, the same elements continue to exist in altered combinations, and when the body decays its constituents live on in other forms. And indeed, we need not question that the elements that go to make up our personalities persist into the indefinite future. But if those elements, like the body's cells, disintegrate and pass into other forms, would there be possible any continuity of memory or purpose? Consciousness, as the name implies, is an organic whole made up of many elements; only the persistence of this *combination* of elements would, apparently, constitute personal immortality. And such a continuity the doctrines above mentioned, even considering them proved, cannot guarantee.

Similarly, the "idealistic" metaphysics, which declares everything to be really "mind," or "spirit," and not "matter" at all, even if granted (and it is granted by but a minority of philosophers to-day), can bring us no farther toward a proof of the survival of the individual. To call the stuff of which the world is made "mental" instead of "material" is rhetorically suggestive; but a "mental" world may be as unconcerned with our personal fortunes as a "material" world. Let the universe be throughout a mass of mind stuff, or even a great consciousness, a World-Soul, or Absolute; grant the immortality of that universal life; and we are yet far from any evidence that you and I shall know each other in the future cycles of that Life, or that the ideals dear to us shall be attained.

(6) The only real attempt to bring forward evidence of a future life is that which has been made by the spiritualists and the societies for psychical research, in their investigations of automatic writing, table-turning, and the other trance phenomena, which are often so puzzling and often so uncanny. The study of these facts is still in its infancy; bulky volumes of "proceedings" have been published, and have convinced a few serious students of the reality of communications from departed spirits. But comparatively few scientifically trained men have been convinced by them, and this for several reasons. In the first place, it is by no means demonstrated that other explanations of the phenomena are untenable. The hypothesis of telepathic communication from living people is held by many to account for all the more puzzling facts. Others hold that they can be explained, so far as they are genuine, in terms of the subject's own subconsciousness. Certainly many of these phenomena that were once held to imply spirit-communication have been definitely relegated to the domain of the psychology of the subconscious, and the presumption is that other phenomena, now inexplicable, will be similarly interpreted as our psychological knowledge widens. A second reason for skepticism lies in the great amount of malobservation and superstition and actual fraud that has been discovered in these matters. Many students become so disgusted with the fraudulent practices in which some of the leading mediums have been caught that they will have nothing more to do with the whole business. In the third place, the sayings and doings of these rapping and squeaking ghosts are, for the most part, so trashy and silly and beneath the dignity of immortal souls, and withal so uncontributive to our knowledge, that serious investigators are apt to lose patience with them. Why do Alexander the Great and Edgar Allan Poe and an Indian Princess (to mention three "spirits" of whose presence, in succession, the writer was once assured) deliver themselves of such closely similar and equally paltry messages?

In reply to these criticisms, the spiritualists admit the existence of much malobservation, and of much fraud; they usually admit the applicability to many cases of the explanations by means of telepathy or the subconsciousness of the subject. But they insist that a residue of genuine phenomena remain, inexplicable save on the spiritistic hypothesis. If the words of the departed seem confused or absurd, it is perhaps because their intrusion into our world is abnormal, and they are unable to send through the veil that separates us more than these hardly articulate messages. It has even been suggested that what we get is their dream-life, which may be as chaotic and absurd as our own. At any rate, we must not reject this mass of unassimilated evidence simply because it is distasteful to us. And if the evidence should point toward a continued existence which is but brief, a gradual fading out of consciousness after death, perhaps, or a future life like that which the ancients imagined, pale, ineffectual, unhappy, at least the actual knowledge that death is not final, that the soul can survive the body's decay, would go far toward encouraging in us the faith toward which we yearn.

In the end, after all our argumentation, pro and con, we must, if we are candid and sincere, admit our ignorance. Eye hath not seen, nor ear heard, aught that takes place beyond the *flamantia mœnia mundi*. We are no better off than the Persian poet who wrote,—

> "Strange, is it not, that of the myriads who
> Before us pass'd the door of Darkness through
> Not one returns to tell us of the Road
> Which to discover we must travel too."

We cannot prove what is the end of all our hearts' desire. If any man think that he can prove it, he is (to echo Kant) just the man we want to see—until we have listened so long to alleged "proofs" that the hope long deferred maketh our hearts sick. Science gives us no evidence; and few philosophers have been able to construct systems that should include personal immortality. Nor is it necessary to believe; our duty is the same in any case. If we cannot believe in a future life, we can set to and make this life brave and glorious. Multitudes of men who have had not even hope in life beyond the grave have found this earthly life full of zest and savor, and have helped to make the lives of their fellows happier and better while they lasted. To sulk, to give way to depression or apathy, because this life were all, would be the part of cowardice and folly; while to give rein to lust and immorality because of a removal of fear of future retribution would be to expose the stupidity and selfishness of a soul that had never grasped the natural worth of virtue or learned to love what is most precious in this life.

42. Is Life After Death Possible?   C. J. Ducasse

The question whether human personality survives death is sometimes asserted to be one upon which reflection is futile. Only empirical evidence, it is said, can be relevant, since the question is purely one of fact.

But no question is purely one of fact until it is clearly understood; and this one is, on the contrary, ambiguous and replete with tacit assumptions. Until the ambiguities have been removed and the assumptions critically examined, we do not really know just what it is we want to know when we ask whether a life after death is possible. Nor, therefore, can we tell until then what bearing on this question various facts empirically known to us may have.

To clarify its meaning is chiefly what I now propose to attempt. I shall ask first why a future life is so generally desired and believed in. Then I shall state, as convincingly as I can in the time available, the arguments commonly advanced to prove that such a life is impossible. After that, I shall consider the logic of these arguments, and show that they quite fail to establish the impossibility. Next, the tacit but arbitrary assumption, which makes them nevertheless appear convincing, will be

From "Is Life After Death Possible?" The Agnes E. and Constantine E. Foerster Lecture, 1947. Copyright by C. J. Ducasse, 1948. Reprinted by permission of The Regents of the University of California.

pointed out. And finally, I shall consider briefly a number of specific forms which a life after death might take, if there is one.

Let us turn to the first of these tasks.

Why Man Desires Life After Death

To begin with, let us note that each of us here has been alive and conscious at all times in the past which he can remember. It is true that sometimes our bodies are in deep sleep, or made inert by anesthetics or injuries. But even at such times we do not experience unconsciousness in ourselves, for to experience it would mean being conscious of being unconscious, and this is a contradiction. The only experience of unconsciousness in ourselves we ever have is, not experience of total unconsciousness, but of unconsciousness *of this or that;* as when we report: "I am not conscious of any pain," or "of any bell-sound," or "of any difference between those two colors," etc. Nor do we ever experience unconsciousness in another person, but only the fact that, sometimes, some or all of the ordinary activities of his body cease to occur. That consciousness itself is extinguished at such times is thus only a hypothesis which we construct to account for certain changes in the behavior of another person's body or to explain in him or in ourselves the eventual lack of memories relating to the given period.

Being alive and conscious is thus, with all men, a lifelong experience and habit; and conscious life is therefore something they naturally— even if tacitly—expect to continue. As J. B. Pratt has pointed out, the child takes the continuity of life for granted. It is the fact of death that has to be taught him. But when he has learned it, and the idea of a future life is then put explicitly before his mind, it seems to him the most natural thing in the world.[1]

The witnessing of death, however, is a rare experience for most of us, and, because it breaks so sharply into our habits, it forces on us the question whether the mind, which until then was manifested by the body now dead, continues somehow to live on, or, on the contrary, has become totally extinct. This question is commonly phrased as concerning "the immortality of the soul," and immortality, strictly speaking, means survival forever. But assurance of survival for some considerable period— say a thousand, or even a hundred, years—would probably have almost as much present psychological value as would assurance of survival strictly forever. Most men would be troubled very little by the idea of extinction at so distant a time—even less troubled than is now a healthy and happy youth by the idea that he will die in fifty or sixty years. Therefore, it is survival for some time, rather than survival specifically forever, that I shall alone consider.

The craving for continued existence is very widespread. Even persons who believe that death means complete extinction of the individual's consciousness often find comfort in various substitute conceptions of

---

[1] J. B. Pratt, *The Religious Consciousness,* p. 225.

survival. They may, for instance, dwell on the continuity of the individual's germ plasm in his descendants. Or they find solace in the thought that, the past being indestructible, their individual life remains eternally an intrinsic part of the history of the world. Also—and more satisfying to one's craving for personal importance—there is the fact that since the acts of one's life have effects, and these in turn further effects, and so on, therefore what one has done goes on forever influencing remotely, and sometimes greatly, the course of future events.

Gratifying to one's vanity, too, is the prospect that, if the achievements of one's life have been great or even only conspicuous, or one's benefactions or evil deeds have been notable, one's name may not only be remembered by acquaintances and relatives for a little while, but may live on in recorded history. But evidently survival in any of these senses is but a consolation prize—but a thin substitute for the continuation of conscious individual life, which may not be a fact, but which most men crave nonetheless.

The roots of this craving are certain desires which death appears to frustrate. For some, the chief of these is for reunion with persons dearly loved. For others, whose lives have been wretched, it is the desire for another chance at the happiness they have missed. For others yet, it is desire for further opportunity to grow in ability, knowledge or character. Often, there is also the desire, already mentioned, to go on counting for something in the affairs of men. And again, a future life for oneself and others is often desired in order that the redressing of the many injustices of this life shall be possible. But it goes without saying that, although desires such as these are often sufficient to cause belief in a future life, they constitute no evidence at all that it is a fact.

In this connection, it may be well to point out that, although both the belief in survival and the belief in the existence of a god or gods are found in most religions, nevertheless there is no necessary connection between the two beliefs. No contradiction would be involved in supposing either that there is a God but no life after death or that there is a life after death but no God. The belief that there is a life after death may be tied to a religion, but it is no more intrinsically religious than would be a belief that there is life on the planet Mars. The after-death world, if it exists, is just another region or dimension of the universe.

But although belief in survival of death is natural and easy and has always been held in one form or another by a large majority of mankind, critical reflection quickly brings forth a number of apparently strong reasons to regard that belief as quite illusory. Let us now review them.

The Arguments Against Survival

There are, first of all, a number of facts which definitely suggest that both the existence and the nature of consciousness wholly depend on the presence of a functioning nervous system. It is pointed out, for example, that wherever consciousness is observed, it is found associated with a living and functioning body. Further, when the body dies, or the head is struck a heavy blow, or some anesthetic is administered, the familiar outward evidences of consciousness terminate, permanently or temporarily. Again, we know well that drugs of various kinds—alcohol, caffein, opium, heroin, and many others—cause specific changes at the time in the nature of a person's mental states. Also, by stimulating in appropriate ways the body's sense organs, corresponding states of consciousness—namely, the various kinds of sensations—can be caused at will. On the other hand, cutting a sensory nerve immediately eliminates a whole range of sensations.

Again, the contents of consciousness, the mental powers, or even the personality, are modified in characteristic ways when certain regions of the brain are destroyed by disease or injury or are disconnected from the rest by such an operation as prefrontal lobotomy. And that the nervous system is the indispensable basis of mind is further suggested by the fact that, in the evolutionary scale, the degree of intelligence of various species of animals keeps pace closely with the degree of development of their brain.

That continued existence of mind after death is impossible has been argued also on the basis of theoretical considerations. It has been contended, for instance, that what we call states of consciousness—or more particularly, ideas, sensations, volitions, feelings, and the like—are really nothing but the minute physical or chemical events which take place in the tissues of the brain. For, it is urged, it would be absurd to suppose that an idea or a volition, if it is not itself a material thing or process, could cause material effects such as contractions of muscles.

Moreover, it is maintained that the possibility of causation of a material event by an immaterial, mental cause is ruled out *a priori* by the principle of the conservation of energy; for such causation would mean that an additional quantity of energy suddenly pops into the nervous system out of nowhere.

Another conception of consciousness, which is more often met with today than the one just mentioned, but which also implies that consciousness cannot survive death, is that "consciousness" is only the name we give to certain types of behavior, which differentiate the higher animals from all other things in nature. According to this view, to say, for example, that an animal is conscious of a difference between two stimuli means nothing more than that it responds to each by different behavior. That is, the difference of *behavior* is what consciousness of difference between the stimuli *consists in;* and is not, as is commonly assumed, only the behavioral *sign* of something mental and not public, called "consciousness that the stimuli are different."

Or again, consciousness, of the typically human sort called thought, is identified with the typically human sort of behavior called speech; and this, again not in the sense that speech *expresses* or *manifests* something different from itself, called "thought," but in the sense that speech—whether uttered or only whispered—*is* thought itself. And obviously, if thought, or any mental activity, is thus but some mode of behavior of the living body, the mind cannot possibly survive death.

Still another difficulty confronting the hypothesis of survival becomes evident when one imagines in some detail what survival would have to include in order to satisfy the desires which cause man to crave it. It would, of course, have to include persistence not alone of consciousness, but also of personality; that is, of the individual's character, acquired knowledge, cultural skills and interests, memories, and awareness of personal identity. But even this would not be enough, for what man desires is not bare survival, but to go on living in some objective way. And this means to go on meeting new situations and, by exerting himself to deal with them, to broaden and deepen his experience and develop his latent capacities.

But it is hard to imagine this possible without a body and an environment for it, upon which to act and from which to receive impressions. And, if a body and an environment were supposed, but not material and corruptible ones, then it is paradoxical to think that, under such radically different conditions, a given personality could persist.[2]

To take a crude but telling analogy, it is past belief that, if the body of any one of us were suddenly changed into that of a shark or an octopus, and placed in the ocean, his personality could, for more than a very short time, if at all, survive intact so radical a change of environment and of bodily form.

The Arguments Examined

Such, in brief, are the chief reasons commonly advanced for holding that survival is impossible. Scrutiny of them, however, will, I think, reveal that they are not as strong as they first seem and far from strong enough to show that there can be no life after death.

Let us consider first the assertion that "thought," or "consciousness," is but another name for subvocal speech, or for some other form of behavior, or for molecular processes in the tissues of the brain. As Paulsen and others have pointed out,[3] no evidence ever is or can be offered to support that assertion, because it is in fact but a disguised proposal to make the words "thought," "feeling," "sensation," "desire," and so on, denote facts quite different from those which these words are commonly employed to denote. To say that those words are but other names for certain chemical or behavioral events is as grossly arbitrary as it would be to say that "wood" is but another name for glass, or "potato" but another name for cabbage. What thought, desire, sensation, and other mental states are like, each of us can observe directly by introspection; and what introspection reveals is that they do not in the least resemble muscular contraction, or glandular secretion, or any other known bodily events. No tampering with language can alter the observable fact that thinking is one thing and muttering quite another; that the feeling called anger has no resemblance to the bodily behavior which usually goes with it; or that an act of will is not in the least like anything we find when we open the skull and examine the brain. Certain mental events are doubtless

---

[2] Cf. Gardner Murphy, "Difficulties Confronting the Survival Hypothesis," *Journal of the American Society for Psychical Research* for April, 1945, p. 72; Corliss Lamont, "The Illusion of Immortality" (New York, 1935), pp. 26 ff.

[3] F. Paulsen, "Introduction to Philosophy" (trans. by F. Thilly, 2d ed.), pp. 82–83.

connected in some way with certain bodily events, but they are not those bodily events themselves. The connection is not identity.

This being clear, let us next consider the arguments offered to show that mental processes, although not identical with bodily processes, nevertheless depend on them. We are told, for instance, that some head injuries, or anesthetics, totally extinguish consciousness for the time being. As already pointed out, however, the strict fact is only that the usual bodily signs of consciousness are then absent. But they are also absent when a person is asleep; and, yet, at the same time, dreams, which are states of consciousness, may be occurring.

It is true that when the person concerned awakens, he often remembers his dreams, whereas the person that has been anesthetized or injured has usually no memories relating to the period of apparent blankness. But this could mean that his consciousness was, for the first time, dissociated from its ordinary channels of manifestation, as was reported of the co-conscious personalities of some of the patients of Dr. Morton Prince.[4] Moreover, it sometimes occurs that a person who has been in an accident reports lack of memories not only for the period during which his body was unresponsive but also for a period of several hours *before* the accident, during which he had given to his associates all the ordinary external signs of being conscious as usual.

But, more generally, if absence of memories relating to a given period proved unconsciousness for that period, this would force us to conclude that we were unconscious during the first few years of our lives, and indeed have been so most of the time since; for the fact is that we have no memories whatever of most of our days. That we were alive and conscious on any long past specific date is, with only a few exceptions, not something we actually remember, but only something which we infer must be true.

Evidence from Psychical Research

Another argument advanced against survival was, it will be remembered, that death must extinguish the mind, since all manifestations of it then cease. But to assert that they invariably then cease is to ignore altogether the considerable amount of evidence to the contrary, gathered over many years and carefully checked by the Society for Psychical Research.* This evidence, which is of a variety of kinds, has been reviewed by Professor Gardner Murphy in an article published in the Journal of the Society.[5] He mentions first the numerous well-authenticated cases of apparition of a dead person to others as yet unaware that he had died or even been ill or in danger. The more strongly evidential cases of apparition are those in which the apparition conveys to the person who

[4] "My Life as a Dissociated Personality" (edited by Morton Prince; Boston: Badger).
[5] An Outline of Survival Evidence," *Journal of the American Society for Psychical Research*, January, 1945.

*[The contention that cases of apparitions have been well authenticated is disputed by a number of scholars. See C. E. M. Hansel, *ESP: A Scientific Evaluation* (New York: Scribners, 1966) and Milbourne Christopher, *ESP, Seers & Psychics* (New York: Crowell, 1970).—Ed.]

sees it specific facts until then secret. An example would be that of the apparition of a girl to her brother nine years after her death, with a conspicuous scratch on her cheek. Their mother then revealed to him that she herself had made that scratch accidentally while preparing her daughter's body for burial, but that she had then at once covered it with powder and never mentioned it to anyone.

Another famous case is that of a father whose apparition some time after death revealed to one of his sons the existence and location of an unsuspected second will, benefiting him, which was then found as indicated. Still another case would be the report by General Barter, then a subaltern in the British Army in India, of the apparition to him of a lieutenant he had not seen for two or three years. The lieutenant's apparition was riding a brown pony with black mane and tail. He was much stouter than at their last meeting, and, whereas formerly clean-shaven, he now wore a peculiar beard in the form of a fringe encircling his face. On inquiry the next day from a person who had known the lieutenant at the time he died, it turned out that he had indeed become very bloated before his death; that he had grown just such a beard while on the sick list; and that he had some time before bought and eventually ridden to death a pony of that very description.

Other striking instances are those of an apparition seen simultaneously by several persons. It is on record that an apparition of a child was perceived first by a dog, that the animal's rushing at it, loudly barking, interrupted the conversation of the several persons present in the room, thus drawing their attention to the apparition, and that the latter then moved through the room for some fifteen seconds, followed by the barking dog.[6]

Another type of empirical evidence of survival consists of communications, purporting to come from the dead, made through the persons commonly called sensitives, mediums, or automatists. Some of the most remarkable of these communications were given by the celebrated American medium, Mrs. Piper, who for many years was studied by the Society for Psychical Research, London, with the most elaborate precautions against all possibility of fraud. Twice, particularly, the evidences of identity supplied by the dead persons who purportedly were thus communicating with the living were the very kinds, and of the same precision and detail, which would ordinarily satisfy a living person of the identity of another living person with whom he was not able to communicate directly, but only through an intermediary, or by letter or telephone.[7]

[6] The documents obtained by the Society for Psychical Research concerning this case, that of the lieutenant's apparition, and that of the girl with the scratch, are reproduced in Sir Ernest Bennett's "Apparitions and Haunted Houses" (London: Faber and Faber, 1945), pp. 334–337, 28–35, and 145–150 respectively.

[7] A summary of some of the most evidential facts may be found in the book by M. Sage, entitled "Mrs. Piper and the Society for Psychical Research" (New York: Scott-Thaw Co., 1904); others of them are related in some detail in Sir Oliver Lodge's "The Survival of Man," Sec. IV (New York: Moffat, Yard and Co., 1909) and in A. M. Robbins' "Both Sides of the Veil," Part II (Boston: Sherman, French, and Co., 1909). The fullest account is in the Proceedings of the Society for Psychical Research.

Again, sometimes the same mark of identity of a dead person, or the same message from him, or complementary parts of one message, are obtained independently from two mediums in different parts of the world.

Of course, when facts of these kinds are recounted, as I have just done, only in abstract summary, they make little if any impression upon us. And the very word "medium" at once brings to our minds the innumerable instances of demonstrated fraud perpetrated by charlatans to extract money from the credulous bereaved. But the modes of trickery and sources of error, which immediately suggest themselves to us as easy, natural explanations of the seemingly extraordinary facts, suggest themselves just as quickly to the members of the research committees of the Society for Psychical Research. Usually, these men have had a good deal more experience than the rest of us with the tricks of conjurers and fraudulent mediums, and take against them precautions far more strict and ingenious than would occur to the average sceptic.[8]

But when, instead of stopping at summaries, one takes the trouble to study the detailed, original reports, it then becomes evident that they cannot all be just laughed off; for to accept the hypothesis of fraud or malobservation would often require more credulity than to accept the facts reported.

To *explain* those facts, however, is quite another thing. Only two hypotheses at all adequate to do so have yet been advanced. One is that the communications really come, as they purport to do, from persons who have died and have survived death. The other is the hypothesis of telepathy—that is, the supposition, itself startling enough, that the medium is able to gather information directly from the minds of others, and that this is the true source of the information communicated. To account for all the facts, however, this hypothesis has to be stretched very far, for some of them require us to suppose that the medium can tap the minds even of persons far way and quite unknown to him, and can tap even the subconscious parts of their minds.

Diverse highly ingenious attempts have been made to devise conditions that would rule out telepathy as a possible explanation of the communications received; but some of the most critical and best-documented investigators still hold that it has not yet been absolutely excluded. Hence, although some of the facts recorded by psychical research constitute, prima facie, strong empirical evidence of survival, they cannot be said to establish it beyond question. But they do show that we need to revise rather radically in some respects our ordinary ideas of what is and is not possible in nature.

Can Mental States Cause Bodily Events?

Let us now turn to another of the arguments against survival. That states of consciousness entirely depend on bodily processes, and therefore

[8]Cf. H. Carrington, "The Psychical Phenomena of Spiritualism, Fraudulent and Genuine" (Boston: Small, Maynard & Co., 1908).

cannot continue when the latter have ceased, is proved, it is argued, by the fact that various states of consciousness—in particular, the several kinds of sensations—can be caused at will by appropriately stimulating the body.

Now, it is very true that sensations and some other mental states can be so caused; but we have just as good and abundant evidence that mental states can cause various bodily events. John Laird mentions, among others, the fact that merely willing to raise one's arm normally suffices to cause it to rise; that a hungry person's mouth is caused to water by the idea of food; that feelings of rage, fear or excitement cause digestion to stop; that anxiety causes changes in the quantity and quality of the milk of a nursing mother; that certain thoughts cause tears, pallor, blushing or fainting; and so on.[9] The evidence we have that the relation is one of cause and effect is exactly the same here as where bodily processes cause mental states.

It is said, of course, that to suppose something non-physical, such as thought, to be capable of causing motion of a physical object, such as the body, is absurd. But I submit that if the heterogeneity of mind and matter makes this absurd, then it makes equally absurd the causation of mental states by stimulation of the body. Yet no absurdity is commonly found in the assertion that cutting the skin causes a feeling of pain, or that alcohol, caffein, bromides, and other drugs, cause characteristic states of consciousness. As David Hume made clear long ago, no kind of causal connection is intrinsically absurd. Anything might cause anything; and only observation can tell us what in fact can cause what.

Somewhat similar remarks would apply to the allegation that the principle of the conservation of energy precludes the possibility of causation of a physical event by a mental event. For if it does, then it equally precludes causation in the converse direction, and this, of course, would leave us totally at a loss to explain the occurrence of sensations. But, as Keeton and others have pointed out,[10] that energy is conserved is not something observation has revealed or could reveal, but only a postulate— a defining postulate for the notion of an "isolated physical system."

That is, conservation of energy is something one has to have if, but only if, one insists on conceiving the physical world as wholly self-contained, independent, isolated. And just because the metaphysics which the natural sciences tacitly assume does insist on so conceiving the physical world, this metaphysics compels them to save conservation by postulations *ad hoc* whenever dissipation of energy is what observation reveals. It postulates, for instance, that something else, which appears at such times but was not until then regarded as energy, is energy too, but it is then said, "in a different form."

Furthermore, as Broad has emphasized, all that the principle of conservation requires is that when a quantity Q of energy disappears at one place in the physical world an equal quantity of it should appear at some other place there. And the supposition that, in some cases, what causes

[9] John Laird, "Our Minds and Their Bodies" (London, 1925), pp. 16–19.
[10] M. T. Keeton, "Some Ambiguities in the Theory of the Conservation of Energy," *Philosophy of Science*, Vol. 8, No. 3, July 1941.

it to disappear here and appear there is some mental event, such perhaps as a volition, does not violate at all the supposition that energy is conserved.[11]

A word, next, on the parallelism between the degree of development of the nervous systems of various animals and the degree of their intelligence. This is alleged to prove that the latter is the product of the former. But the facts lend themselves equally well to the supposition that, on the contrary, an obscurely felt need for greater intelligence in circumstances the animal faced was what brought about the variations which eventually resulted in a more adequate nervous organization.

In the development of the individual, at all events, it seems clear that the specific, highly complex nerve connections which become established in the brain and cerebellum of, for instance, a skilled pianist are the results of his will over many years to acquire the skill.

We must not forget in this context that there is a converse, equally consistent with the facts, for the theory, called epiphenomenalism, that mental states are related to the brain much as the halo is to the saint, that is, as effects but never themselves as causes. The converse theory, which might be called hypophenomenalism, and which is pretty well that of Schopenhauer, is that the instruments which the various mechanisms of the body constitute are the objective products of obscure cravings for the corresponding powers; and, in particular, that the organization of the nervous system is the effect and material isomorph of the variety of mental functions exercised at a given level of animal or human existence. . . .

---

[11] C. D. Broad, "The Mind and Its Place in Nature." pp. 103 ff.

Suggestions
for Further Reading

Anthologies

Anderson, Alan Ross (ed.). *Minds and Machines.* Englewood Cliffs, N.J.: Prentice-Hall, 1964. A collection of interesting contemporary articles on the question of whether men are machines. The articles are difficult but worthwhile reading.

Flew, Anthony (ed.). *Body, Mind, and Death.* New York: Macmillan, 1966. Some important articles on the mind-body problem from Plato to the present day. The introduction and annotated bibliography are excellent.

Hofstadter, Douglas R., and Daniel Dennett (eds.). *The Mind's I.* New York: Basic Books, 1981. Twenty-seven articles on artificial intelligence and the nature of mind with extensive comments by the editors.

Laslett, Peter (ed.). *The Physical Basis of the Mind.* Oxford: Basil Blackwell, 1951. A series of eight radio broadcasts given by British scientists and philosophers. The talks are very clear and interesting.

Individual Works

Adler, Mortimer. *The Difference of Man and the Difference It Makes.* Cleveland: World, 1967. The relation of the problem of the existence of mind to the issue of how men differ from animals. There is also a good discussion of whether men differ essentially from computing machines.

Beloff, John. *The Existence of Mind.* New York: Citadel, 1964. An examination of the arguments for and against dualism.

Dennett, Daniel C. *Brainstorms.* Montgomery, Vt.: Bradford Books, 1978. A series of provocative articles dealing with various aspects of the mind-body controversy.

Dreyfus, Hubert. *What Computers Can't Do: A Critique of Artificial Intelligence.* New York: Harper, 1972. An attack on the claim that computers can duplicate human intelligence.

Ducasse, C. J. *Nature, Mind, and Death.* LaSalle, Ill.: Open Court, 1951. A good discussion of the mind-body problem and its relation to the question of immortality.

Hospers, John. *An Introduction to Philosophical Analysis,* 2nd ed. Englewood Cliffs, N.J.: Prentice-Hall, 1967. Chapter 20 contains a very lucid statement of the main arguments and positions.

Lamont, Corliss. *The Illusion of Immortality,* 2nd ed. London: C. A. Watts, 1952. An attack on the belief in immortality. The book is clearly written but the arguments are not very rigorous.

Taylor, Richard. *Metaphysics,* 2nd ed. Englewood Cliffs, N.J.: Prentice-Hall, 1974. Chapters 2–4 provide a clear discussion of the mind-body controversy and a defense of materialism.

Shaffer, Jerome. *Reality, Knowledge, and Value.* New York: Random, 1971. Chapters 8–14 provide a very readable account of the main issues in the mind-body controversy.

Dictionary of the History of Ideas: Studies of Selected Pivotal Ideas. Philip P. Weiner, editor-in-chief. New York: Scribners, 1973. Substantial and clearly written essays emphasizing the historical development of topics discussed in this part. Designed to inform the nonspecialist, each essay concludes with a select bibliography.

Encyclopedia of Philosophy. Paul Edwards, editor-in-chief. New York: Macmillan, 1967. The student will find many worthwhile articles on the subject treated in this part and excellent bibliographies.

Six:
Knowledge
and Science

Introduction

All men want knowledge, admire it, even revere it. Platitudinous as this statement may appear, it is certainly ambiguous. No doubt this accounts for the fact that so many people think the statement true. For knowledge as something sought, as a value, suggests two quite different things: (1) knowledge as a good or end-in-itself independent of any use to which it may be put; (2) knowledge as a means necessary for the securing of some other value. We call men who dedicate themselves to the disinterested pursuit of knowledge, to the free play of ideas, "intellectuals," and "theoreticians." In this sense, philosophers traditionally have seen themselves and have been seen by others as superintellectuals, as the theoretician's theoretician. Historical legend has it that the first philosopher known to us, Thales of Miletus in Asia Minor (circa 585 B.C.), afflicted with the reproaches of his fellow citizens that he was a man of knowledge but also a poor man (and so what worth did knowledge have?), used his knowledge of nature to predict that the next crop of olives would be a bumper one. Keeping the practical results of his knowledge to himself, as would become a hardheaded businessman, Thales then bought up all of the olive presses in the region, thereby securing a monopoly for himself. When the unusually abundant harvest of olives duly took place, Thales rented out his olive presses at a high price and so made a large amount of money by cornering the market. Philosophers could make money if they wanted to do so, he reportedly declared, but willingly were poor because they valued knowledge above everything else, even wealth. No doubt Thales would never enroll in a business school; however, if he did, he would earn all A's.

Socrates refused to accept money for his teaching, not wishing to be financially dependent on anyone. (No wonder he scorned politicians.) Socrates distrusted wealth; for of what use is wealth but to stimulate and delight the senses, so sapping one's rational energies and distracting one's reason from the pursuit of truth. Refusing to stop asking questions as the price of life and freedom, condemned to death, drinking the hemlock, dying, Socrates has become a symbol of the fearless and unrelenting search for knowledge in spite of the opposition of the ignorant majority. The god Apollo announced that Socrates was the wisest man in Greece. Aristotle, the most influential philosopher in the Western world and the first great biologist, conceived man's highest destiny, because man is the only animal possessing reason, to be the full and unimpeded functioning of that reason, sheer knowing for its own sake. In knowing, man comes closest to being a god. If there are gods, knowing would be the only activity compatible with their exalted status. Practical activities, such as healing broken legs or multiplying loaves and fishes, would be beneath divine dignity. In the seventeenth century, the philosopher Spinoza equated God and Nature. In the glow of his own "intellectual love of God," Spinoza revealed how knowing the unchanging truth for its own sake can elicit all of the traditional religious emotions of devotion to what is greater and worthier than one's self and how knowing for its own sake can satisfy the old religious yearning for triumph over devouring time and for unshakable peace. The pursuit of knowledge as the ultimate Good thus emits cosmic, religious echoes. The devotees of knowing for its own sake have moved with a priestly mien whether they wore the toga or the white laboratory coat of the modern scientist. In our day, Albert Einstein is the symbol of the philosopher-scientist, the pure Knower, the inspired theoretician—Einstein, with the massive brow, the lined face, the flowing white hair suggesting a symphony conductor or other artist, and the luminous eyes through which the universe gazes into you.

Nevertheless, the pursuit of knowledge for its own sake evokes the supreme allegiance of only a small minority of Americans and people in other countries. The great majority values knowledge as technique, as knowhow, as a necessary means to other more important values, such as excitement and amusement. A little over a century ago, a Jewish prophet, who had read Greek and German philosophy, wrote that until his day philosophers had been content to understand the world but that the real task of philosophy was to change the world. Most Americans and all thoroughly modern people of other countries agree with Marx. The great majority of contemporary men and women prize knowledge as power, science as technology, as a kind of magic that works, a cornucopia pouring forth an unending and swelling stream of wealth with its attendant power and luxury. A small minority of intellectuals excepted, most contemporaries know very well what they want—wealth, power, luxury. For them, the problem concerns means: how to produce wealth, power, luxury, and all things dependent on them ever more abundantly. If the cost of that production means a polluted environment, chemically fouled lakes and streams, dying wildlife, and degraded human life, so far we have been willing to pay that cost. And should that cost become exorbitant, even deadly, we are sustained by the faith that the cure for the ills of technology is a bigger and better technology.

Only because science has shown itself so fecund in producing these goods and in progressively eliminating undesirable side effects has it been allowed to develop to its present level. For science, particularly on its theoretical side as a pursuit of knowledge for its own sake, was and is one of the most subversive agents ever invented by man. It is no coincidence that controversy whirls around the figures of Copernicus, Galileo, Darwin, Einstein, and Freud like black clouds rumbling with thunder and flashing with lightning. They symbolize the disturbing fact that science constantly shows us that the world and man really are quite different from what most people thought they were. Hence, for most people the value of knowing for its own sake must be subordinated to other values. Millions of Americans drive automobiles and at the same time reject the proposition that man is a mammal. The pursuit of knowledge is splendid, but such an enterprise must be compatible with national security. Of course we must hold all of our theories tentatively, but we know that any average American is superior in every way to any foreigner.

No, the great majority of men and women tolerate science, admire it, or revere it only to the degree and extent that science is a necessary means to various desired nonscientific ends. When science fails to provide the necessary means, people turn to kinds of "knowledge" other than the scientific. Does scientific psychology look dubiously upon extrasensory perception, does it cast doubt on the claim that those messages really came from beloved Uncle Max dead these many years? Then, scientific psychology is dogmatic, materialistic, too narrow, at best merely partial knowledge. If astronomy won't tell us if we will be lucky or unlucky today, then astrology will. Does science seem to make it difficult to believe God exists? Then our hearts inform us that he does exist. Does science fail to prove convincingly that we should all love one another and stop hating? Then mystical insight will.

This ambiguity of knowledge as an end for its own sake and as a means to realizing other values provides the humus out of which philosophical reflection on knowledge and science grows. Hence, philosophers study and discuss what they technically call *epistemology:* the investigation of the origin, nature, methods, and limits of knowledge. Philosophers wonder about and often answer such questions as: What is the nature of knowledge? What criteria distinguish genuine knowledge from the spurious article? Does all knowledge come from sense experience, or can our reason know that certain propositions must be true independently of sense experience? What is science? What is the scientific method? Is there a scientific method? Is all knowledge that is worthy of the name produced by science and science alone? Is there anything that science cannot find out? More radically, can we know anything at all or is it all merely a matter of shifting opinions, what we call "knowledge" being merely those illusions, or perhaps even delusions, agreed upon?

Obviously, there is no point in trying to find out something unless we doubt we know everything. Socrates claimed to know only that he did not know. Such doubting of the truth of what is claimed to be known, called *skepticism* in philosophy, can be made systematic and pushed farther than Socrates did. Some philosophers have universalized skepticism to include everything, maintaining that nothing exists; or that, if anything does exist, it cannot be known; or that, if anything can be known, it cannot be communicated. In order to be called a philosophy, skepticism must be defended with arguments. For example, consider the claim that we can never learn anything new. This conclusion follows from the proposition that we cannot find something unless we first know what we are looking for. Unless we know what we are seeking, we won't know when we have found it. Therefore, we only can find out what we already know, or we can never learn what we don't know. It is not recommended that students use this argument in answering examination questions. Add to the argument the observation that all men are born ignorant, and you generate the conclusion that no one can ever learn anything. You say you have learned many things? Then refute the argument of the skeptic, or admit that you have been deceived in thinking you've learned many things. The thoroughgoing skeptic argues that we never can be sure that any proposition is true because first we must have reliable criteria to distinguish truth from falsity. But how do we know that we can rely on the criteria? First, the criteria must be justified. But how do we know that we can rely on the justification of the criteria? First, the justification must be justified. And, before that, we must justify the justification of the justification. An infinite regress is generated—that is, no criteria separating truth from falsehood can ever be justified. There are many variations of this kind of argument. Our senses deceive us. Therefore, we appeal to our reason to tell us when our senses are or are not deceiving us. But first we must know whether or not our reason is deceiving us; and so the infinite regress opens before us. Again, some maintain we should only accept as true those propositions confirmed by observation. But why should we accept the principle that we should only accept as true those propositions confirmed by observation? And then why accept the additional principles used to justify that principle? And so on and on and on.

At first one might suppose naively that he could find refuge from the skeptic in divine revelation, mystical insight, or visions induced by LSD and other drugs. However, many of the revelations, insights, and visions contradict one another, to say nothing of common sense and science; and so the question of truth and falsity cannot be evaded permanently. Therefore, the skeptic patiently waits for our inevitable return.

And yet does there not remain one great practical and theoretical refutation of a universal skepticism? That is, does not the great body of modern science and its successful application nearly everywhere in contemporary life clearly prove that we can distinguish truth from falsehood, can know, and can learn?

In the steady light of science, the arguments of the skeptic seem to fade into mere verbal ingenuity, into sleight of hand with language. Indeed, the skeptical arguments, compared with the achievements of science, do not seem worth the trouble needed to expose clearly their logical fallacies. On the contrary, they can simply be dismissed as philosophical curiosities. Or can they?

In the first reading in this part, Bertrand Russell seeks to prove that skepticism finds renewed vigor and sustenance in the very citadel of science, its supposed conqueror. One of the greatest of recent philosophers, Russell throughout a long life sought knowledge for its own sake; he yearned for the Truth, Certainty. But Russell finds that science fails to supply the indubitable truth he seeks. All science ultimately rests on sense perception, on what we see, hear, smell, taste. All sense perception is a matter of cause and effect. All causes differ from their effects because otherwise all causes would be identical with their effects. Whatever we perceive (colors, sounds, smells, and so on) is an effect. Therefore, we never perceive causes. All causes are postulates, entities inferred by inductive reasoning. But in inductive reasoning (that is, any attempt to infer a conclusion on the basis of what we perceive), the evidence is never sufficient to prove the conclusion true beyond any doubt. The conclusion of an inductive argument always may be false. We can never be sure which scientific theories, if any, are true. Consequently, science does not vanquish skepticism, after all. The common, everyday world we perceive—the world of blue sky, green grass and trees, houses, substantial people, beautiful sunsets—turns out to be an illusion whose cause we never can be sure we know. Modern science agrees with Shakespeare's mellow skeptic, Prospero, in *The Tempest:* "We are such stuff as dreams are made on. . . . "

René Descartes, like Bertrand Russell, sought intellectual certainty. To know something is to be unable to doubt its truth. Hence, Descartes searches for a proposition he cannot doubt. If he can discover such a proposition, he can then examine it to learn what characteristics it possesses that make it impervious to any doubt. These characteristics will provide the criteria of certainty. Once we know these criteria of certainty, we can sort out all propositions that satisfy these criteria of certainty from those that do not. Descartes discovers he cannot, in the very act of doubting, doubt the proposition that he is doubting. Since doubting is a kind of thinking, Descartes declares: I think; therefore I am *(Cogito ergo sum.).* Why can't he doubt this? Because it is so clear and distinct to his reason. Clearness and distinctness to one's reason are the criteria of certainty. Descartes soon finds other propositions perfectly clear and distinct, such as: every event has a cause; no cause can be less perfect than its effect; and others. Mathematics, above all, is clear and distinct to our reason. Therefore, mathematical physics must be true. Whatever cannot be treated by mathematical physics must be relegated to the province of faith and subjective opinion. Notice that Descartes' criteria of certainty are clearness and distinctness to reason, not to sense perception. Descartes illustrates a form of philosophical *rationalism* that holds that there are some propositions our reason can know to be true independently of sense experience. Given our supply of propositions known to be true, we can then logically deduce still other propositions that must be true until all of human knowledge stands complete in one vast deductive system. Only in this way can the threat of universal skepticism be overcome successfully, the rationalist claims.

The issue now is focused sharply. Are there truths about the world that our reason can know independently of sense experience? The epistemological *rationalist* answers in the affirmative; the epistemological *empiricist* replies in the negative. John Locke's *Essay Concerning Human Understanding,* from which the selections by him in this book have been excerpted, is one of the great works of philosophy expounding and defending empiricism. Locke tries to work out an explanation of our knowledge in terms of sense experience. Locke's general conclusions about the extent and certainty of our claims to knowledge are much more modest than those of Descartes. Although Locke was willing to admit that we can be intuitively certain of our own existence and can rationally demonstrate God's existence, he claims that beyond these two exceptions we cannot obtain any indubitable information about the physical and spiritual worlds. To Locke, Descartes' ideal conception of science as an absolutely certain and complete understanding of the physical world must forever elude human beings, who therefore must rest content with their imperfect knowledge and accept their inevitable ignorance.

Locke claims that when we scrutinize our understanding, we discover, contrary to the claims of the rationalists, that we possess no innate ideas implanted in our minds and in the minds of all human beings prior to or independent of our sense experience. Rather, one finds that originally one's mind was just a "white paper, void of all characters, without any ideas." When we trace the ideas composing our knowledge back to their origins, we discern that they come from sense experience or from reflecting on the operations of our own minds. Locke divides all of our ideas into two classes: simple ideas and complex ideas. Simple ideas such as the coldness of ice are logically simple in that they are not compounded of any other elements. These simple ideas are presented to us only in sensation and reflection. However, the human mind also has the power to store up, repeat, and combine these simple ideas into complex ideas such as the idea of a city.

Locke faces a major difficulty: from an examination of ideas alone, how do we determine which of our ideas conform with realities outside of our minds and which are but the result of our imaginations? He attempts to resolve this difficulty by grouping our sensations into ideas of primary qualities and ideas of secondary qualities. Primary qualities such as size and shape belong to the objects that we are experiencing, whereas secondary qualities such as color do not belong to actual objects but are "powers" within them, enabling them to produce various sensations in us by their primary qualities, so that, for example, we see them as colored when in fact they have no color. Clearly Locke is trying to draw the distinction between the scientific description of an object—what properties scientists report an object has—and our ordinary experience of an object. Locke attempts to explain how we get our ideas of objects. We cannot conceive of simple ideas as existing without belonging to, or being attached to, some substance that either holds these qualities together or gives rise to them. However, no clear or precise notion of what these substances are can be given. Hence, we can have no certain knowledge of why substances produce the effects they do, only observations and probabilities. In spite of all the doubts raised by the skeptics and by Descartes, we can be pretty sure that some of our experiences are of things that exist outside of our minds, and others are not. Locke thinks we can be sure that all simple ideas represent something outside our minds. We cannot invent simple ideas because, being simple, they cannot be formed out of any ideas we already have. Therefore, they must be the effect of something outside us. Locke also believes we can be sure that secondary qualities are the results of some powers that external things have. Locke admits that it is possible that nothing exists outside our minds, that we're dreaming it all; nevertheless, he insists we have a common-sense assurance of the existence of an external, nonmental world. Although weaker than intuition or demonstration, common-sense experience is sufficient for science and everyday purposes.

"The Detective as Scientist" by Irving M. Copi, an outstanding contemporary logician, provides a clear and authoritative outline of the structure or logic of the process of inquiry that we have come to call "science" or "the scientific method," which has proven so increasingly successful since the seventeenth century. Copi's description reveals how scientific inquiry fruitfully combines elements from philosophic skepticism, rationalism, and empiricism without basing itself wholly on any one of these positions alone.

However, science is not only a problem-solving enterprise; it is a cultural phenomenon of enormous and growing importance. Deprived of science and scientific technologies, our lives would be transformed out of all recognition. Success breeds criticism. The achievement of science is no exception. We may live in a scientific age, as many claim or complain; nonetheless, critics and powerful enemies of science abound in contemporary life and, some fear, steadily mount in numbers and influence. They challenge the value of science, accuse it of doing more harm than good, and champion other methods of obtaining the truth as superior to that of science. In "The Limits and the Value of Scientific Method," two eminent American philosophers of science, Morris Cohen and Ernest Nagel, defend science as "the finest flower and test of a liberal civilization" against its critics and foes.

The contemporary issue of creationism versus evolution puts such abstract themes as the nature, limits, value, and place of science in today's society into concrete focus. Dr. Duane T. Gish, associate director of the Institute for Creation Research, argues that neither creation nor evolution is a valid scientific theory because they have never been observed by human witnesses, are not subject to the experimental method, and are incapable of falsification. He contends that not only are modern formulations of evolutionary mechanisms empty and in conflict with known natural laws, but that the fossil record both falsifies predictions based on evolutionary theory and confirms those of creationism. Dr. Gish urges that public education be reformed so that creation and evolution and the evidence for each are presented in textbooks and classrooms in place of what he sees as the current indoctrination of students in "a mechanistic, humanistic religious philosophy."

In "The Armies of the Night" Isaac Asimov, a biochemist and author of over 200 books, including works of science fiction and others on science, mathematics, history, and the Bible, attacks many of the assertions and arguments of the creationists. He views the advocates of creationism as a very serious threat to science and intellectual freedom, not as mere curiosities or clowns. After criticizing the familiar arguments to design and from common consent, Asimov argues that a scientific theory is not a guess or speculation, as creationists often suggest. He declares that ". . . no theory is better founded, more closely examined, more critically argued and more thoroughly accepted, than the theory of evolution." On the other hand, he writes, there is no scientific evidence supporting creationism; it is a myth—really the biblical story of creation disguised in scientific terminology. The so-called scientific case for creationism, Asimov charges, largely consists of a *non sequitur:* given the imperfections of the evolutionary view and the disagreements over its details among scientists, it does not follow logically that evolution is false and creationism true. The rest of the "scientific" defense of creationism depends on distortions of current science. According to Asimov, creationism long has been discredited in the free and open competition of ideas; but the creationists are poor losers and so are trying to use the government to impose the teaching of their rejected ideas on the public schools. If they actually were in favor of "equal time" for evolution and creationism, they would allow evolution to be taught in their churches. Asimov admits that the creationists might win their educational campaign in this country; but if they do, he prophesies, the United States will degenerate into a backwater among civilized nations.

The physicist John S. Trefil seeks not only to distinguish unorthodox science from pseudoscience but also to offer the "consumer" or scientific layman helpful tips on how to tell the difference. To confuse unorthodox science with pseudoscience would be to throw the baby of new ideas out with the bathwater of error. Novel ideas should be taken seriously; pseudoscientific ones should not be. Professional scientists assume this sound attitude. Trefil offers a brief checklist to aid the layman in appropriately adopting the same stance.

The American philosopher Paul Kurtz discerns a disturbing resurgence of public interest and even acceptance today of various forms of antiscientific and pseudoscientific irrationalism. He seeks to identify the major factors giving rise to this reactionary phenomenon. Although he notes the seemingly perennial conflict between science and religion, reason and passion, and various sociological and cultural theories, he emphasizes "profound psychological factors" and the "confusion about the meaning of science itself." He finds a "tendency toward gullibility" in the human species, a "fascination with mystery and drama," and a "quest for meaning." Antiscience and pseudoscience exploit and abuse these passions and needs. In order to defend ourselves against the seductive blandishments of antiscience and pseudoscience, in a sense to defend ourselves against ourselves, Kurtz recommends the cultivation of a general scientific atti-

tude toward all or most areas of life. There is nothing esoteric about such an attitude; it is continuous with common sense; it is simply critical intelligence in operation. Wherever we lack sufficient evidence for our beliefs, we should, if
possible, suspend judgment. Kurtz sees the basic question to be: How can we
develop this general scientific attitude? Our educational institutions must do
more than merely impart scientific knowledge in a rote manner; they must develop genuinely reflective persons who are skeptical, impartial, objective, free at
last of the Messianic delusion, and yet open to new ideas. Still, the human
yearning for mystery, drama, and meaning cannot be ignored. Man cannot live
by science alone. Kurtz suggests that these human longings can be satisfied by
a deliberate cultivation of the arts in such a way as to richly complement, rather
than destroy, critical intelligence and skepticism.

The Nature of Knowledge

Skepticism

43. Philosophic Doubts   Bertrand Russell

... Philosophy arises from an unusually obstinate attempt to arrive at real knowledge. What passes for knowledge in ordinary life suffers from three defects: it is cocksure, vague, and self-contradictory. The first step towards philosophy consists in becoming aware of these defects, not in order to rest content with a lazy scepticism, but in order to substitute an amended kind of knowledge which shall be tentative, precise, and self-consistent. There is of course another quality which we wish our knowledge to possess, namely, comprehensiveness: we wish the area of our knowledge to be as wide as possible. But this is the business of science rather than philosophy. A man does not necessarily become a better philosopher through knowing more scientific facts; it is principles and methods and general conceptions that he should learn from science if philosophy is what interests him. ...

I mentioned a moment ago three defects in common beliefs, namely, that they are cocksure, vague, and self-contradictory. It is the business of philosophy to correct these defects so far as it can, without throwing over knowledge altogether. To be a good philosopher, a man must have a strong desire to know, combined with great caution in believing that he knows; he must also have logical acumen and the habit of exact thinking. All these, of course, are a matter of degree. Vagueness, in particular, belongs, in some degree, to all human thinking; we can diminish it indefinitely, but we can never abolish it wholly. Philosophy, accordingly, is a continuing activity, not something in which we can achieve final perfection once for all. In this respect, philosophy has suffered from its association with theology. Theological dogmas are fixed, and are regarded by the orthodox as incapable of improvement. Philosophers have too often tried to produce similarly final systems: they have not been content with the gradual approximations that satisfied men of science. In this they seem to me to have been mistaken. Philosophy should be piecemeal and provisional like science; final truth belongs to heaven, not to this world.

The three defects which I have mentioned are interconnected, and by becoming aware of any one we may be led to recognise the other two. I will illustrate all three by a few examples.

Let us take first the belief in common objects, such as tables and chairs and trees. We all feel quite sure about these in ordinary life, and yet our reasons for confidence are really very inadequate. Naïve common sense supposes that they are what they appear to be, but that is impossible, since they do not appear exactly alike to any two simultaneous observers; at least, it is impossible if the object is a single thing, the same for all

From *An Outline of Philosophy* by Bertrand Russell. Reprinted by permission of George Allen & Unwin Ltd., London, 1927.

observers. If we are going to admit that the object is not what we see, we can no longer feel the same assurance that there is an object; this is the first intrusion of doubt. However, we shall speedily recover from this setback, and say that of course the object is "really" what physics says it is. Now physics says that a table or a chair is "really" an incredibly vast system of electrons and protons in rapid motion, with empty space in between. This is all very well. But the physicist, like the ordinary man, is dependent upon his senses for the existence of the physical world. If you go up to him solemnly and say, "Would you be so kind as to tell me, as a physicist, what a chair really is?" you will get a learned answer. But if you say, without preamble, "Is there a chair there?" he will say, "Of course there is; can't you see it?" To this you ought to reply in the negative. You ought to say, "No, I see certain patches of colour, but I don't see any electrons or protons, and you tell me that they are what a chair consists of." He may reply: "Yes, but a large number of electrons and protons close together look like a patch of colour." "What do you mean by 'look like'?" you will then ask. He is ready with an answer. He means that light-waves start from the electrons and protons (or, more probably, are reflected by them from a source of light), reach the eye, have a series of effects upon the rods and cones, the optic nerve, and the brain, and finally produce a sensation. But he has never seen an eye or an optic nerve or a brain, any more than he has seen a chair: he has only seen patches of colour which, he says, are what eyes "look like." That is to say, he thinks that the sensation you have when (as you think) you see a chair, has a series of causes, physical and psychological, but all of them, on his own showing, lie essentially and forever outside experience. Nevertheless, he pretends to base his science upon observation. Obviously there is here a problem for the logician, a problem belonging not to physics, but to quite another kind of study. This is a first example of the way in which the pursuit of precision destroys certainty.

The physicist believes that he infers his electrons and protons from what he perceives. But the inference is never clearly set forth in a logical chain, and, if it were, it might not look sufficiently plausible to warrant much confidence. In actual fact, the whole development from common-sense objects to electrons and protons has been governed by certain beliefs, seldom conscious, but existing in every natural man. These beliefs are not unalterable, but they grow and develop like a tree. We start by thinking that a chair is as it appears to be, and is still there when we are not looking. But we find, by a little reflection, that these two beliefs are incompatible. If the chair is to persist independently of being seen by us, it must be something other that the patch of colour we see, because this is found to depend upon conditions extraneous to the chair, such as how the light falls, whether we are wearing blue spectacles, and so on. This forces the man of science to regard the "real" chair as the cause (or an indispensable part of the cause) of our sensations when we see the chair. Thus we are committed to causation as an *a priori* belief without which we should have no reason for supposing that there is a "real" chair at all. Also, for the sake of permanence we bring in the notion of substance: the "real" chair is a substance, or collection of substances, possessed of permanence and the power to cause sensations. This metaphysical belief has operated, more or less unconsciously, in the inference from sensations to electrons and protons. The philosopher must drag such beliefs into the light of day, and see whether they still survive. Often it will be found that they die on exposure.

Let us now take up another point. The evidence for a physical law, or for any scientific law, always involves both memory and testimony. We have to rely both upon what we remember to have observed on former occasions, and on what others say they have observed. In the very beginnings of science, it may have been possible sometimes to dispense with testimony; but very soon every scientific investigation began to be built upon previously ascertained results, and thus to depend upon what others had recorded. In fact, without the corroboration of testimony we should hardly have had much confidence in the existence of physical objects. Sometimes people suffer from hallucinations, that is to say, they think they perceive physical objects, but are not confirmed in this belief by the testimony of others. In such cases, we decide that they are mistaken. It is the similarity between the perceptions of different people in similar situations that makes us feel confident of the external causation of our perceptions; but for this, whatever naïve beliefs we might have had in physical objects would have been dissipated long ago. Thus memory and testimony are essential to science. Nevertheless, each of these is open to criticism by the sceptic. Even if we succeed, more or less, in meeting his criticism, we shall, if we are rational, be left with a less complete confidence in our original beliefs than we had before. Once more, we shall become less cocksure as we become more accurate.

Both memory and testimony lead us into the sphere of psychology. I shall not at this stage discuss either beyond the point at which it is clear that there are genuine philosophical problems to be solved. I shall begin with memory.

Memory is a word which has a variety of meanings. The kind that I am concerned with at the moment is the recollection of past occurrences. This is so notoriously fallible that every experimenter makes a record of the result of his experiment at the earliest possible moment: he considers the inference from written words to past events less likely to be mistaken than the direct beliefs which constitute memory. But some time, though perhaps only a few seconds, must elapse between the observation and the making of the record, unless the record is so fragmentary that memory is needed to interpret it. Thus we do not escape from the need of trusting memory to some degree. Moreover, without memory we should not think of interpreting records as applying to the past, because we should not know that there was any past. Now, apart from arguments as to the proved fallibility of memory, there is one awkward consideration which the sceptic may urge. Remembering, which occurs now, cannot possibly—he may say—prove that what is remembered occurred at some other time, because the world might have sprung into being five minutes ago, exactly as it then was, full of acts of remembering which were entirely misleading. Opponents of Darwin, such as Edmund Gosse's father, urged a very similar argument against evolution. The world, they said, was created in 4004 B.C., complete with fossils, which were inserted to try our faith. The world was created suddenly, but was made such as it would have been if it had evolved. There is no logical impossibility about this view. And similarly there is no logical impossibility in the view that the world was created five minutes ago, complete with memories and records. This may seem an improbable hypothesis, but it is not logically refutable.

Apart from this argument, which may be thought fantastic, there are reasons of detail for being more or less distrustful of memory. It is obvious that no *direct* confirmation of a belief about a past occurrence is possible, because we cannot make the past recur. We can find confirmation of an indirect kind in the revelations of others and in contemporary records. The latter, as we have seen, involve some degree of memory, but they may involve very little, for instance when a shorthand report of a conversation or speech has been made at the time. But even then, we do not escape wholly from the need of memory extending over a longer stretch of time. Suppose a wholly imaginary conversation were produced for some criminal purpose, we should depend upon the memories of witnesses to establish its fictitious character in a law-court. And all memory which extends over a long period of time is very apt to be mistaken; this is shown by the errors invariably found in autobiographies. Any man who comes across letters which he wrote many years ago can verify the manner in which his memory has falsified past events. For these reasons, the fact that we cannot free ourselves from dependence upon memory in building up knowledge is, *prima facie,* a reason for regarding what passes for knowledge as not quite certain. . . .

Testimony raises even more awkward problems. What makes them so awkward is the fact that testimony is involved in building up our knowledge of physics, and that, conversely, physics is required in establishing the trustworthiness of testimony. Moreover, testimony raises all the problems connected with the relation of mind and matter. Some eminent philosophers, *e.g.* Leibniz, have constructed systems according to which there would be no such thing as testimony, and yet have accepted as true many things which cannot be known without it. I do not think philosophy has quite done justice to this problem, but a few words will, I think, show its gravity.

For our purposes, we may define testimony as noises heard, or shapes seen, analogous to those which we should make if we wished to convey an assertion, and believed by the hearer or seer to be due to someone else's desire to convey an assertion. Let us take a concrete instance: I ask a policeman the way, and he says, "Fourth to the right, third to the left." That is to say, I hear these sounds, and perhaps I see what I interpret as his lips moving. I assume that he has a mind more or less like my own, and has uttered these sounds with the same intention as I should have had if I had uttered them, namely to convey information. In ordinary life, all this is not, in any proper sense, an inference; it is a belief which arises in us on the appropriate occasion. But if we are challenged, we have to substitute inference for spontaneous belief, and the more the inference is examined the more shaky it looks.

The inference that has to be made has two steps, one physical and one psychological. The physical inference is the sort we considered a moment ago, in which we pass from a sensation to a physical occurrence.

We hear noises, and think they proceed from the policeman's body. We see moving shapes, and interpret them as physical motions of his lips. This inference, as we saw earlier, is in part justified by testimony; yet now we find that it has to be made before we can have reason to believe that there is any such thing as testimony. And this inference is certainly sometimes mistaken. Lunatics hear voices which other people do not hear; instead of crediting them with abnormally acute hearing, we lock them up. But if we sometimes hear sentences which have not proceeded from a body, why should this not always be the case? Perhaps our imagination has conjured up all the things that we think others have said to us. But this is part of the general problem of inferring physical objects from sensations, which, difficult as it is, is not the most difficult part of the logical puzzles concerning testimony. The most difficult part is the inference from the policeman's body to his mind. I do not mean any special insult to policemen; I would say the same of politicians and even of philosophers.

The inference to the policeman's mind certainly *may* be wrong. It is clear that a maker of waxworks could make a life-like policeman and put a gramophone inside him, which would cause him periodically to tell visitors the way to the most interesting part of the exhibition at the entrance to which he would stand. They would have just the sort of evidence of his being alive that is found convincing in the case of other policemen. Descartes believed that animals have no minds, but are merely complicated automata. Eighteenth-century materialists extended this doctrine to men. But I am not now concerned with materialism; my problem is a different one. Even a materialist must admit that, when he talks, he means to convey something, that is to say, he uses words as signs, not as mere noises. It may be difficult to decide exactly what is meant by this statement, but it is clear that it means something, and that it is true of one's own remarks. The question is: Are we sure that it is true of the remarks we hear, as well as of those we make? Or are the remarks we hear perhaps just like other noises, merely meaningless disturbances of the air? The chief argument against this is analogy: the remarks we hear are so like those we make that we think they must have similar causes. But although we cannot dispense with analogy as a form of inference, it is by no means demonstrative, and not infrequently leads us astray. We are therefore left, once more, with a *prima facie* reason for uncertainty and doubt.

This question of what we mean ourselves when we speak brings me to another problem, that of introspection. Many philosophers have held that introspection gave the most indubitable of all knowledge; others have held that there is no such thing as introspection. Descartes, after trying to doubt everything, arrived at "I think, therefore I am," as a basis for the rest of knowledge. Dr. John B. Watson the behaviourist holds, on the contrary, that we do not think, but only talk. Dr. Watson, in real life, gives as much evidence of thinking as anyone does, so, if *he* is not convinced that he thinks, we are all in a bad way. At any rate, the mere existence of such an opinion as his, on the part of a competent philosopher, must suffice to show that introspection is not so certain as some people have thought. But let us examine this question a little more closely.

The difference between introspection and what we call perception of external objects seems to me to be connected, not with what is primary in our knowledge, but with what is inferred. We think, at one time, that we are seeing a chair; at another, that we are thinking about philosophy. The first we call perception of an external object; the second we call introspection. Now we have already found reason to doubt external perception, in the full-blooded sense in which common sense accepts it. . . . [W]hat is indubitable in "seeing a chair" is the occurrence of a certain pattern of colours. But this occurrence, we shall find, is connected with me just as much as with the chair; no one except myself can see exactly the pattern that I see. There is thus something subjective and private about what we take to be external perception, but this is concealed by precarious extensions into the physical world. I think introspection, on the contrary, involves precarious extensions into the mental world; shorn of these, it is not very different from external perception shorn of its extensions. To make this clear, I shall try to show what we know to be occurring when, as we say, we think about philosophy.

Suppose, as the result of introspection, you arrive at a belief which you express in the words: "I am now believing that mind is different from matter." What do you know, apart from inferences, in such a case? First of all, you must cut out the word "I": the person who believes is an inference, not part of what you know immediately. In the second place, you must be careful about the word "believing." I am not now concerned with what this word should mean in logic or theory of knowledge; I am concerned with what it can mean when used to describe a direct experience. In such a case, it would seem that it can only describe a certain kind of feeling. And as for the proposition you think you are believing, namely, "mind is different from matter," it is very diffcult to say what is really occurring when you think you believe it. It may be mere words, pronounced, visualised, or in auditory or motor images of what the words "mean," but in that case it will not be at all an accurate representation of the logical content of the proposition. You may have an image of a statue of Newton "voyaging through strange seas of thought alone," and another image of a stone rolling downhill, combined with the words "how different!" Or you may think of the difference between composing a lecture and eating your dinner. It is only when you come to expressing your thought in words that you approach logical precision.

Both in introspection and in external perception, we try to express what we know in words.

We come here, as in the question of testimony, upon the social aspect of knowledge. The purpose of words is to give the same kind of publicity to thought as is claimed for physical objects. A number of people can hear a spoken word or see a written word, because each is a physical occurrence. If I say to you, "mind is different from matter," there may be only a very slight resemblance between the thought that I am trying to express and the thought which is aroused in you, but these two thoughts have just this in common, that they can be expressed by the same words. Similarly, there may be great differences between what you and I see when, as we say, we look at the same chair; nevertheless we can both express our perceptions by the same words.

A thought and a perception are thus not so very different in their own nature. If physics is true, they are different in their correlations: when I see a chair, others have more or less similar perceptions, and it is thought that these are all connected with light-waves coming from the chair, whereas, when I think a thought, others may not be thinking anything similar. But this applies also to feeling a toothache, which would usually be regarded as a case of introspection. On the whole, therefore, there seems no reason to regard introspection as a different *kind* of knowledge from external perception. . . .

As for the *trustworthiness* of introspection, there is again a complete parallelism with the case of external perception. The actual datum, in each case, is unimpeachable, but the extensions which we make instinctively are questionable. Instead of saying, "I am believing that mind is different from matter," you ought to say, "certain images are occurring in a certain relation to each other, accompanied by a certain feeling." No words exist for describing the actual occurrence in all its particularity; all words, even proper names, are general, with the possible exception of "this," which is ambiguous. When you translate the occurrence into words, you are making generalisations and inferences, just as you are when you say "there is a chair." There is really no vital difference between the two cases. In each case, what is really a datum is unutterable, and what can be put into words involves inferences which may be mistaken.

When I say that "inferences" are involved, I am saying something not quite accurate unless carefully interpreted. In "seeing a chair," for instance, we do not first apprehend a coloured pattern, and then proceed to infer a chair: belief in the chair arises spontaneously when we see the coloured pattern. But this belief has causes not only in the present physical stimulus, but also partly in past experience, partly in reflexes. In animals, reflexes play a very large part; in human beings, experience is more important. The infant learns slowly to correlate touch and sight, and to expect others to see what he sees. The habits which are thus formed are essential to our adult notion of an object such as a chair. The perception of a chair by means of sight has a physical stimulus which affects only sight directly, but stimulates ideas of solidity and so on through early experience. The inference might be called "physiological." As inference of this sort is evidence of past correlations, for instance between touch and sight, but may be mistaken in the present instance; you may, for example, mistake a reflection in a large mirror for another room. Similarly in dreams we make mistaken physiological inferences. We cannot therefore feel certainty in regard to things which are in this sense inferred, because, when we try to accept as many of them as possible, we are nevertheless compelled to reject some for the sake of self-consistency.

We arrived a moment ago at what we called "physiological inference" as an essential ingredient in the common-sense notion of a physical object. Physiological inference, in its simplest form, means this: given a stimulus S, to which, by a reflex, we react by a bodily movement R, and a stimulus S′ with a reaction R′, if the two stimuli are frequently experienced together, S will in time produce R'.[1] This is to say, the body will act as if S' were present. Physiological inference is important in theory of knowledge. . . . I have mentioned it partly to prevent it from being confused with logical inference, and partly in order to introduce the problem of *induction.* . . .

Induction raises perhaps the most difficult problem in the whole theory of knowledge. Every scientific law is established by its means, and yet it is difficult to see why we should believe it to be a valid logical process. Induction, in its bare essence, consists of the argument that, because A and B have been often found together and never found apart, therefore, when A is found again, B will probably also be found. This exists first as a "physiological inference," and as such is practised by animals. When we first begin to reflect, we find ourselves making inductions in the physiological sense, for instance, expecting the food we see to have a certain kind of taste. Often we only become aware of this expectation through having it disappointed, for instance if we take salt thinking it is sugar. When mankind took to science, they tried to formulate logical principles justifying this kind of inference. . . . [T]hey seem to me very unsuccessful. I am convinced that induction must have validity of some kind in some degree, but the problem of showing how or why it can be valid remains unsolved. Until it is solved, the rational man will doubt whether his food will nourish him, and whether the sun will rise tomorrow. I am not a rational man in this sense, but for the moment I shall pretend to be. And even if we cannot be completely rational, we should probably all be the better for becoming somewhat more rational than we are. At the lowest estimate, it will be an interesting adventure to see whither reason will lead us.

The problems we have been raising are none of them new, but they suffice to show that our everyday views of the world and of our relations to it are unsatisfactory. . . .

Rationalism

44. Meditations I and II   René Descartes

René Descartes (1596–1650), inventor of analytic geometry and one of the greatest of French philosophers, has affected profoundly the problems, methods, and solutions of modern philosophy.

Meditation I

Of the Things of Which We May Doubt.   Several years have now elapsed since I first became aware that I had accepted, even from my youth,

From *The Meditations and Selections from the Principles of René Descartes,* translated by John Veitch, The Open Court Publishing Co., La Salle, Illinois, 1905.

[1] *E.g.* if you hear a sharp noise and see a bright light simultaneously, often, in time, the noise without the light will cause your pupils to contract.

many false opinions for true, and that consequently what I afterwards based on such principles was highly doubtful; and from that time I was convinced of the necessity of undertaking once in my life to rid myself of all the opinions I had adopted, and of commencing anew the work of building from the foundation, if I desired to establish a firm and abiding superstructure in the sciences. But as this enterprise appeared to me to be one of great magnitude. I waited until I had attained an age so mature as to leave me no hope that at any stage of life more advanced I should be better able to execute my design. On this account, I have delayed so long that I should henceforth consider I was doing wrong were I still to consume in deliberation any of the time that now remains for action. Today, then, since I have opportunely freed my mind from all cares, and am happily disturbed by no passions, and since I am in the secure possession of leisure in a peaceable retirement, I will at length apply myself earnestly and freely to the general overthrow of all my former opinions. But, to this end, it will not be necessary for me to show that the whole of these are false—a point, perhaps, which I shall never reach; but as even now my reason convinces me that I ought not the less carefully to withhold belief from what is not entirely certain and indubitable, than from what is manifestly false, it will be sufficient to justify the rejection of the whole if I shall find in each some ground for doubt. Nor for this purpose will it be necessary even to deal with each belief individually, which would be truly an endless labour; but, as the removal from below of the foundation necessarily involves the downfall of the whole edifice, I will at once approach the criticism of the principles on which all my former beliefs rested.

All that I have, up to this moment, accepted as possessed of the highest truth and certainty, I received either from or through the senses. I observed however, that these sometimes misled us; and it is the part of prudence not to place absolute confidence in that by which we have even once been deceived.

But it may be said, perhaps that, although the senses occasionally mislead us respecting minute objects, and such as are so far removed from us as to be beyond the reach of close observation, there are yet many other of their informations (presentations), of the truth of which it is manifestly impossible to doubt; as for example, that I am in this place, seated by the fire clothed in a winter dressing-gown, that I hold in my hands this piece of paper, with other intimations of the same nature. But how could I deny that I possess these hands and this body, and withal escape being classed with persons in a state of insanity, whose brains are so disordered and clouded by dark bilious vapours as to cause them pertinaciously to assert that they are monarchs when they are in the greatest poverty; or clothed in gold and purple when destitute of any covering; or that their head is made of clay, their body of glass, or that they are gourds? I should certainly be not less insane than they, were I to regulate my procedure according to examples so extravagant.

Though this be true, I must nevertheless here consider that I am a man, and that, consequently, I am in the habit of sleeping, and representing to myself in dreams those same things, or even sometimes others less probable, which the insane think are presented to them in their waking moments. How often have I dreamt that I was in these familiar circumstances,—that I was dressed, and occupied this place by the fire, when I was lying undressed in bed? At the present moment, however, I certainly look upon this paper with eyes wide awake; the head which I now move is not asleep; I extend this hand consciously and with express purpose, and I perceive it; the occurrences in sleep are not so distinct as all this. But I cannot forget that, at other times, I have been deceived in sleep by similar illusions; and, attentively considering those cases, I perceive so clearly that there exist no certain marks by which the state of waking can ever by distinguished from sleep, that I feel greatly astonished; and in amazement I almost persuade myself that I am now dreaming.

Let us suppose, then, that we are dreaming, and that all these particulars—namely, the opening of the eyes, the motion of the head, the forthputting of the hands—are merely illusions; and even that we really possess neither an entire body nor hands such as we see. Nevertheless, it must be admitted at least that the objects which appear to us in sleep are, as it were, painted representations which could not have been formed unless in the likeness of realities; and, therefore, that those general objects, at all events,—namely, eyes, a head, hands, and an entire body—are not simply imaginary, but really existent. For, in truth, painters themselves, even when they study to represent sirens and satyrs by forms the most fantastic and extraordinary, cannot bestow upon them natures absolutely new, but can only make a certain medley of the members of different animals; or if they chance to imagine something so novel that nothing at all similar has ever been before, and such as is, therefore, purely fictitious and absolutely false, it is at least certain that the colours of which this is composed are real.

And on the same principle, although these general objects, viz. a body, eyes, a head, hands, and the like, be imaginary, we are nevertheless absolutely necessitated to admit the reality at least of some other objects still more simple and universal than these, of which, just as of certain real colours, all those images of things, whether true and real, or false and fantastic, that are found in our consciousness, are formed.

To this class of objects seem to belong corporeal nature in general and its extension; the figure of extended things, their quantity or magnitude, and their number, as also the place in, and the item during, which they exist, and other things of the same sort. We will not, therefore, perhaps reason illegitimately if we conclude from this that Physics, Astronomy, Medicine, and all the other sciences that have for their end the consideration of composite objects, are indeed of a doubtful character; but that Arithmetic, Geometry, and the other sciences of the same class, which regard merely the simplest and most general objects, and scarcely inquire whether or not these are really existent, contain somewhat that is certain and indubitable; for whether I am awake or dreaming, it remains true that two and three makes five, and that a square has but four sides; nor does it seem possible that truths so apparent can ever fall under a suspicion of falsity or incertitude.

Nevertheless, the belief that there is a God who is all-powerful, and who created me, such as I am, has, for a long time, obtained steady possession of my mind. How, then, do I know that he has not arranged that there should be neither earth, nor sky, nor any extended thing, nor figure, nor magnitude, nor place, providing at the same time, however, for the rise in me of the perceptions of all these objects, and the persuasion that these do not exist otherwise that as I perceive them? And further, as I sometimes think that others are in error respecting matters of which they believe themselves to possess a perfect knowledge, how do I know that I am not also deceived each time I add together two and three, or number the sides of a square, or form some judgment still more simple, if more simple indeed can be imagined? But perhaps Deity has not been willing that I should be thus deceived, for He is said to be supremely good. If, however, it were repugnant to the goodness of Deity to have created me subject to constant deception, it would seem likewise to be contrary to this goodness to allow me to be occasionally deceived; and yet it is clear that this is permitted. Some, indeed, might perhaps be found who would be disposed rather to deny the existence of a Being so powerful than to believe that there is nothing certain. But let us for the present refrain from opposing this opinion, and grant that all which is here said of a Deity is fabulous; nevertheless in whatever way it be supposed that I reached the state in which I exist, whether by fate, or chance, or by an endless series of antecedents and consequents, or by any other means, it is clear (since to be deceived and to err is a certain defect) that the probability of my being so imperfect as to be the constant victim of deception, will be increased exactly in proportion as the power possessed by the cause, to which they assign my origin, is lessened. To these reasonings I have assuredly nothing to reply, but am constrained at last to avow that there is nothing of all that I formerly believed to be true of which it is impossible to doubt, and that not through thought-lessness or levity, but from cogent and maturely considered reasons; so that henceforward, if I desire to discover anything certain, I ought not the less carefully to refrain from assenting to those same opinions than to what might be shown to be manifestly false.

But it is not sufficient to have made these observations; care must be taken likewise to keep them in remembrance. For those old and customary opinions perpetually recur—long and familiar usage giving them the right to occupying my mind, even almost against my will, and subduing my belief; nor will I lose the habit of deferring to them and confiding in them so long as I shall consider them to be what in truth they are, viz., opinions to some extent doubtful, as I have already shown, but still highly probable, and such as it is much more reasonable to believe than deny. It is for this reason I am persuaded that I shall not be doing wrong, if, taking an opposite judgment of deliberate design, I become my own deceiver, by supposing, for a time, that all those opinions are entirely false and imaginary, until at length, having thus balanced my old by my new prejudices, my judgment shall no longer be turned aside by perverted usage from the path that may conduct to the perception of truth. For I am assured that, meanwhile, there will arise neither peril nor error from this course, and that I cannot for the present yield too much distrust, since the end I now seek is not action but knowledge.

I will suppose, then, not that Deity, who is sovereignly good and the fountain of truth, but that some malignant demon, who is at once exceedingly potent and deceitful, has employed all his artifice to deceive me; I will suppose that the sky, the air, the earth, colours, figures, sounds, and all external things, are nothing better than the illusions of dreams, by means of which this being has laid snares for my credulity; I will consider myself as without hands, eyes, flesh, blood, or any of the senses, and as falsely believing that I am possessed of these; I will continue resolutely fixed in this belief, and if indeed by this means it be not in my power to arrive at the knowledge of truth, I shall at least do what is in my power, viz., suspend by judgment, and guard with settled purpose against giving my assent to what is false, and being imposed upon by this deceiver, whatever by his power and artifice.

But this undertaking is arduous, and a certain indolence insensibly leads me back to my ordinary course of life; and just as the captive, who, perchance, was enjoying in his dreams an imaginary liberty; when he begins to suspect that it is but a vision, dreads awakening, and conspires with the agreeable illusions that the deception may be prolonged; so I, of my own accord, fall back into the train of my former beliefs, and fear to arouse myself from my slumber, lest the time of laborious wakefulness that would succeed this quiet rest, in place of bringing any light of day, should prove inadequate to dispel the darkness that will arise from the difficulties that have now been raised.

Meditation II

Of the Nature of the Human Mind; and That It Is More Easily Known Than the Body.   The Meditation of yesterday has filled my mind with so many doubts, that it is no longer in my power to forget them. Nor do I see, meanwhile, any principle on which they can be resolved; and, just as if I had fallen all of a sudden into very deep water, I am so greatly disconcerted as to be unable either to plant my feet firmly on the bottom or sustain myself by swimming on the surface, I will, nevertheless, make an effort, and try anew the same path on which I had entered yesterday, that is, proceed by casting aside all that admits of the slightest doubt, not less than if I had discovered it to be absolutely false; and I will continue always in this track until I shall find something that is certain, or at least, if I can do nothing more, until I shall know with certainty that there is nothing certain. Archimedes, that he might transport the entire globe from the place it occupied to another, demanded only a point that was firm and immovable; so also, I shall be entitled to entertain the highest expectations, if I am fortunate enough to discover only one thing that is certain and indubitable.

I suppose, accordingly, that all the things which I see are false (fictitious); I believe that none of those objects which my fallacious memory represents ever existed; I suppose that I possess no senses; I believe that body, figure, extension, motion, and place are merely fictions of my mind.

What is there, then, that can be esteemed true? Perhaps this only, that there is absolutely nothing certain.

But how do I know that there is not something different altogether from the objects I have now enumerated, of which it is impossible to entertain the slightest doubt? Is there not a God, or some being, by whatever name I may designate him, who causes these thoughts to arise in my mind? But why suppose such a being, for it may be I myself am capable of producing them? Am I, then, at least not something? But I before denied that I possessed senses or a body; I hesitate, however, for what follows from that? Am I so dependent on the body and the senses that without these I cannot exist? But I had the persuasion that there was absolutely nothing in the world, that there was no sky and no earth, neither minds nor bodies; was I not, therefore, at the same time, persuaded that I did not exist? Far from it; I assuredly existed, since I was persuaded. But there is I know not what being, who is possessed at once of the highest power and the deepest cunning, who is constantly employing all his ingenuity in deceiving me. Doubtless, then, I exist, since I am deceived; and, let him deceive me as he may, he can never bring it about that I am nothing, so long as I shall be conscious that I am something. So that it must, in fine, be maintained, all things being maturely and carefully considered, that this proposition, I am, I exist, is necessarily true each time it is expressed by me, or conceived in my mind.

But I do not yet know with sufficient clearness what I am, though assured that I am; and hence, in the next place, I must take care, lest perchance I inconsiderately substitute some other object in the room for what is properly myself, and thus wander from truth, even in that knowledge which I hold to be of all others the most certain and evident. For this reason, I will now consider anew what I formerly believed myself to be, before I entered on the present train of thought; and of my previous opinion I will retrench all that can in the least be invalidated by the grounds of doubt I have adduced, in order that there may at length remain nothing but what is certain and indubitable. What then did I formerly think I was? Undoubtedly I judged that I was a man. But what is a man? Shall I say a rational animal? Assuredly not; for it would be necessary forthwith to inquire into what is meant by animal, and what by rational, and thus, from a single question, I should insensibly glide into others, and these more difficult than the first; nor do I now possess enough of leisure to warrant me in wasting my time amid subtleties of this sort. I prefer here to attend to the thoughts that sprung up of themselves in my mind, and were inspired by my own nature alone, when I applied myself to the consideration of what I was. In the first place, then, I thought that I possessed a countenance, hands, arms, and all the fabric of members that appears in a corpse, and which I called by the name of body. It further occurred to me that I was nourished, that I walked, perceived, and thought, and all those actions I referred to the soul; but what the soul itself was I either did not stay to consider, or, if I did, I imagined that it was something extremely rare and subtile, like wind, or flame, or ether, spread through my grosser parts. As regarded the body, I did not even doubt of its nature, but thought I distinctly knew it, and if I had wished to describe it according to the notions I then entertained, I should have explained myself in this manner: By body I understand all that can be terminated by a certain figure; that can be comprised in a certain place, and so fill a certain space as therefrom to exclude every other body; that can be perceived either by touch, sight, hearing, taste, or smell; that can be moved in different ways, not indeed of itself, but by something foreign to it by which it is touched and from which it receives the impression; for the power of self-motion, as likewise that of perceiving and thinking, I held as by no means pertaining to the nature of body; on the contrary, I was somewhat astonished to find such faculties existing in some bodies.

But as to myself, what can I now say that I am, since I suppose there exists an extremely powerful, and, if I may so speak, malignant being, whose whole endeavours are directed towards deceiving me? Can I affirm that I possess any one of all those attributes of which I have lately spoken as belonging to the nature of body? After attentively considering them in my own mind, I find none of them that can properly be said to belong to myself. To recount them were idle and tedious. Let us pass, then, to the attributes of the soul. The first mentioned were the powers of nutrition and walking; but, if it be true that I have no body, it is true likewise that I am capable neither of walking nor of being nourished. Perception is another attribute of the soul; but perception too is impossible without the body: besides, I have frequently during sleep, believed that I perceived objects which I afterwards observed I did not in reality perceive. Thinking is another attribute of the soul; and here I discover what properly belongs to myself. This alone is inseparable from me. I am—I exist: this is certain; but how often? As often as I think for perhaps it would even happen, if I should wholly cease to think, that I should at the same time altogether cease to be. I now admit nothing that is not necessarily true: I am therefore, precisely speaking, only a thinking thing, that is, a mind, understanding, or reason,—terms whose signification was before unknown to me. I am, however, a real thing, and really existent; but what thing? The answer was, a thinking thing. The question now arises, am I aught besides? I will stimulate my imagination with a view to discover whether I am not still something more than a thinking being. Now it is plain I am not the assemblage of members called the human body; I am not a thin and penetrating air diffused through all these members, or wind, or flame, or vapour, or breath, or any of all things I can imagine; for I supposed that all these were not, and, without changing the supposition, I find that I still feel assured of my existence.

But it is true, perhaps, that those very things which I suppose to be nonexistent, because they are unknown to me, are not in truth different from myself whom I know. This is a point I cannot determine, and do not now enter into any dispute regarding it. I can only judge of things that are known to me: I am conscious that I exist, and I who know that I exist inquire into what I am. It is, however, perfectly certain that the knowledge of my existence, thus precisely taken, is not dependent on things, the existence of which is as yet unknown to me: and consequently it is not dependent on any of the things I can feign in imagination. Moreover, the phrase itself, I frame an image, reminds me of my error; for I should in truth frame one if I were to imagine myself to be anything, since to imagine is nothing more than to contemplate the figure or image of a corporeal thing; but I already know that I exist, and that it is possible at the same time that all those images, and in general all that relates to the nature of body, are merely dreams or chimeras. From this I discover that it is not more reasonable to say, I will excite my imagination that I may know more distinctly what I am, than to express myself as follows: I am now awake, and perceive something real; but because my perception is not sufficiently clear, I will of express purpose go to sleep that my dreams may represent to me the object of my perception with more truth and clearness. And, therefore, I know that nothing of all that I can embrace in imagination belongs to the knowledge which I have of myself, and that there is need to recall with the utmost care the mind from this mode of thinking, that it may be able to know its own nature with perfect distinctness.

But what, then, am I? A thinking thing, it has been said. But what is a thinking thing? It is a thing that doubts, understands, conceives, affirms, denies, wills, refuses, that imagines also, and perceives. Assuredly it is not little, if all these properties belong to my nature. But why should they not belong to it? Am I not that very being who now doubts of almost everything; who, for all that, understands and conceives certain things; who affirms one alone as true, and denies the others; who desires to know more of them, and does not wish to be deceived; who imagines many things, sometimes even despite his will; and is likewise percipient of many, as if through the medium of the senses. Is there nothing of all this as true as that I am, even although I should be always dreaming, and although he who gave me being employed all his ingenuity to deceive me? Is there also any one of these attributes that can be properly distinguished from my thought, or that can be said to be separate from myself? For it is of itself so evident that it is I who doubt, I who understand, and I who desire, that it is here unnecessary to add anything by way of rendering it more clear. And I am as certainly the same being who imagines; for, although it may be (as I before supposed) that nothing I imagine is true, still the power of imagination does not cease really to exist in me and to form part of my thought. In fine, I am the same being who perceives, that is, who apprehends certain objects as by the organs of sense, since, in truth, I see light, hear a noise, and feel heat. But it will be said that these presentations are false, and that I am dreaming. Let it be so. At all events it is certain that I seem to see light, hear a noise, and feel heat; this cannot be false, and this is what in me is properly called perceiving, which is nothing else than thinking. From this I begin to know what I am with somewhat greater clearness and distinctness than heretofore.

But, nevertheless, it still seems to me, and I cannot help believing, that corporeal things, whose images are formed by thought, which fall under the senses, and are examined by the same, are known with much greater distinctness than that I know what part of myself which is not imaginable; although, in truth, it may seem strange to say that I know and comprehend with greater distinctness things whose existence appears to me doubtful, that are unknown, and do not belong to me, than others of whose reality I am persuaded, that are known to me, and appertain to my proper nature; in a word, than myself. But I see clearly what is the state of the case. My mind is apt to wander, and will not yet submit to be restrained within the limits of truth. Let us therefore leave the mind to itself once more, and, according to it every kind of liberty, permit it to consider the objects that appear to it from without, in order that, having afterwards withdrawn it from these gently and opportunely, and fixed it on the consideration of its being and the properties it finds in itself, it may then be the more easily controlled.

Let us now accordingly consider the objects that are commonly thought to be the most easily, and likewise the most distinctly known, viz., the bodies we touch and see; not, indeed, bodies in general, for these general notions are usually somewhat more confused, but one body in particular. Take, for example, this piece of wax; it is quite fresh, having been but recently taken from the bee-hive; it has not yet lost the sweetness of the honey it contained; it still retains somewhat of the odour of the flowers from which it was gathered; its colour, figure, size, are apparent to the sight, it is hard, cold, easily handled; and sounds when struck upon with the finger. In fine, all that contributes to make a body as distinctly known as possible, is found in the one before us. But, while I am speaking, let it be placed near the fire—what remained of the taste exhales, the smell evaporates, the colour changes, its figure is destroyed, its size increases, it becomes liquid, it grows hot, it can hardly be handled, and, although struck upon, it emits no sound. Does the same wax still remain after this change? It must be admitted that it does remain; no one doubts it or judges otherwise. What, then, was it I knew with so much distinctness in the piece of wax? Assuredly, it could be nothing of all that I observed by means of the senses, since all the things that fell under taste, smell, sight, touch, and hearing are changed, and yet the same wax remains. It was perhaps what I now think, viz., that this wax was neither the sweetness of honey, the pleasant odour of flowers, the whiteness, the figure, nor the sound, but only a body that a little before appeared to me conspicuous under these forms, and which is now perceived under others. But, to speak precisely, what is it that I imagine when I think of it in this way? Let it be attentively considered, and, retrenching all that does not belong to the wax, let us see what remains. There certainly remains nothing, except something extended, flexible, and movable. But what is meant by flexible and movable? Is it not that I imagine that the piece of wax, being round, is capable of becoming square, or of passing from a square into a triangular figure? Assuredly such is not the case, because I conceive that it admits of an infinity of similar changes; and I am, moreover, unable to compass this infinity by imagination, and consequently this conception which I have of the wax is not the product of the faculty of imagination. But what now is this extension? Is it not also unknown? For it becomes greater when the wax is melted, greater when it is boiled, and greater still when the heat increases; and I should not conceive clearly and according to truth, the wax as it is, if I did not suppose that the piece we are considering admitted even of a wider variety of extension that I ever imagined. I must, therefore, admit that I cannot even comprehend by imagination what the piece of wax is, and that it is the mind alone which perceives it. I speak of one piece in particular; for, as to wax in general, this is still more evident. But what is the piece of wax that can be perceived only by the understanding or mind? It is certainly the same which I see, touch, imagine; and, in fine, it is the same which, from the beginning, I believed it to be. But (and this it is of moment to observe) the perception of it is neither an act of sight, of touch, nor of imagination, and never was either of these, though it might formerly seem so, but is simply an intuition of the mind, which may be imperfect and confused, as it formerly was, or very clear and distinct, as it is at present, according as the attention is more or less directed to the elements which it contains, and of which it is composed.

But, meanwhile, I feel greatly astonished when I observe the weakness of my mind, and its proneness to error. For although, without at all giving expression to what I think, I consider all this in my own mind, words yet occasionally impede my progress, and I am almost led into error by the terms of ordinary language. We say, for example, that we see the same wax when it is before us, and not that we judge it to be the same from its retaining the same colour and figure; whence I should forthwith be disposed to conclude that the wax is known by the act of sight, and not by the intuition of the mind alone, were it not for the analogous instance of human beings passing on in the street below, as observed from a window. In this case I do not fail to say that I see the men themselves, just as I say that I see the wax; and yet what do I see from the windows beyond hats and cloaks that might cover artificial machines, whose motions might be determined by springs? But I judge that there are human beings from these appearances, and thus I comprehend, by the faculty of judgment alone which is in the mind, what I believed I saw with my eyes.

The man who makes it his aim to rise to knowledge superior to the common, ought to be ashamed to seek occasions of doubting from the vulgar forms of speech: instead, therefore, of doing this, I shall proceed with the matter in hand, and inquire whether I had a clearer and more perfect perception of the piece of wax when I first saw it, and when I thought I knew it by means of the external sense itself, or, at all events, by the common sense, as it is called, that is, by the imaginative faculty; or whether I rather apprehend it more clearly at present, after having examined with greater care, both what it is, and in what way it can be known. It would certainly be ridiculous to entertain any doubt on this point. For what, in that first perception, was there distinct? What did I perceive which any animal might not have perceived? But when I distinguish the wax from its exterior forms, and when, as if I had stripped it of its vestments, I consider it quite naked, it is certain, although some error may still be found in my judgment, that I cannot, nevertheless, thus apprehend it without possessing a human mind.

But, finally, what shall I say of the mind itself, that is, of myself? For as yet I do not admit that I am anything but mind. What, then! I who seem to possess so distinct an apprehension of the piece of wax,—do I not know myself, both with greater truth and certitude, and also much more distinctly and clearly? For if I judge that the wax exists because I see it, it assuredly follows, much more evidently, that I myself am or exist, for the same reason: for it is possible that what I see may not in truth be wax, and that I do not even possess eyes with which to see anything; but it cannot be that when I see, or, which comes to the same thing, when I think I see, I myself who think am nothing. So likewise, if I judge that the wax exists because I touch it, it will still also follow that I am; and if I determine that my imagination, or any other cause, whatever it be, persuades me of the existence of the wax, I will still draw the same conclusion. And what is here remarked of the piece of wax, is applicable to all the other things that are external to me. And further, if the notion or perception of wax appeared to me more precise and distinct, after that not only sight and touch, but many other causes besides, rendered it manifest to my apprehension, with how much greater distinctions must I not know myself, since all the reasons that contribute to the knowledge of the nature of wax, or of any body whatever, manifest still better the nature of my mind? And there are besides so many other things in the mind itself that contribute to the illustration of its nature, that those dependent on the body, to which I have here referred, scarcely merit to be taken into account.

But, in conclusion, I find I have insensibly reverted to the point I desired; for, since it is now manifest to me that bodies themselves are not properly perceived by the senses nor by the faculty of imagination, but by the intellect alone; and since they are not perceived because they are seen and touched, but only because they are understood or rightly comprehended by thought, I readily discover that there is nothing more easily or clearly apprehended than my own mind. But because it is difficult to rid one's self so promptly of an opinion to which one has been long accustomed, it will be desirable to tarry for some time at this stage, that, by long continued meditation, I may more deeply impress upon my memory this new knowledge.

Empiricism

45. An Empiricist Outlook   John Locke

John Locke (1632–1704) taught philosophy and the classics at Oxford University until he earned a medical degree and became a physician. A member of a group fighting for the overthrow of the government, he was forced to flee England in 1683 because of his subversive activities. While in exile Locke wrote his *Essay Concerning Human Understanding*. With the success of the Glorious Revolution of 1688, he returned to England from Holland and received a government job. However, he spent most of his time defending his philosophical views.

Introduction

1. Since it is the *understanding* that sets man above the rest of sensible beings, and gives him all the advantage and dominion which he has over them; it is certain a subject, even for its nobleness, worth our labour to inquire into. The understanding, like the eye, whilst it makes us see and perceive all other things, takes no notice of itself; and it requires art and pains to set it at a distance and make it its own object. But whatever be the difficulties that lie in the way of this inquiry; whatever it be that keeps us so much in the dark to ourselves; sure I am that all the light we can let in upon our minds, all the acquaintance we can make with our own understandings, will not only be very pleasant, but bring us great advantage, in directing our thoughts in the search of other things.

2. This, therefore, being my purpose—to inquire into the original, certainty, and extent of *human knowledge,* together with the grounds and degrees of *belief, opinion,* and *assent;*—I shall not at present meddle with the physical consideration of the mind; or trouble myself to examine wherein its essence consists; or by what motions of our spirits or alterations of our bodies we come to have any *sensation* by our organs, or any *ideas* in our understandings; and whether those ideas do in their formation, any or all of them, depend on matter or not. These are speculations which, however curious and entertaining, I shall decline, as lying out of my way in the design I am now upon. It shall suffice to my present purpose, to consider the discerning faculties of a man, as they are employed about the objects which they have to do with. And I shall imagine I have not wholly misemployed myself in the thoughts I shall have on this occasion, if, in this historical, plain method, I can give any account of the ways whereby our understandings come to attain those notions of things we have; and can set down any measures of the certainty of our knowledge; or the grounds of those persuasions which are to be found amongst men, so various, different, and wholly contradictory; and yet asserted somewhere or other with such assurance and confidence, that he that shall take a view of the opinions of mankind, observe their opposition, and at the same time consider the fondness and devotion wherewith they are embraced, the resolution and eagerness wherewith they are maintained, may perhaps have reason to suspect, that either there is no such thing as truth at all, or that mankind hath no sufficient means to attain a certain knowledge of it.

3. It is therefore worth while to search out the bounds between opinion and knowledge; and examine by what measures, in things whereof we have no certain knowledge, we ought to regulate our assent and moderate our persuasion. In order whereunto I shall pursue this following method:—

First, I shall inquire into the original of those *ideas,* notions, or whatever else you please to call them, which a man observes, and is conscious to himself he has in his mind; and the ways whereby the understanding comes to be furnished with them.

From *An Essay Concerning Human Understanding* by John Locke (1690).

Secondly, I shall endeavour to show what *knowledge* the understanding hath by those ideas; and the certainty, evidence, and extent of it.

Thirdly, I shall make some inquiry into the nature and grounds of *faith* or *opinion:* whereby I mean that assent which we give to any proposition as true, of whose truth yet we have no certain knowledge. And here we shall have occasion to examine the reasons and degrees of *assent.*

4. If by this inquiry into the nature of the understanding, I can discover the powers thereof; how far they reach; to what things they are in any degree proportionate; and where they fail us, I suppose it may be of use to prevail with the busy mind of man to be more cautious in meddling with things exceeding its comprehension; to stop when it is at the utmost extent of its tether; and to sit down in a quiet ignorance of those things which, upon examination, are found to be beyond the reach of our capacities. We should not then perhaps be so forward, out of an affectation of an universal knowledge, to raise questions, and perplex ourselves and others with disputes about things to which our understandings are not suited; and of which we cannot frame in our minds any clear or distinct perceptions, or whereof (as it has perhaps too often happened) we have not any notions at all. If we can find out how far the understanding can extend its view; how far it has faculties to attain certainty; and in what cases it can only judge and guess, we may learn to content ourselves with what is attainable by us in this state.

5. For though the comprehension of our understandings comes exceeding short of the vast extent of things, yet we shall have cause enough to magnify the bountiful Author of our being, for that proportion and degree of knowledge he has bestowed on us, so far above all the rest of the inhabitants of this our mansion. Men have reason to be well satisfied with what God hath thought fit for them, since he hath given them (as St. Peter says) πάντα πρὸς ζωὴν καὶ εὐσέβειαν, whatsoever is necessary for the conveniences of life and information of virtue; and has put within the reach of their discovery, the comfortable provision for this life, and the way that leads to a better. How short soever their knowledge may come of an universal or perfect comprehension of whatsoever is, it yet secures their great concernments, that they have light enough to lead them to the knowledge of their Maker, and the sight of their own duties. Men may find matter sufficient to busy their heads, and employ their hands with variety, delight, and satisfaction, if they will not boldly quarrel with their own constitution, and throw away the blessings their hands are filled with, because they are not big enough to grasp everything. We shall not have much reason to complain of the narrowness of our minds, if we will but employ them about what may be of use to us; for of that they are very capable. And it will be an unpardonable, as well as childish peevishness, if we undervalue the advantages of our knowledge, and neglect to improve it to the ends for which it was given us, because there are some things that are set out of the reach of it. It will be no excuse to an idle and untoward servant, who would not attend his business by candle light, to plead that he had not broad sunshine. The Candle that is set up in us shines bright enough for all our purposes. The discoveries we can make with this ought to satisfy us; and we shall then use our

understandings right, when we entertain all objects in that way and proportion that they are suited to our faculties, and upon those grounds
they are capable of being proposed to us; and not peremptorily or in-
temperately require demonstration, and demand certainty, where probability only is to be had, and which is sufficient to govern all our concernments. If we will disbelieve everything, because we cannot certainly
know all things, we shall do muchwhat as wisely as he who would not
use his legs; but sit still and perish, because he had no wings to fly.

6. When we know our own strength, we shall the better know what
to undertake with hopes of success; and when we have well surveyed
the *powers* of our own minds, and made some estimate what we may
expect from them, we shall not be inclined either to sit still, and not set
our thoughts on work at all, in despair of knowing anything; nor on the
other side, question everything, and disclaim all knowledge, because some
things are not to be understood. It is of great use to the sailor to know
the length of his line, though he cannot with it fathom all the depths of
the ocean. It is well he knows that it is long enough to reach the bottom,
at such places as are necessary to direct his voyage, and caution him
against running upon shoals that may ruin him. Our business here is
not to know all things, but those which concern our conduct. If we can
find out these measures, whereby a rational creature, put in that state
in which man is in this world, may and ought to govern his opinions,
and actions depending thereon, we need not to be troubled that some
other things escape our knowledge.

7. This was that which gave the first rise to this *Essay* concerning the
understanding. For I thought that the first step towards satisfying several
inquiries the mind of man was very apt to run into, was, to take a survey
of our own understanding, examine our own powers, and see to what
things they were adapted. Till that was done I suspected we began at
the wrong end, and in vain sought for satisfaction in a quiet and sure
possession of truths that most concerned us, whilst we let loose our
thoughts into the vast ocean of Being; as if all that boundless extent were
the natural and undoubted possession of our understandings, wherein
there was nothing exempt from its decisions, or that escaped its comprehension. Thus men, extending their inquiries beyond their capacities,
and letting their thoughts wander into those depths where they can find
no sure footing, it is no wonder that they raise questions and multiply
disputes, which, never coming to any clear resolution, are proper only
to continue and increase their doubts, and to confirm them at last in
perfect scepticism. Whereas, were the capacities of our understandings
well considered, the extent of our knowledge once discovered, and the
horizon found which sets the bounds between the enlightened and dark
parts of things; between what is and what is not comprehensible by us,
men would perhaps with less scruple acquiesce in the avowed ignorance
of the one, and employ their thoughts and discourse with more advantage
and satisfaction in the other.

8. Thus much I thought necessary to say concerning the occasion of
this Inquiry into human Understanding. But, before I proceed on to
what I have thought on this subject, I must here in the entrance beg
pardon of my reader for the frequent use of the word *idea*, which he

will find in the following treatise. It being that term which, I think, serves best to stand for whatsoever is the *object* of the understanding when a man thinks, I have used it to express whatever is meant by *phantasm, notion, species,* or *whatever it is which the mind can be employed about in thinking;* and I could not avoid frequently using it.

I presume it will be easily granted me, that there are such *ideas* in men's minds: every one is conscious of them in himself; and men's words and actions will satisfy him that they are in others.

Our first inquiry then shall be,—how they come into the mind.

No Innate Speculative Principles

1. It is an established opinion amongst some men, that there are in the understanding certain *innate principles;* some primary notions, κοιναὶ ἔννοιαι, characters, as it were stamped upon the mind of man; which the soul receives in its very first being, and brings into the world with it. It would be sufficient to convince unprejudiced readers of the falseness of this supposition, if I should only show (as I hope I shall in the following parts of this Discourse) how men, barely by the use of their natural faculties, may attain to all the knowledge they have, without the help of any innate impressions; and may arrive at certainty, without any such original notions or principles. For I imagine any one will easily grant that it would be impertinent to suppose the ideas of colours innate in a creature to whom God hath given sight, and a power to receive them by the eyes from external objects: and no less unreasonable would it be to attribute several truths to the impressions of nature, and innate characters, when we may observe in ourselves faculties fit to attain as easy and certain knowledge of them as if they were originally imprinted on the mind.

But because a man is not permitted without censure to follow his own thoughts in the search of truth, when they lead him ever so little out of the common road, I shall set down the reasons that made me doubt of the truth of that opinion, as an excuse for my mistake, if I be in one; which I leave to be considered by those who, with me, dispose themselves to embrace truth wherever they find it.

2. There is nothing more commonly taken for granted than that there are certain *principles,* both *speculative* and *practical,* (for they speak of both), universally agreed upon by all mankind: which therefore, they argue, must needs be the constant impressions which the souls of men receive in their first beings, and which they bring into the world with them, as necessarily and really as they do any of their inherent faculties.

3. This argument, drawn from universal consent, has this misfortune in it, that if it were true in matter of fact, that there were certain truths wherein all mankind agreed, it would not prove them innate, if there can be any other way shown how men may come to that universal agreement, in the things they do consent in, which I presume may be done.

4. But, which is worse, this argument of universal consent, which is made use of to prove innate principles, seems to me a demonstration that there are none such: because there are none to which all mankind give an universal assent. I shall begin with the speculative, and instance

in those magnified principles of demonstration, 'Whatsoever is, is,' and 'It is impossible for the same thing to be and not to be'; which, of all others, I think have the most allowed title to innate. These have so settled a reputation of maxims universally received, that it will no doubt be thought strange if any one should seem to question it. But yet I take liberty to say, that these propositions are so far from having an universal assent, that there are a great part of mankind to whom they are not so much as known.

5. For, first, it is evident, that all children and idiots have not the least apprehension or thought of them. And the want of that is enough to destroy that universal assent which must needs be the necessary concomitant of all innate truths: it seeming to me near a contradiction to say, that there are truths imprinted on the soul, which it perceives or understands not: imprinting, if it signify anything, being nothing else but the making certain truths to be perceived. For to imprint anything on the mind without the mind's perceiving it, seems to me hardly intelligible. If therefore children and idiots have souls, have minds, with those impressions upon them, *they* must unavoidably perceive them, and necessarily know and assent to these truths; which since they do not, it is evident that there are no such impressions. For if they are not notions naturally imprinted, how can they be innate? and if they are notions imprinted, how can they be unknown? To say a notion is imprinted on the mind, and yet at the same time to say, that the mind is ignorant of it, and never yet took notice of it, is to make this impression nothing. No proposition can be said to be in the mind which it never yet knew, which it was never yet conscious of. For if any one may, then, by the same reason, all propositions that are true, and the mind is capable ever of assenting to, may be said to be in the mind, and to be imprinted: since, if any one can be said to be in the mind, which it never yet knew, it must be only because it is capable of knowing it; and so the mind is of all truths it ever shall know. Nay, thus truths may be imprinted on the mind which it never did, nor ever shall know; for a man may live long, and die at last in ignorance of many truths which his mind was capable of knowing, and that with certainty. So that if the capacity of knowing be the natural impression contended for, all the truths a man ever comes to know will, by this account, be every one of them innate; and this great point will amount to no more, but only to a very improper way of speaking; which, whilst it pretends to assert the contrary, says nothing different from those who deny innate principles. For nobody, I think, ever denied that the mind was capable of knowing several truths. The capacity, they say, is innate; the knowledge acquired. But then to what end such contest for certain innate maxims? If truths can be imprinted on the understanding without being perceived, I can see no difference there can be between any truths the mind is *capable* of knowing in respect of their original: they must all be innate or all adventitious: in vain shall a man go about to distinguish them. He therefore that talks of innate notions in the understanding, cannot (if he intend thereby any distinct sort of truths) mean such truths to be in the understanding as it never perceived, and is yet wholly ignorant of. For if these words 'to

be in the understanding' have any propriety, they signify to be understood. So that to be in the understanding, and not to be understood; to
be in the mind and never to be perceived, is all one as to say anything
is and is not in the mind or understanding. If therefore these two propositions, 'Whatsoever is, is,' and 'It is impossible for the same thing to
be and not to be,' are by nature imprinted, children cannot be ignorant
of them: infants, and all that have souls, must necessarily have them in
their understandings, know the truth of them, and assent to it.

6. To avoid this, it is usually answered, that all men know and assent
to them, *when they come to the use of reason;* and this is enough to prove
them innate. I answer:

7. Doubtful expressions, that have scarce any significance, go for clear
reasons to those who, being prepossessed, take not the pains to examine
even what they themselves say. For, to apply this answer with any tolerable
sense to our present purpose, it must signify one of these two things:
either that as soon as men come to the use of reason these supposed
native inscriptions come to be known and observed by them; or else,
that the use and exercise of men's reason, assists them in the discovery
of these principles, and certainly makes them known to them.

8. If they mean, that by the use of reason men may discover these
principles, and that this is sufficient to prove them innate; their way of
arguing will stand thus, viz. that whatever truths reason can certainly
discover to us, and make us firmly assent to, those are all naturally imprinted on the mind; since that universal assent, which is made the mark
of them, amounts to no more but this,—that by the use of reason we are
capable to come to a certain knowledge of and assent to them; and, by
this means, there will be no difference between the maxims of the mathematicians, and theorems they deduce from them: all must be equally
allowed innate; they being all discoveries made by the use of reason, and
truths that a rational creature may certainly come to know, if he apply
his thoughts rightly that way.

9. But how can these men think the use of reason necessary to discover
principles that are supposed innate, when reason (if we may believe them)
is nothing else but the faculty of deducing unknown truths from principles or propositions that are already known? That certainly can never
be thought innate which we have need of reason to discover; unless as
I have said, we will have all the certain truths that reason ever teaches
us, to be innate. We may as well think the use of reason necessary to
make our eyes discover visible objects, as that there should be need to
reason, or the exercise thereof, to make the understanding see what is
originally engraven on it, and cannot be in the understanding before it
be perceived by it. So that to make reason discover those truths thus
imprinted, is to say, that the use of reason discovers to a man what he
knew before: and if men have those innate impressed truths originally,
and before the use of reason, and yet are always ignorant of them till
they come to the use of reason, it is in effect to say, that men know and
know them not at the same time.

10. It will here perhaps be said that mathematical demonstrations,
and other truths that are not innate, are not assented to as soon as pro-

posed, wherein they are distinguished from these maxims and other innate truths. I shall have occasion to speak of assent upon the first proposing, more particularly by and by. I shall here only, and that very readily, allow, that these maxims and mathematical demonstrations are in this different: that the one have need of reason, using of proofs, to make them out and to gain our assent; but the other, as soon as understood, are, without any the least reasoning, embraced and assented to. But I withal beg leave to observe, that it lays open the weakness of this subterfuge, which requires the use of reason for the discovery of these general truths: since it must be confessed that in their discovery there is no use made of reasoning at all. And I think those who give this answer will not be forward to affirm that the knowledge of this maxim, 'That it is impossible for the same thing to be and not to be,' is a deduction of our reason. For this would be to destroy that bounty of nature they seem so fond of, whilst they make the knowledge of those principles to depend on the labour of our thoughts. For all reasoning is search, and casting about, and requires pains and application. And how can it with any tolerable sense be supposed, that what was imprinted by nature, as the foundation and guide of our reason, should need the use of reason to discover it?

11. Those who will take the pains to reflect with a little attention on the operations of the understanding, will find that this ready assent of the mind to some truths, depends not, either on native inscription, or the use of reason, but on a faculty of the mind quite distinct from both of them, as we shall see hereafter. Reason, therefore, having nothing to do in procuring our assent to these maxims, if by saying, that 'men know and assent to them, when they come to the use of reason,' be meant, that the use of reason assists us in the knowledge of these maxims, it is utterly false; and were it true, would prove them not to be innate.

12. If by knowing and assenting to them 'when we come to the use of reason,' be meant, that this is the time when they come to be taken notice of by the mind; and that as soon as children come to the use of reason, they come also to know and assent to these maxims; this also is false and frivolous. First, it is false; because it is evident these maxims are not in the mind so early as the use of reason; and therefore the coming to the use of reason is falsely assigned as the time of their discovery. How many instances of the use of reason may we observe in children, a long time before they have any knowledge of this maxim, 'That it is impossible for the same thing to be and not to be?' And a great part of illiterate people and savages pass many years, even of their rational age, without ever thinking on this and the like general propositions. I grant, men come not to the knowledge of these general and more abstract truths, which are thought innate, till they come to the use of reason; and I add, nor then neither. Which is so, because, till after they come to the use of reason, those general abstract ideas are not framed in the mind, about which those general maxims are, which are mistaken for innate principles, but are indeed discoveries made and verities introduced and brought into the mind by the same way, and discovered by the same steps, as several other propositions, which nobody

was ever so extravagant as to suppose innate. This I hope to make plain in the sequel of this Discourse. I allow therefore, a necessity that men should come to the use of reason before they get the knowledge of those general truths; but deny that men's coming to the use of reason is the time of their discovery.

13. In the mean time it is observable, that this saying, that men know and assent to these maxims 'when they come to the use of reason,' amounts in reality of fact to no more but this,—that they are never known nor taken notice of before the use of reason, but may possibly be assented to some time after, during a man's life; but when is uncertain. And so may all other knowable truths, as well as these; which therefore have no advantage nor distinction from others by this note of being known when we come to the use of reason; nor are thereby proved to be innate, but quite the contrary.

14. But, secondly, were it true that the precise time of their being known and assented to were, when men come to the use of reason; neither would that prove them innate. This way of arguing is as frivolous as the supposition itself is false. For, by what kind of logic will it appear that any notion is originally by nature imprinted in the mind in its first constitution, because it comes first to be observed and assented to when a faculty of the mind, which has quite a distinct province, begins to exert itself? And therefore the coming to the use of speech, if it were supposed the time that these maxims are first assented to, (which it may be with as much truth as the time when men come to the use of reason,) would be as good a proof that they were innate, as to say they are innate because men assent to them when they come to the use of reason. I agree then with these men of innate principles, that there is knowledge of these general and self-evident maxims in the mind, till it comes to the exercise of reason: but I deny that the coming to the use of reason is the precise time when they are first taken notice of; and if that were the precise time, I deny that it would prove them innate. All that can with any truth be meant by this proposition, that men 'assent to them when they come to the use of reason,' is no more but this,—that the making of general abstract ideas, and the understanding of general names, being a concomitant of the rational faculty, and growing up with it, children commonly get not those general ideas, nor learn the names that stand for them, till, having for a good while exercised their reason about familiar and more particular ideas, they are, by their ordinary discourse and actions with others, acknowledged to be capable of rational conversation. If assenting to these maxims, when men come to the use of reason, can be true in any other sense, I desire it may be shown; or at least, how in this, or any other sense, it proves them innate.

15. The senses at first let in *particular* ideas, and furnish the yet empty cabinet, and the mind by degrees growing familiar with some of them, they are lodged in the memory, and names got to them. Afterwards, the mind proceeding further, abstracts them, and by degrees learns the use of general names. In this manner the mind comes to be furnished with ideas and language, the *materials* about which to exercise its discursive faculty. And the use of reason becomes daily more visible, as these ma-

terials that give it employment increase. But though the having of general ideas and the use of general words and reason usually grow together, yet I see not how this any way proves them innate. The knowledge of some truths, I confess, is very early in the mind; but in a way that shows them not to be innate. For, if we will observe, we shall find it still to be about ideas, not innate, but acquired; it being about those first which are imprinted by external things, with which infants have earliest to do, which make the most frequent impressions on their senses. In ideas thus got, the mind discovers that some agree and others differ, probably as soon as it has any use of memory; as soon as it is able to retain and perceive distinct ideas. But whether it be then or no, this is certain, it does so long before it has the use of words; or comes to that which we commonly call 'the use of reason.' For a child knows as certainly before it can speak the difference between the ideas of sweet and bitter (i.e. that sweet is not bitter), as it knows afterwards (when it comes to speak) that wormwood and sugarplums are not the same thing. . . .

Of Ideas in General and Their Original

1. Every man being conscious to himself that he thinks; and that which his mind is applied about whilst thinking being the *ideas* that are there, it is past doubt that men have in their minds several ideas,—such as are those expressed by the words *whiteness, hardness, sweetness, thinking, motion, man, elephant, army, drunkenness,* and others: it is in the first place then to be inquired, *How he comes by them?*

I know it is a received doctrine, that men have native ideas, and original characters, stamped upon their minds in their very first being. This opinion I have at large examined already: and, I suppose what I have said in the foregoing Book will be much more easily admitted, when I have shown whence the understanding may get all the ideas it has; and by what ways and degrees they may come into the mind;—for which I shall appeal to every one's own observation and experience.

2. Let us then suppose the mind to be, as we say, white paper, void of all characters, without any ideas:—How comes it to be furnished? Whence comes it by that vast store which the busy and boundless fancy of man has painted on it with an almost endless variety? Whence has it all the *materials* of reason and knowledge? To this I answer, in one word, from EXPERIENCE. In that all our knowledge is founded; and from that it ultimately derives itself. Our observation employed either, about external sensible objects, or about the internal operations of our minds perceived and reflected on by ourselves, is that which supplies our understandings with all the *materials* of thinking. These two are the fountains of knowledge, from whence all the ideas we have, or can naturally have, do spring.

3. First, our Senses, conversant about particular sensible objects, do convey into the mind several distinct perceptions of things, according to those various ways wherein those objects do affect them. And thus we come by those *ideas* we have of *yellow, white, heat, cold, soft, hard, bitter, sweet,* and all those which we call sensible qualities; which when I say the

senses convey into the mind, I mean, they from external objects convey into the mind what produces there those perceptions. This great source of most of the ideas we have, depending wholly upon our senses, and derived by them to the understanding, I call SENSATION.

4. Secondly, the other fountain from which experience furnisheth the understanding with ideas is,—the perception of the operations of our own mind within us, as it is employed about the ideas it has got;—which operations, when the soul comes to reflect on and consider, do furnish the understanding with another set of ideas, which could not be had from things without. And such are *perception, thinking, doubting, believing, reasoning, knowing, willing,* and all the different actings of our own minds;—which we being conscious of, and observing in ourselves, do from these receive into our understandings as distinct ideas as we do from bodies affecting our senses. This source of ideas every man has wholly in himself; and though it be not sense, as having nothing to do with external objects, yet it is very like it, and might properly enough be called *internal sense.* But as I call the other Sensation, so I call this REFLECTION, the ideas it affords being such only as the mind gets by reflecting on its own operations within itself. By reflection then, in the following part of this discourse, I would be understood to mean, that notice which the mind takes of its own operations, and the manner of them, by reason whereof of there come to be ideas of these operations in the understanding. These two, I say, viz. external material things, as the objects of SENSATION, and the operations of our own minds within, as the objects of REFLECTION, are to me the only originals from whence all our ideas take their beginnings. The term *operations* here I use in a large sense, as comprehending not barely the actions of the mind about its ideas, but some sort of passions arising sometimes from them, such as is the satisfaction or uneasiness arising from any thought.

5. The understanding seems to me not to have the least glimmering of any ideas which it doth not receive from one of these two. *External objects* furnish the mind with the ideas of sensible qualities, which are all those different perceptions they produce in us; and *the mind* furnishes the understanding with ideas of its own operations.

These, when we have taken a full survey of them, and their several modes, [combinations, and relations,] we shall find to contain all our whole stock of ideas; and that we have nothing in our minds which did not come in one of these two ways. Let any one examine his own thoughts, and thoroughly search into his understanding; and then let him tell me, whether all the original ideas he has there, are any other than of the objects of his senses, or of the operations of his mind, considered as objects of his reflection. And how great a mass of knowledge soever he imagines to be lodged there, he will, upon taking a strict view, see that he has not any idea in his mind but what one of these two have imprinted;—though perhaps, with infinite variety compounded and enlarged by the understanding, as we shall see hereafter.

6. He that attentively considers the state of a child, at his first coming into the world, will have little reason to think him stored with plenty of ideas, that are to be the matter of his future knowledge. It is *by degrees*

he comes to be furnished with them. And though the ideas of obvious and familiar qualities imprint themselves before the memory begins to keep a register of time or order, yet it is often so late before some unusual qualities come in the way, that there are few men that cannot recollect the beginning of their acquaintance with them. And if it were worth while, no doubt a child might be so ordered as to have but a very few, even of the ordinary ideas, till he were grown up to a man. But all that are born into the world, being surrounded with bodies that perpetually and diversely affect them, variety of ideas, whether care be taken of it or not, are imprinted on the minds of children. Light and colours are busy at hand everywhere, when the eye is but open; sounds and some tangible qualities fail not to solicit their proper senses, and force an entrance to the mind;—but yet, I think, it will be granted easily, that if a child were kept in a place where he never saw any other but black and white till he were a man, he would have no more ideas of scarlet or green, than he that from his childhood never tasted an oyster, or a pineapple, has of those particular relishes.

7. Men then come to be furnished with fewer or more simple ideas from without, according as the objects they converse with afford greater or less variety; and from the operations of their minds within, according as they more or less reflect on them. For, though he that contemplates the operations of his mind, cannot but have plain and clear ideas of them; yet, unless he turn his thoughts that way, and considers them *attentively*, he will no more have clear and distinct ideas of all the operations of his mind, and all that may be observed therein, than he will have all the particular ideas of any landscape, or of the parts and motions of a clock, who will not turn his eyes to it, and with attention heed all the parts of it. The picture, or clock may be so placed, that they may come in his way every day; but yet he will have but a confused idea of all the parts they are made up of, till he applies himself with attention, to consider them each in particular.

8. And hence we see the reason why it is pretty late before most children get ideas of the operations of their own minds; and some have not any very clear or perfect ideas of the greatest part of them all their lives. Because, though they pass there continually, yet, like floating visions, they make not deep impressions enough to leave in their mind clear, distinct, lasting ideas, till the understanding turns inward upon itself, reflects on its own operations, and makes them the objects of its own contemplation. . . .

24. The impressions then that are made on our senses by outward objects that are extrinsical to the mind; and its own operations about these impressions, reflected on by itself, as proper objects to be contemplated by it, are, I conceive, the original of all knowledge. Thus the first capacity of human intellect is,—that the mind is fitted to receive the impressions made on it; either through the senses by outward objects, or by its own operations when it reflects on them. This is the first step a man makes towards the discovery of anything, and the groundwork whereon to build all those notions which ever he shall have naturally in

this world. All those sublime thoughts which tower above the clouds, and reach as high as heaven itself, take their rise and footing here: in all that great extent wherein the mind wanders, in those remote speculations it may seem to be elevated with, it stirs not one jot beyond those ideas which *sense* or *reflection* have offered for its contemplation.

25. In this part the understanding is merely passive; and whether or no it will have these beginnings, and as it were materials of knowledge, is not in its own power. For the objects of our senses do, many of them, obtrude their particular ideas upon our minds whether we will or not; and the operations of our minds will not let us be without, at least, some obscure notions of them. No man can be wholly ignorant of what he does when he thinks. These simple ideas, when offered to the mind, the understanding can no more refuse to have, nor alter when they are im-printed, nor blot them out and make new ones itself, than a mirror can refuse, alter, or obliterate the images or ideas which the objects set before it do therein produce. As the bodies that surround us do diversely affect our organs, the mind is forced to receive the impressions; and cannot avoid the perception of those ideas that are annexed to them.

Of Simple Ideas

1. The better to understand the nature, manner, and extent of our knowledge, one thing is carefully to be observed concerning the ideas we have; and that is, that some of them are *simple* and some *complex.*

Though the qualities that affect our senses are, in the things them-selves so united and blended, that there is no separation, no distance between them; yet it is plain, the ideas they produce in the mind enter by the senses simple and unmixed. For, though the sight and touch often take in from the same object, at the same time, different ideas;—as a man sees at once motion and colour; the hand feels softness and warmth in the same piece of wax: yet the simple ideas thus united in the same subject, are as perfectly distinct as those that come in by different senses. The coldness and hardness which a man feels in a piece of ice being as distinct ideas in the mind as the smell and whiteness of a lily; or as the taste of sugar, and smell of a rose. And there is nothing can be plainer to a man than the clear and distinct perception he has of those simple ideas; which, being each in itself uncompounded, contains in it nothing but *one uniform appearance, or conception in the mind*, and is not distin-guishable into different ideas.

2. These simple ideas, the materials of all our knowledge, are sug-gested and furnished to the mind only by those two ways above men-tioned, viz. sensation and reflection. When the understanding is once stored with these simple ideas, it has the power to repeat, compare, and unite them, even to an almost infinite variety, and so can make at pleasure new complex ideas. But it is not in the power of the most exalted wit, or enlarged understanding, by any quickness or variety of thought, to *invent* or *frame* one new simple idea in the mind, not taken in by the ways before mentioned: nor can any force of the understanding *destroy* those that are there. The dominion of man, in this little world of his own un-

derstanding being muchwhat the same as it is in the great world of visible things; wherein his power, however managed by art and skill, reaches no farther than to compound and divide the materials that are made to his hand; but can do nothing towards the making the least particle of new matter, or destroying one atom of what is already in being. The same inability will every one find in himself, who shall go about in fashion in his understanding one simple idea, not received in by his senses from external objects, or by reflection from the operations of his own mind about them. I would have any one try to fancy any taste which had never affected his palate; or frame the idea of a scent he had never smelt: and when he can do this, I will also conclude that a blind man hath ideas of colours, and a deaf man true distinct notions of sounds.

3. This is the reason why—though we cannot believe it impossible to God to make a creature with other organs, and more ways to convey into the understanding the notice of corporeal things than those five, as they are usually counted, which he has given to man—yet I think it is not possible for any *man* to imagine any other qualities in bodies, howsoever constituted, whereby they can be taken notice of, besides sounds, tastes, smells, visible and tangible qualities. And had mankind been made but with four senses, the qualities then which are the objects of the fifth sense had been as far from our notice, imagination, and conception, as now any belonging to a sixth, seventh, or eighth sense can possibly be;—which, whether yet some other creatures, in some other parts of this vast and stupendous universe, may not have, will be a great presumption to deny. He that will not set himself proudly at the top of all things, but will consider the immensity of this fabric, and the great variety that is to be found in this little and inconsiderable part of it which he has to do with, may be apt to think that, in other mansions of it, there may be other and different intelligent beings, of whose faculties he has as little knowledge or apprehension as a worm shut up in one drawer of a cabinet hath of the senses or understanding of a man; such variety and excellency being suitable to the wisdom and power of the Maker. I have here followed the common opinion of man's having but five senses; though, perhaps, there may be justly counted more;—but either supposition serves equally to my present purpose.

On Truth in General

1. What is truth? was an inquiry many ages since; and it being that which all mankind either do, or pretend to search after, it cannot but be worth our while carefully to examine wherein it consists; and so acquaint ourselves with the nature of it, as to observe how the mind distinguishes it from falsehood.

2. Truth, then, seems to me, in the proper import of the word, to signify nothing but *the joining or separating of Signs, as the Things signified by them do agree or disagree one with another*. The joining or separating of signs here meant, is what by another name we call *proposition*. So that truth properly belongs only to propositions: whereof there are two sorts,

viz. mental and verbal; as there are two sorts of signs commonly made use of, viz. ideas and words.

3. To form a clear notion of truth, it is very necessary to consider truth of thought, and truth of words, distinctly one from another: but yet it is very difficult to treat of them asunder. Because it is unavoidable, in treating of mental propositions, to make use of words: and then the instances given of mental propositions cease immediately to be barely mental, and become verbal. For a *mental proposition* being nothing but a bare consideration of the ideas, as they are in our minds, stripped of names, they lose the nature of purely mental propositions as soon as they are put into words.

4. And that which makes it yet harder to treat of mental and verbal propositions separately is, that most men, if not all, in their thinking and reasonings within themselves, make use of words instead of ideas; at least when the subject of their meditation contains in it complex ideas. Which is a great evidence of the imperfection and uncertainty of our ideas of that kind, and may, if attentively made use of, serve for a mark to show us what are those things we have clear and perfect established ideas of, and what not. For if we will curiously observe the way our mind takes in thinking and reasoning, we shall find, I suppose, that when we make any propositions within our own thoughts about *white* or *black*, *sweet* or *bitter*, a *triangle* or a *circle*, we can and often do frame in our minds the ideas themselves, without reflecting on the names. But when we would consider, or make propositions about the more complex ideas, as of a *man, vitriol, fortitude, glory*, we usually put the name for the idea: because the ideas these names stand for, being for the most part imperfect, confused, and undetermined, we reflect on the names themselves, because they are more clear, certain, and distinct, and readier occur to our thoughts than the pure ideas: and so we make use of the words instead of the ideas themselves, even when we would meditate and reason within ourselves, and make tacit mental propositions. In substances, as has been already noticed, this is occasioned by the imperfections of our ideas: we making the name stand for the real essence, of which we have no idea at all. In modes, it is occasioned by the great number of simple ideas that go to the making them up. For many of them being compounded, the name occurs much easier than the complex idea itself, which requires time and attention to be recollected, and exactly represented to the mind, even in those men who have formerly been at the pains to do it; and is utterly impossible to be done by those who, though they have ready in their memory the greatest part of the common words of that language, yet perhaps never troubled themselves in all their lives to consider what precise ideas the most of them stood for. Some confused or obscure notions have served their turns; and many who talk very much of *religion* and *conscience*, of *church* and *faith*, of *power* and *right*, of *obstructions* and *humours, melancholy* and *choler*, would perhaps have little left in their thoughts and meditations, if one should desire them to think only of the things themselves, and lay by those words with which they so often confound others, and not seldom themselves also.

5. But to return to the consideration of truth: we must, I say, observe two sorts of propositions that we are capable of making:—

First, *mental*, wherein the ideas in our understandings are without the use of words put together, or separated, by the mind perceiving or judging of their agreement or disagreement.

Secondly, *verbal* propositions, which are words, the signs of our ideas, put together or separated in affirmative or negative sentences. By which way of affirming or denying, these signs, made by sounds, are, as it were, put together or separated one from another. So that proposition consists in joining or separating signs; and truth consists in the putting together or separating those signs, according as the things which they stand for agree or disagree.

6. Every one's experience will satisfy him, that the mind, either by perceiving, or supposing, the agreement or disagreement of any of its ideas, does tacitly within itself put them into a kind of proposition affirmative or negative; which I have endeavoured to express by the terms putting together and separating. But this action of the mind, which is so familiar to every thinking and reasoning man, is easier to be conceived by reflecting on what passes in us when we affirm or deny, than to be explained by words. When a man has in his head the idea of two lines, viz. the side and diagonal of a square, whereof the diagonal is an inch long, he may have the idea also of the division of that line into a certain number of equal parts; v.g. into five, ten, a hundred, a thousand, or any other number, and may have the idea of that inch line being divisible, or not divisible, into such equal parts, as a certain number of them will be equal to the sideline. Now, whenever he perceives, believes, or supposes such a kind of divisibility to agree or disagree to his idea of that line, he, as it were, joins or separates those two ideas, viz. the idea of that line, and the idea of that kind of divisibility; and so makes a mental proposition, which is true or false, according as such a kind of divisibility, a divisibility into such *aliquot* parts, does really agree to that line or no. When ideas are so put together, or separated in the mind, as they or the things they stand for do agree or not, that is, as I may call it, *mental truth*. But *truth of words* is something more; and that is the affirming or denying of words one of another, as the ideas they stand for agree or disagree: and this again is two-fold; either purely verbal and trifling, which I shall speak of, (chap. viii.,) or real and instructive; which is the object of that real knowledge which we have spoken of already.

7. But here again will be apt to occur the same doubt about truth, that did about knowledge: and it will be objected, that if truth be nothing but the joining and separating of words in propositions, as the ideas they stand for agree or disagree in men's minds, the knowledge of truth is not so valuable a thing as it is taken to be, nor worth the pains and time men employ in the search of it: since by this account it amounts to no more than the conformity of words to the chimeras of men's brains. Who knows not what odd notions many men's heads are filled with, and what strange ideas all men's brains are capable of? But if we rest here, we know the truth of nothing by this rule, but the visionary words in our own imaginations; nor have other truth, but what as much concerns har-

pies and centaurs, as men and horses. For those, and the like, may be ideas in our heads, and have their agreement or disagreement there, as well as the ideas of real beings, and so have as true propositions made about them. And it will be altogether as true a proposition to say *all centaurs are animals,* as that *all men are animals:* and the certainty of one as great as the other. For in both the propositions, the words are put together according to the agreement of the ideas in our minds: and the agreement of the idea of animal with that of centaur is as clear and visible to the mind, as the agreement of the idea of animal with that of man: and so these two propositions are equally true, equally certain. But of what use is all such truth to us?

8. Though what has been said in the foregoing chapter to distinguish real from imaginary knowledge might suffice here, in answer to this doubt, to distinguish real truth from chimerical, or (if you please) barely nominal, they depending both on the same foundation; yet it may not be amiss here again to consider, that though our words signify nothing but our ideas, yet being designed by them to signify things, the truth they contain when put into propositions will be only verbal, when they stand for ideas in the mind that have not an agreement with the reality of things. And therefore truth as well as knowledge may well come under the distinction of verbal and real; that being only verbal truth, wherein terms are joined according to the agreement or disagreement of the ideas they stand for; without regarding whether our ideas are such as really have, or are capable of having, an existence in nature. But then it is they contain *real truth,* when these signs are joined, as our ideas agree; and when our ideas are such as we know are capable of having an existence in nature: which in substances we cannot know, but by the knowing that such have existed.

9. Truth is the marking down in words the agreement or disagreement of ideas as it is. Falsehood is the marking down in words the agreement or disagreement of ideas otherwise that it is. And so far as these ideas, thus marked by sounds, agree to their archetypes, so far only is the truth real. The knowledge of this truth consists in knowing what ideas the words stand for, and the perception of the agreement or disagreement of those ideas, according as it is marked by those words.

The Independent Existence of Body

7. To discover the nature of our *ideas* the better, and to discourse of them intelligibly, it will be convenient to distinguish them *as they are ideas or perceptions in our minds;* and *as they are modifications of matter in the bodies that cause such perceptions in us:* that so we may not think (as perhaps usually is done) that they are exactly the images and resemblances of something inherent in the subject; most of those of sensation being in the mind no more the likeness of something existing without us, than the names that stand for them are the likeness of our ideas, which yet upon hearing they are apt to excite in us.

8. Whatsoever the mind perceives *in itself,* or is the immediate object of perception, thought, or understanding, that I call *idea;* and the power

to produce any idea in our mind, I call *quality* of the subject wherein that power is. Thus a snowball having the power to produce in us the ideas of white, cold, and round,—the power to produce those ideas in us, as they are in the snowball, I call qualities; and as they are sensations or perceptions in our understandings, I call them ideas; which *ideas*, if I speak of sometimes as in the things themselves, I would be understood to mean those qualities in the objects which produce them in us.

9. [Qualities thus considered in bodies are,

First, such as are utterly inseparable from the body, in what state soever it be]: and such as in all the alterations and changes it suffers, all the force can be used upon it, it constantly keeps; and such as sense constantly finds in every particle of matter which has bulk enough to be perceived; and the mind finds inseparable from every particle of matter, though less than to make itself singly be perceived by our senses: v.g. Take a grain of wheat, divide it into two parts; each part has still solidity, extension, figure, and mobility: divide it again, and it retains still the same qualities; and so divide it on, till the parts become insensible; they must retain still each of them all those qualities. For division (which is all that a mill, or pestle, or any other body, does upon another, in reducing it to insensible parts) can never take away either solidity, extension, figure, or mobility from any body, but only makes two or more distinct separate masses of matter, of that which was but one before; all which distinct masses, reckoned as so many distinct bodies, after division, make a certain number. [These I call *original* or *primary qualities* of body, which I think we may observe to produce simple ideas in us, viz. solidity, extension, figure, motion or rest, and number.

10. *Secondly*, such qualities which in truth are nothing in the objects themselves but powers to produce various sensations in us by their primary qualities, i.e. by the bulk, figure, texture, and motion of their insensible parts, as colours, sounds, tastes, &c. These I call *secondary qualities*. To these might be added a *third* sort, which are allowed to be barely powers; though they are as much real qualities in the subject as those which I, to comply with the common way of speaking, call qualities, but for distinction, secondary qualities. For the power in fire to produce a new colour, or consistency, in *wax* or *clay*,—by its primary qualities, is as much a quality in fire, as the power it has to produce in *me* a new idea or sensation of warmth or burning, which I felt not before,—by the same primary qualities, viz. the bulk, texture, and motion of its insensible parts].

11. [The next thing to be considered is, how bodies produce ideas in us; and that is manifestly by impulse, the only way which we can conceive bodies to operate in].

12. If then external objects be not united to our minds when they produce ideas therein; and yet we perceive these *original* qualities in such of them as singly fall under our senses, it is evident that some motion must be thence continued by our nerves, or animal spirits, by some parts of our bodies, to the brains or the seat of sensation, there to produce in our minds the particular ideas we have of them. And since the extension, figure, number, and motion of bodies of an observable bigness, may be perceived at a distance by the sight, it is evident some singly imperceptible

bodies must come from them to the eyes, and thereby convey to the brain some motion; which produces these ideas which we have of them in us.

13. After the same manner that the ideas of these original qualities are produced in us, we may conceive that the ideas of *secondary* qualities are also produced, viz. by the operation of insensible particles on our senses. For, it being manifest that there are bodies and good store of bodies, each whereof are so small, that we cannot by any of our senses discover either their bulk, figure, or motion,—as is evident in the particles of the air and water, and others extremely smaller than those: perhaps as much smaller than the particles of air and water, as the particles of air and water are smaller than peas or hail-stones;—let us suppose at present that the different motions and figures, bulk and number, of such particles, affecting the several organs of our senses, produce in us those different sensations which we have from the colours and smells of bodies; v.g. that a violet, by the impulse of such insensible particles of matter, of peculiar figures and bulks, and in different degrees and modifications of their motions, causes the ideas of the blue colour, and sweet scent of that flower to be produced in our minds. It being no more impossible to conceive that God should annex such ideas to such motions, with which they have no similitude, than that he should annex the idea of pain to the motion of a piece of steel dividing our flesh, with which that idea hath no resemblance.

14. What I have said concerning colours and smells may be understood also of tastes and sounds, and other the like sensible qualities; which, whatever reality we by mistake attribute to them, are in truth nothing in the objects themselves, but powers to produce various sensations in us; and depend on those primary qualities, viz. bulk, figure, texture, and motion of parts [as I have said].

15. From whence I think it easy to draw this observation,—that the ideas of primary qualities of bodies are resemblances of them, and their patterns do really exist in the bodies themselves, but the ideas produced in us by these secondary qualities have no resemblance of them at all. There is nothing like our ideas, existing in the bodies themselves. They are, in the bodies we denominate from them, only a power to produce those sensations in us: and what is sweet, blue, or warm in idea, is but the certain bulk, figure, and motion of the insensible parts, in the bodies themselves, which we call so.

16. Flame is denominated hot and light; snow, white and cold; and manna, white and sweet, from the ideas they produce in us. Which qualities are commonly thought to be the same in those bodies that those ideas are in us, the one the perfect resemblance of the other, as they are in a mirror, and it would by most men be judged very extravagant if one should say otherwise. And yet he that will consider that the same fire that, at one distance produces in us the sensation of warmth, does, at a nearer approach, produce in us the far different sensation of pain, ought to bethink himself what reason he has to say—that this idea of warmth, which was produced in him by the fire, is *actually in the fire;* and his idea of pain, which the same fire produced in him the same way, is

not in the fire. Why are whiteness and coldness in snow, and pain not, when it produces the one and the other idea in us; and can do neither, but by the bulk, figure, number, and motion of its solid parts?

17. The particular bulk, number, figure, and motion of the parts of fire or snow are really in them,—whether any one's senses perceive them or no: and therefore they may be called *real* qualities, because they really exist in those bodies. But light, heat, whiteness, or coldness, are no more really in them than sickness or pain is in manna. Take away the sensation of them; let not the eyes see light or colours, nor the ears hear sounds; let the palate not taste, nor the nose smell, and all colours, tastes, odours, and sounds, *as they are such particular ideas*, vanish and cease, and are reduced to their causes, i.e. bulk, figure, and motion of parts.

18. A piece of manna of a sensible bulk is able to produce in us the idea of a round or square figure; and by being removed from one place to another, the idea of motion. This idea of motion represents it as it really is in manna moving: a circle or square are the same, whether in idea or existence, in the mind or in the manna. And this, both motion and figure, are really in the manna, whether we take notice of them or no: this everybody is ready to agree to. Besides, manna, by the bulk, figure, texture, and motion of its parts, has a power to produce the sensations of sickness, and sometimes of acute pains or gripings in us. That these ideas of sickness and pain are *not* in the manna, but effects of its operations on us, and are nowhere when we feel them not; this also every one readily agrees to. And yet men are hardly to be brought to think that sweetness and whiteness are not really in manna; which are but the effects of the operations of manna, by the motion, size, and figure of its particles, on the eyes and palate: as the pain and sickness caused by manna are confessedly nothing but the effects of its operations on the stomach and guts, by the size, motion, and figure of its insensible parts, (for by nothing else can a body operate, as has been proved): as if it could not operate on the eyes and palate, and thereby produce in the mind particular distinct ideas, which in itself it has not, as well as we allow it can operate on the guts and stomach, and thereby produce distinct ideas, which in itself it has not. These ideas, being all effects of the operations of manna on several parts of our bodies, by the size, figure, number, and motion of its parts;—why those produced by the eyes and palate should rather be thought to be really in the manna, than those produced by the stomach and guts; or why the pain and sickness, ideas that are the effect of manna, should be thought to be nowhere when they are not felt; and yet the sweetness and whiteness, effects of the same manna on other parts of the body, by ways equally as unknown, should be thought to exist in the manna, when they are not seen or tasted, would need some reason to explain.

19. Let us consider the red and white colours in porphyry. Hinder light from striking on it, and its colours vanish; it no longer produces any such ideas in us: upon the return of light it produces these appearances on us again. Can any one think any real alterations are made in porphyry by the presence or absence of light; and that those ideas of whiteness and redness are really in porphyry in the light, when it is plain

it has no colour in the dark? It has, indeed, such a configuration of particles, both night and day, as are apt, by the rays of light rebounding from some parts of that hard stone, to produce in us the idea of redness, and from others the idea of whiteness; but whiteness or redness are not in it at any time, but such a texture that hath the power to produce such a sensation in us.

20. Pound an almond, and the clear white colour will be altered into a dirty one, and the sweet taste into an oily one. What real alteration can the beating of the pestle make in any body, but an alteration of the texture of it?

21. Ideas being thus distinguished and understood, we may be able to give an account how the same water, at the same time, may produce the idea of cold by one hand and of heat by the other: whereas it is impossible that the same water, if those ideas were really in it, should at the same time be both hot and cold. For, if we imagine *warmth,* as it is in our hands, to be nothing but a certain sort and degree of motion in the minute particles of our nerves or animal spirits, we may understand how it is possible that the same water may, at the same time, produce the sensations of heat in one hand and cold in the other; which yet *figure* never does, that never producing the idea of a square by one hand which has produced the idea of a globe by another. But if the sensation of heat and cold be nothing but the increase or diminution of the motion of the minute parts of our bodies, caused by the corpuscles of any other body, it is easy to be understood, that if that motion be greater in one hand than in the other; if a body be applied to the two hands, which has in its minute particles a greater motion than in those of one of the hands, and a less than in those of the other, it will increase the motion of the one hand and lessen it in the other; and so cause the different sensations of heat and cold that depend thereon.

22. I have in what just goes before been engaged in physical inquiries a little further than perhaps I intended. But, it being necessary to make the nature of sensation a little understood; and to make the difference between the *qualities* in bodies, and the *ideas* produced by them in the mind, to be distinctly conceived, without which it were impossible to discourse intelligibly of them;—I hope I shall be pardoned this little excursion into natural philosophy; it being necessary in our present inquiry to distinguish the *primary* and *real* qualities of bodies, which are always in them (viz. solidity, extension, figure, number, and motion, or rest, and are sometimes perceived by us, viz. when the bodies they are in are big enough singly to be discerned), from those *secondary* and *imputed* qualities, which are but the powers of several combinations of those primary ones, when they operate without being distinctly discerned;— whereby we may also come to know what ideas are, and what are not, resemblances of something really existing in the bodies we denominate from them.

23. The qualities, then, that are in bodies, rightly considered, are of three sorts:—

First, The bulk, figure, number, situation, and motion or rest of their solid parts. Those are in them, whether we perceive them or not; and when they are of that size that we can discover them, we have by these an idea of the thing as it is in itself; as is plain in artificial things. These I call *primary qualities.*

Secondly, The power that is in any body, by reason of its insensible primary qualities, to operate after a peculiar manner on any of our senses, and thereby produce in *us* the different ideas of several colours, sounds, smells, tastes, &c. These are usually called *sensible qualities.*

Thirdly, The power that is in any body, by reason of the particular constitution of its primary qualities, to make such a change in the bulk, figure, texture, and motion of *another body,* as to make it operate on our senses differently from what it did before. Thus the sun has a power to make wax white, and fire to make lead fluid. [These are usually called *powers*].

The first of these, as has been said, I think may be properly called real, original, or primary qualities; because they are in the things themselves, whether they are perceived or not: and upon their different modifications it is that the secondary qualities depend.

The other two are only powers to act differently upon other things: which powers result from the different modifications of those primary qualities.

24. But, though the two latter sorts of qualities are powers barely, and nothing but powers, relating to several other bodies, and resulting from the different modifications of the original qualities, yet they are generally otherwise thought of. For the *second* sort, viz. the powers to produce several ideas in us, by our senses, are looked upon as real qualities in the things thus affecting us: but the *third* sort are called and esteemed barely powers. v.g. The idea of heat or light, which we receive by our eyes, or touch, from the sun, are commonly thought real qualities existing in the sun, and something more than mere powers in it. But when we consider the sun in reference to wax, which it melts or blanches, we look on the whiteness and softness produced in the wax, not as qualities in the sun, but effects produced by powers in it. Whereas, if rightly considered, these qualities of light and warmth, which are perceptions in me when I am warmed or enlightened by the sun, are no otherwise in the sun, than the changes made in the wax, when it is blanched or melted, are in the sun. They are all of them equally *powers in the sun, depending on its primary qualities;* whereby it is able, in the one case, so to alter the bulk, figure, texture, or motion of some of the insensible parts of my eyes or hands, as thereby to produce in me the idea of light or heat; and in the other, it is able so to alter the bulk, figure, texture, or motion of the insensible parts of the wax, as to make them fit to produce in me the distinct ideas of white and fluid.

25. The reason why the one are ordinarily taken for real qualities, and the other only for bare powers, seems to be, because the ideas we have of distinct colours, sounds, &c., containing nothing at all in them of bulk, figure, or motion, we are not apt to think them the effects of these primary qualities; which appear not, to our senses, to operate in their production, and with which they have not any apparent congruity or conceivable connexion. Hence it is that we are so forward to imagine,

that those ideas are the resemblances of something really existing in the objects themselves: since sensation discovers nothing of bulk, figure, or motion of parts in their production; nor can reason show how bodies, *by their bulk, figure, and motion,* should produce in the mind the ideas of blue or yellow, &c. But, in the other case, in the operations of bodies changing the qualities one of another, we plainly discover that the quality produced hath commonly no resemblance with anything in the thing producing it; wherefore we look on it as a bare effect of power. For, through receiving the idea of heat or light from the sun, we are apt to think *it* is a perception and resemblance of such a quality in the sun; yet when we see wax, or a fair face, receive change of colour from the sun, we cannot imagine *that* to be the reception or resemblance of anything in the sun, because we find not those different colours in the sun itself. For, our senses being able to observe a likeness or unlikeness of sensible qualities in two different external objects, we forwardly enough conclude the production of any sensible quality in any subject to be an effect of bare power, and not the communication of any quality which was really in the efficient, when we find no such sensible quality in the thing that produced it. But our senses, not being able to discover any unlikeness between the idea produced in us, and the quality of the object producing it, we are apt to imagine that our ideas are resemblances of something in the objects, and not the effects of certain powers placed in the modification of their primary qualities, with which primary qualities the ideas produced in us have no resemblance.

26. To conclude. Beside those before-mentioned primary qualities in bodies, viz. bulk, figure, extension, number, and motion of their solid parts; all the rest, whereby we take notice of bodies, and distinguish them one from another, are nothing else but several powers in them, depending on those primary qualities; whereby they are fitted, either by immediately operating on our bodies to produce several different ideas in us; or else, by operating on other bodies, so to change their primary qualities as to render them capable of producing ideas in us different from what before they did. The former of these, I think, may be called secondary qualities *immediately perceivable:* the latter, secondary qualities, *mediately perceivable.*

The Nature of Science

46. The Detective as Scientist   Irving M. Copi

Irving Marmer Copi (1917–   ), an American professor of philosophy, has written extensively and lucidly on logic, scientific method, and the philosophy of language.

... A perennial favorite in this connection is the detective, whose problem is not quite the same as that of the pure scientist, but whose approach and technique illustrate the method of science very clearly. The classical example of the astute detective who can solve even the most baffling mystery is A. Conan Doyle's immortal creation, Sherlock Holmes. Holmes, his stature undiminished by the passage of time, will be our hero in the following account:

1. The Problem. Some of our most vivid pictures of Holmes are those in which he is busy with magnifying glass and tape measure, searching out and finding essential clues which had escaped the attention of those stupid bunglers, the "experts" of Scotland Yard. Or those of us who are by temperament less vigorous may think back more fondly on Holmes the thinker, " ... who, when he had an unsolved problem upon his mind, would go for days, and even for a week, without rest, turning it over, rearranging his facts, looking at it from every point of view until he had either fathomed it or convinced himself that his data were insufficient."[1] At one such time, according to Dr. Watson:

> He took off his coat and waistcoat, put on a large blue dressing-gown, and then wandered about the room collecting pillows from his bed and cushions from the sofa and armchairs. With these he constructed a sort of Eastern divan, upon which he perched himself cross-legged, with an ounce of shag tobacco and a box of matches laid out in front of him. In the dim light of the lamp I saw him sitting there, an old briar pipe between his lips, his eyes fixed vacantly upon the corner of the ceiling, the blue smoke curling up from him, silent, motionless, with the light shining upon his strong-set aquiline features. So he sat as I dropped off to sleep, and so he sat when a sudden ejaculation caused me to wake up, and I found the summer sun shining into the apartment. The pipe was still between his lips, the smoke still curled upward, and the room was full of a dense tobacco haze, but nothing remained of the heap of shag which I had seen upon the previous night.[2]

[1] "The Man with the Twisted Lip."
[2] Ibid.

But such memories are incomplete. Holmes was not always searching for clues or pondering over solutions. We all remember those dark periods—especially in the earlier stories—when, much to the good Watson's annoyance, Holmes would drug himself with morphine or cocaine. That would happen, of course, between cases. For when there is no mystery to be unraveled, no man in his right mind would go out to look for clues. Clues, after all, must be clues for something. Nor could Holmes, or anyone else, for that matter, engage in profound thought unless he had something to think about. Sherlock Holmes was a genius at solving problems, but even a genius must have a problem before he can solve it. All reflective thinking, and this term includes criminal investigation as well as scientific research, is a problem-solving activity, as John Dewey and other pragmatists have rightly insisted. There must be a problem felt before either the detective or the scientist can go to work.

Of course the active mind sees problems where the dullard sees only familiar objects. One Christmas season Dr. Watson visited Holmes to find that the latter had been using a lens and forceps to examine " . . . a very seedy and disreputable hard-felt hat, much the worse for wear, and cracked in several places."[3] After they had greeted each other, Holmes said of it to Watson, "I beg that you will look upon it not as a battered billycock but as an intellectual problem."[4] It so happened that the hat led them into one of their most interesting adventures, but it could not have done so had Holmes not seen a problem in it from the start. A problem may be characterized as a fact or group of facts for which we have no acceptable explanation, which seem unusual, or which fail to fit in with our expectations or preconceptions. It should be obvious that *some* prior beliefs are required if anything is to appear problematic. If there are no expectations, there can be no surprises.

Sometimes, of course, problems came to Holmes already labeled. The very first adventure recounted by Dr. Watson began with the following message from Gregson of Scotland Yard:

My Dear Mr. Sherlock Holmes:
   There has been a bad business during the night at 3, Lauriston Gardens, off the Brixton Road. Our man on the beat saw a light there about two in the morning, and as the house was an empty one, suspected that something was amiss. He found the door open, and in the front room, which is bare of furniture, discovered the body of a gentleman, well dressed, and having cards in his pocket bearing the name of 'Enoch J. Drebber, Cleveland, Ohio, U.S.A.' There had been no robbery, nor is there any evidence as to how the man met his death. There are marks of blood in the room, but there is no wound upon his person. We are at a loss as to how he came into the empty house; indeed, the whole affair is a puzzler. If you can come round to the house any time before twelve, you will find me there. I have left everything in statu quo until I hear from you. If you are unable to come, I shall give you fuller details, and

---

[3] "The Adventure of the Blue Carbuncle."
[4] Ibid.

would esteem it a great kindness if you would favour me with your opinion.

Yours faithfully
TOBIAS GREGSON[5]

Here was a problem indeed. A few minutes after receiving the message, Sherlock Holmes and Dr. Watson "were both in a hansom, driving furiously for the Brixton Road."

2. Preliminary Hypotheses. On their ride out Brixton way, Holmes "prattled away about Cremona fiddles and the difference between a Stradivarius and an Amati." Dr. Watson chided Holmes for not giving much thought to the matter at hand, and Holmes replied: "No data yet . . . It is a capital mistake to theorize before you have all the evidence. It biases the judgment."[6] This point of view was expressed by Holmes again and again. On one occasion he admonished a younger detective that "The temptation to form premature theories upon insufficient data is the bane of our profession."[7] Yet for all of his confidence about the matter, on this one issue Holmes was completely mistaken. Of course one should not reach a *final judgment* until a great deal of evidence has been considered, but this procedure is quite different from *not theorizing*. As a matter of fact, it is strictly impossible to make any serious attempt to collect evidence unless one *has* theorized beforehand. As Charles Darwin, the great biologist and author of the modern theory of evolution, observed: " . . . all observation must be for or against some view, if it is to be of any service." The point is that there are too many particular facts, too many data in the world, for anyone to try to become acquainted with them all. Everyone, even the most patient and thorough investigator, must pick and choose, deciding which facts to study and which to pass over. He must have some working hypothesis for or against which to collect relevant data. It need not be a *complete* theory, but at least the rough outline must be there. Otherwise how could one decide what facts to select for consideration out of the totality of all facts, which is too vast even to begin to sift?

Holmes' actions were wiser than his words in this connection. After all, the words were spoken in a hansom speeding towards the scene of the crime. If Holmes really had no theory about the matter, why go to Brixton Road? If facts and data were all that he wanted, any old facts and any old data, with no hypotheses to guide him in their selection, why should he have left Baker Street at all? There were plenty of facts in the rooms at 221-B, Baker Street. Holmes might just as well have spent his time counting all the words on the pages of all the books there, or perhaps making very accurate measurements of the distances between each separate pair of articles of furniture in the house. He could have gathered data to his heart's content and saved himself cab fare into the bargain!

---

[5] *A Study in Scarlet.*
[6] Ibid.
[7] *The Valley of Fear.*

It may be objected that the facts to be gathered at Baker Street have nothing to do with the case, whereas those which awaited Holmes at the scene of the crime were valuable clues for solving the problem. It was, of course, just this consideration which led Holmes to ignore the "data" at Baker Street and hurry away to collect those off Brixton Road. It must be insisted, however, that the greater relevance of the latter could not be *known* beforehand but only conjectured on the basis of previous experience with crimes and clues. It was in fact a *hypothesis* which led Holmes to look in one place rather than another for his facts, the hypothesis that there was a murder, that the crime was committed at the place where the body was found, and the murderer had left some trace or clue which could lead to his discovery. Some such hypothesis is always required to guide the investigator in his search for relevant data, for in the absence of any preliminary hypothesis, there are simply too many facts in this world to examine. The preliminary hypothesis ought to be highly tentative, and it must be based on previous knowledge. But a preliminary hypothesis is as necessary as the existence of a problem for any serious inquiry to begin.

It must be emphasized that a preliminary hypothesis, as here conceived, need not be a complete solution to the problem. The hypothesis that the man was murdered by someone who had left some clues to his identity on or near the body of his victim was what led Holmes to Brixton Road. This hypothesis is clearly incomplete: it does not say who committed the crime, or how it was done, or why. Such a preliminary hypothesis may be very different from the final solution to the problem. It will never be complete: it may be a tentative explanation of only part of the problem. But however partial and however tentative, a preliminary hypothesis is required for any investigation to proceed.

3. Collecting Additional Facts. Every serious investigation begins with some fact or group of facts which strike the investigator as problematic and which initiate the whole process of inquiry. The initial facts which constitute the problem are usually too meagre to suggest a wholly satisfactory explanation for themselves, but they will suggest—to the competent investigator—some preliminary hypotheses which lead him to search out additional facts. These additional facts, it is hoped, will serve as clues to the final solution. The inexperienced or bungling investigator will overlook or ignore all but the most obvious of them; but the careful worker will aim at completeness in his examination of the additional facts to which his preliminary hypotheses lead him. Holmes, of course, was the most careful and painstaking of investigators.

Holmes insisted on dismounting from the hansom a hundred yards or so from their destination and approached the house on foot, looking carefully at its surroundings and especially at the pathway leading up to it. When Holmes and Watson entered the house, they were shown the body by the Scotland Yard operatives, Gregson and Lestrade. ("There is no clue," said Gregson. "None at all," chimed in Lestrade.) But Holmes had already started his own search for additional facts, looking first at the body:

... his nimble fingers were flying here, there, and everywhere, feeling, pressing, unbuttoning, examining. ... So swiftly was examination made, that one would hardly have guessed the minuteness with which it was conducted. Finally, he sniffed the dead man's lips, and then glanced at the soles of his patent leather boots.[8]

Then turning his attention to the room itself,

... he whipped a tape measure and a large round magnifying glass from his pocket. With these two implements he trotted noiselessly about the room, sometimes stopping, occasionally kneeling, and once lying flat upon his face. So engrossed was he with his occupation that he appeared to have forgotten our presence, for he chattered away to himself under his breath the whole time, keeping up a running fire of exclamations, groans, whistles, and little cries suggestive of encouragement and of hope. As I watched him I was irresistibly reminded of a pure-blooded, well-trained foxhound as it dashes backward and forward through the covert, whining in its eagerness, until it comes across the lost scent. For twenty minutes or more he continued his researches, measuring with the most exact care the distance between marks which were entirely invisible to me, and occasionally applying his tape to the walls in an equally incomprehensible manner. In one place he gathered up very carefully a little pile of gray dust from the floor and packed it away in an envelope. Finally, he examined with his glass the word upon the wall, going over every letter of it with the most minute exactness. This done, he appeared to be satisfied, for he replaced his tape and his glass in his pocket.

"They say that genius is an infinite capacity for taking pains," he remarked with a smile. "It's a very bad definition, but it does apply to detective work."[9]

One matter deserves to be emphasized very strongly. Steps 2 and 3 are not completely separable but are usually very intimately connected and interdependent. True enough, we require a preliminary hypothesis to begin any intelligent examination of facts, but the additional facts may themselves suggest new hypotheses, which may lead to new facts, which suggest still other hypotheses, which lead to still other additional facts, and so on. Thus having made his careful examination of the facts available in the house off Brixton Road, Holmes was led to formulate a further hypothesis which required the taking of testimony from the constable who found the body. The man was off duty at the moment, and Lestrade gave Holmes the constable's name and address.

Holmes took a note of the address.

"Come along, Doctor," he said: "we shall go and look him up. I'll tell you one thing which may help you in the case," he continued, turning to the two detectives. "There has been murder done, and the murderer was a man. He was more than six feet high, was in the prime of life, had small feet for his height, wore coarse, square-toed boots and smoked a Trichinopoly cigar. He came here with his victim in a four-wheel cab, which was drawn by a horse with three old shoes and one new one on his off fore-leg. In all probability the murderer had a florid face, and

---

[8] *A Study in Scarlet.*
[9] Ibid.

the fingernails of his right hand were remarkably long. These are only a few indications, but they may assist you."

Lestrade and Gregson glanced at each other with an incredulous smile.

"If this man was murdered, how was it done?" asked the former.

"Poison," said Sherlock Holmes curtly, and strode off.[10]

4. Formulating the Hypothesis. At some stage or other of his investigation, any man—whether detective, scientist, or ordinary mortal—will get the feeling that he has all the facts needed for his solution. He has his "2 and 2," so to speak, but the task still remains of "putting them together." At such a time Sherlock Holmes might sit up all night, consuming pipe after pipe of tobacco, trying to think things through. The result or end product of such thinking, if it is successful, is a hypothesis which accounts for all the data, both the original set of facts which constituted the problem, and the additional facts to which the preliminary hypotheses pointed. The actual discovery of such an explanatory hypothesis is a process of creation, in which imagination as well as knowledge is involved. Holmes, who was a genius at inventing hypotheses, described the process as reasoning "backward." As he put it,

> Most people if you describe a train of events to them, will tell you what the result would be. They can put those events together in their minds, and argue from them that something will come to pass. There are few people, however, who, if you told them a result, would be able to evolve from their own inner consciousness what the steps were which led up to that result.[11]

Here is Holmes' description of the process of formulating an explanatory hypothesis. However that may be, when a hypothesis has been proposed, its evaluation must be along the lines that were sketched in Section III [omitted here]. Granted its relevance and testability, and its compatibility with other well-attested beliefs, the ultimate criterion for evaluating a hypothesis is its predictive power.

5. Deducing Further Consequences. A really fruitful hypothesis will not only explain the facts which originally inspired it, but will explain many others in addition. A good hypothesis will point beyond the initial facts in the direction of new ones whose existence might otherwise not have been suspected. And of course the verification of those further consequences will tend to confirm the hypothesis which led to them. Holmes' hypothesis that the murdered man had been poisoned was soon put to such a test. A few days later the murdered man's secretary and traveling companion was also found murdered. Holmes asked Lestrade, who had discovered the second body, whether he had found anything in the room which could furnish a clue to the murderer. Lestrade answered, "Nothing," and went on to mention a few quite ordinary effects. Holmes was not satisfied and pressed him, asking, "And was there nothing else?" Lestrade answered "Nothing of any importance,"and named a few more

[10] Ibid.
[11] Ibid.

details, the last of which was "a small chip ointment box containing a couple of pills." At this information,

> Sherlock Holmes sprang from his chair with an exclamation of delight. "The last links," he cried, exultantly. "My case is complete."
>
> The two detectives stared at him in amazement.
>
> "I have now in my hands," my companion said, confidently, "all the threads which have formed such a tangle. . . . I will give you a proof of my knowledge. Could you lay your hands upon those pills?"
>
> "I have them," said Lestrade, producing a small white box. . . .[12]

On the basis of his hypothesis about the original crime, Holmes was able to predict that the pills found at the scene of the second crime must contain poison. Here deduction has an essential role in the process of any scientific or inductive inquiry. The ultimate value of any hypothesis lies in its predictive or explanatory power, which means that additional facts must be deducible from an adequate hypothesis. From his theory that the first man was poisoned and that the second victim met his death at the hands of the same murderer, Holmes inferred that the pills found by Lestrade must be poison. His theory, however sure he may have felt about it, was only a theory and needed further confirmation. He obtained that confirmation by testing the consequences deduced from the hypothesis and finding them to be true. Having used deduction to make a prediction, his next step was to test it.

6. Testing the Consequences. The consequences of a hypothesis, that is, the predictions made on the basis of that hypothesis, may require various means for their testing. Some require only observation. In some cases, Holmes needed only to watch and wait—for the bank robbers to break into the vault, in the "Adventure of the Red-headed League," or for Dr. Roylott to slip a venomous snake through a dummy ventilator, in the "Adventure of the Speckled Band." In the present case, however, an experiment had to be performed.

Holmes asked Dr. Watson to fetch the landlady's old and ailing terrier, which she had asked to have put out of its misery the day before. Holmes then cut one of the pills in two, dissolved it in a wineglass of water, added some milk, and

> . . . turned the contents of the wineglass into a saucer and placed it in front of the terrier, who speedily licked it dry. Sherlock Holmes's earnest demeanour had so far convinced us that we all sat in silence, watching the animal intently, and expecting some startling effect. None such appeared, however. The dog continued to lie stretched upon the cushion, breathing in a laboured way, but apparently neither the better nor the worse for its draught.
>
> Holmes had taken out his watch, and as minute followed minute without result, an expression of the utmost chagrin and disappointment appeared upon his features. He gnawed his lip, drummed his fingers upon the table, and showed every other symptom of acute impatience. So great

[12] Ibid.

was his emotion that I felt sincerely sorry for him, while the two detectives smiled derisively, by no means displeased at this check which he had met.

"It can't be a coincidence," he cried, at last springing from his chair and pacing wildly up and down the room: "it is impossible that it should be a mere coincidence. The very pills which I suspected in the case of Drebber are actually found after the death of Stangerson. And yet they are inert. What can it mean? Surely my whole chain of reasoning cannot have been false. It is impossible! And yet this wretched dog is none the worse. Ah, I have it! I have it!" With a perfect shriek of delight he rushed to the box, cut the other pill in two, dissolved it, added milk, and presented it to the terrier. The unfortunate creature's tongue seemed hardly to have been moistened in it before it gave a convulsive shiver in every limb, and lay as rigid and lifeless as if it had been struck by lightning.

Sherlock Holmes drew a long breath, and wiped the perspiration from his forehead.[13]

By the favorable outcome of his experiment, Holmes' hypothesis had received dramatic and convincing confirmation.

7. *Application.* The detective's concern, after all, is a practical one. Given a crime to solve, he has not merely to explain the facts but to apprehend and arrest the criminal. The latter involves making application of his theory, using it to predict where the criminal can be found and how he may be caught. He must deduce still further consequences from the hypothesis, not for the sake of additional confirmation but for practical use. From his general hypothesis Holmes was able to infer that the murderer was acting the role of a cabman. We have already seen that Holmes had formed a pretty clear description of the man's appearance. He sent out his army of "Baker Street Irregulars," street urchins of the neighborhood, to search out and summon the cab driven by just that man. The successful "application" of this hypothesis can be described again in Dr. Watson's words. A few minutes after the terrier's death,

. . . there was a tap at the door, and the spokesman of the street Arabs, young Wiggins, introduced his insignificant and unsavoury person.

"Please, sir," he said touching his forelock, "I have the cab downstairs."

"Good boy," said Holmes, blandly. "Why don't you introduce this pattern at Scotland Yard?" he continued, taking a pair of steel handcuffs from a drawer. "See how beautifully the spring works. They fasten in an instant."

"The old pattern is good enough," remarked Lestrade, "if we can only find the man to put them on."

"Very good, very good," said Holmes, smiling. "The cabman may as well help me with my boxes. Just ask him to step in, Wiggins."

I was surprised to find my companion speaking as though he were about to set out on a journey, since he had not said anything to me about it. There was a small portmanteau in the room, and this he pulled out and began to strap. He has busily engaged at it when the cabman entered the room.

"Just give me a help with this buckle, cabman," he said, kneeling over his task, and never turning his head.

---

[13] Ibid.

The fellow came forward with a somewhat sullen, defiant air, and put down his hands to assist. At that instant there was a sharp click, the jangling of metal, and Sherlock Holmes sprang to his feet again.

"Gentlemen," he cried, with flashing eyes, "let me introduce you to Mr. Jefferson Hope, the murderer of Enoch Drebber and of Joseph Stangerson."[14]

Here we have a picture of the detective as scientist, reasoning from observed facts to a testable hypothesis which not only explains the facts but permits of practical application.

47. The Limits and the Value of Scientific Method
Morris R. Cohen and Ernest Nagel

Morris Raphael Cohen (1880–1947), American philosopher and logician, was profes- sor of philosophy at the College of the City of New York for many years, then at the University of Chicago. He was a tireless champion of reason, scientific naturalism, and liberalism against all forms of irrationalism, supernaturalism and dogmatism.

Ernest Nagel (1901–   ), an internationally known American philosopher of science, is now university Professor Emeritus, Columbia University. From 1955 to 1966 he was John Dewey Professor of Philosophy at the same institution. As was Morris Cohen, he is an unwavering defender of reason, scientific naturalism, and liberalism.

The desire for knowledge for its own sake is more widespread than is generally recognized by anti-intellectualists. It has its roots in the animal curiosity which shows itself in the cosmological questions of children and in the gossip of adults. No ulterior utilitarian motive makes people want to know about the private lives of their neighbors, the great, or the no- torious. There is also a certain zest which makes people engage in various intellectual games or exercises in which one is required to find out some- thing. But while the desire to know is wide, it is seldom strong enough to overcome the more powerful organic desires, and few indeed have both the inclination and the ability to face the arduous difficulties of scientific method in more than one special field. The desire to know is not often strong enough to sustain critical inquiry. Men generally are interested in the results, in the story or romance of science, not in the technical methods whereby these results are obtained and their truth continually is tested and qualified. Our first impulse is to accept the plausible as true and to reject the uncongenial as false. We have not the time, inclination, or energy to investigate everything. Indeed, the call to

[14] Ibid.

do so is often felt as irksome and joy-killing. And when we are asked to treat our cherished beliefs as mere hypotheses, we rebel as violently as when those dear to us are insulted. This provides the ground for various movements that are hostile to rational scientific procedure (though their promoters do not often admit that it is science to which they are hostile).

Mystics, intuitionists, authoritarians, voluntarists, and fictionalists are all trying to undermine respect for the rational methods of science. These attacks have always met with wide acclaim and are bound to continue to do so, for they strike a responsive note in human nature. Unfortunately they do not offer any reliable alternative method for obtaining verifiable knowledge. The great French writer Pascal opposed to logic the spirit of subtlety or finesse (*esprit géometrique and esprit de finesse*) and urged that the heart has its reasons as well as the mind, reasons that cannot be accurately formulated but which subtle spirits apprehend none the less. Men as diverse as James Russell Lowell and George Santayana are agreed that:

> "The soul is oracular still,"

and

> "It is wisdom to trust the heart . . .
> To trust the soul's invincible surmise."

Now it is true that in the absence of omniscience we must trust our soul's surmise; and great men are those whose surmises or intuitions are deep or penetrating. It is only by acting on our surmise that we can procure the evidence in its favor. But only havoc can result from confusing a surmise with a proposition for which there is already evidence. Are all the reasons of the heart sound? Do all oracles tell the truth? The sad history of human experience is distinctly discouraging to any such claim. Mystic intuition may give men absolute subjective certainty, but can give no proof that contrary intuitions are erroneous. It is obvious that when authorities conflict we must weigh the evidence in their favor logically if we are to make a rational choice. Certainly, when a truth is questioned it is no answer to say, "I am convinced," or, "I prefer to rely on this rather than on another authority." The view that physical science is no guide to proof, but is a mere fiction, fails to explain why it has enabled us to anticipate phenomena of nature and to control them. These attacks on scientific method receive a certain color of plausibility because of some indefensible claims made by uncritical enthusiasts. But it is of the essence of scientific method to limit its own pretension. Recognizing that we do not know everything, it does not claim the ability to solve all of our practical problems. It is an error to suppose, as is often done, that science denies the truth of all unverified propositions. For that which is unverified today may be verified tomorrow. We may get at truth by guessing or in other ways. Scientific method, however, is concerned with verification. Admittedly the wisdom of those engaged in this process has not been popularly ranked as high as that of the sage, the prophet, or the poet. Admittedly, also, we know of no way of supplying creative intelligence to those who lack it. Scientists, like all other human beings, may get into ruts and apply their techniques regardless of varying circumstances. There will always be formal procedures which are fruitless. Definitions and formal distinctions may be a sharpening of tools without the wit to use them properly, and statistical information may conform to the highest technical standards and yet be irrelevant and inconclusive. Nevertheless, scientific method is the only way to increase the general body of tested and verified truth and to eliminate arbitrary opinion. It is well to clarify our ideas by asking for the precise meaning of our words, and to try to check our favorite ideas by applying them to accurately formulated propositions.

In raising the question as to the social need for scientific method, it is well to recognize that the suspension of judgment which is essential to that method is difficult or impossible when we are pressed by the demands of immediate action. When my house is on fire, I must act quickly and promptly—I cannot stop to consider the possible causes, nor even to estimate the exact probabilities involved in the various alternative ways of reacting. For this reason, those who are bent upon some specific course of action often despise those devoted to reflection; and certain ultramodernists seem to argue as if the need for action guaranteed the truth of our decision. But the fact that I must either vote for candidate X or refrain from doing so does not of itself give me adequate knowledge. The frequency of our regrets makes this obvious. Wisely ordered society is therefore provided with means for deliberation and reflection *before* the pressure of action becomes irresistible. In order to assure the most thorough investigation, all possible views must be canvassed, and this means toleration of views that are *prima facie* most repugnant to us.

In general the chief social condition of scientific method is a widespread desire for truth that is strong enough to withstand the powerful forces which made us cling tenaciously to old views or else embrace every novelty because it is a change. Those who are engaged in scientific work need not only leisure for reflection and material for their experiments, but also a community that respects the pursuit of truth and allows freedom for the expression of intellectual doubt as to its most sacred or established institutions. Fear of offending established dogmas has been an obstacle to the growth of astronomy and geology and other physical sciences; and the fear of offending patriotic or respected sentiment is perhaps one of the strongest hindrances to scholarly history and social science. On the other hand, when a community indiscriminately acclaims every new doctrine the love of truth becomes subordinated to the desire for novel formulations.

On the whole it may be said that the safety of science depends on there being men who care more for the justice of their methods than for any results obtained by their use. For this reason it is unfortunate when scientific research in the social field is largely in the hands of those not in a favorable position to oppose established or popular opinion.

We may put it the other way by saying that the physical sciences can be more liberal because we are sure that foolish opinions will be readily eliminated by the shock of facts. In the social field, however, no one can tell what harm may come of foolish ideas before the foolishness is finally, if ever, demonstrated. None of the precautions of scientific method can prevent human life from being an adventure, and no scientific investigator knows whether he will reach his goal. But scientific method does enable large numbers to walk with surer step. By analyzing the possibilities of any step or plan, it becomes possible to anticipate the future and adjust ourselves to it in advance. Scientific method thus minimizes the shock of novelty and the uncertainty of life. It enables us to frame policies of action and of moral judgment fit for a wider outlook than those of immediate physical stimulus or organic response.

Scientific method is the only effective way of strengthening the love of truth. It develops the intellectual courage to face difficulties and to overcome illusions that are pleasant temporarily but destructive ultimately. It settles differences without any external force by appealing to our common rational nature. The way of science, even if it is up a steep mountain, is open to all. Hence, while sectarian and partisan faiths are based on personal choice or temperament and divide men, scientific procedure unites men in something nobly devoid of all pettiness. Because it requires detachment, disinterestedness, it is the finest flower and test of a liberal civilization.

Contemporary Issues

Creationism vs. Evolution

48. Creation, Evolution and Public Education   Duane Tolbert Gish

Duane T. Gish (1921–   ) is associate director of the Institute for Creation Research, El Cajon, California. He has degrees from both the University of California at Los Angeles and the University of California at Berkeley (Ph.D., biochemistry), as well as 18 years of experience in biochemical and biomedical research at Berkeley, Cornell University, and the Upjohn Company. He has authored numerous books and articles on scientific creation, including booklets for high school and college students.

It is commonly believed that the theory of evolution is the only scientific explanation of origins and that the theory of special creation is based solely on religious beliefs. It is further widely accepted that the theory of evolution is supported by such a vast body of scientific evidence, while encountering so few contradictions, that evolution should be accepted as an established fact. As a consequence, it is maintained by many educators that the theory of evolution should be included in science textbooks as the sole explanation for origins but that the theory of special creation, if taught at all, must be restricted to social science courses.

As a matter of fact, neither evolution nor creation qualifies as a scientific theory. Furthermore, it is become increasingly apparent that there are a number of irresolvable contradictions between evolution theory and the facts of science, and that the mechanism postulated for the evolutionary process could account for no more than trivial changes.

It would be well at this point to define what we mean by creation and evolution. By *Creation* we are referring to the theory that the universe and all life forms came into existence by the direct creative acts of a Creator external to and independent of the natural universe. It is postulated that the basic plant and animal kinds were separately created, and that any variation or speciation that has occurred since creation has been limited within the circumscribed boundaries of these created kinds. It is further postulated that the earth has suffered at least one great world-wide catastrophic event or flood which would account for the mass death, destruction, and extinction found on such a monumental scale in geological deposits.

By *Evolution* we are referring to the General Theory of Evolution. This is the theory that all living things have arisen by naturalistic, mechanistic processes from a single primeval cell, which in turn had arisen by similar processes from a dead, inanimate world. This evolutionary process is postulated to have occurred over a period of many hundreds of millions of years. It is further postulated that all major geological formations can be explained by present processes acting essentially at present rates without resort to any world-wide catastrophe(s).

Reprinted by permission of Duane T. Gish, Ph.D., Institute for Creation Research, El Cajon, CA 92021.

Creation has not been observed by human witnesses. Since creation would have involved unique, unrepeatable historical events, creation is not subject to the experimental method. Furthermore, creation as a theory is non-falsifiable. That is, it is impossible to conceive an experiment that could disprove the possibility of creation. Creation thus does not fulfill the criteria of a scientific theory. That does not say anything about its ultimate validity, of course. Furthermore, creation theory* can be used to correlate and explain data, particularly that available from the fossil record, and is thus subject to test in the same manner that other alleged historical events are subject to test—by comparison with historical evidence.

Evolution theory also fails to meet the criteria of a scientific theory. Evolution has never been witnessed by human observers; evolution is not subject to the experimental method; and as formulated by present-day evolutionists, it has become non-falsifiable.

It is obvious that no one has ever witnessed the type of evolutionary changes postulated by the general theory of evolution. No one, for example, witnessed the origin of the universe or the origin of life. No one has ever seen a fish evolve into an amphibian, nor has anyone observed an ape evolve into a man. No one, as a matter of fact, has ever witnessed a significant evolutionary change of any kind.

The example of the peppered moth in England has been cited by such authorities as H. B. D. Kettlewell[1] and Sir Gavin de Beer[2] as the most striking evolutionary change ever witnessed by man. Prior to the industrial revolution in England, the peppered moth, *Biston betularia*, consisted predominantly of a light-colored variety, with a dark-colored form comprising a small minority of the population. This was so because predators (birds) could more easily detect the dark-colored variety as these moths rested during the day on light-colored tree trunks and lichen-covered rocks. With the on-set of the industrial revolution and resultant air pollution, the tree trunks and rocks became progressively darker. As a consequence, the dark-colored variety of moths became more and more difficult to detect, while the light-colored variety ultimately became an easy prey. Birds, therefore, began eating more light-colored than dark-colored moths, and today over 95% of the peppered moths in the industrial areas of England are of the darker-colored variety.

Although, as noted above, this shift in populations of peppered moths has been described as the most striking example of evolution ever observed by man, it is obvious that no significant evolutionary change of any kind has occurred among these peppered moths, certainly not the type required to substantiate the general theory of evolution. For however the populations may have shifted in their proportions of the light and dark forms, all of the moths remained from beginning to end peppered moths, *Biston betularia*. It seems evident, then, that if this example is the

---

*An idea or set of ideas may be called a theory even though it does not qualify as a *scientific* theory. The term "model" is, however, a better expression than "theory" for the concept of creation or evolution, although "theory" and "model" will be used interchangeably in this paper.

most striking example of evolution witnessed by man, no real evolution of any kind has even been observed.

The world-famous evolutionist, Theodosius Dobzhansky, while endeavoring to proclaim his faith in evolution, admitted that no real evolutionary change has ever been observed by man when he said, ". . . the occurrence of the evolution of life in the history of the earth is established about as well as events *not witnessed by human observers can be*."[3] It can be said with certainty, then, that evolution in the present world has never been observed. It remains as far outside the pale of human observation as the origin of the universe or the origin of life. Evolution has been *postulated* but *never observed*.

Since evolution cannot be observed, it is not amenable to the methods of experimental science. This has been acknowledged by Dobzhansky when he stated, "These evolutionary happenings are unique, unrepeatable, and irreversible. It is as impossible to turn a land vertibrate into a fish as it is to effect the reverse transformation. The applicability of the experimental method to the study of such unique historical processes is severely restricted before all else by the time intervals involved, which far exceed the lifetime of any human experimenter. And yet it is just such *impossibility* that is demanded by antievolutionists when they ask for 'proofs' of evolution which they would magnanimously accept as satisfactory."[4]

Please note that Dobzhansky has said that the applicability of the experimental method to the study of evolution is an impossibility! It is obvious, then, that evolution fails to qualify as a scientific theory, for it is certain that a theory that cannot be subjected to experimental test is not a scientific theory.

Furthermore, modern evolution theory has become so plastic, it is non-falsifiable. It can be used to prove anything and everything. Thus, Murray Eden, a professor at Massachusetts Institute of Technology and an evolutionist, has said, with reference to the falsifiability of evolution theory, "This cannot be done in evolution, taking it in its broad sense, and this is really all I meant when I called it tautologous in the first place. It can, indeed, explain anything. You may be ingenious or not in proposing a mechanism which looks plausible to human beings and mechanisms which are consistent with other mechanisms which you have discovered, but it is still an unfalsifiable theory."[5]

Paul Ehrlich and L. C. Birch, biologists at Stanford University and the University of Sidney, respectively, have said, "Our theory of evolution has become . . . one which cannot be refuted by any possible observations. Every conceivable observation can be fitted into it. It is thus 'outside of empirical science' but not necessarily false. No one can think of ways in which to test it. Ideas, either without basis or based on a few laboratory experiments carried out in extremely simplified systems, have attained currency far beyond their validity. They have become part of an evolutionary dogma accepted by most of us as part of our training."[6]

Some evolutionists have been candid enough to admit that evolution is really no more scientific than is creation. In an article in which he states his conviction that the modern neo-Darwinian theory of evolution is based on axioms, Harris says " . . . the axiomatic nature of the neo-Darwinian theory places the debate between evolutionists and creationists in a new perspective. Evolutionists have often challenged creationists to provide experimental proof that species have been fashioned *de novo*. Creationists have often demanded that evolutionists show how chance mutations can lead to adaptability, or to explain why natural selection allows apparently detrimental organs to persist. We may now recognize that either challenge is fair. If the neo-Darwinian theory is axiomatic, it is not valid for creationists to demand proof of the axioms, and it is not valid for evolutionists to dismiss special creation as unproved so long as it is stated as an axiom."[7]

In his introduction to a 1971 edition of Charles Darwin's *Origin of Species,* Matthews states, "In accepting evolution as a fact, how many biologists pause to reflect that science is built upon theories that have been proved by experiment to be correct, or remember that the theory of animal evolution has never been thus proved? . . . The fact of evolution is the backbone of biology, and biology is thus in the peculiar position of being a science founded on an unproved theory—is it then a science or a faith? Belief in the theory of evolution is thus exactly parallel to belief in creation—both are concepts which believers know to be true but neither, up to the present, has been capable of proof."[8]

It can be seen from the above discussion, taken from the scientific literature published by leading evolutionary authorities, that evolution has never been observed and is outside the limits of experimental science. Evolution theory is, therefore, no more scientific than creation theory. That does not make it necessarily false, and it can be tested in the same way that creation theory can be tested—by its ability to correlate and explain historical data, that is, the fossil record. Furthermore, since evolution is supposed to have occurred by processes still operating today, the theory must not contradict natural laws.

Evolutionists protest, of course, that these weaknesses of evolution as a theory are not necessarily due to weaknesses of the theory, per se, but are inherent in the very nature of the evolutionary process. It is claimed that the evolutionary process is so slow that it simply cannot be observed during the lifetime of a human experimenter, or, as a matter of fact, during the combined observations of all recorded human experience. Thus, as noted above, Dobzhansky is incensed that creationists should demand that evolution be subjected to the experimental method before any consideration could be given to evolution as an established process.

It must be emphasized, however, that it is for precisely this reason that evolutionists insist that creation must be excluded from science textbooks or, for that matter, from the whole realm of science, as a viable alternative to evolution. They insist that creation must be excluded from possible consideration as a scientific explanation for origins because creation theory cannot be tested by the experimental method. It is evident, however, that this is a characteristic that it shares in common with evolution theory. Thus, if creation must be excluded from science texts and discussions, then evolution must likewise be excluded.

Evolutionists insist that, in any case, the teaching of the creation model would constitute the teaching of religion because creation requires a Creator. The teaching about the creation model and the scientific evidence supporting it, however, can be done without reference to any religious literature. Furthermore, belief in evolution is as intrinsically religious as is belief in creation.

If creation must be excluded from science in general and from science textbooks and science classrooms in particular because it involves the supernatural, it is obvious that theistic evolution must be excluded for exactly the same reason. Thus the only theory that can be taught according to this reasoning, and in fact, the only theory that is being taught in almost all public schools and universities and in the texts they use, is a purely mechanistic, naturalistic, and thus atheistic, theory of evolution. But atheism, the antithesis of theism, is itself a religious belief.

The late Sir Julian Huxley, British evolutionist and biologist, has said that "Gods are peripheral phenomena produced by evolution."[9] What Huxley meant was that the idea of God merely evolved as man evolved from lower animals. Huxley desired to establish a humanistic religion based on evolution. Humanism has been defined as "the belief that man shapes his own destiny. It is a constructive philosophy, a *non-theistic religion*, a way of life."[10] This same publication quotes Huxley as saying, "I use the word 'Humanist' to mean someone who believes that man is just as much a natural phenomenon as an animal or plant; that his body, mind, and soul were not supernaturally created but are products of *evolution*, and that he is not under the control or guidance of any supernatural being or beings, but has to rely on himself and his own powers."[10] The inseparable link between this non-theistic humanistic religion and belief in evolution is evident.

George Gaylord Simpson, Professor of Vertebrate Paleontology at Harvard University until his retirement and one of the world's best-known evolutionists, has said that the Christian faith, which he calls the "higher superstition" (in contrast to the "lower superstition" of pagan tribes of South America and Africa) is intellectually unacceptable.[11] Simpson concludes his book, *Life of the Past*,[12] with what Sir Julian Huxley has called "a splendid assertion of evolutionist view of man."[13] "Man," Simpson writes, "stands alone in the universe, a unique product of a long, unconscious, impersonal, material process with unique understanding and potentialities. These he owes to no one but himself, and it is to himself that he is responsible. He is not the creature of uncontrollable and undeterminable forces, but his own master. He can and must decide and manage his own destiny."[12]

Thus, according to Simpson, man is alone in the Universe (there is no God), he is the result of an impersonal, unconscious process (no one directed his origin or creation), and he is his own master and must manage his own destiny (there is no God to determine man's destiny). That, according to Simpson and Huxley, is the evolutionist's view of man. That this is the philosophy held by most biologists has been recently emphasized by Dobzhansky. In his review of Monod's book, *Chance and Necessity*,

Dobzhansky said, "He has stated with admirable clarity, and eloquence often verging on pathos, the mechanistic materialist philosophy shared by most of the present 'establishment' in the biological sciences."[14]

No doubt a majority of the scientific community embraces the mechanistic materialistic philosophy of Simpson, Huxley, and Monod. Many of these men are highly intelligent, and they have woven the fabric of evolution theory in an ingenious fashion. They have then combined this evolution theory with humanistic philosophy and have clothed the whole with the term "science." The product, a non-theistic religion, with evolutionary philosophy as its creed under the guise of "science," is being taught in most public schools, colleges and universities of the United States. It has become our unofficial state-sanctioned religion.

Furthermore, a growing number of scientists are becoming convinced that there are basic contradictions between evolution theory and empirical scientific data as well as known scientific laws. On the other hand, these scientists believe special creation provides an excellent model for explaining the correlating data related to origins which is free of such contradictions. Even some evolutionists are beginning to realize that the formulations of modern evolution theory are really incapable of explaining anything and that an adequate scientific theory of evolution, if ever attainable, must await the discovery of as yet unknown natural laws.

The core of modern evolution theory, known as the neo-Darwinian theory of evolution, or the modern synthetic theory, is the hypothesis that the evolutionary process has occurred through natural selection of random mutational changes in the genetic material, selection being in accordance with alterations in the environment. Natural selection, itself, is not a chance process, but the material it must act on, mutant genes, is produced by random, chance processes.

It is an astounding fact that while at the time Darwin popularized it, the concept of natural selection seemed to explain so much, today there is a growing realization that the presently accepted concept of natural selection really explains nothing. It is a mere tautology, that is, it involves circular reasoning.

In modern theory, natural selection is defined in terms of differential reproduction. In fact, according to Lewontin, differential reproduction *is* natural selection.[15] When it is asked, what survives, the answer is, the fittest. But when it is asked, what are the fittest, the answer is, those that survive! Natural selection thus collapses into a tautology, devoid of explanatory value. It is not possible to explain *why* some varieties live to reproduce more offspring—it is only known that they do.

In discussing Richard Levins' concept of fitness set analysis, Hamilton stated, "This criticism amounts to restating what I think is the admission of most evolutionists, that we do not yet know what natural selection maximizes."[16] Now if evolutionists do not know what natural selection maximizes, they do not know what natural selection selects.

In a review of the thinking in French scientific circles, it was stated, "Even if they do not publicly take a definite stand, almost all French specialists hold today strong mental reservations as to the validity of natural selection."[17] Creationists maintain that indeed natural selection could not result in increased complexity or convert a plant or animal into another basic kind. It can only act to eliminate the unfit.

Macbeth has recently published an especially incisive criticism of evolution theory and of the concept of natural selection as used by evolutionists.[18] He points out that although evolutionists have abandoned classical Darwinism, the modern synthetic theory they have proposed as a substitute is equally inadequate to explain progressive change as the result of natural selection, and, as a matter of fact, they cannot even define natural selection in non-tautological terms. Inadequacies of the present theory and failure of the fossil record to substantiate predictions based on the theory leave macro-evolution, and even micro-evolution, intractable mysteries according to Macbeth. Macbeth suggests that no theory at all may be preferable to the present theory of evolution.

Using Macbeth's work as the starting point for his own investigation of modern evolution theory, Bethell, a graduate of Oxford with a major in philosophy, has expressed his complete dissatisfaction with the present formulations of evolution theory and natural selection from the viewpoint of the philosophy of science.[19] Both Macbeth and Bethell present excellent reviews of the thinking of leading evolutionists concerning the relationship of natural selection to evolution theory. While both are highly critical, neither profess to be creationists.

According to modern evolutionary theory, ultimately all of evolution is due to mutations.[20] Mutations are random changes in the genes or chromosomes which are highly ordered structures. Any process that occurs by random chance events is subject to the laws of probability.

It is possible to estimate mutation rates. It is also possible to estimate how many favorable mutations would be required to bring about certain evolutionary changes. Assuming that these mutations are produced in a random, chance manner, as is true in the neo-Darwinian interpretation of evolution, it is possible to calculate how long such an evolutionary process would have required to convert an amoeba into a man. When this is done, according to a group of mathematicians, all of whom are evolutionists, the answer turns out to be billions of times longer than the assumed five billion years of earth history![21]

One of these mathematicians, Murray Eden, stated, "It is our contention that if 'random' is given a serious and crucial interpretation from a probabilistic point of view, the randomness postulate is highly implausible and that an *adequate scientific theory of evolution must await the discovery and elucidation of new natural laws—physical, physico-chemical, and biological.*"[22] What Eden and these mathematicians are saying is that the modern neo-Darwinian theory of evolution is totally inadequate to explain more than trivial change and thus we simply have no basis at present for attempting to explain how evolution may have occurred. As a matter of fact, based on the assumption that the evolutionary process was dependent upon random chance processes, we can simply state that evolution would have been impossible.

Furthermore, evolution theory contradicts one of the most firmly established laws known to science, the Second Law of Thermodynamics.

The obvious contradiction between evolution and the Second Law of Thermodynamics becomes evident when we compare the definition of this Law and its consequences by several scientists (all of whom, as far as we know, accept evolutionary philosophy) with the definition of evolution by Sir Julian Huxley, biologist and one of the best-known spokesmen for evolution theory.

> "There is a general natural tendency of all observed systems to go from order to disorder, reflecting dissipation of energy available for future transformations—the law of increasing entropy."[23]

> "All real processes go with an increase of entropy. The entropy also measures the randomness, or lack of orderliness of the system: the greater the randomness, the greater the entropy."[24]

> "Another way of stating the second law then is: 'The universe is constantly getting more disorderly!' Viewed that way, we can see the second law all about us. We have to work hard to straighten a room, but left to itself it becomes a mess again very quickly and very easily. Even if we never enter it, it becomes dusty and musty. How difficult to maintain houses, and machinery, and our own bodies in perfect working order: how easy to let them deteriorate. In fact, all we have to do is nothing, and everything deteriorates, collapses, breaks down, wears out, all by itself—and that is what the second law is all about."[25]

Now compare these definitions or consequences of the Second Law of Thermodynamics to the theory of evolution as defined by Huxley:

> "Evolution in the extended sense can be defined as a directional and essentially irreversible process occurring in time, which in its course gives rise to an increase of variety and an increasingly high level of organization in its products. Our present knowledge indeed forces us to the view that the whole of reality is evolution—a single process of self-transformation."[26]

There is a natural tendency, then, for all observed natural systems to go from order to disorder, towards increasing randomness. This is true throughout the entire known universe, both at the micro and macro levels. This tendency is so invariant that it has never been observed to fail. It is a natural law—the Second Law of Thermodynamics.

On the other hand, according to the general theory of evolution, as defined by Huxley, there is a general tendency of natural systems to go from disorder to order, towards an ever higher and higher level of complexity. This tendency supposedly operates in every corner of the universe, both at the micro and macro levels. As a consequence, it is believed, particles have evolved into people.

It is difficult to understand how a discerning person could fail to see the basic contradiction between these two processes. It seems apparent that both cannot be true, but no modern scientist would dare challenge the validity of the Second Law of Thermodynamics.

The usual, but exceedingly naive, answer given by evolutionists to this dilemma is that the Second Law of Thermodynamics applies only to closed systems. If the system is open to an external source of energy, it is asserted, complexity can be generated and maintained within this system at the expense of the energy supplied to it from the outside.

Thus, our solar system is an open system, and energy is supplied to the earth from the sun. The decrease in entropy, or increase in order, on the earth during the evolutionary process, it is said, has been more than compensated by the increase in entropy, or decrease in order, on the sun. The overall result has been a net decrease in order, so the Second Law of Thermodynamics has not been violated, we are told.

An open system and an adequate external source of energy are necessary *but not sufficient* conditions, however, for order to be generated and maintained, since raw, undirected, uncontrolled energy is destructive, not constructive. For example, without the protective layer of ozone in the upper atmosphere which absorbs most of the ultraviolet light coming from the sun, life on earth would be impossible. Bacterial cells exposed to such radiation die within seconds. This is because ultraviolet light, or irradiation of any kind, breaks chemical bonds and thus randomizes and destroys the highly complex structures found in biologically active macromolecules, such as proteins and DNA. Biological activity of these vitally important molecules is destroyed and death rapidly follows.

That much more than merely an external energy source is required to form complex molecules and systems from simpler ones is evident from the following statement by Simpson and Beck: ". . . the simple expenditure of energy is not sufficient to develop and maintain order. A bull in a china shop performs work, but he neither creates nor maintains organization. The work needed is *particular* work; it must follow specifications; it requires information on how to proceed."[27]

Thus a green plant, utilizing the highly complex photosynthetic system it possesses, can trap light energy from the sun and convert this light energy into chemical energy. A series of other complex systems within the green plant allows the utilization of this energy to build up complex molecules and systems from simple starting material. Of equal importance is the fact that the green plant possesses a system for directing, maintaining, and replicating these complex energy conversion mechanisms— an incredibly complex genetic system. Without the genetic system, no specifications on how to proceed would exist, chaos would result, and life would be impossible.

For complexity to be generated within a system, then, four conditions must be met:

1. The system must be an open system.
2. An adequate external energy source must be available.
3. The system must possess energy conversion mechanisms.
4. A control mechanism must exist within the system for directing, maintaining, and replicating these energy conversion mechanisms.

The seemingly irresolvable dilemma, from an evolutionary point of view, is, how such complex energy conversion mechanisms and genetic systems arose in the *absence* of such systems, when there is a general natural tendency to go from order to disorder, a tendency so universal it can be stated as a natural law, the Second Law of Thermodynamics.

Simply stated, machines are required to build machines, and something or somebody must operate the machinery.

The creationist thus opposes the wholly unscientific evolutionary hypothesis that the natural universe with all of its incredible complexity, was capable of generating itself, and maintains that there must exist, external to the natural universe, a Creator, or supernatural Agent, who was responsible for introducing, or creating, the high degree of order found within this natural universe. While creationism is extra-scientific, it is not anti-scientific, as is the evolutionary hypothesis which contradicts one of the most well-established laws of science.

Finally, but of utmost significance, is the fact that the fossil record is actually hostile to the evolution model, but conforms remarkably well to predictions based on the creation model.[28] Complex forms of life appear abruptly in the fossil record in the so-called Cambrian sedimentary deposits or rocks. Although these animals, which include such highly complex and diverse forms of life as brachiopods, trilobites, worms, jellyfish, sponges, sea urchins, and sea cucumbers, as well as other crustaceans and molluscs, supposedly required about two to three billion years to evolve, not a single ancestor for any of these animals can be found anywhere on the face of the earth.[28-31] George Gaylord Simpson has characterized the absence of Precambrian fossils as "the major mystery of the history of life."[32] This fact of the fossil record, incomprehensible in the light of the evolution model, is exactly as predicted on the basis of the creation model.

The remainder of the fossil record reveals a remarkable absence of the many transitional forms demanded by the theory of evolution.[28] Gaps between all higher categories of plants and animals, which creationists believe constituted the created kinds, are systematic. For example, Simpson has admitted that "Gaps among known orders, classes, and phyla are systematic and almost always large."[33] Richard B. Goldschmidt, well-known geneticist and a rabid evolutionist, acknowledged that "practically all orders or families known appear suddenly and without any apparent transitions."[34] E. J. H. Corner, Cambridge University botanist and an evolutionist, stated, " . . . I still think, to the unprejudiced, the fossil record of plants is in favor of special creation."[35]

Recently, the well-known evolutionary paleontologist, David B. Kitts, stated, "Despite the bright promise that paleontology provides a means of 'seeing' evolution, it has presented some nasty difficulties for evolutionists the most notorious of which is the presence of 'gaps' in the fossil record. *Evolution requires intermediate forms between species and paleontology does not provide them. . . .* "[36]

Lord Solly Zuckerman, for many years the head of the Department of Anatomy at the University of Birmingham, was first knighted and then later raised to the peerage as recognition of his distinguished career as a research scientist. After over 15 years of research on the subject, with a team that rarely included less than four scientists, Lord Zuckerman concluded that *Australopithecus* did not walk upright, he was not intermediate between ape and man, but that he was merely an anthropoid ape. *Australopithecus* (Louis Leakey's "Nutcracker Man," and Donald Johanson's "Lucy") is an extinct ape-like creature that almost all evolutionists believe walked erect and showed many characteristics intermediate between ape and man. Lord Zuckerman, although not a creationist, believes there is very little, if any, science in the search for man's fossil ancestry. Lord Zuckerman states his conviction, based on a life-time of investigation, that if man has evolved from an ape-like creature he did so without leaving any trace of the transformation in the fossil record.[37] This directly contradicts the popular idea that paleontologists have found numerous evidences of ape-like ancestors for man, but rather suggests they have found none at all.

The explosive appearance of highly complex forms of life in Cambrian and other rocks with the absence of required ancestors, and the abrupt appearance of each major plant and animal kind without apparent transitional forms are the facts of greatest importance derivable from a study of the fossil record. These facts are highly contradictory to predictions based on the evolution model, but are just as predicted on the basis of the creation model of origins.

The facts described above are some of the reasons why creationists maintain that, on the basis of available scientific evidence, the creation model is not only a viable alternative to the evolution model, but is actually a far superior model. Furthermore, after more than a century of effort to establish Darwinian evolution, even some evolutionists are beginning to express doubts. This is evidently true, for example, of Pierre P. Grassé, one of the most distinguished of French scientists. In his review of Grassé's book, *L'Evolution du Vivant*,[38] Dobzhansky states, "The book of Pierre P. Grassé is a frontal attack on all kinds of 'Darwinism.' Its purpose is 'to destroy the myth of evolution as a simple, understood, and explained phenomenon,' and to show that evolution is a mystery about which little is, and perhaps can be, known. Now, one can disagree with Grassé but not ignore him. He is the most distinguished of French zoologists, the editor of the 28 volumes of 'Traite de Zoologie,' author of numerous original investigations, and ex-president of the Academie des Sciences. His knowledge of the living world is encyclopedic. . . . "[39] In the closing sentence of his review, Dobzhansky says, "The sentence with which Grassé ends his book is disturbing: 'It is possible that in this domain biology, impotent, yields the floor to metaphysics.' "[40] Grassé thus closes his book with the statement that biology is powerless to explain the origin of living things and that it may possibly have to yield to metaphysics (supernatural creation of some kind).

In his Presidential Address to the Linnaean Society of London, "A Little on Lung-fishes," Errol White said, "But whatever ideas authorities may have on the subject, the lung-fishes, like every other major group of fishes I know, have their origin firmly based in *nothing*. . . . " He then said, "I have often said how little I should like to have to prove organic evolution in a court of law." He closed his address by saying, "We still do not know the mechanics of evolution in spite of the over-confident claims in some quarters, nor are we likely to make further progress in this by the classical methods of paleontology or biology: and we shall certainly not advance matters by jumping up and down shrilling 'Darwin is God and I, So-and-so, am his prophet'—the recent researches of workers like Dean and Hinshelwood (1964) already suggest the possibility of incipient cracks in the seemingly monolithic walls of the Neo-Darwinian Jericho."[41] White thus seems to be suggesting that the modern neo-Darwinian theory of evolution is in danger of crashing down just as did the walls of Jericho!

Thus, today we have a most astounding situation. Evolution has never been observed by human witnesses. Evolution cannot be subjected to the experimental method. The most sacred tenet of Darwinism—natural selection—in modern formulation is incapable of explaining anything. Furthermore, even some evolutionists are conceding that the mechanism of evolution proposed by evolutionary biologists could account for no more than trivial change in the time believed to have been available, and that an adequate scientific theory of evolution, based on present knowledge, seems impossible. Finally, the major features of the fossil record accord in an amazing fashion with the predictions based on special creation, but contradict the most fundamental predictions generated by the theory of evolution. And yet the demand is unceasing that evolution theory be accepted as the only scientific explanation for origins, even as an established fact, while excluding creation as a mere religious concept!

This rigid indoctrination in evolutionary dogma, with the exclusion of the competing concept of special creation, results in young people being indoctrinated in a non-theistic, naturalistic, humanistic religious philosophy in the guise of science. Science is perverted, academic freedom is denied, the educational process suffers, and constitutional guarantees of religious freedom are violated.

This unhealthy situation could be corrected by presenting students with the two competing models for origins, the creation model and the evolution model, with all supporting evidence for each model. This would permit an evaluation of the students of the strengths and weaknesses of each model. This is the course true education should pursue rather than following the present process of brainwashing students in evolutionary philosophy.

References

1. H. B. D. Kettlewell, *Scientific American,* Vol. 200, No. 3, p. 48 (1959).
2. Gavin de Beer, *Nature,* Vol. 206, p. 331 (1965).
3. T. Dobzhansky, *Science,* Vol. 127, p. 1091 (1958).
4. T. Dobzhansky, *American Scientist,* Vol. 45, p. 388, (1957).
5. M. Eden, *Mathematical Challenges to the Neo-Darwinian Interpretation of Evolution,* P. S. Moorehead and M. M. Kaplan, Eds., Wistar Institute Press, Philadelphia, p. 71 (1967).
6. P. Ehrlich and L. C. Birch, *Nature,* Vol. 214, p. 352 (1967).
7. C. Leon Harris, *Perspectives in Biology and Medicine,* Winter 1975, pp. 179–184.
8. L. Harrison Matthews, Introduction to *The Origin of Species,* Charles Darwin, J. M. Dent and Sons, Ltd., London, pp. X, XI (1971).

9. J. Huxley, *The Observer,* July 17, 1960, p. 17.

10. *What Is Humanism?,* The Humanist Community of San Jose, San Jose, California 95106.

11. G. G. Simpson, *Science,* Vol. 131, p. 966 (1960).

12. G. G. Simpson, *Life of the Past,* Yale University Press, New Haven (1953).

13. J. Huxley, *Scientific American,* Vol. 189, p. 90 (1953).

14. T. Dobzhansky, *Science,* Vol. 175, p. 49 (1972).

15. R. C. Lewontin, "Selection in and of Populations" in *Ideas in Modern Biology,* Natural History Press, Garden City, New York, p. 304 (1965).

16. W. D. Hamilton, *Science,* Vol. 167, p. 1478 (1970).

17. Z. Litynski, *Science Digest,* Vol. 50, p. 61 (1961).

18. N. Macbeth, *Darwin Retried,* Gambit, Inc., Boston, 1971.

19. T. Bethell, *Harper's Magazine,* February, 1976, p. 70.

20. See for example, G. L. Stebbins, *Processes of Organic Evolution,* 2nd Ed., Prentice-Hall, Inc., Englewood Cliffs, N. J., 1971, p. 3; E. Mayr, *Animal Species and Evolution,* Harvard University Press, Cambridge, p. 176. (1966).

21. R. Bernhard, *Scientific Research,* November, 1967, p. 59; P. S. Moorhead and M. M. Kaplan, Eds., *Mathematical Challenges to the Neo-Darwinian Interpretation of Evolution,* Wistar Institute Press, Philadelphia, 1967.

22. M. Eden, in *Mathematical Challenges to the Neo-Darwinian Interpretation of Evolution,* p. 109.

23. R. B. Lindsay, *American Scientist,* Vol. 56, p. 100 (1968).

24. H. Blum, *American Scientist,* Vol. 43, p. 595 (1955).

25. I. Asimov, *Smithsonian Institute Journal,* June, 1970, p. 6.

26. J. Huxley, "Evolution and Genetics," in *What Is Science?,* J. R. Newman, Ed., Simon and Schuster, New York, p. 272 (1955).

27. G. G. Simpson and W. S. Beck, *Life: An Introduction to Biology,* 2nd Ed., Harcourt, Brace & World, Inc., New York, p. 466 (1965).

28. D. T. Gish, *Evolution: The Fossils Say No!,* Creation-Life Publishers, San Diego, 1973.

29. Preston Cloud, *Geology,* Vol. 1, p. 123 (1973).

30. D. Axelrod, *Science,* Vol. 128, p. 7 (1958).

31. T. N. George, *Science Progress,* Vol. 48, p. 5 (1960).

32. G. G. Simpson, *The Meaning of Evolution,* Yale University Press, New Haven, p. 18 (1953).

33. G. G. Simpson, in *The Evolution of Life,* Sol Tax, Ed., University of Chicago Press, Chicago, p. 149 (1960).

34. R. B. Goldschmidt, *American Scientist,* Vol. 40, p. 97 (1952).

35. E. J. H. Corner, in *Contemporary Botanical Thought,* A. M. MacLeod and L. S. Cobley, Eds., Quadrangle Books, Chicago, p. 97 (1961).

36. David B. Kitts, *Evolution,* Vol. 28, p. 467 (1974).

37. S. Zuckerman, *Beyond the Ivory Tower,* Taplinger Pub. Co., New York, 1970, p. 64; see also *Journal of the Royal College of Surgeons of Edinburgh,* Vol. 11, pp. 87–115 (1966).

38. Editions Albin Michel, Paris, 1973.

39. T. Dobzhansky, *Evolution,* Vol. 29, p. 376 (1975).

40. Reference 39, p. 378.

41. E. White, *Proceedings Linnean Society of London,* Vol. 177, p. 8 (1966).

49. The Armies of the Night   Isaac Asimov

Isaac Asimov (1920–) was born in Russia and came to the United States in 1923. A professor of biochemistry, he is a polymath and prolific author reminiscent of the philosopher Democritus in the ancient world. An indefatigable interpreter of science to the general public and annotator of the Bible, Shakespeare, and other literary works, among the laity he probably is best known as a writer, critic, and anthologer of SF or science fiction. In the 1982–1983 *Who's Who in America,* Professor Asimov writes " . . . I have published 237 books as of now and am well-thought of in consequence. As you see, none of this is to my credit. I am the beneficiary of a lucky break in the genetic-sweepstakes."

Scientists thought it was settled.

The universe, they had decided, is about 20 billion years old, and Earth itself is 4.5 billion years old. Simple forms of life came into being more than three billion years ago, having formed spontaneously from nonliving matter. They grew more complex through slow evolutionary processes and the first hominid ancestors of humanity appeared more than four million years ago. Homo sapiens itself—the present human species, people like you and me—has walked the earth for at least 50,000 years.

But apparently it isn't settled. There are Americans who believe that the earth is only about 6,000 years old; that human beings and all other species were brought into existence by a divine Creator as eternally separate varieties of beings, and that there has been no evolutionary process.

They are creationists—they call themselves "scientific" creationists— and they are a growing power in the land, demanding that schools be forced to teach their views. State legislatures, mindful of votes, are beginning to succumb to the pressure. In perhaps 15 states, bills have been introduced, putting forth the creationist point of view, and in others, strong movements are gaining momentum. In Arkansas, a law requiring that the teaching of creationism receive equal time was passed this spring and is scheduled to go into effect in September 1982, though the American Civil Liberties Union has filed suit on behalf of a group of clergymen, teachers and parents to overturn it. And a California father named Kelly Segraves, the director of the Creation-Science Research Center, sued to have public-school science classes taught that there are other theories of creation besides evolution, and that one of them was the Biblical version. The suit came to trial in March, and the judge ruled that educators must distribute a policy statement to schools and textbook publishers explaining that the theory of evolution should not be seen as "the ultimate cause of origins." Even in New York, the Board of Education has delayed since January in making a final decision, expected this month, on whether

From *The New York Times Magazine,* June 14, 1981, where it appeared under the title "The 'Threat' of Creationism." Reprinted with permission of the author.

schools will be required to include the teaching of creationism in their curriculums.

The Rev. Jerry Falwell, the head of the Moral Majority, who supports the creationist view from his television pulpit, claims that he has 17 million to 25 million viewers (though Arbitron places the figure at a much more modest 1.6 million). But there are 66 electronic ministries which have a total audience of about 20 million. And in parts of the country where the Fundamentalists predominate—the so-called Bible Belt—creationists are in the majority.

They make up a fervid and dedicated group, convinced beyond agrument of both their rightness and righteousness. Faced with an apathetic and falsely secure majority, smaller groups have used intense pressure and forceful campaigning—as the creationists do—and have succeeded in disrupting and taking over whole societies.

Yet, though creationists seem to accept the literal truth of the Biblical story of creation, this does not mean that all religious people are creationists. There are millions of Catholics, Protestants and Jews who think of the Bible as a source of spiritual truth and accept much of it as symbolically rather than literally true. They do not consider the Bible to be a textbook of science, even in intent, and have no problem teaching evolution in their secular institutions.

To those who are trained in science, creationism seems like a bad dream, a sudden reliving of a nightmare, a renewed march of an army of the night risen to challenge free thought and enlightenment.

The scientific evidence for the age of the earth and for the evolutionary development of life seems overwhelming to scientists. How can anyone question it? What are the arguments the creationists use? What is the "science" that makes their views "scientific"? Here are some of them:

The Argument from Analogy

A watch implies a watchmaker, say the creationists. If you were to find a beautifully intricate watch in the desert, far from habitation, you would be sure that it had been fashioned by human hands and somehow left there. It would pass the bounds of credibility that it had simply formed, spontaneously, from the sands of the desert.

By analogy, then, if you consider humanity, life, earth and the universe, all infinitely more intricate than a watch, you can believe far less easily that it "just happened." It, too, like the watch, must have been fashioned, but by more-than-human hands—in short by a divine Creator.

This argument seems unanswerable, and it has been used (even though not often explicitly expressed) ever since the dawn of consciousness. To have explained to prescientific human beings that the wind and the rain and the sun follow the laws of nature and do so blindly and without a guiding hand would have been utterly unconvincing to them. In fact, it might well have gotten you stoned to death as a blasphemer.

There are many aspects of the universe that still cannot be explained satisfactorily by science; but ignorance implies only ignorance that may someday be conquered. To surrender to ignorance and call it God has always been premature, and it remains premature today.

In short, the complexity of the universe—and one's inability to explain it in full—is not in itself an argument for a Creator.

The Argument from General Consent

Some creationists point out that belief in a Creator is general among all peoples and all cultures. Surely this unanimous craving hints at a great truth. There would be no unanimous belief in a lie.

General belief, however, is not really surprising. Nearly every people on earth that considers the existence of the world assumes it to have been created by a god or gods. And each group invents full details for the story. No two creation tales are alike. The Greeks, the Norsemen, the Japanese, the Hindus, the American Indians and so on and so on all have their own creation myths, and all of these are recognized by Americans of Judeo-Christian heritage as "just myths."

The ancient Hebrews also had a creation tale—two of them, in fact. There is a primitive Adam-and-Eve-in-Paradise story, with man created first, then animals, then woman. There is also a poetic tale of God fashioning the universe in six days, with animals preceding man, and man and woman created together.

These Hebrew myths are not inherently more credible than any of the others, but they are our myths. General consent, of course, proves nothing: There can be a unanimous belief in something that isn't so. The universal opinion over thousands of years that the earth was flat never flattened its spherical shape by one inch.

The Argument by Belittlement

Creationists frequently stress the fact that evolution is "only a theory," giving the impression that a theory is an idle guess. A scientist, one gathers, arising one morning with nothing particular to do, decides that perhaps the moon is made of Roquefort cheese and instantly advances the Roquefort-cheese theory.

A theory (as the word is used by scientists) is a detailed description of some facet of the universe's workings that is based on long observation and, where possible, experiment. It is the result of careful reasoning from those observations and experiments and has survived the critical study of scientists generally.

For example, we have the description of the cellular nature of living organisms (the "cell theory"); of objects attracting each other according to a fixed rule (the "theory of gravitation"); of energy behaving in discrete bits (the "quantum theory"); of light traveling through a vacuum at a fixed measurable velocity (the "theory of relativity"), and so on.

All are theories; all are firmly founded; all are accepted as valid descriptions of this or that aspect of the universe. They are neither guesses nor speculations. And no theory is better founded, more closely examined, more critically argued and more thoroughly accepted, than the theory of evolution. If it is "only" a theory, that is all it has to be.

Creationism, on the other hand, is not a theory. There is no evidence, in the scientific sense, that supports it. Creationism, or at least the particular variety accepted by many Americans, is an expression of early Middle Eastern legend. It is fairly described as "only a myth."

The Argument from Imperfection

Creationists, in recent years, have stressed the "scientific" background of their beliefs. They point out that there are scientists who base their creationists beliefs on a careful study of geology, paleontology and biology and produce "textbooks" that embody those beliefs.

Virtually the whole scientific corpus of creationism, however, consists of the pointing out of imperfections in the evolutionary view. The creationists insist, for example, that evolutionists cannot show true transition states between species in the fossil evidence; that age determinations through radioactive breakdown are uncertain; that alternate interpretations of this or that piece of evidence are possible, and so on.

Because the evolutionary view is not perfect and is not agreed upon in every detail by all scientists, creationists argue that evolution is false and that scientists, in supporting evolution, are basing their views on blind faith and dogmatism.

To an extent, the creationists are right here. The details of evolution are not perfectly known. Scientists have been adjusting and modifying Charles Darwin's suggestions since he advanced this theory of the origin of species through natural selection back in 1859. After all, much has been learned about the fossil record and about physiology, microbiology, biochemistry, ethology and various other branches in life science in the last 125 years, and it is to be expected that we can improve on Darwin. In fact, we have improved on him.

Nor is the process finished. It can never be, as long as human beings continue to question and to strive for better answers.

The details of evolutionary theory are in dispute precisely because scientists are not devotees of blind faith and dogmatism. They do not accept even as great a thinker as Darwin without question, nor do they accept any idea, new or old, without thorough argument. Even after accepting an idea, they stand ready to overrule it, if appropriate new evidence arrives. If, however, we grant that a theory is imperfect and that details remain in dispute, does that disprove the theory as a whole?

Consider. I drive a car, and you drive a car. I do not know exactly how an engine works. Perhaps you do not either. And it may be that our hazy and approximate ideas of the workings of an automobile are in conflict. Must we then conclude from this disagreement that an automobile does not run, or that it does not exist? Or, if our senses force us to conclude that an automobile does exist and run, does that mean it is pulled by an invisible horse, since our engine theory is imperfect?

However much scientists argue their differing beliefs in details of evolutionary theory, or in the interpretation of the necessarily imperfect fossil record, they firmly accept the evolutionary process itself.

The Argument from Distorted Science

Creationists have learned enough scientific terminology to use it in their attempts to disprove evolution. They do this in numerous ways, but the most common example, at least in the mail I receive, is the repeated assertion that the second law of thermodynamics demonstrates the evolutionary process to be impossible.

In kindergarten terms, the second law of thermodynamics says that all spontaneous change is in the direction of increasing disorder—that is, in a "downhill" direction. There can be no spontaneous buildup of the complex from the simple, therefore, because that would be moving "uphill." According to the creationist argument, since, by the evolutionary process, complex forms of life evolve from simple forms, that process defies the second law, so creationism must be true.

Such an argument implies that this clearly visible fallacy is somehow invisible to scientists, who must therefore be flying in the face of the second law through sheer perversity.

Scientists, however, do know about the second law and they are not blind. It's just that an argument based on kindergarten terms is suitable only for kindergartens.

To lift the argument a notch above the kindergarten level, the second law of thermodynamics applies to a "closed system"—that is, to a system that does not gain energy from without, or lose energy to the outside. The only truly closed system we know of is the universe as a whole.

Within a closed system, there are subsystems that can gain complexity spontaneously, provided there is a greater loss of complexity in another interlocking subsystem. The overall change then is a complexity loss in line with the dictates of the second law.

Evolution can proceed and build up the complex from the simple, thus moving uphill, without violating the second law, as long as another interlocking part of the system—the sun, which delivers energy to the earth continually—moves downhill (as it does) at a much faster rate than evolution moves uphill.

If the sun were to cease shining, evolution would stop and so, eventually, would life.

Unfortunately, the second law is a subtle concept which most people are not accustomed to dealing with, and it is not easy to see the fallacy in the creationist distortion.

There are many other "scientific" arguments used by creationists, some taking quite clever advantage of present areas of dispute in evolutionary theory, but every one of them is as disingenuous as the second-law argument.

The "scientific" arguments are organized into special creationist textbooks, which have all the surface appearance of the real thing, and which school systems are being heavily pressured to accept. They are written by people who have not made any mark as scientists, and, while they discuss geology, paleontology and biology with correct scientific terminology, they are devoted almost entirely to raising doubts over the legitimacy of the evidence and reasoning underlying evolutionary thinking on the assumption that this leaves creationism as the only possible alternative.

Evidence actually in favor of creationism is not presented, of course, because none exists other than the word of the Bible, which it is current creationist strategy not to use.

The Argument from Irrelevance

Some creationists put all matters of scientific evidence to one side and consider all such things irrelevant. The Creator, they say, brought life and the earth and the entire universe into being 6,000 years ago or so, complete with all the evidence for an eons-long evolutionary development. The fossil record, the decaying radioactivity, the receding galaxies were all created as they are, and the evidence they present is an illusion.

Of course, this argument is itself irrelevant, for it can neither be proved nor disproved. It is not an argument, actually, but a statement. I can say that the entire universe was created two minutes ago, complete with all its history books describing a nonexistent past in detail, and with every living person equipped with a full memory: you, for instance, in the process of reading this article in midstream with a memory of what you had read in the beginning—which you had not really read.

What kind of a Creator would produce a universe containing so intricate an illusion? It would mean that the Creator formed a universe that contained human beings whom He had endowed with the faculty of curiosity and the ability to reason. He supplied those human beings with an enormous amount of subtle and cleverly consistent evidence designed to mislead them and cause them to be convinced that the universe was created 20 billion years ago and developed by evolutionary processes that included the creation and development of life on Earth.

Why?

Does the Creator take pleasure in fooling us? Does it amuse Him to watch us go wrong? Is it part of a test to see if human beings will deny their senses and their reason in order to cling to myth? Can it be that the Creator is a cruel and malicious prankster, with a vicious and adolescent sense of humor?

The Argument from Authority

The Bible says that God created the world in six days, and the Bible is the inspired word of God. To the average creationist this is all that counts. All other arguments are merely a tedious way of countering the propaganda of all those wicked humanists, agnostics and atheists who are not satisfied with the clear word of the Lord.

The creationist leaders do not actually use that argument because that would make their argument a religious one, and they would not be able to use it in fighting a secular school system. They have to borrow the clothing of science, no matter how badly it fits and call themselves "scientific" creationists. They also speak only of the "Creator," and never mention that this Creator is the God of the Bible.

We cannot, however, take this sheep's clothing seriously. However much the creationist leaders might hammer away at their "scientific" and "philosophical" points, they would be helpless and a laughing stock if that were all they had.

It is religion that recruits their squadrons. Tens of millions of Americans, who neither know or understand the actual arguments for—or even against—evolution, march in the army of the night with their Bibles held high. And they are a strong and frightening force, impervious to, and immunized against, the feeble lance of mere reason.

Even if I am right and the evolutionists' case is very strong, have not creationists, whatever the emptiness of their case, a right to be heard?

If their case is empty, isn't it perfectly safe to discuss it since the emptiness would then be apparent?

Why, then, are evolutionists so reluctant to have creationism taught in the public schools on an equal basis with evolutionary theory? Can it be that the evolutionists are not as confident of their case as they pretend. Are they afraid to allow youngsters a clear choice?

First, the creationists are somewhat less than honest in their demand for equal time. It is not their views that are repressed: Schools are by no means the only place in which the dispute between creationism and evolutionary theory is played out.

There are the churches, for instance, which are a much more serious influence on most Americans than the schools are. To be sure, many churches are quite liberal, have made their peace with science and find it easy to live with scientific advance—even with evolution. But many of the less modish and citified churches are bastions of creationism.

The influence of the church is naturally felt in the home, in the newspapers and in all of surrounding society. It makes itself felt in the nation as a whole, even religiously liberal areas, in thousands of subtle ways: in the nature of holiday observance, in expressions of patriotic fervor, even in total irrelevancies. In 1968, for example, a team of astronauts circling the moon were instructed to read the first few verses of Genesis as though NASA felt it had to placate the public lest they rage against the violation of the firmament. At the present time, even the current President of the United States has expressed his creationist sympathies.

It is only in school that American youngsters in general are ever likely to hear any reasoned exposition of the evolutionary viewpoint. They might find such a viewpoint in books, magazines, newspapers or even, on occasion, on television. But church and family can easily censor printed matter or television. Only the school is beyond their control.

But only just barely beyond. Even though schools are now allowed to teach evolution, teachers are beginning to be apologetic about it, knowing full well their jobs are at the mercy of school boards upon which creationists are a stronger and stronger influence.

Then, too, in schools, students are not required to believe what they learn about evolution—merely to parrot it back on tests. If they fail to do so, their punishment is nothing more than the loss of a few points on a test or two.

In the creationist churches, however, the congregation is required to believe. Impressionable youngsters, taught that they will go to hell if they listen to the evolutionary doctrine, are not likely to listen in comfort or to believe if they do.

Therefore, creationists, who control the church and the society they live in and who face the public school as the only place where evolution is even briefly mentioned in a possibly favorable way, find they cannot stand even so minuscule a competition and demand "equal time."

Do you suppose their devotion to "fairness" is such that they will give equal time to evolution in their churches?

Second, the real danger is the manner in which creationists want their "equal time."

In the scientific world, there is free and open competition of ideas, and even a scientist whose suggestions are not accepted is nevertheless free to continue to argue his case.

In this free and open competition of ideas, creationism has clearly lost. In has been losing in fact, since the time of Copernicus four and a half centuries ago. But creationists, placing myth above reason, refuse to accept the decision and are now calling on the Government to force their views on the schools in lieu of the free expression of ideas. Teachers must be forced to present creationism as though it has equal intellectual respectability with evolutionary doctrine.

What a precedent this sets.

If the Government can mobilize its policemen and its prisons to make certain that teachers give creationism equal time, they can next use force to make sure that teachers declare creationism the victor so that evolution will be evicted from the classroom altogether.

We will have established the full groundwork, in other words, for legally enforced ignorance and for totalitarian thought control.

And what if the creationists win? They might, you know, for there are millions who, faced with the choice between science and their interpretation of the Bible, will choose the Bible and reject science, regardless of the evidence.

This is not entirely because of a traditional and unthinking reverence for the literal words of the Bible; there is also a pervasive uneasiness—even an actual fear—of science that will drive even those who care little for Fundamentalism into the arms of the creationists. For one thing, science is uncertain. Theories are subject to revision; observations are open to a variety of interpretations, and scientists quarrel among themselves. This is disillusioning for those untrained in the scientific method, who thus turn to the rigid certainty of the Bible instead. There is something comfortable about a view that allows for no deviation and that spares you the painful necessity of having to think.

Second, science is complex and chilling. The mathematical language of science is understood by very few. The vistas it presents are scary—an enormous universe ruled by chance and impersonal rules, empty and uncaring, ungraspable and vertiginous. How comfortable to turn instead to a small world, only a few thousand years old, and under God's personal and immediate care; a world in which you are His peculiar concern and where He will not consign you to hell if you are careful to follow every word of the Bible as interpreted for you by your television preacher.

Third, science is dangerous. There is no question but that poison gas, genetic engineering and nuclear weapons and power stations are terrifying. It may be that civilization is falling apart and the world we know is coming to an end. In that case, why not turn to religion and look forward to the Day of Judgment, in which you and your fellow believers will be lifted into external bliss and have the added joy of watching the scoffers and disbelievers writhe forever in torment.

So why might they not win?

There are numerous cases of societies in which the armies of the night have ridden triumphantly over minorities in order to establish a powerful orthodoxy which dictates official thought. Invariably, the triumphant ride is toward long-range disaster.

Spain dominated Europe and the world in the 16th century, but in Spain orthodoxy came first, and all divergence of opinion was ruthlessly suppressed. The result was that Spain settled back into blankness and did not share in the scientific, technological and commercial ferment that bubbled up in other nations of Western Europe. Spain remained an intellectual backwater for centuries.

In the late 17th century, France in the name of orthodoxy revoked the Edict of Nantes and drove out many thousands of Huguenots, who added their intellectual vigor to lands of refuge such as Great Britain, the Netherlands and Prussia, while France was permanently weakened.

In more recent times, Germany hounded out the Jewish scientists of Europe. They arrived in the United States and contributed immeasurably to scientific advancement here, while Germany lost so heavily that there is no telling how long it will take to regain its former scientific eminence. The Soviet Union, in its fascination with Lysenko, destroyed its geneticists, and set back its biological sciences for decades. China, during the Cultural Revolution, turned against Western science and is still laboring to overcome the devastation that resulted.

Are we now, with all these examples before us, to ride backward into the past under the same tattered banner of orthodoxy? With creationism in the saddle, American science will wither. We will raise a generation of ignoramuses ill-equipped to run the industry of tomorrow, much less to generate the new advances of the days after tomorrow.

We will inevitably recede into the backwater of civilization and those nations that retain open scientific thought will take over the leadership of the world and the cutting edge of human advancement.

I don't suppose that the creationists really plan the decline of the United States, but their loudly expressed patriotism is as simple-minded as their "science." If they succeed, they will, in their folly, achieve the opposite of what they say they wish.

Pseudoscience and Science

50. A Consumer's Guide to Pseudoscience   James S. Trefil

James S. Trefil (1938–   ) is professor of physics at the University of Virginia.

I have mixed feelings about the current boom in things parascientific—movies like *Star Wars* and *Close Encounters of the Third Kind,* TV shows about weekly UFO landings, and books about spaceships that descended to earth in prehistoric times. As a physicist, I realize that today's flights of fancy may well be tomorrow's scientific orthodoxy. But it worries me that a public ill equipped to distinguish between razzle-dazzle and sound speculation is swallowing whole many pseudoscientific notions that strike me as silly at best and as a species of intellectual junk food at worst.

My concern here is not, incidentally, altogether cool and disinterested; I still brood about the time several years ago when my son, then ten, was watching a TV "documentary" about ancient civilizations that had been visited by extraterrestrials. When I ventured something mildly skeptical about the show, my son turned on me and cried, "But didn't you *see*? They *proved* it!"

Repeated experiences like this with my children, my students, and my contemporaries have left me convinced that the world could use a kind of do-it-yourself guide to getting one's bearings in the Alice-in-Wonderland realm of unorthodox scientific claims. Before launching into this guide, however, I'd like to make some general remarks about offbeat claims and mention some concrete examples.

As I said above, it's important to realize that unorthodox views are not alien to conventional science. When you come down to it, every accepted scientific principle started out in life as an unorthodox thought in the mind of one man. It follows, then, that in every living science there is a frontier area where new basic principles are being sought and where innovative ideas can gain a hearing. In my own field of physics there are several frontier areas, the most wide-open one being the study of elementary particles (the subatomic objects that in some way contain the key to the ultimate structure of matter). So newness in itself is not now and never has been a basis for the rejection of an idea by the scientific community.

One can visualize the situation in science in terms of concentric circles: At the *center* is that body of time-tested, universally accepted ideas that are set forth in school and college texts. The first circle out from the center is the *frontier,* which interacts constantly with the center, feeding it new ideas that the center, after lengthy testing, adopts and assimilates.

If we move beyond the frontier region of a science, however, we come to a hazy outer circle area that I like to call the *fringe.* The fringe is characterized by a scarcity of hard data and by a general fuzziness of ideas that make the average scientist very uncomfortable. It is a zone in which neither accepted scientific writ nor reasonable extrapolations of

From *The Saturday Review,* April 29, 1978. Reprinted with permission of *The Saturday Review.*

scientific knowledge seem to apply. For these reasons, it is an area that scientists generally prefer to avoid.

Yet the fringe has its uses, for it feeds ideas to the frontier, much as the frontier feeds ideas to the center. Fifty years ago, the notion that we should attempt to communicate with extraterrestrial intelligences would most emphatically have been a fringe concept. Yet today this idea has moved into the more respectable frontier circle. (Incidentally, this move illustrates an important point about the ideas contained within both the fringe and the frontier. The soundest, most useful of them keep gravitating inward, ring by ring, toward the orthodox center.)

Now there is only one thing that will make the average scientist more uneasy than talking about what lies beyond his particular frontier and that is having someone express doubts about the validity of ideas that he considers to be established at the center of his discipline and therefore no longer open to question. For example, in the time of Isaac Newton the law of gravity was a frontier subject, but now it is regarded as a principle that has been validated by centuries of experiment and use. This law has passed from the frontier of science and is firmly ensconced within the vital center. Anyone who suggests that the law ought to be abandoned or modified is not going to get a sympathetic hearing unless he presents a very convincing argument.

The progression of scientific ideas from frontier circle to "center" acceptance isn't always smooth. The germ theory of disease and the theory of continental drift are examples of ideas that were considered too "fringy" when they were first introduced. Only long, often acrimonious campaigns won them official recognition.

There have of course been thousands of fringe ideas that never made it to the frontier and thousands of frontier ideas that never gained centrist respectability. The basic problems, then, that anyone, scientist or layman, faces when confronted with a new theory are how to decide where it belongs on the concentric-circle scale and how to determine its chances of eventual acceptance.

In making such judgments, scientists have to keep two criteria in mind: A new idea may be rejected because it is too far beyond the frontier—for instance, too fringy and unprovable; or it may be rejected because it is too far behind the frontier—for instance, a clumsy, complicated way of accomplishing ends already being accomplished by simple, efficient, economical centrist theories. Thus, an overly elaborate, hard-to-prove, Rube Goldberg-like notion could be rejected because it might be at once to fringy and too inefficient in comparison with well-established centrist theories.

With this framework in mind, let's look at some current offbeat theories and the problems they pose for the citizen who is wondering whether to accept or reject their striking claims.

Velikovsky and *Worlds in Collision*

In 1950 Immanuel Velikovsky, a Russian-born psychoanalyst, published a book called *Worlds in Collision* that touched off a minor tempest among astronomers and served as a model for an entire generation of pseudoscientific writing. The premise of his work was that the recent history of our solar system has been marked by a series of catastrophic events and that these events are faithfully recorded in ancient writings. Thus, according to Velikovsky the planet we now know as Venus was ejected from Jupiter about 5,000 years ago (an event recorded in Greek mythology). Thereafter, Venus wandered about the solar system as a comet, experiencing several close encounters with our earth before settling into its present orbit. One of these encounters coincided with the parting of the Red Sea for the Israelites and another, with the stopping of the rotation of the earth for the benefit of the ancient Hebrew leader Joshua. Both of these events and other "catastrophes" too numerous to mention are recorded in the Old Testament.

To substantiate these claims, Velikovsky cited examples from other legends about massive floods and about days when the sun stood still in the sky. He also used the ancient writings to predict the properties of the planets. For example, since the manna that fell on the Israelites during their wanderings in the desert was supposed to have been material from the Venusian comet, he predicted that hydrocarbons (or many carbohydrates—the distinction between the two isn't clear in the book) would be found in the Venusian atmosphere. He also predicted that Venus would be found to be "candescent."

When these claims were made, very little was known about planetary science, so they could be classified as fringe ideas. At the same time, they required that known physical laws (such as the conservation of energy) had to have been violated at some time in the past or the events Velikovsky described would have been impossible. Thus, the scientific community rejected his thesis because his ideas were both too far ahead and too far behind the frontier. (Velikovsky's followers also claim that a group of professors tried to suppress publication of the book. If this is true, I can only say that professors have less clout now than in the early Fifties.)

Velikovsky's claims are set forth in a book that runs to 389 pages in the paperback edition. Faced with this avalanche of fact and hypothesis, what is the reader supposed to do? Well, in Velikovsky's case we're lucky because his book caused so much furor that a number of refutations have been written. The most recent of these refutations is the published proceedings of a symposium held in 1973 by the American Association for the Advancement of Science (AAAS) (Donald Goldsmith, ed., "Scientists Confront Velikovsky," Cornell University Press, 1977). A quick look at the *Reader's Guide to Periodical Literature* or at the card catalog of a public library will turn up other books and articles contra Velikovsky. The counterarguments fall into three categories: questions of fact, questions of logical consistency, and questions of alternative explanations.

Let's take the category of factual questions. As we noted above, Velikovsky claimed flatly that hydrocarbon-based manna from Venus fell upon the Israelites during their desert wanderings. Yet National Aeronautics and Space Administration space probes have turned up no evidence of hydrocarbons in the atmosphere of Venus—although once a scientist was misquoted as saying that an early probe did find such evidence—and the temperature of the planet is about what you'd expect on the basis of the greenhouse effect. (Certainly it's not hot enough to make the surface candescent.) Such evidence helps to clear the air, but it's hardly the kind of knowledge that most of us would have at our fingertips. In keeping with my goal of providing a do-it-yourself system for analyzing theories then, I'll have to turn to the other two categories, logical consistency and alternative explanations.

About logical consistency: If you look over Velikovsky's argument, it becomes apparent that the central point is his idea that ancient writings are supposed to be taken as literal, eyewitness accounts of celestial events. Fair enough. But when I read the Bible's account of the Israelites' wanderings, I find that the manna fell from heaven daily *except for the Sabbath.* Now I can imagine a comet whose tail contains edible material, and I can even conceive of this edible material falling only on one small area of the earth for an extended period, but I cannot for the life of me imagine a comet that keeps the Sabbath. That doesn't seem to me "logically consistent." This sort of example can be multiplied ad infinitum by anyone who looks seriously into the thousands of statements in *Worlds in Collision.*

In the same way—and here we come to the category of alternative explanations—we can ask if it's really necessary to suspend the laws of nature in order to explain the accounts of natural disasters in ancient writings. Isn't there some less complicated way of interpreting these phenomena? Surely disaster is one experience that has been shared, at one time or another, by the entire human race. And of course, the idea that ancient writers never took liberties with facts in order to achieve literary effect is a notion that doesn't stand scrutiny very well. If it did, we'd be faced with trying to explain why ancient writers were so different from their modern counterparts.

Erich von Daniken and *Chariots of the Gods*

If there is ever a prize established for the most rhetorical questions per page, Erich von Daniken will win it hands down. Using this device, he theorizes that mythological references to flying gods actually refer to extraterrestrial visitors to earth and that many of the achievements of ancient civilizations were realized with the help of advanced technology made available by ancient space-faring astronauts. Because so many claims are made in a short space of time, the reader's rational circuits overload and he just floats along. Being unable to challenge every claim, he is reduced to the state of challenging none.

The way to cope with this blizzard of assertions and rhetorical questions (which is fairly common in pseudoscientific writing) is to resist the temptation of allowing the verbal avalanche to bury you. Instead, pick out one or two claims and look into them thoroughly. For example, here's a quote from Von Daniken about the Egyptian pyramids:

> Is it really a coincidence that the height of the pyramids multiplied by a thousand million corresponds approximately to the distance between the earth and the sun? Is it a coincidence that a meridian running through the pyramids divides continents and oceans into two exactly equal halves?

Is it coincidence that the area of the base of a pyramid divided by twice its height gives the celebrated figure $\pi = 3.14159$? Is it coincidence that calculations of the weight of the earth were found and is it also coincidence that the rocky ground on which the structure stands is carefully and accurately leveled?

Confronted with a paragraph like this, it would be an unusual reader who would not become intimidated and move on to the next paragraph, carrying with him the definite impression that the Egyptians could never have built the pyramids without outside help—even though this claim is not made explicitly. But instead, let's stop for a moment. There are five claims made in this paragraph, and checking all of them could occupy the better part of a day. Few people would want to spend that much time investigating one paragraph in a book full of such paragraphs.

So let's not. Let's pick one claim at random and check it out. For example, in Volume 18 of the *Encyclopaedia Britannica* (Plastics–Razin) I find the information that the pyramids were originally built to be 146.59 meters high and to have a square base of 230 meters to a side. A quick check shows that the claim about π can't be right (actually, any student in a freshman physics class could have told us that you can't get a dimensionless number like π when you divide an area by a height). In the interest of fairness, though, I tried a few combinations and came up with the fact that twice the length of a side of the Pyramid of Cheops divided by the structure's height is 3.138, which differs from π by only 0.1 percent. Assuming that this is what Von Daniken meant, doesn't this bit of research confirm the claim implicit in his rhetorical question?

Not necessarily. Let's take the idea one step farther. If the ancient astronauts intended to have this number be exactly π, it means they mismeasured the side of the pyramid by 0.1 percent. (For reference, 0.1 percent of 230 meters is about 9 inches.) A check through some books on surveying at the library revealed that run-of-the-mill commercial surveying is usually accurate to .01 percent (10 times more precise than the measurements done at the pyramid). A call to a man who teaches surveying yielded the information that beginning college level surveying students routinely get an accuracy of 0.05 percent; not commercial quality but still better than that at the pyramid. What I found therefore was that although an accuracy of 0.1 percent sounds very good, it is actually pretty poor by modern standards. (As an interesting aside, it turns out that all of the dimensions of the pyramid were surveyed with about this accuracy.)

So what do we have? Either the numbers quoted by Von Daniken are the result of the Egyptians' building to plan as best they could, or we have a race of ancient astronauts who could assemble and operate a spaceship but who would have flunked freshman surveying. Take your pick.

This example illustrates one important weapon in the consumer's arsenal. If you ignore an author's invitation to slide over a series of glib claims and instead take a few statements and follow them to their logical conclusion, you can get a pretty good idea of how much weight should be given to the claims that you don't verify. In the case of Von Daniken's rhetorical questions, this probably isn't much.

The pyramid-measuring example also brings up a question that is frequently asked about the pseudosciences: If they're wrong, why aren't they refuted by reputable scientists? The answer is that it would simply take too much time. It took me the better part of a morning to chase down this claim, and an exhaustive analysis of even a single chapter in this one book would take months. Very few scientists have this much time to spare for a project that will not advance their professional standing in any way and that will in all likelihood gain them nothing but a lot of crank mail. They prefer to remain silent (though disapproving) and will only do something if they are irritated beyond endurance (as they eventually were in the case of Velikovsky).

ETI and UFO Phenomena

If I had been writing this article 10 years ago, the field of extraterrestrial intelligence (ETI) and unidentified flying objects (UFOs) would have been relegated to the farthest reaches of the fringe. The whole thing reeked of little green men and bug-eyed monsters, and the Condon report had pretty well established that the great majority of UFO sightings could be assigned a perfectly natural (although sometimes complex) explanation. There seemed to be nothing more to say on the subject.

In the past few years, however, a number of developments have occurred to alter this picture. Astronomers have started to give serious thought to the idea that radio telescopes might be able to "listen in" on signals from other planetary systems. In fact, the search for evidence of ETI has already begun with existing telescopes, and proposals are in the wind to build new ones just for this purpose. In a sense, the interest in ETI constitutes a success story in which a formerly unacceptable idea has moved into the realm of serious scientific consideration.

Although the UFO phenomenon hasn't achieved this sort of status, in recent years a few reputable scientists have been willing to look into UFO sightings to see if there might be something there beyond optical illusion. The results to date are not impressive, but the fact that some scientists are willing to take the time to examine the question is itself significant. I know it may sound terribly elitist to say so, but one of the best indicators of the soundness of a new idea is the willingness of scientists to devote their time to developing it.

Most scientists aren't wealthy, so about the only things they can invest in their career are the time and effort that go into research. Like an investor looking through stock offerings, each scientist has to make a judgment as to where his energies should go to produce the maximum return. Thus, when a scientist passes up "sure thing" conventional research to devote his time to something like listening with a radio telescope for extraterrestrial signals, he's doing the equivalent of putting his money where his mouth is.

Of course, the presence of reputable scientists in a field doesn't guarantee that the idea being investigated will turn out to be right. On the other hand, there are a lot of conventional research projects that don't prove out either. So although the ETI-UFO subject still has a very fringy flavor to it, the past few years have seen some parts of it move tentatively into the legitimate frontier area of conventional science.

Pyramid Power

This whole pyramid-power business is so far out that I wasn't going to deal with it at all. I changed my mind when I saw the following ad in the catalog of a respected scientific-supplies company.

> CAN THE GREAT PYRAMID UNLOCK THE MYSTERIES OF ENERGY & AGING?. . . Did the ancient Egyptians build Cheops's Pyramid in such a way that the laws of nature are contradicted? Some people have been using exact scale models of the pyramids and are claiming all kinds of things . . . meat doesn't rot, razor blades stay sharp, things don't rust, and other strange phenomena. All these claims are based on energy resonating in an exact scale model of Cheop's Pyramid oriented to magnetic North.

From this ad, it's clear we're dealing with something firmly established behind the frontier. Oh well, back to Volume 18 of the *Britannica* for the pyramid dimensions. Assemble, as I did, a cardboard pyramid. Put a piece of hamburger inside and line the pyramid up with a compass. Wait a few days. Whew!

Do-It-Yourself Checklist

On the basis of the foregoing examples, I think we can now try to list general techniques that anyone can use when confronted with the next plausibly presented arguments for God-only-knows-what new idea. Here are some useful questions to ask:

Are the facts really what the author says they are? Further (and more to the point), has someone already been sufficiently irritated by the author's claims to answer this question for you?
Some of the "facts" presented in any argument just might be wrong, but it's not always convenient to check them out yourself. It's always easier if someone else does the work. For example, trying to run down all the half-truths, rumors, and inaccuracies about the Bermuda Triangle would be a prodigious task. Fortunately, you don't have to do it because it's been done and the results published by Lawrence Kusche in *The Bermuda Triangle Mystery—Solved* (Harper & Row, 1975). In a similar vein, the proceedings of the AAAS symposium mentioned previously give a pretty good overall critique of Velikovsky, so you don't have to go searching around for scattered articles.
Therefore the first thing to do is to check your local library listings on the subject you want to look into.

Is the author trying to overload your circuits?

Although Erich von Daniken is the best (or worst) example of this technique of bludgeoning the reader into quiescence, all such authors that I have read use it. The only defense against the ploy is to pick out a few statements made about a field you know something of and look into them thoroughly. The chances are that if the author hasn't gotten those right, he hasn't done too good a job on the material you don't check.

Given the author's facts, is there a simpler explanation of them?

If I had to pick the single failing that characterizes pseudoscientific theories, I would choose their tendency *to propose complex solutions to simple problems.* We have already seen in the case of Velikovsky that the existence of old manuscripts describing cataclysmic events can easily be explained in terms of shared human experiences and of the known tendency of writers to exaggerate. What are we to do then when given the choice between revising almost the whole body of physics and astronomy and accepting as literal truth "facts" that may be only-too-human exaggerations? It seems to me that the most sensible path is to take the explanation that does the least amount of damage to other ideas.

I can't resist mentioning another example of how this criterion works. In the ancient-astronaut documentary mentioned earlier, there was an episode in which a subterranean vault with painted walls was shown. The announcer made a big point of claiming that there was no evidence of soot (such as a torch would have left) anywhere in the vault. The program's conclusion was that the ancient Egyptians must have had access to electric lights and hence had been visited by extraterrestrials.

Now, even assuming that it is correct that this chamber was put together without any soot being left behind by the workmen, does it necessarily follow that the Egyptians were visited by astronauts? Putting it another way, if you were an Egyptian engineer, could you think of a way to get a chamber built without leaving deposits of soot? A few minutes' reflection turns up (1) washing the soot off after the work is finished, (2) sinking a shaft to the chamber to let smoke out and light in, (3) doing it all with mirrors.

The interested citizen should always take a little time to play devil's advocate on such questions because the penchant for ignoring the very existence of a simpler explanation of the facts—an explanation that doesn't require a wildly complicated set of theories—is the besetting weakness of almost all pseudoscience.

Does the whole thing boil down to being unable to prove a negative?

It is impossible to prove that there are no unicorns. All we can prove is that we've found none so far. If the end result of a long argument (the "bottom line," if you prefer) is nothing more than the statement that a particular theory can't be disproved, you are probably safe putting it in the same class as unicorns.

Are established scientists putting time in on the phenomenon?

In the case of UFOs and ETIs, discussed above, one element in our considerations was the fact that a number of reputable scientists have been willing to bet their valuable time that the idea has something to it. While this doesn't guarantee that an idea is right, it does mean that someone has looked into it thoroughly and has come up with the conclusion that it's worth looking into a little more.

Having said this, let me hasten to add a caveat. There is no proposition on God's green earth so silly that it can't find at least one Ph.D. to support it. If you're going to use this criterion in judging a theory, find out who the scientists are. A quick check in *American Men and Women of Science* or in *Who's Who* will give you some idea of the credentials of the person involved. If you want a standard of comparison, look up Peter Sturrock of Stanford University—he's one of the people with sound credentials who are investigating UFO sightings these days.

Finally, you have to realize that this "credentials" criterion is only one of several you should use in making a judgment. If the theory sounds fishy to you, if you feel that the conclusions are unreasonable, and if the arguments of the scientists don't convince you, then so be it. In the final analysis, you have to make up your own mind anyway.

Can you test the theory yourself?

If you have a mechanical turn of mind, you can occasionally check out a claim yourself, as I did with the pyramid-power test.

Ask such simple questions as those on the checklist when you're reading the next book that reveals the secret of the ages—they will help you decide whether you're looking at a genuine scientific breakthrough or at just another addition to the fringe. There are two areas in which such questioning will be of little help, however, and we might as well get them straight right now. If outright fraud is involved—as it is reputed to have been in the famous "demonstration" by Uri Geller at the Stanford Research Institute—going through this sort of questioning will do you little good. There is no way that fraud can be detected secondhand by the layman, and there is probably no one more ill equipped than the average scientist to deal with outright duplicity. Also, the test questions really don't apply to writings that are specifically nonrational, such as the mystical and drug-oriented books that were so common a few years ago. Such books aren't playing the same game as those by the pseudoscientists and therefore can't be judged by the same rules.

No discussion of pseudoscience would be complete without some comment on its social implications. I am well aware that many of my colleagues regard modern pseudoscience as the forerunner of an antirational swing in our society and denounce it in terms that are worthy of that doom-crying German philosopher Oswald Spengler. I feel that this is something of an overreaction. Pseudoscience has been around at least as long as (and perhaps even longer than) conventional science. Perhaps it serves some deep need of human beings to believe that there is still some mystery—something unknown—left in life. Maybe the unknown thrives because people like to see the pompous scientific establishment discomfited ("Okay, Mr. Know-it-all, explain *this* one"). Or

A Compact (and Highly Personal) Guide to the Frontier and the Fringe Beyond

★★★★*Is moving into a respectable frontier position.*

★★★*Still does not have wide acceptance, but it's moving that way.*

★★*Probably will never amount to anything, but you might want to keep an eye on it.*

★*Forget it.*

★*Immanuel Velikovsky and* Worlds in Collision: The space program has pretty well taken the shine off this one.

★★★*ESP:* Started life on the far fringe but is moving toward respectability as more hard data is collected.

★★*UFOs:* This old favorite is moving up in the rankings on the basis of new interest by a few scientists, but it could move down again just as fast.

★*Ancient Astronauts:* If the UFOs are here now, they may have been here before, but that doesn't mean one of their crews built the pyramids.

★★★★*Extraterrestrial Intelligence:* There's a reasonable amount of effort and (more important) money going into listening for signals from space. So this subject has pretty well moved into the frontier regions of astronomy.

★*Bermuda Triangle:* It turns out there are no more mysterious disappearances than you'd expect for an ocean area often hit by hurricanes and other storms.

★*Lost Atlantis:* Another group that didn't build the pyramids.

★★*Water Witching (Dowsing):* Ordinarily I'd give this one star, but a student recently showed me not only that he could locate an underground water pipe but that I could too. There's probably a neurological explanation.

★*Pollen Power:* Pollen collected by honeybees is supposed to be very healthful. But since the pollen is taken from the bees before they go into the hives, why not just eat the flowers and eliminate the middleman?

★★★*Acupuncture:* It shouldn't work, but it seems to.

★*Biorhythms:* People are marketing calculators that will allow you to keep separate track of your three cycles (mental, emotional, physical) according to your birth date. But statistical studies show as many successes at the low points as at the high. Another numerological fad.

★*Horoscopes, Phrenology, and Palmistry:* These can be fun if you don't take them too seriously.

★*Perpetual Motion Machines:* Interest in these devices, the ultimate in energy saving, has dropped considerably since the patent office began requiring a working model with each application.

★*Fingertip Reading:* A few years ago the Russians caused quite a stir when they announced that they had found a woman who could read with her fingertips while blindfolded. Various professors at American universities promptly made headlines by claiming they too had located women fingertip readers. When the blindfolds were improved according to instructions from stage magicians, the powers mysteriously vanished, both here and in the U.S.S.R.

★★*Bigfoot, the Abominable Snowman, and All That:* Undoubtedly there's a measure of hoaxing here, but the discovery of something like these creatures wouldn't violate any scientific principles.

★*Loch Ness Monster:* The failures of searches in a small place have pretty well ruled this one out. I draw this conclusion with regret because I was rooting for Nessie.

★*Psychic Phenomena a la Uri Geller:* As far as the various key-bending, spoon-twisting, and remote-reading tricks are concerned, I'll believe them when they are done in front of a panel that includes at least one magician.

maybe it's just that P. T. Barnum was right about a sucker being born every minute. None of these interpretations constitutes a threat to conventional science.

After all, Luigi Galvani's "animal electricity" cures in the nineteenth century didn't impair the development of the science of electricity. Mme. Blavatsky's theosophy certainly had little effect on American science. And despite the apocalyptic terms with which it was greeted, it would be hard to show that Velikovsky's *Worlds in Collision* has had much of an effect on modern astronomy. At its worst, pseudoscience is a minor inconvenience of the cocktail party variety; and at its best, it is good entertainment. I certainly make no apology for the fact that I enjoyed reading Velikovsky and Von Daniken, even though I think they are wrong.

On balance, I'd say the best attitude to have toward pseudoscience is the one reflected in the story (probably apocryphal) about the time Groucho Marx attended a séance. After the usual hand holding, table thumping, and light dimming, the medium announced in funereal tones that she was now in contact with the spirit world and that the participants could ask any questions they liked: Nothing, she said, was hidden from the spirits. Without hesitation, Groucho shot back, "What's the capital of North Dakota?"

51. The Scientific Attitude vs. Antiscience and Pseudoscience
Paul Kurtz

Paul Kurtz (1925–   ) is professor of philosophy at the State University of New York at Buffalo and chairman of the Committee for the Scientific Investigation of Claims of the Paranormal. He also serves on the editorial board of *The Skeptical Inquirer,* a publication devoted to a fair and forthrightly critical examination of paranormal claims.

There has been a long-standing conflict in the history of culture between science and religion, reason and passion. Theologians have incessantly argued that there are "limits" to scientific inquiry and that it cannot penetrate the "transcendental realm"; and poets have decried deductive logic and the experimental method, which they claim denude experience of its sensuous qualities. The running controversy between the two cultures of science and the humanities is thus familiar.

This classic critique notwithstanding, the scientific enterprise has made remarkable progress in the past three centuries, resolving problems that were allegedly beyond the reach of its methodology; and the scientific revolution which first began in the natural sciences, has been extended to the biological, social, and behavioral sciences, with enormous benefits

From *The Humanist,* July/August 1976. Reprinted with permission of the author.

to humankind. Since the Enlightenment, it has been commonly believed that with the achievement of universal education, the scientific outlook would eventually triumph and would emancipate humankind from superstition. Progress was thought to be correlative with the growth of science.

This confidence in science, however, has been badly shaken in recent years. Even supposedly advanced societies are inundated by cults of unreason and other forms of nonsense. Earlier in this century we witnessed the emergence of fanatic ideological cults, such as Nazism and Stalinism. Today, Western democratic societies are being swept by other forms of irrationalism, often blatantly antiscientific and pseudoscientific in character. There are various manifestations of this new assault on reason.

A good illustration of the trend is the growth of astrology; but it is only the tip of the iceberg. For if one surveys the current state of belief, one finds that large numbers of people are apparently ready and able to believe in a wide variety of things, however outrageous, without sufficient evidence or proof. Even a random cataloging of some of the bizarre cults and gurus illustrates the point: Krishna consciousness, the Maharaj Ji, Aikido, the Maharishi Mahesh Yogi and various forms of transcendental meditation, the Unification Church, the Process, Gurjievians, Zen, Arica, the Children of God, the I-Ching, and Jeane Dixon. From the standpoint of the skeptical, scientific humanist, these cults are no more irrational than orthodox religious groups. Why are the preachings of the latest guru more nonsensical than a dead and risen diety, Mohammed's visitation by the angel Gabriel, Joseph Smith and his trek westward, Mary Baker Eddy and Christian Science, Theosophy, the Rosicrucians, or the canonization of saints for alleged miracles? The traditional religions strain the credulity as much as or more than the newer exotic mystery religions imported from Asia; but the former have been around longer and are considered to be part of the established social system. What is apparent is the tenacious endurance of irrational beliefs throughout history down to the present day—and in spite of the scientific revolution.

Take the phenomenon of "nouveau witches," as Marcello Truzzi has called them, and the revival of interest in exorcism. Only a few years ago it would have been rare to have encountered any college students who believed in witches. Yet today, belief in a host of witches and demons, even the devil, has become fashionable in some circles. This is the age of monsters, in which Frankenstein, Dracula, and werewolves become real for impressionable minds. The novel and the film *The Exorcist* stimulated belief in exorcism; and some people were unable to distinguish truth from fiction. Thus we are confronted with a plethora of flourishing myths, cultivated by a very profitable publishing and media industry. There is a new sacred church—the visual media—that feeds the imagination and outstrips any requirements for evidence.

This is all symptomatic of the current rejection of reason and objectivity. Whereas a decade ago there was a general consensus that at least some rules of evidence existed, today the very existence of objective criteria for judging truth claims is being seriously questioned. One hears over and over again that "one belief is as good as the next" and that there is a kind of "subjective truth" immune to rational or evidential criticism. One even finds proponents of forms of subjectivity among the philosophers of science, those who claim that historical conditions or psychological factors are largely responsible for revolutions in scientific thinking.

This reaction against rigorous standards assumed another form in the 1960s in the assault of the New Left and the counterculture upon the intellect. The current growth of cults of unreason is perhaps only a consequence of that phenomenon. We were told then that we needed to break loose from the demands of logic and evidence, and to "expand our consciousness" by drugs or other methods. Theodore Roszak spelled out such a position in his widely read book *Making of a Counter-Culture* (New York: Doubleday, 1969). Now in a new, equally subjective book, *Unfinished Animal: The Aquarian Frontier and the Evolution of Consciousness* (New York: Harper & Row, 1975) he says:

> Within the past few years, I have found myself more and more in the company of people like my former student: bright, widely read, well-educated people whose style it has become to accept and endorse all things occultly marvelous. In such circles, skepticism is a dead language, intellectual caution an outdated fashion. That Edgar Cayce could diagnose the illnesses of distant patients and predict earthquakes by psychic readings . . . that the pyramids were built by ancient astronauts . . . that orgone boxes can trap the life energy of the universe . . . that the continents of the earth were settled by the migrations from lost Lemuria . . . one does not question these reports, but, calmly letting the boundary between fact and fairy tale blur, one *uses* them—uses them to stretch one's powers of amazement. One listens through them to hear still another intimation of astounding possibilities, a shared conviction which allows one to say, "Yes, you feel it too, don't you?" That we are at the turning point, the Kairos, where the orders of reality shift and the impossible happens as naturally as the changing of seasons. (Page 2)

The counterculture insisted that objectivity was impossible, either because of class or professional biases or because we were locked into the categories of our scientific world view. One doesn't hear as much today of the Marxist critique, but one does hear a good deal that the existing scientific outlook is confining. And so there is an attempt to break out into newer forms of experience, of which the occult is only a part: people are willing to accept any and all novel departures in experience. Yesterday it was encounter groups; today it is apt to be mantras, meditation, bioenergetics, yoga, organic gardening, Kirlian photography, or ESP.

This exists beside another mood that is increasingly evident today— an aversion to technological culture itself. Science and technology are often indiscriminately blamed for the present world situation. We hear on all sides about the dangers of technology: the destruction of the natural ecology, pollution, resource depletion, the misuses of energy, the threat of nuclear power plants, and so on. Many of these concerns are genuine. Yet the critical stance is often not simply against technology but against science and scientific research itself. There are those on the fundamentalist right who still vehemently oppose, on ethical or religious grounds, the teaching of theories of evolution, comparative social-studies courses, and sexual education. But in addition, the scientist is often viewed by some on the left as a kind of demon—if he engages in human experimentation or behavior modification, or if he participates in genetic research or wishes to test the genetic basis of I.Q. And there is a growing body of opinion that views medical doctors and psychiatrists as evil high priests or voodoo men.

We are confronted today with a form of moral righteousness and anti-intellectualism—often bordering on hysteria—that indicts hard science as dehumanizing, brutalizing, and destructive of human freedom and value. This attitude is paradoxical, for it seems to occur most virulently in affluent societies, which have made the greatest strides in scientific research and technology. What was once considered to have the highest promise for humankind is now viewed by many as its greatest threat. Some would even have us repeal contemporary society and return to simpler modes of romantic existence.

Should we assume that the scientific revolution, which began in the sixteenth century, is continuous? Or will it be overwhelmed by the forces of unreason? The picture I am drawing must not be overstated. Alongside the critics of science are its defenders. And vast resources are plowed into scientific education, research, organizations, and publications. Science is still highly regarded by much of the public.

Indeed, the fact that science is essential to our technological civilization is well recognized by some of the critics of science—which brings me to still another dimension of the growth of irrationality: the proliferation of pseudoscience. Those who are not tempted by the occult can always find chariots of the gods, UFOs, Bermuda triangles, or lost continents to beguile them. The new prophets seek to have their speculative theories cloaked in the mantle of scientific legitimacy; they include von Däniken and those associated with dianetics, Scientology, and recent efforts to develop a "scientific astrology."

The growth of pseudoscience can be seen in many other areas. There is, for example, an effort to explore the so-called parapsychological realm. Psychic phenomena, which were carefully studied in the late nineteenth century by the Society for Psychical Research in England, and parapsychology, which was researched for many years by J. B. Rhine at Duke University, have now become the rage. Uri Geller has been examined by "scientific experts" and found to possess amazing "psychic powers." His feats have been duplicated by magicians such as James Randi, using traditional magic tricks. Students and professors alike announce new investigations of clairvoyance, precognition, dream telepathy, out-of-body experiences, reincarnation, communication with spirits of the dead, psychic healing, poltergeists, and physical aura. Some enthusiasts claim to have discovered "leaks from the transcendental realm" and new dimensions of reality. The enemy is always the "behaviorist," "experimentalist," or "mechanist," who is allegedly closed to such inquiries. We are, some maintain, at a revolutionary stage in the history of science, which has seen the emergence of new paradigms of explanation. Critics insist that our usual scientific categories and methods are too narrow and limiting.

I am not denying the constant need to examine evidence and to maintain an open mind. Indeed, I would insist that it is essential that scientists be willing to investigate claims of new phenomena. Science cannot be censorial and intolerant, nor cut itself off from new discoveries by making judgments antecedent to inquiry. Extreme forms of scientists can be as dogmatic as subjectivism. There is a difference, however, between the careful use of research methods on the one hand, and the tendency to hasty generalizations based upon slender evidence on the other. Regretfully, there is all too often a tendency for the credulous to latch onto the most meager data and frame vast conjectures, or to insist that their speculations have been conclusively confirmed, when they have not been.

Serious questions can be raised about the current scene: Is the level of irrationality greater or less than in previous times, or has the level of nonsense remained fairly constant in human culture and only assumed different forms? Why does irrationality persist, even in advanced societies?

There are, no doubt, many sociological and cultural hypotheses that can be introduced to explain the phenomenon of the growth of irrational beliefs. In recent years the mass media have grown in influence: the image of the scientist is drawn by journalists, novelists, and dramatists, not by scientists themselves; and what science is or does has been misconstrued and given a bad name. Or again, it is estimated that half of all the support in the world for scientific research is for weapons development, and most of the rest is for industrial and pragmatic purposes. Scientific research all too often has been controlled by private interests for their profit or by governments for indoctrination and control. The free, creative scientific inquirer often has to depend for his financial support on the power structure; and what happens to the fruits of his labor is beyond his control.

All of these explanations are no doubt true. But there are also, in my judgment, profound psychological factors at work; and there is much confusion about the meaning of science itself. The persistence of irrationality in modern culture suggests something about the peculiar nature of the human species. At the very least it suggests that there is a tendency in the human animal toward gullibility—that is, a psychological readiness to accept untested beliefs, to be gulled into assent. This tendency seems to be so deeply ingrained in human behavior that few are without it in some measure. We are tempted to swallow as the gospel truth what others offer us. I am not talking simply of stupidity and ignorance but of uncritical näiveté about some matters.

Undoubtedly there are individuals who specialize in deceiving others and who play to the gullible galleries. They are purveyors of false gods and empty services, the perpetrators of fraud and distortion. But there are no doubt also sincere believers who delude themselves, who are willing to believe ideas without adequate evidence, and who seek to convert others to their misconceptions. What is at work here is not conscious fraud, but self-deception. The curious thing is that, if a psychotic repeats himself often enough, in time others will come to believe him, and like lemmings, even follow him to the sea. Moreover, if an untruth is exaggerated sufficiently, people are more apt to believe it. Many would rather believe a liar who promises them wondrous things than a nay-saying debunker; the heretic always risks being burned at the stake, especially after the new mythology becomes institutionalized as official doctrine.

As I have written elsewhere, one form of gullibility is nincompoopery. If *gullibility* refers to descriptive beliefs about the world, then *nincompoopery* refers to our normative values. The nincompoop, like the gull, uncritically accepts as true what he is fed, but he goes on to base his deeds upon it. He infuses his life-style with undigested falsehoods; they become his "faith," his salvation, his guide, and his whole existence is built around a myth. It permeates his very being, his moral values and social attitudes. Some gulls today reject orthodox religion, yet they are willing to follow every fad and fashion that appears and be taken in by antiscience and pseudoscience.

Why is this so?

There is, I think, still another tendency in human behavior that feeds on gullibility—the fascination with mystery and drama. Life for many persons is humdrum and boring. Daily existence for them is often a burden, with the same pattern repeated day in and day out. Overcome by ennui and the tyranny of trivia, they may seek to escape this world by the use of drugs or alcohol, by dulling or suppressing their consciousness. Release into nothingness is their goal.

Another method of diversion is the quest for hedonistic pleasures and thrills. Still another is the role of the imagination in widening our world. The arts of literature and drama give free play to the creative imagination, as does religion. It is often difficult for many individuals to be able to distinguish truth from falsity, fiction from reality. The cults of unreason and the paranormal attract and fascinate. They enable one to skirt the boundaries of the unknown. For the ordinary person, there is the everyday world—and the possibility of escape to another. And so they look elsewhere—for another universe and another reality.

Thus there is a search that is fundamental to our being: the quest for meaning. The human mind has a genuine desire to plumb the depths of the unspoken, to find deeper significance and truth, to reach out to another realm of existence. Life is without meaning for many, especially for the poor, the sick, the forsaken, and those who have failed or have little hope. The imagination offers salvation from the trials and tribulations encountered in this life. Thus, belief in reincarnation or ideological religions; the means of salvation is the utopian vision of the perfect society in the future. The soul cries out for something more, farther beyond, deeper, more lasting, and more perfect than our contingent and transient world of experience.

Accordingly, the persistence of faith may be explained in part by something within our nature: gullibility, the lure of mystery, the quest for meaning. People will take the least shred of evidence and construct a mythological system. They will pervert their logic and abandon their senses, all for the Promised Land. Some will gladly barter their freedom to the most authoritarian of systems in order to achieve comfort and security. The cults of unreason promise solace; they seek to invest the solitary individual, who often feels estranged and alone, with an important role in the universe. The transcendent reality offers soothing balm for the ache of living. Though it transcends evidence and reason, it speaks to a passionate hunger that has its roots within the very depths of human beings.

What can science say about such passions and needs? Have we perhaps left the domain of science entirely and moved into that of philosophy? Science should have something to say, for what is at stake is the nature of science itself.

There are many meanings of the word *science*. Some who talk about science refer to specialties in a specific field, such as endocrinology, microbiology, or econometrics. Scientific researchers in their fields undoubtedly endeavor to use careful methods to test their explanatory hypotheses. Others who talk about science have in mind the technological and experimental applications of scientific theories to concrete problems. Yet these views of science are overly narrow; for it is possible for a society to make massive progress in certain narrowly technical fields and yet miss the whole point of the scientific enterprise. The totalitarian societies of our time have invested vast sums in technical research and have achieved a high level of scientific competence in certain fields, but the scientific outlook has not prevailed in them. Merely training people to be scientific specialists is not enough. A culture can be full of scientific technicians, yet still be dominated by the irrational. We must distinguish science as a narrow technical enterprise from the *scientific attitude*. It is here that I think we have not yet fulfilled an important goal. Unfortunately, to have scientific credentials in one field does not mean that a person will incorporate a scientific attitude into other parts of his life.

The best therapy for gullibility and unbridled imagination is the development of the critical use of the scientific attitude, as it applies not only to one's specialized field of expertise but to the wider questions of life itself. But we have failed in our society to make clear the role of the scientific attitude. It is evident that one can be a scientific specialist but a cultural barbarian, an expert technologist in a particular field but broadly miseducated outside of it.

If we are to meet the growth of irrationality, we need to develop an appreciation for the scientific attitude as part of culture. We must make it clear that the key methodological principle of science is that one is not justified in affirming a truth claim unless one can support it by evidence or reason. It is not enough to be inwardly convinced of the truth of one's beliefs. They must at some point be objectively verifiable by other, impartial investigators. A belief that is warranted is not so because it is "subjectively true," as Kierkegaard thought; if it is true, it is so because it has been confirmed by a community of inquirers. To believe validly that something is true is to relate one's beliefs to a rational justification; it is to make a claim about the world, independent of one's wishes.

Although the specific criteria for testing a belief depend upon the subject under consideration, there are certain general criteria that we must take into account. We need to examine the *evidence*. Here I am referring to observation of data that are reproducible by independent observers and that can be examined experimentally in test cases. This is familiarly called the empiricist or experimentalist criterion. A belief is true if, and only if, it has been confirmed, directly or indirectly, by reference to observable evidence. A belief is also validated by offering supporting *reasons*. Here there are logical considerations that are relevant. A belief is related to a set of other beliefs that have been established by previous inquiries. This criterion is that of logical consistency. A belief is invalid if it contradicts other well-grounded beliefs within a framework. We also evaluate our beliefs in part by their observed *consequences* in practice and by their effect upon conduct. This is the utilitarian or pragmatic criterion: the utility of a belief is judged by reference to its function and its value. However, one cannot claim that a belief is true simply because it has utility; independent evidence and rational considerations are essential. Nevertheless, reference to the results of a belief, particularly to those of a normative belief, is important.

These general criteria are, of course, familiar in logic and the philosophy of science. It is the hypothetical-deductive method of testing hypotheses that I am talking about. But this method should not be narrowly construed, for the scientific method is continuous with common sense; it is not some esoteric art available only to the initiated. Science employs the same methods of critical intelligence that the ordinary man uses in formulating beliefs about his practical world; and it is the method one has to use, to some extent, if he is to live and function, to make plans and choices. To deviate from objective thinking is to be out of touch with cognitive reality; and we cannot avoid using it if we are to deal with the concrete problems that we encounter in the world.

The paradox is that so many people are willing to abandon the use of their practical intelligence when they enter fields of religion or ethics, or to throw caution to the wind when they flirt with so-called transcendental matters.

In any case there is a need to develop a general scientific attitude for all or most areas in life, to use, as far as possible, our critical intelligence to appraise beliefs, and to insist that they be based upon evidential grounds. The chief corollary to this is the criterion that *where we do not have sufficient evidence, we ought, if possible, to suspend judgment.* Our beliefs should be considered tentative hypotheses based on degrees of probability. They should not be considered absolute or final. We ought to be committed to the principle of fallibilism (as Charles Peirce long ago pointed out), which considers that our beliefs can be erroneous. We should be willing to revise them, if need be, in the light of new evidence and new theories.

The scientific attitude thus does not foreclose on a priori grounds any examination of claims about the transcendental. It is committed to continued free and open inquiry. It cannot refuse to engage in research, say, for example, into paranormal phenomena. But it does claim the right to ask that such research not be outstripped by conjecture, nor the conclusions based upon the will to believe.

The basic question here is, How we can cultivate the scientific attitude? The most vital institution in society for developing an appreciation for the scientific attitude is the school. It is not enough, however, for educational institutions to simply inform young people of the facts or to disseminate a body of knowledge. Education of that sort may be nothing more than role learning or indoctrination. Rather, a key purpose of education should be to develop within individuals the use of *critical intelligence* and *skepticism*. It is not enough to get people to memorize a subject matter, amass facts, pass examinations, or even to master a specialty or profession or be trained as citizens. If we do that and nothing more, we have not educated fully; the central task is to cultivate the ability to test beliefs, evaluate hypotheses, appraise arguments—in short, to develop an attitude of objectivity and impartiality. The tremendous information explosion today has bombarded us with competing truth claims. It is vital that individuals develop some understanding of the effective criteria for judging these claims. I refer not only to our ability to examine claims of knowledge about the world but also to our ability to develop some skills in appraising value judgments and ethical principles. The goal of education should be to develop reflective persons—skeptical, yet receptive to new ideas; always willing to examine new departures in thought, yet insisting that they be tested before they are accepted.

Education is not achieved when we transmit a finished subject matter or discipline to students—only when we stimulate a living process of inquiry. This goal is appreciated today in some educational institutions that do attempt to cultivate reflective intelligence. But education is not complete unless we can extend our concern to other important educative institutions in society. If we are to raise the level of critical intelligence and promote the scientific attitude, it is important that we concern ourselves with the media of mass communication—television, radio, the cinema, newspapers, magazines, and book publishing. An especially serious problem with the electronic media is that they employ visual images rather than written symbols, immediate impressions instead of sustained analyses. How can we stimulate reflective criticism in viewers given this form of information?

I have no easy solution to offer. What I do wish to suggest is that we ought not to assume, simply because ours is an advanced scientific-technological society, that irrational thinking will be overcome. The evidence suggests that that is far from being the case. Indeed, there is always the danger that science itself may be engulfed by those forces of unreason.

If we are to deal with the problem, what we need, at the very least, is to be clear about the nature of the scientific enterprise itself and to recognize that it presupposes a basic attitude about evidential criteria. Unless we can impart through the educative institutions in society some sense of the skeptical approach to life—as therapeutic and corrective—then I am afraid we will be constantly confronted by new forms of "know-nothingism," and as soon as one myth is discarded individuals will all too readily seek to replace them with others.

If we are to make progress in overcoming irrationality, however, we must go still further. We must perhaps try to satisfy the need for mystery and drama and the hunger for meaning. The growth of education and science in the modern world is a marvel to behold, and we should do whatever we can to further its development. But we have learned that an increase in the sum of knowledge by itself will not necessarily overturn superstition, dogma, and gullibility, because these are nourished by other sources in the human psyche.

One point often overlooked in satisfying our fascination with mystery and drama is the possible role of imagination in the sciences. Science can only proceed by being open to creative explorations in thought. The breakthroughs in science are astounding, and they will continue as we probe further into the microworld of matter and life, and into the universe at large. The space age is the beginning of a new epoch for humankind, as we leave our solar system and explore the universe for extraterrestrial life. Perhaps there will be no more exciting excursion that we will take. We need to disseminate an appreciation for the adventure of scientific enterprise. Unfortunately, for some, science fiction is a substitute for science. The religion of the future may be a space-age religion, in which the new prophets are not the scientists, but the science-fiction writers.

Thus science has a double focus: objectivity and creativity. The arts are essential in keeping alive the dramatic qualities of experience; poetry, music, and literature express our passionate natures. Man does not live by reason alone; and science is often viewed by its critics as cold and rational. People hunger for something more. Our aesthetic impulses and our delight in beauty need cultivation. The arts are the deepest expression of our "spiritual" interests, but we need to make a distinction between art and truth; for though we may appreciate aesthetic form, knowledge claims require rigorous testing.

In any case, we need poetry and symbol, creativity and drama, passion and emotion, love and devotion. We need to appeal to the whole person, not simply his cerebellum. We need to celebrate life and its potential goods, to find joy and happiness as part of it, and to satisfy the quest for meaning. It is this craving for ethereal meaning that, I think, leads to the psychotic disorientation found in the cults of unreason. "Follow me," say the cults of irrationality. "I am the light, the truth, and the way." And people are willing to abandon all standards of critical judgment in the process.

I wish to make it clear that there is a need today for developing alternative normative institutions. I cannot say in detail, in an already long article, what such a normative program would entail. I have attempted to do so elsewhere. I would only suggest here that such a program would not build systems with beliefs that are patently false or irrational or that violate the evidence of the sciences; yet it would seek to address itself to the other dimensions of human experience, and it would give the arts, philosophy, and ethics powerful roles in helping fulfill our human needs.

Suggestions
for Further Reading

Anthologies

Ammerman, Robert, R., and Marcus G. Singer (eds.). *Belief, Knowledge and Truth.* New York: Scribners, 1970. A rich selection, ranging from elementary to difficult, from philosophical writings on skepticism, empiricism, rationalism, and other issues in the theory of knowledge from ancient Greece to the present. An extensive bibliography of books and articles.

Braybrooke, David (ed.). *Philosophical Problems of the Social Sciences.* New York: Macmillan, Sources in Philosophy Series, 1965. Contains a substantial introductory essay by the editor and a selection of recent philosophical writings treating problems suggested by psychology, history, economics, and the other social sciences. This book of readings is designed for the beginning student.

Frazier, Kendrick (ed.). *Paranormal Borderlands of Science.* Buffalo, N.Y.: Prometheus Books, 1981. This anthology consists of 47 articles written by Isaac Asimov, Paul Kurtz, and others, which originally appeared in *The Skeptical Inquirer,* a magazine devoted to the critical investigation of pseudoscience from a scientific viewpoint.

Gardner, Martin (ed.). *Great Essays in Science.* New York: Pocket Books, 1957. A highly readable collection of writings on the nature of science and its social implications by scientists and philosophers. This book is more entertaining than many novels.

Klemke, E. D., Robert Hollinger, and A. David Kline. *Introductory Readings in the Philosophy of Science.* Buffalo, N.Y.: Prometheus Books, 1981. In addition to such standard subjects as explanation and confirmation of theories, this anthology for the beginning student contains sections on science and pseudoscience and science and values.

Shapere, Dudley (ed.). *Philosophical Problems of Natural Science.* New York: Macmillan, Sources in Philosophy Series, 1965. Contains a substantial introductory essay by the editor and a selection of recent philosophical writings dealing with the structural and historical analyses of science. This book of readings is designed for the beginning student.

Individual Works

Ayer, A. J. *The Problem of Knowledge.* Baltimore: Penguin, 1956. A more advanced yet clearly written philosophical investigation of the nature, scope, and limits of human knowledge. This book was designed not only for the professional philosopher but for the general reader as well. Particular attention is called to Chapter 2, "Skepticism and Certainty."

Cohen, Morris R. *Reason and Nature,* 2nd ed. New York: Free Press, 1964. A classic work by an American philosopher who was a champion of the supremacy of critical reason in human life. Cohen devotes considerable attention to the ethical, legal, religious, and historic implications of scientific knowledge and method. A scholarly work, yet written so lucidly that the beginning student can read it with pleasure.

Eldredge, Niles. *The Monkey Business: A Scientist Looks at Creationism.* New York: Washington Square Press, 1982. A curator at the American Museum of Natural History vigorously attacks creationism and forcefully defends the continuing teaching of evolution.

Gardner, Martin. *Fads and Fallacies in the Name of Science,* 2nd ed. New York: Dover, 1957. A fascinating examination of extrasensory perception, the hollow earth hypothesis, dianetics, orgone boxes, and other theories and devices that the author criticizes as being pseudoscience.

————. *Science: Good, Bad, and Bogus.* Buffalo, N.Y.: Prometheus Books, 1981. A recent collection of Gardner's essays, book reviews, and other writings that attack fraud, hoax, and self-delusion when practiced in the name of science.

Gish, Duane T. *Evolution? The Fossils Say No!* San Diego: Institute for Creation Research, 1973. A leading advocate of creationism attacks evolutionary philosophy.

Hospers, John. *An Introduction to Philosophical Analysis,* 2nd ed. Englewood Cliffs, N.J.: Prentice-Hall, 1967. This expository text contains a clear, contemporary, and elementary discussion of rationalism and empiricism for the beginning student.

Huxley, Thomas Henry. *Selections from the Essays of T. H. Huxley,* edited by Alburey Castell. New York: Appleton, 1948. A collection of some of the most famous essays treating such topics as science and education, science and religion, and science and ethics.

Nagel, Ernest. *The Structure of Science.* New York: Harcourt, 1961. A recent comprehensive treatment of the nature of explanation in the natural and social sciences by an outstanding American philosopher of science. A book for the more advanced student.

Otto, Max C. *Science and the Moral Life.* New York: New American Library, Mentor Book, 1949. An unusually felicitous defense of a scientific humanism in the tradition of William James and John Dewey. With a sophistication developed to the point of simplicity, this book is designed for the layman in philosophy.

Ravetz, Jerome R. *Scientific Knowledge and Its Social Problems.* New York: Oxford U.P.: 1973. A recent and influential discussion of the nature of science and its impact on society and nature.

Russell, Bertrand. *The Scientific Outlook,* New York: Norton, 1962. The first two parts of this book deal with the natures of scientific knowledge and scientific technique. In the third part, entitled "The Scientific Society," Russell rewrites and updates Plato's *Republic.* In the course of his philosophical critique of the scientific society, Russell discusses all of the objections to such a society to be found in George Orwell's *1984*, Aldous Huxley's *Brave New World,* and other similar fictional and nonfictional critiques.

Stapledon, Olaf. *Last and First Men* and *Star Maker.* New York: Dover, 1968. Two science fiction novels by a philosopher, which convey the haunting beauty and disturbing strangeness of the world revealed by science better than most abstract treatises. These powerfully imaginative works reveal why many people find the scientific understanding and manipulation of the world and man so fascinating and hopeful and many others find it so appalling and depressing.

Dictionary of the History of Ideas: Studies of Selected Pivotal Ideas. Philip P. Wiener, editor-in-chief. New York: Scribners, 1973. Substantial and clearly written essays emphasizing the historical development of topics discussed in this part. Designed to inform the nonspecialist, each essay concludes with a select bibliography.

Encyclopedia of Philosophy. Paul Edwards, editor-in-chief, New York: Macmillan, 1967. The beginning student will find many worthwhile articles on the subjects treated in this part and excellent bibliographies.

Epilogue

In 1918, Clarence Darrow delivered a high school commencement address remarkable for its brevity and Socratic wisdom. While waiting to speak, Darrow suffered through a verbose and preposterously flattering introduction depicting him as a perfect model whom young people should emulate. Finally the introductory speech came to an end, and Darrow ambled to the lectern, smiled, and gave probably one of the shortest commencement addresses ever given.

> That was as fine a lot of bunk as I ever heard in my life and I know darned well you youngsters didn't believe a word of it. You're no more fit to go forth and serve than the man in the moon. You're just a bunch of ignorant kids, full of the devil, and you've learned practically nothing to show for the years you spent here. You can't fool me, for I once spent four years in such a place.

If, after reading this book and reflecting on what he has read, the student now knows he is ignorant, he will be a true friend of Socrates.